JAVA
PROGRAMMING

JAVA

PROGRAMMING

EXPLORER

Steve Simkin

Neil Bartlett

Alex Leslie

CORIOLIS GROUP BOOKS

Publisher	*Keith Weiskamp*
Editor	*Scott Palmer*
Proofreader	*Jenni Aloi and Diane Green Cook*
Cover Design	*Gary Smith*
Interior Design	*Bradley Grannis*
Layout Production	*Kim Eoff*
Indexer	*Nicole Stock*

The Coriolis Group
7339 E. Acoma Drive, Suite 7
Scottsdale, AZ 85260
Phone: (602) 483-0192
Fax: (602) 483-0193
Web address: www.coriolis.com

ISBN 1-883577-81-0 : $39.99

Printed in the United States of America

10 9 8 7 6 5 4 3 2 1

To Mary, who made it possible and worthwhile.
  Neil Bartlett

To my long suffering wife Robin,
  my neglected daughter Sierra,
and my new daughter Rachel
    who I can finally get to know.

Your husband and father is back!
  Alex Leslie

To my darling wife,
    "...This is my beloved, and this is my friend..."
(Song of Songs 5:16)
  Steve Simkin

About the Authors

Neil Bartlett is a member of the Toronto Java Users Group and a judge for the Java Applet Rating Service (JARS). He currently runs Great Explorer Software Consulting, Ltd., whose clients include Northern Telecom, IBM, and the Toronto Stock Exchange. He is also a partner in NetExcel, an Internet consulting and training company.

Alex Leslie has been immersed in Java and HotJava since the alpha test stage and is a member of the Toronto Java User's Group. He owns a software development company and his clients include Citibank, Nortel, and Southam Information Systems. He is also a partner in NetExcel.

Steve Simkin has been a professional software developer for 13 years. In his current incarnation, he develops object-oriented manufacturing and engineering applications at Northern Telecom. He is a member of the Toronto Java Users Group.

CONTENTS

Chapter 3 A Java Programming Tutorial 41

Chapter 4   Basic Ingredients of a Potent Brew   73

Chapter 22   Interfacing with C   743

Acknowledgments

Thanks to Keith Weiskamp, our publisher at the Coriolis Group. He deserves much credit for having faith in three guys he'd never met and only talked to on the phone a couple of times. With a man like Keith at the helm, it's no wonder Coriolis is the success it is.

To Scott Palmer, for stepping up to the editor's plate towards the end of the game and hitting a home run. Thanks, Scott, for your patience and for contributing from your own years of experience as an author.

Neil Bartlett

Thanks to my wife, Mary. Finally, we can celebrate Christmas and New Years together. It is only one month late. I now know why authors thank their wives so much. Thanks is such a small word, considering how much you deserve.

Alex and Steve. Dudes—it was hard work, but we did it.

A big hello to all my friends, especially David Janes and Mike Fischer. There is probably some part of a conversation with you in this book—unless it was cut! Just as big a hello to all my sailing buddies and, naturally, Jacques and Janet—my "Summer family."

Thanks to Bread & Roses and The Second Cup of Bloor West Village, Toronto, for providing good food and a pleasant atmosphere to work in during the day. I'm the guy who sits in the corner earnestly scribbling on pieces of paper and consuming Java by the tankful.

Finally, I would like to say hello to my parents, whom I have not seen for several years. I will be home this year. I promise—I need to rest!

Alex Leslie

First and foremost, I thank my loving wife Robin for her patient support throughout this project. Neither of us knew exactly what we were getting into when we first began the odyssey, but she shared my excitement and offered encouragement every day. For her, it meant becoming *a single parent* for several months, but she did it gracefully. At the time the concept for this book was just hatching, we already had a loving and playful one-year-old daughter, Sierra. But in September 1995, Rachel graced our family with her happy arrival. Unfortunately, it was just about the time activity on this book began in earnest and I disappeared into my study. The months to follow were certainly action-packed for us all! But now with the fruit of our sacrifice before me, I look forward to rewarding my family for being my home team.

This book would not exist without the dedication and vision of Neil Bartlett. He deserves much praise for his boldness in daring to ask "why not?" He laid down the outline for this book, back in August 1995, entirely on his own and, surprisingly, we have held quite faithfully to it since. He approached Steve and me, and we became believers overnight—Java has that effect. There have been no regrets. Not only did Neil have the vision, but he also proved to be the organizational force during the long months while we coded and wrote and coded and wrote and February 1996 seemed so far off. Thanks, Neil!

Thanks to Steve for rounding out our authorship. He was able to bring a unique set of skills to the table that made the difference in the end. Writing a book with three authors could be a recipe for disaster and conflict but, in fact, our shared goals—and shared pressures—had a beneficial effect and brought us closer together. It is very special when that happens.

Finally, thanks to all the staff at Coriolis who contributed in some way to the success of this book. I hope to one day thank you in person.

Steve Simkin

Growing up, I learned to translate Ecclesiastes 12:12 as "of making many books there is no end." Now I know better.

I picture King Solomon at 1:00 a.m., just two verses to go in a book that will instruct the masses in the meaning of life. Decades of accumulated wisdom captured on parchment, and just two more verses! The phone rings. It's the royal editor. Chapter 3 must be rewritten with a twelve-point quill, and don't forget the italics on "A time for *this* and a time for *that*...." Oh, and stick in some tabs, makes the page more eye-catching.

Wearily the king opens another bottle of ink and scrawls verse 12, whose proper translation I now present for the first time anywhere: "Making books is greatly endless."

I'd like to thank Neil Bartlett for inviting me to join him and Alex in this project. It has been a marvelous opportunity. It is especially rare for an opportunity to march up to one's door and bang on it, demanding entry.

I was able to open the door to it only with my wife's support and cooperation. For more than three months, she allowed me the time required for extended periods of solitude with my word processor and the Java Virtual Machine. Java's great, but I'm looking forward to returning as a presence on the domestic front. My spouse is looking forward to the ski trip I promised her.

There's time to be made up with the kids, too. "Will the book *ever* come out of your computer?" they ask. I must admit, I've wondered the same thing myself a few times. Thanks for your patience, Michael, Haya, and Hanan. Quality time is just around the corner.

Finally, I'd like to thank the intelligent twelve-year-old. When I first joined the project, a friend told me to imagine teaching Java to an intelligent twelve-year-old, someone loaded with brains, but with no background in the subject. As I've struggled with explanations of Java concepts, I've often pictured this child (looking remarkably like my intelligent ten year-old), sitting across the desk from me, waiting to be enlightened in all things Java. To the intelligent twelve-year-old I say, "So long. It's time for me to get back to my real children. I know you'll return someday, but for now, enjoy your vacation. You've earned it."

A Taste of Java

Steve Simkin

Our journey of a thousand miles begins with a single chat over coffee. We look at Java, its history, its current state, and the revolution it might cause. In short, here's why you should learn Java now.

Imagine a world free of pressure to increase your disk space, expand your memory, accelerate your CPU, and replace your whole system every two years. Imagine not having to support the latest swollen version of the spreadsheet program you were comfortable with four years ago, which now offers hundreds of features you don't need, demands five times the disk space and four times the memory, and costs three times the price. Or being able to pay just a few pennies for those features you want to use on a one-time basis. Imagine being able to test-drive the latest and greatest without having to commit to purchase and installation. Or to mix-and-match this word processor with that spell checker and somebody else's drawing tool.

Think of enhancing your home page with eye-catching animation that attracts prospective buyers to your products. Or using the Internet to publish a 3D simulation of the new medical technique pioneered by your department, enabling other practitioners to learn about the technique and try it on simulated patients.

1

Picture yourself a multimedia innovator who has just invented the next killer app that relies on files in a brand new format. You don't need to worry about publicizing where users can find your software or hope that it will become popular enough for Netscape to incorporate into their next release. Instead, you deliver files in your new format with the player program bundled right in. This makes your users' lives easier, too, because they no longer have to download and install the software just to have a peek at the new file type. And besides that, you only need to write a single version of your killer app, because it will run on the full range of computers people use to connect to the Internet. Think of lowering the entry barriers to the global software market by using the Internet as both your distribution channel and your billing mechanism. Think how much more time you could devote to creating quality applications.

What would it be like if you could have your software update itself transparently as new versions were released?

Utopia? Hardly. True, most of the developments we've described haven't happened yet, but they are all possible and have come significantly closer to being realized thanks to a new software environment called Java. Java promises to revolutionize the way we think of software use, extending the limits of our computers by making available the resources of the Internet. Java is a wake-up call.

Java is a complete environment, composed of a programming language, development tools, and a runtime system that allows any Java program to run on any platform to which the runtime library has been ported. Whatever roles you play in the software community—whether developer, provider, or user— Java has important implications for the way you use computers. We can ease your entry into this exciting new world.

To appreciate the importance of Java, and what Java may mean to you, it's important to understand the Java philosophy. The best way to start is by reviewing the origins of Java.

A THEMATIC HISTORY OF JAVA

The history of Java is full of creative personalities letting loose, business missteps, near disasters, recriminations, grand visions, and shortsightedness. Any of these aspects could serve (and has served) as the theme of a history of the Java environment. But for the Java developer, the most important angle on the Java story is the idea of Java. What was the original conception of Java's designers, and how did that conception change during the ups and downs of the Java project? The answers to these questions serve as a first step for any potential Java developer trying to appreciate the Java philosophy.

Java traces its origins to a group of disgruntled engineers and programmers at Sun Microsystems. In 1990, this group envisioned a computing environment different from what they had encountered at Sun. The group included James Gosling, a master programmer who would eventually create the Java language, and Patrick Naughton, who would go on to design the visual interfaces used to promote the Java environment. But in the spring of 1990, these achievements were yet to come, and Gosling and Naughton's group, which Sun code-named *Green*, was still establishing guidelines for the environment they hoped to create.

The environment would be designed with consumers—normal people, not computer nerds—in mind. It would be small, simple, and compact. And it would run on a number of different devices, including some not normally thought of as computers. So the earliest ruminations of the Green team already put in place some of the buzzwords from the Java white paper definition. The environment must be simple, so that nontechnical people could quickly master the devices running it. It must be portable, so that it could run on the different devices envisioned for it. And, as a corollary, it must be architecture-neutral, in order to not limit the design of those devices by imposing an architecture on them. The Green team received enthusiastic backing and support from Scott McNealy, Sun's CEO.

The first area of application envisioned by the team was consumer electronics. The complexity of tasks, such as programming a household thermostat or coordinating a VCR and TV, was recognized as what a digital environment should *not* be. The Green team proposed connecting household appliances to a network that would be run by a single controller. This controller would feature an intuitive user interface using animation to portray the devices connected to it and the user's options. In the spring of 1991, the team produced a paper called *Behind the Green Door*, which included the following mission statement: "To develop and license an operating environment for consumer devices that enables services and information to be persuasively presented via the emerging digital infrastructure." The proposed environment would thus be distributed, a network of totally dissimilar devices, using bytestreams to communicate with the controller. This bytestream would be interpretable by toasters, VCRs, and house alarms.

Until this time, Gosling had been trying to implement the environment by extending the C++ language. Eventually he realized that C++ could not meet his needs. The reasons for this inadequacy were the direct memory management so central to C++, the fragility of the relationships among the components of a C++ program, and the fact the C++ does not enforce object-oriented programming. We will explore these issues when we discuss the nature of the Java language, since Gosling concluded that together they made it impossible for him to adapt C++ to the demands of his new environment.

Gosling set about inventing a new language. The new language would take memory management out of the hands of the application programmer by eliminating pointers and address arithmetic entirely. This one feature of the language would greatly enhance the robustness of the new environment. The new language would also resolve references among classes at runtime instead of compile-time. A superclass could be changed without adversely affecting the software that uses it. This would make the new environment truly dynamic, because changes to underlying software could be implemented on demand without having to recompile and re-release anything else.

While Gosling was inventing his new language, Naughton was working on the controller device for the networked household. He thought of visually representing the household on this device by using animation that the user could manipulate in the virtual space in order to send marching orders to her electronic troops. For example, the user could open a cartoon TV Guide, select a movie, then drop the TV Guide onto a cartoon VCR, thus instructing her real VCR to record the selected movie when it is broadcast. Gosling quickly got the animation working in his new language, which he called Oak, after a tree outside his office window.

From a programming point of view, Gosling was able to accomplish this cooperation of cartoon image, controller device, network, and VCR by designing a language that was purely object-oriented. This means that the sole unit of expression was by means of objects (called *classes* in Oak). It was these classes that got passed around the domestic network, and every device knew how to interpret them and how to create them and send them back to the controller. For example, there may have been a VCR class that included a method of saying to the VCR, "Record channel 3 for the next two hours, please." Here again, C++ could not serve Gosling's needs. It facilitated object-oriented programming but did not enforce it.

The Green team, now incorporated as FirstPerson, Inc., a wholly owned subsidiary of Sun, spent 1993 looking for business applications for their exciting new technology. They came close to licensing it to several other companies in applications as diverse as cellular phones, industrial automation systems, interactive television, CD-ROMs, and commercial online services. But each time the deal fell through. Amazingly, they never thought of the Internet, even though Sun was the leading provider of Internet hosts, a major source of its revenue.

In early 1994, Bill Joy and Eric Schmidt thought Oak and the Net would make a perfect match. Joy was a Net old-timer, having developed the Berkeley version of the Unix operating system, which was widely used on the Net. Schmidt was Sun's chief technology officer. Together they encouraged Gosling and Naughton to adapt Oak for the Internet. Around this time, Oak was renamed Java. Once again, Gosling worked on the language, extending it with Internet functionality, while Naughton developed a user interface. By the end of the year, Naughton had come up with a Web browser with a built-in Java interpreter. He named the browser HotJava.

In January 1995, Sun began to distribute Java and HotJava for free on the Internet. Sun was intent on establishing Java as the programming language of the Net and hoped that profits would follow once Java gained a foothold. Java encouraged developers to write small applications, called *applets*, which would be included on their home pages but would run on the machine of whoever visited the page—assuming the visitor was using HotJava as a Web browser, that is. Java got a big boost when Marc Andreessen of Netscape endorsed it, and an even bigger boost in August 1995, when Netscape included a Java interpreter in release 2.0 of the Netscape Navigator. More than anything else, the alliance with Netscape has advanced Sun's quest to make Java the programming standard of the Internet.

WHY DOES THE INTERNET NEED A LANGUAGE?

Those of you who have been using the Internet for a few years know what a tremendous boon the World Wide Web has been. Before the introduction of the Web, all Internet activity was conducted in the command line. If you wanted to email someone, you had to invoke your email application, remembering the set of commands for composing, addressing, sending, reading, and organizing messages. If you wanted to retrieve a file from an FTP site, you brought up your FTP app and used it to logon to the FTP host, remembering the user ID and password, negotiating a directory hierarchy, locating the file you were interested in, remembering to set transfer mode to ASCII or binary as appropriate, and finally pulling the file. If you wanted to check out a newsgroup you needed yet another application, with its own list of com-

mands you had to learn in order to review, reply, post, and save the latest exchanges to your hard drive. The beauty of Unix is that a typing mistake at any stage in one of these processes could have irrevocable, disastrous results. Living with that danger certainly conferred a feeling of superiority on those mortals who braved the network, but it also preserved the Net as the private property of the privileged few. Some liked it that way.

Then the Web came along. Suddenly the Net could serve up graphics and sound, and your mouse could lead you around the world with a point and a click. No more arcane line-mode commands, no more specialized little applications for each Net activity. The Net became the province of normal people. As long as you kept to the file formats supported by your Web browser, you could travel where you liked, enjoy the files that you liked, and communicate and download freely, all without having to leave your browser and with a minimum of keystrokes.

Of course, if the author of a Web page provided content in a format that wasn't part of your browser, you would have to hunt around for software that could understand the file format and could run on your computer. You would then have to download the software and install it and identify it to your browser as a helper application. Highly inconvenient, especially if all you wanted from the Web site was to have a peek.

The developers of Web browsers tried to reduce this inconvenience by teaching their browsers to handle a greater variety of file formats. Since their inception, Web browsers had bundled in mailers and FTP apps and newsgroup readers. Over time they also increasingly included viewers and players for the more common multimedia formats as well. As the variety of these file formats increased, so did the disk space and memory needed to store and run the browsers. Browser developers didn't dare step off this carousel for fear that their products would become obsolete. But neither they nor their users could have been happy to see Web browsers join the trend toward the "bloatware" that characterized the rest of the software industry. Bloatware refers to software products that grow substantially with each release, usually by adding features most users don't need. As it swells, bloatware makes increasing demands on the user's hardware, practically forcing her to upgrade every couple of years just to keep running the same old word processors and spreadsheets she was satisfied with three releases ago. For Web browsers, there seemed no way out of this vicious cycle, as people introduced ever more file formats that required ever more programs to make use of them.

At that time, the greatest deficiency of the Web browsers was that for the most part, Web-surfing remained a passive activity. Sure, the Web sparkled and sang, but the user was still a passive consumer of content prepared by someone else. There were very few means to let the user actually *do* something on the Net. Of course, he could press a button to vote in an online referendum, or "Get the latest release here," but his sphere of activity was extremely limited.

This passive paradigm of Internet activity was really the source of the limitations of the Web that we've mentioned. As long as the Web remained a mere peddler of passive content, innovators of new file formats had no choice but to distribute a separate software package that understood the format of files themselves. Anyone who wanted to make use of these files would have to download and install the software before getting the file itself. If the new format became popular, developers of browsers would be pressured to incorporate its software into their next release, thus bloating the browser. The only escape from this trap would be a mechanism to make software, as well as content, available to users requesting a file. The helper application would be transparently loaded onto the user's computer and remain there for the duration of the user's session with the file he requested. At the end of the session, the helper application would disappear.

The ability to load programs over the Net would solve the passivity problem. Once the mechanism for loading software was in place, there would be no limit on the types of programs that could be loaded. It might be a multimedia player, or it might just as easily be a word processor or a graphics package with just the feature the user needs right now, or a little animation to make a Web author's home page more eye-catching. The Internet would then become more than a source of content. It would be a truly global applications server.

Sounds great, but do we really need a whole new language to make it happen? Think for a moment of all the different users who access the net. Try to picture them at their desks, pointing and clicking away. The first thing I notice is the number of different machines they are running on. I see Unix boxes, PCs, and Macs, and a few others running operating systems that never caught on in the market but whose devotees make up in zeal for what they lack in numbers. So the first challenge to any developer writing for the Net is to keep all those people happy. Of course, he or she could develop software on one platform, port it to the others, and decorate a home page with buttons reading, "To enjoy this concert on a Mac, click here," and "To tour my gallery under Windows/NT, press here." Sounds unaesthetic, and far more trouble than it's worth. Suddenly the words *architecture neutral* echo a little more loudly in my mind. If a toaster and a sprinkler can engage in meaningful dialogue, surely I can run a single version of a program on both a PC and a Mac.

As long as applications are written in traditional languages and compiled on traditional compilers, architecture neutrality is impossible. An executable for a Windows environment is meaningless to a Mac or Unix machine. The Java developers solved this problem by making Java an *interpreted* language. The Java program sits on the Net in a form that can be interpreted and run on any platform. The user's machine (known as the *client*) must have a single piece of software, the Java interpreter, that translates the Java program into machine instructions that are meaningful to the client's native operating system. Yes, you must download one more program. But having done so, any program written in Java will run on your machine.

But couldn't interpreters have been written for an existing language, so we wouldn't need to learn yet another syntax, yet another list of keywords? Possibly, but there would have been a heavy price to pay. Returning to C++, we see a number of language features that would be a burden on an interpreter. Foremost among these is memory management. In C++, the programmer must explicitly allocate memory and remember to delete it when it's no longer needed. These activities are done differently under different operating systems, and anyone adapting C++ to architecture neutrality would be hard pressed to make them neutral. The solution would probably be to invent a "vanilla" memory management library, which would be implemented by the interpreter for each client operating system. Similar vanillifying would be needed for window management and anything else specific to operating systems. In its current implementation, components of C++ applications rely on knowledge of each other's exact memory layout when they reference each other. In an interpreted implementation, running on who knows what operating systems, this reliance would be impossible. Therefore yet another significant feature of C++ would have to be redesigned in order to run over the Net. Even the memory allocated to standard data types is implementation dependent in C++. Variations in the meaning of "int" would also have to be neutralized in our interpreted environment. I could go on, but I think you get the idea.

In retrospect, the enthusiasm that greeted the introduction of Java for the Internet vindicated the decision to create a new language. Netscape Navigator, the most popular Web browser, now includes a Java interpreter. Together with Sun, Netscape has introduced JavaScript, a simple scripting language to enable nonprogrammers to create Java applications. Java's biggest coup is probably that Microsoft, which is developing a competing language, has signed a Java source license and will be working with Sun to optimize Java for Windows. Microsoft is incorporating Java into its Web browser, the Internet Explorer, which will also support JavaScript. This will immeasurably enlarge the Java user base and bring even closer the establishment of Java as the de facto Internet programming standard.

Java has brought other Sun rivals, namely Silicon Graphics and Macromedia, to cooperate with it. The companies will be working together to develop standards for 3D interactive applications based on Java and Silicon Graphics' Virtual Reality Markup Language (VRML). IBM has also licensed Java and is working on porting it to all its major nonmainframe operating systems. Many other developers have licensed Java with the intention of integrating it into their existing software tools.

Java clearly answered a deeply felt need throughout the Internet community. Let's take a few pages to review the white paper definition of Java, with an emphasis on just what makes Java the answer to the problems of programming for the Internet.

WHAT IS JAVA?

Now that we have some background to the problems Java came to solve, it's worth reviewing the white paper definition of Java, term by term. We'll begin with Java itself.

Java is a simple, object-oriented, distributed, interpreted, robust, secure, architecture-neutral, portable, high-performance, multithreaded, and dynamic language.

In one respect, James Gosling did acknowledge the popularity of C++ when he created the Java language. He made the syntax of Java, its "look and feel," as close as possible to that of C++. This reduces training time for experienced C++ programmers and allows them to take advantage of C++ experience when designing Java programs. However, a number of C++ features were simply eliminated from Java. These fall into two categories. The first consists of features that Gosling felt to be sources of trouble in C++ programs. Features in the first category include operator overloading, multiple inheritance, and automatic coercions between data types. These features are all confusing to programmers, and their misuse is a common source of program errors.

The second category of eliminated features is related to memory management. Java takes memory management out of the hands of the programmer. Memory is allocated when objects are created and remains available as long as the created object continues to be referenced. When Java detects that an object is finished being referenced, the object is freed by automatic garbage collection. Eliminating memory management simultaneously frees the programmer to concentrate on the application and removes a major source of bugs. We'll talk about this at more length when we discuss the *robustness* of the Java language.

Java's similarity to C++, combined with the elimination of problematic features, makes Java a **simple** programming language. Its simplicity also keeps it small enough to be implemented on a phone or a VCR. So it shouldn't put too much strain on your computer.

Java was designed as a purely **object-oriented** language. When we reviewed the history of Oak we mentioned the importance of the class as the single unit of expression. A Java class is a representation of an entity (an "object"). The essence of a Java class is the set of data that collectively describes the object. These sets of data are accessible through a set of interfaces that controls who gets what type of access to them and what operations can be performed on them. The data, together with a description of the set of interfaces to it, make up the class. When you run a Java program that resides on somebody's Web site, the site where the program is located (the *host* computer) sends one or more class descriptions to your client computer. Class descriptions are the only thing that can travel between the host computer and the Java interpreter. This greatly simplifies the interpreter's work, since the only message it needs to know how to receive takes the form, "I'm a class called so-and-so. Here are my variables, and here are my methods for accessing them." This is another advantage over C++; C++ combines features of both object-oriented and procedural languages, greatly complicating the work of an interpreter. Over the course of this book, we will return to object-oriented theory and practice, because it is the soul and the beauty of the Java environment.

When James Gosling extended the original Oak language to function on the Net, he gave it a library of classes for Internet access. You can use objects from anywhere on the Net to compose your application, or create an object that can be freely accessed and manipulated by other developers' software. You can even create a class that is dependent on a class that resides on the Net, thus being assured of always picking up the latest copy of the remote class. This Net functionality makes Java a truly **distributed** environment.

The Java team settled upon an **interpreted** environment as its solution to the problem of functioning in a multi-platform environment. The Java compiler reads source files and from them produces *bytecode*. Bytecode is an intermediate stage between source code and machine code, as close as possible to machine code without becoming platform-specific. More precisely, bytecode really is machine code but not for any machine that actually exists physically. Bytecode runs on the *Java Virtual Machine*, a mythical machine whose behaviors were precisely defined at Sun Microsystems. The Java Virtual Machine (JVM) specification describes the behavior expected of any physical machine running any given bytecode. Conformance to JVM specifications is what ensures the portability of Java programs.

To execute a Java program, you must be running a Java interpreter, either as a standalone or as part of a Web browser. The interpreter reads the bytecode as a stream of bytes and executes the appropriate machine instructions on the platform where it's running. Initially, only the class responsible for the application's overall behavior is loaded, along with a set of system classes needed by the interpreter and for housekeeping tasks like garbage collection. Other classes are loaded as needed by the program, from either the client machine or an Internet site. Thus, unlike the practice with compiled languages, linking in Java is deferred until runtime. Type information needed for correctness checking is written into the compiled bytecode to allow the linker to repeat those tests. The implications for performance of this interpreted approach will be discussed when we talk about *high performance*.

The dynamic approach to linking has a couple of pleasant side effects. One is that compile-time is much quicker than for traditional compiled languages. First, the compilation process itself is shorter, because it stops "part way through." Second, you don't have to wait for your program to link. The compiler checks all references to other classes for type correctness, but doesn't spend time assembling all the program's objects into a single executable. Another side effect of dynamic linking is that your program will always link in the latest release of the classes it uses. You don't need to recompile just because your underlying classes have changed. As long as the interfaces to those classes remain constant, you can continue to use them without making any changes to your code. I'll explain why this is in a few paragraphs, when we talk about *robustness*. If, on the other hand, the interfaces do change, the linker will catch the incompatibility when it does its type checking and issue a clear error message, which simplifies debugging.

The combination of bytecodes and dynamic linking makes Java's interpreted environment highly functional in the distributed, multi-platform world of the Internet.

When Gosling decided that his new environment demanded a new language, he cited a number of deficiencies in C++. These deficiencies tended to under-

mine software quality even when the programs were being written with a specific operating system in mind. In a multi-platform, environment the danger posed by these flaws could only be exaggerated.

We've already talked about how direct memory management is central to C++. And we've mentioned the dangers of making the programmer responsible for allocating and freeing memory. Leaving memory management in the hands of the application programmer often leads to failure to free allocated memory, or, even worse, the attempt to access previously freed memory.

There is a second risk in giving programmers direct access to memory. In C++, the programmer uses pointers to access memory locations directly. This allows lots of wonderful low-level manipulations and allows programs to run at the fastest possible speed. But it also has many less desirable consequences. For one thing, nothing stops a pointer being used to populate an array from populating right past the end of the array into other data structures. Potentially more damaging is the possibility of crashing the system by directly accessing the areas of memory reserved for system use. Most operating systems will prevent application programs from overwriting these areas, but there's nothing in the C++ language to prevent it. Any memory-related error can result in very subtle bugs. It is debatable whether the execution time saved by pointer manipulation equals the programming time lost to marathon debugging sessions trying to isolate the source of corrupted memory.

In addition to automatic garbage collection, Java protects developers from memory-related errors in a couple of ways. First, there is no pointer arithmetic in Java. There is no way to reference any memory address explicitly. When a Java program creates an object, it is handed a pointer to that object. But the only use it can make of the pointer is to reference the members of the object itself. It cannot increment the pointer, calculate a displacement from, or engage in any other activity that refers to actual memory locations rather than their symbolic names. As for arrays, they are objects in their own right, and every access to them is subjected to runtime bounds checking. The only way to access an array member is by name and occurrence number, and any attempt to slip in an occurrence number outside the allocated range of the array will result in an out-of-bounds exception.

A second source of program fragility in C++ derives from its treatment of data types. C++ allows implicit data type coercions, as well as implied procedure declarations. Implicit coercions can lead to an unintentional loss of precision or even complete corruption of numeric data. In Java, conversions of values from one data type to another can only be accomplished via explicit casting, ensuring that the programmer is made aware, at least, of the potential for corruption. There are no implicit declarations in Java. Thus programmers are forced to match their arguments exactly against an existing explicit method declaration. Bad values can still be passed to methods, but at least the compiler won't make kindly assumptions about your intentions when you try invoke a method with an argument list of incorrect types. These type checks are repeated at runtime to guard against discrepancies that might have crept in.

When we discussed the Java interpreter, I told you how Java links dynamically, loading in the classes it needs as it needs them. This overcomes another problem with C++—the fragility of the relationships among different components of a program. In C++, subclasses (program elements that extend or refine more basic elements, known as superclasses) depend on the exact memory layout of their superclasses. Thus, if a superclass definition changes, the subclass must be recompiled before relinking, or the software will break. This leads to extreme fragility on large projects where class definitions come from many sources, and it is difficult to coordinate dependencies to ensure that every executable was linked from totally compatible versions.

An acute example of how dangerous this can be occurs when a program uses third-party class libraries. The developers of the program have no control over the distribution of these libraries. C++ developers are always vulnerable to a new release of a class library that could break their program. In the Java environment, memory mapping of superclasses is deferred until runtime. This means that changes to superclasses have no effect on their subclasses, which will continue to work with no recompilation needed. Another C++ dragon slain.

By taking over memory management responsibilities, eliminating pointers, making arrays into true objects, tightening up type-checking, and linking dynamically, the Java environment promotes the development of software **robust** enough to run in a multi-platform environment.

By now you're probably asking a number of questions about potential problems introduced by the Java environment. Foremost among your questions is surely security. "Do you really expect system administrators to allow applications from anywhere to just pop onto their machines for a visit? Isn't that an invitation to Trojan horses?" The Java environment includes several features to protect your machine against destructive intruders.

First, the Java interpreter itself stands between Java applications and your system. The interpreter restricts Java programs to an acceptable range of behavior. There are no Java methods for low-level mischief and no ways to link in compiled code to perform mischief by proxy. Java tests files for access permissions before allowing applications to open them. The interpreter verifies bytecode, using a technique based on public-key encryption, to detect tampering with compiled code. This verification would also foil someone who wrote a Java compiler that did allow pointer manipulation or low-level system calls. By deferring memory mapping to runtime, Java prevents hackers from forging data structures. The absence of pointers makes it impossible to peek at restricted addresses. The interpreter also keeps track of the origin of every piece of code that it runs. It always loads the classes that are built in to the Java environment from the local machine (which *do* contain system calls). This means that a hacked, dangerous version from the Internet will never get the chance to masquerade as the built-in class.

Together, these features should reassure system administrators that the Java environment is **secure**, and that they can go ahead and install it on their systems.

For the software developer, interpreted bytecode has advantages that could only be dreamed about until now. The first advantage is that you only have to develop one version of your program! Think: no more porting efforts between PC and Mac. No more variations to take advantage of the architecture of different processors. Your programs will even run on Unix, which you might not have considered before. Once again, Java helps you concentrate on your application without wasting time on details of platform porting.

And the end user's days of waiting for the latest-and-greatest to be ported to his or her platform are over. Only the Java runtime system itself needs to be ported to the user's system. Once it's equipped with Java, any Java app is ready for the clicking.

For a local network administrator, especially if the network connects a variety of machines, Java could form the basis of a new applications server. If every machine on your network can run the Java interpreter, you only need to administer a single library of applications. No need to maintain parallel application directory structures for each platform on your network.

No matter where you are located on the continuum of software development and use, Java's **architecture-neutral** interpreted bytecodes are a boon.

Another one of the drawbacks of C++ as the language for a network environment is its inconsistency. For example, the memory occupied by short, integer, and long variables is implementation dependent in C++. As a consequence, the range of permissible values in each of these data types varies between platforms. For a multi-platform application, this inconsistency is unacceptable. Data types must have unambiguous meanings independent of the architecture where they are implemented. The Java Virtual Machine specification provides just such consistency. The range of values in Java data types are controlled by the JVM, and the Java interpreter worries about memory allocation on any given platform.

When it comes to user-interface design and window management, the variation among PCs, Macs, and Unix machines is even more confusing. The Java environment relieves the developer of having to concern himself with any of these details. Java has its own windowing interfaces that provide development tools for creating user interfaces. The developer only has to ensure that his or her GUIs will work on the JVM, and Java will make sure that they are properly implemented on real machines.

The architecture neutrality of Java bytecode thus extends considerably beyond machine code translation. It includes all aspects of software that must be examined and rewritten during a software port. By standardizing data types and windowing, and leaving their implementation to the interpreter, Java makes your applications truly **portable**.

By now you may be thinking that an interpreted environment, with linking, memory-mapping, and type-checking deferred to runtime, and automatic garbage collection to boot, must run like a snail. You may have memories of laid-back BASIC and REXX interpreters. You can forget about them. While it is true that a compiled executable will run faster than interpreted bytecode, the difference is smaller than you may think. The Java interpreter includes a number of features that narrow the performance gap between compiled and interpreted code.

The most basic of these is the bytecode itself. Bytecode was designed to be as close as possible to machine code, so translation is surprisingly simple, efficient, and quick. Another performance booster is the fact that garbage collection and other housekeeping tasks run as separate threads from the application itself. Unless you run out of unallocated memory, Java waits for free CPU cycles to do its garbage collection, and you needn't feel any effect.

There is a performance penalty to be paid as each new class is loaded and verified, and as method invocations pass type-checking. But classes are generally small, and type-checking is quick. Most of the time you won't feel much difference between a Java application and an equivalent C++ program. The designers of Java have done their best to ensure the **high performance** of the Java environment.

In the Java system, multiple processes (known as *threads*) execute simultaneously with Java itself apportioning system resources to each of these threads. Java was written to take advantage of the pre-emptive, **multithreaded** capabilities of the modern operating systems on which it's been implemented. Preemptive here means that the various threads don't share an equal claim on the CPU's attention but rather are prioritized. A high-priority task can hog the CPU, relinquishing it only when it's ready to pause, for example while waiting for data from an I/O device. The high-priority task is said to *pre-empt* competing tasks. This allows low-priority tasks, such as garbage collection, to run in the background, waiting for available CPU cycles in order to do their work.

Java doesn't restrict its multithreadedness to system tasks. It also provides the developer with synchronization primitives to simplify explicit thread management. This facilitates the development of applications that model real-world behavior. For example, a program may simulate a physics experiment where multiple processes affecting the progress of the experiment occur simultaneously and interact with each other.

As we've seen, Java's multithreaded capabilities enhance both the system and applications sides of the Java environment.

We've described how Java's practice of dynamic linking, as we've mentioned a couple of times, allows applications to work on an ongoing basis with the latest releases of their underlying classes. It also allows a more flexible use of classes than is possible in C++. For example, you can dynamically populate a string variable with the name of a class, and then create an object of that class type. The dynamic linker will look for that class's description and load it.

Java has several other features that facilitate flexible (but robust) class usage. One is the Java interface. In the Java language, an interface is a collection of method specifications with no implementations. For example, you may have an application with several kinds of objects whose color is relevant. These objects need methods for examining an object's color and changing it under certain circumstances. In C++, the solution would probably be to create a class called Color, which would define how an object's color would be represented, and how it could be manipulated. The Color class would be defined as an additional superclass of all those classes for which color is relevant. That is, all these objects would now have two superclasses, their appropriate superclass, plus Color. This practice is known as multiple inheritance. It is the source of much confusion and fragility in programs that use it. Confusion because it opens up the possibility of conflict among inherited variable and method names; and fragility because the dependency on memory representation of superclasses grows exponentially as multiple superclasses are introduced.

Java eliminated multiple inheritance. Instead, Color would be declared as an interface, which would be implemented by any class whose color is relevant. This enforces discipline in color management among all classes in an application, without introducing variable or method name confusion. In fact, it promotes clarity, because any class wishing to query or modify another class' color knows the protocol for doing so, without having to take the other class' type into consideration. No fragility is introduced either, because an interface has no instance variables or any other data structure that could break the class that implements it. Thanks to interfaces, we see clarity in place of confusion, stability in place of fragility.

In C++, classes can masquerade as each other through a technique known as *casting*. Casting instructs the compiler to treat an object of one class as if it were an instance of a different class. The C++ compiler allows the programmer to do this, shrugging its shoulders and assuming that she knows what she's doing. This masquerading is a potent source of errors, as is the fact that in C++ there's no facility for asking an object, "Who are you, really, underneath the cast?" Java handles both of these points differently. In Java, there are strict rules for casting that make it harder for a class to dress up as a different class in a way that will prove disastrous. On the other hand, Java has a command for querying the true identity of a class, which facilitates writing generalized routines that accept a superclass as an argument and then decide on appropriate processing by asking, "Which child are you?"

Java's linking practices, combined with its flexible but strict class usage, make it **dynamic** enough to function reliably in an evolving environment.

As we've seen, the catchy terms in the white paper definition actually have meaning. Together they describe a language and an operating environment that should help the Internet take its next major step forward. But how can you, the prospective Java developer, start living in this wondrous new world? Why, though the JDK, of course.

WHAT IS THE JDK?

When you downloaded Java, you probably noticed the files were referred to as the Java Developer's Kit, or JDK. The JDK defines the Java world you are about to enter. It includes all the class libraries and tools you need to start creating and running Java programs. Let's take a tour of the facilities offered by the JDK, starting with its class libraries.

Along with the Java language itself, the JDK gives you the basic class libraries that implement the general data types and services you are likely to need as you start to program in Java. Again, we see how Java frees programmers to concentrate on what is special about their application without having to design a hash table implementation or write a routine to inspect the contents of a character array. The presence of the JDK class libraries on your system comes in handy at runtime as well. As we've seen, an applet (Internet application) that arrives over the Net and starts running on your machine will load the classes it needs dynamically. It will look for those classes on your (i.e. the client) machine first, and only if it fails to find them there will it reach back over the Net to look for them on the host it came from. Because any applet is likely to make use of the JDK classes, their presence on the client system results in speedy loading and minimal disruption to execution. What a clever environment. Table 1.1 contains a list of the JDK class libraries and a general description of the services they provide.

I will be your guide to **lang**, where the nuts and bolts of the Java language are defined. There you'll see that Java itself is a small, simple language. Its interactions with your file system and operating system are implemented in the **io** library, so we'll go there next. There you'll learn how to think of files and your system as objects, and how to access their services in an object-oriented environment.

Neil will be your main instructor for graphic interface layout. He'll take you through the buttons, menus, and text areas of the awt library and help you to combine them effectively.

Table 1.1 *The Java Developer's Kit Class Libraries*

Package	Content
applet	defines the superclass for all applets (Internet applications)
awt	"Abstract Windowing Toolkit" provides windowing and GUI services
io	provides IO and operating system services
lang	defines the basic elements of the Java language, plus objects for wrapping up basic elements with their most commonly needed services
net	provides Internet and communications services
util	provides utilities for commonly needed data structures and services such as hash tables, stacks, etc.

Alex will connect you to the **net**, reviewing the Internet services offered in that class library and the applet prototype class in **applet**. He will also reveal the intricacies of Java multithreading services, which are defined in **lang**. We'll all dip into **util** from time to time.

The second component of the JDK is a set of tools for compiling and running Java applets and standalone applications. Actually, the JDK gives you even more than this. There are also tools for debugging programs, generating documentation, and analyzing Java programs. Table 1.2 lists the JDK tools and their purposes.

These tools are all you need to function in the Java environment. In this book, we'll teach you how to use them.

We will spend a lot of time on the Java compiler. It has many options, some of them are extremely useful. I won't simply list the options and what they are supposed to do. I will let you benefit from my many hours of sometimes frustrating experience trying to use them. This may be the biggest favor the three of us can do for you. We want to share our enthusiasm for the Java language and environment, but we also want to share our real experiences with you. Our experience can save you time and make sure your involvement with Java is rewarding.

We will also discuss the Java interpreter and appletviewer. You will use these tools constantly, and although they are simple to use, there are a few pointers that will help you. The Java documentation generator is one of the unifiers of the Java community. By standardizing the format of Java documentation, javadoc will help to quickly keep Java APIs comprehensible to prospective users. This will help weave together the members of the Web community.

Table 1.2   *The Java Developer's Kit Tools*

Tool	Purpose
appletviewer	runs applets on your machine outside the context of a Web browser
java	Java interpreter: interprets and executes bytecodes
javac	Java compiler: compiles source files into bytecodes
javadoc	generates API documentation from Java source files
javah	generates C-language header and source files to connect Java programs with native compiled C code.
javap	disassembles compiled byte code into its component variables and methods
jdb	Java debugger: a dbx-like interactive debugger

Sadly, the Java debugger is still in an alpha state. I will discuss the debugger and give you some pointers on getting it running. I'll also describe how to use some features that will work in a future release. But it sure would have been great to have it working now.

Native methods (linking compiled C code into Java applications) have received a great deal of attention in the Java newsgroups. Native methods present special problems to the Java philosophy and a special challenge to security. The javah tool will be examined in the context of a mostly philosophical discussion of these issues.

We've had a look at the main features of the Java language, its development tools, and the Java Virtual Machine. We've talked in general terms about the features of the Java environment which make it suitable for Internet programming. But in practical terms, what should we expect from Java?

THE STATE OF THE APPLET WORLD: A TOUR

Expect to be amazed! The quality and creative content packed into many Java applets already circulating around the Web is remarkable. With only limited documentation available—until books like this came along—it couldn't have been easy for the applet authors to figure out Java, but they did it with panache. Some of these applets are literally works of art. I can only imagine what kind of applets will be zipping through cyberspace once suitable documentation and mature development environments are commonplace.

The emergence of Java crystallized an idea about the Net that I think few appreciate. Java could not have become lodged in the hearts and minds of so many so quickly if not for the Internet. Java aside for a moment, I really believe that the rate of technological development will hit hyperwarp as all time lag of distribution is eliminated. The world is only as far away as your computer. Oh, the future's so bright!

Java's rise has been meteoric. But was it really any surprise? After all, the ingredients for the explosion were there from the start, as I mentioned earlier. Remember, Java only made its debut—in an alpha state no less—in May 1995. It didn't take long for the alluring scent wafting through cyberspace at the speed of light to arouse the interest of more than a few. Maybe you too sensed it from the first time you set eyes on it. Java wasn't just another half-baked prototype posing as some kind of breakthrough technology. It was the real thing. Now that Java has finally reached version 1.0—post-beta—get ready to feel the reverberations. Java's going to shape the world of computers in the months to come.

I first encountered Java during the summer of 1995. And the past few months have be a whirlwind dance with it. Along the way I've come across some examples of Java applets that will get you really excited if you're not already. I've seen the future and these applets are a taste of it. What I've done in this section is selected a small number of Java applets that are exemplary in one way or another. Each represents a separate category. Of course, I've included the URL so you can check them out for yourself. Java is all about participation don't ya know? Screen shots are in there, too. These applets are my favorites so you'll have to excuse me if I can't help gushing about them as I give you the play-by-plays.

Art

Who said you're either born with artist talent or you're not? It's simply not true. At least not if you use this Java applet. You too will be creating some inspired works in no time.

The hyper-creative gang at Silicon Graphics Inc. are already well-known as masters of the digital graphics age. As soon as Java moved into their sights, they picked it up and started producing some stunning applets. Head to

```
http://reality.sgi.com/employees/paul_asd/impression/imppaint.html
```

to access this applet.

The one that stands out among the field of excellent applets is called The Impressionist. The names actually refer to you as you'll soon see! Check out Figure 1.1.

You start simply enough by choosing one of several small thumbprint images along the top of the screen. Some you might recognize, even though they're only about as tall as your cursor. But that's not the point. Actually, it's better if you don't even know what's in the picture. It's for you to find out creatively.

Your job is to give expression to the image. See, nothing visible happens after you pick your picture but it's hiding there nevertheless. The next step is to create a brush to use. You've got full control over size and shape. That done, just start painting. Note you can always go back and pick a different brush so don't get hung up on trying to choose the perfect one.

Figure 1.1 *The Impressionist applet from Silicon Graphics.*

Gradually the masterpiece emerges. But what about the color? Note that you didn't even pick the color of the brush. Ah, there's a catch. The color that appears on the canvas is the color that would appear on that exact part of that underlying image you selected earlier.

No, you won't end up just redrawing that original image either. The blotches of color that get laid down on the canvas depend on your brush and that you chose yourself. So, if you are inspired by the works of Seurat you can reveal the image with a dotted brush. If Monet's works are more to your liking, grab some other shaped brush and start slapping away at the canvas.

I encourage you to access the site and try it for yourself. It's an awful lot of fun—and you don't have to tell anybody that there was a famous picture under there to begin with.

Business

I just knew I should have sunk my life savings into Sun Microsystems Inc. the day I first saw Java. But I didn't. Oh, I can just hear you savvy investors laughing at me. Now, I've been forced to earn my living by the honest sweat of my brow that falls and short-circuits my keyboard.

So what are you going to do with the million bucks you're going to make writing Java applets? The Stock Market would be an excellent place to sock it away. If you're smart, as I'm sure you are, you'll try tracking your portfolio with a powerful Java applet from BulletProof. It's called WallStreetWeb, and it's the first in a wave of advanced business and finance Java applets that are about to appear. This service was free for a time but now you've got to ante up some coin each month to get the goods. It's an example of a real client/ server, if that means anything to you. What makes it so special is that, unlike an applet like The Impressionist, this applet communicates with home base. All the data that you want to graph has to come from somewhere, right? What happens is that you can make ticker selections and get interactive charts displayed on the fly with real data. The applet—which is the service client transmits your requests back to a database at BulletProof. There, another application—the server—grabs the data you'll need, packages it up, and bangs it back to you. Your client applet takes the data and generates all the colorful graphs you could imagine. That's the benefit of client/server. The graphing processing is performed by the applet. Alternative systems would have required the server to send not data but prepared graphs. Java really makes it easy as you'll see in the Java Internet chapter coming later in the book.

Go ahead, see how Sun Microsystems Inc. has been doing lately, I'll look away. Feast your eyes on Figure 1.2.

WallStreetWeb is a little different from some of the other Web applets you'll meet. It demonstrates how instead of always being integrated into an HTML page, a Java applet can be written to live in its own new window which has all the properties of any other window. You can resize it, close it, move it, whatever. This was a necessary design decision for WallStreetWeb because their service is accessed via several different applets. Java makes a way for them all to be in their own windows. You can then organize your screen layout according to your whims.

The WallStreetWeb interface is one of the best in any category. The design is elegant and functional. It makes excellent use of the screen real estate. You have a single column of fields and a scrollable area. The fields all have handy

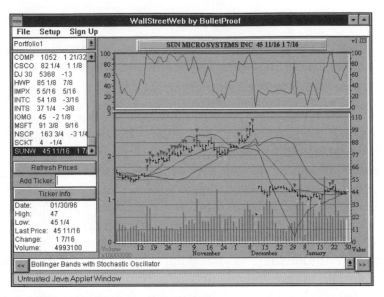

Figure 1.2   *WallStreetWeb tracks Sun's financial progress.*

little drop-down combo boxes with lists of choices. The right side of the applet is dominated by a graphing area. The graphs that appear are very professional looking and make excellent use of different colors. All in all, WallStreetWeb is one of the most attractive applets you'll meet. You'll find it at:

```
http://www.bulletproof.com/WallStreetWeb
```

Education

Don't you just wish you were back in school now. The kids these days won't believe you if you tell them about the hard old days when it was just you, a pen, and a piece of paper. Many people are starting to realize the pedagogical potential of Java applets. Figure 1.3 illustrates just one such initiative taken recently to harness Java for the presentation of teaching material.

Michael McCool and the gang at The University of Waterloo in Canada have been busy prototyping an exciting new concept in multimedia teaching using Java. The result is called MetaMedia. You can access their homepage at:

```
http://www.meta.cgl.uwaterloo.ca
```

The goal of the project is to develop a flexible media tool that can easily adapt to different arbitrary media. That's what they call structured networked ex-

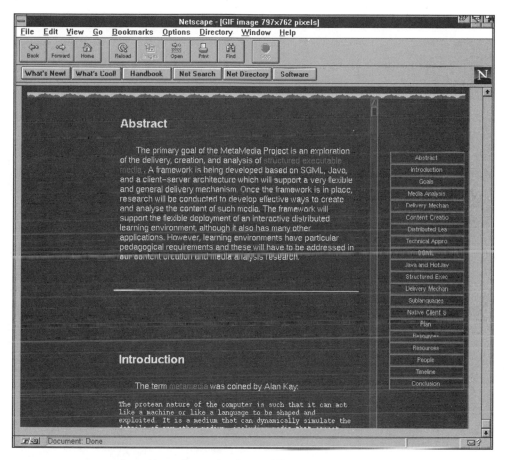

Figure 1.3 *MetaMedia is designed to easily adapt to different arbitrary media.*

ecutable media. Java is enabling them to build a tool that will support collaboration, multimedia, symbolic mathematics, computer graphics, and other specialized forms of computation.

Homepages

The granddaddies of Rock and Roll have a hit with their new Web homepage. Premier showmen as always, The Rolling Stones were exceptionally quick to integrate Java into their Web presence. It's one of those sites you've just got to visit to experience. Unfortunately, you'll need to use Sun's HotJava rather than Netscape. You'll be entertained with show-stopping animation, clever games, nifty puzzles, sounds, and images. There's a whole lot packed into it. You'll actually be running several different applets at once. The combination makes for one helluva slick homepage. Rock on in Figure 1.4.

If you didn't guess it already, The Stones have their homepage at:

http://www.stones.com

Fun and Games

You thought the Web was distracting already? Get ready for an explosion of all kinds of Internet-based Java Web games. One of the rockets that is propelling Java to such heights is its handy built-in toolkit of software components. The toolkit contains a wealth of code you can practically just plug together to create your own game applets. It's got everything for programming graphics all the way to programming for the Internet and tons in between. The details are what this book is all about so get ready to face the challenge in chapters to come.

The applet I've chosen to highlight is strictly single-player. But that's just the nature of this outstanding game. Other games you're likely to see soon will

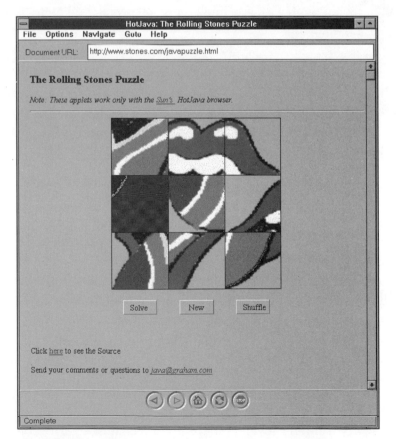

Figure 1.4   *The Rolling Stones homepage provides lots of fun for aging rockers.*

enable multiple players to test their wits against each other in cyberspace. Sure, you've seen a few other notable games that do that already. But do you realize that it's really within your reach with Java today?

You've seen already how The Rolling Stones homepage jumped up and down and shouted *Try me!* It was Irresistible! Fun and games often serve a valuable purpose. Even commercial applets need to have some degree of playfulness to be enticing. The same magic that makes a well-designed game successful needs to find its way into your more mundane applets, too. Despite being some of the toughest code to write, if you mix a smile or two into your applet brews they'll be tastier than ever.

DISCLAIMER: The authors of this book cannot be held responsible for any job losses, marriage breakups, or course failures that result from becoming addicted to the Java applet introduced in this section. Blame Viacom NewMedia instead. Zoop is the name. Maddeningly addictive fun is the game.

Zoop is a phenomenon. The ambitious marketers at Viacom NewMedia have unleashed upon the unsuspecting masses a game that has a place already reserved in the pantheon of legendarily addictive games. First, you were kid-napped by Pac-Man but you escaped. Perhaps more recently, your life has consisted of perfecting your ability to juggle a rain of colored blocks. Don't drop the counseling sessions because you'll need them for Zoop. Check out the gameboard in Figure 1.5.

You're all alone on an island, and you're under attack from all sides. Start blasting away. Careful though because, as you'll soon find out, indiscriminate fire may as well be directed at your own foot. Sorry, but I'm not going to explain anymore. You're just going to have to visit the site. If you dare, punch

http://www.zoop.com

into Netscape and say good-bye to the rest of the world for a few weeks. I hope you have pre-arranged checking and an understanding boss.

The Cutting Edge

We're exploring the outer reaches of Java endeavor with this applet. It's innocent enough, but that simplicity belies the revolution that it represents.

The applet consists of two clocks on your screen. Both are ticking away. And unless you've just been privy by some remarkable coincidence, they'll display

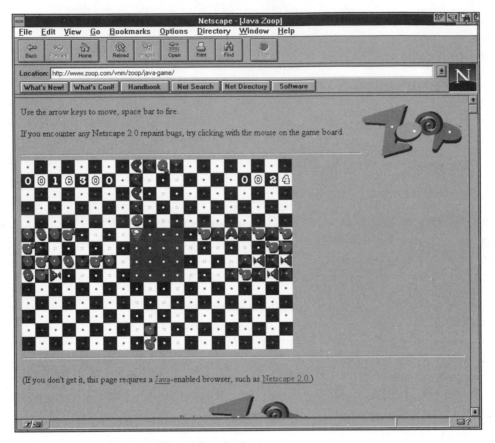

Figure 1.5 *Zoop may be the demise of mankind.*

different times. The top clock is one you should recognize. Just look at your watch. The second clock will bear a significance to readers with friends or family in Japan. You no longer have to incur those excruciatingly expensive phone calls to the Tokyo Time Service. You've got it right on your screen. You can have it by accessing:

```
http://ring.etl.go.jp/openlab/horb
```

Maybe you're thinking that this is no big deal. That might be true unless you appreciate the fact that each second a message is being transmitted across the Internet to the applet running in your browser. That message contains the time information for Japan. Wow! Tell me that's not amazing! Here it is in Figure 1.6.

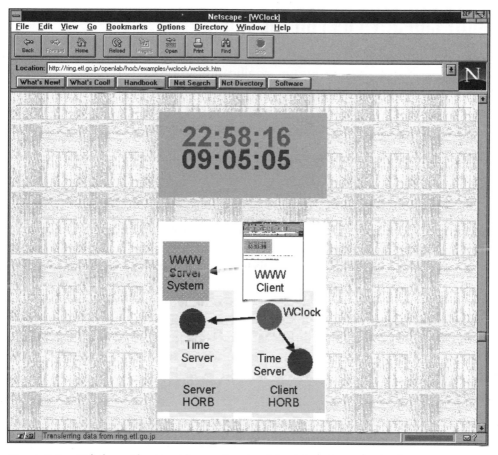

Figure 1.6   *Wclock provides you with up-to-the-second time information—local and Japanese.*

Where's This All Heading?

Remember that as innovative as these applets are, they just begin to scratch the surface of what's possible with Java. The first Java applets all seemed to feature dancing text or something similarly obscure. But even to see something simple, like text moving around on a browser once populated solely by immobile text and images, has a serious *WOW* factor.

The applets profiled in this section are certainly not trivial. They're still relatively simple and prototypical. Java is just now getting out of diapers, but the toddler will run sooner than you can imagine. Serious, hardcore applet development has already started in earnest in shops all over the world. The trickle of applets has become a flow. The flow will become a tidal wave that crashes down upon the status quo that has existed for so long.

WHAT CAN JAVA DO FOR THE WORLD?

At the beginning of this chapter, I outlined a number of scenarios that describe a world of software usage significantly improved from today's. Now that we have some grounding in the Java philosophy, let's review those scenarios, highlighting those elements that are already real and expanding on how Java can help to make the other elements a reality.

The applets available today have not yet reached the stage of an industrial-strength, general-purpose program, such as word processors or graphics packages. But that day is approaching. When it arrives, you will no longer need the 50 MB or more of disk space that some of these applications require. You will also not need all the memory demanded by the latest feature-burdened version of your word processor, if you use it mostly for typing memos. Instead of paying hundreds of dollars to purchase office suites, you will rent the programs you need. These programs will double as word processors and taxi meters, reporting the length of your session to the home office when you are done using them. In a truly refined world, they would even track which features you used, charging an extra penny or two for math equation parsers and other esoteric goodies. Java's dynamic linking and object-oriented architecture will help to make this kind of accounting possible.

How likely is this scenario? Well, Sun, Oracle, and other companies are working on inexpensive "Internet devices," Java-powered computers with little disk space, and high-speed communications capabilities, optimized to work almost exclusively in a "rent-an-app" world. Of all the possibilities suggested by Java, this could be the most revolutionary for the software business.

Eye-catching animations to enhance your home page are already a reality, and in a couple of pages I'll show you just how easy it is to add them. The 3D medical demo is a little ways off, but the folks at Sun, Silicon Graphics, and Netscape are cooperating to bring it about.

Java already has a facility for bundling data together with programs for interpreting the data. These programs are known as "content handlers," and they are launched transparently when an applet is told to read a file of the type recognized by the content handler. By transparently, I mean that the user doesn't need to take any special action to trigger the program; it is done automatically when he asks for the file. We will teach you how to write content handlers and attach them to your files. As for single-version software development, by now you know that it is at the very heart of Java. The Java interpreter will be ported to the Mac soon, and IBM and others are working on other platforms. The day is very close when your programs will work on most machines connected to the Net. That takes care of distribution. Billing still has to be worked out.

As for self-updating software, it's already possible. A good candidate for self-renewal would be the Java interpreter itself. It could be built to run a background thread that would pull down the latest version the first time the interpreter is run after a new release.

WHAT'S IN THIS BOOK?

We've had a lovely chat. So far we've discussed Java's potential to shift the paradigm of software usage and software economics. We've discussed the qualities that make Java ideally suited to Internet programming. We've had a history lesson. And we've poked around the Web to see what other people have already done in Java. Now it's time to do something ourselves.

This book now makes a decided turn for the practical. Chapter 2 shows how you can start using Java to liven up your home page right away, *without having to program a single line of code!* After that, the tutorial in Chapter 3 will teach you to program applications in the Java language, and how to use the tools in the Java Developer's Kit to get your creation up and running.

Chapters 4 and 5 go deeper into the details of the Java language. Chapter 4 explains the Java approach to the features common to all programming languages: data representation and logic flow control. It also explores the object-oriented side of the Java language: classes, objects, and methods. Chapter 5 continues with an explanation of Java's special facilities for handling exceptions, also known as "Things That Go Wrong." Java's coping mechanisms are intricate enough to merit a chapter of their own!

In Chapter 6, we return briefly to the theoretical plain. There, Alex will give you a crash course in object-oriented software development (usually referred to as OOP). This short chapter is the background you need to take advantage of the power of Java.

Much of that power is demonstrated by the Java Developer's Kit. The next four chapters show you how to harness that power. Chapter 7 concentrates on string manipulation and other data-related services offered by the JDK. Chapter 8 introduces file I/O, Java-style. Chapter 9 will familiarize you with the JDK's ready-made data structures. And Chapter 10 will help you manage time, at least in your programs!

Chapter 11 combines many of the techniques you've learned to create a sophisticated Java program. And a useful one, too. You'll leave this chapter with knowledge in your head and a handy utility on your hard drive.

And now the moment you've all been waiting for: graphics. The tutorial in Chapter 12 will guide you through the process of creating your own Java applet. Put this on your home page refrigerator so your mother can admire it.

The tutorial was nice, but when do *you* get to be creative? Right now. The next seven chapters give you the raw materials for creating your own masterpiece. Chapter 13 is another tutorial. It will introduce you to the JavaUser Interface. It may be fingerpainting, but every artist has to start somewhere. Chapter 14 examines the graphical components of the JDK and how to combine them. Chapter 15 helps you decorate your work with color, drawings, and fonts.

In Chapter 16, you'll become interactive by learning to respond to the mouse and keyboard. Chapter 17 adds the "multi" to the "media" when it shows you how to give your creation motion and sound. Chapter 18 gives some guidelines on layout, so you can display your creations to their best advantage. Chapter 19 explains how to soup up the JDK's basic graphical components by creating your own.

Chapter 20 reveals the secrets of multithreading. This is one of the most intricate and error-prone areas of Java programming. We can make it easier, so you'll want to pay close attention.

Chapter 21 may be the reason you bought this book. It breaks out of your machine to teach you how to program the Internet. URLs, client/server communications, the works. This chapter will help you realize the Java vision.

If you have hand-crafted C-code libraries left over from a previous life, and you'd like to use them in your Java apps, Chapter 22 is for you. There we teach you how to call native methods from Java.

We flesh out the book with three appendices on supplementary topics. Appendix A details the differences between the Java language and C++. Appendix B tells you where to get Java, and where to find more Java resources (just in case this book isn't absolutely enough). Appendix C explains how to use the CD-ROM that comes with this book.

These topics are all you need to launch your Java career. Have fun, and get ready to enjoy the programming world's most refreshing new taste in years.

Spicing Up Your Home Page

Steve Simkin

For some readers, this little chapter ("*chaplet*"?) will be all the Java you need. Once you've read these few pages, you'll know how to liven up your home page with any applet on the Net.

Start using Java now without writing a line of code! Ride on the shoulders of the Java giants by sprinkling existing applets onto your home page. If you weren't a cool dude before, you are now!

HTML

HTML stands for "HyperText Markup Language." It is used to write pages on the Web. The language is made up of a combination of content and *tags*. The tags consist of matched pairs of instructions to your Web browser, enclosed in angle brackets. These instructions tell your browser how to format the content they enclose. For example, **<h1>Welcome to my home page!</h1>** tells your browser to present the "Welcome" greeting as a big bold heading. As in this example, the closing tag always consists of the opening tag preceded by a slash.

 **Just Enough HTML...**

This chapter teaches you just enough HTML for you to incorporate Java applets into your Web pages. If you need a more complete tutorial about how to write Web pages with HTML, see the *Netscape & HTML EXplorer* by Urban A. LeJeune and Jeff Duntemann (Coriolis Group Books, 1995).

HTML is made up of a standard set of tags, which are understood by every browser. In addition, browsers such as HotJava and Netscape Navigator version 2.0 recognize an *applet* tag, which means—you guessed it—"Put an applet here, please." You can use the applet tag to embed any applet into your home page in just minutes.

 **What If I Don't Have a Home Page?**

If you don't have a home page, you can still use the techniques in this chapter. Just use the Open File option of your browser's File menu item to open the HTML files you create.

GETTING STARTED: THE APPLET TAG

One of the demo applets that comes with the JDK is called "NervousText." NervousText puts whatever text you pass it into your home page, in big block letters that jump around, well, *nervously*—threatening to jumble their order. You can use it to put a little energy into the main topic of your page, or to make your signature more eye-catching. Or just to let off steam, as shown in Figure 2.1.

The screen capture doesn't do justice to the full frantic effect of this applet, so try jiggling the book around for a few seconds. To add NervousText to your home page, just copy the NervousText.class file from the java/demo/NervousText directory in your JDK installation to the directory where your HTML file is. The page in the screen capture is described in the HTML file shown in Listing 2.1.

Listing 2.1 HTML File with NervousText

```
<title> Steve's Nervous Home Page </title>
<h1> Boy, am I </h1>
<applet code="NervousText"width=200 height=50>
<param name=text value="Nervous!">
</applet>
```

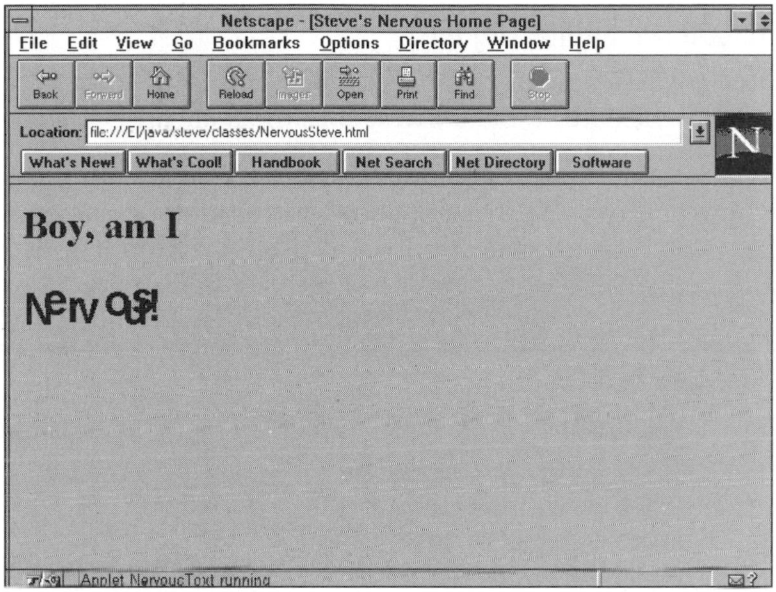

Figure 2.1   The NervousText applet.

Let's look more closely at how your Web browser interprets this file. The **applet** HTML tag instructs your Web browser to launch an applet, and the **code** argument gives the browser the name of a compiled Java file that defines the applet. **width** and **height** specify the dimensions of the rectangle on the home page where the applet will be displayed.

After the **applet** tag comes a line starting with **<param**. The **param** tag is a special tag containing information that is used by the applet, not by your browser. Each piece of information that your HTML page makes available to the applet is called a *parameter*. Since an applet can accept several pieces of information, each one has both a *name* and a *value*. As you can see in Listing 2.1, the parameter's name and value are indicated by the words **name=text** and **value="Nervous!"**, which are enclosed in angle brackets together with the **param** tag.

Every applet has its own set of parameters. If the applet's creator was considerate, you will find documentation along with the applet. If not, you can see how other pages use the applet by using the Document Source option of the View menu item in Netscape. This option displays the page's HTML code. At least you'll know what parameters somebody else gave to the applet.

What Else Can the Applet Tag Do?

The **applet** tag has several options to make applet placement on your Web page more flexible. Table 2.1 describes them all, and indicates which are required.

Let's see how you can use these options to liven up your home page. In Listing 2.2, I used the **align=left** option to place the **UnderConstruction** applet (also in the JDK) on the left side of my new home page.

Table 2.1   *The Applet Tag Options*

Option	Description	Required/Optional
code	The name of the file containing the applet. This will usually be the applet name with ".class" on the end. If you use the codebase option, the code filename will be relative to the value of codebase. Otherwise, it will be relative to the directory where the HTML file is located.	required
width	Initial width of the applet in pixels.	required
height	Initial height of the applet in pixels.	required
codebase	The base Internet address (URL) of the applet. You can omit this if the applet's address is the same as that of the HTML page that specified the applet. Your can use this option to embed an applet from anywhere on the Internet into your home page!	optional
alt	Alternate text that will be displayed by text-only browsers.	optional
name	Symbolic name of the applet. This name can be used by other applets on the same HTML page.	optional
align	The alignment of the applet. The following values are valid: left, right, top, texttop, middle, absmiddle, baseline, bottom, absbottom.	optional
vspace	The vertical space around the applet. This option is only valid when align is set to left or right.	optional
hspace	The horizontal space around the applet. This option is only valid when align is set to left or right.	optional

Listing 2.2   An HTML File That Uses the align Option

```
<title>Steve's Bumpy Home Page</title>
I was so nervous after that last home page that I thought I'd better drive home.
But the winters in Toronto are so brutal that
<applet code="JackhammerDuke.class"width=300 height=100 align=left>
<p>To see Duke at work, get a Java-enabled browser<p>
</applet>
the highway was full of potholes. They sent an emergency repair
team to fix the road, but still I bumped and I bumped and I bumped and I bumped
and I bumped and I bumped and I bumped and I bumped and I bumped and I bumped
and I bumped and I bumped and I bumped and I bumped and I bumped and I bumped
and I bumped and I bumped and I bumped and I bumped and I bumped and I bumped
and I bumped and I bumped and I bumped and I bumped and I bumped and I bumped
and I bumped and I bumped and I bumped and I bumped and I bumped and I bumped
all the way around the applet.
<p>
<a href="JackhammerDuke.java">The source </a>
```

I entered all that bumpy text to demonstrate a byproduct of the **align** option. It allows text to flow around the applet, giving a sense of continuity to the page, as you can see in Figure 2.2.

I made use of one other feature of the **applet** tag. Any standard HTML content enclosed within the **applet** tag is ignored by Java. But it will be picked

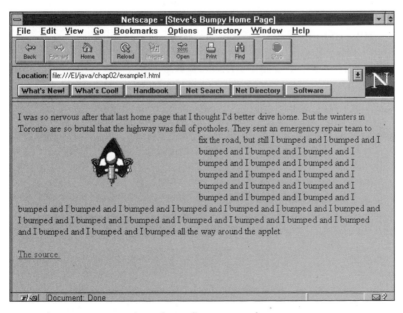

Figure 2.2   *UnderConstruction applet with text flowing around.*

up by any non-Java-enabled browser, which doesn't recognize the **applet** tag. In other words, old browsers will display this content because they don't know any better! This is a good place to insert abusive messages for anyone still using a Stone Age browser.

As a mark of my good manners, I added a link to the applet's source code at the end of the page. The Java community is a cooperative one, and many applet creators are happy to share their techniques.

WHERE CAN I GET SOME?

Of course, you're not restricted to the applets that came with the JDK. Here are two places to look for the coolest and greatest.

JARS

The Java Applet Rating Service (JARS) is dedicated to searching out the finest applets on the Web. JARS ranks applets, so you can hop straight to the top 1percent. They also have an "Applet Bank." Go ahead and make a few withdrawals. And before I forget, Neil asked me to mention that he's on the JARS panel of judges. Nevertheless, their taste is pretty good. You can connect with JARS at **http://www.surinam.net/java/jars**.

Gamelan is another great source of Java treasures. Gamelan can keep you up to date about Java developments—news, programming tools, and, of course, applets. Gamelan's address is **http://www.gamelan.com**.

Take a few hours to Java-surf. When you're done, think about what you've seen. What did you like? Why did you like it? Have you already pointed to it from your home page? If you're like me, surveying other people's work has given you a few ideas about what you might do yourself—if only you knew how.

Which is where we come in, of course. Starting with Chapter 3, you'll be learning to brew it yourself. Have a good time. I look forward to pilfering some of your ideas from the global applet bank (a.k.a. the Internet).

A Java Programming Tutorial

Steve Simkin

We start learning to program with a simple, bare-bones, no-nonsense program. We take it apart, look at it from all angles, and put it back together so it runs smoothly.

I remember the first time I stared at a page of Braille. On the table in front of me lay a brown piece of paper, covered with rows of raised dots. Some of the dots were alone or in pairs, some seemed bunched or clumped into larger groups. There were a few off by themselves in the corner of the page. But mostly it was row after row, with no pattern I could detect. When I ran my fingers over them, the situation seemed even more hopeless. How could a human finger tip ever distinguish among all those dots? How would my daughter Haya, who is blind, ever know how many dots she was feeling, or whether a pair of dots slanted this way or that? For that matter, how would I ever make sense of it all, even inspecting the dots visually?

Haya's teacher showed us that Braille is composed of a grid, two columns wide by three rows tall. There is a basic progression in the use of the top two rows, which recurs three times, with slight variations, over the course of the alphabet, varying the second and third time by the addition of dots from the bottom row. My wife and I dutifully learned the alphabet and came back to class the next week, thinking we had learned Braille. That's when the teacher hit us with contractions. You see, reading Braille is a very slow process, and to speed it up, Braille users have developed an extensive set of contractions for common combinations of letters. "Sh" is a single letter in Braille, for example, as are "ed" and "ing." So home we went, and we learned the contractions.

We came back the following week, thinking that this time we had learned Braille. And that's when we learned about abbreviations. It seems that to streamline the process even further, every letter of the alphabet is an abbreviation for a commonly used word. "B" means "but," "c" means "can." Even poor "x" didn't escape. An "x" by itself means "it" ("I" was already taken). The week after that, we learned how the letters "A" through "J" do double duty as digits when they are preceded by yet another character called the "number sign." And so on. All together, there are over 200 characters and meaningful pairs of characters in Braille in the English language! We haven't mastered them all, but we're functional.

I learned a couple of things from my Braille course. The most important was the Braille alphabet itself. It's great to be on Haya's wavelength when she asks me "What's dot-5-W?" and I can toss back, "Work." But beyond learning the material, I learned the importance of presentation. My wife and I could easily have drowned in a sea of detail without the careful structuring that Haya's teacher gave to the material.

That kind of structuring is the goal of this chapter. I don't know what kind of programming background you are bringing to our book. You might be an ace C++ programmer ready to swallow Java whole and publish the next killer applet. Or you might be a casual HTML writer who is looking to Java liven up your home page. Either way, it's our job to make Java accessible to you so that you can get on with achieving your programming goals.

This chapter will introduce you to Java programming. You'll learn to create Java programs and use the tools in the Java Developer's Kit (JDK) to run them. I'll also show you where to find complete documentation of everything the JDK has to offer. In addition you'll learn how to generate your own Web-ready documentation, plus a little bit about the interactive debugger that came with your Java installation.

All the source code for this chapter can be found on the CD-ROM in the directory\source\chap03.

FIRST STEPS: A SIMPLE JAVA PROGRAM

We programmers are a tradition-bound lot. For all the talk of the Java revolution, of a radically new software paradigm, of defining software economics afresh, there is no better entry into the world of Java than that old standby, HelloWorld. For the benefit of those of you who have never programmed before, I'll explain that HelloWorld is traditionally the first program programmers write when they learn a new language. Tradition also dictates that you type in (or "enter") HelloWorld by rote, copying it from a book and seeing it run, before you get an explanation of what it is you've done. So the first thing you need to do is get into a text editor (such as vi in Unix, the MS-DOS editor, or even Notepad in Windows) and enter the exact text that appears in Listing 3.1.

Listing 3.1   Minimal HelloWorld Program

```
class MinimalHelloWorld {

  public static void main( String args[] ) {

    System.out.println( "Hello, World!" );

  }
}
```

These five lines define an *entire* Java program. When you finish entering them (exactly!), save them in a file called MinimalHelloWorld.java. Remember which directory you saved it in. Then go to an operating system prompt (in Windows, this means double-clicking the "MS-DOS Command Prompt" icon in your Main program group). At the prompt, change directories to the directory where you saved the program. Your prompt should look something like:

```
cmd>
```

Do You Have to Use a Long File Name?

Java doesn't require you to use long filenames, however, Java is currently available only on systems that support long file names. If you have an older MS-DOS or Windows 3.x system, you'll probably have to upgrade if you want to use Java.

Compiling the Application

Now enter the following command by typing on the remainder of the line following the prompt, known as the *command line* (Remember to press Enter after each command):

```
cmd> javac MinimalHelloWorld.java
```

At this point, you might see a message that looks something like:

```
MinimalHelloWorld.java:3: Method printl(java.lang.String) not found in class
java.io.PrintStream.
    System.out.printl("Hello, World.");
                     ^
1 error
```

If so, congratulations! You just survived your very first Java *compiler error*. A *compiler* is a program that converts source code into instructions that the computer can understand, known as *machine instructions*. Javac is a compiler for Java source code. One of the first things it does when it reads a program is to ensure that the program's contents conform exactly to the rules of the Java language. After all, if the source code contains misspelled names or syntax errors, there's no way for the compiler to know exactly which machine instructions to generate. When it detects an error of this sort, javac displays messages designed to let you, the programmer, know the nature and location of the error. By and large, Java's compiler error messages are well written, and are meaningful even to inexperienced programmers.

After a compiler error, take a deep breath and count your blessings. You're still breathing, you're computer hasn't melted down, and no one has broadcast your Visa number all over the Internet. The error does mean, however, that you didn't copy MinimalHelloWorld.java *exactly* as it appears in Listing 3.1. Check your work, save the file again, and try that javac command again. Eventually, you should get your operating system prompt back with no messages. In this case, no news is definitely good news. It means that you successfully compiled your first Java program. Go treat yourself to a cappuccino. I'll wait here.

If, after several tries, you still get error messages, use the copy of MinimalHelloWorld.java that's included on the CD-ROM that comes with this book. There's no use wasting too much time overcoming typing errors. Plenty of time for that later!

What? You Didn't Install Java Yet?

I'm assuming that you have Java successfully installed, and that you've added the directory containing the Java tools to your path. If you haven't, and you know how to change your path, then do so now. The tools are in the java\bin directory wherever you chose to install the JDK. If you don't know how to change your path, or if you have any other problem getting things to work, please contact the nearest Java User Group (JUG). There may be a JUG in your city. If you can't find it, then you might try sending your question to the Java mailing list (java-interest@java.sun.com) or to the Toronto JUG (jug@solect.com). If you know how to use Internet newsgroups, you can post your question to the java newsgroup, which is called *comp.lang.java*.

Now that you have the prompt back, ask for a list of files in the directory (the **dir** command, if you're using DOS). In addition to MinimalHelloWorld.java, your response should include a file called MinimalHelloWorld.class.

You should recognize MinimalHelloWorld.java. After all, you just created it. But where did MinimalHelloWorld.class come from? The answer is that you just created it as well! Here's how: MinimalHelloWorld.java is what's known as a *source file*, which is a file made up of characters from the English alphabet, containing Java statements that you can enter using your keyboard. The contents of a source file, the stuff that you typed and saved, is called *source code*. Source code bears a vague resemblance to languages used by normal human beings. When you spend enough time with them, you become able to read them as comfortably as you would the morning paper. By that point, you will also bear only a vague resemblance to a normal human being. But I guess that's what you want, or you wouldn't be reading this book. So press on.

Running the Application

The javac program takes your source file, and converts your lovely code into truly unintelligible stuff. The proper name for this stuff is *bytecodes*. Bytecodes describe your program in a format unintelligible to you, but completely comprehensible to Java. The Java compiler puts the bytecodes it produces into files that end with *.class*, in this case MinimalHelloWorld.class. If you have a class file, you're ready to run your program! At your operating system prompt, enter:

```
cmd> java MinimalHelloWorld
```

What happened? If you did just as you were told, your computer should display the following sincere greeting on the line after the prompt:

```
Hello, World!
```

If you got anything other than this greeting, it must be an error message. Go back and check your spelling. Make sure you didn't enter "java MinimalHelloWorld.class" or "java MinimalHelloWorld.java."

The java command runs the Java *interpreter*, which is a program that is responsible for running your program. The Java interpreter looks in your current directory for a file called MinimalHelloWorld.class. That is, it takes whatever word you enter after the command java, tacks ."class" onto the end of it, and looks for a file of that name.

Applications vs. Applets

If you have gotten this far, you really do deserve congratulations. You've entered the source code for an entire Java program, compiled it, and run it. More specifically, the program you created and ran is called an *application*. You may remember from Chapter 1, *A Taste of Java*, that there are two broad categories of Java programs. Programs that are run directly by the Java interpreter are called applications. Applications are very easy to write and run, which makes them well-suited for experimenting with the Java language. Later on, you'll start writing programs that will run under the supervision of a browser such as Netscape or HotJava. Those programs are called *applets*. Most of you are probably anxious to get going on applets. You will soon, after you've mastered a few basics.

So you've created a working Java application. In order to do this, you've learned to use the two most important tools in the JDK. If you haven't ordered that cappuccino yet, now is certainly the time.

What's in MinimalHelloWorld.java?

You've learned how to use a couple of Java tools, but what of the Java language itself. What is in that source code that you entered so obediently?

Let's start where the program itself starts when it runs. Look at the second line of MinimalHelloWorld.java. Do you see where it says **main (String args[])**? Well, that word **main** indicates the *entry point* to your application. **main** is where your program starts. In Java terminology, this starting place is known as the application's *main method*.

Notice how the line ends with an open curly bracket ("{"). If you look down two lines, you'll see a matching close curly bracket ("}"). When the Java interpreter runs an application, it starts with the line of source code after the main method's open curly, and proceeds until it hits the matching close curly. The lines of source code between the curlies are known as the method's body. I hope you'll excuse me if I hold off for a while before I explain the rest of the words on the second line. Their meaning will be more apparent a little later.

Line three contains the code that actually displays the greeting, "Hello, World!" You're going to be seeing a lot of **System.out.println()**, so you may as well get to know it now. **System.out.println()** will display everything between its parentheses. No, I'm not talking dirty. I'm just letting you know that this is the most common way of getting a message to the user. The message can be a greeting, as in the program you just entered, or a request for information ("What's your astrological sign?"), a warning ("Unauthorized user attempting to launch nuclear missile!"), or debugging information ("MinimalHelloWorld run at 0100 by Steve Simkin").

The semicolon (";") after **System.out.println** is the terminator for lines of Java code that do things, as opposed to controlling what gets done (like the main method). Semicolons separate Java statements the way periods separate English sentences. One of the most frequent compiler errors you are likely to see is

```
MinimalHello.java:3: ';' expected.
    System.out.println("Hello, World.")
                                                    ^
1 error
```

meaning that you forgot the semicolon at the end of line 3.

You have now seen all the parts of MinimalHelloWorld.java that actually do any work. The word main provides an entry point and matching exit, while **System.out.println()** displays a message. But there is one more part to this program. Look at the first line of the program, where it says **class MinimalHelloWorld** {. Do you see how the entire program is enclosed by the curly brackets that open on this line and close on the very last line? Everything in Java is contained in classes. You can think of classes as containers for the code that actually does the work in Java programs. If you want to push the metaphor, you can even think of the enclosing curly brackets as the container's walls. So the class statement in MinimalHelloWorld.java accomplishes a couple of things: It creates a container for all the *working code* in the program, and it gives that container a name. The Java compiler creates a *.class* file whose name matches that of the class.

I bet you noticed how I indented the second, third, and fourth lines for MinimalHelloWorld.java? This indentation is of no significance in the Java language. By this I mean that the computer is indifferent to it. On the other hand, it is extremely helpful to human beings when they're trying to read your source code. By matching the indentation of close curly brackets with the lines where they open, you can help your human reader to appreciate the logic of your program. Indenting all the lines between open and close curlies also indicates which code belongs to which logical units.

Recap

Let's put together what we've learned so far in order to get a fuller picture of what happens when you run a Java application. When you enter the java command, followed by a word, the Java interpreter makes a few assumptions. First, it assumes that the word is the name of a class. Second, it assumes that the class is defined in a file whose name matches the class name, with *.class* tacked on the end. Third, it assumes that the class in the file has a **main** method. If any of these assumptions prove false, you'll get a nice clear error message. But if they're all correct, the Java interpreter will start running your program.

Figure 3.1 shows the entire process of entering Java source code, compiling it into bytecodes in a class file, and running the Java application.

ADDING A METHOD

Enter the program shown in Listing 3.2, and save it as HelloWorld.java. Try compiling it and running it.

Listing 3.2   Hello World Program with Two Methods

```
class HelloWorld {

  public static void main(String args[]) {
    SayHello("World");
  }

  public static void SayHello(String recipient) {
    System.out.println("Hello, " + recipient + "!");
  }

}
```

What response did you get? If you entered everything correctly, you got the same "Hello, World!" message that you got from MinimalHelloWorld. But a

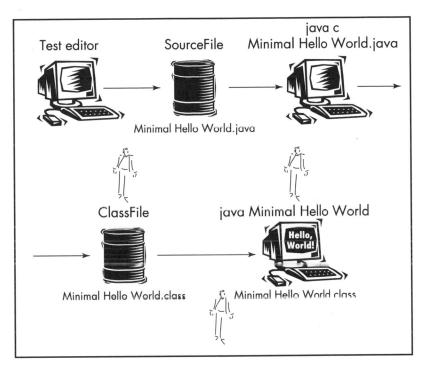

Figure 3.1   *Entering, compiling, and running a Java application.*

first glance at the listing rcvcals that "Hello," and "World" are in two separate parts of the program. How did they get together in the message? The answer to this question will require a second, third, and fourth glance at the listing.

Constants and Their Types

The first line of code in the body of the **HelloWorld** class is immediately recognizable as the program's main method, so let's start there. **HelloWorld's** main method consists of the single line of code:

```
SayHello("World");
```

We know what "World" is, or at least we think we do. Actually, in Java words like "World," or numbers such as "2.45," have a special status. They are known as *constants*, because they have values that cannot be changed. It may never have occurred to you to try to change the value of the number "3," but trust me that you can't. This may seem like a trivial observation, but its significance will become apparent very soon.

Java treats constants differently, depending on their value. People do, too. For example, in daily life we don't usually do arithmetic with words and letters, but we do put them in sequence to form sentences. We do one kind of arithmetic with dollars and cents, and quite a different kind of arithmetic with hours and minutes. When we encounter a value such as "Michael," we assume that it represents a first name, and could be used for calling a child to dinner, but probably not for introducing oneself to the CEO of a large corporation. Most of the time, we are barely conscious of this categorization of values, and without even knowing it, we've made a decision about what we can and can't do with them. If we were to articulate the rules of how we use constants, we would have to invent categories such as "time of day," "sum of money," or "surname." For each category, we would have to describe the criteria for determining that a given value belongs to that category, as well as the set of activities a value of that kind can be used for.

Java does the same thing. When it encounters the value "World," it use the term *String* to describe what kind of value "World" is, and what it can be used for. In Java, these categories are known as *types*. You will be hearing a great deal about types throughout this book.

The Calling of Methods Is a Simple Thing

If you look through the whole listing, you'll see that the word **SayHello** appears twice; once in the line we've been looking at, and a second time a few lines later. The line where it makes its second appearance is virtually identical to the line that introduces the **main** method, with **SayHello** substituted for **main**, and one other minor difference.

SayHello is the name of an independent section of HelloWorld.java, separate from the main method. You can match up pairs of curly brackets to verify this point. Each of these sections enclosed in curly brackets is called a *method*. A method is a unit of Java code that performs a specific task. Every method has a name, and is contained by a class. It is said to belong to the class that contains it.

You already know, from MinimalHelloWorld.java, that every Java application has a main method, which the Java interpreter uses as an entry point. Now you see that an application can have more than one method.

When the line of code in the main method used the name **SayHello**, it was asking the **SayHello** method to perform its task. This is known as *calling* the method. By placing the constant **"World"** between parentheses when it called **SayHello**, main made it available to **SayHello**. This enabled **SayHello** to use the value **"World"** while performing its appointed task, which happens to be display the "Hello, World!" message. When a program makes values available while calling a method, it is said to *pass* the values to the method.

We've made great progress toward answering the question we started with: how do "Hello," and "World" get together in the message? But we still have a few gaps to fill in our understanding of value passing.

Passing Arguments to a Method

In the statement that introduces the **SayHello** method (known as its *declaration*), the name of the method is followed by parentheses containing the words **String recipient**. In fact, in every method declaration, the method name is followed by parentheses containing a list of values the method expects to receive whenever it is called. This list is called the method's *argument list*. The argument list specifies the number of values (or *arguments*) the method expects to receive, as well as each value's type and the name the method will use to refer to it.

SayHello's argument list tells us that it expects a single value of type **String**. When we look back to the **SayHello** method call in main, we see that main passes a single value of type **String**. It's a perfect match! It had better be, because if it weren't a perfect match, HelloWorld.java would not compile. Figure 3.2 illustrates method calls and argument passing.

Methods Also Have Types

We now have a pretty good understanding of how to pass values to methods. But there's a flip side to the story. Methods frequently pass values back to the program that calls them. For example, a method called CelToFar, which accepts a temperature in Celsius and calculates the equivalent temperature in Fahrenheit, needs a way of letting the calling program know the result of its calculation. To this end, every method has a type, indicating the kind of value the method will pass back (or *return*) to the calling program.

A method's type appears immediately before its name in the method declaration. Looking at HelloWorld.java, we see that both **main** and **SayHello** have a type of **void**. Normally, methods return values to the calling program. You hand them some parameters, and they hand you something back. But **void** is a special type that indicates a method that doesn't return any value. You may wonder about the need for a type that means, "No value here." The **void** type derives from the Java philosophy of never making assumptions about the programmer's intention. *You must indicate every method's type explicitly,* even if the method doesn't return anything at all.

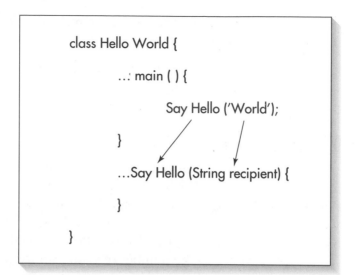

Figure 3.2   Method calls and argument passing.

Variables

Like main, **SayHello** contains a single line of code:

```
System.out.println("Hello, " + recipient + "!");
```

The only part of this statement that we haven't seen before is the word **re-cipient,**" surrounded by plus signs. We know that **recipient** is the name the argument list used to refer to the value **"World,"** which was passed to **SayHello** from main. Since **SayHello** has no way of knowing what value it will receive when it is called, it uses the name recipient as an indirect way of getting access to the value of the argument. Symbols such as recipient, which represent values, are called *variables*. In Java, every variable has a name, a value, and (yes, them too) a type. The type of a variable limits the legal types of values that the variable can hold. For instance, a numeric variable will simply refuse to accept a value of type **String**.

Java attaches the variable recipient to the constants **"Hello,"** and **"!"** by using plus signs in a very unusual way. In Java, when a plus sign appears between two **String** values, it has the effect of joining the **String**s together into one big **String**. Joining **String**s end-to-end in this way is called *concatenation*. You can learn more about this unusual use of the plus sign, and a whole lot more about the behavior of **String**s, in Chapter 7.

Recap

There you have it. The mystery is solved. The **String** value **"World"** was passed as an argument to the **SayHello** method, which concatenated the argument into a big **String** containing the "Hello, World!" message, and then used **System.out.println** to display the message.

GREETING A USER

HelloWorld has always seemed a little impersonal to me. With all the hype about Java and its interactivity, surely there's a way to give HelloWorld a more personal touch. To learn how, enter the program shown in Listing 3.3 and save it as HelloUser.java.

Listing 3.3   HelloUser Program Using Command Line Arguments

```
class HelloUser {

  public static void main(String args[]) {
    SayHello(args[0]);
  }

  public static void SayHello(String recipient) {
    System.out.println("Hello, " + recipient + "!");
  }

}
```

Compile the application, but when you run it, add your name after the word HelloUser, like this:

```
cmd > java HelloUser Steve
```

If your name is Steve, your computer just gave you the following greeting:

```
Hello, Steve!
```

Command Line Arguments

Now that's what I call user friendly! Let's see how HelloUser.java did that. The only difference between HelloUser.java and HelloWorld.java is in the call to **SayHello**. Instead of passing **"World,"** as the argument which HelloUser passes **args[0].** is HelloUser.java's name for whatever value you entered after the word HelloUser when you ran the program. Values that you enter in this way are called *command line arguments*, and they work just like the arguments passed by calling methods inside a program.

Earlier, I referred to an application's main method as its entry point. It's time to refine that definition. When you run the Java interpreter, it divides the command line arguments into two groups. The first group consists of the first word you entered after the java command. As you know, the interpreter assumes that this word is really a class name. The second group consists of everything on the command line to the right of the class name. The interpreter itself isn't interested in the "everything else." It just makes a method call to the main method of the class you named, and passes the "everything else" to main as arguments.

Arrays

An application's main method always has an argument list of **String args[]**. The square brackets mean that main will accept a group of **Strings**. In Java, groups of variables with the same type are called *arrays*. Each variable in an array is called an *element* of the array. The argument list to the main method is a **String** array. Arrays are a Java type in their own right, and have their own set of rules and behavior beyond that of whatever type of variables they contain. For example, the following line from HelloUser.java shows how to refer to the first element in an array:

```
SayHello(args[0]);
```

args[0] means "the value of the **String** variable 0 elements away from the beginning of the args array." You might think it would have been simpler to call the first element in the array args[1], but that would have been thinking like a human instead of like a computer. You wouldn't want to do that, would you? The numeric value inside the square brackets is called an *index*.

 ### An Array's First Slot Is Always Numbered 0

Remember that the first element in an array is always referred to by the array index 0, *not* 1. As a result, you have to make adjustments when you refer to elements in an array. For example, when you refer to the first element in an array named *ThisArray[]*, you'd type *ThisArray[0]*. That much is obvious. What isn't quite so obvious—at least, until you've messed it up a few times in your code—is that in general, you refer to the nth array element by the array index $n-1$. Thus, to refer to the 10th array element, you'd type *ThisArray[9]*, and so on.

When you run the Java interpreter, each word you enter after the class name becomes a new element of the args **String** array. We'll see a great use for this fact in a few pages, but first we have a problem to solve.

TROUBLE IN PARADISE

How sweet to have a working application, an application that calls you by name. Sweet, that is, until in your euphoria you forget to add your name when you run HelloUser. You innocently enter

```
cmd> java HelloUser
```

and to your horror, you see something like this:

```
Exception in thread "main" java.lang.ArrayIndexOutOfBoundsException: 0
at HelloUser.main(HelloUser.java:17)
```

What went wrong? The term *ArrayIndexOutOfBoundsException: 0* which appears in the error message gives us a pretty good indication that our problem is that we forgot to pass a command line argument. By and large, Java's error messages are clear and helpful.

Suppose, though, that you encountered this problem and didn't understand the error message. What resources are available to help you in your hour of confusion? There are a few.

Inserting Debug Code

The most widely used technique (in Java and in most other programming languages) consists of strategically placed **System.out.println** statements that display the values of variables which you think will indicate the source of the error. You could, for example, insert the following statement into HelloUser's main method, right before the call to **SayHello:**

```
System.out.println("args contains " + args.length + "elements");
```

args.length is a variable that belongs to the **args** array. Its value is always the number of elements in the array it belongs to. If you add this print statement to HelloUser.java, it will always tell you how many command line arguments you entered. If you run HelloUser without any arguments, you will see:

```
args contains 0 elements
```

And then—Boom! You get the **ArrayIndexOutOfBoundsError** message again. But at least this time you know why.

The Java Interactive Debugger

If you don't have much experience with other programming languages, you should probably skip this section. Jump ahead to the section called "How to Fix It." Those of you who have already spent time tracking down bugs may want to know about a tool called *jdb* that comes in the Java Developer's Kit.

jdb is the Java interactive debugger. It is a little, well, immature, but it is useful in some situations. To trap the error we mentioned, you might conduct a session similar to the one recorded in Listing 3.4.

Listing 3.4   A Typical jdb Session

```
cmd> jdb
>run HelloUser
 running ...
main[1] Uncaught exception: java.lang.ArrayIndexOutOfBoundsException 0
at HelloUser.main(HelloUser.java:17)
at sun.tools.debug.MainThread.run(Agent.java:48)

main[1] list
13    }
14
15    public class HelloUser {
16      static public void main(String args[]) {
17=>      SayHello(args[0]);
18      }
19    }
main[1] locals
Local variables and arguments:
  args = class[0]
main[1] quit
```

As I said, the Java debugger is itself a little shaky, a little buggy, so I won't spend any more of our precious tutorial time on it. Suffice it to say that the world is ripe for a robust Java development environment.

How to Fix It

Now that we've diagnosed the flaw in HelloUser.java, the question remains of how to fix it. Listing 3.5 shows an improved version of the application that shows how we can control the sequence of statements that get executed by the interpreter in order to protect HelloUser from a user who forgets his name.

Listing 3.5   HelloUser Using Logic Flow Control

```
class HelloUser {

  public static void main(String args[]) {
    if (args.length == 0) {
      SayHello("World");
    }
    else {
      SayHello(args[0]);
    }
  }

  public static void SayHello(String recipient) {
    System.out.println("Hello, " + recipient + "!");
  }

}
```

The If Statement

The new, improved HelloUser.java uses the following statement to test whether or not the user entered a command line argument:

```
if (args.length == 0) {
```

Not surprisingly, this statement is called an *if statement*. The parentheses of an **if** statement always contain something that is either true or false. In this case, they contain the assertion that **args.length** equals 0. Notice the double equal sign. Whenever you are testing whether two things are equal, use a double equal sign. The single equal sign means something else, as you'll soon see.

The Java interpreter *evaluates* the contents of the **if** statement's parentheses. If **args.length** does equal 0, the assertion is evaluated as true, and the interpreter performs the statement enclosed by the curly brackets following the parentheses. In our example, this would result in the constant **"World"** being passed to **SayHello**, which would display the message

```
Hello, World!
```

If, on the other hand, the user entered a command line argument, the assertion **args.length == 0** would evaluate false, and the interpreter would skip ahead to the word **else** and execute the statement enclosed by its curlies. **SayHello** would then display your personalized greeting.

What's This "==" Stuff?

In Listing 3.5, you might have noticed that we used a double equal sign to test whether or not **args.length** was equal to 0. The == operator, inherited from the C and C++ languages, is Java's version of the garden-variety equal sign.

Logic Flow Control

The sequence of statements executed by the interpreter is known as a program's *logic flow*. By controlling the flow of your application's logic, you can help your program respond more flexibly, sensibly, and robustly to whatever conditions it encounters. You can determine that a set of statements should be executed only if a given condition is true. You can have your program repeat a set of statements until the condition becomes false. Or, as in HelloUser.java, you can make your program choose between two sets of statements. We'll examine logic flow control very closely in Chapter 4.

Expressions

A series of terms that gets evaluated, such as **args.length == 0** is called an *expression*. Like variables and methods, expressions have types, which is actually the type of the result of evaluation. For example, we know that the contents of the parentheses in an **if** statement must evaluate to true or false. True and false are the only legitimate values for a Java type called boolean, named after George Boole, a 19th-century mathematician. So when I say that the contents of the parentheses must evaluate to true or false, I'm really saying that the parentheses must contain a boolean expression.

Recap

The user can pass command line arguments to a Java application by typing them after the class name when he runs the Java interpreter. Each argument is an element in the **String** array accepted by the main method.

An **if** statement tests whether a condition is true, and uses the result of the test to determine which set of statements to execute. By controlling the flow of logic in this way, we can help our programs respond correctly to whatever conditions they encounter.

GREETING ALL YOUR FRIENDS

Not to complain, but programming can be a lonely business. Let's broaden the scope of the HelloUser class to send greetings to friends and loved ones. Enter the application shown in Listing 3.6, and save it as GreetFriends.java.

Listing 3.6 GreetFriends Greets a Whole Array of Friends

```
class GreetFriends {

  public static void main(String args[]) {

    for (int i = 0; i < args.length; ++i)
        SayHello(args[i]);
  }

  static void SayHello (String greeting) {
    System.out.println("Hello, " + greeting + "!");
  }


}
```

Compile the application, and run it with as many command line arguments as you like. If I enter

```
cmd > java GreetFriends Michael Haya Hanan
```

I'll get the following response:

```
Hello, Michael!
Hello, Haya!
Hello, Hanan!
```

I can greet all my children in just one command. Now that's power!

What happens if I don't enter any command line arguments? Nothing. Well, not literally. But GreetFriends doesn't display any messages, and it doesn't crash either.

Looking at the listing for GreetFriends.java, we see that there is still exactly one call to **SayHello**. Yet we've seen that sometimes GreetFriends displays lots of messages, and sometimes it doesn't display any. Let's figure out why.

 **You Have No Friends? Try This.**

If you couldn't think of any friends whose names you could use with the GreetFriends application, then you need a hug from your computer. Try using the **if** statement to modify the GreetFriends application so that if the user doesn't enter any names, the program displays a message of sympathy.

Variable Declaration and Initialization

Sift through the first line of GreetFriends.java's main method, looking for the statement **int i = 0**; This statement does two things. First, the terms **int i** create a variable of type **int** called **i**. The **int** type is used for variables with integer values.

When you create a variable by stating the variable's type followed by its name, you are said to *declare* the variable. Notice that variable declarations take the same form as members of method argument lists, which makes sense since they communicate the same information.

Once **i** is created, the second half of the statement (**= 0**) assigns it a value of 0. Assigning an initial value to a variable, before it is processed at all, is called *initialization*. If the Java compiler catches you referring to a variable without having initialized it, it will issue an error. You've been warned.

The Increment Operator

Later in that same line, the expression **++i** appears. Together, the two plus signs perform a special task: they *increment*, or add one to the value of the variable they are attached to. In this case, they increase the value of **i** by one. Any symbol, such as + or < or ==, that can be combined with variables to form an expression, is called an *operator*. The double plus sign is known as the *increment operator*. There are two varieties of increment operator: *prefix* (**++i**) and *postfix* (**i++**). You can find out the difference between them in Chapter 4.

For Loops

In GreetFriends.java, the call to **SayHello** is enclosed by a statement that starts:

```
for (int i = 0; i < args.length; ++i)
```

This statement controls the number of times main calls **SayHello**. It consists of the word **for** and some stuff in parentheses. This structure is known as a *for loop*. The stuff in parentheses has three parts, separated by semicolons. These three parts, known as the *head* of the **for** loop, cooperate to ensure that the body of the **for** loop (the statements enclosed by the curlies) is executed the right number of times.

Each of the three parts has a specific role to play in managing the **for** loop. The first part is the variable declaration and initialization statement we discussed a few paragraphs ago. As the first part of a **for** loop's head, it performs a different kind of initialization. It initializes the control conditions of the loop. That is, the first part of the **for** loop's head is responsible for setting variables to whatever values they must have when the loop starts. Once it has done this, the first part of the **for** loop head is never executed again, no matter how many times the body is repeated.

Now we know that when the **for** loop starts, the **int** variable **i** equals 0. The second part of a for loop head, **i < args.length;** is a boolean expression that controls how many times the body of the **for** loop will be executed. As long as the expression evaluates to true, the body will be executed again. They don't call this structure a loop for nothing. In this case, the expression means that the body of the **for** loop will be executed for as long as **i** is less than the number of elements in the **args** array.

On first hearing, the effect of that expression may not be clear. We know that if there are three command line arguments, there will be three elements in the **args[]** array. So the **for** loop will repeat for as long as **i** is less than 3. We also know that if there are three command line arguments, we want the **for** loop to execute exactly three times. We also know that **i** starts at 0. Something must happen to ensure that after three message have been displayed, the value of **i** is no longer less than 3.

The third part of the for loop head takes care of that. It consists of an expression that is evaluated following each repetition of the loop. Only after evaluating part three of the **for** loop head does Java evaluate part two to decide whether to repeat the loop. Figure 3.3 shows how **for** loops control repetition.

GreetFriends.java illustrates an extremely common use of the third part of the **for** loop head. We already know that **++i** means "increment the value of **i** by 1." Now we know that after each repetition of the **for** loop, the value of **i** gets closer to the cutoff value of **args.length**. A quick count on my fingers tells me

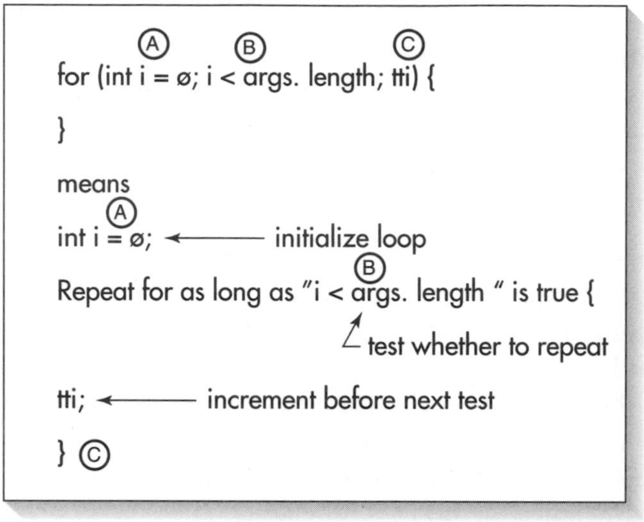

```
           Ⓐ        Ⓑ              Ⓒ
for (int i = ø; i < args. length; ++i) {

}

means
           Ⓐ
int i = ø;  ◄────── initialize loop
           Ⓑ
Repeat for as long as "i < args. length " is true {
                        ╱
                       └ test whether to repeat

++i;  ◄────── increment before next test

} Ⓒ
```

Figure 3.3 *For loops.*

that after the third repetition of the **for** loop, the value of **i** will reach 3. Then **i** will cease being less than 3, and the program will leave the **for** loop and go to the first statement after the **for** loop's closing curly brackets.

Now we understand why the **for** loop is repeated exactly three times when there are three command line arguments. We also know what happens when there are no command line arguments. **i** gets set to 0, and immediately fails the "less than **args.length**" test. The body of the **for** loop is never executed!

Stepping through Arrays

We've learned how the **for** loop structure controls the number of times the loop is repeated. But we still need to explain how it passes each successive command line argument to **SayHello**. The call to **SayHello** looks like this:

```
SayHello(args[i]);
```

This statement calls **SayHello**, passing it the element of the **args** array at index **i**. Since the value of **i** starts at 0, and increases by 1 with each repetition, this has the effect of stepping through the array, passing each element in turn to **SayHello**. A simple mechanism, and one that you will use constantly.

Recap

The **for** loop is a powerful tool for controlling the flow of a program's logic. It is well suited to stepping through arrays and other situations where the same logic must be applied to a succession of values. See the discussion of Enumerations in Chapter 9 for another common **for** loop structure.

USING OBJECTS

You've gone a long time without a cappuccino. I strongly recommend that you order one now, for a couple of reasons. First, because you've earned it. If you've absorbed all of the concepts I've presented so far in this chapter, you're well along the road to becoming a Java programmer. The second reason to order a drink now is that you may want something to sip on while you contemplate the last sample program. Before you start drinking, though, enter the program in Listing 3.7 and save it as FancyGreetFriends.java.

Listing 3.7   FancyGreetFriends.java Uses Objects

```java
import java.lang.*;

/**
 * FancyGreetFriends introduces readers of the Java Programming
 * Explorer to objects
 * @author Steve Simkin
 */
class FancyGreetFriends {

  public static void main(String args[]) {

    for (int i = 0; i < args.length; ++i)  {
      SayHello sh = new SayHello(args[i]);
      sh.GreetFriend();
    }

  }
}

class SayHello {
  String recipient;

/**
 * The SayHello constructor assigns the value of s to recipient
 * @param s a String containing the recipient of the greeting
 */
  SayHello(String s) {
    recipient = s;
  }
```

```
  void GreetFriend() {
    System.out.println("Hello, " + recipient + "!");
  }
}
```

Compile and run FancyGreetFriends exactly as you did GreetFriends. You should get the same responses, whether you enter many command line arguments or none. Of what use, then, is this long and complicated program that mimics the behavior of a short and simple one? Of purely pedagogic use, I admit. But this program demonstrates the last major feature of Java you should be exposed to before you step out of this tutorial into the real world.

In FancyGreetFriends.java, **SayHello** is declared as a distinct class, not as a method. In fact, if you list the contents of your directory, you'll find two separate class files: FancyGreetFriends.class and SayHello.class. **SayHello** has now become a completely independent entity.

This change forces the **FancyGreetFriends** class to change the way it asks **SayHello** to perform its task. In order to understand how this program works, we must broaden our understanding of the nature of classes.

When I introduced classes, I described them as containers for methods, the code that actually does the work in Java. Later we saw that classes can contain more than one method. We also saw how a class' main method could call its other methods, asking them to perform their tasks. As long as the classes we created were essentially collections of services, these explanations were sufficient. But classes can be much more than that.

Classes can represent things in the real world, things such as subatomic particles, baseball bats, and airplane wings. The **BaseballBat** class would contain methods describing all the services one might conceivably request of a baseball bat (I'll leave as an exercise for the reader the identification of what those might be). It would also contain all the pieces of information needed to describe a particular bat. Let's assume that one of these pieces of information is a variable called **SerialNumber**.

If the **BaseballBat** class contains information that uniquely identifies a bat, we programmers are faced with the problem of how to use the class to represent more than one bat simultaneously. After all, **SerialNumber** can't contain two values at the same time! In these situations, Java uses *objects* to solve the problem.

You can think of objects—also known as an *instances* of the class—as incarnations of the idea the class describes. The **BaseballBat** class describes the nature and behavior of bats as a group, but in order to represent a specific bat, Java must create a **BaseballBat** object. The act of creating an object is called *instantiation*. Each object has its own variables (such as **SerialNumber**), its own methods, and its own name. It is, in fact, a variable whose type is the class that it instantiates. If this talk of objects, classes and instantiation sounds like so much gobbledygook, I suggest you take a break from this chapter and read Chapter 6. There, Neil gives a fuller explanation of these terms and the ideas they represent.

Before the **FancyGreetFriends** class can ask **SayHello** to display a message, it has to create a **SayHello** object. It does this as follows:

```
SayHello sh = new SayHello(args[i]);
```

The **new** operator is used to instantiate the class name following it. The class name is followed by parentheses, which contain the variable **args[i]**. In fact, the use of the class name here looks suspiciously like a method call. We'll see why in a few paragraphs.

To the left of the parentheses, we see the variable declaration **SayHello sh**, meaning "Create a variable called sh of type **SayHello**." The equal sign initializes **sh** to the **SayHello** object created by **new**. So far, so good. We have an object, and the object has a name.

Constructors and Instance Variables

Let's follow **args[i]** over to the SayHello class, and find out what happened to it.

SayHello contains two methods. The first is named *SayHello*, and accepts a single **String** argument, **s**. The name and argument list match the *method call* in the statement in main that created the **SayHello** object.

Java programs, like those in C++, always use special methods whose names match that of the class which contains them—such as SayHello—to instantiate the class. These methods are known as *constructors*. A **new** statement always calls a constructor method in order to create an object.

Like all constructors, the **SayHello** method declaration has no type before its method name. But it certainly does return something: the object it created. The **SayHello** *constructor method* returns a **SayHello** *object* back to main, so that main can assign it to the variable **sh**.

There is no *object creation* code in the body of the **SayHello** constructor. The actual creation of the object takes place behind the scenes just before the Java interpreter executes statements in the body of the constructor. For you, this means that your constructor code can refer to the variables and classes in the object as if they already exist—because they do! All your constructor needs to do is to initialize the object to the state you want it in before the calling method receives it.

Which is precisely what the **SayHello** constructor is doing when it assigns the value of **s** to another **String** variable, **recipient**. Let's take a look at **recipient**. It is declared outside of either of the methods in the **SayHello** class. Until now, we've only seen variables that existed inside methods, and were used only by the method in which they appeared. **recipient**, on the other hand, is used by both methods in the **SayHello** class. Variables that belong to an object, and that are available to every method in the object, are called *instance variables*. Figure 3.4 depicts the relationship among a calling method, a constructor method, and a few objects.

Calling Instance Methods

Once main has its **SayHello** object, it calls the object's **GreetFriend** method in order to display the greeting:

```
sh.GreetFriend();
```

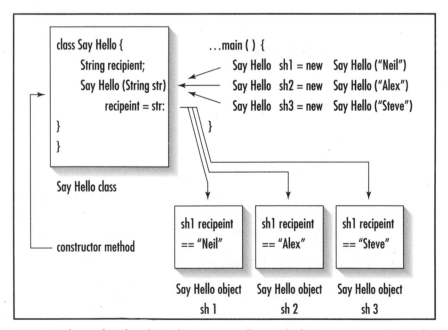

Figure 3.4   *Understanding the relationship among a calling method, a constructor, and some objects.*

Let's analyze this code. **GreetFriend** is a method that belongs to an instance of the **SayHello** class (methods that belong to objects are called *instance methods*). Remember that you could easily have many instances of a class in your program, so the method call must indicate which **SayHello** object's **GreetFriend** method you want to call. As we see in FancyGreetFriends.java, the pattern for calling an instance method is: *variablename.methodname(argumentlist)*.

The call to **GreetFriend** works out to be particularly simple. **GreetFriend** has an empty argument list, so there's nothing to put between the parentheses; and it has a return type of void, so there's no variable to assign.

As for the **GreetFriend** method itself, it just displays the greeting, using **System.out.println**, and concatenating the instance variable recipient right into the message. Hey, this is getting easy!

Recap

Constructors are a special kind of method responsible for instantiating classes. The body of a constructor method initializes the object, which Java created behind the scenes. It returns the object to the calling method, where it must be assigned to a variable in order for the calling method to use it.

Other methods belonging to an object (instance methods) are called using the pattern *variablename.methodname(argumentlist)*.

Objects can have variables, called instance variables, which exist outside of any method. Instance variables can be used by any constructor method or instance method.

A TOUR OF THE JDK

I still haven't discussed the very first statement of FancyGreetFriends.java, which reads:

```
import java.lang.*;
```

The **import** statement makes the services offered by the JDK available to my program. These services are actually methods, which, as we know, are defined in classes. Classes, in turn, are kept in groups known as *packages*. By importing **java.lang.*** I let Java know that I intended to use methods defined in the classes of the lang package. For example, **System** is a class defined in lang. **System.out.println** is a method in the **System** class. In order to use it, we need to help Java make the connection between the **System** class in our program and the **System** class defined in the lang package. The **import** statement does just that. You're probably asking, "How have I managed to use **System.out.println** until now, without putting **import** statements into my programs?" Good question, and I hope you thought of it. The answer is that the **lang** class is a kind of freebie. It is implicitly imported into every Java program. I included it in NewGreetUser.java just so I could show it to you. I'm just that kind of guy.

Usually, all the classes in a package are related in some way—by function or by project, for example. The JDK itself is a great example of the use of packages. In Chapter 1 I showed you a table listing all the packages in the JDK. Let's take a more detailed look at the contents of each package.

The *applet* package contains a class called **Applet** plus a couple of others which provide the foundation for the applets you will soon create.

The *awt package* stands for "Abstract Windowing Toolkit" and it contains classes you can use to describe such screen elements as choice lists, buttons, and scroll bars: all the building blocks you need to construct winning applets.

As its name implies, the *io* package contains a variety of classes suitable for many varied kinds of data access. Generally that data will be associated with a file. The package starts with the simplest possible conception of what a file is, and builds on that foundation until it offers us a comprehensive set of input-output services.

You may not know it, but you have been making use of the *lang* package since the first lesson in this tutorial. This package contains definitions of many of the most basic elements of the Java language. It also includes more sophisticated classes, which offer many services that are frequently needed in order to take full advantage of the more basic elements. You've used one of these services when you joined two strings using a plus sign. That little plus sign hides a frenzy of activity on Java's part, as you'll learn in Chapter 7.

You've seen the articles, heard the hype, maybe even read Chapter 1. So by now you know that Java is a programming language for the Internet. More than likely, that's why you're reading this book. If so, then you'll want to study the contents of the *net* package very carefully. This package contains classes that enable your applets to function on the Net. URLs, sockets, content handlers, and the other features that make the Internet so exciting are all defined in classes in the net package. See Chapter 21 for complete instructions on how to use them effectively.

The *util* package is a kind of grab bag for all kinds of services commonly needed by programs. The general purpose classes that provide these services are known as *utilities*. They include hashtables and system properties, which may be unfamiliar terms right now, as well as time and date services. No, a date service won't find you someone to go to a movie with on Saturday night, but it will let you know what time your computer thinks it is right now. Small consolation perhaps, but between you and me, I would never even think of taking a recommendation for a date from something that describes itself as object-oriented.

How Can I Learn More about the Contents of the JDK?

For all our talent as educators, there's no way that Neil, Alex, and I can answer every question you'll have about the classes and methods in the JDK. You can find complete documentation of the contents of each package in the JDK at Sun Microsystems' Java site on the World Wide Web. Just go to the following location:

```
http://java.sun.com/JDK-beta2/api/packages.html
```

From there you can find your way to the package or class you're interested in. Figure 3.5 shows what one of the Sun documentation pages looks like.

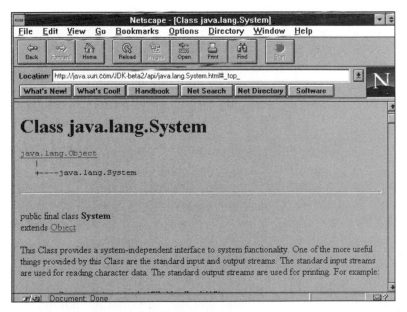

Figure 3.5 *A Sun Microsystems online documentation page.*

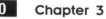

GROWING YOUR OWN [DOCUMENTATION THAT IS]

As you look things up in the documentation at Sun's Web site, you may notice its standardized format. Looking ahead to when you publish your first applet on the Net, you may even wish that you could create documentation just like Sun's to let people know how to use your creation. If so, you'll be pleased to learn about *javadoc*, another of the tools that comes in the JDK.

We'll start our javadoc lesson by examining the last unexplained element of FancyGreetFriends.java. Take a look at these lines:

```
/**
 * FancyGreetFriends introduces readers of the Java Programming
 * Explorer to objects
 * @author Steve Simkin
 */
```

Adding Comments to Your Code

Java regards any text contained between /** and */ as a *comment*. When javac reads your sou1rce file, it ignores all comments, so you can put anything you want in them. Use comments to make your programs more understandable to human readers.

Java actually has three different ways of setting comments off from the source code itself. One is a pair of slashes, //. The Java compiler ignores anything to the right of a pair of slashes:

```
s.SayHello();  // call the SayHello method
```

Another way to delineate comments is by enclosing them between /* and */:

```
/* call the SayHelloClass constructor method */
SayHelloClass s = new SayHelloClass(str);
```

Notice that there is only one asterisk after the first slash. The comments in FancyGreetFriends have two asterisks after the first slash. They are examples of a special kind of, known as *doc comments*, which are used by *javadoc*, the Java documentation generator.

Javadoc reads Java source files, locating the doc comments and matching them with the classes and methods they describe. Once it has gathered all these elements, it makes them look just like the documentation you saw at

Sun's Web site. It saves the documentation in HTML files. (HTML, or HyperText Markup Language, is the language used to describe the format of home pages on the World Wide Web).

You can run javadoc by typing:

```
cmd> javadoc FancyGreetFriends.java
```

You should see the following message:

```
generating documentation for class FancyGreetFriends
generating documentation for class SayHello
```

Now when you list the contents of your directory, you should see a couple of new HTML files: FancyGreetFriends.html and SayHello.html.

Try entering your own name instead of mine as author of FancyGreetFriends.java. The word **@author** has special meaning to javadoc. It causes javadoc to use specific HTML commands highlighting your name as author of the program. There are several of these special symbols, known as *javadoc tags*. javadoc tags help javadoc create online documentation with the "look and feel" you saw at Sun's Web site. Figures 3.6 and 3.7 show what the results look like.

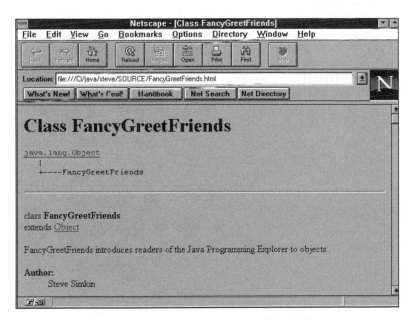

Figure 3.6   *FancyGreetFriends online documentation generated by javadoc.*

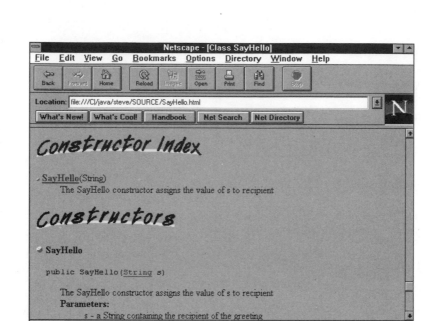

Figure 3.7   *SayHello constructor documentation generated by javadoc.*

Pretty nifty, huh? You can find the full HTML files containing the documentation for FancyGreetFriends.java on the CD-ROM that comes with this book. There, you'll also find a directory called *images* containing the files that define the little colored balls and other graphical elements you see in these figures.

ONE FOR THE ROAD

You've come a long way. You've entered, compiled, and run three Java source files. You've debugged one program, and generated documentation for another. You've also seen how Java programs use the services of the JDK. Perhaps most importantly, you've been introduced to the fundamental concepts of Java programming. The remainder of this book is an elaboration of those concepts, and how you can use them to create the Java app of your dreams. Take a breather, pour yourself a cuppa java (the hot brown stuff), and prepare to go further into Java programming.

Basic Ingredients of a Potent Brew

Steve Simkin

We've enjoyed the aroma and the taste of Java. We know what we can do. Now let's brew our own.

On the way home from a camping trip last summer, we passed the hours by playing "The Animal Game." The Animal Game is really twenty questions, except that the object of the questioning is always an animal. My nine year-old son and seven year-old daughter have settled on a pretty systematic pattern of questioning: "Can it fly?" "Is it a bird?" "Is it a bird of prey?" But Hanan, my four year old son, has his own categorization system. "Does it wiggle?" he asks. Or better yet, "Does it scatter?" Does it what? "Scatter, Dad. Does it scatter?" I had to think for a good long time before the meaning of his question dawned on me. If the Simkin family is having a picnic, and a flock or herd of the mystery animal comes along and surrounds the picnickers, and I, Hanan, run shrieking into the middle of the flock, waving my arms and kicking, *DOES IT SCATTER?* From this we learn that in life, context is all, and so it is in Java.

IT'S SOMETHING IN THE AIR

My wife tells me that the more bread one bakes in a kitchen, the better the bread from that kitchen gets. Something about yeast in the air that enriches subsequent baking efforts. . . .

In Java, too, there are enriching things in the air, so to speak. By this I refer to elements of the language that take up no space in compiled applications, but nevertheless contribute greatly to their success. The invisible yeast molecules, floating in the air of the Java bistro, imparting taste to each brew, are the *Unicode character set*, the *names* used to identify anything that can be named, and the *comments* that explain the programmer's intent.

The Unicode Character Set

The very smallest Java units (Java atoms, if you will) are the characters used to write Java source code. These characters are defined by the Unicode character set. The Unicode character set is an emerging standard that associates the complete character sets of as many scripts as possible, both living and historical, with 16-bit character values. There are 34,168 defined characters in the Unicode character set. However, most of us think in terms of the basic letters, digits and punctuation used in normal English which make up the *ASCII* character set. The examples in this book restrict themselves to the ASCII character set. For the sake of completeness, however, I include instructions on how to use the other Unicode characters, but I never discuss them beyond that.

Naming Rules for Java Identifiers

Variables, methods, classes, and packages all have names. Try to choose names that clearly indicate the nature and purpose of the named item. There are exceptions, of course. For example, a well established programming convention gives single-letter names (usually **i**) to integer variables used for menial tasks such as stepping through arrays. But in general, variables, and certainly more complex entities, should be given meaningful names.

You're not completely free to name things at will, however. There are rules. Java names (more properly known as *identifiers*) must start with a letter, underscore (_) or dollar sign ($). By "letter," I mean any of the letters in the English alphabet (upper-or lowercase), plus any Unicode character above hex 0C00. If you don't understand what "hex 0C00" is, that's okay. You probably have no immediate needs that won't be satisfied by the ASCII character set, so don't worry about it. After the first character, identifiers can continue with any of the symbols mentioned previously, as well as digits (0 through 9). Listing 4.1 gives examples of legal and illegal identifiers. Note, of course, that an identifier's data type (*for example,* int) isn't part of the name, even though it appears on the same line where the identifier is declared.

Listing 4.1   Examples of Legal and Illegal Identifiers

```
// legal indentifier, starts with underscore
int  _newIntIdentifier = 0;

// all legal identifiers, start with dollar sign or letters
public abstract void  $MethodName(int  argl, String  Arg2);

// illegal identifier, starts with digit
int   2ndInt = 0;

// illegal identifier, contains illegal character ('<')
class A<B {
```

Comments

Comments are the third category of Java yeast, if you will. Remember that anything contained in a *comment* appears in the source code, but is ignored by the compiler. There are three ways of writing comments in Java:

- The double slash (//), used earlier in Listing 4.1 to describe the legality of the identifiers in the Java code. Anything on a line to the right of double slashes is a comment. This type of comment syntax is also used in C++.
- The slash-asterisk (/*) followed by an asterisk-slash (*/). Anything between the slash-asterisk and the asterisk-slash is included in the comment. This style of comment can stretch over several lines. This type of comment syntax is inherited from C. Both the double slash and the slash-asterisk can be used anywhere in a program.
- The slash-double-asterisk (/**) followed by an asterisk-slash, just like the second style of comment. Anything between the /** and the */ is included in the comment. This type of comment, called a *"doc comment,"* only has significance when it immediately precedes declarations. The Java documentation generator, *javadoc*, inserts doc comments into the online documentation it creates for packages, classes, and methods.

YOUR BASIC BEANS: SIMPLE TYPES

In Chapter 3, we introduced the notion of *types*. There we learned that every entity that can be used in a Java program—constants, variables, expressions, methods and objects—has a type. The entity's type determines the nature of the value it can have, as well as its permissible behavior. For example, an integer variable can only have an integer value, while a **String** variable cannot be used for arithmetic.

Java recognizes two kinds of types: simple and composite. Simple types are those that cannot be broken down into their components. They include integer, floating-point, character, and boolean types. Composite types are composed of simple types in combination. They include classes and interfaces, which will be described later in the chapter.

The following section reviews all the simple types in the Java language. For each type, it lists the nature and range of permissible values, and gives examples of notation for constants of that type. It then demonstrates commonly used operators for that type, with examples of how expressions employing those operators would be evaluated.

Numeric Types

The numeric types in Java can be divided into two groups, each with its own convention for expressing constant values, its own set of operators, and its own default type for expressions. From the programmer's point of view, the standard arithmetic operators have the same meaning for all numeric types. For example, **a + b** means "the sum of **a** and **b**," regardless of **a**'s and **b**'s specific numeric type. From Java's point of view, the types of the values it is adding makes a big difference. If **a** and **b** have values of 3 and 5 respectively, Java adds them differently than if either of them has a value of 3.28. Nevertheless, when I discuss these operators, I will describe them as operating on "numeric" values, unless I'm saying something that applies only to one particular group of numeric types.

Integer Types

The first family of numeric types is used to represent whole numbers, or integers. There are four integer types in Java. Table 4.1 lists the integer types, along with their minimum and maximum values.

Table 4.1 *Java Integer Types*

Type	Minimum Value	Maximum Value
byte	-256	255
short	-32768	32767
int	-2147483648	2147483647
long	-9223372036854775808	9223372036854775807

Unlike the situation in C++, integer variables in Java have no "unsigned" attribute available to them. If your variable needs to accommodate positive integers ranging up to 256, you'll have to use a **short** instead of a **byte**.

The Results of Integer Arithmetic

When performing integer arithmetic operations, be careful to use a type large enough to contain the largest possible results. For example, multiplying two **byte** variables can yield a result requiring an **int** to hold it: 100 and 150 can both be byte values, but the result of 100 * 150 cannot!

Failure to allow for maximum potential size requirements can result in a very subtle error. The Java program will not indicate the overflow condition. It will simply reduce the value of the result to the remainder that would result from dividing the real result by the maximum value the result's type can hold. Beware.

Integer Constants

The easiest way to insert an integer value into a Java program is to type it straight in. When you do that, you create what is known as an *integer constant*. As we discussed in Chapter 3, a constant (also called a *literal*) is a direct representation of a value. It has no name, and cannot be manipulated. The example I gave in the tutorial was the number three (written in your program as **3**). It can't be referred to by another name, and its value cannot be changed.

As we saw in the previous paragraph, the simplest way to express an integer constant is to write the number as is in decimal format: 0, 17 -929. But you do have other options for writing integer constants. Optionally, integer values can be expressed in octal or hexadecimal. To write the number in octal, prefix it with a 0 (zero); in hex, prefix it with 0x. In each case, values are restricted to digits in the base corresponding to the format. For octal, this means 0 through 7; for decimal, 0 through 9; and for hex, 0 through 9 plus A through F. Thus, the number 110 could be represented as any of the following:

```
int octalInt = 0156; // integer literal in octal format
int decimalInt = 110; // integer literal in decimal format
int hexInt = 0x6E; // integer literal in hexadecimal format
```

It is important to remember that constants have types. They can be used in all situations where data items of a specific type are required, such as passing arguments to a method (remember passing "World" to the **SayHello** method in Chapter 3?).

Integer literals have a type of **int** unless their value is outside of **int**'s range limits, in which case they are of type **long**. You can force a literal to type **long** by appending an "L" (upper- or lowercase), as shown in this code line:

```
long longOfLittleValue = 2L; // integer literal forced to long type
```

Operators for Integers

As you would expect, the operators for integers perform either arithmetic operations or arithmetic comparisons. Most of these are familiar to you from grade school arithmetic, although the names they get in a computer programming context may be new. Others are more obscure. My examples will come mostly from the familiar ones, which I'll demonstrate both to show you what they look like in action, and to help you get used to their "nerd names." I have listed bit operations in the tables of operators, but I will not be discussing them at all. If you are already familiar with them from other languages, you can transfer your knowledge directly to Java: they work the same way as you'd expect.

Operators are commonly classified by the number of values (or *operands*) they operate on. This distinction is useful because many operators have different (though related) meanings, depending on whether they are combined with two operands or just one.

For example, ever since you took algebra in grade school, you've known that you can use "-x" as the equivalent of "0 -x". The minus sign acts on the single numeric value, performing an operation known as *negation*. An operator—such as the minus sign in this example—that acts upon a single operand, is known as a *unary* operator. Thus, the operation performed by the minus sign is more properly called *unary negation*.

On the other hand, if you place the minus sign between two numeric values, it performs a different operation: subtraction. When used for subtraction, the minus sign is acting as a *binary* operator; that is, an operator that acts on two operands.

In Java, the operators and operands combine to form *expressions*. If the operands are integers, the expression will usually evaluate to a result of type **int**.

In the following example, **-i** is an expression of type **int**.

```
int i = 6;
System.out.println(-i);  // displays "-6"
```

Unary Integer Operators

There are four unary integer operators, as shown in Table 4.2. Listing 4.2 shows some examples of their use.

Listing 4.2   Using Unary Integer Operators

```
int i = 20,
    j = -i;  // unary negation, j = -20
    i++;   // increment, i = 21
```

 **The Increment Operator: Prefix (++i) or Postfix (i++)?**

We saw the increment operator in action in Chapter 3, when we used **++i** to increment the index of an array in the head of a **for** loop. There, I mentioned that you can place the increment operator either before or after the integer variable. Either way, the variable's value is incremented by one. The difference is in the value of the expression.

If the increment operator is placed before the variable, the expression will be evaluated *after* the variable has been incremented; if the increment operator is placed after the varialbe, the expression will be evaluated *before* the variable is incremented. For example, if **i** has a value of six, the expression **++i** has a value of seven, while **i++** has a value of six. Either way, once the expression has been evaluated, **i** has a value of seven.

Binary Integer Operators

By now you've seen plus signs used to join **Strings**, equal signs used to assign values, and double equal signs used to test for equality. With that kind

---

Table 4.2   *Unary Integer Operators*

Operator	Operation
-	unary negation
~	bitwise complement
++	increment
—	decrement

of preparation, you may be approaching the binary operators with some trepidation. What could Java possibly throw at you, when all you want is to add *a* and *b*? For once, you can relax. The Java arithmetic operators behave just like the operators in regular arithmetic. The algebraic expression "*a* + *b*" would be expressed in Java as **a + b**.

Aside from the bit operators, the only operator in the list that you might not be familiar with is the *modulus* operator, **%**. Modulus is a fancy word for remainder. If you divide one number into another, the modulus value is what's left over. For example, **100 % 10** (spoken as "100 mod 10") equals 0 because 10 divides 100 evenly, leaving no remainder. On the other hand, **63 % 10** equals 3 because when you divide 63 by 10, you get a remainder of 3. Here's how it would look in Java code:

```
int a = 63, b = 10, c = 0;
c = a % b;  // c == 3
```

Table 4.3 lists the binary integer operators. Listing 4.3 gives a few more examples of their use.

Listing 4.3   Using Binary Numeric Operators

```
int a, b, c, d;

a = b * c;  // multiplication

d = 11 % 3;  // modulus operation, d = 2

a = 15-12;

b = a >> 2;  //sign-propogating right shift, b = -3
```

Op =operators

From C, Java inherits a neat shorthand version of each of the binary operators. The shorthand versions are used when you want the value of the expression to be assigned to one of the operands. For example, you may want to increase the value of the variable **currentValue** by 5. If you're into verbose code, you could write:

```
currentValue = currentValue + 5;
```

On the other hand, the following code line means the same thing and requires less typing:

```
currentValue += 5;
```

Table 4.3 *The Binary Integer Operators*

Operator	Operation
+	addition
-	subtraction
*	multiplication
/	division
%	modulus
&	bitwise AND
|	bitwise OR
^	bitwise XOR
<<	left shift
>>	sign-propagating right shift
>>>	zero-fill right shift

Yes, here we go again, using familiar symbols in strange ways. But once you get used to this notation, you'll find it much clearer than **currentValue = currentValue + 5;**. Any binary operator can be combined with an equal sign in this way. Collectively, this family of operators are known as *op=* operators. Listing 4.4 shows more examples of *op=* operators in use.

Listing 4.4   Using the op= Operators

```
int a = 3;

a += 4;    // add 4 to a, a = 7

a <<= 1;   // shift a left one byte, a = 14
```

Handling Expressions with Large Values

If any operand in an integer equation is **long**, the result is of type **long**. Otherwise, it is **int**, regardless of the types of the operands. What happens if a pair of **int**s is mulitplied, yielding a value that requires a **long** to hold it? The result will be reduced by modulus the range of **int** (4244967296), and Java will not indicate an error condition! What can you do to prevent this hard-to-trace error? You must do two things: First, your result field must be of type **long**; second, you must cast the expression to force it to type **long**, as follows:

```
long resultField = (long) int1 * int2;
```

Relational Operators

In addition to manipulating arithmetic values, we frequently need to compare them. In Chapter 3, I used **i < args.length** as the termination condition in the head of a **for** loop. I explained there that this expression evaluates to either **true** or **false**. In fact, it is exactly equivalent to the slightly more complex expression **(i < args.length) == true**. As we'll discuss shortly, Java has a special type, **boolean**, whose values are either **true** or **false**.

Operators, such as <, which compare numeric values, are called *relational* operators. Relational operators combine with the numeric values they compare to produce **boolean** expressions. There are six integer relational operators, and the familiar ones mean just what you'd expect from middle-school algebra: <, >, ==, !=, <= and >=.

You saw == in the tutorial, where you learned that it just means what we normally mean when say "equals." There we saw that if you want to say "if *a* equals *b*" in Java, you have to write **if (a == b)**. != means "not equals." Yes, we programmers do find new and creative things to do with punctuation. <= means "less than or equal to." At least that one makes sense, as much sense as offering your guests "coffetea." Listing 4.5 demonstrates the Java relational operators, and describes the results they yield.

Listing 4.5   Using Relational Operators

```
int a = 3;
. . .
a > 5 // yields boolean "false" value
a < 20 // yields boolean "true" value
a >= 3 // yields boolean "true" value
a == 3 // yields boolean "true" value
a != 3 // yields boolean "false" value

... (a == 4) ...  // yields boolean "false" value
if ((a == 4) == false)  // equivalent to "if (a != 4)"
```

The Char Type

Java has a special type for holding character values. Character values include all the letters, numbers, and punctuation marks. This can be a little confusing when discussing numbers. We don't usually distinguish between the *number* six and the *character* "6," at least not consciously. But the fact that "six" and "6" both represent the same numeric value indicates that we recognize a distinction between a symbol and its underlying value. In any event, Java has different values for the character "6" and the number six. It uses the type **char** for character values.

The **char** type is actually an unsigned integer that can hold values ranging from zero to 65535. It can thus accommodate all 34,168 Unicode characters that have been assigned so far, plus all that could potentially be assigned. You may wonder why a type for representing characters would be numeric. The answer is that this allows you to do arithmetic on **char** values. For example, you might want to step through the alphabet by incrementing a **char** variable from "a" through "z."

To use a character constant in a program, enclose its value in single quotes. For example, to declare a character variable called "c" and assign it the value of the letter "b," you would code this:

```
char c = 'b';  // Note the single quotes
```

Knowing that, we can code our stroll through the lowercase alphabet as follows:

```
for (char c = 'a'; c <= 'z'; c++) { . . .}
```

 **Using Chars in Numeric Expressions**

It is legal to use **char** variables in binary numeric expressions. For example, if **c** is a **char** variable, **javac** will accept the expression **c + 1**. However, the result will not be what you expect. As with the proverbial apples and oranges, Java will only add similar items. Therefore, before adding a **char** and an **int**, Java changes the **char's** type to **int**. The resulting expression is also an **int**, and If you display it, you will see a number. You can get around this problem by casting the entire expression back to **char** as follows:

```
System.out.println((char) (c + 1));
```

If you're unfamiliar with *casting*, see the discussion of it at the end of the "Types" section of this chapter.

Special Characters

Unicode characters outside of the ASCII character set are coded identically to ASCII characters by enclosing them in single quotes. If the Unicode character you're coding requires two characters, just enclose both in single quotes.

There are a few commonly used characters outside of the "printable" ASCII character set. For example, when you hit Enter or Tab on your keyboard, you actually enter a non-printing character into the text you are typing. Your computer and printer know how to interpret those characters when they are displaying or printing the text. These commonly used characters—as well as a few obscure ones—are called *special characters*. In order to let Java know that you're entering a special character, you precede it with a backslash ("\"). A newline character, for instance, is written "\n." The backslash followed by a character, combined as a special character, is called an *escape sequence*. The backslash allows the character that follows to *escape* its normal value.

Escape sequences allow you to express the character value of the single-quote, as well as of the backslash itself. You can also use them to enter values in formats other than normal character values.

Table 4.4 lists the characters and formats requiring escape sequences.

Floating-Point Types

The second group of numeric types is used to represent non-integer values, such as "98.6" or "-7.0." Values whose precision is expressed beyond the decimal point are called floating-point values. This is true even if there are only zeroes to the right of the decimal point. In other words, "6" and "6.0" are not the same thing! Java is smart enough to recognize that they have the same value, however, so **6 == 6.0** evaluates to **true**. Phew!

There are two floating-point types in Java: **float** and **double**. Their range and precision are shown in Table 4.5.

Table 4.4   *Characters Requiring Escape Sequences*

Value or Format	Escape Sequence
new-line NL(LF)	\n
horizontal tab HT	\t
back space BS	\b
carriage return CR	\r
form feed FF	\f
backslash \	\\
single quote '	\'
double quote "	\"
octal bit pattern 0ddd	\ddd
hex bit pattern 0xdd	\xdd
unicode char 0xdddd	\udddd

Table 4.5   *Java Floating-Point Types*

Type	Maximum Absolute Value of Mantissa	Minimum Value of Exponent	Maximum Value of Exponent
float	2^24	-149	104
double	2^53	-1045	1000

 **The Results of Floating-Point Arithmetic**

As with integer types, you should pay attention to the type of variables receiving the results of computations involving floating-point values. A binary operation on two **float** operands returns a **float**; if either operand is a **double**, the result is a **double**.

Floating-Point Constants

Like integer constants, you can enter floating-point constants in the same format you would use in normal writing: "3.7" or "-65.89." However, floating-point constants give you many more format options than integer constants do. They can have up to five different parts (as shown in Figure 4.1): a leading decimal integer, a decimal point, a fraction, an exponent (consisting of the letter E plus an integer), and a type suffix.

The literal (which, as I said earlier, is another word for *constant*) must have at least one digit plus either an exponent or a decimal point. Floating-point constants have an implied type of **double**. You can force their type by appending D (double) or F (float). Listing 4.6 gives some examples of floating-point literals in different formats.

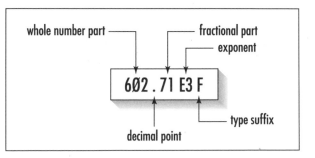

Figure 4.1   *Floating-Point constant format.*

Listing 4.6 Examples of Floating-Point Literals

```
// minimal configuration, decimal point plus integer
double  firstDouble = .1,

// minimal configuration, integer plus exponent
double secondDouble = 2E-1,

// full configuration, integer, decimal point, fraction, exponent
// plus type suffix
float firstFloat = -47.852E12F;
```

Operators for Floating-Point Values

All of the operators available to integer values are available to floating-point values, except for bit-level operators (complement, shifts, AND, and OR) and operators that depend on a value having a clearly defined successor or predecessor (such as the increment and decrement operators). All the relational operators are available. As mentioned previously, expressions that involve exclusively **float** operands produce **float** results. If either operand (or both, of course) is a **double**, the result of the expression is a **double**.

Reaching Infinity in Your Lifetime

Floating-point operations never cause arithmetic exceptions. Overflow and divide-by-zero by produce **Inf**, a special floating-point value recognized by Java as a symbol for infinity.

Boolean Type

By this point in the book, you've seen plenty of examples of the **boolean** type. For example, you know that the parentheses of an **if** statement must contain a **boolean** expression. The **boolean** type can have a value of either **true** or **false**. Note that **true** and **false** are *reserved words* in Java, meaning that they have special significance to the compiler. Make sure to write them without quotation marks. You'll find a list of all the reserved words in the Java language at the end of this chapter.

You can use **boolean** variables in place of **boolean** expressions. For example, if you have a **boolean** variable called **ready**, then **if (ready)** is equivalent to **if (ready == true)**; and **if (!ready)** is equivalent to **if (ready == false)**.

Operators for Boolean Values

There is one unary **boolean** operator, **boolean** negation: '!'.

```
if (!(2>3)) {}  // tests whether expression is false
```

You can combine **boolean** expressions using **&&** to mean "and" and **||** to mean "or." The "and" operator is shown in the code snippet below:

```
char c = 'c';
if (c >= 'A' && c <= 'Z')  // tests for a capital letter
```

What about Strings?

There is no simple Java type for representing strings. Strings can only be represented by **String** objects, which are described in detail in Chapter 7. **String** objects have one feature, however, that should be mentioned in this chapter. By enclosing characters in quotes, you implicitly create a **String** object, which can be used as a constant. We used this feature of strings in the tutorial, when we wrote: **System.out.println("Hello, World!");**. The greeting is a string constant. Listing 4.7 gives more examples of String constants.

Listing 4.7   Examples of String Constant

```
"This is a string"
""    // This is an empty string
"This is a string " +
    "split between two lines"  // (actually two concatenated strings)
```

Casting

When I introduced the floating-point types, I mentioned that floating-point constants have a default type of **double**. What happens if you want to declare a **float** and initialize it using a constant? If you enter **float f = 3.5;**, you will get the following compiler error:

```
test.java:3: Incompatible type for declaration. Explicit cast
needed to convert double to float.
    float f = 3.5;
          ^
1 error
```

You could force the constant's type to **float** by appending "F," but suffixes won't help you fix the following statement:

```
float floatVal = f * 3.5;  // will cause a compiler error
```

The value of a multiplication expression is a **double**, and can't be assigned to a **float** variable. To solve this problem, Java allows limited conversions of numeric values between types through a technique known as *casting*. To cast a variable or expression, precede it with the type you want it converted to, enclosed in parentheses. To fix the erroneous multiplication statement in the last example, just write:

```
float floatVal = (float) (f * 3.5);
```

The parentheses around the expression ensure that the cast is applied to the value of the expression. Without them, it would apply to the variable **f** only. The expression would still be of type **double**.

Conversion by casting can be done between any numeric types. By casting a floating-point value to an integer value, for example, you can assign the result of a floating-point expression to an integer variable (with the fraction truncated, of course):

```
int intVar = (int) (4.83 / 5.5E-1);
```

THE BREW THICKENS: FLOW CONTROL

So far we've explored the syntax for individual statements that create and manipulate values of various types. The next step is to control the execution of groups of statements. Java gives you complete control over when—and how many times—your program executes each group (or *block*) of statements.

In the tutorial, I introduced the concept of *logic flow*. I mentioned there that by controlling the flow of your application's logic, you can help your program respond more flexibly, sensibly, and robustly to whatever conditions it encounters. I also mentioned in passing the basic structures of logic flow control: sequential execution, conditional execution, alternate paths, and repetition. Figure 4.2 illustrates these four basic structures. Let's take a minute to expand on each of them, and then go on to see how Java helps you to use them.

Sequential execution is a time-manager's dream. Get up in the morning, look at the "to-do" list you compiled before you went to bed the previous night, and spend the day checking each item off the list. Not much to talk about here. Just pray that nothing upsets your schedule, demanding that you make a decision.

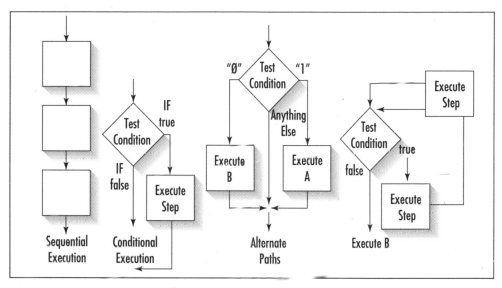

Figure 4.2 *The four basic logic flow structures.*

Conditional execution means that before starting an activity on your "to-do" list, you test whether a prerequisite condition has been fulfilled: "If the zucchini seeds arrive, plant them." Otherwise, there's nothing to do, so you move on to the next step on your list. Notice that "If the zucchini seeds arrive" is a **boolean** expression.

Alternate paths refer to a choice among alternatives. A simple choice might be between two alternatives: "If my weight is up, order salad; otherwise, order cheesecake." More complex circumstances might demand a choice among several available paths: "If I have to deposit checks on the way home from work, drive home on Eglinton Ave; if I need beer, drive home on Wilson Ave.; otherwise, take Highway 401." The condition that determines which path I take (literally) is no longer purely **boolean**. That is, the expression "errand I must do on the way home from work" can have multiple values.

Finally, my "to-do" list can inform me of tasks that have to be repeated for as long as a condition remains true: "Make frivolous purchases until you exceed your credit card limit." Checking off this item might take some time (well, not that long!), but at least it would be fun.

Sequential Execution

Most of the methods we used in Chapter 3 executed sequentially. The interpreter started at the open curlies, and executed through the close curlies with no digressions or distractions. OK, many of those methods had only one statement in them. The point is that nothing in the method could prevent the statement from being executed, or make it execute more than once. Simple is as simple does.

Conditional Execution

In the tutorial, we used an **if** statement to test whether the user entered command-line arguments after the java command. In order to cope with either possible result of that test, we matched the **if** with an **else**. However, you can also use **if** statements without **else** to write strictly conditional logic ("If the zucchini seeds arrive, plant them."). In fact, Listing 4.8 shows how we could have written the main method of HelloUser.java without using an **else** clause.

Listing 4.8   HelloUser without an else Clause

```
class HelloUser {

  public static void main(String args[]) {
    String recipient = "World";

    if (args.length > 0) recipient = args[0];
    SayHello(recipient);
  }
  SayHello method
}
```

Notice how I wrote **if (args.length > 0) recipient = args[0];** all on one line, with no enclosing curly brackets around **recipient = args[0];**. These are two separate features of the Java language. First, it demonstrates that line placement is irrelevant. When it groups source statements, the compiler looks at content and punctuation, not at page layout. Which brings me to the lack of curlies. If there are no curlies enclosing a block of statements following an **if** statement, the compiler causes a single statement to be executed if the expression in parentheses evaluates to **true**.

Personally, I usually use curly brackets and new lines even when my program executes only a single statement as the result of an **if**. I think it makes the program easier to read. Whatever you choose, your criterion should be clarity. Make it as easy as possible for a stranger to understand your programs. Even if you're the only one who will ever see your programs, have a little mercy on yourself. You'd be amazed at how incomprehensible your own brilliant logic can be when you haven't seen it in six months. Spreading it out on the page, and using curlies to delineate even single-statement blocks of code can help.

Whether it is paired with an **else** clause or not, the expression tested by an **if** statement must have a type of **boolean**. This throws a favorite C-language technique out the window. In C, a variable of any data type can be tested in an **if** statement for value/non-value, regardless of the way nonvalue is expressed for that particular data type (0, NULL, or whatever), simply by enclosing it in parentheses. In Java, as in life, you can say "if" only about things that are either true or false. This might force you into a few extra keystrokes, anathema to the C programmer. But it results in greater clarity, which is also anathema to some C programmers! So if you want to know whether the integer variable intVar has been assigned a non-zero value, you'll have to ask explicitly, as in Listing 4.9.

Listing 4.9 Testing an Integer Variable for Non-zero Value

```
if (intVar != 0) statement;
else {
  block of statements;
}
```

Alternate Paths

For responding to truly **boolean** conditions, the **if...else...** structure you learned in the tutorial is sufficient.

You might find yourself embedding **if** statements inside other **if** statements. That's fine. But make sure that your **else**s are alternatives to the right **if**. The rule is that the compiler matches **else**s to the last **else**-less **if** in the same block. Look at the code snippet below. According to this rule, the **else** in example one matches the first **if**, while the **else** in example two matches the second **if**. Don't let the indentation fool you.

```
// example one
if (...) {
  if (...) statement;
}
  else statement;
// example two
if (...) {
  if (...) {
    statement;
  }
else statement;
}
```

The Conditional Operator "?:"

Under certain circumstances, you can use a very shorthand version of the **if** statement to indicate alternate paths through code. The two examples in Listing 4.10 demonstrate just how compact this shorthand really is. The two examples there are exactly equivalent:

Listing 4.10 The Conditional Operator

```
// example one: in shorthand
boolean KeepGoing = i < args.length ? true : false;

// example two: not short at all
boolean KeepGoing;
if (i < args.length) KeepGoing = true;
else KeepGoing = false;
```

Together, the question mark/colon (? :) are called the *conditional operator*. The conditional operator consists of three expressions, separated by the two punctuation marks, combining to create one big expression. Figure 4.3 shows the parts of a conditional operator expression.

The first expression (the one before the question mark) must be **boolean**. The question mark means, in effect, "Is the first expression true or false?" If the first expression evaluates to **true**; the second expression (the one between the question mark and the colon) is evaluated; if the first expression evaluates to **false**, the third expression (the one after the colon) is evaluated. Now here's the fun part: the entire expression takes on the value of whichever of the last two expressions gets evaluated. In other words, if the first expression is **true**, the entire expression takes on the value of the second expression.

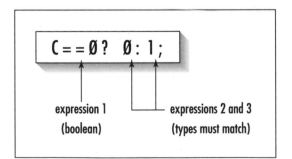

Figure 4.3 *A conditional operator expression.*

The second and third expressions do not have to be **boolean**. They can also be numeric. But they must be of the same type as each other. Thus, you could use the following statement to assign a value to an **int**:

```
int intVal = i < args.length ? 1 : -1;
```

As you can see, conditional expressions are only suitable where you want to return one of two values depending on the value of a **boolean** expression. But when they do fit, their compactness can save you a lot of typing. And once you get used to their notation, you'll find them clearer to read than long-winded declarations followed by **if...else...** constructions.

Multiple Alternate Paths

What if an expression could evaluate to more than two values, each requiring its own logic? For example, suppose you had to examine a field called **empCode**, which represents an employee's category. For the purposes of our example, **empCode** can have three relevant values: zero, one, and anything else. You could code a series of **if...else...** structures until you covered all the possibilities, but by the second **else**, the program would become tiresome and confusing. Java provides a different structure—the **switch** structure—for just such situations. **switch** statements provide a simple way to code any number of logic paths to be taken based on the value of a single expression, as Listing 4.11 demonstrates.

Listing 4.11   The switch Structure

```
int empCode;

... code to populate empCode ...

switch (empCode) {
  case(0): statement;
  case(1): {
    statement;
    statement;
    break;
  }
  default: statement;
}
```

Let's look at this a little more closely. The **switch** statement is followed by an integer type expression. This expression is evaluated and matched against the integer expressions of each of the **case** conditions. At the first match, Java starts to execute the statements associated with the matching condition. Execution continues from that point, even if that includes "falling through" subsequent conditions. The **break** statement is used to force control out of the block enclosing the **switch** conditions. Thus, in our example, if **empCode** has a value of 0, the statement associated with the 0 condition will execute, but so will the statements associated with the 1 condition. Execution will continue until the **break** statement at the end of the statements associated with the 1 condition. A value of 1 will cause only the statements associated with the 1 condition to be executed. Any other value will be caught by the **default** condition, and the statement associated with it will be executed.

Repetition

Repetitive structures all involve repeating a series of actions for as long as a condition remains true (*for example,* "Make frivolous purchases until you exceed your credit card limit"). The **while** statement is the simplest way to represent this kind of structure in Java. For an example, I'm going to borrow from Chapter 8, which makes heavy use of **while** statements to control the repetitive act of reading a file. Listing 4.12 is a paraphrase of one of the programs from Chapter 8.

Listing 4.12   The while Loop

```
boolean done = false;

int rc = System.in.read(ba);  // This statement reads stuff
if (rc == -1) done = true;
while (!done) {
  System.out.write(ba, 0, rc);  // This statement displays stuff
  rc = System.in.read(ba);  // This statement reads more stuff
  if (rc == -1) done = true;
}
```

This excerpt tests a **boolean** variable—**done**—to control repetition of the **while** loop. For now, you can ignore the **read** and **write** statements themselves. All you need to know at this point is that the **read** method returns a positive integer following a successful read operation, and "-1" when it reaches the end of the file it's reading. The value returned by **read** is stored in the **int** variable **rc**. After each of the two **read** statements, there is an **if** statement that sets **done** to **true** if **rc** equals -1, indicating the end of the file. Before each repetition (including the first one), the **while** statement tests whether **done** equals **true**. Thus, if the very first attempt to read the file indicates that the file is empty, the loop is never executed.

There are situations where you'll want to execute the body of a loop at least once before testing whether to repeat. For example, you might be examining a **string** array, looking for the index of the first element that equals "Eureka!" Listing 4.13 shows a variation on the **while** statement you can use to control the repetition.

Listing 4.13   The do...while Loop

```
boolean done = false;
int i = 0;

do {
  if (args[i] == "Eureka!") {
    done = true;
    i++;
  }
} while (!done);
```

The For Loop

Here's an exercise for you: try to rewrite the example of the **do...while** loop more simply, using the **for** loop structure you learned in the tutorial. If you think it through, you can get all of the logic into the head of the **for** loop, leaving the body of the loop empty! You don't even need the curlies. Just write the head of the loop followed by a semicolon.

This exercise should give you a sense of the power of the **for** statement. Like the conditional operator you learned a few pages ago, the syntax of the **for** statement is a little complicated, but once you master it, watch out! The **for** loop head brings together in one place all the logic for controlling repetition, combining compactness and clarity.

Variable Scope in for Loops

Be careful where you declare the variables you use in a **for** loop. The scope of any integer declared in the **for** loop's head is the body of the loop. Thus, the code in the following example would result in a compile-time error.

```
int j = 10;
for (int i = 0; i < 10; i++) {
  statement;
}
j += i;  // invalid: i out of scope
```

Labels

Java supplies a simple way of avoiding one of the trickier maneuvers in the C language: breaking out of multiple enclosing loops. If, for example, I am using embedded loops to search a two-dimensional array for a value, I may want to jump straight to the next iteration of the outer loop after finding the value and executing some code. In Java, I can do this gracefully by labeling the outer loop and naming the label in my continue statement, as shown in Listing 4.14.

Listing 4.14   Using Labels to Exit Embedded Loops

```
int intArray = new int[10][10];

... code to populate intArray ...

outer: for (int i = 0; i < 10; i++) {
  for (int j = 0; j < 10; j++) {
    if (intArray[i][j] == 6) {
      statement A;
      continue outer;
    }
    statement B;
  }
  statement C;
}
```

Without the label, the **continue** statement would succeed in bypassing **statement B**, but would get caught in **statement C**. Of course, you could set a condition around **statement A**, and then test for it before executing statement C, but that quickly gets messy. By labeling the enclosing loop, you can have precise, simple, elegant control over the scope of your **continue** statement.

You can use the same mechanism with a **break** statement to break out of an arbitrary number of levels of nested **if**s, as shown in Listing 4.15.

Listing 4.15   Using Labels to Escape Nested ifs

```
int intVar = 20;

outer: if (intVar > 5) {
  middle: if (intVar > 10) {
    inner: if (intVar > 15) {
      System.out.print("This is ");
      break middle;
    }  // closes inner block
    System.out.print("really ");
```

```
  }  // closes middle block
  System.out.print("big!");
}  // closes outer block
```

This will cause the phrase "This is big!" to be written to the console. Really.

The Return Statement

In the tutorial, we learned that methods have types, meaning that they promise to *return* a value of a specific type to any method that calls them. However, all the methods we met in that chapter had a type of **void**. We never saw a method actually return anything. Methods that return values use the **return** statement to pass the value back to the calling method. It also has the effect of passing logic flow control back to the calling method. This means that if the interpreter encounters a **return** statement in the middle of a method, as in Listing 4.16, it exits the method immediately, and the rest of the method never gets executed.

Listing 4.16   The return Statement

```
boolean exampleMethod(int age) {
  if (age > 10)  return true;
  else return false;
}
```

Exception Handling

The Java language has built in mechanisms for handling things that go wrong. But the subject is intricate, and Neil does such a good job covering it in Chapter 5, that I'll simply refer you to that discussion.

CLASSES AND INTERFACES

Classes are the basic unit of object-oriented programming. They are the very essence of the definitions you need to work out before you can write a Java application. In Chapter 6, Alex will give you the conceptual background you need to start working with objects (which are classes incarnate). But I'll lighten Alex's load a little by teaching you the syntax of class definition now, with just enough theory to explain the language elements.

Let's say we've defined a class called **musicalEnsemble**, which represents the attributes and behaviors common to all configurations of musicians playing together. We won't go into details here, because some musical ensembles exhibit behavior which, believe me, you don't want to know about. So our **musicalEnsemble** class is, for the most part, a black box. One thing we know, though, is that some types of ensembles have attributes and behaviors that are simply not relevant to others. For example, we may decide that it's useful to distinguish between large and small ensembles by agreeing that large ensembles have conductors, while small ones don't. So we'll define two new classes based upon **musicalEnsemble**: **orchestra** (large ensembles) and **chamberEnsemble** (small ensembles). Figure 4.4 illustrates the relationships among **musicalEnsemble, orchestra,** and **chamberEnsemble**.

For purposes of Java programming, we need to learn the following terms: **musicalEnsemble** is known as the *superclass* of **orchestra** and **chamberEnsemble**. They are said to be the *subclasses* of **musicalEnsemble**. Another way of expressing this relationship is to say that the subclasses are *derived* from the superclass. To declare the **musicalEnsemble** and **orchestra** classes in a way that expresses their relationship, as well as indicating that only orchestras have conductors, we would write the code shown in Listing 4.17.

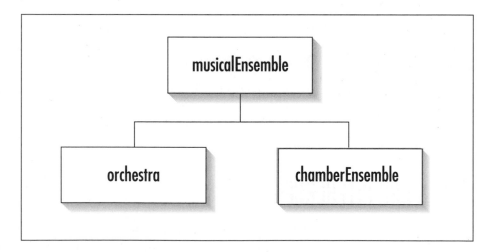

Figure 4.4   *musicalEnsemble and its subclasses.*

Listing 4.17   The orchestra Class, with Its Variable, conductor

```
/**
 * The musicalEnsemble class represents attributes and behavior
 * common to all musical ensembles
 */
public class musicalEnsemble {
  int members;
  int totalWeight;
  int gigsYearToDate;
  ...
}

/** The orchestra class represents the attributes and behaviour
 *specific to large ensembles
 */
public class orchestra extends musicalEnsemble {
  String conductor;
  ...
}
```

The **musicalEnsemble** class gives us variables for storing the statistics we simply must know about every musical ensemble, such as total weight. The **orchestra** class has only one variable in its own right, a **String** object for storing the name of the group's conductor. Declaring that **orchestra** extends **musicalEnsemble** enables us to let Java know that **orchestra** is a subclass of **musicalEnsemble**. The implication of this is that every **orchestra** object automatically has its own members, **totalWeight** and **gigsYearToDate** variables. This property of automatically endowing subclasses with all the attributes and behaviors of their superclasses (as well as of the superclasses of their superclasses, and so on, up to **Object** the superclass of all superclasses), is called *inheritance*. The subclass is said to inherit all the variables and methods (i.e. attributes and behaviors) of its superclass.

Do you remember back near the beginning of the chapter, when I described the three styles of comments in Java? I mentioned there that the third style was specific to declarations, and promised to demonstrate it when we got to class declarations. Well, here we are! And true to my word, before each of the class declarations in the last example, I placed a comment line that starts with a slash and two asterisks (/**). This special comment indicator tells documentation generation programs to include the comment in any documentation of the declaration that follows it.

Java regards classes as new types. Thus, you can use any class you have declared as a type for a variable. Variables of class types are known as "objects" and are the subject of Chapter 6. You can perform operations on these objects, and assign them values, just as you can do to variables of any other type. And here I must make good on another promise. When we discussed operators and expressions, I mentioned that there is an operator called **instanceof**, which operates on any object. The **instanceof** operator allows you to query the type of any object, enabling you to make decisions about how to proceed with processing, as shown in Listing 4.18.

Listing 4.18   Using the instanceof Operator

```
String StringObject;
NewClass NewClassObject;
Object ObjectObject;

...   code which manipulates objects of different types ...
if (boolean expression) {
  ObjectObject = (Object) StringObject;
}
else {
  ObjectObject = (Object) NewClassObject;
}
...   code generic to objects of all types   ...
if (ObjectObject instanceof String) {
  String tempStringObject = (String) ObjectObject;
  ...
}
else if (ObjectObject instanceof NewClass) {
  NewClass tempNewClassObject = (NewClass) ObjectObject;
  ...
}
```

Given an **Object** object that is actually an instance of some subclass (or subsubsubsubsubclass), **instanceof** lets you test the mystery object's true identity. This approach allows you to write extremely generic code that can accept any type of object as input, and perform appropriate manipulations.

Casting between Classes

Did you notice how I cast **StringObject** and **NewClassObject** to the **Object** class, and then cast them back after using **instanceof** to identify their type? Java supports casting between types, but only in accordance with these restrictions:

- An object can always be cast to a superclass (all the way up to **Object**, as we've seen).

- An object can be cast to a subclass *if* it is actually an instance of that subclass, or one of the subclass' subclasses (as far down as the hierarchy goes).

Casting an object to its superclass makes unavailable any attributes and behaviors specific to the subclass. For example, if I casted an **orchestra** object to the **musicalEnsemble** class, the casted object would have no access to the value of the **orchestra**'s conductor variable.

Listing 4.19 demonstrates one last complication of casting between classes.

Listing 4.19   The Effect of Casting Classes on Variable Access

```
class musicalEnsemble {

  String type = "musicalEnsemble";
  ...
}

class orchestra extends musicalEnsemble {
  ...
  String type = "orchestra";
  ...
}

public class classCastDemo {
  public static void main() {
    orchestra orchObject;
    musicalEnsemble ensObject = (musicalEnsemble) orchObject;

    System.out.println(orchObject.type); // prints "orchestra"
    System.out.println(ensObject.type); // prints "musicalEnsemble"
  }
}
```

See what happened? Both **musicalEnsemble** and **orchestra** have a **String** object called **type**. When **orchObject** is cast to the **musicalEnsemble** class, not only does it lose access to its own **type** variable, but it gains access to **musicalEnsemble**'s **type** variable. If you can't be good, be careful.

Every object can refer to itself, its attributes and behaviors in either of two ways. A variable called **this** is automatically created for every object. It refers to the object itself, and has the object's type. In addition, every object has a variable called **super**, which also refers to the object itself, but whose type is that of the object's superclass. Variables and methods with no class qualification have an implicit **this** in front of them. Print lines similar to the ones at the end of the previous example could thus be written as shown in Listing 4.20.

Listing 4.20   Using this

```
class orchestra extends musicalEnsemble {
  ...
  public void printType() {
    System.out.println(this.type);  // prints "orchestra"
    System.out.println(type);  // prints "orchestra"
                               // (implicit "this." prepended to
                               // variable reference)
    System.out.println(super.type);  // prints "musicalEnsemble"
    return;
  }
}
```

METHODS

I've used the phrase "attributes and behaviors" several times in this chapter. We've seen that attributes are represented as variables belonging to a class. Behavior is represented by the class' methods. Methods are the user-defined operations that can be performed on a class (or objects of that class). All Java code that "does" anything is implemented in the form of methods.

In the control flow section of this chapter, we discussed the **return** statement, which passes control back to whoever invoked a method, and with it passes a value of the type expected by the calling method. With one exception (which we'll discuss shortly), every method has a type, which is the type of the value that anyone calling the method expects to receive when the method returns control. This type is part of the method's declaration. A method that returns no value has a **void** type.

Method declaration statements also define the number and types of arguments expected by the method. Listing 4.21 contains some tiny methods, which demonstrate the syntax of method declaration.

Listing 4.21   Method Declaration Syntax

```
/** Declaration comments can precede method declarations as well
 * as class declarations
 */
// accepts arguments, returns a value
int total(int intVar1, int intVar2) { return intVar1 + intVar2; }
// accepts arguments, returns no value
public void doNothingReturnNothing(float floatVar,
    boolean booleanVar) { return; }
// accepts no arguments, returns a value
static boolean noArgs() { return true; }
```

The terms **public** and **static** are called *modifiers*. They are optional, and we'll discuss them when we learn about access. After the modifiers comes the return type, which is mandatory. Following that is the name of the method, also mandatory. Following that, in parentheses, is the parameter list, also mandatory. As you can see from the third example, if the method accepts no arguments (like my boss), an empty pair of parentheses is required as a place holder. Finally, between curly brackets comes the body of the method, the code that actually does the work. Unless the method's type is **void**, the body must contain at least one **return** statement, which must return a value of the appropriate type.

Classes can have multiple methods with the same name. Java uses their parameter lists to distinguish among them. It uses both number and types of arguments. Thus two methods with the same name but different parameter lists are considered different methods. This is known as *overloading* the method name. Overloading is usually used to group methods that perform essentially the same task, but must accept a variety of argument combinations.

Overload by Argument List, Not by Return Type

While methods can be overloaded by varying the number and type of arguments, they cannot be overloaded by varying the type returned. This will result in a compile-time error. Two methods with the same name cannot be distinguished only by their return types: for overloading to work, their parameter lists have to be different.

Overriding Methods

A class and its subclass can both have methods with identical names, return types and parameter lists. In this case, the subclass method is said to override the method in the superclass. Listing 4.22 shows an example of method overriding.

Listing 4.22   Method Overriding

```
class musicalEnsemble {
  int members = 65;
  public int getMembers() {
    return members;
  }
}
```

```
class orchestra extends musicalEnsemble {
  public int getMembers() {
    // assume the conductor is not considered a member
    return members + 1;
  }
  void overrideDemo() {
    System.out.println(this.getMembers());  // prints "66"-calls
              // orchestra.getMembers() for the current object
    System.out.println(getMembers());  // prints "66"-
              // equivalent to this.getMembers()
    System.out.println(super.getMembers());  // prints "65"
              // -calls musicalEnsemble.getMembers() for the
              // current object
}
```

Constructors

A few paragraphs ago I said that there is one exception to the rule that every method has a type, indicating the type of the value it returns. The exception is the category of methods known as *constructors*. Constructors are the methods responsible for creating objects and initializing their variables. They always have the same name as the class they create, and as I mentioned, they don't return a value of any type.

What does it take to create an orchestra? More than I can describe in the course of a programming language tutorial. Luckily, our task is an easier one. We just have to initialize part of a computer's memory to values that represent an orchestra. Let's say that, at a minimum, we need to know the number of members, the name of the conductor, and the length in centimeters of an unraveled bassoon. We could code the program shown in Listing 4.23.

Listing 4.23   The orchestra Class' Constructor Method

```
class orchestra extends musicalEnsemble {
  String conductor;
  int bassoonLength;

  // constructor method-has same name as class
  orchestra(int members, String conductor, int bassoonLength) {
    // uses members variable that it inherits from musicalEnsemble
    this.members = members;
    this.condutor = conductor;
    this.bassoonLength = bassoonLength;
  }
  orchestra(int members) {  // constructor with just one argument
    this(members, "Leonard Bernstein", 100);
  }
}
```

If the constructor method has no return type, how do you call it, and what do you get back? Constructors are invoked by means of the new statement, as follows:

```
orchestra myOrch = new orchestra(55, "Kazuyoshi Akiyama", 256);
```

Let's look at this more closely. This statement declares a variable, **myOrch**, of type **orchestra**. It uses **new** to invoke the constructor method for the **orchestra** class and to pass it three argument values. The constructor does its work, and the object it created is the value assigned to the **myOrch** variable.

But what's with the second constructor method, the one with only one argument? This is an example of overloading a method name. In this case, the constructor invokes the first constructor we saw, passing it the one argument it received, as well as default values for the two missing arguments. Thus, the following two statements are equivalent:

```
orchestra myOrch = new orchestra(65);
```

```
orchestra myOrch = new orchestra(65, "Leonard Bernstein", 100);
```

We've seen how a constructor method can initialize variables that are declared in the constructor's superclass. This raises an interesting question. How much control does a constructor method have over its elements that are actually declared in its superclass hierarchy? To our relief, the answer is as much control as we care to exercise. So far we've talked about constructor methods for the **orchestra** class without considering how attributes of the **musicalEnsemble** class get initialized if they're not handled explicitly by the **orchestra** constructor. So in Listing 4.24 we'll revisit these classes, expanding them a bit, and see what happens to their constructors.

Listing 4.24 Implicit Call to the Superclass' Constructor Method

```
class musicalEnsemble {
  int members;
  int category;  // code indicating classical, jazz, polka-fusion,
                 // etc.  Default should be 1 (classical)
  musicalEnsemble() {
    members = 65;
    category = 1;
  }
  musicalEnsemble(int members, int category) {
    this.members = members;
    this.category = category;
```

```
  }
}

class orchestra extends musicalEnsemble {
  String conductor;
  int bassoonLength;

  // constructor method - has same name as class
  orchestra(int members, String conductor, int bassoonLength) {
    // uses members variable that it inherits from musicalEnsemble
    this.members = members;
    this.condutor = conductor;
    this.bassoonLength = bassoonLength;
  }
}
```

Same old **orchestra** constructor, with nary a reference to **musicalEnsemble**. What value, if any, would the **category** variable get when the **orchestra** constructor is invoked? The answer is that, unless otherwise stated, every constructor begins with an implicit invocation of its superclass' constructor method with an empty argument list. Knowing this, we can quickly check the empty-argument-list **musicalEnsemble** constructor and discover that the **category** variable will be assigned a value of 1.

Two questions arise from this knowledge: 1) Can I define a **chamber Orchestra** class that extends **orchestra**? If so, how will it cope with **orchestra's** lack of an empty argument-list constructor? 2) Suppose I don't want the default values for the variables that belong to **musicalEnsemble**. Do I have to go through them one by one, overriding the values assigned by the empty argument-list constructor, as I did for members in the previous example?

A wise man answers questions in order, so: 1) If an empty argument-list constructor is not defined for a class, Java defines an implicit one that sets all variables to zeroes and nulls. So, not to worry. 2) Any constructor method may invoke any of its superclass' constructor methods. This invocation must be the first statement in the constructor. Thus, I could rewrite the **orchestra** constructor as shown in Listing 4.25.

Listing 4.25   Explicit Call to the Superclass' Constructor Method

```
// constructor method - has same name as class
orchestra(int members, String conductor, int bassoonLength) {

  // call superclass constructor, passing arguments to populate
```

```
    // members and category variables
    super(members, 1);
    this.condutor = conductor;
    this.bassoonLength = bassoonLength;
}
```

Class vs. Object: Static Attributes and Behavior

So far, we've seen methods and variables that belong to objects. Methods and variables associated with an object are known as *instance* methods or variables (remember that an object is also known as an "instance" of its class). But often you will want to define methods and variables that are associated with the class itself, not with any particular instance of the class. For example, I may decide that **musicalEnsemble** is just the place to provide a service that will return the name of the ensemble made up of any given number of musicians. Listing 4.26 shows what such a method would look like. It would be inappropriate for that type of method to belong to a specific orchestra object. It is more properly a service performed by the class itself, independent of whether an **orchestra** object has even been instantiated in whatever application happens to be running. Methods associated with a class, rather than with an object, are known in Java as *static* methods.

Listing 4.26   A static Method

```
class musicalEnsemble {
    ...
    public static String getEnsembleType(int members) {
        String ensembleType;
        switch(members) {
            case (0):ensembleType = "John Cage";
break;
            case(1):ensembleType = "Solo";
break;
            case(2)ensembleType = "Duo";
... etc. ...
        }
    }
}
```

The method was declared static by placing a modifier, **static**, before the method name. An additional modifier, **public**, makes it accessible to the public, but we'll wait a couple of pages to explore that.

Not only methods, but variables and the code to initialize them, can also be declared static. As with methods, the static modifier associates the variables and code with the class, rather than with any object of that class. You may

have a class that keeps tally of how may times it has been instantiated in the current application. After all, too many orchestras could get on one's nerves. Listing 4.27 shows how to implement a static counter variable.

Listing 4.27   A static Variable

```
class orchestra {
  static int numberOfOrchs; // static variable
  static { // static initialization code
    numberOfOrchs = 0;
  }
  orchestra() {
    numberOfOrchs++;
    System.out.println("There are " + numberOfOrchs
        + " in this corner of the virtual universe.");
  }
}
```

Static variables must be declared outside of any method. They are initialized by a block of code marked with the **static** modifier, which also resides outside of any method.

Access Specifiers

In addition to the **static** modifier, there is a group of modifiers which control access to variables and methods. Table 4.6 describes the four levels of access in Java.

The need for these levels of access is best left to Chapter 6. Listing 4.28 shows a quickie example of how you might put them to use.

Table 4.6   *Java Access Modifiers*

Access Name	Applies to	Description
public	classes, methods, variables	Can be accessed from anywhere by anyone
private	methods, variables	Can be accessed only from within the class in which the method or variable is declared
protected	methods, variables	Can be accessed from within the same class or its subclasses, even if the subclass is declared in a different package from its superclass
(unspecified)	classes	Can be accessed only from within the same package in which the class is declared

Listing 4.28   Using Access Methods

```
public class orchestra {
  private static int numberOfOrchs; // can't catch me

  // You want to know how many orchestras?  You'll have to call me.
  public static int getNumberOfOrchs(){
    return numberOfOrchs;
  }
}
```

The only access the outside world gets to the **numberOfOrchs** variable is via the **getNumberOfOrchs** method. I'll leave it to Alex to explain what's so great about that.

The final Modifier

Classes, methods, and variables can also be marked as **final**. The meaning of the **final** modifier varies, depending on context, as detailed in Table 4.7.

Remember when we were discussing overriding methods, and I gave an example of **getMembers**, which was declared in the **musicalEnsemble** class and overridden in the **orchestra** class? Remember? Well suppose you don't like conductors, you're very picky about accounting methods, and you simply don't want anybody coming along, extending your class and deciding for himself how he's going to count the members of one of **musicalEnsemble**'s children. One little word in the right place is all you need, as Listing 4.29 demonstrates.

Listing 4.29   Using the final Modifier

```
public class musicalEnsemble {
  ... appropriate declaration of members variable

  // "final" prevents subclasses from overriding this method
  public final int getMembers() {
    return members;
  }
}
```

Table 4.7   *The final Modifier*

Context	Meaning
class	Class can not have subclasses
method	Method can not be overridden
variable	Variable's inital value can not be changed

Synchronization

In the very first chapter of this book, when I reviewed the features that make Java so suitable for Internet programming, one of the traits I emphasized is that the Java environment is *multithreaded*. This support for threads extends right into the language. However, the syntactic support for threads is inseparable from the Java environment's general approach to threads, which is too complicated to include in this language chapter. I am therefore leaving the entire subject of threads to Chapter 20, where Alex will enlighten you about all aspects of thread programming in Java.

Abstract Classes and Methods

Our **musicalEnsemble** class is very general. We may well make a design decision that **musicalEnsemble** will never represent any actual musical group, but rather will serve purely as a skeleton, or protocol definition, for its subclasses. Such a class is called an *abstract* class. You can tell an abstract class by the presence of abstract methods. Abstract methods are marked with the **abstract** keyword, and have no body, as demonstrated in Listing 4.30.

Listing 4.30   An Abstract Class (with Abstract Methods)

```
class musicalEnsemble {
  private int members;
  abstract int getMembers(); // abstract method declaration
}
```

The declaration of the abstract **getMembers()** method mandates any subclass of **musicalEnsemble** to implement a **getMembers()** method. Without it, your Java compilation will fail. If your class hierarchy is very deep, you can put the implementation in **musicalEnsemble**'s grandchildren instead of its children. The implication of this is that **musicalEnsemble**'s children will also be considered abstract classes, and so on through the generations until all abstract methods are resolved.

Interfaces

Musical ensembles are examples of cultural institutions, or at least we hope so. If we're defining a system representing a variety of cultural institutions, we may decide that all cultural institutions should be capable of a certain set of behaviors. This is a civilized world, after all. We could define a class, **culturalInstitution**, of which **musicalEnsemble** would be a subclass. But that may interfere with other design decisions we've made, and may violate the modeling of a subset of reality that we've tried to capture in our design. Chapter 6 will explore the conceptual background of these dilemmas in greater depth. I just wanted to present a problem, and the Java language's facility for solving the problem. Listing 4.31 is an example of an interface.

Listing 4.31 An Interface

```
public interface culturalInstitution {
  Date getDateofNextFundraiserCostumeBall() ;
  int getNumberofTuxesToRent(int members, int females,
      int malesWhoOwnTuxes);
  void lobbyGovernmentForFunding(String levelOfGovernment);
}

class orchestra extends musicalEnsemble
    implements culturalInstitution { // implementation of interface
  Date getDateofNextFundraiserCostumeBall()  {
    ...    implementation code
  }
  ...    and so on and so forth for the other methods in the interface
}
```

An interface is a collection of method declarations, but without implementations. They are used to define a set of protocols that can be shared by otherwise unrelated classes. In our case, we declared methods that are surely ·
essential for any cultural institution. We determined the types of arguments these methods should accept, and the type of value they should return. We also made a decision that many musical ensembles are not worthy of the name "cultural institution," but that orchestras are. Therefore, when declaring the **orchestra** class, in addition to saying that it extends **musicalEnsemble**, we said that it implements **culturalInstitution**. By adding those words, we committed the **orchestra** class to implementing all the methods described in the **interface**.

interfaces can be used as types in the same way that classes can, as shown in Listing 4.32.

Listing 4.32   Using an Interface as a Type

```
class culturalInstitutionManager {

  // culturalInstitution (an interface) is used as argument type
  public static void lobbyEverybody(culturalInstitution CIobj) {
    CIobj.lobbyGovernmentForFunding("City");
    CIobj.lobbyGovernmentForFunding("State");
    CIobj.lobbyGovernmentForFunding("Feds");
  }
}
```

"Interface managers," such as **culturalInstitutionManager**, can save you a lot of redundant coding.

A few quick points about interface rules in Java:

- A class can implement multiple interfaces.
- Interfaces can extend each other.
- Variables in interfaces are by definition **final**, **public,** and **static**. They must be initialized.

ARRAYS, AND LIFE WITHOUT POINTERS

The sounds you hear are the cheering of giddy C programmers, relieved of ever having to worry about pointers to unallocated memory. Java has no, I repeat no, pointer variables that are directly manipulated by the programmer. It does have arrays, which are genuine objects, with methods in place to prevent you from going out of bounds, and no possibility of keeping the array variable in existence after you've freed the memory it points to. Java also has automatic garbage collection, so just relax and enjoy your clean new home.

If arrays are objects, they must be created using the **new** operator:

```
int intArray[] = new int[10];
```

You can also create arrays of arrays:

```
int intArray[][] = new int[10][5]; // this defines an array of 10
                                    // arrays, each of which is an
                                    // array of 5 ints
int intArray[][] = new int[10][]; // this defines an array of 10
                                   // arrays.  The dimensions of
                                   // each of these 10 arrays will
                                   // be allocated individually
intArray[0] = new int[5];
intArray[1] = new int[20];
```

Java has a class called **Array**, which is a subclass of **Object**. Every primitive data type and every class, whether user-defined or part of Java, has a corresponding subclass of **Array**. For example, if we define **musicalEnsemble**, and its subclass **orchestra**, Java automatically defines **musicalEnsemble[]**, and its subclass **orchestra[]**. These classes have one instance variable, **length**, whose value is the number of members in the array. Thus, we can use length to traverse an array, as shown in Listing 4.33.

Listing 4.33   Using an Array's length Variable

```
int members;
...    code to populate members    ...
int membersSalariesArray[] = new int[members];
for (int i = 0; i < membersSalariesArray.length; i++) {
    ...    code to populate membersSalariesArray    ...
}
```

Passing Values by Reference

What's a C programmer to do? There are simply situations where you feel you absolutely must pass by reference. One possibility is to pass an array, whose members would then be available to the called method. A second would be to wrap the piece of data in a class with setting-and-getting methods.

Garbage Collection and Finalization

I mentioned that Java manages garbage collection automatically. However, it does not manage reclamation of other resources, such as file descriptors. You can release these explicitly when you're finished with them. You can also write an instance method with the following protocol:

```
void finalize() {
    ...    code to release resources    ...
}
```

Any resources that cannot be accessed by any active object, and which belong to an object whose class includes an implementation of **finalize()**, will be released automatically by Java through an invocation of the **finalize()** method. This invocation will occur at an unspecified point in processing, so you can't depend on its timing. But it does ensure that resources are eventually returned to Java, which can improve performance.

PACKAGES AND COMPILATION UNITS

Earlier, we learned about compilation units and packages, the largest logical unit in Java. To indicate that a compilation unit belongs to a certain package, the first non-comment statement in the package must be a **package** statement:

```
package explorer;  // This compilation unit belongs to the Java
                   // programming explorer package!
```

Using Definitions from Other Packages

There are two ways you can specify classes or interfaces defined in other classes:

```
java.long.System.out.println("These two examples are equivalent.");
```

```
import java.long.*;
```

```
System.out.println("These two examples are equivalent.");
```

In the first example, I fully qualified the package (java.long) and class (System) name as part of the specification. In the second, I imported all classes in the java.long package, which makes all their names available to me without further qualification. What if by importing a class I create a potential ambiguity? Does Java have any mechanism for resolving ambiguous class references? Absolutely not. Ambiguous class references will not pass compilation. So if you have two identically named classes, you *must* qualify all references to them. Listing 4.34 is an example of a program with an ambiguous class reference: it is a *bad, bad* thing.

Listing 4.34   Ambiguous Reference: Don't Do This!

```
package explorer;
import java.long.*;

private class System { // please don't engage in this stupidity
    ...    System class implementation    ...
}

System mySystem = new System(); // This will fail compilation

// This will pass compilation, but please don't do it
explorer.System mySystem = new explorer.System;
```

In order to know where to look for imported classes, Java makes use of an environment variable called CLASSPATH. This variable must be defined in your operating system before you try to compile Java code.

Order of Declarations and Initialization

The order of declarations of classes, methods, and variables is irrelevant. This means that, unlike in C, you can refer to a method in the same class that has not been defined yet in the source code.

There are two general principles regarding order of initialization: 1) Static initializations precede in lexical order, unless 2) they are dependent on the static code of a class that hasn't been loaded yet. In this case, the second class is loaded and initialized before initialization of the first class can continue. If a cycle is created among classes that are dependent on each other, Java throws a **NoClassDefFoundException**.

Name Resolution

We've seen examples where local variables within a method had the same names as their object's instance variables. How does Java cope with this? Very simply, on the basis of proximity. Any searches for unqualified variable names within the current block of code, expanding the scope of its search outward until the entire current method is covered. If the name has not been found, Java examines class variables, and if necessary ascends the class hierarchy until it resolves the name.

For method names, the resolution process is more complicated. If a method name has been overloaded, Java searches the method name's set of over loaded declarations for an exact match by number and type of arguments (no matching is done on return type!). If it finds an exact match, the matching implementation is chosen. If not, Java determines which of the implementations with the same number of arguments "costs" the least to convert the data types in the invocation to the data types in the declaration. The exact algorithm for calculating the conversion cost can be found in the Java Language Specification. My advice: keep control of your code by matching method argument types exactly. Use explicit casting to control conversions, if necessary.

WHAT ISN'T IN JAVA

Earlier in the chapter, I promised you a list of reserved words in the Java language. You can find it in Table 4.8. Look it over. As we approach the end of our perusal of the menu at the Java bistro, you may be wondering what happened to a couple of things you expected to see on the menu. Like I/O, for instance. I/O, and many other elements needed to make the Java language good for anything at all, are not part of the language per se. They are implemented in the Java language as part of the Java Developer's Kit, made available by Sun Microsystems. We'll spend most of the book explaining how to use the classes in the JDK, but it's important to be

Table 4.8 *Java Language Reserved Words*

abstract	boolean	break	byte	case	cast	catch
char	class	const	continue	default	do	double
else	extends	final	finally	float	for	future
generic	goto	if	implements	import	inner	instanceof
int	interface	long	native	new	null	operator
outer	package	private	protected	public	rest	return
short	static	super	switch	synchronized	this	throw
throws	transient	try	var	void	volatile	while

aware that the JDK is not Java, but rather a set of classes defined by Sun that both facilitate the creation of applets, and circumscribe the range of behavior acceptable in applets. But that's a lecture for another day.

Exceptions: What to Do When Things Go Wrong

Neil Bartlett

Sometimes, things go wrong: Murphy's law is a universal invariant. We see how Java lets you cope with programming errors and keeps you on the path toward a program that works.

I am having one of those vivid flashbacks of a time and place. It is not a flashback of any momentous occasion in my life. I am sitting in a lecture theater at university and my friends and I are being taught about the mysteries of programming compilers. The lecturer, a bushy bearded man named Tony Davie, is telling us about the design of a local computer language called S-ALGOL. The flashback is quite strong. I can even see and smell the lecture hall—which is quite unfortunate because the aroma is none too savory.

S-ALGOL is one of those languages nowadays called a teaching language. No one ever uses it in the real world, which is sad because I missed S-ALGOL when I left the university. I remember being quite fascinated by the technique used to compile this language. The technique, a common one, was called recursive descent compiling. I really loved the simplicity of it. Recursive descent compiling made the tricky business of compiling a language seem almost easy. Throughout the lecture course, I became more and more enamored of writing compilers. The language constructs, via a recursive descent compiler, seemed to just compile themselves. It all made so much logical sense.

It was not long before my rosy-eyed view was challenged.

I managed to get hold of the source code for the S-ALGOL compiler. I was amazed to read this program, which was unrecognizable as the program we had learned about during lectures. Okay—maybe I exaggerate somewhat, but let me exaggerate some more. Like Jeff Goldblum in the film "The Fly," the neat logical compiling principle we had learned in lectures had been transformed into a monster. Sure, like Jeff and the fly, there were the remnants of the original still visible. What remained, though, was not a pretty sight.

And what had caused this monstrous change? None other than error handling: trying to cope with the many problems that occur—especially when those damn programmers type in incorrect programs. In the S-ALGOL compiler, I saw the real world pulling down the nicely erected walls of academy.

Yes, error handling is the seamy side of programming computers, but equally it is much of what programming is about.

The plain fact is that if you don't do error handling well, you will probably end up with a buggy, hard-to-maintain program. As it happens, and I must say this before I get calls from my Alma Mater revoking my degree, the S-ALGOL compiler was actually a well-written program. It had been written from the beginning with error handling firmly in mind. Even so, the code read as a hymn to error handling.

Since this subject of error handling is so important, this chapter is designed to help you with its thorny issues. In the course of the chapter, we will see one of the reasons Java is such a good language: it truly does provide you with state of the art error handling facilities.

If you are a C++ programmer, you will recognize the error handling mechanism used by Java. It's based on an idea proposed by Stroustroup in his book, *The C++ Programming Language, second edition.* The main difference is that the Java compiler, unlike many C++ compilers, actually implements the proposal! Beware though that there are a number of subtle differences between C++ and Java. The differences are subtle and numerous enough to trap the unwary.

THE BASICS

First, the basics. Like, er, what *are* errors and exceptions, anyway?

An *error* is something that happens which shouldn't. Imagine that we have a piece of code designed to open a file. The code is designed to open a file using a filename supplied by a user. If the user supplies the code with the name of a file that does not exist—that is an error. The code is designed to open the file, but the error is that there is no file to open. We can blame the user all we want, but our program still must be able to cope with this type and other types of errors.

Errors then are just things that can go wrong with a program.

Our job as programmers is to try to anticipate these errors and write code that will not crash and burn. We want to be able to write code that will, for the above example, detect that the user entered an incorrect filename and print out a useful message. It won't stop in its tracks or run around in loops looking for a file that is not there. We call this writing *robust* code.

There are many techniques for handling errors. The recommended Java way of doing things is to use *exceptions*. An exception is a way of detecting an error and jumping directly to a piece of code that is designed to *handle* that error.

Traditional techniques for handling errors, such as return code passing, are not normally so direct at finding the code to handle the error. These traditional techniques keep plowing on even after an error has been found. They plow right into the code that follows the error expecting that code to handle any problems caused by the error. The net effect is that all the code you write must be prepared to be in the path of an error. You end up with a lot of **if** statements that ask the previous piece of code if it was in error. Typically even small pieces of code can become so bloated with these tests for previous errors that the actual code that does the real work is lost inside of the code that does the error handling.

The great thing about exceptions, then, is that as soon as an error is found, the exception can bypass any code that comes after the code that found the error and jump straight to the exception handler code. Now you can see the wood for the trees. There is no bulky error code to gum things up. There is the code that finds the error and the code that handles the error.

You Throw, I'll Catch

The basic concepts of exception handling are *throwing* and *catching*. The code that finds an error will throw an exception, the code that handles the error will catch the exception.

The throwing and catching metaphor is very apt. When an error is detected, an *exception object* is created and thrown to the catch code that handles the error. You really can imagine that exception object is a ball thrown between the code that detects the error and the code that catches the error. Just like in a game of catch the ball does not touch the ground (assuming you threw it well enough) until the catcher touches it. In other words, the exception goes over the head of the code that you see written between the code that throws and the code that catches.

To throw an exception, a object derived from the **Exception** class is created. The object is then thrown using the **throw** keyword, as shown in this code snippet:

```
throw new FileNotFoundException();
```

To catch the exception, the code that is likely to throw an exception is placed in a **try** clause. The **catch** exception handler is tacked on to the end of the try clause, as shown in Listing 5.1.

Listing 5.1   The catch Exception Handler

```
try {
    if (!fileFound)
        throw new FileNotFoundException();

    doSomething();

} catch(FileNotFoundException e) {

    System.out.println("File not found");

}
```

If the boolean variable **fileFound** is false, the **throw** clause will throw the **FileNotFoundException**. This causes the processing to jump to the end of the **try** clause looking for a catch handler that matches the **FileNotFoundException**. The **doSomething** method will not be called.

The **catch** clause explicitly names the exception it wants to catch. In this case, it will catch the **FileNotFoundException**.

Built-in Exceptions

Generally when you first start out programming the JDK, you will only be catching exceptions. When a JDK method internally encounters an error, it will throw an exception. The exception is thrown out of the JDK method and into your code. All you have to do is worry about catching it.

For example, when you open a file for input, the **FileInputStream** constructor requires you to take into account that the file you named may not exist. You do this by enclosing the code that opens the file in a **try** statement, and following the **try** statement with a **catch** statement to trap the error condition thrown by a failed construction of a **FileInputStream**. The coding looks like Listing 5.2.

Listing 5.2   Trapping an Error

```
try {

      inifile = new DataInputStream(new FileInputStream(path));

} catch(FileNotFoundException e) {

      System.out.println(filename + " not found in file system.");
      System.exit(0);

}
```

Of course, Listing 5.2 shows a very simple example on just a couple of methods being called inside of the **try** clause. Typically a number of methods will be called inside of the try statement. In effect, the **try** statement will contain the program that would have been written if you did not care about exception handling and were truly optimistic enough to believe that errors don't happen to you; they only happen to other programmers. Meanwhile the catch statement will implement all the code that the belt and braces people will want to write.

When you read some Java code with **try** and **catch** statements in it, also read the try code as the program that the programmer wanted to write and the catch code as the code that deals with the problems the programmer thinks will occur. This makes it quite simple to spot if the programmer forgot to deal with a problem. If there is no **catch** statement for the problem at the **try** statement, the exception will not be handled correctly.

Big Glove

Of course you don't just have to catch just one exception at the end of the **try** clause you can catch as many as you need to. If you want to catch a whole bunch of exceptions, you can nest exception handlers at the end of a **try** clause, as shown in the code snippet below:

```
try {
} catch (..) {
} catch (...) {
} catch (...) {
}
```

If an exception is thrown, it will be matched against the first exception handler, then the second, and so on until a match is found. For this reason, you should arrange the order of the exception handlers so that the most specific exception classes are at the top and the least specific at the bottom.

Ensuring a Catch

If a catch handler wants to catch any exception that is thrown, it can catch objects of the **Exception** class, as shown in the code snippet below:

```
catch(Exception e) {
}
```

If this were placed at the top of the list of exception handlers, it would always catch any exception that was thrown inside of the **try** clause.

THE EXCEPTION HIERARCHY

Actually, there are rather a lot of exception objects that can be thrown. All exceptions are ultimately derived from the **Throwable** class. An object must be descended from the **Throwable** class in order to be thrown using the **throw** keyword.

Figure 5.1 shows the complete hierarchy of exceptions thrown by the JDK methods. At the top is the **Throwable** class and immediately descended from that is the **Exception** class. Then come all manner of exception classes. You can tell what the exception is for by looking at the name. For example the **StringIndexOutOfBoundsException** is thrown, when an index to a string it either less than zero or beyond the end of the string.

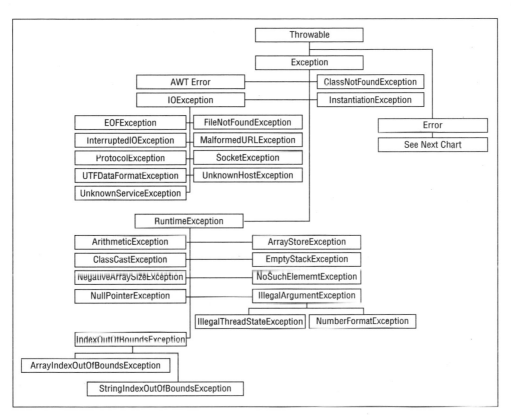

Figure 5.1 *The Java exception hierarchy.*

When you use a method from the JDK, you should check with the JDK API documentation to find out which exceptions the method might throw. You should write code like that shown in Listing 5.2 to catch the exceptions thrown by the methods you are using.

Making an Exception of Yourself

But you don't have to wait for a JDK method to throw an exception. You can throw your own! Go ahead! Try the code in Listing 5.3.

Listing 5.3 Throwing an Exception

```
void readfile() throws FileNotFoundException {

    if (! file_exists)
        throw new FileNotFoundException();

    doread();
}
```

The method in the listing throws the **FileNotFoundException**. When the exception is thrown, the end of the method is jumped to, and the **doread()** method is not called.

The **throws** keyword tells the Java compiler that the method may throw the given exception. If the method can throw more than one exception, then the name of each exception should be listed separated by commas. If the compiler encounters a throw of an exception inside of a method that does not list the exception in the list following the **throws** keyword, the compiler will get nasty, give out a message and refuse to compile the file. This little bit of accounting might seem bothersome, but it is a small price to pay for all the benefits that exceptions can bring.

Throwing Back in Relay

If you write a method that throws an exception, then the Java compiler will require that you do one of two things: you must either declare that the method throws the exception using the **throws** keyword, or else you must provide a catch exception handler to catch that exception. The Java compiler does not allow an exception to be thrown without you being very clear that you have either passed the exception out of the method to the code that called the method, or that you have dealt with the exception completely inside of the method.

If you throw the exception out of the method who deals with it?

Why the code that calls the method, naturally. Now since the code that calls the method is also inside a method itself, the code will have to handle this exception. It is faced with the same choices as the originating method—it can either pass it on or it can catch the exception and handle it locally. If this method decided to throw the exception, the method it calls is faced with the same problem. Listing 5.4 shows this in operation.

Listing 5.4   Passing on an Exception

```
import java.lang.*;
import java.io.*;

public class except {

    void methodA()  throws FileNotFoundException {
        throw new FileNotFoundException();
    }

    void methodB()  throws FileNotFoundException {
```

```
        methodA();
    }

    void methodC() {
        try {
            methodB();
        } catch (FileNotFoundException e) {
            System.out.println(e.toString());
        }
    }

    public static void main(String args[]) {
        except e = new except();
        e.methodC();
    }
}
```

In Listing 5.4, **methodA** throws a **FileNotFoundException** therefore it declares that it throws the **FileNotFoundException**. **methodB** calls **methodA**. **methodB** does not install an exception handler to catch the **FileNotFoundException**; therefore it must declare that it throws the **FileNotFoundException**. **MethodC**, however, installs an exception handler, so **methodC** does not declare itself to throw the **FileNotFoundException**.

Why So Much Bother?

The idea is to make the exception handling system into an active thing. Rather than passively ignoring exceptions you have to actively ignore them. At the very least, you are forced to place an empty exception handler at the end of the **try** block, as shown in the code snippet below:

```
try {
    throw new FileNotFoundException();
}catch (FileNotFoundException e) {
}
```

This type of enforcement puts exception handling high on the agenda when it comes to programming Java. You can't ignore it. Hopefully, this will result in more robust and "bulletproof" pieces of code.

THE RUNTIME EXCEPTION CLASS

Now we have seen that if you throw exceptions you must make sure that you either pass the exception on or that you catch it. You might be wondering then why a lot of code you will see does not have any mention of exceptions in it at all—no **throws** keywords and no catches. After all, we know that a lot of the JDK methods throw exceptions so why aren't we forced to provide **catch** exception handlers for all of them?

Well, the JDK developers decided to allow a special case. The special case is that all exceptions derived from the **RuntimeException** class are exempt from having to be thrown or caught. If a method — any method not just a JDK method—throws an exception derived from the **RuntimeException** class, then it and all the methods that call it do not *have* to write code that deals with the exception.

This special privilege is provided to prevent typical code that uses the Java language from being completely cluttered with exception handlers and throws statements. You will appreciate this when you realize that even an innocent **i++** can eventually overflow the **i** variable and consequently throw an exception. Imagine every **for** loop having to protect itself with a **try** clause and an exception handler.

Having **RuntimeException**s is very useful, then. It does raise the issue, though, of being able to circumvent the entire throws/catch enforcement.

As we will see in a moment, you can create your own exception classes. However, if you create your own exceptions by deriving them from the **RuntimeException**, you have a "get out of jail free" card. You will not have to implement all the throws and catches. This may sound like good news, but it isn't. It is not recommended at all that you derive your exceptions from the **RuntimeException** class. If you do so, you will find that you have defeated much of the purpose of the exception handling system.

As you can see, the **RuntimeException** class kind of gives with one hand and takes with the other if you use it wrongly.

So That's Why My Programs Crash!

Yeah, programs crash because the Java runtime throws an exception that is not caught and the program exits. Typically these exceptions will be derived from the **RuntimeException** class. Conveniently, Java runtime installs an exception handler that prints a stack trace when the program does not trap an exception.

As we will see at the end of the chapter, there is another **Throwable** class called **Error**. Classes derived from **Error** are also thrown and typically not caught by programs.

Throwing Baggage Around

Often, an exception will contain information about itself.

As we saw when we threw the **FileNotFoundException**, the exception is just an instance of a class. An exception class, like any other class, can contain data. Actually all exceptions support the concept of a message string that can be passed into the constructor of the exception, as shown in the code snippet below:

```
throw new FileNotFoundException("data.txt");
```

The **catch** statement can then extract the message using the **getMessage** method, as shown in the code snippet below:

```
catch(FileNotFoundException e) {
    System.out.println("Unable to find file "+e.getMessage);
}
```

MAKING YOUR OWN EXCEPTIONS

There is nothing sacred about the predefined exception classes. You are free to create your own exception classes to meet your own needs. Naturally, it is useful to use the predefined exception classes if they fit your needs.

The process of creating an exception is simple. You create a class that derives from **exception** or one of **exception's** child classes. For example, Listing 5.5 shows an exception called **MyException** being defined. It is parented directly by the **Exception** class itself.

Listing 5.5   Deriving an Exception Class

```
class MyException extends Exception {

    public MyException() {
    super();
    }
}
```

There is not much to the exception code. You can now throw this exception just like any other exception, as shown in the code snippet below.

```
throw new MyException();
```

Making Public Exceptions

If you want to share exceptions outside of the current package, you will need to declare the exception as a **public** class. Also, since the compiler forces public classes to be in a file of their own, you will need to put your exception definition in a separate file.

Choosing a Parent

When you write your own exception it is a good idea to carefully choose which class to derive the exception from.

The **Throwable** class does not make a good choice. Often, programmers will implement catch-all exception handlers that just catch objects of the **Exception** class. If you derive from **Throwable**, programmers cannot do this to your exception. This may be seen as as non-conforming code. Essentially, the **Exception** class acts as the categorizing class for all exceptions.

Deriving from lower down the hierarchy might make sense. For instance, **IOException** might make a good candidate. However, you should only make this type of decision after careful investigation of the circumstances under which the exceptions will be thrown. If you categorize the exception as an **IOException**, it had best be clear to programmers that your new exception is, indeed, an **IOException**.

As we mentioned earlier, you should not derive from **RuntimeException** or one of its descendants.

Carrying Baggage

If we want our exception to pass around data, we can simply add class variables to contain the information, as shown in Listing 5.6.

Listing 5.6   Adding Class Variables

```
class MyAWTExeption extends AWTException {
    Public Point p;

    public MyException(int x, int y) {
        p = new Point(x, y);
    super();
    }
}

class user {
```

```
void method() {
    try {
        // do some stuff
        if (problem)
            throw new MyAWTException(10, 20);
        // do some more stuff
    } catch (MyAWTException e) {
        System.out.println(e.p.toString());
    }
}
}
```

MyAWTException is an exception that will pass around some point information. Presumably we are defining this exception to throw an exception when a point is in error. We want the **catch** exception handler to be able to extract the point information and do something useful with it.

When to Create Your Own Exceptions

As a general rule of thumb, if you have an error condition that is generated by your program, you should create you own exception and that exception should be derived directly from the **Exception** class.

You can break this rule only if you feel that an existing exception is thrown in exactly the same circumstances you need.

If you do not create your own exception, you run the risk of not being able to distinguish your error condition from a system error condition. If you are writing a package for external use, then you should make doubly sure that you use you own exception classes; otherwise, you might run the risk of conflicting with other packages.

USING EXCEPTIONS FOR DEBUGGING

Obviously, when an exception is thrown, the code will eventually hit an exception handler.

If you want to find out what the stack trace is when the exception is caught, you can use the **printStackTrace** method which is available to all classes derived from **Throwable**, as shown in Listing 5.7.

Listing 5.7   Using the printStackTrace Method

```
import java.lang.*;
import java.io.*;
```

```
public class printstack {

    void methodA()  throws FileNotFoundException {
        throw new FileNotFoundException();
    }

    void methodB() {
        try {
            methodA();
        } catch (FileNotFoundException e) {
            e.printStackTrace();
        }
    }

    public static void main(String args[]) {
        printstack p = new printstack();
        for (int i = 0; i < 2; i++)
            p.methodB();
    }
}
```

This will print out two stack traces when the program is run, as shown in Listing 5.8.

Listing 5.8   Printing Out Two Stack Traces

```
cmdn>java printstack
java.io.FileNotFoundException
        at printstack.methodA(printstack.java:7)
        at printstack.methodB(printstack.java:12)
        at printstack.main(printstack.java:21)
java.io.FileNotFoundException
        at printstack.methodA(printstack.java:7)
        at printstack.methodB(printstack.java:12)
        at printstack.main(printstack.java:21)
```

This technique can be useful when you have a program where unusual exceptions are being thrown, but where you want to continue with the program.

WHY USE EXCEPTIONS?

Now that you've seen how Java wants you to do things, maybe it is useful to understand why it is good to use exceptions for error handling. I suppose you can consider this section a justification of using exceptions. At the beginning of this chapter we mentioned some traditional techniques for dealing with errors. Let's look at one of these techniques and see how exceptions hold up against it.

Error Return Codes

There are a number of techniques for dealing with errors. The most common technique is probably to use error return codes. This technique uses a return value from a method to tell the calling method whether the called method had an error.

Let's look at the use of error return codes and try to get a feel for how to use them. Listing 5.9 shows an example.

Listing 5.9   Using Error Return Codes

```
class test {

    boolean openfile(string name) {

        if( canreadfile(name) == 0)
            return False;

        open( name );

        return True;
    }

    public void caller(String name) {

        if ( ! openfile( name ) )
            System.out.println("File not found");
    }
}
```

Take a look at the example. It features a class called **test** that has two functions in it. One method, **caller**, is a public method which uses an internal method **openfile** to open a file of the given name. The two functions communicate using an error code system. In this case, **openfile** returns a boolean True if it opened a file, and False otherwise. If you have read the chapter on I/O, you will realize that I have taken a few liberties with the code here. This is not the best way of doing things in Java.

One thing I hope will be apparent is that already, even with this simple example, we are a long way from the actual intended code. The intended code *sans* error handling would be something like that shown in the code snippet below:

```
class test {

    void caller(String name) {
```

```
        open( name);
    }
}
```

One of the problems of error codes is percolating the error code. As you can see from our bit of sample code, we use a method **canreadfile** to determine if the file is really on disk. We use the error code from **canreadfile** to determine an error code for **openfile**. In essence, we are layering the error codes one on top of the other. For all we know, **canreadfile** may use error codes from another method.

So why is this percolation a problem? Well, in a simple phrase: human error. We frail humans might forget to pass on an error code on the caller code, or more likely, we might forget to pass on information. This can be tough for functions which need that information. For example, suppose **canreadfile** did more than just return a boolean value and returned an **int**, which encoded the reason for the failure. This is a very common type of error code scheme. The error codes typically do more than just return true or false—they try to record why the error happened so that later code might better know how to handle the situation. They do this encoding by assigning numbers to different errors. Suppose **canreadfile** returns the values shown in Table 5.1.

Now, the error code from **openfile** might be misleading: **caller** might print out the message "File not found" when in fact the file exists, but is just not readable by the user.

Okay, this last problem is fixable. We just make sure that **openfile** returns the full range of error codes from **canreadfile**. Then, **caller** can make a better assessment of the error.

This is just the start of our problems. Besides the fact that we are starting to burden ourselves with a lot of work, we have not considered the problem of conflicting error codes. Suppose for instance that **openfile** uses another support method called **validatefilename** in addition to **canreadfile**. **Validatefilename** checks that the given name is indeed a file name and not

Table 5.1 *Encoded Return Codes for* **canreadfile**

Value	Meaning
-1	file does not exists
-2	file exists but is not readable by this user

just a random string of characters. Let's update the code for **openfile** to use this technique, as shown in Listing 5.10.

Listing 5.10   Updating the openfile Code

```
int openfile(string name) {

    int i = validatefilename(name) ;
    if (i < 0)
        return i;

    i = canreadfile(name);
    if (i < 0)
        return i;

    open( name );

    return 1;
}
```

Now further suppose that **validatefilename** has the potential return codes shown in Table 5.2.

Notice a problem? The potential error codes from **validatefilename** are the same potential error codes as canreadfile! We can't tell if a error code of -1 from **openfile** means "name too long" or "file does not exist."

As you can see, we are starting to get into some very murky water. We will have to work out some scheme of combining the error codes from canreadfile and from **validatefilename** so that the caller can get the full information. We will probably have to design a conversion scheme to covert the error codes to different numbers.

Without knowing it, we have backed ourselves into a design and maintenance wall. The error handling has far outstripped the original code in size and cost to design and maintain. We are rapidly moving into the situation where we have obscured the original code and we have a spaghetti mess of error codes.

Table 5.2   *Encoded Return Codes for* **validateFilename**

Value	Meaning
-1	name too long
-2	name contains invalid characters

The problem is we are trying to do the right thing. We are trying to write robust, error-handled code. It is no wonder that some programmers give up and write code that allows errors to go by.

So How Are We Doing?

So how does the exceptions stuff improve upon the error code mechanism? Well, for a start, it solves the biggest problems we encountered when using error codes.

We don't have to do any conversion of the error codes to allow us to use two functions and we don't have to remember to pass the exceptions up to caller functions. In essence, the error handling runs itself; our job now is simply to shape it to our needs, not to implement it.

What I really like about exceptions is their optimism. The main code is clean and uncluttered with the realities of the world. All the nastiness is handled outside away from the main code. That is the most compelling distinction between code and error handling.

Choosing Exceptions Versus Error Return Codes

So I have battered error codes and praised exceptions throughout this section. Are error codes dead? Actually, no. Error codes very much have their place. In localized areas, they are often used to maintain readability — especially where algorithms are concerned.

Take, as an example, the **match** method from the regular expression package: how would you choose to run it as an algorithm? Would you use an exception handling error code system, as I did, or system? Actually, I deliberately used both techniques! Notice that when parsing the structure, I used exceptions to deal with errors that might arise.

So why did I chose error codes in one place and exceptions in another?

Well, the answer is personal and style related. There are no hard and fast rules. I use error codes generally where the "error" is part of the algorithm. For instance, is backtracking an error situation? I have decided that it is not; it is actually rather likely to happen even when the programmer has entered a good regular expression and the user has passed in a string to be matched. Therefore, I chose error codes to implement it. However, for forming the parser, I decided that the pattern should be well formed: it's a programming error if it is not. For me, this is the right place for an exception. However, I could very well have used exceptions for both.

A minor point is that exceptions do carry some overhead: the classes need to be constructed and so on. If the exception is likely to be thrown a lot, then it starts to become an issue.

Exceptions stop code slipping into the high entropy abyss. They are not necessarily the thing to use for algorithms.

THE ERROR CLASS

I must confess that I have been a little loose with "the error word" in this chapter.

The problem is that the JDK has a class called **Error**. To make matters worse, **Error** is a kind of exception—note the small "e"—but it is a cousin of the class **Exception**—with the capital "E." My dilemma when writing this chapter was: should I go with using "the error word" as I am accustomed to using it, or should I go with the JDK word? I resolved to use the error word, and then explain my way out of it later. So this section is my attempt to set the record straight.

An **Error** is a kind of exception. Errors are exceptions that are thrown by the Java runtime. There is no real difference between Errors and Exceptions: they both derive from the **Throwable** class. The main difference lies in their intended use. The idea is that typical end-user programs should not try to catch exceptions derived from the **Error** class. Figure 5.2 shows the class hierarchy of Errors. Compare this to the class hierarchy of Exceptions shown in Figure 5.1

At runtime, Java installs exception handlers for exceptions of the **Error** class. Typically, it installs a simple stack trace printer. It is not advisable to install your own exception handlers for classes derived from **Error**. You run the grave danger of running off into system crashspace.

AND FINALLY...

If you think about it very, very carefully you will notice a tiny gap in the team's defense.

Suppose we have something that must be guaranteed to happen after a **try**— no matter what happens during the **try**. We can handle this, can't we? Well, no! At least not using **try** and **catch**.

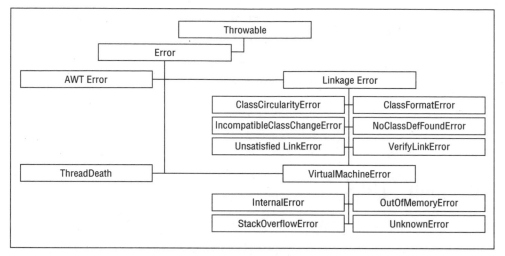

Figure 5.2 Class hierarchy of Errors.

First, consider placing the code you want to run after the **try**. Does this work? No. If an exception is thrown, the code will not necessarily be called. Okay, now: consider placing the code in an exception handler—**catch** statement— does that work? Again, no. If an exception is not thrown, then the catch code is not called.

It seems we have a Catch-22 (sorry, I could not resist the pun) here: either we have to duplicate code after the **try** and in a generic **catchall**, or we are out of luck.

This is where the **finally** clause comes in. It guarantees to execute no matter what.

We can tack a **finally** clause onto the end of some **try** and **catch** clauses and it will execute no matter what. It doesn't matter if an exception is thrown or not thrown, as shown in Listing 5.11.

Listing 5.11   Using a finally Clause

```
void func() {

    try {
        openExternalService();
    } catch {
        System.out.println("External service not available");
        return;
    }
```

```
try {
    doSomethingUseful();
} catch {
    System.out.println("Problem happened");
} finally {
    closeExternalService();
}

}
```

The code for the method **func()** demonstrates how this execution occurs. The **finally** clause saves us having to duplicate the **closeExternalService** method. Admittedly, small potatoes in this example, but useful when clean-up becomes more messy.

LET'S RECAP

Exceptions are the recommended error handling technique for Java programs. Exceptions enable us to jump straight from the problem code to the code that can clean up the error. We use the **throw** keyword to jump to the clean up code and we use the **catch** keyword to define where the clean-up code is.

An Object-Oriented Primer

Alex Leslle

Every day, you're immersed in a world full of complexity. I'll show you how to make sense of the challenges of Java programming, at least, by adopting an object-oriented approach.

The only common denominator for readers such as yourself is that you all share a desire to learn Java. That's the kind of grass-roots enthusiasm that has been driving the popularity of Java all along. However, it means we have to deal with a wide range of programming experience.

Maybe you're an HTML writer trying to get a handle on a new way of jazzing up your home pages. Maybe you're an accomplished Visual Basic programmer looking to do a bit of Web programming. Or maybe you're an old C++ hack checking out a new language that you've heard bears some similarities to C++.

Whatever your bias or background, if you want to learn to program Java, you must appreciate the implications of the statement from Chapter 1: *Java is an object-oriented language.*

To program in Java, you need to understand at least the fundamentals of object-oriented programming (OOP). It is a fact of Java life that all Java programs rely to some degree on object-oriented techniques, and understanding the JDK will require some appreciation of those techniques. Even reading this book demands some knowledge of them.

You're going to encounter some new1 words and concepts. If you think that polymorphism is a character in a children's television program, or inheritance is what you get when a rich uncle dies, then this chapter is for you. We are going on a fast, streamlined dash into OOP territory.

This chapter is a primer taking you through OOP concepts and the jargon. I assume that you have read Chapter 4, which introduced the basic concepts of Java. I'll be repeating some of them here, but with a new, object-oriented spin. You certainly can't expect to become an object-oriented guru without designing Java programs and trying to implement your designs—and sometimes falling flat on your face. A few missteps are inevitable as you gain experience and develop your skills. However, after reading this chapter, you will at least have earned your OOP cadet badge. Hopefully, the design missteps you suffer will be few and not too painful. You should also be able to read most of this book while appreciating the object-oriented techniques that are usually mixed into the examples.

One final word of encouragement before we begin: If you are a programmer and have not yet worked with an object-oriented language, you'll encounter some new concepts that might clash with your current programming style. It might be tougher to rid yourself of old habits than you think. Cut the negative thoughts immediately. Just look in the mirror, smile, and say "Every day, in every way, I'm programming better and better."

OOP WITHOUT PROGRAMMING

Forget about programming for a minute. Look around you. What you see are *objects* that, in various ways, respond to external events—that is, objects that can exhibit *behaviors*. Each object contains within itself all the information it needs to react to the various events that might happen to it. The dog is hairy, affectionate, and knows how to beg for its supper. The VCR is cool, metallic, and knows how to send video signals to a coaxial cable. The table is heavy, solid, and knows how to stub your toe when you walk into it in the dark.

That world is significantly different from the world we model in traditional procedural programming. In the programming world, we enforce a strict separation between data and procedures—that is, if you wish, between *things* and *actions*. Data just sits there, waiting for an algorithm to come along and do something to it. And algorithms themselves are off in a world of Platonic forms, waiting for some data to give substance to their existence.

To model a world of objects that have built-in behaviors, object-oriented programming is significantly clearer than old-style procedural programming. Oh, the old concepts are all still there—information hiding, air-tight subroutines, and the like—but data is no longer passive. Instead of waiting for algorithms to come and act on it, data (objects) now has its own *built-in* algorithms.

Basic Concepts of Object-Oriented Programming

Now that we've talked about the "real world," let's talk about the world of programming—specifically, the world of object-oriented programming. If you've programmed before, you'll find that object orientation embodies some familiar ideas, but takes them further than you've seen them go before. This type of programming is based on several key concepts:

- **Objects.** An object is a data item that includes its own methods. Instead of passing the data item to an external subroutine for processing, you send a message to the data item, telling it to call one of its own methods to manipulate its data. An object is defined by a class, which is similar to a C **struct**, a Pascal **record**, or a Visual Basic **type**—except with its own methods added. This is probably the hardest idea for experienced procedural programmers to grasp, because it requires a complete shift in how they think about designing programs. But it's similar to the real world: Just like a table or a toaster, an object has *properties* (data members) and *behaviors* (methods that react to events).

- **Encapsulation.** This just means that an object's data and methods are kept together inside the object itself. In a way, this is just "information hiding" applied to objects. Just as a global function can't access local variables inside another function—an example of information hiding in traditional programming—so the data inside an object is normally hidden from code outside the object. To manipulate the data, other parts of the program have to ask the object to call its own encapsulated methods, which can return values to the calling subroutines. As you would expect, the internal details of the object type are normally invisible to the rest of the program. If you change the implementation of an object class, then as long as its "interface" to the outside world stays the same, you don't need to change anything else in your program.

- **Inheritance.** Just as a child inherits traits from its parents, so a class (which defines a type of program object) can inherit traits—data members and methods—from its ancestors. For example, if you have a class that defines an **ElectricGizmo** object type, this class will have certain data members and methods of its own (for example, a boolean field to show if the gizmo is turned on, and a method to change the value of the field). If you then define a new class as a descendent of **ElectricGizmo**, such as **CDPlayer**, the new class automatically inherits all the data members and methods of its ancestor class. This saves you the trouble of "reinventing the wheel" with respect to inherited class features. Instead, you can focus your work on the *new* features required by the **CDPlayer** class. This concept is discussed in more detail later in this chapter.

- **Polymorphism.** This is the ability of different objects to respond differently to the same message. Because each class encapsulates its own methods, and these methods are hidden from the rest of the program, different classes can have some methods with the same names. For example, suppose that you had an ancestor class called **Shape**, on which you based the descendent classes **Circle**, **Square**, **Triangle**, and **Trapezoid**. Each class would have its own **draw** method, so that you could send the same message—"Draw yourself"—to objects of the four different types, and get an appropriate result each time. An object of type **Circle** will not get confused and draw itself as a triangle. That's polymorphism in action. It's made possible by encapsulation and information hiding.

How Do You Know What You Know?

It's believed that most of the neural pathways in a human being are laid down before age five. There is one essential skill that we all develop naturally during our earliest years; it is a fundamental key to being able to understand and interact with the world.

To a newborn, the world is a jumble of sensory stimulations—a complex chaos of information. With sufficient exposure and repetition, a baby begins to recognize correlations and similarities. As it grows and learns, it learns to create *abstractions*. Abstraction just means recognizing and focusing on similarities between objects while ignoring differences. The baby learns to recognize its mother and then perhaps its father. The human face is learned exceptionally early. There are a series of black-and-white toys that have been used with children when they were just newborns. All of the images are abstract shapes, but one, which is a stylized human face—not a real human face. It is astonishing to see how strong an affinity a baby appears to have with the human face—even simplified. The baby has already successfully abstracted the human face. Two dots for eyes and a dot for a nose and a curved line for a mouth already trigger the thought: face.

The process of abstraction is generally goal-oriented. An object used for a different purpose would need to be abstracted differently. A baby's first priority is securing a reliable source of food. It pays to be able to recognize people since they are the only care-givers. Dogs might be good at washing your face, but they hardly ever bring you food. Slippers, maybe. Cigars, possibly, but since most infants aren't allowed to smoke cigars, that's kind of a non-issue.

Dogs and Cats

I have a one-year-old daughter. It is eye-opening to share her learning experiences. A few months ago, she was at a stage where (among animals) she recognized only dogs and cats. She didn't yet know what other animals were. Frequent, first-hand encounters with both domestic animals probably made deep impressions. We own two cats, so she was very good at differentiating between cats and large dogs immediately. However, some small dogs, at first, were still embarrassed by this little child calling them *Cat* in public. With more examples and corrections, she soon fine tuned her identification abilities.

Even so, further errors showed up. Horses and other apparently dog-like animals—at least in terms of form rather than size—were commonly mistaken for dogs. Again, with encouragement and exposure to more examples, her recognition was refined. Next came the distinction between zebras and horses. The refinement continues. As her abilities improve, I find that my own abilities to describe the essential differences are challenged. Most of us would recognize the differences between a common dog and a wolf. However, have you ever tried to explain the differences in terms that a one-year-old can understand?

With enough examples, she will continue to learn which features are important to correct identification, and which features are simple variations within a type and can be ignored. In fact, that process never ends. Every learning process, including the learning expedition you're on right now, is taxing your abilities to make sense of what you are seeing. You have to abstract before you can understand.

Black Boxes

I'm proud of my daughter, without a doubt. Though she hasn't corrected the time on the VCR to match Daylight Savings Time, she does know how to play her favorite *Barney* video. And she knows to rewind once Barney starts to say his *Goodbyes*. She's comfortable with the CD player, too. She hasn't got to my computer yet—but only because it has been off-limits during the past several months while I've been writing this book.

The first thing she learned was the power button. She recognized instantly the temporal relationship between pressing that button on any appliance and an instant change in the state of the appliance: on or off.

The next thing to capture her interest was more subtle. The Play button had slightly differing behaviors on each appliance. She was able to ignore the slight differences and master the abstraction. Rewind was, and still is, a bit mysterious to her. Without a concept of a linear tape, it's understandable. Though after too many Barney re-runs, I'm sometimes tempted to sacrifice one to her education and my sanity.

Obviously, she has no clue what actually goes on inside either appliance but she doesn't care. She is a client of the appliance. It provides her with a limited set of services from which she chooses by pressing one of several buttons.

She's already learned that the same sorts of buttons show up on different appliances. Everything has an "on" button, for instance. The interfaces of many different appliances have some elements in common. Perhaps she's grasped how on and off have much more general relevance than to just specific appliances. She's starting to form a mental hierarchy of behavior and function.

Interfaces

The point: We all deal with the world through interfaces that hide details we need not know. The interface is often the product of an abstraction. In most modern appliances, the level of complexity in the inner workings is astonishing. I've read that the average television set has tens of thousands of lines of software and obviously a lot of advanced hardware too. One thing most of us have in common with a one-year-old is ignorance of the implementation details of most appliances.

I didn't need to cite the example of a modern appliance. A dog has an interface. It has a physical manifestation and a pattern of behavior. One of the reasons that you would teach a child the difference between a dog and a wolf has to do with their different behavioral interfaces. Petting a dog is fun and reduces stress—petting a wolf is inappropriate and threatens injury. Correct recognition of a dog implies that you can be comfortable in making assumptions about its behavior. An animal that manifests itself as a dog suggests a certain behavior contract. A dog is expected to behave properly. Dogs that behave like wolves and bite people are often destroyed. That's because people feel deceived. No longer can the dog be trusted. The dog betrayed the contract of what being a dog involves.

People can interact with and enjoy the company of a dog for years without an appreciation of its biochemistry. For the purpose of keeping a dog as a pet, biochemistry is not important as long as you have a good veterinarian and a reliable brand of dog food. There are people involved in medical research on dogs, however, for whom a detailed knowledge of their inner workings is very important. It's their job not to ignore the secret processes, but to study and learn about them. It all has to do with purpose. You hide or ignore what's not important for the purpose at hand.

The world is full of cases in which an abstraction *encapsulates* the implementation details that are simply not necessary to comprehend simply to use the familiar interface the object provides. It's just a way of dealing with complexity.

JAVA PROGRAMMING AND OOP

Earlier, we took a brief look at the basic concepts of object-oriented programming. This section explores those concepts in more detail, particularly as they apply to Java. I'll even dip into the JDK to illustrate the concepts with concrete examples.

I avoided all mention of programming in the previous section because I really believe that the concepts in an object-oriented approach transcend programming. Programming is mechanics, or should be—if it is the result of a thorough analysis and design. Solving a programming problem is not much different from solving any real-world problem. Only the medium is different. You still have to study the problem carefully, establish requirements for the solution, and then design a solution that satisfies the requirements. Problem solving is so natural that you're likely not conscious of the steps you take—because they run together and are not very distinct.

Don't get me wrong. That doesn't mean programming with an object-oriented approach will be easy at first. There's no shortcut to mastering it. It's one thing to appreciate and quite another to implement. Design is design, no matter what the methodology. It is also the hard work that must be tackled first every time.

I hope that as the programming part of the discussion unfolds and you see exactly how to implement the concepts in Java, you'll come to appreciate the value of investing so much effort in object-oriented deign. In this section, I'll securely connect the abstract concepts to their specific programming counterparts. And I'll discuss the programming implications of each concept.

Abstraction

I imagine you're just brimming with ideas for new applications you want to write with Java. You have images of graphical user interfaces floating in your mind already. But my job is to pull your feet back to earth—back to the details.

 **The Devil's in the Details**

The time spent analyzing a programming problem, combined with the time spent designing a solution, is not wasted. It's really the most important stage. Resist the temptation to avoid it and skip straight to the programming. If you do quality analysis and design up front, the programming will be a breeze—especially with the object-oriented approach.

Most applications exist in order to solve a perceived problem. During a thorough analysis, you need to totally pick apart the problem at hand. You must grasp the essence of the problem. You must not be satisfied until you understand the problem intimately. What you're looking for is more information than you'll eventually use. It's a lot like doing research for a paper. You end up creating something new by taking away. It's like sculpting with information. With all the information gathered, you will evaluate what you end up with. You'll discard that which bears little value while retaining details that are critical to a successful solution to the problem.

Even if object-oriented programming is totally new to you, if you've ever programmed, you'll agree that *divide-and-conquer* is a reliable technique for taming complexity. It is necessary to organize the details. When the time comes to design your application, you're going to come face-to-face with the opportunity to organize the program into discrete parts. The object-oriented approach stresses certain valuable techniques.

In Java or any other object-oriented programming language, you are encouraged to think of those application parts as objects. The application then becomes the product of a cooperative effort of a collection of objects.

Object = Data + Methods

In traditional programming, data just sits there, waiting for some algorithms to come and do things to it. That "procedural" paradigm has served us well for a couple of decades. Now, however, object orientation has provided us with a better paradigm—one that incorporates all the good ideas in the procedural approach, but adds new ideas to improve on it.

In object-oriented programming, data is *active*, including its own algorithms (in Java, called "methods") to manipulate itself. No longer is unprotected data passed among functions that could corrupt it. Data is always packaged with its own sets of methods. These methods, custom-designed for the specific data to which they are bound, ensure that access to the data is controlled and that the correct state of the data is always maintained.

Instead of passing data to a separate method, you simply send a message to the data, telling it to activate one of its own methods and do something—just as you might tell (send a message to) your dog (an object) to "heel" (perform a specific behavior). Figure 6.1 emphasizes graphically how you should wrap data in a shell of methods that provide the sole access to your object data.

The objects you choose can really represent anything at all. Sometimes they'll represent real objects in the problem. Sometimes the representation will be of more abstract things. The objects are abstract models of the things they represent. They don't include every detail of the thing—just what is appropriate for the use you have intended for it in the application.

Object Orientation Is How the Real World Operates

Notice that the object-oriented paradigm is much closer to how we think in the "real world" than is the old procedural paradigm. In the real world, we deal with objects, each of which has a set of properties and behaviors—just like the objects in a Java program.

In Java, objects are represented by classes. Let's start trying to model a CD player with a new Java class, as shown in Listing 6.1.

Listing 6.1 A Rudimentary CDPlayer Class

```
class CDPlayer {
    boolean isTrayIn;
    boolean isPlaying;
    int        trackBeingPlayed;
    int        totalTracks;
    float      timeInCurrentTrack;
}
```

The class is pretty limited, but it's a good beginning. It has the name **CDPlayer** and encloses five variables of different types. You can guess the purpose of each variable from its name. This class includes enough information to enable

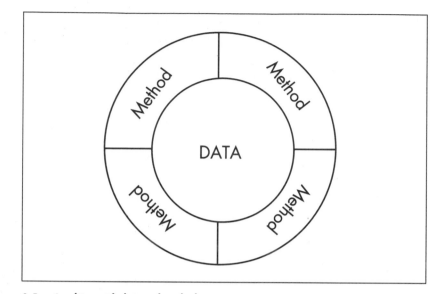

Figure 6.1 · *An object with data and methods.*

you to create the front panel LED display for an onscreen **CDPlayer**. Note that this class is just one possible class you could have created for CD players in general.

The class variables in Listing 6.1 would be insufficient if you needed to identify one particular **CDPlayer**. The color, serial number, and retail price are all characteristics of a CD player, but they were not included in the original example. They were discarded because they were unnecessary. You really don't need to know the retail price of a CD player in order to create an onscreen display.

If, on the other hand, you were writing an application that would be used by an Internet electronics vendor, this **CDPlayer** class would fail horribly. The abstraction is all wrong. Different classes are necessary for different purposes, even for the same object

Listing 6.2 shows a **CDPlayer** class that might do a better job.

Listing 6.2   An Improved CDPlayer Class

```
class CDPlayer {
    String brand;
    String model;
    String color;
    float    listPrice;
    public CDPlayer() {
  }
}
```

Instantiating Classes

Classes are like templates. They define the characteristics of program objects, but are not the objects themselves. When you create an object based on a class—that is, when you instantiate the class—you've created a real thing you can use in your program. Only an instance of a class is a real thing. Merely defining a class doesn't create any objects of that type.

I'll make an instance of a CD player for myself based on the class **CDPlayer.** This is shown in the code line below:

```
CDPlayer myPlayer = new CDPlayer();
```

Here's how the code line breaks down:

- **CDPlayer:** This, the first item on the code line, gives the *type* of the object variable that's being created.
- **myPlayer:** This gives the *name* of the object variable that's being created.
- **new:** This tells Java to create a new object variable.
- **CDPlayer():** This is the constructor for the **CDPlayer** class. It initializes the data members of the variable and does other setup work.

That new instance, **myPlayer,** has inside it all the variables that were described in its class. Recall you need to both define a class and declare an instance variable. Both are being done in this one line. The bit to the left of the equal sign is the definition: **myPlayer** is an instance of a **CDPlayer**. While the bit including the equal sign to the right is the declaration. The definition tells what the instance is capable of referencing. The declaration gives it something concrete to reference.

Since I haven't defined any methods to do it for me, I'll have to set the values of my object's variables one by one, as shown in the snippet below:

```
myPlayer.isTrayIn              = true;
myPlayer.isPlaying             = true;
myPlayer.trackBeingPlayed      = 3;
myPlayer.timeInCurrentTrack    = 1.5;
myPlayer.totalTracks           = 12;
```

To review: programming objects are abstracted and become established as classes. The classes need to be instantiated before they can be used.

Encapsulation

Maybe some of you feel that it is unnatural to be asked to put every last bit of code in a class somewhere. Do you feel you're being asked to hide your code away in some sort of Houdini box of torture when programming with an object-oriented language? But like Houdini and his magic boxes, enclosing and hiding are really to your advantage. Houdini needed to be hidden so that his secret techniques weren't visible to his audiences or his competitors. That would spoil the mystery of the magic.

Encapsulation is also a form of information hiding. Like Houdini, your code is not visible to other objects unless you make it visible. You have explicit control right down to a variable-by-variable basis. You expose only what is absolutely necessary and then only give access to selected variables via methods. You retain the right of implementation specifics. Nobody knows how you perform your programming magic. There are several implications of this. First, as long as your class continues to behave as originally advertised, you are free to change or even improve the "hidden" implementations without affecting anyone who is using your code. This is especially important with a language such as Java that allows you to load classes remotely.

If you've already been programming with Java, you have employed abstraction and encapsulation already. In Java, it is mandatory that all methods and variables be included in classes. The compiler will not accept any alternatives. If you've been successful in getting your Java programs to compile, then you were in compliance.

Data Members

Data members are simple. They are just the variables that are included in any class. In the previous example, you already saw how several variables were used to identify an instance of a class.

Methods

Being able to store information in objects is fine, but real world objects *do* things. For instance, we can tell our CD player to change tracks or to stop playing. We want to give our objects that ability too. We want to be able to tell our objects what to do. It's also not recommended to give users of your object direct access to its variables. It limits your ability to keep the contents of the object from getting incorrectly changed. A user would only be limited by the range of the type of the variable. That range usually includes values that are inappropriate for the object. You need a way to change an object's variables, but in a way that's verified and known to be correct.

To do this, we use what is called a *method*. I hope you are familiar with the concept of a function or a subroutine, because that is what a method is. It's just a function that belongs to a class. When the method executes, it has available to it all the information about the object.

Listing 6.3 shows an upgrade of our original **CDPlayer** class. This upgrade adds a few methods.

Listing 6.3 CDPlayer Class with Methods

```
class CDPLayer {
    boolean isTrayIn;
    boolean isPlaying;
    int        trackBeingPlayed;
    int        totalTracks;
    float      timeInCurrentTrack;

    public void Play() {
        isPlaying - True,
    }

    public void NextTrack() {
        if (trackBeingPLayed <= totalTracksOnCD)
            trackBeingPlayed++;
    }

    public void PreviousTrack() {
        if (trackBeingPlayed > 1)
            trackBeingPlayed-;
    }
}
```

Suppose that your CD player is different from mine. Perhaps you have a more sophisticated model—one that can be loaded with multiple CDs at the same time. How can you model this situation based on your experience with **CDPlayer** class I just designed?

Inheritance

Inheritance picks up where abstraction leaves off. An abstraction itself is a means of dealing with the inherent complexity of objects. It is successful because it is goal-oriented and purposeful. However, even abstraction can introduce a new form of complexity. It is the complexity that arises from generating numerous independent abstractions.

A great thing about the human mind is its ability to group things together—to see some fundamental similarities between things and be able to treat these things in a consistent manner. At first, you used abstraction to organize the complexity of numerous qualitative and quantitative characteristics of objects. Now, you'll have to use inheritance to organize the abstractions themselves according to common characteristics you recognize.

Cutting Through the Inheritance Jargon
One of the aspects of inheritance that can be confusing is the terminology. You get words like base class, ancestor, superclass, and such used interchangeably whenever programmers gather. Well, they do all mean the same thing! The problem is that, like spoken human languages, OOP evolved from a number of different sources and directions, so naturally, each source created its own terms for inheritance. The following terms are synonymous: super, ancestor, base, and parent. Likewise, these terms are all synonymous: subclass, descendent, derived, and child.

Now that we have considered what objects are, let's look at how we might manage relationships among them. To see an example of this in action, let's look at a simple extension of a previous example. I have a CD player but I want a multi-CD player. If you were writing lots of code for CD players, wouldn't it be great if when you wrote the code for a multi-CD player you could just build on the foundation of the code that you had already written for a simple CD player? You can do it!

Let's say that **multiCDPlayer** inherits from **CDPlayer**, as shown in Listing 6.4.

Listing 6.4   Inheriting from CDPlayer

```
class CDPlayer {
    int track;

    void play() {
        // some clever code
    }
}

class multiCDPlayer extends CDPlayer{
    int currentCD;

    void selectCD( int i ) {
        currentCD = I;
    }
```

```
}
// ...
{
    // ...
    multiCDPlayer m;

    m.selectCD( 1 );
    m.play();
    // ...
}
```

Java uses the **extends** keyword to express inheritance of one class from another. You simply tag it on the end of the class definition and, voilà, instant code reuse. Now a user can call methods that were defined in **CDPlayer** as if they had been defined in **multiCDplayer**. The user is none the wiser. It really makes no difference, because all a user cares about is that the CD gets played.

Remember our previous discussion about classes and objects? Classes provide the template—instances fill in the values in the template. In Java, inheritance is class-based. Suppose, for example, that we have a class called ElectricGizmo with the properties **On/Off** and plugged_in. From that class, we could create descendent classes for **CDPlayer**, **AirConditioner**, and **ElectricToothbrush**. All of these descendant classes would add their own properties to those inherited from their ancestor class, **ElectricGizmo**.

Any object variable that instantiated, for instance, the **CDPlayer** class would automatically have all the properties (data members) and behaviors (methods) of its class, and it would *also* automatically have all the properties and behaviors that its class inherited from the ancestor class.

Of course the inheritance does not have to be restricted to one level. You are free to add as long a chain of ancestors and descendents as you need. It is quite common to start with an ancestor class that is very abstract and provides very little in the way of functionality—maybe it just provides a name so that we can ask any object its name—and then add successive levels of classes, each providing more detail. You'll be introduced to the easy-to-overlook class called **Object** later in this chapter that does just that.

Java does not allow multiple inheritance—meaning, a particular class cannot have multiple ancestors that are unrelated to each other. Each descendent class can only have one immediate ancestor class. However, each ancestor can have multiple descendents. This means that we can have lots of different types of CD players derived from the **CDPlayer** class. We might have portable CD players, multi-CD players, CD-ROM players, etc. You might hear Java disparaged for its lack of multiple inheritance. The truth is that multiple inheritance can be very problematic in inexperienced hands. The Java designers made a conscious decision to omit it. Besides, Java provides other techniques, such as interfaces, which are better suited to the role. Interfaces deal with the cases where multiple inheritance would normally be used in other object-oriented programming languages.

Access and Visibility

So far, our view of encapsulation has been rather like one of those old fashioned carriage clocks—you can see what's going on inside. You can plainly see all the gears and springs and how they join together. You can see all the cogs rotating. That's fine for ornamental clocks, but let's suppose we want to design some other kind of clock. Do you really want the whole world to see what is going on inside? Maybe you want the freedom to be able to switch the internal mechanism of the clock. Maybe we find that an electronic timing system is more accurate than the old cogs and sprockets.

Java puts control in your hands. You can control access to the various parts of any class you write: the class itself, its variables, and its methods. Access control is possible with three *access specifiers* built into Java. They are simple keywords that are placed before the thing to be controlled.

Java provides three main keywords to help you regulate the encapsulation of an object. We have seen one: **public**. The other two are **protected** and **private**.

Visibility Is Not What It Appears

A variable or method is visible to other objects only if the rules of access allow it. Good design dictates that only as much should be visible as is necessary—and no more. Encapsulation is preserved with the judicious use of the access specifiers: **public**, **protected**, and **private**. When not preceded by one of these access modifiers, variables and methods default to being visible only to other classes in their own package. Resist the temptation to use **public** when **protected** or **private** would be more suitable. Why waste an opportunity to strengthen your design? Learn to use the access modifiers.

Public means that the class, method, or variable is visible by objects of other classes anywhere. That means wide-open visibility.

In contrast, **private** means that only the current object can access those variables and methods.

Protected provides an in-between level of access. It is like **public** to children that inherit from the class. To all other classes in other packages it is as good as **private**.

A unique quirk about access specifiers, or the lack of them, is that classes, methods, and variables are neither **public**, **protected**, nor **private** by default. In other words, if you don't put **public**, **protected**, or **private** in front of, say, a method, then the method is only visible to other classes contained in the same package.

If you're fuzzy on the concept of a "package," see Chapter 4. Briefly, a package is a group of classes that have been explicitly bundled together, usually because they play roles in a cooperative process. By default, Java files compiled in the same directory are part of one package. So it is likely that all of your classes are part of the same package if you are doing all of your Java development in one directory.

Polymorphism

Polymorphism has a reputation as one of the more difficult object-oriented concepts to understand. Actually, polymorphism is really just a natural extension of the other concepts you've just learned. They weren't too difficult. You'll be surprised how easy it is to understand polymorphism.

Polymorphism follows as a natural consequence of inheritance. By the way, the term polymorphism is derived from two Greek words: *poly* meaning many and *morph* meaning form. Therefore polymorphism has to do with multiple forms of something.

Polymorphic CD Players

I don't know if you noticed, but when I was describing the simple inheritance example of the **multiCDplayer** inheriting from the **CDplayer**, I kind of glossed over a few things. For instance, what happens if **multiCDplayer** needs to do some prep work before a CD can be played? In that case, the **multiCDPlayer** has no way to influence the **play** method's behavior. If the **CDPlayer play** method is insufficient for the demands of the **multiCDPlayer**, then the **multiCDPlayer** won't work. If this troubled you, then you have already recognized the need for polymorphism.

Polymorphism allows a derived class to change what a method does. It is a way of putting more specialized code into the base class so that the derived class does not have to do exactly what the base class does. To implement polymorphism in Java, the derived class will be created with a method with exactly the same name, return value, and parameters as the base class.

This doesn't seem to be that much of an advantage until you realize that you can now create an object of a derived class, treat it as an instance of its base class, and yet still have a method in the derived class available when you make the appropriate call. In other words, if we had different implementations of the **play** method in both the **multiCDPlayer** and the **CDPlayer** classes, we could create an object of the class **multiCDPlayer** and pass it to a user who only knew about **CDPlayer** classes. The user could call the **play** method and end up calling not the **play** method of a **CDPlayer** but a **multiCDPlayer**'s **play** method. Note that the calling class still does not know about **multiCDPlayer** class even though it ends up calling one of its methods.

This technique is very useful because it means that we can write our **CDPlayer** class today. We can write code that uses the **CDPlayer** class. Then later we can create more classes that derive from **CDPlayer** and still satisfy the interface contract of the **CDPlayer**. This is a truly superb example of reuse! Perhaps eventually, we have completely changed instances and are not even using a **CDPlayer** instance anymore. The user of the class doesn't care, as long as whatever derived class is masquerading as just a **CDPlayer** satisfies the interface.

Furthermore, the user can use the keyword **instanceof** to determine if the **CDPlayer** instance is instead a full-blown **multiCDPlayer** instance. If so, the program can use the appropriate methods. Listing 6.5 shows a concrete example.

Listing 6.5   Using the instanceof Operator

```
class Shape {
    void draw( int x, int y ) {
        // do nothing
    }
}

class Circle extends Shape {
    void draw( int x, int y ) {
        // circle-specific drawing code
    }
}
class Square extends Shape {
    void draw( int x, int y ) {
```

```
        // square-specific drawing code
    }
}

class Palette {
    Shape getRandomShape() {
        Shape shape;

        if( ... ) {
            shape = new Circle();
        } else {
            shape = new Square();
        }

        return shape;
    }
}

// ....
Shape shape = new Palette().getRandomShape();
shape.draw( x, y );
// ...
```

It appears that the **draw** method of class **Shape** is being called. But that code does nothing. In fact, there isn't even any body code at all. But if you were to run this code fragment, you would find that something does get drawn. That's because before running **Shape.draw**, the interpreter effectively asks the **Shape** object, "What are you, really?" It then invokes the appropriate class' **draw** method. In this case, it was unnecessary to know any more than that you were dealing with a **Shape**. Remember what I said about "need-to-know."

This is an example of what's called *dynamic typing*. Despite the name, it's a simple concept. *Typing* pertains to the kinds of rules governing class interchange. That just means it has to do with whether it's legal to assign something of one type to something of another type. Java is *strongly typed*, which means there are strict rules that must be followed when it comes to data types. You won't get through a compile without adherence to those rules. Before I explain dynamic typing, let's look at something more familiar: *static typing*.

In the examples we've seen so far, the compiler has always been able to determine what code will get executed even before the code is run. By extension, that means that the compiler can check that only valid object assignments are attempted in the program. Since the compiler is doing it, it is called compile-time checking. That's static typing. This applies equally to most simple Java code, too. Static typing is helpful for several reasons, not the least of which is that the compiler is able to highlight errors that you can repair before running the program.

However, the previous example illustrates something distinctly different. The compiler has no way of knowing beforehand exactly which **draw** method is going to get called. That means it can't determine which code gets executed. You'll have to wait until runtime to find out if you've done something wrong. That's the cost you incur for being able to use polymorphism. It's really a small price to pay for the benefit of code reuse, though.

Abstract Methods and Classes

In the previous example, **Shape** is a real class that you certainly could instantiate. It won't do anything, but it would be legal. Why is it necessary to define the method **draw** with a body since its body should never be executed? The answer is that it's not necessary. In fact, the method should be **abstract**. That means that the class needs to be **abstract** as well, since it will have at least one **abstract** method. Here's the new **Shape** class:

```
abstract class Shape {
    abstract void draw( int x, int y );
}
```

That's not too much different, except that **draw** now has no body at all. It's not even legal for an **abstract** method to have a body. **Abstract** classes are similar to another vehicle for defining Java classes: **interfaces**. When we learn about **interfaces**, I will outline the differences between them and **abstract** classes.

Polymorphism still has a few more wrinkles. Another kind of polymorphism is *method overloading*.

Method Overloading

Suppose that every time you needed a method to print different types of values, you had to write a separate method with a different name. Ugh! Your code would end up littered with stuff like that shown in the code snippet below:

```
printInt(x);
printString(s);
printBoolean(b);
```

Besides cluttering your code with numerous methods that all do roughly the same thing, the user of the class is always forced to determine which method to use, depending on what type of data is to be printed. Fortunately, you can avoid all this and create several methods with the same name but which operate on different data types!

Method overloading lets you call a group of similar methods with identical names but which take different parameters. Suppose you have an output class and you want it to print out the value of any variable you give it. You want to be able just to say *print* and the name of the variable, regardless of the type of the variable, will print. The variable might be a **string** or it might be an **int** or a **boolean**. Additional **print** methods could be written to accept any other parameters.

This is how method overloading will tidy things up. The caller does not need to know a different method for each type, but can simply call the method by the same name and provide a different parameter list. Java will work out the precise method to call for you. Overloaded methods are shown in Listing 6.6.

Listing 6.6 Defining Overloaded Methods

```
class output {
    void print( String s )  {
        // code to display a String
    }

    void print( int i ) {
        // code to display an integer
    }

    void print( boolean b ) {
        // code to display a boolean
    }
}
```

Now you can simply call **print** for each of the different variables, as shown in Listing 6.7.

Listing 6.7 Overloaded Methods in Action

```
int     x = 6;
String  s = " Hi There" ;
boolean b = false;

print( x );
print( s );
print( b );
```

What Are You?

You'll soon find a need to distinguish the lineage of a particular object. Java provides you a way of doing this by using the **instanceof** keyword.

Let's suppose you are writing a shape library. You have a class called **Shape**.

From **Shape**, you derive several other classes such as **Square**, **Ellipse**, and **Triangle**. You have also set it up so that all shapes support an **equality** method. The **equality** method lets you determine if two **Shape** objects are the same.

Now, the first thing we have to do is make a polymorphic method that captures the idea of equality. Each instance of **Square**, **Ellipse**, or **Triangle** will have its own implementation of the **equality** method. The method will take a shape and determine first if the comparison is even possible: squares can only be compared with squares, and so on. However, the **equality** method is passed a **Shape** object. How can it find out more precisely what kind of shape the object is?

Fortunately, we can use the **instanceof** operation. Listing 6.8 shows the **equality** method for the rectangle shape.

Listing 6.8   Using the instanceof Operator

```
class Rect extends Shape {
    boolean equality(Shape s) {
    if ((shape != null) && (shape instanceof Boolean)) {
        return (height == ((Rect)shape.height). && width == ((Rect)shape.width);
    }
    return false;
    }
}
```

The **instanceof** operator is indispensable when you begin to use polymorphism.

this and super

The Java keywords **this** and **super** are special. You can think of them as representing a class and that class' parent.

You use **this** as the name of an instance within an instance. I imagine some of you are wondering why you'd ever need to refer to yourself that way. After all, methods in a class can call other methods in that class without prefixing the method name with the name of any particular instance. A class defaults to calling its own methods. That's true generally. But there are some cases where it is necessary to use **this** to eliminate confusion that can arise when both a class and its parent class have methods of the same name.

The keyword **super** refers to the immediate parent of the class. Similarly, it's used to specifically access methods or data of your parent class. In the constructor for a class that derives from a parent class whose constructor takes parameters, you must explicitly call your parent class' constructor using **super** and the series of parameters that are appropriate. You've likely never had to pass parameters to the parent class' constructor and have probably grown accustomed to the parameter-less parent class constructor being called automatically. Note that, if used, the **super** call must appear on the first line of the derived class' constructor.

Interfaces

Sometimes, you run into a problem with inheritance. You want to write a class that seems to be the descendent of several of ancestor classes. You want to combine a little of this class and a little of that class. What you're actually trying for is *multiple inheritance*. But remember that I said that Java doesn't support it.

As a simple example, let's return to the world of animals. Actually I really dislike animal examples. Virtually every book you'll ever read on OOP reads like a tribute to Carolus Linnaeus, the man who originally started categorizing the animal kingdom into genus, species, and so on.

Consider the following animals: bats, birds, and bees. If you follow a straightforward genus inheritance, each of these animals would fall into a very different part of your animal kingdom inheritance tree. However, each of these animals could also be categorized as a flying animal. Maybe that one ability is of central importance to you. Maybe you would like to write common code for such flying animals, but you don't want to break the established hierarchy of the animal kingdom classes.

The Java solution to this problem is to use **interfaces**, which let you specify a set of methods that a class must implement. You specify that a class must conform by using the **implements** keyword. The **bat** class might look like the code snippet below:

```
interface flyingAnimal {
    int numberOfWings();
    void fly();
}

class bat extends mammal implements flyingAnimal {
    int numberOfWings() { return 2; }
}
```

A class can implement more than one **interface** if necessary.

Multiple inheritance problems are not the only reason, nor even the most common reason, for using the **interface** technique. You can think of an

interface rather like a specification that says what a class' responsibilities are in terms of services that must be provided. It does not, however, include any information about *how* the class is to implement the service. This provides you with a lot of freedom. You are not forced to provide any more details. Implementation details are often distracting at such an early design stage. This kind of thing might sound like a small gain, but you'll eventually appreciate it.

Providing **interfaces** rather than classes as the way of controlling access to the functionality of a library is a very useful and powerful mechanism. It also allows you to reserve the right to make changes to the underlying structure of the library as long as the *interface contract* with users is respected. **Abstract** classes and Java **interfaces** are quite similar, but have a few important differences. An **abstract** class may still have other non-abstract methods. This is not possible with an **interface**. However, while several **interfaces** can be mixed together in the implementation of a class, **abstract** classes are bound by the same limitation as other classes, and must be the sole parent of any class derived from them. Just remember that an **interface** is just a template of services, while a class—even an **abstract** one—is an abstraction of some object. The distinction is fine but important to understand.

THE ROOT OF ALL CLASSES

The **Object** class is the root of the entire Java class hierarchy. All classes are implicitly derived from the **Object** class. You don't have to do anything for your classes to be beneficiaries of a surprisingly indispensable set of methods. Check out the code snippet below:

```
class ASimpleClass {
}
```

Do you realize that even this class is derived from the **Object** class? It's easy to overlook. I didn't even have to extend the **Object** class to create the class! Now, if there are some who don't believe me I'll add a little meat to the bone, as shown in Listing 6.9.

Listing 6.9   All Objects Extend Object

```
class ASimpleClass {
};

class SomeOtherClass {
    public static void main( String args[] ) {
```

```
        ASimpleClass simpleClass = new ASimpleClass();
        String          className =
            simpleClass.getClass().getName();
    }
};
```

The variable className will be assigned the name of the class. You can guess what it is. This just illustrates simply that every class shares a common ancestry. There are some **Object** methods you can use unchanged; others must be overridden, making them more specific and hence more useful.

Exploring the Basic Methods

Think of some of the things you would expect every class to be able to do. Many of the methods that the **Object** class offers are obvious if you think about it. A few others require some additional explanation.

One important method that **Object** contains lets you make more of a good thing. It's called **clone**. This is shown in Listing 6.10.

Listing 6.10   Using the clone Method

```
class DerivedClass {
    String instanceName;

    DerivedClass( String name ) {
        instanceName = name;
    }

    String getInstanceName() {
        return instanceName;
    }

    public void specialFunction() {
        // something only a DerivedClass can do
    }
}

class TestBed {
    public static void main( String args[] ) {
        DerivedClass derivedClass      =
            new DerivedClass( " derivedClass1" );
        DerivedClass derivedClassClone =
            ( DerivedClass )derivedClass.clone();

        derivedClassClone.specialFunction();
    }
}
```

Note that **clone** returns an **Object**. But since you started with a **DerivedClass**, you're asking: "What's the point of cloning if all you ever end up with is a plain old **Object**?" The answer is that with the appropriate cast you can get what you need. See Chapter 4 for much more about the language specifics. I leave it up to you to check out a method similar to **clone**, called **copy**.

Now, after all this talk about copying and cloning, remember that all classes are not identical. That wouldn't be too useful: "strength through diversity" and all that. It's the clever interaction between different classes that gives object-oriented software its smarts, after all.

In order to compare instances, **Object** has an **equals** method. Just like primitive types such as integers or longs, instance variables of more sophisticated classes can be compared. Listing 6.11 extends my favorite example.

Listing 6.11   Using the equals Method

```
class DerivedClass {
    String instanceName;

    DerivedClass( String name ) {
        instanceName = name;
    }
}

class TestBed {
    public static void main( String args[] ) {
        DerivedClass derivedClass =
            new DerivedClass( " derivedClass1" );
        DerivedClass derivedClass2 =
            derivedClass;
        DerivedClass derivedClassClone =
            ( DerivedClass )derivedClass.clone();
        DerivedClass anotherDerivedClass =
            new DerivedClass( " DerivedClass2" );

        if( derivedClass.equals( derivedClass2 )) {
            // ...
        }
        if( derivedClass.equals( derivedClassClone )) {
            // ...
        }
        if( derivedClass.equals( anotherDerivedClass )) {
            // ...
        }
    }
}
```

Not surprisingly, the only statement that succeeds is the **if** statement comparing **derivedClass** and **derivedClass2**. Equality is more than the sum of the parts. Check out the signature of the equals method, shown in the code line below:

```
public boolean equals( Object obj )
```

Unlike several of **Object**'s methods, **equals** is not final. It can be overridden. The method **equals** is important in the **Object** class because it is one of the two methods—**hashCode** being the other—that are central to the operation of all other derived classes!

Let's go back to the introductory example. It's always good to be able to ask a class to identify itself. A variation of **getClass** is common to the base class of nearly all class hierarchies. Some of you might recognize it as something called "runtime type information" that's used in other programming languages.

getClass's return variable is of type **Class**. That's right—a class called **Class**. **Class** is a class, but it operates more like a **meta-class**. A meta-class is a class that just contains information about some other class. I used **Class**' method **getName** because I wanted a string to display. Interestingly enough, code could still be written that would do the same thing without the availability of **getName**. There's another method of **Class** called **toString** that also returns a string. It gets called automatically if an instance of a class is passed as a parameter to something that is looking for a **String**.

Let's take a closer look at the class **Class**. We used it to get the name of the class. How about the name of the class' superclass?

Check out the signature for **getClass**, shown in the following code line:

```
public final native Class getClass()
```

Final. That's it—that's all. You cannot override this method. It works great and doesn't need fixing. What could you even do to improve it? I'm just pointing that out in case you ever try. Most of the other **Object** class methods can, in fact, be overridden. For many, like **toString**, it is even necessary in order to give them more specific behavior.

Sometimes it's possible to get away with more compact expression that doesn't even use **getClass**. Check out the use of **instanceof**, shown in Listing 6.12.

Listing 6.12   Another Example of instanceof

```
class DerivedClass {
}

class TestBed {
    public static void main( String args[] ) {
        DerivedClass derivedClass = new DerivedClass();

        if( derivedClass instanceOf DerivedClass ) {
            System.out.println( " Yes! I' m an instance of a DerivedClass" );
        }
    }
}
```

Ever heard of hashcodes? They have more to do with codes than with hash. A hashcode is a numerical value that is the result of some mathematical function applied to the contents of a class.

The whole point is to generate discrete values that will make it possible to index a set of classes for quicker retrieval from a data structure. This is just what goes on inside the **Hashtable** in the java.util package.

Remember that a clone is not equal to the instance from which it was cloned. Well, neither is its hashcode equal, as shown in this code snippet:

```
DerivedClass derivedClass = new DerivedClass();
DerivedClass derivedClassClone = ( DerivedClass )derivedClass.clone();

long derivedClassHashcode = derivedClass.hashcode();
long ClonesHashcode        = derivedClassClone.hashcode();
```

Finally, **Object** has several other methods that are totally beyond the scope of this chapter. They will be introduced in other chapters as they are needed. Just appreciate that there are methods like **toString** or **copy** that will appear in several Java classes. Now you know where they're coming from.

OBJECT CLASSES IN THE JDK

The Java Developer's Kit consists of the central hierarchy of classes and interfaces that you'll use programming with Java. Some of you might recognize it as a sort of library of pre-designed classes. Learning to program Java consists of two parts: learning the language—its keywords, their use, and all the other syntactical details—while the other part is learning the JDK. The JDK is not a part of the language, but you'll always need to use it.

The contents of the JDK have been a source of controversy from the beginning. It's not surprising. It really harks back to the saying: "You can please some of the people some of the time, but you can't please all of the people all of the time." With version 1.0, Java is full-fledged—alpha and beta incarnations are left far behind. This means, like it or not, the current contents of the JDK are standardized as-is. Those still arguing heatedly in the Internet's comp.lang.java newsgroup about why this or that feature should have been included or excluded just don't get it. The bottom line is that at least what's already published won't change except through the addition of new classes. You're safe to go ahead and write Java programs with the JDK and its classes without worrying that in the next version they'll suddenly be nowhere to be found. Don't laugh. That happened as Java progressed from alpha to beta. But it was really a shakedown period and to be expected.

The JDK is divided into nine distinct parts. The naming convention for each of the parts is described in Chapter 4, but briefly: the name of a part is taken from the path to that part of the JDK from the root of your Java development directory hierarchy. If you just substitute backslashes for the dots in the name, you'll have the path. These parts are identified below:

- java.applet
- java.awt
- java.awt.image
- java.awt.peer
- java.io
- java.lang
- java.net
- java.util
- sun.tools.debug

Appendix C contains diagrams that list the entire hierarchy of classes in each part of the JDK. They will be indispensable as you gain familiarity with how each class fits into the overall structure.

OOP DESIGN

By this point, maybe I've got you all fired up and ready to code like a demon; or maybe I've frightened the semicolons out of you. Either way, stick with me a little while longer. In this section, I give you some guidelines that might help you avoid some pitfalls in object-oriented programming.

Don't Bypass Analysis

The step that precedes design is analysis. Analysis time is often short-changed in favor of design and even programming. There is still a common feeling that unless you're pounding keys you're not being productive. That's far from the truth. In fact, programming that follows a well laid-out analysis and design should be almost as obvious as paint-by-numbers. All the details should have been analyzed, and solutions to anticipated problems already specified.

A thorough and thoughtful analysis is key to all that follows. Think of it as laying a foundation. You certainly wouldn't build a house on a shaky foundation. Don't deprive your inspired Java applications of a solid beginning.

Don't Bloat Your Objects

A very common object-oriented failure is trying to pack too much into one class. After even a dozen methods, excluding constructors, you should start to wonder whether such a class needs to be further refined. This problem is often labeled "bloated objects." Nip it in the bud and spare yourself grief later. You have several methods for addressing the problem. A good rule of thumb is that if what a class represents can't be expressed briefly in normal English, your original concept for the class is unclear and a poor design.

Often, it's best to break the class into two or maybe even three or more separate classes. Make sure that the resulting classes make sense, or else you'll be stepping into the territory of another pitfall mentioned later.

Sometimes it's possible to move methods up or down the inheritance hierarchy. This works as long as they really belong in those other classes in the first place. Beware of just jamming them in somewhere for no good reason.

The final solution is to totally scrap the class and redesign it. This is a common method of solving a design problem. It's often easy to err too much on the side of avoiding the inevitable. Be brave and prepared to bite the bullet when the truth is staring you in the face. What's more important—learning to repair flawed class designs, or learning to design a class right the first time—it is up to you to decide.

Don't Slight OOP Design

Closely related to the problem of bloated objects is the problem of a lack of focus. Its progenitor is an abstraction that's not up to the task. Often an incomplete analysis and design is to blame. It again underscores the importance of a complete and consistent design. In this case, you can scrap what you have or you can muddle through. However, as I warned earlier, you'll not escape the ill effects of sticking with an incoherent design.

You structured-approach programmers will feel a temptation to give little thought to design, and just collect up the functions in a module and tag them as methods of a new class. You'll end up with a pseudo-random mishmash, and you'll only get so far with that solution. It might work, as long as your goal is simply to port an existing application. But in that case, you're only going through the motions. It is possible to write programs in Java or any other object-oriented language without the programming being really object oriented!

If you use this approach, you'll inevitably find it impossible to use the classes that you've created for anything but their original purpose. You'll not be able to reap the conceptual benefits of inheritance or polymorphism. And class reuse is simply not going to happen. You'll recognize no real benefits and you might be tempted to bad-mouth the object-oriented approach in general.

So make the investment in up-front, disciplined OOP analysis and design. Eventually, you'll develop the insights necessary to design simple applications well, without thinking directly about making it object oriented.

Be Careful When Extending

Once you've got something working, the next thing you'll want to do is to extend the application and include new functionality. You must beware of a pitfall that might get you still.

The simple act of tweaking an OOP-designed application beyond the design intentions can de-focus the design. This happens because your once-clear design begins to take on the characteristics of a poorly designed one. Maybe you start adding methods that subtly clash with the abstraction the class embodies.

Another problem is that you can end up making the class too specific to solve one problem. Generally, this is what's happening when you feel compelled to add more methods. What you might not realize is that you are subtly changing the class. You might protest by saying that the original methods are still there and can be used as before. But you know as well as I that you won't be able to resist the temptation of exploiting the new methods that you have added. Soon, the class will no longer be applied to the purpose for which it was designed. This problem is insidious, so beware!

These guidelines just scratch the surface of what you'll learn best through doing—so roll up your sleeves and get busy designing.

I am sure that if OOP is new to you and you have managed to reach this far in the chapter, then you are fairly exhausted. We have covered a lot of ground. The good news is that you now have covered all the basic principles you need to read the rest of this book. In fact, we have covered most of the essential details of object-oriented programming.

IF YOU LIKED THIS, YOU'LL LOVE THESE

If you are interested in knowing more, then I strongly recommend a few resources.

Object Oriented Analysis and Design

Pick up the book *Object Oriented Analysis and Design* by Grady Booch. It is a useful reference and still one of the better books on the practical application of object-oriented techniques. It begins simply, and provides an excellent introduction and description of the motivation behind the object-oriented approach.

Design Patterns

A must-have book, in my opinion, is *Design Patterns—Elements of Reusable object-oriented Software* by Erich Gamma, Richard Helm, Ralph Johnson, and John Vlissides. It is an advanced book, so be forewarned. But it introduces you to the concept of a consistent vocabulary of object-oriented design techniques. When you're ready for it, you'll appreciate it.

LET'S REVIEW

I wouldn't even go as far as to say that you've been exposed to one-tenth of what OOP is all about. I focused on a few points that are important as you begin to program Java. This is necessary because you can't avoid OOP with Java. It's object oriented all the way to its roots.

I've said it before, and I'll repeat it here: you must gain experience by doing. So dust off that fabulous Java application idea you had. Start carefully planning and trying to think in terms of objects that comprise data and methods. Experiment with simple prototypes. Learn from your failures—there'll be a few, for sure. Finally, build on what seems to work.

11

A Few of My Favorite Strings

CHAPTER 7

Steve Simkin

Although we discussed strings in Chapter 3, we only scratched the surface. In this chapter we will be learning to join up the letters and write in full sentences.

Back in college (and long before I punched my first FORTRAN statement onto an 80-character card), I was in awe of two things: a perfectly crafted solo by the great alto saxophonist Charlie Parker, and its verbal equivalent, lively Shakespearean dialogue. The interplay of character, wit, and spontaneity, grounded in an underlying fixed rhythm, seemed to me the very essence of greatness. Just the right note, just the right word, in just the right context. Nothing in my current work can match the sublime magic of that creative activity, of course. But the drive to get just the right words permeates this chapter. The existence of the classes described here is solely for the sake of helping us hacks put the exact words we need exactly where we need them—and then tinker with them if we have to. The immortal Bard must have anticipated our desire to send perfectly chosen bits of verbiage over the Web when he wrote:

"To write with idle spider's strings."

Measure for Measure, Act III Scene 2

171

And remember, just like spider webs, character arrays won't leave smudges on your fingers.

The source code for this chapter can be found on the CD-ROM in the directory SOURCE\CHAPØ7\.

ARRAYS IN JAVA

We've mentioned the simple data types that are used to represent elementary data items in Java. These include the various numeric types, plus boolean and character types. Before we can get into the really interesting classes that are used to represent strings, we should review a few points about arrays.

You may remember from our discussion of arrays in Chapter 3 that in addition to being sets of similar items, arrays in Java are full objects. They have an instance variable, **length**, containing the size of the array.

What does this have to do with strings? Very simply, the easiest way to represent a sequence of characters in Java is by using a character array. It has the advantages of being able to query its length, and of being protected from range errors. Quite the opposite of string manipulation in languages such as C, where nothing's to stop you from trampling other data by appending characters beyond the end of memory allocated to a character array.

However, it's clear that Java character arrays by themselves aren't nearly sufficient to give us the range of operations we need to create, inspect, and manipulate strings. For example, think of the amount of bookkeeping it would take to implement a method to insert the contents of one character array into the middle of another. You would have to make sure that the target array is large enough to contain the combined contents, and handle a new array allocation if it isn't. You would have to code shifting the trailing characters of the old content by the length the new content, and then insert the new content at the proper location. A lot of work. But once again, Java comes equipped to handle these situations.

THE STRING AND STRINGBUFFER CLASSES

Java provides not one, but two classes for bundling character arrays up with the most common methods needed to create, inspect, and manipulate them. These methods protect the array from direct access by prying outsiders, and provide appropriate error checking of the arguments to each method. For example, the implementation of the intimidating insertion operation contemplated earlier would include the necessary test to ensure that the allocated array is capable of containing the result of the insertion. It would also test that the location we choose for insertion is actually within the current content of the array. Both of these classes store the actual value of the string in a private instance variable, a character array called (what else?) **value**.

Why two classes? Very simply, the **String** class is used for constant strings, while **StringBuffer** is used for dynamic strings. Thus, in addition to the character array itself, **String** makes available a set of methods for *inspecting* the contents of the character array. In Java these are called *accessor methods*.

If it's OK for the outside world to fool around with our **String**, we can repackage it as a **StringBuffer**. In addition to the accessor methods available from **String**, **StringBuffer** provides the programmer with a number of methods for manipulating the contents of the character array.

At the heart of both of these classes sits a character array, which contains the object's actual value. But we outsiders can never touch it, and thus we are saved from many difficult-to-debug errors.

There are also classes for bundling up the other simple types (numerics, character, and boolean), but **String** and **StringBuffer** are by far the richest of the data type classes, and we'll spend most of the chapter examining their use. We'll also look at a class that is useful for string parsing: **StringTokenizer**.

The String Class

As I said, the **String** class is used for creating and examining constant strings. So let's roll up our sleeves, and do just that. Most commonly, you'll create **String** objects implicitly, as in the following example:

```
"This is a String object."
```

And that's all there is to it. Java automatically creates a **String** object for any quoted string. This feature of the language can come in handy, because it makes available to you all the methods that accept **String** object as arguments. As a trivial example, you could use the **String** class' **length** method, and say

```
int len = "This is a String object".length();
```

which would return the number of characters in your string. The application of this property of quoted strings may not be immediately apparent, but as we get into concatenation, you will appreciate the usefulness of Java's treating quoted items as **String** objects. We'll look more closely at **length()** in a couple of pages.

What if you want to create a **String** object explicitly? You can certainly do that, in a number of ways. For example, the most intuitive way to wrap your string in a **String** object might seem to be the following:

```
String newString = new String("This is a string.");
```

Would it work? Yes, it's 100 percent legal. The **String** class definition includes a constructor that accepts a **String** object as its argument and creates a new **String** object with the same contents as the one passed to it.

However, there's a problem with this "explicit" approach: it's not very efficient. Before it can pass the quoted string to the **String** class constructor, Java actually creates a **String** object and then passes it to the constructor, which creates an identical **String** object.

In most cases, using an implicitly declared **String** class will work just fine. Sometimes, of course, the most elegant solution to a coding problem will require declaring a few superfluous **String** objects. Listing 7.1 is an example from a baseball scorecard application, which receives an integer representing the player's position, and returns a **String** naming the position. For simplicity's sake, we'll lump infielders and outfielders together.

Listing 7.1   A Baseball Scorecard Application

```
package explorer;

/**
 * Position class represents a simplified version of generic
 * positions on a baseball team
 * @see lang.String
 */
public
class Position {
// integer constants representing all the positions in our
// simplified game
  private final static int pitcher=1;
  private final static int catcher=2;
  private final static int infield=3;
  private final static int outfield=4;

/**
 * getPositionName returns String name of position represented by
 * integer positionCode
 * @param positionCode integer code corresponding to position on
 * baseball team
```

```
 * @return String name of position corresponding to positionCode
 */
  public static String getPositionName(int positionCode) {
    String positionName;

    switch (positionCode) {
      case pitcher:
    positionName = "Pitcher";
    break;
      case catcher:
    positionName = "Catcher";
    break;
      case infield:
    positionName = "Infielder";
    break;
      case outfield:
    positionName = "Outfielder";
    break;
      default:
    positionName = "Get the bum off the field";
    }
    return positionName;
  }
}
```

Here's a little application that includes the **Position** class and calls **getPositionName()**. Together with the output it produces:

```
import explorer.*;

class testPosition {
  public static void main(String args[]) {
    System.out.println(Position.getPositionName(1));
    System.out.println(Position.getPositionName(8));
  }
}
```

```
c:\java> java testPosition
Pitcher
Get the bum off the field
```

Creating Null Strings

What happens if you do this?

```
String nullString = new String();
```

As the name I gave to my **String** variable suggests, this command will create a null **String**. A null **String** exhibits all the attributes and behavior of a **String** object, but its internal value is a character array with zero length. The code snippet above is the exact equivalent of

```
String nullString = "";
```

but is entirely different from:

```
String nullString;
```

This last snippet declares a **String** object that defaults to a null value. That is, it would return true if I asked:

```
if (nullString == null) . . .
```

The first two snippets would return false. They describe fully instantiated **String** objects, which happen to have empty character arrays for their values.

Once your **String** object has been created, how can others find out what you've got in there? By using the **String** class' accessor methods, of course. In this chapter I describe the methods I've found most useful, but you can find a complete list of the **String** class' methods in Table 7.1.

Table 7.1 *String Class Methods*

Method Signature	Description
String()	Null String constructor
String(String value)	Constructor with String argument
String(char value[])	Constructor with character array argument
String(char value[], int offset, int count)	Constructor with subarray of characters argument
	offset = offset within char array
	count = length of the value of the String object
String(byte ascii[], int hibyte)	Constructor with byte array argument
	hibyte = value of high order Unicode byte
String(byte ascii[], int hibyte, int offset, int count)	Constructor with subarray of bytes argument
	hibyte = value of high order Unicode byte
	offset = offset within char array
	count = length of the value of the String object
int length()	returns length of String
char charAt(int index)	returns char at offset index

Continued

Table 7.1 *String Class Methods (Continued)*

void getChars(int srcBegin, int srcEnd, char dst[], int dstBegin)	copies characters from String into dst srcBegin = offset in String.value to begin copying srcEnd = end of characters to copy dst = destingation character array dstBegin = offset within dst to start copying to
void getBytes(int srcBegin, int srcEnd, byte dst[], int dstBegin)	copies characters from String into dst srcBegin = offset in String.value to begin copying srcEnd = end of characters to copy dst = destination byte array dstBegin = offset within dst to start copying to
boolean equals(Object anObject)	compares String to another object (returns true if Object argument is a String and both values of both Strings are equal)
boolean equalsIgnoreCase(String anotherString)	returns true if Strings are equal after folding uppercase to lower case
int compareTo(String anotherString)	compares Strings, returning integer indicating less than, equal to, or greater than
boolean regionMatches(int toffset, String other, int ooffset, int len)	compares a region of this String to a region of another String toffset = where to start comparing in this String other = other String ooffset = where to start comparing in the other String len = how many characters to compare
boolean regionMatches(boolean ignoreCase, int toffset, String other, int ooffset, int len)	compares a region of this String to a region of another String, with option to ignore case ignoreCase = if true, ignore case toffset = where to start comparing in this String other = other String ooffset = where to start comparing in the other String len = how many characters to compare
boolean startsWith(String prefix)	tests whether Start begins with specified prefix prefix = String to look for

Continued

Table 7.1   *String Class Methods (Continued)*

boolean startsWith(String prefix, int toffset)	test whether Start ends with specified prefix, starting search at specified offset prefix = String to look for toffset = where in String to start looking
boolean endsWith(String suffix)	tests whether Start ends with specified suffix suffix = String to look for
int hashcode()	returns a hashcode for the String
int indexOf(int ch)	returns offset of first occurrence of ch (-1 if not found)
int indexOf(int ch, int fromIndex)	returns offset of first occurrence of ch, starting at fromIndex (-1 if not found)
int indexOf(String str)	returns offset of first occurrence of str (-1 if not found)
int indexOf(String str, int fromIndex)	returns offset of first occurrence of str, starting at fromIndex (-1 if not found)
int lastIndexOf(int ch)	returns offset of last occurrence of ch (-1 if not found)
int lastIndexOf(int ch, int fromIndex)	returns offset of last occurrence of ch, starting at fromIndex (-1 if not found)
int lastIndexOf(String str)	returns offset of last occurrence of str (-1 if not found)
int lastIndexOf(String str, int fromIndex)	returns offset of last occurrence of str, starting at fromIndex (-1 if not found)
String substring(int beginIndex)	returns substring, starting at beginIndex through end of String
String substring(int beginIndex, int endIndex)	returns substring, starting at beginIndex through endIndex
String concat(String str)	returns String object consisting of *this* + *str*
String replace(char oldChar, char newChar)	returns String with all occurences of oldChar replaced by newChar
String toLowerCase()	returns String with all characters converted to lower case
String toUpperCase()	returns String with all characters converted to uppercase
String trim()	returns String with leading and trailing whitespace removed

Continued

Table 7.1 *String Class Methods (Continued)*

String toString()	returns the String itself
char[] toCharArray()	returns a new character array equal to String's value
static String valueOf(Object obj)	returns obj's toString()
static String valueOf(char data[])	returns String whose value is data (i.e. not equal to data, but the thing itself)
static String valueOf(char data[], int offset, int count)	returns String whose value is a subarray of data (i.e. not equal to data, but the thing itself)
static String copyValueOf(char data[])	returns String whose value is equal to data
static String copyValueOf(char data[], int offset, int count)	returns String whose value is equal to a subarray of data
static String valueOf(boolean b)	returns String object whose value is character representation of b
static String valueOf(char c)	returns String object whose value is character representation of c
static String valueOf(int i)	returns String object whose value is character representation of i
static String valueOf(long l)	returns String object whose value is character representation of l
static String valueOf(float f)	returns String object whose value is character representation of f
static String valueOf(double d)	returns String object whose value is character representation of d
String intern()	returns a String equal to *this* but which is guaranteed to be from the unique String pool

---

Special Characters in String Objects

Listing 7.2 shows a simple program that uses three of the handiest accessor methods to parse a string into words and print them one line at a time. For the purposes of this program, we'll define a word as any character or group of characters separated from other characters by *whitespace*. Whitespace refers to characters that are commonly used as separators between groups of other characters. The most common whitespace character is *space* (the invisible character that prints when you hit the spacebar on your keyboard). Others include *newline* and *tab*. Newline refers to the character that gets inserted into text when you press Enter to advance to a new line while typing text. It is represented in a string by "\n" (backslash-n). Tab refers to the character that gets inserted when you press Tab. It is represented by "\t" (backslash-t). Newline and tab are known as *special characters*, and their backslashed representations are known as *excape sequences*. You can find a complete list of Java special characters in Chapter 3.

Listing 7.2 Parsing a String with Accessor Methods

Each word within the string, seperated from its neighbors by specific delimiting characters, is known as a token. And a program that parses the string into tokens is called a tokenizer.

```
package explorer;
/**
 * tokenMethods provides simple tokenizing services to demonstrate
 * compound String method invocations
 * @see lang.String
 */
public
class tokenMethods {

/**
 * print each token (seperated by space, newline, carriage return or tab)
 * on a line
 * @param str String to be tokenized
 */
  public static void printlnPerToken(String str) {
    int currentPosition = 0;
    int strLength = str.length();
    int inWhitespace = 0;
    String whitespaceChars = " \n\r\t";

    while (currentPosition < strLength) {
      while (whitespaceChars.indexOf(str.charAt(currentPosition))
          >= 0) {
  currentPosition++;
      }
      int placeHolder = currentPosition;
      while ((currentPosition < strLength) &&
          (whitespaceChars.indexOf(str.charAt(currentPosition))
              < 0)) {
        currentPosition++;
      }
      System.out.println(str.substring(placeHolder,
          currentPosition));
    }
  }
}
```

How does this listing work? I'll restrict myself to a description of the use of **String** accessor methods, except to point out the use of a public static method.

I'll discuss static methods later in the chapter when we talk about wrapper classes, but for now I'll just say that static methods are services provided by classes that don't require an instantiation of that class. For C programmers, think of them as the equivalent of library functions.

We saw **length()** earlier in the chapter. Here, it's used to record the length of our **String** argument in an integer variable in order to save access time. Because we use this value as part of the termination condition of our **while** statement, it would be very expensive to invoke the **length()** method on each iteration. So we invoke it once at the outset and we're on our way.

The following expression might look a little complicated:

```
whitespaceChars.indexOf(str.charAt(currentPosition))
```

Let's break it down. First, the **charAt()** function accepts an int argument, indicating a displacement into the string. After error checking, **charAt()** returns a char indicating the character found at that displacement within the string. **indexOf()** works in the other direction. It accepts a char argument and returns an int, indicating the displacement of the first occurrence of that character in the string. So, our complex expression passes the value of the character at **currentPosition** to the **indexOf()** method of a string consisting of the whitespace characters. If **indexOf()** returns a value of zero or more, it means that the character at **currentPosition** is a whitespace character. Otherwise, it will return a negative value to indicate "not found." So as long as the compound expression returns "not found," we know that the current character in the string that we're parsing is not one of the characters we defined in the **whitespaceChars** string.

Two methods useful for record parsing and formatting are **substring()** and **getBytes()**. As you would expect, **substring()** returns a string whose content is a portion of the string it belongs to. Which portion is indicated by the two int arguments passed to it. Yes, you can omit the second argument to mean "get me the trailing characters of the string." In the tokenizer program I just described, I used **str.substring(placeHolder, currentPosition)** to isolate the token with the larger string.

Like **substring()**, the **getBytes()** method copies a specified portion of a string's value. However, instead of returning a **String** object, it copies the contents of the string's value (a private character array, remember?) to another character array. **getBytes()** is just the thing for formatting output records. Let's say you're writing to an address book file whose records contain three fields with the following format:

Firstname	20 bytes
Lastname	20 bytes
Address	100 bytes

Listing 7.3 shows how to populate the output records before writing them (we'll leave the I/O code to the next chapter).

Listing 7.3 Populating Output Records with getBytes()

```
String firstname;
String lastname;
String address;
int recordLength = 140;
byte outputRecord[] = new byte[recordLength];

. . . code that populates firstname, lastname, and address   . . .

int firstnameLength = firstname.length();
int lastnameLength = lastname.length();
int addressLength = address.length();

// initialize outputRecord to spaces
for (int i = 0; i < outputRecord.length; i++) {
  outputRecord[i] = ' ';
}

// populate outputRecord in correct format
firstname.getBytes(0, firstnameLength, outputRecord, 0);
lastname.getBytes(0, lastnameLength, outputRecord, 20);
address.getBytes(0, addressLength, outputRecord, 40);
```

getBytes() copies the value of a string (or part of it) to a specified displacement within a byte array. So once the entire output record is initialized to blanks, **getBytes()** is used to overlay it with the contents of each field at the correct displacement. How? **getBytes()** accepts four arguments. First, the displacement within the source string to start copying from. Second, the displacement within the source string where **getBytes()** should stop copying. Third, the name of the destination byte array. And finally, the displacement within the byte array to start copying into. So by using this statement, for example

```
lastname.getBytes(0, lastnameLength, outputRecord, 20);
```

we're saying "Copy the entire content of lastname into outputRecord, starting from outputRecord's 20th byte." It may not have the sparkle of C's fprintf, but it works. Besides, this is a string chapter. I/O comes later.

What if you want to treat a numeric value as a **String**? You may be tempted to cast an int to a **String** as follows:

```
int intVal = 3;
String str = (String) intVal;
```

Resist the temptation. Java will not let you cast a numeric value to a **String**. However, every numeric type has a corresponding wrapper class, which offers a static **toString()** method for converting primitive types to **Strings**. We'll discuss wrappers classes later, but I'll save you the suspense of waiting to find out how to convert your int to a **String**:

```
String str = Integer.toString(intVal);
```

There are, however, a couple of situations in which you can use numeric values freely. The **print()** and **println()** methods print the value of any Java primitive type, or any object for which **toString()** has been implemented. This allows you to print the value of an int very simply:

```
int intVal = class.methodReturningInteger();
System.out.println(intVal);
```

Don't worry. Using the implied **toString()** method won't corrupt the "integerness" of your variable. It just creates a temporary **String** object whose value is the character representation of the integer variable's value. This **String** object is used by the method to which it's passed, and then cleaned up by Java's automatic garbage collection.

Joining Strings Together

The "+" operation has been implemented for the **String** class to achieve *concatenation*—joining to strings together.

```
String s = new String( "Hello "+"world");
```

The previous example is the same as saying

```
String s = new String("Hello world");
```

There is an implicit conversion of numeric values to strings during string concatenation. Like the print methods, the string concatenator accepts all Java primitive types, or objects for which **toString()** has been implemented. This makes displaying debugging or error messages as simple as:

```
int numAttempts = this.tryToDialin();

System.out.println("Dial-in failed after "+numAttempts+" trys.");
```

You can also use string concatenation to tack some characters onto the end of an existing string:

```
String str = "prefix";
str += "suffix";
```

At this point, you may be wondering about my claim that the **String** class is for constant values. How does a constant object get concatenated? Behind the scenes, Java converts **str** to a **StringBuffer**, **uses StringBuffer's append()** methods, and substitutes the concatenated character array for the value of **str.** That's a lot to hide behind one little plus sign! It also gives us a taste of using **StringBuffers** to modify strings.

The StringBuffer Class

In the introduction to this chapter I mentioned that a **StringBuffer** contains a variable string, that is, a **String** equipped with methods allowing manipulation of its contents by outsiders. Let's take a closer look at what that means.

The documentation in the **StringBuffer** class code describes it as a "growable buffer for characters." What's meant by "growable" is that the class methods themselves include mechanisms for allocating additional memory when necessary. For example, the **append()** method has to deal with the possibility that the memory allocated for the **StringBuffer** may be insufficient to contain the new contents resulting from the **append()** operation. It does this as you might expect, allocating a new, larger buffer, copying the old contents to the new buffer, appending the additional characters, and instructing the **StringBuffer** object that its value is now the new character array. This prevents lots of C-type boundary errors, but at a price.

*Note: Memory allocation is time consuming. Make an effort to guess well when you first allocate the size of your **StringBuffer** object.*

 ## Understanding Synchronization

All the methods that access the character buffer containing the **StringBuffer's** value are *synchronized.* This means that before acting, these methods put a lock on the **StringBuffer** object, preventing anyone else from accessing the object's resources. Anyone attempting to do so will be put on hold until the prior method finishes and releases the object's lock. This approach prevents the possibility of one method accessing the object's value while another method is updating it, or, even worse, of simultaneous multiple updates to the character array containing the object's value. This protection is necessary because of Java multithreading capabilities.

Java gives you two ways of letting it know how your **StringBuffer** should get its start in life. You can tell Java how much empty space to set aside for the character array that will contain the object's value, or you can initialize the array, and let Java worry about how much space to set aside:

```
StringBuffer initializedBySize = new StringBuffer(256);
StringBuffer initializedByContent = new StringBuffer("Use this String.");
```

The first of these statements would create an empty **StringBuffer** with a capacity of 256 characters. The second would create a StringBuffer initialized to the value "Use this String." (As a matter of interest, its size would be 32 characters— the length of "Use this String." + 16 characters added for good measure.)

Once again, I'm going to discuss only those **StringBuffer** methods I have found most useful. Table 7.2, however, contains a complete list of public **StringBuffer** methods.

After that introduction to **StringBuffer**s and how to create them, Listing 7.4 shows EditStringBuffer, a class which extends the functionality of **StringBuffer** by adding methods that perform simple editing tasks. Because **StringBuffer**

Table 7.2 *Public StringBuffer Methods Class*

Method Signature	Description
StringBuffer()	constructs empty StringBuffer of default length
StringBuffer(int length)	constructs empty StringBuffer of specified length
StringVUffer(String str)	constructs StringBuffer with value equal to String
int length()	returns character count o value
int capacity()	returns size of value array
void copyWhenShared()	copies value to new array if it is shared (preparatory to updating, so as not to disturb other object)
void ensureCapacity(int minimum Capacity)	makes sure buffer is at least minimumCapacity in size
void setLength(int newLength)	sets length of value to newLength, truncating or null-padding if necessary

Continued

Table 7.2   *Public StringBuffer Methods Class (Continued)*

char charAt(int index)	returns character at offset index
void getChars(int srcBegin, int srcEnd, char dst[], int dstBegin	copies characters from String into dst
	srcBegin = offset in String.value to begin copying
	srcEnd = end of characters to copy
	dst = destingation character array
	dstBegin = offset within dst to start copying to
void setCharAt(int index, char ch)	changes character at index to ch
StringBuffer append(Object obj)	appends obj's String representation to StringBuffer
StringBuffer append(String str)	appends String to StringBuffer
StringBuffer append(char str[])	appends str's String representation to StringBuffer
StringBuffer append(char str[], int offset, len)	appends subarray of str's String representation to int StringBuffer
StringBuffer append(boolean b)	appends b's String representation to StringBuffer
StringBuffer append(char c)	appends c's String representation to StringBuffer
StringBuffer append(int i)	appends i's String representation to StringBuffer
StringBuffer append(long l)	appends l's String representation to StringBuffer
StringBuffer append(float f)	appends f's String representation to StringBuffer
StringBuffer append(double d)	appends d's String representation to StringBuffer
StringBuffer insert(int offset, Object obj)	inserts obj's String representation to StringBuffer at offset
StringBuffer insert(int offset, String str)	inserts String to StringBuffer at offset
StringBuffer insert(int offset, char str[])	inserts str's String representation to StringBuffer at offset
StringBuffer insert(int offset, char str[], offset, int len)	inserts subarray of str's String representation to int StringBuffer at offset
StringBuffer insert(int offset, boolean b)	inserts b's String representation to StringBuffer at offset
StringBuffer insert(int offset, char c)	inserts c's String representation to StringBuffer at offset
StringBuffer insert(int offset, int i)	inserts i's String representation to StringBuffer at offset
StringBuffer insert(int offset, long l)	inserts l's String representation to StringBuffer at offset
StringBuffer insert(int offset, float f)	inserts f's String representation to StringBuffer at offset
StringBuffer insert(int offset, double d)	inserts d's String representation to StringBuffer at offset

is a final class, EditStringBuffer can't extend it directly. Instead, it encapsulates a **StringBuffer** variable—ESBStringBuffer—whose methods it combines to provide the added functionality.

Listing 7.4 Extending StringBuffer

```
package explorer;

/**
 * EditStringBuffer adds two useful editing methods to StringBuffer
 * <pre>
 *    EditStringBuffer ESB
 *        = new EditStringBuffer("Put this in buffer and smoke it");
 * </pre>
 * @see lang.StringBuffer
 */
public class EditStringBuffer {

  private StringBuffer ESBStringBuffer = null;
  private int ESBcount;

/**
 * constructor
 * @ param str String with content to be edited
 */

  public EditStringBuffer(String str) {
    ESBStringBuffer = new StringBuffer(str);
    ESBcount = ESBStringBuffer.length();
  }

/**
 * replaceChar replaces every occurrence of oldChar with newChar
 * @param oldChar character to be replaced
 * @param newChar character to replace it with
 */
  public synchronized void replaceChar(char oldChar, char newChar)
  {
    for (int j = 0; j < ESBcount; j++) {
      if (ESBStringBuffer.charAt(j) == oldChar) {
    ESBStringBuffer.setCharAt(j, newChar);
      }
    }
  }

/**
 * insertBeforeChar inserts insertionString before every occurrence
 *    of targetChar
 * @param targetChar character you should insert before
 * @param insertionString String for insertion
 * @return EditStringBuffer, which may be new and expanded
 */
  public synchronized void
```

```
    insertBeforeChar(char targetChar, String insertionString) {
      for (int j = 0; j < ESBcount; j++) {
        if (ESBStringBuffer.charAt(j) == targetChar) {
          ESBStringBuffer.insert(j, insertionString);
          j += insertionString.length();
          ESBcount = ESBStringBuffer.length();
        }
      }
    }

/**
 * toString returns the contents of ESBStringBuffer
 * @return ESBStringBuffer.toString
 */
  public String toString() {
    return ESBStringBuffer.toString();
  }
}
```

EditStringBuffer's second instance variable is ESBCount, which records the number of characters in ESBStringBuffer. It is populated by calling ESBStringBuffer's length method. There is a tradeoff involved in using this variable. On the one hand, accessing an instance variable gives a slight performance improvement over repeated calls to **StringBuffer.length**. On the other hand, it also imposes on EditStringBuffer the responsibility of keeping ESBCount current. Any EditStringBuffer method that can change the number of characters in ESBStringBuffer must immediately refresh ESBCount.

The first thing EditStringBuffer's constructor does is to call **StringBuffer**'s constructor, passing on the String argument it itself received. It then sets ESBCount and returns.

Both of EditStringBuffer's editing methods use the method ESBStringBuffer.charAt to examine the contents of each successive location in ESBStringBuffer's character array. charAt accepts an **int** argument and returns the character value at that displacement within the array. **replaceChar** then uses ESBStringBuffer.setCharAt to change the value at that location from oldChar to newChar.

The insertBeforeChar method uses ESBStringBuffer.insert to insert insertionString into the array. The **StringBuffer** insert method is extremely handy. You can use it to insert the String representation of any data type into the middle of a **StringBuffer**. It also handles additional memory allocation, if necessary. After each insertion operation, I advance j by the length of insertionString. This ensures that the value examined in the next iteration of the loop is indeed the next character in the contents of the character array as they were before I updated them. Finally, I use ESBStringBuffer.length to update ESBcount.

A StringBuffer's "Length" Compared to "Its "Capacity'

Speaking of length and count, I should mention a second method that could be confused with length. This is the capacity method, which returns the size of a **StringBuffer**'s character array, for example, the number of allocated characters, as opposed to the number of characters actually in use.

The last method in EditStringBuffer is an implementation of **toString**, which returns the EditStringBuffer object's value as a String. The implementation is extremely simple, consisting of a single call to ESBStringBuffer.toString.

Like all data type classes, **StringBuffer** has a **toString()** method that returns the object's value as a **String** object. This method does not copy the character array containing the value, but rather, creates a new **String** object whose value is the same character array as the **StringBuffer**'s value. Remember that both **String** and **StringBuffer** are full-fledged objects whose value is contained in a private character array. In this case, the **toString()** method results in two objects with character arrays at the same address. I can hear you thinking, "If **Strings** are constant, and **StringBuffers** are variable, and they store their values in the same memory addresses, what happens when I want to update my **StringBuffer**?" Great question. Luckily, Java thought of it too. The **StringBuffer's toString()** method marks the character array as "shared." This flag lets any subsequent update operations know that the **StringBuffer's** character array is being shared with a **String** object. Before updating the object's value, the update methods will copy the value to a new character array and reset the "shared" flag. Updates are performed on the new array and our **String** can live in peace, unaware that its stability was briefly threatened.

What about parsing strings? I'm very proud of the **printlnPerToken()** implementation I showed you earlier, but unless displaying a whitespace-delimited token on every line is exactly what you need, it won't do much for you. Luckily, Java has once again anticipated your needs.

The StringTokenizer Class

When I presented **printlnPerToken()**, I mentioned that tokens are groups of meaningful characters separated by specified delimiter characters. Java has a class that provides comprehensive, flexible tokenization services.

The **StringTokenizer** class facilitates the breakup of a **String** into tokens. You can declare a set of delimiters (default is whitespace) at creation time, or you can define them as you go. Each token is returned as a **String**, and you don't have to print them. **StringTokenizer** is an implementation of Java's Enumeration interface, which is discussed at greater length in Chapter 9, *Data Structures*. Remember that an interface is a collection of method declarations without implementations. Any class that implements an interface is responsible for implementing all the methods in the interface. In our case, Enumeration is an interface that's useful for (surprise!) counting things. It declares two methods: "boolean hasMoreElements()" and "Object nextElement()". **StringTokenizer** implements these methods, plus a few more. The advantage to me, the Java programmer, of knowing that **StringTokenizer** implements Enumeration, is that I can expect a basic set of behaviors, plus a predictable programming interface, without having to know anything about **StringTokenizer's** particular implementation. Alex discusses the Enumeration interface at length in his chapter on data structures.

I work in a shop that frequently passes data between applications in ASCII files in which the fields in each record are delimited by ^ characters. Could I use **StringTokenizer** to parse these files? Did Bill Clinton inhale?

```
// for each record, retrieve each hat-delimited token
// and - oh well - display it
String currentRecord;
. . . input operation populating currentRecord . . .
StringTokenizer currentRecordST
    = new StringTokenizer(currentRecord, "^");

while (currentRecordST.hasMoreTokens()) {
  System.out.println(currentRecordST.nextToken());
}
```

Well, that was easy!

If you need to count the tokens remaining in a **String**, you could, of course, use **nextToken()** and tally the number of calls until **hasMoreTokens()** returned false. But **StringTokenizer** provides you with a much quicker and simpler method. A single call to **countTokens()** returns an integer containing just what you're looking for.

USING WRAPPER CLASSES

What classes? *Wrapper* classes. These are classes that wrap the simple numeric, character, and boolean types in objects. As I mentioned, this approach has the advantages of preventing outsiders from having direct access to the data items, and of automatically providing the most common services needed for creating, inspecting, and manipulating the item. In the case of the wrapper classes, data transformations are among the most important of these services. For example, use of the **Boolean** class ensures that the **String** equivalents of boolean values will always be "true" and "false." No chance for failed matches because of case discrepancies. Wrapper classes are the "things" of "String and Things." I put them in this chapter because their behavior and usage is very similar to those of the **String** class. The major difference between them is that while the value of a wrapper object is a primitive Java data type, the value of a **String** object is another object. From the programmer's point of view, this makes no difference, and all these classes belong to the same family.

Wrapping your data in an object makes the full range of Java utilities available to you. Many Java utilities must be passed objects as arguments. For example, the **Vector** class is terrific for managing variable-sized arrays of any kind of object. So if you wrap your data items in objects, you're eligible.

Using Static Methods

The wrapper classes make heavy use of *static methods*. Static methods are methods that apply to a class, rather than to an instance of that class. The data transformation methods I mentioned a couple of paragraphs ago are a good example. If I make use of **Integer.toString(3)** to transform the number 3 to the String 3, there's no need for that method to be associated with any particular **Integer** object. In fact, there's no need for the **Integer** class to have been instantiated at all in my program. So within the **Integer** class, **toString()** is a static method. It exists because the class exists.

All of the wrapper classes implement **toString()**, a static method that returns a string representation of the object's value. They also implement *type*Value methods (e.g. booleanValue(), intValue(), etc.). These methods return the object's value as a simple data item. We'll see that the type of the data item returned doesn't always have to match that of the class. The *type*Value methods are *instance* methods, that is, they apply to a particular instance of the class.

The syntax of the constructors for all the wrapper classes is straightforward. For example, to create an **Integer** object whose value is equal to that of an int variable, you could write:

```
int intVariable = someOtherIntVariable * 2;
Integer intObject = new Integer(intVariable);
```

Number Class and Other Numeric Classes

The numeric classes, Integer, Long, Float, and Double, are all subclasses of a class called Number. Number is an *abstract* class. This means that it cannot be instantiated in its own right, but only by subclasses which extend it. It can be used, as in this case, to impose uniformity of behavior on a family of subclasses. In our case, Number declares four abstract methods: **intValue()**, **longValue()**, **floatValue()**, and **doubleValue()**. By declaring them here, Number is mandating its subclasses to implement these four methods. For us programmers, this guarantees that any numeric wrapper class will return its value to us as a simple data item, converted to any of the four numeric types.

 **How to Extend Numeric Classes**

The numeric subclasses are all *final* classes, which means that they cannot be extended. So if you want to create your own "myFloat" class, give it an instance variable which is itself a Float object.

In addition to **toString()**, the numeric classes all implement **valueOf()**. **valueOf()** is a static method which does the opposite of **toString()**. That is, it accepts a **String** argument, and returns a numeric object (not just a simple data item), after appropriate format checking of the argument.

Here are some examples of numeric data conversions using methods in the numeric wrapper classes:

```
int intVal1 = 3, intVal2 = 5;
String str = Integer.toString(intVal1 + intVal2);  // str = "8"

float floatVal = Float.valueOf("3.51");

double doubleVal1 = 4.3, doubleVal2 = 5.8;
Double DoubleObject = new Double(doubleVal1 / doubleVal2);
float floatVal = Double.floatVal();
```

The **Integer** and **Long** classes have methods - parseInt() and parseLong() - which are useful for parsing user input. They accept a **String** argument, test it for numeric content, and return an int or long. If the value of the **String** does not represent an integer, the methods throw a **NumberFormatException**. Here's how to use them:

```
int intVal = 0;
String str = null;
  . . . code to populate str . . .
```

```
try {
  intVal = Integer.parseInt(str);
}
catch (NumberFormatException e) {
  System.out.println("Enter a number next time!");
}
```

The Boolean and Character Classes

By this point, the last two wrapper classes, **Boolean** and **Character**, will seem extremely simple. We've already mentioned that **Boolean.toString()** returns "true" and "false".

In addition to the methods common to all the wrapper classes, Character has methods for identifying the standard character classifications, and for case adjustment. The following example could benefit from an acquaintance with **StringTokenizer**, but it demonstrates the use of these methods:

```
/**
 * MakeTitle capitalizes the first letter of every word in a
 * string
 * @param sb StringBuffer for "title-ization"
 */
public static void MakeTitle(StringBuffer sb) {
    boolean inWhitespace = false;

    for (int i = 0; i < sb.length(); i++) {
      char c = sb.charAt(i);
      if (Character.isSpace(c)) {
        inWhitespace = true;
      }
      else {
        if (inWhitespace) {
      sb.setCharAt(i, Character.toUpperCase(c));
        }
        inWhitespace = false;
      }
    }
  }
```

Crude, perhaps, but it does the job. **isSpace()** determines whether each character equals one of the standard whitespace values. If so, it turns on the **inWhitespace flag**. Otherwise, it looks to see whether **inWhitespace** is on. If so, it uses the following line to set the current character to its upper case value:

```
sb.setCharAt(j, Character.toUpperCase(c));
```

Character.toUpperCase(c) returns the upper case value of c. **setCharAt()** sets the character at location i to that value. The effect is to capitalize the first non-whitespace character following any whitespace character. In other words, a simple title-generating algorithm. Note that I included **MakeTitle** as a method in the TokenMethods.java file on the distribution disk.

So this:

```
StringBuffer BardsStringBuffer
    = new StringBuffer("To write with idle spider's strings");
TokenMethods.MakeTitle(BardsStringBuffer);
System.out.println(BardsStringBuffer));
```

will yield "To Write With Idle Spider's Strings".

Happy stringing!

CHAPTER 8

Input, Output, And System

Steve Simkin

The file system can be a daunting thing to beginning Java users. This chapter shows you how to get to the file system without it getting to you.

And the LORD called to Moses, and spoke to him out of the Tent of Meeting. . . .

Leviticus 1:1

And when Moses came into the Tent of Meeting to speak with Him, he heard the voice speaking to him from upon the covering that was on the ark of Testimony. . .

Numbers 7:89

. . . from between the cherubs it spoke to him.

ibid.

From an object-oriented perspective, the Almighty was engaging in a practice which, many centuries later, would come to be known as chaining output classes. This technique, of endowing a single output object with multiple patterns of behavior, served to adapt the Voice to varying configurations of Moses' location within the camp and the current state of the Tent of Meeting. As we'll see, we can use it, too. But first, a few words of introduction.

CAN YOU STAND ANOTHER "HELLO, WORLD" PROGRAM?

Can you stand another "Hello, world" program? There really is a point to this —I promise. Take a look Listing 8.1.

Listing 8.1   Hello World.java

```
/**
 * HelloWorld says hi
 */
class HelloWorld {
  public static void main (String args[]) {

  System.out.println("Hello, world!");
  }
}
```

You saw this program in the tutorial, where we used it to learn about program structure in Java. But it can also teach us plenty about I/O programming in Java.

First of all, let's break down the line that actually does the writing. It's shown here:

```
System.out.println("Hello, world.");
```

Java syntax tells us that **System** must be a class, **out** must be an object belonging to that class, and **println** must be a method, accepting a **String** argument, implemented for **System.out**'s class.

We will discuss the **System** class in detail after we've mastered I/O, by which time it will seem straightforward. For now, it's enough to say that **System** is an abstract class; that is, one that can never be instantiated. It provides many operating system services commonly needed by applications, including input/output operations between the application and the console.

Java I/O is based on byte streams. You can think of a byte stream as just that: an unformatted series of bytes which originates somewhere, and flows into your application. From Java's point of view, it doesn't matter what the origin of the stream actually is. The stream could be from a file on disk, or the console, or a modem. Java allows you to ignore the physical characteristics of the byte stream's origin and concentrate on the stream of bytes.

Another useful metaphor for understanding byte streams is to think of a byte stream as a firehose, which you have the fun of yanking off the reel. You can yank and yank until, finally, you yank one too many times and the hose doesn't move. When you reach the "end-of-hose condition," the recoil sends a burning twinge through your elbow. Applied to a byte stream, this is known as an "end-of-file condition," and the recoil is called a *return code*. Alternatively, you might pull the hose right off the reel and be left empty-handed. This is known as a "null pointer condition." Depending on which method you use to read your byte stream, reaching the end of the stream will return one or the other of these conditions, and you'd better test for them or your program will die in a hurry.

In actuality, of course, Java is working hard to maintain that illusion of a simple byte stream. For a file on disk, Java maintains a pointer to its current position within the file, and **read** copies one or more bytes from the disk into memory, then updates the pointer. Shades of Assembler! Glad to have the Java elves relieve me of that responsibility.

Just in case you've forgotten, by convention there are three streams provided by the operating system for passing data between your program and the console. Console is a term from the old days, when people used to run programs in line—mode entering data as they were prompted for it, and waiting for lines of output to be displayed. In our modern, graphical world, people don't use consoles to communicate with computers very often (or at least they don't admit it). But for learning I/O programming in Java, it's a good place to start.

So what are these three streams provided by the operating system? The first is an input stream called *standard input* or *stdin*. Standard input is usually used to accept user-entered input from the console. The second stream is an output stream called *standard output* or *stdout*. Standard output is generally used to display messages and formatted data to the console. Finally, there is a second output stream called *standard error* or *stderr*. Standard error is used for displaying—you guessed it—error messages. If you've programmed in C or C++, this is old home week.

Why do we need two different output streams—one for data and informational messages, and one for errors—when both are written to the same destination? The answer lies in another facility provided by the operating system: *redirection*. Redirection is the ability to read from a file in place of standard input, or write to a file instead of standard output or standard error. The way you do this varies depending on the operating system, but in each case you can redirect standard output and standard error independently. The result is that error messages can be appended to a log file, for example, while standard output can be redirected to a data file for later processing elsewhere.

The **System** class provides access to the three standard streams. In Java, standard input is known as **System.in**, standard output is known as **System.out** and standard error is known as **System.error**. By looking at how these objects are implemented, we can learn a lot about I/O programming in Java. But first, a necessary disclaimer. My analysis of the Java classes is based on an early release of the Java source code. While I don't expect the interfaces or behavior of the Java classes to change, the details of their implementation might. The purpose of this analysis, however, is more to explore possibilities in Java coding and to demonstrate good Java style than it is to explain the actual internals of Java. To that end, the examples I am using will remain good even if Java itself changes.

System.out is declared and created as in this code snippet:

```
public static PrintStream out;

out = new PrintStream(new BufferedOutputStream(new
    FileOutputStream(1), 128), true);
```

By the time we've puzzled through these two lines, we'll know a great deal about output in Java. Let's look at each of the three classes mentioned here, and then see how they are compounded to define **System.out**. To help us on our journey of discovery, take a look at Figure 8.1. It shows the class relationships that together make up **System.out**.

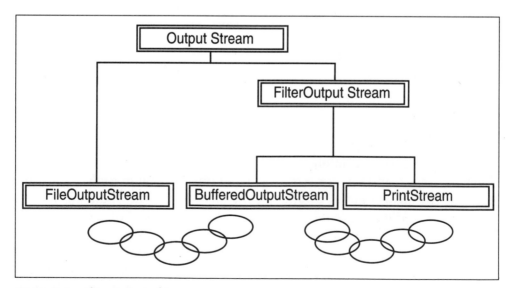

Figure 8.1   *Class structure of System.out.*

PrintStream and **BufferedOutputStream** both extend **FilterOutputStream**, which in turn extends **OutputStream** (don't you love OOP?), so let's look at the last two first.

OutputStream is the highest level output class on which all other output classes are based. It is an abstract class representing an output stream of bytes. It includes the following declaration:

```
public abstract void write(int b) throws IOException;
```

This declaration mandates any extension of **OutputStream** to implement a low-level, system-dependent operation writing a single byte to the output stream. It also implements two methods for writing byte arrays, but both of them ultimately call the low-level single byte abstract method. This relationship is at the heart if Java's approach to I/O programming. Somewhere, there must be a native method that handles the actual system-dependent operation, but that method is mostly used as a building block in implementations of more sophisticated operations. Frequently, these higher-level methods are in turn used in implementations of even more sophisticated operations. We'll see how effectively this arrangement can be used to create powerful composite classes from relatively simple components.

OutputStream also includes the following methods:

```
public void flush() throws IOException {}

public void close() throws IOException{}
```

flush() writes any buffered output bytes to the output device, while **close()** releases any resources associated with the stream and closes it. Seems straightforward enough. But there's something strange about their implementations. These are public, not abstract, methods, and yet their bodies have no content. The intention is to allow extensions of **OutputStream** that don't implement these methods. These classes will work as long as no one tries to invoke either **flush()** or **close()**. Anyone unfortunate enough to call either of these classes will immediately be tossed to the mercies of **IOException**.

In its documentation, **FilterOutputStream** describes itself as an "abstract class representing a filtered output stream of bytes." This description merits closer examination, first of all for its inaccuracy. Strictly speaking, **FilterOutputStream** is not an abstract class. It is a public class whose only data element is a protected **OutputStream** object. The constructor's declaration looks like this:

```
public FilterOutputStream(OutputStream out) {
    this.out = out;
}
```

So all the constructor does is chain its own **OutputStream** object to an existing **OutputStream** object. The fact that out is protected means that the constructor can only be invoked by one of **FilterOutputStream**'s subclasses, rendering **FilterOutputStream** an abstract class in effect, if not in essence.

What's the rationale for devising such a class? Precisely its attribute of chaining an existing **OutputStream** object to a subclass of **FilterOutputStream**! This creates the possibility of attaching methods to the existing object, thus expanding its range of behaviors. You could then create groups of related behaviors, and mix and match the groups as needed within a single class. **System.out** is an example of how this can work in practice.

As we said earlier, **BufferedOutputStream** is a subclass of **FilterOutputStream**. It provides a mechanism for buffering output before writing it to the actual output device. **BufferedOutputStream** makes use of its child relationship to **FilterOutputStream** in two ways. One is in its constructor, which accepts an **OutputStream** argument: **out**. The first line of the constructor reads:

```
super(out);
```

The **super()** method invokes the current class' superclass. In this case, that means calling **FilterOutputStream**'s constructor, which, as we saw, is only legal from one of its subclasses, so we're okay. The effect of the **super()** call is purely to chain the attributes of a **BufferedOutputStream** to the existing **OutputStream** object by identifying it (the **OutputStream**) with the **BufferedOutputStream**'s inherited variable **out**. Got that? Now say it three times without breathing. If your brain wasn't object-oriented before, it is now. I hear that it's irreversible. Don't worry. You can still have a productive and happy life, as long as you don't mind drooling on your shoes every now and then.

But **System.out** was declared as a **PrintStream** object, and we haven't even mentioned that yet. So let's go. **PrintStream** is also an extension of **FilterOutputStream**. Instead of providing buffering services, it provides printing services. Basically, this means that every Java type, or any object, can be passed to either one of two methods: **print()** and **println()**. **print()** will print the **String** value of the item or object, while **println()** will also append a newline character. Handy, no? So here we find the implementation of the methods that allow any application to write anything to standard output. The following two examples are equivalent:

```
int x = 10;

System.out.print("x = ");
System.out.println(x);

System.out.println("x = " + x);    // Remember String concatenation?
```

So we're starting to see daylight. At least we know where in all this chaining and inheritance we can find the method we needed in order to display "Hello, world." on the console. But how does it hang together? And where does the actual low-level write operation get implemented? Let's go back to the line of code used to create **System.out** in the first place:

```
out = new PrintStream(new BufferedOutputStream(new
    FileOutputStream(1), 128), true);
```

We see that there's an element there we haven't even talked about yet: **FileOutputStream**. **FileOutputStream**, as its name suggests, provides the services needed to associate a byte stream with an output device. Its constructors can be passed a **String** containing a system-dependent file name, or a **File** object (more about that later), or an integer equal to the value of a system-dependent file descriptor. By convention, standard input has a file descriptor of 0, standard output has a file descriptor of 1, and standard error has a file descriptor of 2. So we see in the line of code shown above that the **FileOutputStream**'s constructor is invoked with an integer argument of 1.

If we go any lower in our code analysis, we'll hit the native method that actually opens standard output. So this is where we stop. **FileOutputStream** is also where we find the native implementations of **open()**, **write()**, and **close()**. Remember when I spoke before about successively more sophisticated building blocks? Well, **FileOutputStream** is the foundry for the smallest bricks. The real work gets done here.

Has the line of code creating **System.out** become comprehensible? Let's see. The first constructor to be invoked is **new FileOutputStream(1)**, which opens standard output. The **FileOutputStream** object is passed to **BufferedOutputStream**, along with the integer 128, indicating the size of the desired buffer. We said that **BufferedOutputStream** accepts an **OutputStream** argument, however, any object can be used as an instance of its superclass. There are certain consequences that you must be aware of, but you're probably confused enough by now.

As we saw, **BufferedOutputStream** invokes the **FilterOutputStream** constructor to chain its resources to the existing object. The resulting bundle is then passed to **PrintStream**, along with a boolean true value, which in this case tells **PrintStream** to *autoflush* the object. Autoflush means to write the contents of the buffer to the output device every time a newline is encountered. **PrintStream** calls the **FilterOutputStream** constructor once again in order to chain the new set of variables and behaviors to the existing object. The result is a bundle that combines low-level output abilities with buffering and printing behavior. The best thing about it is that in order to use **System.out**, we don't have to know any of what we just learned. We need only pass just about anything to **System.out.print()** or **System.out.println()**. However, everything we've gone through puts us well on the way to writing our own file I/O routines.

LET THE WORLD SAY HELLO BACK

What about input from the console? We quickly discover **System.in** to be a similar creature to **System.out**, but simpler. Witness the following line from System.java, which creates **System.in**:

```
in = new BufferedInputStream(new FileInputStream(0), 128);
```

No sweat. We see immediately that **FileInputStream** opens standard input and get its hands dirty with operating system functions, while **BufferedInputStream** gives the object buffering capabilities. So how would you write code to read from standard input? Listing 8.2 shows you a way.

Listing 8.2   Letting the World Say "Hello"

```
import java.io.*;

/**
 * echo echoes user input, demonstrating use of System.in
 */
public class echo {
  public static void main(String args[]) {
  boolean done = false;
    // a byte array to hold input for echoing
    byte ba[] = new byte[120]
    int rc = 0;
    try {
```

```
      rc = System.in.read(ba);
    }
  catch(IOException e) {
    System.out.println("Error reading from System.in");
    done = true;
  }
  if (rc == -1) done = true;
  while (!done) {
    System.out.write(ba, 0, rc);
    try {
      rc = System.in.read(ba);
    }
    catch(IOException e) {
      System.out.println("Error reading from System.in");
      done = true;
    }
    if (rc == -1) done = true;
  }
 }
}
```

System.in.read() is a native method, implemented in **FileInputStream**, which accepts a byte array as an argument, and reads bytes from the input stream until the array is full.

Notice the use of error-catching in Java. Any input error encountered by **System.in.read()** will throw an **IOException** condition. **IOException** is the superclass of more specific exception conditions, so in the absence of more specific catch statements, it will be triggered. What about an EOF (end-of-file) condition? Unlike some other input operations in Java, **System.in.read()** never throws one.

In order to detect EOF, I coded:

```
if (rc == -1) done = true;
```

This is because **System.in.read()** returns an integer indicating the number of bytes that were read by a successful input operation, or -1 in the event of an EOF condition.

The output operation for echoing our byte array to the console is:

```
System.out.write(ba, 0, rc);
```

This line means "write *rc* bytes to the output stream from byte array *ba*, starting from displacement *0* (the beginning of the array)." Remember that

the earlier read operation populated *ba*, and set *rc* to the number of bytes read. This includes the end-of-line character from the end of each sourceFile record.

Since the value of *rc* figures so prominently in both the input and output operations, you can easily use it both to dictate how many bytes to write in output operations, and as an elegant way to control a simple read loop. This technique is shown in Listing 8.3.

Listing 8.3   Using a Return Code to Control a Loop

```
FileInputStream inputFile=new FileInputStream("sourceFile1.java");
byte ba[] = new byte[10000];
int rc = 0;

rc = inputFile.read(ba);
while (rc != -1) {
  System.out.write(b, 0, rc);
  rc = inputFile.read(ba);
}
```

Each **inputFile.read** statement must be enclosed in the appropriate **try. . . catch** code (**see echo.java above**). I omitted it here in order not to obscure the simple structure of the read loop.

FILE I/O

Our knowledge of writing for standard input and output can easily be extended to files. We could base a primitive **copyFile** class on the echo class we just wrote. Take a look at Listing 8.4.

Listing 8.4   A Primitive File Copying Class

```
import java.io.*;

/**
 * copyFile demostrates sequential file I/O
 */
public class copyFile {
  public static void main(String args[]) {
     // args[0] = source file, args[1] = destination file
    boolean done = false;
    byte ba[] = new byte[120];
    int rc = 0;
    FileInputStream sourceFile = null;
    FileOutputStream destFile = null;
```

```java
// open source file for input
    try {
        sourceFile = new FileInputStream(args[0]);
    }
    catch(FileNotFoundException e) {
      System.out.println("Source file " + args[0] + " not found");
      System.exit(0);
    }
    catch(IOException e) {
      System.out.println("Error opening " + args[0]);
      System.exit(0);
    }

// open destination file for output
    try {
        destFile = new FileOutputStream(args[1]);
    }
    catch(IOException e) {
      System.out.println("Error opening " + args[1]);
      System.exit(0);
    }

    // initial read followed by write-and-read loop
    try {
      rc = sourceFile.read(ba);
    }
    catch (IOException e) {
      System.out.println("Error reading " + sourceFile);
      done = true;
    }
    if (rc == -1) done = true;
    while (!done) {
      try {
          destFile.write(ba, 0, rc);
      } catch (IOException e) {
          System.out.println("Error writing to " + destFile);
           done = true;
      }
      try {
          rc = sourceFile.read(ba);
      }
      catch (IOException e) {
          System.out.println("Error reading " + sourceFile);
          done = true;
      }
      if (rc == -1) done = true;
    }
  }
}
```

A Note to C++ People

Notice I declared the two file objects in copyFile.java. C++ style allows delaying a variable's declaration until the variable is used. Syntactically, I could have done that, but it would have limited the scope of the variables to the **try** statements in which each file was opened. So learn from my debugging, and declare your file objects up top.

I'll leave you the exercise of error-checking the input arguments. As it stands, **copyFile** trusts that arguments one and two are valid file names. The statement

```
FileInputStream sourceFile = new FileInputStream(args[0]);
```

calls the **FileInputStream** class constructor, which accepts a **String** argument. This constructor attempts to open the filename passed to it, and throws a **FileNotFoundException** if it has any problems. Similarly, the **FileOutputStream** constructor accepts a **String** object containing the destination filename as an argument, and opens it for output.

The structure of initial-read-followed-by-write-and-read-loop is the same as we saw in the echo class. By comparing them we see how Java treats *stdin* and *stdout* identically to data-system files.

Pop quiz question one: What would I have needed to do in order to use the more convenient print function? Question two: Why did I say **print** and not **println**? Answer one: In order to use **print**, I would have had to do a few things. First, I would have had to turn my byte array into a **String**, the only argument type accepted by **print**. Since a byte array is not an object, and therefore has no easy **toString()** method, I would have had to call a **String** constructor that accepts byte arrays as arguments. By sheer chance, such a constructor exists, and you could embed it in a **print** command like this:

```
System.out.print(new String(ba, 0, 0, rc));
```

This means "Create a **String** whose value equals *ba*, copying *rc* bytes starting from the beginning of the array (indicated by the second zero)." The first zero indicates the value to be placed in the high-order byte when converting from a one-byte byte array to two-byte Unicode characters.

For **copyFile**, the second thing you would need to do would be to chain a **PrintStream** object to **destFile** with a compound creation statement such as we saw when examining **System.out**. Answer two: I didn't use **println** because the end of file character at the end of each record was already in ba. **println** would have generated a blank line between each output record.

FORMATTED I/O

Applications frequently need to read or write files with fixed-format records. Java can handle fixed-format files in a couple of different ways, depending on whether the data is represented in ASCII (American Standard Code for Information Interchange, common on PCs) or in the actual Java data types: Unicode data handling is exactly parallel to ASCII. For example, suppose we had to write a Java program to read a file in the format (ASCII characters) shown in Listing 8.5.

Listing 8.5   A File to Read

```
Position   Field Name Type
1-10 Name byte array
11-12 Rank  short
13-16 ID integer

Sample records:
Bartlett   430001
Leslie  390002
Simkin  550003
```

The basic strategy would be to read each record into a **String** object, and then populate each data item with the corresponding substring. The **DataInputStream** class has a **readLine()** method, which is convenient for just such situations. Listing 8.6 shows the completed class.

Listing 8.6   Echoing the Personnel File

```java
import java.io.*;

/**
 * echoPersonnelFile demonstrates DataInputStream functionality
 */
public class echoPersonnelFile {
  public static void main(String args[]) {
    // args[0] = source file
    boolean done = false;
    String name = null;
    Integer rank = null;
    Integer id = null;
    int rc = 0;
    DataInputStream personnelFile = null;
```

```
    String personnelFileRec = null;

    // open source file for input
    try {
      personnelFile =
    new DataInputStream(new BufferedInputStream(new
            FileInputStream(args[0]), 128));
    }
    catch(FileNotFoundException e) {
      System.out.println("Source file " + args[0] + " not found");
      System.exit(0);
    }
    catch(IOException e) {
      System.out.println("Error opening " + args[0]);
      System.exit(0);
    }

    // initial read of personnel file
    try {
      personnelFileRec = personnelFile.readLine();
    }
    catch (IOException e) {
      System.out.println("Error reading " + personnelFile);
      done = true;
    }
    if (personnelFileRec == null) done = true;
    else {
      name = personnelFileRec.substring(0, 10);
      rank = new Integer(personnelFileRec.substring(10, 12));
      id = new Integer(personnelFileRec.substring(12, 16));
    }

    // read loop: echo and read until done
    while (!done) {
      System.out.println("Name: " + name + " Rank: " + rank
          + " Id: " + id);
      try {
        personnelFileRec = personnelFile.readLine();
      }
      catch (IOException e) {
        System.out.println("Error reading " + personnelFile);
        done = true;
      }
      if (personnelFileRec == null) done = true;
      else {
        name = personnelFileRec.substring(0, 10);
        rank = new Integer(personnelFileRec.substring(10, 12));
        id = new Integer(personnelFileRec.substring(12, 16));
      }
    }
  }
}
```

I used the **DataInputStream**'s **readLine()** method to read the input record into a **String** object. **readLine()** returns a **String** object whose value is the series of bytes received from the input stream, up to (but not including) the newline, carriage return, or EOF. This opens before us the whole world of string manipulation we explored in the last chapter. Our Java skills are starting to come together. In this case, we can use **String**'s **substring()** method to break the input record down and populate its component data items. You may remember from Chapter 7 that **String.substring()** returns a **String** object, which can be passed to the constructor of the wrapper class for any Java type.

The true versatility of **DataInputStream**'s read methods finds expression when the data is stored in Java-recognizable primitive data types. These are the portable, archtitecture-neutral types I described in the language chapter. If your personnel file is intended for use solely by Java applications, you might want to use Java primitive type representation. This approach allows you to populate your data item objects directly from the input stream, bypassing the intermediate **personnelFileRecord** string. Don't forget that in such a case, there would be no need for the newline character after each record, since the file wouldn't be intended for visual inspection. The code to read the file and populate the data item objects would look like Listing 8.7.

Listing 8.7 Fragment of echoPrimitivesFile Class

```
byte name[] = new byte[10];
// notice that read() returns a byte
// array, while readShort() and
// readInt() return primitive short
// or int items
short rank = 0;
int id = 0;
try {
    if (personnelFile.read(name, 0, 10) == -1) done = true;
    else {
      rank = personnelFile.readShort();
      id = personnelFile.readInt();
    }
  }
  catch (IOException e) {
    System.out.println("Error reading " + personnelFile);
    done = true;
  }
```

You can find the complete program from which this fragment was taken in echoPrimitivesFile.java on the book's CD-ROM. I used the integer return code from **read()** to test whether I'd reached end of file, and proceeded with the second and third read operations only on condition that **read()** was successful.

I used the following statement to create the **personnelFile** object:

```
DataInputStream personnelFile =
    new DataInputStream(new BufferedInputStream(new
        FileInputStream(args[0]), 128));
```

This has the effect of chaining both data conversion functionality and buffering functionality to the **FileInputStream** object. The buffering activity is especially important in light of the recurring reads of two and four bytes from the byte stream. By chaining these two classes, we can enjoy the benefits of actual file I/O only every 128 bytes, while picking small groups of bytes out of the buffer at leisure.

Another useful **DataInputStream** method is **readLine()**, which accepts bytes from the input stream until it encounters \n, \r, \r\n, or EOF. **readLine()** returns a **String** object whose value is the series of bytes received from the input stream, up to (but not including) the newline character, carriage return, or EOF. This technique opens before you the whole world of string manipulation we explored in the last chapter. Our Java skills are starting to come together.

There is, of course, a corresponding output class, **DataOutputStream**, which is useful for writing the contents of data items of different types to an output byte stream. We've seen that **print()** and **println()** will accept all of the Java types as arguments, but they offer no control over output format. When fixed-format output is required, especially if you're using Java primitive data representation, **DataOutputStream** may be just the thing, as shown in Listing 8.8.

Listing 8.8   Using DataOutputStream

```
byte  ba[] = new byte[10];
int   i = 0;
short s = 0;

DataOutputStream personnelFile =
    new DataOutputStream(new BufferedOutputStream(new
        FileOutputStream("personnel.new"), 128));

. . .     code to populate ba, I and s    . . .

  try {
    formattedFile.writeBytes(name);
    formattedFile.writeShort(rank.intValue());
```

```
    formattedFile.writeInt(id.intValue());
}
catch (IOException e) {
  System.out.println("Error writing to personnel.new");
  done = true;
}
```

Forcing Out the Output

I included **BufferedOutputStream** in the chain of output classes that make up **personnelFile**. This approach prevents continuous real I/O operations involving small numbers of bytes, but it also carries the danger of leaving unwritten data in the output buffer at the end of the program. This data will not get written to the output device automatically! You must add code to flush the buffer:

```
try {
  formattedFile.flush();
}
catch (IOException e) {
  System.out.println("Error flushing personnel.new");
  done = true;
}
```

There is another way to handle the population of fixed-format data records, especially if the data is represented in ASCII characters. You can create a buffer the size of your output record, populate the whole thing with data, and write it to the output stream as a single byte array. Using this method, the code in Listing 8.8 could be rewritten as shown in Listing 8.9.

Listing 8.9   Fragment of writePersonnelFile.java

```
byte  ba[] = new byte[10];
byte  outputRecord = new byte[16];
int  i = 0;
int  j = 0;
short  s = 0;

//  String object for staging int values
//  before copying them into outputRecord
String  intString;
//  records length of value of intString
int  intStringLength = 0;

DataOutputStream personnelFile =
    new DataOutputStream(new BufferedOutputStream(new
        FileOutputStream("personnel.new"), 128));
```

```
    . . .       code to populate ba, i and s       . . .
// Fill byte areas of outputRecord with blanks and int areas of
// outputRecord with zeroes
    for (int i = 0; i < 10; i++) {
      outputRec[i] = ' ';
    }
    for (int i = 10; i < 16; i++) {
      outputRec[i] = '0';
    }
    name.getBytes(0, 9, outputRec, 0);
    String rankString = rank.toString();
    rankString.getBytes(0, rankString.length(), outputRec,
        12 - rankString.length());
    String idString = id.toString();
    idString.getBytes(0, idString.length(), outputRec,
        16 - idString.length());
    try {
      personnelFile.write(outputRec, 0, 16);
    }
    catch (IOException e) {
      System.out.println("Error writing to personnel.new");
      done = true;
    }
```

The program that includes this code fragment is called writePersonnelFile.java, and is included on the book's CD-ROM. This method of output record formatting has the advantage of allowing the inspection and manipulation of the output record as an entity in its own right. If you have to do a lot of error-trapping around each write operation, then this method will also look neater and be easier to maintain. If you're more confident of the integrity of your data, and can get by with less error-trapping code, then the first method will be more maintainable. But the main determinant of which to use is the data representation in the output file.

The **DataOutputString** equivalent of **DataInputString.readLine()** is **writeBytes**, which accepts a **String** argument. Be careful, though. **writeBytes()** doesn't append a newline or carriage return character to your **String**. You'll have to manage that yourself:

```
String riddlerThreat = new String("Take that, Batman!");

DataOutputStream famousLastWords =
    new DataOutputStream(new BufferedOutputStream(new
        FileOutputStream("super.heroes"), 128));

famousLastWords.writeBytes(riddlerThreat + "\n");
```

RANDOM ACCESS FILES

Often, we need more complex file access than simple sequential read or write operations. We may need to position an application within a file, or provide both read and write operations against a single file. The **RandomAccessFile** class addresses many of these requirements. It provides basic security by requiring an access method specifier (either "r" or "rw") in its constructor. It has its own implementation of all the **DataInput** and **DataOutput** methods, and a **seek()** method for positioning within the file. These can be combined to create simple data entry and display applications, as shown in Listing 8.10.

Listing 8.10   Gathering Personnel Information from the User

```java
import java.io.*;

/**
 * collectPersonnelData demonstrates RandomAccessFile functions
 */
public class collectPersonnelData {
  public static void main(String args[]) {
    int i;    // counter
    int outputBufLength = 100;
    byte outputBuf[] = new byte[outputBufLength];
    boolean done = false;
    String name = null, rank = null, id = null;
    String rankRules = "Rank must be numeric value below 100";
    String idRules = "ID must be numeric value below 100";
    String nameRules = "Name may not exceed 10 characters";
    int nameCap = 10;
        // capability (i.e. maximum length) of name field
    int nameLength = 0, rankLength = 0, idLength = 0;

    try {
      RandomAccessFile personnelFile = new
          RandomAccessFile("personnel.dat", "rw");
      DataInputStream dataIn = new DataInputStream(System.in);

      try {
System.out.print("Enter name:   ");
System.out.flush();
name = dataIn.readLine();
      }
      catch (IOException e) {
        System.out.println("Error accepting name");
      }
      if ((name == null) || (name.length() == 0)) done = true;
      else {
nameLength = name.length();
System.out.print("Enter rank:   ");
```

```
            System.out.flush();
            rank = dataIn.readLine();
            rankLength = rank.length();
            System.out.print("Enter id:  ");
            System.out.flush();
            id = dataIn.readLine();
            idLength = id.length();
                }
writeLoop:        while (!done) {  // labeled loop
        if (nameLength > 10) {  // data validation
          System.out.println(nameRules);
          done = true;
          break writeLoop;
        }
        if (rankLength > 2) {
          System.out.println(rankRules);
          done = true;
          break writeLoop;
        }
        for (i = 0; i < rankLength; i++) {
          if (!Character.isDigit(rank.charAt(i))) {
            System.out.println(rankRules);
            done = true;
            break writeLoop;
          }
        }
        if (idLength > 4) {
          System.out.println(idRules);
          done = true;
          break writeLoop;
        }
        for (i = 0; i < idLength; i++) {
          if (!Character.isDigit(id.charAt(i))) {
            System.out.println(idRules);
            done = true;
            break writeLoop;
          }
        }
            // initialize alpha fields to ' '
        for (i = 0; i < nameCap; i++) {
          outputBuf[i] = ' ';
        }
            // initialize numeric fields to zero
        for (i = nameCap; i < 16; i++) {
          outputBuf[i] = '0';
        }
        name.getBytes(0, nameLength, outputBuf, 0);
        rank.getBytes(0, rankLength, outputBuf, 12 - rankLength);
        id.getBytes(0, idLength, outputBuf, 16 - idLength);
        personnelFile.seek(personnelFile.length());
        personnelFile.write(outputBuf, 0, 16);
        try {
          System.out.print("Enter name:  ");
```

```
        System.out.flush();
        name = dataIn.readLine();
            }
            catch(IOException e) {
        done = true;
            }
            if ((name == null) || (name.length() == 0)) done = true;
            else {
        nameLength = name.length();
        System.out.print("Enter rank:   ");
        System.out.flush();
        rank = dataIn.readLine();
        rankLength = rank.length();
        System.out.print("Enter id:   ");
        System.out.flush();
        id = dataIn.readLine();
        idLength = id.length();
    }
        }
    }
    catch (IOException e) {
      System.out.println("Can't open personnel.dat for dynamic " +
          "access.");
    }
  }
}
```

This program demonstrates a few useful techniques. The first technique is the chaining of the **DataInputStream** class to **System.in**. Remember that as far as Java is concerned, **System.in** is just another input stream, and will therefore tolerate most of the manipulations we would perform on any file. In this case, chaining **DataInputStream** to **System.in** allows us to use **readLine()** to read a line of data from the console, which is especially important for the name field, which may contain spaces.

Second, notice how I used **String.getBytes()** to populate the output record. You may recall from the previous chapter that **getBytes()** copies a subset of a **String**'s value's bytes to a displacement within a specified character array. That was very straightforward for **name**, since I was copying the entire value of name to the beginning of **outputBuf**. But **rank** and **id** were a little trickier. Since these are numeric values that are likely to be entered by users without leading zeroes, we first initialize all characters in these fields to 0. Then, we can take the value entered by the user, and use its length to determine the displacement from the beginning of **outputBuf** needed to right-justify it, as shown in this code line:

```
rank.getBytes(0, rankLength, outputBuf, 12 - rankLength);
```

As for coding the append itself, let's take a second look. It's shown in the following code snippet:

```
personnelFile.seek(personnelFile.length());
personnelFile.write(outputBuf, 0, 16);
```

I used **RandomAccessFile.length()** to first position the file pointer to the end of the file, and then **RandomAccessFile.write()** to write the new record beginning at that position.

The last thing I wanted to point out in this class is the error checking. I labeled the validation-write-read loop **writeLoop**. Labeling the loop allowed me to escape from it by using the **break** command. Setting done to true before exiting is redundant but it makes the intention of the break clearer. The error checking itself used **String** and **Character** methods to test the length and content of each input item. The numeric test used the following loop:

```
for (i = 0; i < idLength; i+) {
  if (!Character.isDigit(rank.charAt(i)) {
  . . .
  }
}
```

In the previous chapter, we mentioned the **Character** class' static methods, which identify a character with the common character classifications (digit, whitespace, etc.). I used one of these methods to validate the **rank** and **id** items entered by the user as numeric. **rank.charAt(i)** returns the character at displacement **i** within **rank**, which **Character.isDigit()** accepts as an argument. **Character.isDigit()** returns a boolean indicator. If this indicator comes back false, **break writeLoop** takes us out of the loop.

THE FILE CLASS

We've talked about classes that enable us to manipulate byte streams for input and output, but we often have to look at files from the outside, as entities in a file system. These entities have properties apart from their content. The **File** class enables us to examine and manipulate those properties. The **File** class consists of a **String** representing the name of a file on the host file system, plus a set of methods for setting and determining system-dependent properties.

The simplest use of the **File** class is to test the existence and access authorization of a given filename, as shown in Listing 8.11.

Listing 8.11   A Class to List a Directory

```java
import java.io.*;

/**
 * listDir accepts a directory name from stdin.  It then lists
 * the names and attributes of all the files
 * in the directory.
 */
class listDir {
  public static void main (String args[]) {
    int MAXFILES = 100; // maximum files per directory

    if (args.length < 1) {
      System.out.println("Usage: Java listDir dirName");
      return;
    }

    File dirName = new File(args[0]);

    if (!dirName.exists()) {
      // dirName must be a directory on the file system
      System.out.println(args[0] + " does not exist on system");
      return;
    }
    if (!dirName.isDirectory()) {
      System.out.println(args[0] + " is not a directory");
      return;
    }

    System.out.print("Files in directory: "
        + dirName.getAbsolutePath() + "\n\n\n"); // in case user
                                // entered relative path name

    String fileArr[] = new String[MAXFILES];
    try {
      fileArr = dirName.list();   // list files in dirName
    }
    catch (IOException e) {
      System.out.println("Error listing contents of " + dirName);
      System.exit(0);
    }

    // for each file in directory, concatenate fully qualified
    // file name, and query file type and permissions
    for (int i = 0; i < fileArr.length; i++) {
      File filename = new File(args[0]
          + System.getProperty("file.separator") + fileArr[i]);
      System.out.println(" Filename: " + fileArr[i]);
      if (filename.exists()) {
  if (filename.isFile()) {
    System.out.println("    Is a file");
  }
```

```
    if (filename.isDirectory()) {
      System.out.println("   Is a directory");
    }
    if (filename.canWrite()) {
      System.out.println("   You have write permission");
    }
    if (filename.canRead()) {
      System.out.println("   You have read permission");
    }
      }
      else {
  System.out.println("   Does not exist");
      }
    System.out.println("");
    }
  }
}
```

I used **exists()** and **isDirectory()** to validate the directory name entered by the user. **list()** returns a string array of all the files in the directory. It was then a matter of examining and reporting the attributes of each one. To compose the header line, I used the following code:

```
System.out.print("Files in directory: " +
        dirName.getAbsolutePath() + "\n\n\n");
```

These lines handle the case where the user enters a directory with a relative pathname.

The **File** class has methods for manipulating, as well as inspecting file attributes. For example, the code in Listing 8.12 could be used to change the file extensions on a group of files in a directory.

Listing 8.12   A Class to Change File Extensions

```
import java.io.*;

/**
 * renameFile replaces "awk" suffix with "bat"
 */
class renameFile {
  public static void main (String args[]) {
    int MAXFILES = 100; // maximum files per directory

    if (args.length < 1) {
      System.out.println("Usage: Java listDir dirName");
      return;
    }
```

```
    File dirName = new File(args[0]);
    if (!dirName.exists()) {  // dirName must be a directory on
                             // the file system
      System.out.println(args[0] + " does not exist on system");
      return;
    }
    if (!dirName.isDirectory()) {
      System.out.println(args[0] + " is not a directory");
      return;
    }

    String fileArr[] = new String[MAXFILES];
    try {
      fileArr = dirName.list();    // list files in dirName
    }
    catch (IOException e) {
      System.out.println("Error listing contents of " + dirName);
      System.exit(0);
    }

    for (int i = 0; i < fileArr.length; i++) {
      File filename = new File(args[0]
          + System.getProperty("file.separator") + fileArr[i]);
      if (fileArr[i].endsWith(".awk")) {
        System.out.println(" filename: " + fileArr[i]);
        StringBuffer filenameString = new StringBuffer(args[0]
            + System.getProperty("file.separator") + fileArr[i]);
        filenameString.setCharAt(filenameString.length() - 3, 'b');
        filenameString.setCharAt(filenameString.length() - 2, 'a');
        filenameString.setCharAt(filenameString.length() - 1, 't');
        File newFilename = new File(filenameString.toString());
        try {
          filename.renameTo(newFilename);
        }
        catch(IOException e) {
          System.out.println(" could not be renamed");
        }
        System.out.println(" renamed as " + filenameString);
      }
    }
  }
}
```

This program scans the array returned by **list()**. Each filename is retrieved and stored in a **String**. Any filename that ends in "awk" is copied to a **StringBuffer** in order to use **StringBuffer**'s manipulation methods. That required me to use **StringBuffer.toString()** when I wanted to feed the altered name to the **File** constructor that created the **newFilename** object. I used **getPath()** here because I want to mimic the path usage of user. In other words, whether the user entered a relative or an absolute path, I want to do the same when I try to rename the file, in order to keep it in the same directory.

THE SYSTEM CLASS

We've made extensive use of **System.in** and **System.out**, and made a passing reference to **System.err**. But what is the **System** class?

System is a class that provides an interface to system functionality. In addition, to standard input and output operations, **System** provides access to system properties (such as file separator and current working directory), system time, garbage collection, and return code passing.

All **System** methods are defined as static; that is, they operate on the class level and not on the instance level. In fact, a glance at the **System** class source code reveals a technique that's worth noting. The **System** class is defined as a final class, meaning that it won't allow subclasses. As a double safeguard, the **System** class constructor is defined as shown in this code line:

```
private System() {}
```

Not only was this constructor implemented with no body, but its declaration as private prevents outsiders from invoking the constructor at all. **System** cannot be instantiated, and cannot beget children! **System**, then, is the prime moving spirit of Java activity, but is never actually incarnated. Oh, the power wielded by this ephemeral presence! But I digress.

The **System** class has a **SecurityManager** object. **SecurityManager** is an abstract class whose subclasses are responsible for implementing security policy. In **System**'s case, there is a method, **setSecurityManager()**, that accepts a **SecurityManager** argument. The first thing **setSecurityManager()** does is to check whether it has been invoked before. If it has, it throws an error. This means that in any application, you can extend **SecurityManager** to implement your security policy, and call **setSecurityManager()** (but just once!) to set it for your application.

Listing 8.13 shows an example of one of the more interesting methods in the **System** class. Let's say we have a startup file, java.ini, that contains a set of variable names and their values, delineated by an equals sign. Later on we'll see a proper *.INI file parser, but for now, we'll just read each line, copying the variable names to one byte array, and their values to another. Just to make sure that our simple parsing worked, we'll display the results.

Listing 8.13   An INI File Parser

```
import java.io.*;
class displayINIFile {
```

```
public static void main (String args[]) {
  String iniRecord = null,
           variableName = null,
           variableValue = null;
  // number of characters returned by read operation
  int numRead = 0,
       equalsPos = 0;
  boolean done = false;
  DataInputStream iniFile = null;

  try {
      iniFile = new DataInputStream(new
      FileInputStream("java.ini"));
  }
  catch(IOException e) {
    System.out.println("Error opening java.ini");
    System.exit(0);
  }
  try {
    iniRecord = iniFile.readLine();
  }
  catch(IOException e) {
    done = true;
  }
  if (iniRecord == null) done = true;
  while (!done) {
    equalsPos = iniRecord.indexOf('=');
    if (equalsPos > 0) {
      variableName = iniRecord.substring(0, equalsPos);
      variableValue = iniRecord.substring(equalsPos + 1);
      System.out.println("Variable name: " + variableName
          + "   Variable value: " + variableValue);
    }
    else {
      System.out.println(iniRecord);
    }
    try {
iniRecord = iniFile.readLine();
    }
    catch(IOException e) {
      done = true;
    }
    if (iniRecord == null) done = true;
  }
 }
}
```

The only thing here we haven't seen before is **System.arraycopy()**. This method copies members between arrays. The destination array must be allocated before **arraycopy()** is called.

We mentioned before that the **System** class allows access to system properties. You can retrieve these properties as follows:

```
// retrieve current working directory
String cwd = System.getProperty("user.dir");
```

THE PROPERTIES CLASS

Underlying the **System.getProperty** is a mechanism for storing a collection of variable names and their values. This mechanism is the **Properties** class. The **Properties** class is essentially a hashtable associating the name of the system property with its value. The name of the property is known as the *index* to the **Properties** object.

You can get a list of the properties available using the code shown in Listing 8.14.

Listing 8.14   Class to List the Property Settings

```
import java.lang.*;
import java.util.*;

class prop {
    public static void main(String argv[]) {
        Properties p = System.getProperties();
        p.list(System.out);
    }
}
```

When I compiled and ran this on my machine using Java I got the results shown in Listing 8.15.

Listing 8.15   Result of Running Properties Listing 8.14

```
cmd>>java prop
— listing properties —
java.home=d:\java\bin\..
awt.toolkit=sun.awt.win32.MToolkit
java.version=1.0beta2
file.separator=\
line.separator=

java.vendor=Sun Microsystems Inc.
user.name=Neil
os.arch=x86
os.name=Windows NT
java.vendor.url=http://www.sun.com/
user.dir=D:\java.dev\iosystem
```

```
java.class.path=.;d:\java\bin\..\classes;d:\java\bin\...
java.class.version=45.3
os.version=3.50
path.separator=;
user.home=F:\users\default
```

You can also set your own properties on the fly. You can use the -D switch of the runtime interpreter to do this. For instance,

```
cmd>java -Dtemp=/temp prop
```

will add

```
temp=/temp
```

to the current property settings.

An INI File Reader

We can use this mechanism in other situations as well. Let's look at an example using the **Properties** class. Suppose we want to refer to the contents of WIN.INI or some other startup file with a similar structure.

For those used to other operating systems, Windows 3.1 uses a number of files with an extension of .INI to set control variable values when as it starts up. These files consist of a number of sections. Each section is demarcated by a header enclosed in square brackets. Within each section, records consist of a variable name and its value, delineated by an equals sign. Comment lines start with a semicolon. Listing 8.16 shows an example of one section of an .INI file:

Listing 8.16   Part of an INI File

```
[Paintbrush]
;Comment about paintbrush control variables goes here
width=480
height=384
clear=COLOR
```

Listing 8.17 shows a program that reads a specified startup file, stores its values in a **Properties** object, and allows retrieval of selected values.

Listing 8.17   A Program to Read INI Files

```
import java.io.*;
import java.util.*;
```

```
class INIFile {

Properties INIProperties = new Properties();

/**
/* INIFile class represents a file with standard *.ini structure.
/* It is read into a Properties object and can be referenced by
/* applications.
*/

public INIFile(String filename, String directory) {
    DataInputStream inifile = null;   // inifile input stream
    String path = null,        // full qualified name of inifile
           iniRecord = null,   // inifile record
           section = null,    // current inifile section name
           vname = null,    // variable name
           vvalue = null;   // variable value
    boolean done = false;
    int equalIndex = 0;

    if (filename.length() == 0) {
      // validate arguments and supply defaults
      System.out.println("INIFile requires filename argument");
      System.exit(0);
    }
    if (directory.length() == 0) {
      directory = new String("c:\\windows");
    }
    if (filename.indexOf(".") < 0) {
      // if filename has no extension, append ".ini"
      filename = new String(filename + ".ini");
    }
    // concatenate directory and stream,
    // separated by system-dependent file separator
    path = new String(directory +
               System.getProperty("file.separator") + filename);
    // open file for input
    try {
      inifile = new DataInputStream(new FileInputStream(path));
    }
    catch(FileNotFoundException e) {
      System.out.println(filename + " not found in file system.");
      System.exit(0);
    }
    // initial read
    try {
      iniRecord = inifile.readLine();
    }
    catch(IOException e) {
      done = true;
    }
    while (!done && iniRecord != null) {
      if (iniRecord.startsWith("[")) {
        // if section header, capture section name
```

```
            section = iniRecord.substring(1,
                        iniRecord.lastIndexOf("]"));
      }
      else if (!iniRecord.startsWith(";")) {
         // if not comment record AND record contains '=', parse it
    equalIndex = iniRecord.indexOf("=");
    if (equalIndex > 0) {
      vname = new String(section + "." +
                      iniRecord.substring(0, equalIndex));
      vvalue = new String(iniRecord.substring(equalIndex + 1));
          // add property to Properties object
      INIProperties.put(vname, vvalue);
    }
      }
      try {
      iniRecord = inifile.readLine();
      }
      catch(IOException e) {
        done = true;
      }
    }
  }

  // constructor with just filename argument
  // use current directory
  public INIFile(String filename) {
    this(filename, System.getProperty("user.dir"));
  }

  // retrieve property value; if not found, return default
  public String getINIVar(String key, String defaultValue) {
    return INIProperties.getProperty(key, defaultValue);
  }

  // retrieve property value; if not found, return null
  public String getINIVar(String key) {
    return INIProperties.getProperty(key);
  }
}
```

I used an instance variable of the **Properties** class to contain the keys and their values. Note that the class constructor never takes an argument. Every **Properties** object is initialized empty. To promote uniqueness, the key names consist of the section name plus the variable name, separated by a period. I make heavy use of the **String** comparison methods to distinguish among section, comment and variable records. Once I have a property key and value, I add a new property to my object, as shown in this code line:

```
INIProperties.put(vname, vvalue);
```

That's all there is to it.

INIFile variables can be retrieved by calling **getINIVar**, which accepts the property key, as well as an optionally default value to return in case the key is not defined for that object. The way I've written the class, the calling application is responsible for concatenating the section and variable names. I'll leave it as an exercise for the reader to move the intelligence to do that inside the class, while preserving the optional default value.

I/O, I/O, IT'S OFF TO WORK WE GO

The techniques we've seen here should be enough to get you and your system communicating happily. Good luck getting the message out!

Data Structures

Alex Leslie

A stitch in time saves nine, or so the saying goes. You couldn't imagine life without an appointment book, so schedule some time now to learn the nuts and bolts of organizing data in Java.

"Where did I put that list?"

Does that sound familiar? I'd bet that once in a while, you're like most of us. You let things pile up. Of course, you have the best intentions of organizing it all later. But one day, you turn around and the pile on your desk has taken on distinctly mountainous proportions. Often, it's not until the papers have reached the *maximum angle of repose* and start sliding off the desk before you feel compelled to start excavating. Hey, it happens to me too.

Organizing is all about making the most of the information or data you have. You put what's worth keeping into some place safe and then you trash everything else. Whatever is the ultimate destination for the stuff you keep—whether hanging files, notebook, album, etc.—part of the organization process is to make sure that you are able to find the stuff you want promptly at a later time.

But maybe you're comforted by a mess. Maybe you defend yourself by quoting someone famous.

Wasn't it Einstein who said that a messy desk was the sign of a creative mind? And you're keeping it that way to express yourself. It's like a line from "Wild at Heart," an offbeat movie of a few years ago: this mess "...is a symbol of my individuality and my belief in personal freedom."

Sad to say, what might pass with personal habits of organization just won't wash when it comes to organizing data in programs. If you've programmed before, you already know that programs are a lot less accommodating than spouses.

The whole issue of keeping things organized is intimately related to programming. Programs process data, and that data must be organized; otherwise, the program will be inefficient or even crash. The whole function of a program is data processing. Data processing itself involves retrieving data, manipulating it, and then returning it to some organized storage area. Think of this as a kind of *data cycle*. The graphic in Figure 9.1 illustrates the simple concept.

Programmers long ago recognized the need to keep the data in their programs well organized. At first they would just *roll their own* clever organization techniques. But it wasn't long until a serious analysis was made into the different ways data was handled in programs. The results of these analyses suggested a series of discrete ways to arrange storage and access. A set of definitions emerged. Those definitions outline several different structures for data to be stored, and the operations that can be performed to manipulate

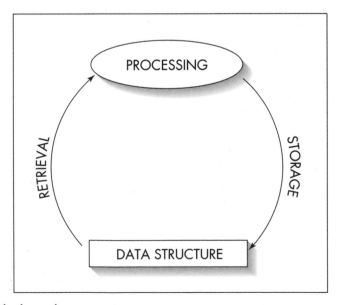

Figure 9.1 *The data cycle.*

that data. By design, each structure has different strengths and weaknesses, depending on the data organization task it is to perform. Collectively, the structures are called *data structures*.

Most computer languages have already implemented each data structure as a program module. Java, too, has a set of data structures built-in. Actually, Java has a subset of the traditional data structures. Table 9.1 lists the Java data structures. Despite the fact that several traditional data structures are omitted in the Java Developer's Kit, what Java provides is likely all you'll ever need.

If you do outgrow them, you can always write your own. It's not difficult. In fact, I write a new data structure called a Queue later on in the chapter.

But before we dive into Java's data structures, let's imagine a world without them.

A SHOPPING LIST

Let's go shopping. But before we can, we have to make a list and, like Santa, we need to check it twice.

Take a look at Listing 9.1. It's a simple Java program that accepts shopping list items from the command line and stores them in an array. They are then just recited back. Sure, it's simple, but it'll get the ball rolling.

Listing 9.1   Using an Array

```
public class ShoppingList1 {
    static String[] shoppingList = new String[ 5 ];

    public static void main( String args[] ) {
        int length = args.length;

        for( int i = 0; i < length; ++i ) {
            shoppingList[ i ] = args[ i ];
        }

        System.out.println( "The shopping list:" );
        for( int i = 0; i < length; ++i ) {
            System.out.println( shoppingList[ i ] );
        }
    }
}
```

Table 9.1   *Java's Data Structures*

Name	Vector	Dictionary	Hashtable	Stack

Now just in case you've already forgotten *which way's up* with arrays, I'll quickly review. All arrays are defined with a size and a type. The size controls the number of slots that get created in the array. The slots are called array entries. The entries are numbered sequentially: the first entry is numbered as zero. Finally, all the entries in the array must be either of the type specified in the array's definition or be a descendent of that type. If you are uncertain about arrays, check Chapter 3 for more information.

This first program is simple enough. There is just one method in this public class. The **main** method will be executed when ShoppingList1 is run. This program requires you to enter some typical shopping list items on the command line. The command-line parameters are passed into the **main** method in an array of **Strings**. ShoppingList1 has its own static array of **Strings** to which the command-line parameters are immediately copied. Once a determination is made as to just how many items you are planning to buy—using the array member **length**—the items are simply listed back using an index into the **String** array via **System.out.println**.

When we run the program, it seems to work fine:

```
cmd> java ShoppingList1 milk eggs bread
The shopping list:
milk
eggs
bread
```

No surprises until the time comes to go on a really big shopping trip:

```
cmd> java ShoppingList milk eggs bread ice-cream apples hamburger soup Coke
java.lang.ArrayIndexOutOfBoundsException: 5
        at ShoppingList.main(ShoppingList.java:8)
```

We were going to shop for a few more items than we had previously, but this time the program crashed. According to the **ArrayIndexOutOfBounds Exception** that was thrown, we have a problem with an index into an array going out of range. We only have one array so it must have to do with the number of items we entered on the command line.

What happened exactly is we forgot to abide by one of the strict limitations of arrays. The legal indices (slot numbers) you can use with an array must fall into the range of zero to one-less-than the length of the array. There are no ifs, ands, or buts. Our list had eight items, three greater than the size the array was defined to handle. Our program choked as soon as it saw the sixth item—using item number five—as the error message indicates.

Maybe you're looking back at the program, thinking "Sure, it failed" because it only had room for five items. I could have increased the size to accommodate eight items and there would be no problem. But what about an even bigger shopping list next time? The fact is that you never know how many to expect. That's a critical problem with this approach using arrays. Arrays are fine when you know beforehand the size required; otherwise, they can be awkward.

You might be able to cobble together a solution. You can check whether the array is full before you add an item. If it is, you can create a larger array and copy all the items from the smaller array into it. But that gets ridiculous pretty soon. Why bother anyway? You're much better off acquainting yourself with a Java class called **Vector**. In uncertain times, **Vector** proves a much more reliable friend, as you'll see in Listing 9.2.

Listing 9.2   Using a Vector

```java
import java.util.*;

public class ShoppingList2 {
    static Vector shoppingList = new Vector();

    public static void main( String args[] ) {
        int length = args.length;

        for( int i = 0; i < length; ++i ) {
            shoppingList.addElement( args[ i ] );
        }

        System.out.println( "The shopping list:" );
        for( Enumeration e = shoppingList.elements(); e.hasMoreElements(); ) {
            System.out.println( e.nextElement() );
        }
    }
}
```

You've probably noticed that this new example is very similar to Listing 9.1. What is different is that **shoppingList** is no longer implemented as an array, but as a **Vector**. And since we're now using a **Vector**, there is a new way of putting the shopping list items into the data structure and an especially different way of retrieving the list items for display.

Since the items are added to a **Vector** object, you must use the appropriate method: **addElement**. Note with pleasure that you no longer have to keep track of the array slot into which each item is to be placed. You can make extensive use of a **Vector** object without the necessity of dealing with indices. That's good, because indices can get screwed up without proper care.

A strange new Java interface called **Enumeration** was *snuck in* and used, though I imagine you can intuit how it works in this example. It is just an efficient and elegant way of stepping through the contents of a **Vector**. In fact, this technique is available to you with *every* Java data structure, so pay particular attention to it.

When we run the program, we find all our problems are solved. As shown in the snippet below, we can now shop for as many items as we want—with no fear of crashing anything but our weekly budget.

```
cmd> java ShoppingList2 milk eggs bread ice-cream apples hamburger soup Coke
The shopping list:
milk
eggs
bread
ice-cream
apples
hamburger
soup
Coke
```

Even if you had a thousand items to buy, this solution, using a **Vector**, would work without modification.

You might find it remarkable that whereas the array was declared with a certain size, this **Vector** doesn't even have an explicit size specified any-where. Even so, it was able to accommodate an unknown number of items. The mystery will be explained later.

VECTOR

You've already cut your data-structure teeth with **Vector**, but there's tons more to be explored. It is the most method-rich data structure available to you in Java. Learn to use it because it is also the single most important one you've got at your disposal. It will likely also serve as the basis for any other data structures that you develop on your own.

What's Your Vector, Victor?

I bet what jumps into your mind is a short line segment on an air traffic controller's display representing an imaginary intersection of coordinates in the sky. A brief encoded label is all that identifies your plane. Blip! The screens go blank. Somewhere in the bowels of the airport, an electrician accidentally slices through fragile data cables. Then you wake up, relieved that you're not sitting at an altitude of 35,000 feet.

A Physics Analogy

A line on an air traffic controller's display is certainly one example of a vector (a direction and a velocity). It's a physics kind of vector, really. Now, since we live in a 3-dimensional space—you know x,y,z or up/down, left/right, back/forth—a simple physics vector can be expressed with just the coordinates of two points in space. See Figure 9.2 to see what I mean. The vector described is a list of coordinates. You'll soon find out that Java's **Vector** is just a glorified list too.

A list, after all, is simple enough. It's just a collection of items. It could really contain anything, though usually, the contents of the list are related. Otherwise, what's the point of storing them together? In the ShoppingList example, all the items were Java **Strings** containing the names of the items you planned to buy.

The items in a list might or might not be organized in some special way. If they are all character strings, it would make sense to store them alphabetically. If they are headers from email messages you've received, perhaps you would sort by date instead. We could even have ordered our shopping list to match the layout of the store in which we were to shop.

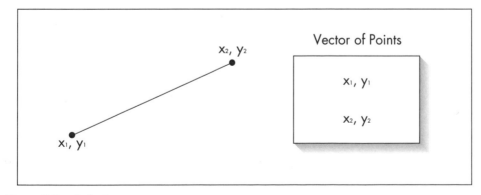

Figure 9.2 *A physics vector.*

Now, what's the ultimate point of the list anyway? If you took the trouble to store data carefully in a list, you're likely doing it so that you can retrieve the data at some later time. When you do attempt retrieval, you likely have an idea of how you want the contents returned. We didn't really care specifically with our shopping list, because the **Enumeration** would return the list of items in the same order in which they were originally added to the list. I guess this is a good time to actually tell you what an **Enumeration** is.

Enumeration Explanation

I exploited a **Vector** method called **elements** in the ShoppingList example without explaining much about it. Actually, all Java data structures provide a method that returns an object implementing an **Enumeration** interface. Usually that method is called **elements**. You use that method to *enumerate* the contents of the data structure. That just means you can use it to step element-by-element through the list of items in the data structure.

Note that **Enumeration** is not a class. The return value of the method **elements**, in the case of **Vector**, is definitely an instance variable. But the only two methods you will ever employ on that variable are those provided by **Enumeration**. And you will always employ them as I did in Listing 9.2. The relevant code appears in this snippet:

```
for( Enumeration e = list.elements(); e.hasMoreElements(); ) {
    Object object = e.nextElement();
    // usually object will be cast to some other class and
    // processing using the element will be performed.
}
```

Remember that there are three sections in the first line of a for loop. The first performs *once-only* initializations before the for loop begins. In this case, the return value of the **elements** method is assigned to an instance variable that you might just as well call e for compactness.

The second section contains an expression that is evaluated each time the for loop iterates. The method **hasMoreElements** is called against the **Enumeration** variable. Not surprisingly, it will return true as long as there are more elements available to be assigned to e.

The third section can be left blank. Conventionally, it contains an expression that will update the value of the *loop variable* that is checked in the second section. You can leave it blank because generally you will call **nextElement**—the second of **Enumeration**'s methods—in the same line as the assignment to some variable.

In the previous code snippet, I have made an assignment to a variable of class **Object** because that's what **nextElement** returns. Generally, however, you will check to see if that variable is an instance of some other class—which will nearly always be true—since the list will likely contain data that is *derived from Object*, not just straight instances of **Object** class itself. In Listing 9.2, I got away without any explicit cast because the return value of **nextElement** was passed directly to **System.out.println**, which was expecting a Java **String**. It didn't get one, but it took what it was passed and converted it into a **String**.

There might be no need to check the type of the items returned if the list only contains one type of data and you know for sure what it is. In that case, you could immediately cast **e.nextElement** to the appropriate class and make an assignment in the same line. Nevertheless, it is safer to check whether the object is an instance of the class that you want to assign it to. That eliminates the possibility of a runtime error.

Some data structures do provide methods that return an array containing the contents of the data structure. You'll use that method occasionally, too. Copying the contents of the data structure into an array is significantly more expensive than the alternative. Also, manipulation of the elements in an array is somewhat more verbose and a lot more cumbersome than using **Enumeration**.

Nevertheless, Listing 9.3 shows you how to dump the contents of a **Vector** into an array.

Listing 9.3   Dumping a Vector to an Array

```
import java.util.*;

public class ShoppingList3 {
    static Vector shoppingList = new Vector();

    public static void main( String args[] ) {
        int length = args.length;

        for( int i = 0; i < length; ++i ) {
            shoppingList.addElement( args[ i ] );
        }
```

```
        int size = shoppingList.size();
        String itemArray[] = new String[ size ];
        shoppingList.copyInto( itemArray );

        System.out.println( "The shopping list:" );
        for( int i = 0; i < size; ++i ) {
            String name = itemArray[ i ];
            System.out.println( name );
        }
    }
}
```

Remember: there's no beating the compactness of the code and the efficiency possible with **Enumeration**. You'll use the technique repeatedly.

Vector Capacity

I know I'm not going to get away without an explanation of how it is that a **Vector**—constructed parameterless—is able to accommodate items seemingly without limit. The truth is that there are two limits to consider. It's just that you never realize that you're running through the first one. The second one, however, is unmistakable. What I'm talking about will be clearer after we run through the program in Listing 9.4.

Listing 9.4   A Vector Limit

```
import java.util.*;

public class CapacityTest {
    public static void main( String args[] ) {
        Vector vector = new Vector();
        System.out.println( "vector's capacity: " + vector.capacity() );
    }
}
```

I don't know what you expect to see when we ask the vector just how much capacity it has. I did say that thousands of items could be added safely.

```
cmd> java CapacityTest
vector's capacity: 10
```

What? I can tell that suspicious stares are being directed my way. I know I'm just going to have to prove what I claimed.

In Listing 9.5, I've coded up another simple program that will add the thousands of items I promised a **Vector** object could swallow without gagging.

Actually I go an order of magnitude better than that, adding *ten* thousand items. They're just going to be **Integer** objects this time, because they can be automatically created. I wouldn't ask you to do all that typing.

Listing 9.5   Adding 10,000 Items

```
import java.util.*;

public class CapacityTest {
    public static void main( String args[] ) {
        Vector vector = new Vector();
        System.out.println( "vector's capacity: " + vector.capacity() );

        for( int i = 0; i < 10000; ++i ) {
            vector.addElement( new Integer( i ));
        }

        System.out.println( "vector's new capacity: " + vector.capacity() );
    }
}
```

If the **Vector** object only had a capacity of 10, then what happened when the eleventh item was added? The snippet below shows that the vector contains far more than 10 items.

```
cmd> java AThousandItems
vector's capacity: 10
vector's new capacity: 10240
```

Well, there's certainly something going on behind the scenes! How would *you* implement a vector? You could either allocate no space initially and then just add a new slot everytime a slot was needed. Alternatively, you could allocate some reasonable number of slots. You'd have to come up with a compromise between the waste involved in allocating slots that never ended up used—if too many were set aside—and the processing cost of having none set aside and having to grow the **Vector** upon each insertion.

A Java **Vector** just so happens to start with a capacity of 10. Maybe the Java designers thought that if 10 is a good number of fingers, it'll be a great number for initial **Vector** capacity. When that capacity is exhausted, another block of capacity is brought online automatically in the form of a capacity increment. In fact, all of the Java data structures will increase capacity automatically to accommodate new items.

Let's compare the performance of a **Vector** created with this default capacity and one that was created with one of **Vector**'s other constructors that allow you to specify a larger capacity. There should be some improvement in the case where the **Vector** doesn't have to go through repeated increments as it finds out that you are trying to stuff yet more into it. But let's find out for sure.

It's time for a showdown between the alternatives. The code is in Listing 9.6 below:

Listing 9.6   A Vector Showdown

```java
import java.util.*;

public class VectorShowdown {
    public static void main( String args[] ) {
        Vector vector1 = new Vector();
        Vector vector2 = new Vector( 10000 );

        System.out.println( "Timing vector1" );
        long time;
        time = System.currentTimeMillis();
        for( int i = 0; i < 10000; ++i ) {
            vector1.addElement( new Integer( i ));
        }
        System.out.println( "time: " +
            (System.currentTimeMillis() - time ) +
            " milliseconds" );

        System.out.println( "Timing vector2" );
        time = System.currentTimeMillis();
        for( int i = 0; i < 10000; ++i ) {
            vector2.addElement( new Integer( i ));
        }
        System.out.println( "time: " +
            (System.currentTimeMillis() - time ) +
            " milliseconds" );
    }
}
```

You run the program expecting some performance improvement and, perhaps, are disappointed by the results. You'll often find that they are neck-and-neck or even—God forbid—reversed performance from what you'd expect.

```
cmd> java VectorShowdown
Timing vector1
time: 1252 milliseconds
Timing vector2
time: 1222 milliseconds
```

My recommendation is to do some experimenting until you are convinced that there is something to be gained by specifying an initial increment other than the default. There's another **Vector** constructor that I didn't introduce. In addition to an initial capacity, you can specify the increment size that will be automatically added every time you blow through the current capacity. But again, experiment with the performance before you bother using it.

 **Initial Vector Capacity Seems to Be Insignificant**

There seems to be very little measurable difference in performance between adding large numbers of items to a Vector that was created with the default constructor—and hence the default capacity of 10—and adding the same number to a vector that was constructed with a much larger capacity. Maximum performance improvements appear to be less than 10 percent. That margin can easily be erased by other factors during a Java program execution.

Oh, before I forget: That second limit on the number of items you can put into a vector is a limit due to available memory on your computer. If you create a monstrous **Vector** and use up all your computer memory you'll get an **OutOfMemoryError**. Listing 9.7 contains a very short program that shows you how to use the **Runtime** class to check exactly how much memory you have available.

Listing 9.7   MemoryCheck.java

```java
public class MemoryCheck {
    public static void main( String args[] ) {
        Runtime runtime = Runtime.getRuntime();

        System.out.println( "Free memory: " +
            runtime.freeMemory() + " bytes" );
        System.out.println( "Total memory: " +
            runtime.totalMemory() + " bytes" );
    }
}
```

There'll certainly be a lot of variations in free and total system memory available, depending on your computer, as shown in the snippet below:

```
cmd> java MemoryCheck
Free Memory: 3136792 bytes
Total Memory: 3145720 bytes
```

Enough said about this topic. Let's continue on into the **Vector** methods that really let you do something meaningful.

Adding Data to a Vector

By now you've already seen numerous examples of adding an item to a **Vector** object with the method **addElement**. In every example, it was either a **String** or **Integer** instance that was added. Have you ever considered what happens if you try to add a primitive data type such as an **int**? You don't even get past the compile without a error message like this:

```
AddInteger.java:7: No method matching addElement(int) found in class
java.util.Vector.
        v.addElement( i );
```

Let this serve as a reminder that any object you add to a **Vector** must be derived from **Object**. You always have to create non-primitive class instances out of the primitive types that you want to store in the **Vector**. That means, for example, making an **Integer** out of an **int**.

Note that whatever you add to a **Vector**, the added element goes to the end of the **Vector**. If you pull out the last element in the **Vector**, you'll find the one you just added. Listing 9.8 shows you what I mean.

Listing 9.8   At the End of a Vector

```
import java.util.*;

public class ShoppingList4 {
    static Vector shoppingList = new Vector();

    public static void main( String args[] ) {
        int length = args.length;

        for( int i = 0; i < length; ++i ) {
            shoppingList.addElement( args[ i ] );
        }

        System.out.println( "The last item is: " +
            shoppingList.elementAt( length-1 ));
    }
}
```

```
cmd> java ShoppingList4 milk eggs bread ice-cream apples hamburger soup Coke
The last item is: Coke
```

Note that the index of items in a **Vector** begins at zero. This is consistent with most other data structures you will encounter, both in Java and elsewhere.

So far, all the items that have been added to the shopping list have been going to the bottom of the list. That is the normal way that you prepare a list on paper. But suppose for a moment that each item you provide on the command line has a higher purchase priority than the one immediately preceding it. What then? Listing 9.9 shows how to use a new **Vector** method to do just that.

Listing 9.9   Adding to the Top of a Vector

```
import java.util.*;

public class ShoppingList5 {
    static Vector shoppingList = new Vector();

    public static void main( String args[] ) {
        int length = args.length;

        for( int i = 0; i < length; ++i ) {
            shoppingList.insertElementAt( args[ i ], 0 );
        }

        System.out.println( "The shopping list:" );
        for( Enumeration e = shoppingList.elements(); e.hasMoreElements(); ) {
            System.out.println( e.nextElement() );
        }
    }
}
```
```
cmd> java ShoppingList5 milk bread eggs ice-cream
The shopping list:
ice-cream
eggs
bread
milk
```

Good to see you have your priorities straight and aren't going to forget the ice cream!

The method **insertElementAt** can be used to insert at locations other than the top of the **Vector**. You must make sure that the index you give falls within the range zero to one-less-than the size of the **Vector**. Oh, I almost forgot to mention something that I've already taken for granted. You use a method called **size** to determine the number of elements in a **Vector** object. I told you it was obvious.

Finally, I'll demonstrate the use of the last main **Vector** method to add items. See Listing 9.10.

Listing 9.10   One More Way to Add Items

```
import java.util.*;

public class ReplaceAnItem {
```

```
public static void main( String args[] ) {
    Vector vector = new Vector();

    String s = args[ 0 ];
    String p = args[ 1 ];
    int    position = 0;

    try {
        position = new Integer( p ).intValue();
    } catch( NumberFormatException e ) {
    }

    char[] c = {'A'};
    for( int i = 0; i < 26; ++i ) {
        vector.addElement( new String( c ));
        c[ 0 ] += 1;
    }

    try {
        vector.setElementAt( s, position );
    } catch( ArrayIndexOutOfBoundsException e ) {
    }

    System.out.println( "The contents:" );
    for( Enumeration e = vector.elements(); e.hasMoreElements(); ) {
        System.out.println( e.nextElement() );
    }
}
}
```

How about replacing a letter of the alphabet with the name of our favorite programming language?

```
cmd> java ReplaceAnItem.Java 12
The contents:
A
B
C
D
E
F
G
H
I
J
K
L
Java
N
O
P
Q
```

R
S
T
U
V
X
Y
Z

It's now time to look at what it is exactly that gives a **Vector**—or any other Java data structure—the ability to keep track of all those items.

HashCode and Equals

I want to point out two important methods of the class **Object**. They are crucial to any Java data structure's ability to store, organize, and retrieve data. They are called **hashCode** and **equals**.

Equals is an obvious method that every non-primitive class has to provide. The **equals** method should implement a class-specific way of determining whether two variables are equivalent. This function is indispensable. In order to be able to match an instance against all the contents of a data structure, some comparison mechanism must exist. The second half of the story is about the **hashCode** method and it requires a little more explanation.

The **hashCode** method for a class is another class-specific function. It calculates a value that is expressed as a long. The calculation is based on the data in the instance of the class. Obviously, different instances should end up with different **hashCode**s: the **equals** method relies on it. The **hashCode** then serves as a standard index that can be used to sort data in the data structure. Note that the **hashCode** is used internally. It is just a long value and wouldn't mean much to you if you saw it displayed. **hashCode** is necessary in every class because a standard index is commonly required.

I bet you're thinking about strings and wondering why data couldn't just be sorted alphabetically. The **hashCode** for **String** could very well be implemented to encode the alphabetical value of the **String** into the long value. That would then mean that **String** data stored in a data structure would implicitly be stored in alphabetical order. But what about data that is not a **String**? **HashCode** solves the problem because the **hashCode** method of all non-primitive classes must return a long value. That provides a standard baseline that makes it possible to add objects of very different classes to the same data structure!

OK, so we've figured out how to put data into a **Vector**. But how do we get it out again?

Getting Data Out of a Vector

So far, your only taste of data retrieval has been with that handy **Enumeration** technique. But there are several other methods that you can use to probe the contents of a **Vector** and retrieve items.

First, however, there are two distinctions that need to be drawn. Some methods retrieve a copy of the data but do not actually remove the data from the **Vector**. Other methods remove the data altogether. It is sometimes necessary to use both types in conjunction. For instance, you often need to compare a candidate item against some other item before you know it's really the one to be removed from the **Vector**.

You've already met the **Vector** methods **first** and **last**. I've also already beaten the standard order of addition into your head so you already know which items **first** and **last** will come home with. Note that neither of these methods actually removes data from the **Vector**.

One of the most powerful aspects of a **Vector** is its ability to search its contents for a specified item. Let's look at the example in Listing 9.11.

Listing 9.11   Searching a Vector's Contents

```
import java.util.*;

public class LetterSearch {
    public static void main( String args[] ) {
        Vector vector = new Vector();

        String letter = args[ 0 ];

        char[] c = {'A'};
        for( int i = 0; i < 26; ++i ) {
            vector.addElement( new String( c ));
            c[ 0 ] += 1;
        }

        int index = vector.indexOf( letter );
        if( index != -1 ) {
            System.out.println( "The letter " + letter +
                " is at location " + index +
                " in the alphabet" );
            if( letter.equals( vector.elementAt( index ))) {
                System.out.println( "Confirmed" );
```

```
        }
    }
    else
        System.out.println( "Sorry, incorrect input" );
    }
}
```

```
cmd> java LetterSearch Y
The letter Y is at location 25 in the alphabet
Confirmed
```

First of all, just as in Listing 9.10, the **Vector** object is filled with the letters of the alphabet. The program is expecting a single command-line argument. That argument should be a capital letter of the alphabet. The **Vector** method **indexOf** is used to find the index of the letter you entered. If you don't abide by these instructions and enter something other than a letter, the **indexOf** method returns a -1, indicating a failure to find any matching entry. Note that the search proceeds from index zero in the **Vector** to the end of the **Vector**. The first match is returned. There's a complementary method called **lastIndexOf** which starts at the opposite end. I'll leave it up to you to explore the variations of these two methods, which take additional parameters that can be used to specify some other search starting indices.

One time you'll need the index methods is when you are using **Vector** to implement some other data structure. Remember that there's a lot more burden placed on you to write careful code when you're manipulating the **Vector** contents with an index. An element's index is dynamic and the addition of new elements can change the real index of an entry which you may have retrieved just before the newest addition.

Just to be sure about the results of **indexOf**, I used the method **elementAt** to confirm that the letter at position twenty-five was indeed *Y*.

But what about removing items altogether? So far, I've left that up to the Java garbage collector, which cleans up the **Vector** object as the program ends.

None of the methods covered above actually removes data. You will often want to retrieve data and then immediately remove that data. You have three methods at your disposal: **removeElement**, **removeElementAt**, and **removeAll**. I think you already know enough about all the other methods to figure out how to use them, so I'll dispense with any trivial examples. Just note that a **Vector** object collapses down as elements are removed. Holes are not left in the **Vector** object.

Odds and Ends

One method that I have found useful is **clone**. You'll often find situations where you want to keep a pristine, unmodified **Vector** of data. But what if you need to modify it? **clone** to the rescue: you can **clone** the **Vector** and then you have your own copy to do with as you please. Any changes you make to that copy will not affect the original.

I've used **clone** when I wanted to remove items from a **Vector** in different random orders. I wanted to do this repeatedly, so I needed to keep an un-adulterated **Vector** around.

Clone is said to be a *shallow-copy* because while you are free to manipulate the **Vector** however you please, the items in the **Vector** are the same items as in the original. And if you modify them, the changes will show up universally.

It's time for alphabet soup! See Listing 9.12.

Listing 9.12   Eat Your Alphabet Soup

```java
import java.util.*;

public class AlphabetSoup {
    public static void main( String args[] ) {
        Vector alphabet = new Vector();

        char[] c = {'A'};
        for( int i = 0; i < 26; ++i ) {
            alphabet.addElement( new String( c ));
            c[ 0 ] += 1;
        }

        Vector soup     = ( Vector )alphabet.clone();
        int    soupSize = soup.size();

        Random r = new Random();

        System.out.println("Making alphabet soup:");
        for( int i = 0; i < soupSize; ++i ) {
            int index = ( int )( (soup.size()-1)*r.nextFloat() );
            System.out.println( soup.elementAt( index ));
            soup.removeElementAt( index );
        }

        if( soup.isEmpty() )
            System.out.println( "The soup is empty" );
    }
}

Making alphabet soup:
```

```
T
G
E
Y
J
W
I
H
F
L
B
A
N
V
X
P
K
S
D
U
R
C
O
U
M
Z
The soup is empty
```

The **clone** cast is necessary because **clone** is defined from **Object** and overloaded by **Vector**. I also introduced the check method called **isEmpty**. No surprise what it does.

Believe it or not, by now you should have all the knowledge of **Vector** methods that you'll likely ever need. As I said, **Vector** is the most method-rich data structure and makes an excellent base for extension. In fact, the Java class **Stack**—which I'm about to introduce—is, in fact, derived from **Vector**. Go figure!

STACK

An excellent way to understand what a stack is is to think: *cafeteria trays.* You come along and always grab the top tray. As trays are washed by the staff, they, too, are replaced onto the top of the stack. Everything happens at the top. Makes you think that there must be some trays at the bottom of the stack in amazingly pristine condition, since all the trays above must be popped off to get to them. But we'll probably never find out unless the tray washer is lazy and the stack becomes empty. Now, if you replace the trays in the example with data objects you'll start to see the light.

Do you know there's already a stack in your computer? "A stack of what?" you ask. It's actually a stack of bytes. It's an essential part of the processor in nearly every computer architecture. It's just implemented with fast computer memory. Your processor uses it as a temporary storage place while it performs computations.

Can you guess what LIFO stands for? It stands for *Last In, First Out.* Stick to the cafeteria tray example and you'll understand. The last tray placed on the stack by the washing staff will be the first tray that a customer picks up as he or she enters the cafeteria.

You readers clutching HP calculators are onto this LIFO thing already. Maybe you've never used such a calculator and, hence, don't know what I'm talking about. Most HP calculators require you to phrase mathematical expressions in RPN. RPN stands for *Reverse Polish Notation*—for what it's worth, though you're no better off understanding what it means.

Did you ever ask someone in school for a calculator and were handed some cryptic monstrosity that didn't even have an *equals* button on it? You probably handed it back politely and said: *thanks but no thanks,* and looked elsewhere. Besides the fact that the owner of the calculator has likely founded a multi-million-dollar high-tech company since then, you also had a close brush with a stack without realizing it.

If instead, you had bravely asked for a couple of words of instruction for using the calculator, you would now be privy to a secret about stacks. Ever notice that HP calculators, in addition to missing *equals* signs, didn't sport *round braces* either? That's because there's no need for them. With a stack, keeping all the intermediate figures during the calculation of some expression is disarmingly elegant. See Figure 9.3 for a diagram illustrating the operation of a stack.

A stack is so elegant that I have chosen a slight variation to illustrate how to use the methods of Java's **Stack** class. I've already mentioned that **Stack** is derived from **Vector**. You probably realize that since **Stack** is derived from **Vector**, all of **Vector**'s functions are still available. Though using native **Vector** methods against a **Stack** object is certainly legal, it is a violation of the design intention of **Stack**. If you really need to use those **Vector** methods, perhaps you would be better off using a **Vector** object instead.

A simple cousin to an HP calculator using **Stack** is shown in Listing 9.13.

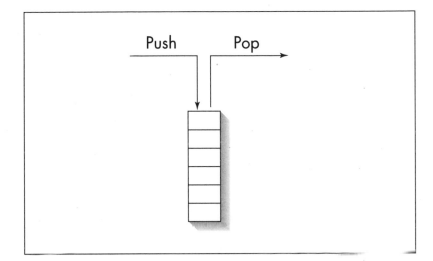

Figure 9.3 *Understanding the operation of a Stack.*

Listing 9.13   Using a Stack

```
import java.util.*;

class Processor {

    Stack    stack;
    String[] args;
    int      value = 0;

    Processor( Stack s, String[] a ) {
        stack = s;
        args  = a;
    }

    public double run() {
        int length = args.length;

        for( int i = 0; i < length; i++ ) {
            String s = args[ i ];

            if( s.compareTo( "+" ) == 0 ) {
                System.out.println( "operation: add" );
                int a = 0;
                int b = 0;

                try {
                    a = (( Integer )stack.pop()).intValue();
                } catch( EmptyStackException se ) {
                }

                try {
```

```
                        b = (( Integer )stack.pop()).intValue();
                        value = a + b;
                    } catch( EmptyStackException se ) {
                        value += a;
                    }

                    stack.push( new Integer( value ));
                    System.out.println( "partial sum: " + value );
                } else if( s.compareTo( "-" ) == 0 ) {
                    System.out.println( "operation: subtract" );
                    int a = 0;
                    int b = 0;

                    try {
                        a = (( Integer )stack.pop()).intValue();
                    } catch( EmptyStackException se ) {
                    }

                    try {
                        b = (( Integer )stack.pop()).intValue();
                        value = b - a;
                    } catch( EmptyStackException se ) {
                        value -= a;
                    }

                    stack.push( new Integer( value ));
                    System.out.println( "partial sum: " + value );
                } else {
                    try {
                        Integer x = new Integer( s );
                        System.out.println( "operand: " + x );
                        stack.push( x );
                    } catch( NumberFormatException e ) {
                    }
                }
            }

        return value;
    }
}

public class RPNCalc {
    static Stack stack;

    public static void main( String[] args ) {
        stack = new Stack();
        double value = new Processor( stack, args ).run();
        System.out.println( "Output: " + value );
    }
}
```

The program only adds and subtracts, but that will still allow us to string together a rather complicated expression. Fortunately, it spits out partial sums along the way to help you understand what operations are being performed at each step. The process is shown in the snippet below.

```
cmd> java RPNCalc 3 6 + 4 + 5 8 1 - - +
operand: 3
operand: 6
operation: add
partial sum: 9
operand: 4
operation: add
partial sum: 13
operand: 5
operand: 8
operand: 1
operation: subtract
partial sum: 7
operation: subtract
partial sum: -2
operation: add
partial sum: 11
Output: 11
```

It's not as difficult to understand as it appears. In the program, a **Stack** object is created. The parameters on the command line are stepped through one by one. If a number is found, it is pushed onto the **Stack**. As you can see from the example, you can enter a series of numbers unpunctuated by an operation such as + or -.

When an operation is recognized by the program, two numbers are popped off the **Stack** and that operation is performed on them. The result of the operation is then pushed back on the **Stack** to be available for the next operation that needs to pop operands. That's all there is to it!

Unfortunately, you only got a taste of the **Stack** class' **push** and **pop** methods in the example. There are a few others, which are all used in Listing 9.14.

Listing 9.14   Stack Methods Demonstrated

```java
import java.util.*;

public class StackProbe {
    private static Stack s = new Stack();

    public static void main( String args[] ) {
        for( int i = 0; i < args.length; ++i ) {
            s.push( args[ i ] );
        }

        if( s.empty() ) {
```

```
        System.out.println( "Ante up some numbers" );
    } else {
        System.out.println( "The top item: " + s.peek() );
        System.out.println( "A 2 is found " +
            s.search( "2" ) + " down in the stack" );
    }
  }
}
```

The **peek** method differs from **pop** in that it does not actually remove the top item from the stack, it just takes a peek. The method **search** is handy because it is the only way to probe the contents of the stack without removing all the items and checking them one by one. The process is shown in the snippet below:

```
cmd> java StackProbe 1 2 3 4 5
The top item: 5
A 2 is found 4 down in the stack.
```

It is important to realize that there is nothing equivalent to the **getElementAt** method of **Vector** for a **Stack**. This may make **Stack** limited, but for the appropriate uses of a **Stack**, the methods are sufficient. With a **Stack**, all insertions and deletions are made at the top of the list: the idea of getting a stack element "at" some other location contradicts the whole idea of having a stack.

You will find the greatest use for **Stack** in keeping track of data that represents some sort of *nested* operation. That's the very reason that your computer has a stack. As the processor executes code, it periodically encounters instructions to jump to some other subroutine rather than continue executing instructions in order. The processor must keep track of where it is before it jumps, in order to be able to return later. Many such jumps may occur before any return trips are attempted. It's like that indispensable list of places you've been browsing on the Web that Netscape stores for you under the Go pull-down menu. The jumps are said to be *nested* because each is encompassed entirely by some other. A stack preserves the order in the correct way so that when it comes time to return, a series of **pop**s off the **Stack** will produce the return addresses in the correct order. The same reason holds true for the RPN calculator example, except in that case, it's temporary sums rather than code addresses. **Stack** is simply the right data structure for the job in both cases.

The next two Java data structures are not derived from **Vector**. They are especially important structures to learn because they give you the ability to store data that is referenced with a key that can be later used for fast retrieval. Let's start with **Dictionary**.

DICTIONARY

You use a normal dictionary to find a definition for a word. You find the definition by using the word as a key to the contents of the dictionary. The dictionary is ordered to make the task of finding the word easy.

This is roughly how the Java data structure **Dictionary** works, too. It contains data items that each have an associated key. The data is ordered internally, based on that key, so that retrieval of the data is possible by key alone. Dictionaries are also identified as *associative arrays* because they associate a key with some data.

Dictionary is an abstract class. Thus, what we are really interested in is the class **Hashtable** that is derived from **Dictionary** and implements all of **Dictionary**'s abstract methods. A hashtable is a dictionary.

HASHTABLE

The **Object** methods **hashCode** and **equals** are especially important to the operation of the Java **Hashtable** class. Each **Hashtable** object contains a series of key/data pairs sorted by the key. It's the **hashCode** function that is applied to each key that sorts them. Individual keys can be identified using the key's **equals** function since the key object must be derived from **Object**.

Hashtable Inheritance

Note that **Hashtable** is not derived from **Vector**. The **Vector** methods that you have become familiar with are not available as they were with a class like **Stack**, which was derived from **Vector**.

You can use a **Hashtable** as a simple database. In Listing 9.15, I have included a Vehicle Registration application that could be used to look up a license plate number and retrieve the associated ownership record.

The application consists of a simple form that includes fields for license plate number and other vehicle information, as well as owner information. There is a row of buttons at the bottom. The function of each should be obvious. Note that when adding a new entry, the only mandatory field is the license plate field. Also, the search function uses only the license plate number as a key. It is not possible to search by owner's name or any other field. However, if that were needed, it would be easy to extend the application.

The instance variables of the class **Vehicle Record** are put into the **Hashtable** called **register**.

Listing 9.15   A Vehicle Record Hashtable

```java
import java.awt.*;
import java.util.*;

class VehicleRecord {

    protected String license;
    protected String make;
    protected String model;
    protected String year;
    protected String fName;
    protected String lName;

    VehicleRecord( String l, String mk, String mdl, String yr,
                   String fn, String ln ) {
        license = l;
        make    = mk;
        model   = mdl;
        year    = yr;
        fName   = fn;
        lName   = ln;
    }
}

class VehicleRegistrationManager extends Frame implements Runnable {

    Thread manager;
    Panel  dataEntryPanel;
    Panel  buttonPanel;

    Hashtable register;

    TextField licenseField;
    TextField makeField;
    TextField modelField;
    TextField yearField;
    TextField fNameField;
    TextField lNameField;

    VehicleRegistrationManager() {

        super( "Vehicle Registration" );
```

```
    register = new Hashtable();

    setLayout( new BorderLayout());
    dataEntryPanel = new Panel();
    dataEntryPanel.setLayout( new GridLayout( 6, 2 ));
    dataEntryPanel.add( new Label( "License Plate #" ));
    dataEntryPanel.add( licenseField = new TextField() );
    dataEntryPanel.add( new Label( "Make" ));
    dataEntryPanel.add( makeField   = new TextField() );
    dataEntryPanel.add( new Label( "Model" ));
    dataEntryPanel.add( modelField  = new TextField() );
    dataEntryPanel.add( new Label( "Year" ));
    dataEntryPanel.add( yearField   = new TextField() );
    dataEntryPanel.add( new Label( "First Name" ));
    dataEntryPanel.add( fNameField  = new TextField() );
    dataEntryPanel.add( new Label( "Last Name" ));
    dataEntryPanel.add( lNameField  = new TextField() );

    buttonPanel = new Panel();
    buttonPanel.setLayout( new GridLayout( 1, 5 ));
    buttonPanel.add( new Button( "Clear" ));
    buttonPanel.add( new Button( "Add"    ));
    buttonPanel.add( new Button( "Delete" ));
    buttonPanel.add( new Button( "Search" ));
    buttonPanel.add( new Button( "Quit"   ));

    add( "Center", dataEntryPanel );
    add( "South",  buttonPanel     );

    resize( 250, 150 );
    show();
}

public void run() {
}

public void start() {
    if( manager == null ) {
        manager = new Thread( this );
        manager.start();
    }
}

public void stop() {
    if( manager != null ) {
        manager.stop();
        manager = null;
    }
}

public void clearFields() {
    licenseField.setText( "" );
```

```
        makeField.setText   ( "" );
        modelField.setText  ( "" );
        yearField.setText   ( "" );
        fNameField.setText  ( "" );
        lNameField.setText  ( "" );
}

public boolean action( Event evt, Object obj ) {
if( evt.target instanceof Button ) {
    String label = ( String )obj;

        if( label == "Quit" ) {
            System.exit( 0 );
        }
        else if( label == "Clear" ) {
            clearFields();
        }
        else if( label == "Add" ) {
            String licenseKey = licenseField.getText();

            if( licenseKey != null ) {
                VehicleRecord vehicleRecord =
                        new VehicleRecord( licenseKey,
                                           makeField.getText(),
                                           modelField.getText(),
                                           yearField.getText(),
                                           fNameField.getText(),
                                           lNameField.getText()));

                register.put( licenseKey, vehicleRecord );
                clearFields();
            } else {
                // Need a key in order to add a record
            }
        }
        else if( label == "Search" ) {
            String licenseKey = licenseField.getText();
            Object object     = register.get( licenseKey );

            if( object != null ) {
                VehicleRecord record = ( VehicleRecord )object;

                makeField.setText ( record.make  );
                modelField.setText( record.model );
                yearField.setText ( record.year  );
                fNameField.setText( record.fName );
                lNameField.setText( record.lName );
            } else {
                // Key not found
            }
        }
        else if( label == "Delete" ) {
            String licenseKey = licenseField.getText();
```

```
                    if( register.remove( licenseKey ) != null ) {
                        clearFields();
                    }
                }
            }
        }

        return true;
    }
}

public class VehicleReg {

    VehicleRegistrationManager manager;

    VehicleReg() {
        manager = new VehicleRegistrationManager();
    }

    public static void main( String args[] ) {
        new VehicleReg();
    }
}
```

licenseKey is the only key used in this example. **licenseKey** is a string and it provides a **hashCode** method that the **Hashtable** can use to index the contents. In order to use several keys, it would be necessary to start using multiple **Hashtable**s.

A new **VehicleRecord** is created based on the information that can be extracted from the form.

The next line puts the **VehicleRecord** variable containing all the vehicle and owner information that you provided in the form into the **Hashtable**. The **vehicleRecord** includes the **licenseKey**, too. The **licenseKey** is the key to the **Hashtable** of **VehicleRecords**.

In order to attempt to retrieve a record, the license key from the form is retrieved and used to access the **Hashtable**. If successful, the result of the search is cast to a **VehicleRecord**. This is safe in this case because the **Hashtable** contains only **VehicleRecords**. In situations where the type of the **Hashtable**'s contents is uncertain, I recommend that you use **instanceof** to determine their type. The fields of the retrieved **VehicleRecord** are copied into the form fields.

Removing an entry from the **Hashtable** is as simple as providing the key. Only the first matching object is removed: that car registration information might not necessarily be for the first car entered in order. Thus, in the unlawful case of two cars registered with the same license plate number, you don't know for certain which car registration information will actually be removed.

Closer Look at Hashtable

You've already encountered the methods **put** and **get** in Listing 9.15, so there will only be brief mention of them here.

After each call to the **put** method, the **Hashtable** is re-sorted based on the hashcode values of the keys. Remember that this doesn't necessarily mean, for instance, that strings will be sorted alphabetically. It's really not important, because when it comes time to retrieve data objects from the **Hashtable**, there will be a one-to-one correspondence between key and data object, and retrieval will be assured.

The **get** method doesn't actually remove the data from the **Hashtable**. You need the **remove** method for that.

Finally, there is a set of methods that you first saw in Vector, together with a few closely related ones. The methods you've seen have the same names and functions as in **Vector**. They have been given the same names safely because **Hashtable** is not derived from **Vector**. Therefore, there is no danger of any of **Vector**'s methods being hidden.

There is a **contains** method which is identical to that for **Vector**. However, since key/data pairs are stored in **Hashtable**s there's also a method called **containsKey**.

Enumeration Again

You'll find that there's a method **elements** in **Hashtable** too. But because we're dealing with keys—and not just data entries—there is another method tagging along. It's called **keys**. Though it's hardly worth it, here's a little code snippet that illustrates its use:

```
for( Enumeration e = table.keys(); e.hasMoreElements(); ) {
    String license = ( String )e.nextElement();
    // ...
}
```

The methods **isEmpty** and **size** should not be strangers to you, either.

Removal and Cleanup

To clean up a **Hashtable**, you can remove elements one at a time with code as in this snippet:

```
for( Enumeration e = table.elements(); e.hasMoreElements(); ) {
    table.remove( e.nextElement () );
}
```

Finally, you can clean out the entire contents of a **Hashtable** all at once with the method **clear**.

We've covered all of the Java classes that could be strictly defined as data structures. I develop a new data structure called Queue next.

DO-IT-YOURSELF DATA STRUCTURES

Probably 99 percent of the time you need to use a data structure, one of Java's built-in data structures will satisfy your requirements.

If you do need to hand-craft a special data structure, you're more than able to do it in Java. In this section, I've developed a data structure called **Queue**. Note that a Queue is not a Java data structure like **Vector** or **Stack**. However, a Queue is very similar to a stack—as you can see in Figure 9.4.

You're probably wondering why we couldn't just be content with a stack or even just a vector and avoid developing something totally new. The fact is that Queue isn't some totally new data structure I've cooked up. Besides being a traditional cornerstone data structure, this Queue is based on the Java **Vector** class, so we're still in familiar territory. As I've already mentioned, **Vector** provides an excellent set of methods to implement any new data structures. That's exactly what I'll be doing below.

The Queue

One of the best developments since drive-thru coffee joints is bank-by-phone. My bank is only as far as the nearest phone and I know when I call that I'll be

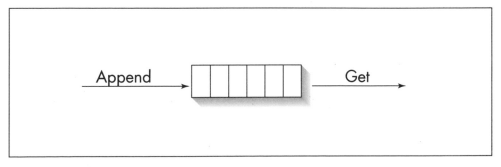

Figure 9.4   *A Queue.*

able to get all I want done quickly. I don't have to spend time waiting in queues for other earlier people to get served before me. Queues are efficient, you'll have to admit, but I think you'd all agree you'd rather never have to wait in one. Maybe we're not so bad off. I once read that before the fall of Communism in the Soviet Union, the average citizen spent four hours per day waiting in queues!

A queue is a data structure, but one you've not yet met. It was named for the kind of queues you find in a bank, so you're already quite familiar with how it works. It implements a *FIFO* policy. No, that's not the name of some unfortunate dog named by an owner whose mouth was full of food at the time. It means *First In, First Out*. Just like the bank queues we all hate. And just like the bank, you wait your turn in the queue, progressing one position at a time towards the teller as each customer ahead of you is serviced.

In a queue, data is manipulated in nearly the same way. Like a bank, where prompt people who arrive early go straight to the front of the empty queue, and the rest of us pile in behind, in the order in which we arrive, the data first added to the queue will be the first pulled out of the queue. That's the essence of it. You assume when you use a queue that all the items in the queue are of equal priority and that the order of insertion needs to be preserved. In fact, the order of insertion serves as the only means of assigning priority. Queues may be de-humanizing to some people, but at an organizational level, they are simple and equitable.

In a program, a queue typically serves as a temporary holding place for data that is being shared by two or more functions. It can sit between them and *queue up* requests for services that may come in bursts, and that would otherwise overload the server function's ability to accept them. The order of the requests is preserved, so they can be pulled out of the queue later and processed in order. If this describes a programming problem you're facing, a queue is the right tool for the job.

Listing 9.16 has an example of a Queue implemented based on **Vector**.

Listing 9.16   Example of a Queue

```
import java.util.*;

interface Queue {

    public void    clear();
    public int     entries();
```

```java
        public Object first();
        public Object last();

        public Enumeration elements();
        public Object get();

        public Object append( Object obj );
        public Object insert( Object obj );

    }

    public class MyQueue implements Queue {
        private Vector myVector;

        public MyQueue() {
            myVector = new Vector();
        }

        public MyQueue( Object obj ) {
            myVector = new Vector();
            myVector.addElement( obj );
        }

        public Object append( Object obj ) {
            myVector.addElement( obj );
            return obj;
        }

        public void clear() {
            myVector.removeAllElements();
        }

        public int entries() {
            return myVector.size();
        }

        public Object first() {
            return myVector.firstElement();
        }

        public Object get() {
            Object object = null;
            try {
                object = myVector.firstElement();
                myVector.removeElementAt( 0 );
            } catch( ArrayIndexOutOfBoundsException e ) {
            }
            return object;
        }

        public Object insert( Object obj ) {
            try {
```

```
        myVector.insertElementAt( obj, 0 );
    } catch( ArrayIndexOutOfBoundsException e ) {
    }
    return obj;
}

public Object last() {
    return myVector.lastElement();
}

public Enumeration elements() {
    return myVector.elements();
}
}
```

Once you've learned how to use **Vector** effectively, you'll be tempted never to stray from it.

Are you disappointed to see that **MyQueue** is implemented solely with an internal **Vector** object? "Why not just use a **Vector** directly and dispense with all the trouble of developing a new data structure like a queue?"

There are several good reasons why I recommend you consider writing your own data structure. But first, I want to highlight some details about this queue implementation that you likely don't appreciate. When designing this queue, I had the choice of either deriving a new queue class from **Vector** class or creating an **interface** of queue methods and then implementing that **interface**. I chose the second of these options.

An internal **Vector** object that is private to the implementation is used in **MyQueue**. The subtlety is nearly beyond the scope of this chapter, but the essence is this: it is better to do what I have done because you hide the implementation details. By deriving from **Vector**, you are implying that a queue *is a* **Vector**, but that's not true. It just so happens that I have chosen to use a **Vector** because it is so handy. I could instead have decided to inflict some torture on myself and implement it all with arrays, as we started to do early in this chapter with the ShoppingList example.

As a consequence of my design decision, **Queue** just *has a* **Vector**. The **Vector** is encapsulated in the **MyQueue** implementation. That's recommended style because obviously you have a need in mind that is specifically suited to the methods a standard queue provides—no more, no less. A **Queue** class that was an extension of a **Vector** would still give users of your class access to all those **Vector** methods. The temptation would be difficult to resist, and soon the users could start using **Vector** methods directly. That would undermine your queue concept. Finally, I have illustrated an exemplary use of an **interface**. The queue **interface** lists succinctly all the methods that anything posing as a queue must provide. Also it limits the access of any class implementing the **interface** to the specific methods declared in the **interface** definition. Got all that?

Whoa! I guess I almost got away without detailing a queue's methods. Note that the methods in this queue are the basics. You'll probably encounter other queue implementations that have many more methods. But you can count on these few being common to all, though they might be named differently. Listing 9.17 is a little program that takes **MyQueue** for a spin.

Listing 9.17   Demonstrating the Queue

```
import java.util.*;
import MyQueue;

public class MyQueueTester {
    public static void main( String args[] ) {
        MyQueue queue = new MyQueue();

        for( int i = 0; i < args.length; ++i ) {
            queue.append( args[ i ] );
        }

        System.out.println( "At first the queue contains:" );
        for( Enumeration e = queue.elements();
                        e.hasMoreElements(); ) {
            System.out.println( e.nextElement() );
        }

        System.out.println( "ALPHA is inserted" );
        System.out.println( "OMEGA is appended" );
        queue.insert( "ALPHA" );
        queue.append( "OMEGA" );

        System.out.println( "The queue contains " +
                        queue.entries() + " entries" );
        System.out.println( "The first is " + queue.first() );
        System.out.println( "The last is " + queue.last() );

        System.out.println( "the queue now contains:" );
        for( Enumeration e = queue.elements();
                        e.hasMoreElements(); ) {
            System.out.println( e.nextElement() );
        }
    }
}
```

Is it any surprise that **MyQueue** works just as designed? The only nuance you might have missed is the difference between the methods **insert** and **append**. The method **append** is the usual means of adding an item to a queue. The item goes to the end. However, the **insert** method is provided to let an item *jump the queue*. The process is shown in the snippet below.

```
cmd> java MyQueueTester a b c
At first the queue contains:
a
b
c
ALPHA is inserted
OMEGA is appended
The queue contains 5 entries
The first is ALPHA
the last is OMEGA
the queue now contains:
ALPHA
a
b
c
OMEGA
```

Don't Reinvent Any Wheels

I recommend that you first acquaint yourself with some of the traditional data structure designs that have been developed. When you encounter a programming problem, you'll be able to quickly recognize which particular data structure is the right tool for the job. You can either locate a reliable data structure package containing the data structure you need, or you can write your own based on the standard specification of that data structure.

Have fun, but play safe!

SERIALIZATION OF A DATA STRUCTURE

First of all, serialization is just the process of converting data to a format that can be saved to and read from an input or output stream. But the only serialization you've likely ever heard of is in regards to turning a large book into a series of smaller magazine articles or even a run of TV shows. The concept in either case is actually similar to data serialization. You might think of some data in your program as a monolithic block much like a large tome. Magazines are only equipped to publish articles that don't exceed a few thousand words. In order to make a book fit the magazine format, it must be broken down into smaller chunks. The story in the book will then be spread out over a series of months.

The reader waits anxiously each month for the next installment, so that he or she can put one more piece of the story together. Data, too, has to be chopped into pieces to the passed through an input or output stream.

But why does data need to be chopped up—can't it just be saved as it is? The answer, of course, is no. When you are saving data to and retrieving data from a file you'll need to use a stream. There's no other way. Fortunately, however, you just read all about streams in Chapter 8, so you're well prepared for a quick, cursory example. In Listing 9.18, I present a simple example of a program that accepts a list of strings from the command line. It then saves them in a **Vector** object. That object is then taken and squeezed out serially into a stream that is connected to a file. The file is closed and re-opened and another new **Vector** object is constructed based on the data read.

Listing 9.18   Serializing Data

```java
import java.io.*;
import java.util.*;

public class SerializeVector {
    static Vector list = new Vector();

    public static void main( String args[] ) {
        int length = args.length;

        for( int i = 0; i < length; ++i ) {
            list.addElement( args[ i ] );
        }

        System.out.println( "The original vector:" );
        for( Enumeration e = list.elements();
                        e.hasMoreElements(); ) {
            System.out.println( e.nextElement() );
        }


        File vectorFile = new File( "AList" );

        //
        // Output
        //
        FileOutputStream fos = null;
        try {
            fos = new FileOutputStream( vectorFile );

        } catch( IOException e1 ) {
        }
        for( Enumeration e = list.elements();
                        e.hasMoreElements(); ) {
            String itemString = ( String )e.nextElement();
            int itemStringLength = itemString.length();
```

```
        byte[] itemByteArray = new byte[ itemStringLength ];
        itemString.getBytes( 0, itemStringLength,
                               itemByteArray, 0 );
        try {
           fos.write( itemByteArray );
           fos.write( ' ' );
        } catch( IOException e2 ) {
        }
    }


    //
    // Input
    //
    Vector newList = new Vector();

    FileInputStream  fis = null;
    byte[] inputArray = null;
    try{
        fis = new FileInputStream( vectorFile );
        inputArray = new byte[ fis.available() ];
        fis.read( inputArray );
    } catch( IOException e3 ) {
    }

    String inputString = new String( inputArray, 0 );
    StringTokenizer t = new StringTokenizer( inputString );

    while( t.hasMoreTokens() ) {
        newList.addElement(( String )t.nextToken() );
    }

    System.out.println( "The new vector:" );
    for( Enumeration e = newList.elements();
                     e.hasMoreElements(); ) {
        System.out.println( e.nextElement() );
    }
    }
  }
}
```

Let's run the thing and see what goes on. The results are shown in the snippet below.

```
cmd> java SerializeVector a b c
The original vector:
a
b
c
The new vector:
a
b
c
```

No surprises here. The **Vector** object was written out to a file. Then that same file was read back into a newly created **Vector**. You'll have to remember that a little file named Alist will get created to contain the list. You can take a look into it with an editor or just blow it away.

This example was simple, but you can see that serialization is not so difficult to implement for a **Vector**. You'll really have no more difficulty with serializing any other data structures either.

Include Data Structure Type Information

It's wise to encode the type of the data structure in the data file too. You can't always safely assume you're going to know the type of data structure to which the later-read data belongs.

The use of standard data structures such as you've just met is something that, until recently, has been haphazardly applied. Data structures are not particularly difficult to throw together, and that's just what has happened. It's spooky how much software is out there running with homemade data structures. The wheel has certainly been reinvented several times. But Java helps to improve the situation and I'll explore how after some background.

REUSABLE CODE

Software engineering is an example of an industry just emerging from the *cottage industry* stage. This is the explanation for the prominent large-system failures that have occurred over the years. Scientists looking at the problems have found that despite the availability of proven, consistent, and reliable software components, they are not yet a focus of standard software development.

Mechanical manufacturing essentially passed out of cottage industry stage nearly a hundred years ago. There was a time when manufacturers couldn't buy standard components. All the constituent parts of any product had to be manufactured in-house. So if you were a gun-maker, you would have to make your own screws, for instance. Every manufacturer that needed screws made screws. Some made better screws than others. There was no consistency. There was no way for a manufacturer to focus on its specific area of manufacture regardless of whether it was gun-smithing or buggy-making. That made it hard to make better guns or better buggies.

In retrospect, it easy to see how such a system was just crying out for specialization. Of course, now, only screw-makers concentrate on making better screws. Other manufacturers produce better products because they have better screws than if they had to make them themselves. Manufacturing is now focused and, hence, more productive, yielding higher-quality goods.

Programmers are often still making screws—so to speak. Some of the most common programming structures that are reinvented are data structures. Several standard data structures have been developed over the years. One of the positive things about Java is that it provides in the Java Developer's Kit a rich set of classes that most developers will use right away. The basics are already provided, so there's not much need to improvise. This sort of large-scale code reuse is a big positive and should help to ensure the quality of Java software.

LET'S REVIEW

Java data structures are powerful and indispensible, yet simple to use. **Vector** is the universal data structure that you will use most often. Whenever you need to index your data, you'll use a **Hashtable**. **Stack** is a built-in Java data structure that is derived from **Vector**. It's good for keeping track of nested operations.

In this chapter, I developed another data structure called **Queue**. It was a taste of what you might need to do if you have a very specific requirement that the available Java data structures don't satisfy. The rich set of methods that **Vector** provides makes it possible to define new data structures such as **Queue**. Whenever you do derive a new data structure from **Vector**, it is wise to implement the structure as an interface and encapsulate a **Vector** object inside the new class. It makes the design consistent, and users are prevented from circumventing your design.

There's certainly a great deal that this chapter didn't deal with. You're still going to have to experiment with the different data structures until you are familiar with them and are able to quickly implement a program solution using them. You might care to do some reading into other data structures in order to broaden your experience.

A DATA STRUCTURE TO LOVE

Doug Lea, a professor in the Computer Science Department at the State University of New York at Oswego, has done some interesting work with collections. He defines a collection as an object that holds other objects that are accessed, placed, and maintained according to some set of rules. You might recognize that as a data structure. Either way, check out: http://g.oswego.edu/dl/classes/collections/index.html

DATE AND TIME

CHAPTER 10

Alex Leslie

We stop off at the millenium to check out what is happening. If your watch is broken, don't worry. We'll show you how to build a new one.

Not surprisingly, this chapter is about handling dates and times in Java programs. Date and time are important concepts. You will find that they are integral parts of many Java programs you'll write. I've added a simple, little Java applet to my home page that displays your time and date accurate to the second. I think it's pretty nifty. Seeing the seconds tick by emphasizes the dynamic nature of what Java brings to programming—especially with applets that are downloaded over the Net.

Java dates and times need to be formatted to be useful. With Java, you need to write the code that formats dates and times yourself. I have included example code that does a lot of the date and time formatting for you and the code is easy to extend for your own needs.

With Java so intimately related to the Internet, your date and time displays could appear on a computer screen anywhere in the world. You'll look just that much better if your applets are able to adapt to different locales and are able to display

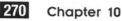

dates and times according to local customs. I discuss the issue of localization briefly but locale is one area in which Java is currently weak.

Finally, dates and times are certainly not static entities. I'll show you how to use Java threads to keep a clock ticking accurately.

Time will fly and soon you'll be a Java date and time whiz.

31 DECEMBER 1999 11:59:57...11:59:58...11:59:59... OOOPS!

We all regard times and dates rather casually, but there is a date crisis looming over our heads all because some programmers got a little too relaxed while writing applications that process dates.

"Crisis, what crisis! I'm just looking forward to one hell of a great party!"

The new millennium is only four years away. Reports of plans for outrageous end-of-the-millennium parties are starting to appear in the press nearly every-day. Even Disneyland is already booked solid, so you're out of luck if you thought it might be nice to bring the kids. There are even cults that have been founded on suicide pacts and populated by those fearful of what the next millennium will hold in store. It's the sort of doom-and-gloom talk that most sane people casually ignore. However, there is one real issue regarding the year 2000 that can't be ignored any longer. It has been lying in wait for years—waiting for the clock to strike 12:00.

Imagine if you will: computer programs all over the world—programs that only days before had been operating reliably—suddenly start spitting out wrong answers to standard calculations. Calculations that all share one common element: they all involve calculations with dates.

If you were to say 95 instead of 1995 nobody would have any problem understanding what you mean—unless, of course, you're writing a history textbook. But what if you see 00. What does that mean? To many computer applications out there, it means 1900 not 2000. The distinction is critical.

All modern computer programming has taken place within 50 years of the year 2000. In a shortsighted attempt to be efficient, many programmers have coded their applications to handle years with two digits instead of four. It's an example of "penny wise and pound foolish." Perhaps the designers of computer applications just couldn't dream how long-lived their programs would be.

It's not like anyone really has a handle on which lines of which modules of which applications even contain the flaw. The cost to hunt down and repair this serious problem world-wide is enormous. Estimates range from $300- to $600-million. And there are still a lot of applications containing the flaw that will go unnoticed until it's too late and fixes have to be implemented in panic-mode.

Just imagine if one of these flawed applications calculates something like Social Security checks or bond yields. Calculations will simply fail. You can be sure that it won't be long until somebody's phone is ringing off the hook. We'll let somebody else worry about the 2000 problem. Let's start with the absolute simplest way to get the time out of Java—though its not what you're likely expecting.

SYSTEM AND TIME

System sure is handy.

```
System.out.println( "Hello World" );
```

You're probably pretty comfortable with this statement already. It just prints out the now-familiar "Hello World"—a brief affirmation popularized in a still wildly popular book on C by Kernigan and Ritchie and which now seems to appear as the first example in almost every introductory computer language book.

System is a real grab-bag of system-oriented functionality. It gives you access to many system features in a way that is independent of your computing platform. One of those features just happens to be a function that produces your computer's system date. Every computer you're likely to use has included among all its other hardware a clock. That clock runs on a recharge able battery that is recharged during computer use so that time settings can be maintained even while the computer is turned off and even unplugged from the wall for periods of time. The clock keeps track of time in milliseconds— that is, thousandths of a second. In fact, the only information that your computer's clock can give you is a tally of milliseconds representing the actual number of milliseconds that have elapsed since a universally—at least for computers—recognized time and date in history, called "the epoch." That special date is introduced in a few moments.

The one specific **System** method that I want you to take note of is this:

```
public static native long currentTimeMillis();
```

That's the one and only way that any of your Java programs can get a hold of the system time. The **Date** class, which we'll discuss soon, even uses the method **currentTimeMillis**.

The **currentTimeMillis** method is public and static because it's available to any other classes outside of its own package but cannot be overridden. It is implemented as a native method, which means it is really a wrapper around some other platform-specific system function that actually retrieves the current system time.

currentTimeMillis returns a long and takes no parameters—it simply goes and gets the time. The time it does return is expressed as a long. When was the last time that *you* wrote the time as a long? Probably never! The way the long expresses the time—and the date too—is in milliseconds. Maybe you could have guessed that from the name of the method itself. That just happens to be the greatest possible time precision you can get from Java.

"But milliseconds are not what I need—I need something I can display on the screen!"

The Java **Date** class is what you need. You will use the **Date** class rather than **currentTimeMillis** for most of the kinds of dates and times in your Java programming.

Understanding Dates

1 January 1970. The epoch. It has an important-sounding ring to it. It's a very special date in the history of computers. If you've never heard of it, you're not alone. I've seen more than one question posted in a newsgroup asking what it was. It's just one of those things that are taken for granted by people who write computer applications.

Its significance lies in the fact that it is the date from which computer time is measured. What I mean is that the clock inside your computer is counting milliseconds. It has a tally especially for that total. And if you were to count backwards all the way to zero milliseconds from that total in your computer right now, you would have counted all the way back to 1 January 1970 at 12:00 am.

It's just a standard baseline, chosen for no better reason than setting one meter as a standard of length or measuring one second as so many vibrations of some rare atomic isotope. The epoch could have been set at any time in the past. It could have been set at the boundary between "B.C." and "A.D," which would have made sense since we in the Western world are already comfortable measuring years from that date. But then again, a lot more milliseconds have elapsed between then and now. Most computers use a long integer to count the milliseconds. As I write this, about

62125900000000 milliseconds have elapsed between the "year zero" and January 1, 1970. That's a lot of overhead to be included on every date used in a computer. It's really unnecessary considering nothing important happened before 1970 anyway. Unless, that is, you count Jimi Hendrix and Janis Joplin.

CAN YOU GET ME A DATE?

Milliseconds may score big for precision, but they sure are inadequate if you need a readable date and time. You could work out the math yourself—but why bother? The Java **Date** class rescues you from the unwieldy milliseconds.

Your computer counts milliseconds but you're looking to display a string of characters. **Date** gets you nearly there. It won't produce a neatly formatted date and time string, but it does offer a complete set of methods that, individually, give you access to all the constituent parts of any date and time. Most of the methods just return integers but it's relatively easy to piece them together and produce a date and time string in any format you want.

The **Date** class converts between your dates and times, and your computer's system time and back again.

The Pickup Lines

In Java, you have five choices if you want to get yourself a date. Table 10.1 lists the constructors for **Date**. The first constructor is special in that it takes no parameters. A **Date** variable instantiated in this way will read your computer's system date and time and convert it to the years, months, days, hours, minutes,

---

Table 10.1 *Date Constructors*

Constructor	Description
Date()	Accurate to the millisecond
Date(long V)	As identified below, you can't use just any long
Date(int year, int month, int date)	Specific to the day
Date(int year, int month, int date, int hrs, int min)	Specific to the minute
Date(int year, int month, int date, int hrs, int min, int sec)	Specific to the second

---

and seconds you are more familiar with. You would use the remaining constructors if you want to set a **Date** variable with some other date and time other than the current system time.

Note that no constructor method that accepts parameters takes anything finer than a second. The milliseconds are always zeroed.

Say you want to set a date accurately to 8:35:06 and 123 milliseconds am on July 4, 1996 . Here's a way to do it:

```
Date date = new Date( 96, 6, 4, 8, 35, 6 );
date.setTime( date.getTime() + 123 );
```

Now let's take a step back and introduce each constructor.

First of all, the easiest way to get a date is to be sincere and just ask:

```
Date date = new Date();
```

Presto, you got yourself a **Date**. And that date is now accurate to the millisecond.

Actually, that constructor calls another constructor which takes long milliseconds with the return value of **System.currentTimeMillis**. Remember what I said about the method **currentTimeMillis** being integral to time and date. You can call **Date** with a long yourself, too by using the second constructor shown in Table 10.1. But be careful:

```
Date date = new Date( 1234567890 );
```

This code line *looks* plausible enough, but it doesn't work:

```
Exception in thread "main" java.lang.IllegalArgumentException:
time out of range for timezone calculation.
at java.util.Date.getYear(Date.java:387)
```

No matter how tempting, you can't just use any old long or it'll throw an **IllegalArgumentException** your way.

If you're satisfied with finding only the year, month, and day—for instance, 23 May 1996—you'll use the third constructor shown in Table 10.1:

```
Date date = new Date( 96, 5, 23 );
```

Date chokes on negative years, so don't try it.

I can hear it now, "Hey, wait a minute! Aren't you introducing the year 2000 date problem mentioned earlier?"

Though it may look as if I have, I really haven't. The 96 is an integer not a string like "96." That's the important distinction. The year 2000 and 1900 can't be confused because to express the year 2000 you'd use 100 not 0, which is used to represent 1900. You use the number of years after 1900 expressed as an integer whenever a constructor is looking for a year.

You can add a specific time to your request by using the fifth constructor listed in Table 10.1:

```
Date date = new Date( 96, 5, 23, 10, 31, 15 );
```

And you can construct a **Date** without the seconds by using the fourth constructor. That's almost it for the constructors.

Parse This!

Date may not be able to produce a formatted time and date string for you, but it does accept a string containing a date. In this case, you must pass the string to **Date** via the **parse** method.

Let's say you called **Date** like this:

```
Date date = new Date( "Sat, 12 Aug 1995 13:30:00 GMT" );
```

The **Date** constructor turns around and fires the string off to one of its methods called **parse**. The method **parse** has a lot of smarts built into it. It's able to read and decipher a variety of date formats. By the way, the process of taking a string and extracting it's constituent parts is called *parsing*. Certainly, there are limitations to the method's abilities.

We'll discuss some of those limitations in a bit. Never pass a **null String** or you'll get another **IllegalArgumentException**.

How does the method **parse** convert a time and date string to a **Date**? First of all, days of the week are ignored; they are redundant. Your date and time string will need to include the numerical date. The method **parse** then steps through the string character-by-character. It ignores any leading blanks, commas, and dashes. Comments enclosed in parentheses are also ignored. It is legal to nest comments. I don't know why you would, but feel free.

The method **parse** starts working once it hits a digit, a forward slash, a colon, a plus sign, or a non-leading dash, or really any other character that looks interesting. The **parse** method processes a string of digits and interprets it based on the previous non-digit character. If that character is a plus or minus sign, the digits are considered timezone offsets, as shown in Table 10.2.

There are a set of timezone abbreviations that North Americans take for granted. Those of you living in other parts of the world may not even recognize them. Table 10.2 includes two timezone abbreviations. You may be familiar with GMT (Greenwich Mean Time). It serves as the baseline for all other timezones. Most of the world uses hour offsets from GMT to express their local timezones. EST is a North American timezone. It stands for Eastern Standard Time Zone and includes approximately the eastern third of North America. It's entry in the table is invalid.

The **parse** method interprets any number that is greater than or equal to 70 as the year. Remember the epoch? The year must be followed by a blank space, a comma, a forward slash, or the end of the **string**. Simple enough.

The **parse** method expects only hours and minutes to be followed by colons. Seconds can be added at your discretion but remember the colon.

If you want to express the month, date, and year with forward slashes, the month must precede the date as the hour must precede the minutes. Also, the forward slash may only come after the month and the date.

If a character other than a comma, a blank space, or a dash is encountered while parsing a date, an **IllegalArgumentException** will be thrown.

Finally, the **parse** method can recognize the month expressed in text and the timezone, as we already covered.

Table 10.2 *Offsets from Greenwich Mean Time*

Valid	String	Description
Yes	GMT-3	3 hours west of GMT
Yes	GMT-0430	4 hours and 30 minutes west of GMT
No	EST-0430	1 hour west of EST. You can only make timezone adjustments to any timezone but GMT

Timezones Revealed

Timezones might be something that you seldom encounter. Most of Europe is included in one timezone, for instance. Many timezones have been drawn up to include regional areas. Unless you interact with people living outside your local region, timezones are not something you give much thought to.

Timezones divide the world up into twenty-four uneven segments, some of which are shown in Table 10.3. They are necessary so that everyone in the world can conduct their lives according to a consistent set of hours. It's just natural to expect the sun to reach its zenith in the sky around 12:00 pm no matter where you live.

EST has already been introduced. You probably know your own timezone, too. **parse** can handle a set of North American timezones—though Alaskans and just about everyone else in the world will feel left out.

Some regions of the world, like most of North America recognize Daylight Savings Time between March and October. The original motivation was to save electricity by shifting people's schedules during the winter into periods with more daylight. No great downside as long as you remember each bi-annual clock adjustment.

The timezones in Java are North American-centric. It's up to you to write your own more robust parser if you want to handle other timezone abbreviations.

Table 10.3 *Some World Time Zones*

Abbreviation	Time Zone	Time Adjustment
GMT	Greenwich Mean Time	0:00 hr
EST	Eastern Standard Time	+5:00 hr
EDT	Eastern Daylight Time	+4:00 hr
CST	Central Standard Time	+6:00 hr
CDT	Central Daylight Time	+5:00 hr
MST	Mountain Standard Time	+7:00 hr
MDT	Mountain Daylight Time	+6:00 hr
PST	Pacific Standard Time	+8:00 hr
PDT	Pacific Daylight Time	+7:00 hr

DO-IT-YOURSELF FORMATTING

It's finally time to tackle the issue of formatting a time and date string. You're going to have to roll up your sleeves and get down to work because formatting dates and times is left strictly up to you in Java. There is no formatting mechanism built-in. But I'm sure you'll want to be able to produce a date and time string formatted appropriately.

All **Date** provides is a series of get/set methods. Remember that I said that **Date** won't do all your work for you. There is a get method for each date or time component, as shown in Table 10.4. They return integers, which is fine for everything except months and days. Both of those need to be converted to the appropriate string separately.

The corresponding set methods, also shown in Table 10.4, perform exactly the opposite functions that the get methods do. It's good to know that even after a Date is created with one of the constructors you have the set methods available to later change it.

These methods are all you need to build a simple digital clock just like the one gracing my home page. But first, we'll start out with the essential formatter.

First, you've got to decide what to display with the clock. I've already written a little Java code, shown in Listing 10.1, that does just that and I'll explain the details later in this chapter.

Table 10.4 *Using Date Functions*

Date Component	Input	Output	Return Value or Parameter
Year	int getYear()	void setYear(int year)	Years after 1900
Month	int getMonth()	void setMonth(int month)	Month (0-11)
Date	int getDate()	void setDate(int date)	Day Date (0-31) - 29,30,31 may roll forward for shorter months
Hours	int getHours()	void setHours(int hour)	Hours (0-23) - midnight is 0
Minutes	int getMinutes()	void setMinutes(int minutes)	Minutes (0-59)
Seconds	int getSeconds()	void setSeconds(int seconds)	Seconds (0-59)
Day	int getDay()	void setDay(int day)	Day (0-6) - Monday? is 0

Listing 10.1   Formatting a Date and Time String

```java
import java.util.*;

class TimeAndDateFormatter {

    String formattedDate;

    String  daysOfWeek[]   = { "Sunday",
                               "Monday",
                               "Tuesday",
                               "Wednesday",
                               "Thursday",
                               "Friday",
                               "Saturday" };

    String  monthsOfYear[] = { "January",
                               "February",
                               "March",
                               "April",
                               "May",
                               "June",
                               "July",
                               "August",
                               "September",
                               "October",
                               "November",
                               "December"  };

    TimeAndDateFormatter( Date date ) {

        int h = date.getHours();
        int m = date.getMinutes();
        int s = date.getSeconds();

        int dy = date.getDay();
        int dt = date.getDate();
        int mn = date.getMonth();
        int yr = date.getYear();

        String hours, minutes, seconds, am_pm;
        String day, numericalDate, month, year;

        if( h == 0 ) {
            hours = new String( "12" );
            am_pm = new String( "am" );
        } else if( h > 12 ) {
            hours = new String( "" + (h-12) );
            am_pm = new String( "pm"       );
        } else {
            hours = new String( "" + h );
            am_pm = new String( "am"   );
        }
```

```
        if( m < 10 ) {
            minutes = new String( "0" + m );
        } else {
            minutes = new String( ""  + m );
        }

        if( s < 10 ) {
            seconds = new String( "0" + s );
        } else {
            seconds = new String( ""  + s );
        }

        day = daysOfWeek[ dy ];

        numericalDate = new String( "" + dt );

        month = monthsOfYear[ mn ];

        year  = new String( "" + (1900 + yr) );

        formattedDate = new String( hours   + ":" +
                                    minutes + ":" +
                                    seconds + am_pm + "   " +
                                    day + ", " +
                                    numericalDate + " " +
                                    month + " " +
                                    year );
    }

    public String toString() {
        return formattedDate;
    }
}

public class TimeAndDateDriver {

    public static void main( String args[] ) {
        Date date = new Date();

        TimeAndDateFormatter formattedTimeAndDate =
            new TimeAndDateFormatter( date );

        System.out.println( "Current Time and Date: " +
                            formattedTimeAndDate );
    }
}
```

The time and date line you're going to display will need to include the numerical date, the month, and the year as well as the hours, minutes, and seconds. The idea behind the program is shown in Figure 10.1. Unfortunately, you need to use a separate method to retrieve each element. A

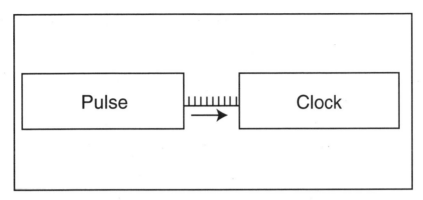

Figure 10.1 *Conceptual diagram of the clock program.*

series of **Date** gets is what you're looking at. The particular format that you use will depend on cultural convention or even just personal preference. The format I've used in this example code is standard in North America.

Since the **Date** method **getDay** returns an integer not a String, you'll usually need to have one String array handy with the days of the week and another one with the months of the year. The integers that do get returned from the methods **getDay** and **getMonth**, respectively, will be used as the index into the appropriate array.

Let's define two arrays:

```
String  daysOfWeek[]  = { "Sunday",
                          "Monday",
                          "Tuesday",
                          "Wednesday",
                          "Thursday",
                          "Friday",
                          "Saturday" };

String  monthsOfYear[] = { "January",
                           "February",
                           "March",
                           "April",
                           "May",
                           "June",
                           "July",
                           "August",
                           "September",
                           "October",
                           "November",
                           "December"  };
```

Let's discuss the sort of formatting that you will always need to do. For this example, we'll use a common time and date format: "HH:MM:SSam/pm DAY, DD MONTH YY".

The first step is to extract the time and date components. There's simply no escaping it.

```
int h  = date.getHours();
int m  = date.getMinutes();
int s  = date.getSeconds();
int dy = date.getDay();
int dt = date.getDate();
int mn = date.getMonth();
int yr = date.getYear();
```

Now, we're going to exploit the power of Java Strings. Each time and date component will be an instance of the class **String**.

Formatting is simple because **String** provides the "+" operator, which I'll use to concatenate strings together.

```
String hours, minutes, seconds, am_pm;
String day, numericalDate, month, year;
```

This code is necessary to handle all the different formatting issues that arise during twenty-four hours. Note the *""+s* trick I used to coerce an int into a **String**. Steve discusses this trick in Chapter 7: *Strings and Things*.

```
if( h == 0 ) {
    hours = new String( "12"  );
    am_pm = new String( " am" );
} else if( h > 12 ) {
    hours = new String( "" + (h-12) );
    am_pm = new String( " pm"      );
} else {
    hours = new String( "" + h );
    am_pm = new String( " am"  );
}

if( m < 10 ) {
    minutes = new String( "0" + m );
} else {
    minutes = new String( ""   + m );
}

if( s < 10 ) {
    seconds = new String( "0" + s );
```

```
} else {
    seconds = new String( "" + s );
}
numericalDate = new String( "" + dt );
year  = new String( "" + (1900 + yr) );
```

It is equally simple to extract the appropriate day or month string from the arrays that were defined earlier. Just use the integer that was return as the index into the array.

```
day   = daysOfWeek[ dy ];
month = monthsOfYear[ mn ];
```

The formatted **String** containing the date and time is created by constructing a new **String** and adding together all the elements that compose the date and time.

```
formattedDate = new String( hours   + ":" +
                            minutes + ":" +
                            seconds + am_pm + "   " +
                            day + ", " +
                            numericalDate + " " +
                            month + " " +
                            year );
```

WORLDWIDE TIME AND DATE

As I have said, there's currently no way to define a formatted string in Java. There is no clever date formatter to complement the **parse** method. You simply have to build any date strings yourself. This brings up the issue of different formats. Living in North America, it is sometimes easy to forget the rest of the world out there. We often assume that the way we do or write things is standard or even "the right way." That's rather naive. The Internet is bringing people together from all over the globe. The fact is that many countries and cultures of the world do have surprisingly diverse ways of expressing dates, time, and even currency values.

Maybe you are already concerned with issues of internationalization. That's great! On the Net, who knows who might access your site?

Java has no internationalization features and no concept of locale. To Java, locale is just a standard way of identifying a set of date, time, currency formats in which you prefer to have information presented. Locale and the National Language System are two hot topics that you will certainly face if you want to communicate effectively over the Internet.

Locale can be represented by something as simple as an environment variable. Any application or applet—in this case—can access that variable and format it accordingly.

"How can I go ahead and implement a sort of locale if I wanted to?"

First you'd need to create a local property called **locale** that can be referenced. **Locale** could be put into the system properties since it applies to every application. (Properties are another one of those things included under the System umbrella.)

```
Properties properties = System.getProperties();
properties.put( "locale", "US" );
```

And when you need to determine the locale in use hopefully it has been defined.

```
Properties properties = System.getProperties();
String locale = propertiest.get( "locale" );
```

That's easy enough. Remember that Java yet has no concept of locale so this solution is therefore imperfect. For locale to work across the Internet, for instance, a standard locale property needs to be established. In the future, Java will include locale.

TIME AND DATE COMPARISONS

You can use the method **getTime** to return the number of milliseconds between the stored date and the epoch. Likewise, it can be set with the method **setTime** if you already have a valid time value long expressing milliseconds since the epoch.

The following code using **getTime**

```
Date date = new Date();
long millis = date.getTime();
```

is equivalent to:

```
long millis = System.currentTimeMillis();
```

Finally, **Date** includes three important methods: **before**, **after**, and **equals**. The following sample code shows how to process a date into before, after, and now segments.

```
Date someOtherDate = ...
Date date           = new Date();

if( date.before( someOtherDate )) {
    // ...
} else if( date.after( someOtherDate )) {
    // ...
} else if( date.equals( someOtherDate )) {
    // this better be true!
}
```

A REALTIME CLOCK

Now, let's build a realtime clock application, as shown in Figure 10.2. You could put this applet on your own home page.

It's called a realtime clock because the time display will be automatically updated and will show your local computer system time accurate to the seconds. If you wait until midnight, you'll even see the date display advance. The code for this applet is shown in Listing 10.2.

The source code for the realtime clock applet can be found in the file java.dev/ datetime/ClockOnPageApplet.java.

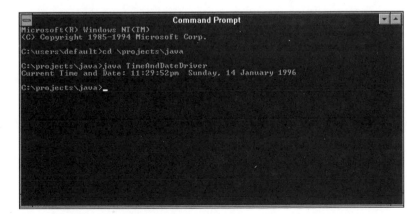

Figure 10.2 *A realtime clock application.*

Listing 10.2   Realtime Clock Application

```java
import java.applet.*;
import java.awt.*;
import java.util.*;

abstract interface ClockDisplay {
    public abstract void updateTime();
}

class SimpleClockDisplay extends Label implements ClockDisplay {
    Pulse p;

    public SimpleClockDisplay() {
        setFont( new Font( "Helvetica", Font.BOLD, 20 ));
        setAlignment( CENTER );
        setForeground( Color.yellow );
        setBackground( Color.black );

        p = new Pulse(this);
        p.init();
    }

    public void updateTime() {
        Date date   = new Date();

        int h = date.getHours();
        int m = date.getMinutes();
        int s = date.getSeconds();

        String hours, minutes, seconds, am_pm;

        if( h == 0 ) {
            hours = new String( "12" );
            am_pm = new String( "am" );
        } else if( h > 12 ) {
            hours = new String( "" + (h-12) );
            am_pm = new String( "pm"    );
        } else {
            hours = new String( "" + h );
            am_pm = new String( "am"   );
        }

        if( m < 10 ) {
            minutes = new String( "0" + m );
        } else {
            minutes = new String( ""   + m );
        }

        if( s < 10 ) {
            seconds = new String( "0" + s );
```

```
        } else {
            seconds = new String( ""  + s );
        }

        setText( new String( hours   + ":" +
                             minutes + ":" +
                             seconds + am_pm ));
    }
}

class Pulse implements Runnable {

    public ClockDisplay clock;

    public Pulse( ClockDisplay c ) {
        clock = c;
    }

    public void init() {
        clock.updateTime();
        new Thread( this ).start();
    }

    private synchronized void tick() {
        try {
            wait( 1000 ),
            clock.updateTime();
        } catch( InterruptedException e ) {
        }
    }

    public void run() {
        while( true ) {
            tick();
        }
    }
}

public class ClockOnPageApplet extends Applet {

    public void init() {
        add(new SimpleClockDisplay());
    resize(200, 75);
    }

    public void start() {
    }

    public void stop() {
    }
}
```

You will also need to write an HTML file that uses the clock. Here is a sample file:

```
<title>Simple Clock Test</title>
<hr>
<applet code="ClockOnPageApplet.class" width=200 height=200>
</applet>
<hr>
<a href="ClockOnPageApplet.java">The source.</a>
```

To build the applet use the command:

```
cmd> javac ClockOnPageApplet.java
```

You can run the program using the appletviewer:

```
cmd> appletviewer SimpleClockTest.html
```

Alternatively, you can put the HTML on your home page and view it with your favorite Web browser.

The source code uses two techniques—thread and applet programming—that we have not covered so far in the book. If you find yourself getting confused by some of the code in this example, take a look at the chapters on thread and applet programming.

The program uses the class **SimpleClockDisplay** to display a realtime clock, which displays the time in a label. Labels are the graphical equivalent of a System.out.println. We cover labels in Chapter 15.

The time is formatted by the **updateTime** method of the **SimpleClockDisplay** class. This works in a broadly similar fashion to the date and time formatter we looked at earlier. However, it just formats a time not a date. You should be able to work out how it formats the time.

The inner workings of the clock will appear a little mysterious. The ticking of the clock is provided by the class called **Pulse**. It generates a regular time signal for the clock. It makes sure that the time and date displayed are accurate.

Pulse is implemented using a *thread*. Threads are an essential concept to Java programming. They let different pieces of code in the same program run as if they were in separate programs. This allows pulse to tick away.

Pulse is created and initialized with these lines in the constructor for the **SimpleClockDisplay**:

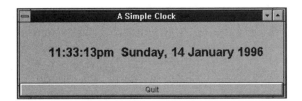

Figure 10.3   Diagram of pulse.

```
p = new Pulse(this);
p.init();
```

The **init** method of **Pulse** is short a contains the line that actually starts the pulse thread ticking.

```
new Thread( this ).start();
```

The only part of the pulse mechanism that you need to understand are the run and tick methods of **Pulse**. These form an infinite loop that ticks away. The loop waits for 1000 milliseconds—or one second—between each tick. This gives the effect of the clock time being changed once a second, as illustrated in Figure 10.3.

TIME'S UP!

Needless to say dates and especially times are going to show up in many of the applications that you write. Java provides you with a collection of simple methods that are easy to use. Unfortunately, Java date and time capabilities are limited and you are going to find it necessary to write routines such as internationalization or any other dynamic formatting for yourself. Java is continuously being improved and is evolving and it's likely that date and time is one area that will see enhancements in the future.

GREP: A Real-World Application

Neil Bartlett

We show you a real-world, "hard core" application that uses the Java techniques you've learned up to this point.

We have now covered most of the important topics about programming the Java language. Before we move on to look at the cool topics of using Java for multimedia and applet programming, I want to present a major project that will use most of the stuff we have learned up till now. It will hone your programming skills and show you some of the issues involved in putting together a real application using Java.

This chapter is what you might term an advanced chapter. It's a no-holds barred discussion on using Java to program an application. We pull no punches in this chapter. We develop a tool that you can use everyday. It will take a lot of code to develop the tool, and some of that code will demand work on your part to understand it. I will be holding your hand, but we will be walking high above the ground—so don't look down. If you are sitting comfortably and you feel that you are ready to be stretched, then read on. Otherwise, take your time: you might wish to skip this chapter and read it when you have read more of the book and developed a stronger understanding of Java.

The tool we are going to develop is called Grep. The source code for this chapter can be found on the CD-ROM in the directory \SOURCE\CHAP11\.

WHAT IS GREP?

Grep is a file searching utility. It will search a file for a string and print out lines in the file that match the string. Grep is used from the command line. The version of Grep we are going to write will only read its input from the computer's standard input device, so if we want search a file we will need to redirect it in to Grep. To search the file file.txt for the word "public," we use:

```
grep "public"<file.txt
```

Grep, though, does more than get an exact match on a string. It allows you to specify pattern matches. Just like you can pattern match a file in a directory list using asterisk, grep allows you to perform sophisticated searches. For instance, if you want to find all lines in a file beginning with the word "public", you can use Grep like this:

```
grep "^public" < file.txt
```

The ^ is a special directive that says "only match the public word if it is at the beginning of a line." There are a number of different directives that grep supports. The directives are called regular expressions.

A Grep utility is commonly provided as part of the Unix programing system, so this might not light your fire if you are currently running on a Unix box, but stick with it. The journey is the thing; not the end point. There is plenty to be learned about Java programming along the way.

OVERVIEW

We need to put a fair amount of discussion into some of the concepts before we can actually get down to the coding of the grep tool. Here is how this chapter is going to unfold.

First of all, we are going to look at what regular expressions are. Then once we have a firm handle on regular expressions, we are going to develop some code to implement them. It is important to understand that unlike some languages such as Perl, Java itself does not support or provide any code for regular expressions. We will have to write all the code ourselves.

Finally, once we have developed our regular expression package, we will design the Grep tool using the regular expression package.

WHAT THE [A-Z] ARE REGULAR EXPRESSIONS?

So what are regular expressions? Well I have one word for you: *wildcards*. Ever play poker where deuces were wild, and in your hand you held a 10, Jack, Queen, King of Diamonds, and a deuce? Well if you were so lucky, your hand was a regular expression for a Royal Flush. The deuce was a wildcard for the Ace of Diamonds. Your reward for recognizing the regular expression was probably a fair number of your fellow poker player's, um, *matchsticks*.

The truth is that you probably use regular expressions everyday.

Another commonly encountered regular expression is the open dialog file name. This regular expression is the description of the file using a combination of dots, letters, and asterisks. For example, to find all files with the ending .bmp we would use:

```
*.bmp
```

Regular expressions are a little more sophisticated than just mere wildcards.

Let's take a look at a more complicated regular expression—a description of all U.S. local telephone numbers.

```
[0-9]{3}-[0-9]{4}
```

Pretty cryptic, huh? We can certainly see some numbers in there, but the square and curly brackets don't seem to belong in a phone number. Moreover, there seem to be too many hyphens for a simple U.S. domestic phone number. But remember: we are using the regular expression to *describe* telephone numbers. The regular expression is not, itself, a telephone number. The cryptic string of the regular expression is a *rule* that we can use to check if a number is actually a telephone number.

Let's break this apart and try to understand it.

First off, notice the **[0-9]** bit—it appears twice. This is regular expression shorthand for the numbers between 0 and 9. It means match any number between 0 and 9. What about {3}? It is a multiplier value. It says take the previous valve and use it exactly three times. So **[0-9]{3}** is a cryptic way of saying match exactly three numbers! In other words, it is the exchange part of the telephone number: the available characters are 0 .. 9, and you have three slots to put them in. And what of **[0-9]{4}**? Well, I am sure that your pattern-matching skills are now honed well enough to recognize it as four digits in a row—or the line part of the phone number.

So now we have explained the **[0-9]{3}** and the **[0-9]{4}**sections. But what about the dash? Does it means subtract the left hand part from the right hand part? No actually it means only match a dash character and only the dash character. It is called a *literal* that is, the character must match literally.

Note, by the way, that the dash has two different meanings, depending on the part of the expression in which it appears. When it appears *within* the brackets, as in **[0-9]**, it denotes a *range;* when it appears *outside* the brackets, it denotes a literal. Naturally with something as expressive as regular expressions, dash is not the only literal. You can use any character as a literal if you need it. Here we just needed the dash.

So if we had a telephone number, say 555-1234, we would say that it matched the regular expression **[0-9]{3}-[0-9]{4}**. We could announce, triumphantly, that 555-1234 is indeed a U.S. telephone number.

Regular expressions are very simple rules: rules that even a computer can follow. This makes them ideal for describing things like telephone numbers or file names or, in our case, search strings for Greps.

Never Meta Character I Didn't Like

All these symbols such as **[** and {, are called *meta-characters.* In other words they are characters that have special meanings.

In Tables 11.1 through 11.3, I've listed the meta-characters we are going to use to develop our regular expression package. The meta-characters are based on those supported by the Unix version of grep, the tool we are going to develop using the regular expression package.

Each meta-character has its own special meaning. The meta-characters are joined together to form the regular expressions. Take a good look at the tables to get an idea of the types of things you can express using the meta-

Table 11.1   *Character Matchers*

Character	Description
match	The character itself is used to match a character explicitly. For example, *a* will exactly the character *a*. This form of match is called a literal. The character match works unless it is one of the meta-characters. If you want to match a meta-character, you will need to prefix the meta-character with \, the escape character. Thus \. is used to represent the dot character.
.	Naturally you can string together as many characters are you want. The dot will match any single character. *a.b* will match the character *a*, followed by any character followed by the character *b*. The characters matched by the dot do not have to be alphabetic or numeric. They can be any symbol.
[]	The square brackets are used to match individually listed characters. For example, [atz] will match any of the characters *a, t, or z*.
[x-y]	As a shorthand the hyphen character can be used inside the square brackets to represent a range of characters. For example, [a-c] represents the characters from *a* to *c*. The range uses the character order of unicode. The character on the left of the range must be less in unicode order than the character on the right. To negate the list—that is, to only match characters that are not in the list—use the ^ symbol as the first character in the box. For example, [^a-c] matches any character apart from *a, b,* or *c*.
[^]	To use ^, -, or] within the square brackets as a character rather than as a special symbol, use the escape character \ before the character, for example, [\]] will match the] character.
(x|y)	The round brackets and the bar character allow you to find sets of characters. For example, (abc|def|xyz) will match *abc, def,* or *xyz*. Note: unlike [abc]{3}, which will match any combination of *a, b,* and *c*, (abc) will only match *a* followed by *b* followed by *c*.

characters. There are three types of meta-characters. The first are character matches. These will match a single character. For instance, **[a-c]** will match one character—either *a* or *b* or *c*. The second type are multipliers. These apply to the character matchers. They control how many times to apply the preceding character matcher. We have already seen how **{3}** can be used to control the number of preceding characters. Finally, there are the positional meta-characters. These are used to anchor the characters at a place in a string. For instance using ∧ will force Grep to start matching at the beginning of the string.

Table 11.2 *Multiplying Meta-Characters*

Character	Description
+	There must be at least one or more of the previous thing in the regular expression. For example, a+, matches one or more a characters.
*	This character is similar to + except that it includes zero matches. For example, [a-z]*, matches zero or more letters from a to z.
{number}	There must be exactly the given number of the previous thing. For example a{3}, matches exactly three a characters.

Table 11.3 *Positional Meta-Characters*

Character	Description
^	The caret is used to match the beginning of the string. For example, ^abc, matches string beginning with the characters *abc*.
$	The dollar sign is used to match the end of the string. For example, ^a$, matches a string consisting only of the character *a*.

Here are a few more examples to help you get a better feel for regular expressions.

[A-Z][a-z]* will match all words with a leading capital letter. In other words, it will match all words, where the first letter is a capital and the rest of the word is in lowercase.

(sci | the)[a-z]+logy will match words like *scientology* or *theology*.

At this point, you might recall that earlier we mentioned that ***.bmp** was a regular expression to match all filenames with the extension, .bmp. You might think that this does not seem to fit with the meta-characters I have listed. And yes, you would be quite right.

One of the problems with regular expressions is that there is no standardized definition of the meta-characters. In fact, there are a number of different regular expression usages. Not only do they not agree on what meta-characters to use, they don't agree on what the meta-characters do or how many meta-characters are required. This makes the regular expression business somewhat confusing.

Regular expressions tend to be tuned to particular applications. For example, the filename-tuned regular expressions tend to concentrate on being easy to express things you do a lot with files, for example, finding file names with a given extension. It is much easier to say **f*.bmp** to get all bitmap files beginning with *f* than it is to say **f.*\.bmp**. The regular expression set shown in Tables 11.1 through 11.3 is based more on string searching than it is on filename searching. This approach will make its ideal for writing a Grep utility.

We've had a good long look at what regular expressions are. I hope you are now comfortable enough with them to move on. We'll look at designing some code to turn regular expressions into code that can be used as the search engine for our Grep tool.

Our Regular Expression Package

Before we get to describing the design of the regular expression package, let's look how it is going to be used.

We have covered in depth the regular expressions our Grep utility will support, and we have seen the telephone number regular expression, **[0-9]{3}-[0-9]{4}**. Now let's see a piece of code (Listing 11.1) that can be used to take that regular expression and check an incoming string against the expression.

Listing 11.1   Using Our Regular Expression Package

```
import explorer.regexp.*;
public class PhoneCheck {

    static RegExp telephoneRegExp = new RegExp("[0-9]{3}-[0-9]{4}");

    static boolean IsTelephoneNumber(String s) {
        return telephoneRegExp.match(s);
    }

    public static void main(String a[]) {
        if (PhoneCheck.IsTelephoneNumber(args[0]))
            System.out.println(a[0]+" is a telephone number");
        else
            System.out.println(a[0]+" is not a telephone number");
    }
}
```

The string to be matched is passed in on the command line. The program is run using

```
java PhoneCheck 555-1874
```

This command will try to match the number *555-1874* against our telephone number regular expression. It will print out a message if there is a match.

The listing starts with **import**, which imports our regular expression package. We have named our package **explorer.regexp**. In other words, it is part of the explorer set of packages.

The Regular expression is created by constructing an object of the **RegExp** class. Here the object is called **telephoneRegExp**. The **telephoneRegExp** object will hold the regular expression ready and waiting to be given a string to match against.

The string comes in via the **main** method. The **main** method calls **isTelephoneNumber**, which calls **telephoneRegExp.match** to match the incoming string against the regular expression.

Our regular expression package is designed so that we can reuse the **telephoneRexExp.match** method any number of times in the same program. If we had a whole batch of telephone numbers to test, we could pass them one at a time to **telephoneRexExp.match** without having to construct another regular expression object.

The RegExp Class

As you can see, the **RegExp** class is the class we use to represent the regular expression. Below I describe the public methods that can be used. There are only three. Two we have seen already. The third—**enumeration**—will need some explaining. Methods of the **RegExp** class are shown in Table 11.4.

Previously we saw that the **match** method will check the regular expression against the test string. However suppose the test string was something a little longer than a telephone number—suppose it was a list of names and telephone

Table 11.4 *RegExp Methods*

Member Function Use

RegExp(String) throws RegExpCompileException	Create a regular expression object using the given String as the pattern for the regular expression. If the regular expression is in error, the RegExpCompileException exception is thrown.
boolean match(String)	Match the given String against the regular expression given when the regular expression object was created. If the given String contains one or more matches, the match method returns the boolean value true.
Enumeration enumeration()	This method returns an enumeration that can be used to enumerate through the matches, after the match method returns true.

numbers. The **match** method is written so that it will find every single match in the string. It will not stop at one, it will keep searching until it has tried to match every character in the test string against the regular expression. The **enumeration** method is used to find out how many matches **match** found. You can use it just as if you are enumerating through a vector or similar data structure.

Regular expressions have many uses beyond a Grep utility. For instance, we might want to write an editor with a search tool in it rather than a Grep tool. For this reason, we have packaged the **RegExp** class and the other classes used to make the regular expression package into a package of its own. This means that to use the regular expression package we have to import the appropriate classes.

Implementing the Regular Expression Package

When I first decided to write the Grep tool, I scanned the Net for a suitable set of Java regular expression classes. I didn't find any. I was disappointed. I did not really want to write my own set of regular expression classes. I figured it would be time-consuming and hard. In the end, after a long search, I bit the bullet and decided to implement my own.

To my surprise, though, it was the process of writing this set of classes that convinced me how cool a language Java is.

I had already bought into the idea of the browser technology. I though it was great to be able to download programs to dynamically upgrade the abilities of the browser. I had not yet bought into the idea of Java itself. I thought it was *YAAAATL—Yet Another Attempt At A Language*. Also, it bore a certain similarity to C++, which to me made it seem even more suspicious. My initial programs had not really brought out the advantages of Java.

In writing these classes, though, I was very surprised at how everything came together so easily, and as an added bonus, the core code worked almost without problems the first time. That's not to deny that I tweaked the code a fair amount to get things working, but the tweaks were more my poor attempts at coming to grips with regular expression matching than Java's support for programming. Java seems to combine the best of interpreted languages along with the best of compiled languages. It's kind of "rapid development with a safety net."

So enough of praising Java's virtues. Let's design these classes.

We're going to take a fairly simple approach one that will not cause too headache, to understand. It will not be as fast as the very best implementations,

but it will have the nice property of being relatively simple and straightforward. I have seen a number of regular expression packages written in languages like C and C++, and most of them are sacrifices on the altar of obfuscated code: members of the species *Spaghettius Horriblis*. This makes them difficult to understand and very difficult to check for correctness.

The majority of code for the regular expression package is not printed in this chapter. The space to print the listing would have exceeded the current running length of the chapter. So before we proceed let's put the code in perspective. All the code that you see comes from the RegExp.java source file unless otherwise noted.

Putting It in a Package

All the regular expression stuff is placed in the package explorer.regexp by placing the line

```
package explorer.regexp
```

As the first line of the RegExp.java file and any other file that will be needed by the regular expression package.

When packaging stuff as a library it is a good idea to use the built-in Java documentation system. For this reason, in the source code file that contains the code for **RegExp**, I have use the Java documentation comment mechanism. Listing 11.2 shows the **RegExp** class in the correct format.

Listing 11.2   The RegExp Class

```java
/**
 * A regular expression class to enable pattern
 * matching of a string against a regular expression
 * @version 1.6 08/12/95
 * @author  Neil Bartlett
 */

public class RegExp {
    /**
     * Match the given String against the regular expression
     * given when the regular expression object was created.
     * If the given String contains one or more matches,
     * the match method returns the boolean value true.
     * @param s the string to match against
     */

    public synchronized boolean match(String s) {
```

To keep things short, Listing 11.2 is only a fragment of the **RegExp** source file.

We can process the file using the javadoc tool.—javadoc RegExp.java. This will generate the complete documentation in HTML format. We can then use this to publish the documentation for our package by simply including a link to the HTML in our home page.

Building the Regular Expression Package

To build the regular expression package, go to the java.dev/regexp directory and use the following commands to build the package:

```
cmd> javac -d . RegExpCompileException.java
cmd> javac -d . RegExpNonMultiableToken.java
cmd> javac -d . RegExp.java
```

These commands will build the package files in the local directory. If you want the package put elsewhere, use a directory path on the -d switch.

Design Overview

Before we proceed with the design proper let's introduce the cast of characters. We have already seen **RegExp**. That is the class to use to access the regular expression package. It provides the method that is used to match the incoming strings against the regular expression.

The **match** method can get quite complicated, so to help things out, **RegExp** will take the regular expression and digest it into a format that will help **match** do its work. In a simple process, which is similar to how a compiler compiles source code into object code, the **RegExp** constructor will take the regular expression string and compile it in to a more useful format.

That more useful format is a list of regular expression tokens. A token in this sense is a codifed version of the regular expression. For instance, the dot meta-character will form the token **REany**, while the dot meta-character followed by any of the multiplier meta-characters such as + or * will form the **REmultiAny** token. See Tables 11.1 through 11.3 if you need a refresher on any of these meta-characters.

The tokens save the **match** method some work each time **match** is called. For instance, this approach without the **match** method would need to keep looking at the string and working out meta-characters like the dot meta-character are followed by a multiplier meta-character. When you see how **match** works, you will appreciate that this would be a lot of overhead and would slow down the matching process considerably.

The process of converting to tokens also helps us with error checking. We can check for badly formed regular expressions once when we do the conversion. We don't have to do it each time the **match** method is called.

Constructing the List of Tokens

First of all, then, let's look at how the regular expression string is turned into list of tokens. The basic idea is to inspect each character of the regular expression string in turn and convert it into the appropriate token. Then we add the token to a list of tokens. The list of tokens is stored in the vector called **tokens.**

The conversion process is made a little more difficult because we don't actually know what the exact token will be until we have processed a few characters, but we will look at an elegant mechanism to solve that problem in a moment.

Listing 11.3 shows a fragment of the code from the **RegExp** class from the RegExp.java file. It consists of the constructor, which converts the regular expression into a list of tokens, and a few variables. After the listing we will discuss what is going on.

Listing 11.3   Code from the RegExp Class

```
final char multiOChar='*';
Vector tokens = new Vector();

public RegExp(String original) throws RegExpCompileException {
    try {
        String s = new String(original);
        while (s.length() != 0) {
        switch (s.charAt(0)) {
                case multiOChar:
                    RegExpToken tok = RemoveLastToken();
                    addToken(tok.makeMulti(0, Integer.MAX_VALUE));
                    break;
                default:
                    addToken(new REliteral(s.substring(0,1)));
                    break;
            }
        s = s.substring(1, s.length());
        }
    } catch (StringIndexOutOfBoundsException e) {
        throw new RegExpCompileException();
    }
}
```

```
void addToken(RegExpToken t) {
    tokens.addElement(t);
}

RegExpToken RemoveLastToken() throws RegExpCompileException {
    if (tokens.isEmpty()) throw new RegExpCompileException();
    RegExpToken token = (RegExpToken) tokens.lastElement();
    tokens.removeElement(token);
    return token;
}
```

Obviously, this code does not create the tokens for every single meta-character. The code would just be too darn big to print and I don't want to bore you (at least not too much!). So in the interest of saving time, I have cut to the chase and shown only the code that creates two of the tokens: **RELiteral** and **REmultiLiteral**.

We will be sticking with these two tokens for the rest of the explanation on regular expressions. Bear in mind though that all the code for each meta-character is contained in the RegExp.java file. I'm simply using **RELiteral** and the **REmultiLiteral** because they illustrate all of the salient points.

In the constructor of the **RegExp** class we parse the pattern, creating appropriate tokens for each meta-character we find.

The heart of the parse is a **while** loop that steps through the string one character at a time, comparing the character against the meta characters. Let's ignore the **multi0Char** test for the moment. If the regular expression string consists of a plain set of literals such as *abc*, then the then code will create a **RELiteral** token for each of the three meta-characters. Each of the tokens is then added to the list of tokens using the **addToken** method.

The interesting thing is what happens if we receive the **multi0Char**, *. For instance, suppose we have the regular expression, **a***. First we will create the **RELiteral** token for the a character and add it to the list, then we will decode the *. We pop the **RELiteral** token off the list using the **removeLastToken** method and we call the removed token's **makeMulti** method. All tokens have a special **makeMulti** method, which will turn the token into a multi version of the token—in this case, **REmultiLiteral**. The **REmultiLiteral** token is then added to the list of tokens. This means that at the end of the parse the token list only has the one token—**REmultiLiteral**.

```
class RELiteral extends RegExpToken {

    final public RegExpToken makeMulti(int min, int max)
                         throws RegExpCompileException {
```

```
        return new REmultiLiteral(min, max, literal);
    }
}
```

This listing is a code fragment from the **REliteral** class. It shows the **makeMulti** method, which creates a token for multi class corresponding the the token. In this case, it creates the **REmultiLiteral** class.

The reason for this seemingly perverse way of doing things is that multipliers such as * and + do not just multiply the literal meta-character, they can be used to multiply most of the meta-characters. To shorten the code, and to avoid having to code up special case combinations for each of the possible meta-character/multiplier meta-character pairs, we use the **makeMulti** method. It works the same way for each multiplier, so there is only one piece of code to write for each meta-character.

As another part of the compression of the listing to fit into the book, I have only shown the code for the **multi0Char**, *. The other multipliers, such as + and {3}, work similarly.

You might noticed a class called **RegExpToken**, which is used as a cast in the **removeLastToken** method. As we will be seeing in a moment, this is the abstract class for all of the token classes. It is the **RegExpToken** class that insists that all tokens provide methods such as the **makeMulti** method.

Coding for Errors

If at any stage a problem is encountered—for example, if there is no token to remove when a multi is found, or if a token cannot be made into a multi-token— then a **RegExpCompileException** is thrown. The **RegExpCompileException** is a public exception because it needs to be caught by code outside of the package. For example, code using the **RegExp** class will need to catch this exception to determine if a pattern was malformed:

```
package explorer.regexp;

public class RegExpCompileException extends Exception {
    public RegExpCompileException() {
    super();
    }
}
```

The definition of this exception, which needs to be public because it can be passed back to the code that calls the **RegExp** class, can be found in the file RegExpCompileException.java in the same directory as the RegExp.java file.

RegExp.match—The Engine

The heart of the regular expression system is the **match** algorithm. It takes a string and compares it to the token list form of the regular expression and tries to match as many patterns in the string as it can. It does not accept partial matches of the regular expression. Once it has found every pattern it can, it stops.

When programming the engine, I had a number of choices. Given that I had decided to keep things simple, I decided to write a simple non-recursive version of the code. I could have considered a recursive version, but recursion does tend to suffer from data dependencies, so I opted for non-recursive. Also, the typical implementation method is to use what are known as FSAs (Finite State Automata). I did not want to deal with such things in this book so I put together a fairly straightforward search loop with a backtracking mechanism. It is not as fast as it could be, and it definitely has a lot of pathologically slow search times, but I am fairly certain it works—always a bonus!

Listing 11.4 shows the complete **match** method of the **RegExp** class. Given what we have seen of regular expressions, I hope that you are surprised by the simplicity of the match engine.

Listing 11.4   A Match Method

```
Vector tokens - new Vector();
Vector matches;

public synchronized boolean match(String s) {
    RegExpToken token;
    matches - new Vector();

    for (int index - 0; index < s.length(); ++index) {
        int i-0, p - index;

        for (i-0; i < tokens.size(); ++i) {
            token - (RegExpToken)tokens.elementAt(i);
            p - token.match(s, p);
            if (p == RegExpToken.MATCH_FAILED)
                for (; i >= 0; —i) {
                    token - (RegExpToken)tokens.elementAt(i);
                    p - token.backtrack();
                    if (p != RegExpToken.MATCH_FAILED)
                        break;
                }
            if (i < 0)
                break;
        }

        if (i > 0 && p > index) {
            matches.addElement(s.substring(index, p));
```

```
            index = p-1;
        }
    }
    return matches.size() != 0;
}
```

As I said earlier, the regular expression token list is stored as the **tokens** vector. The **match** method will take each of the tokens and test them one at a time against the string. If a token matches, we move on to the next token and try to match it against the next position in the string after the match occurred.

The outer **for** loop is used to move through each character in the string. We use the **index** variable to keep track of where we are in the string.

The inner **for** loops are used to keep track of the token we are dealing with. We use the **i** variable to keep track of where we are in the vector of tokens.

I want to take an optimistic view for the first pass through this description and assume that the token match does not fail, the algorithm works like this: The outer **for** loop chooses the first character from the incoming test string, the inner **for** loop picks the first token from the list of tokens. The token's **match** method, which tests if a character can match the individual token, is used to compare if the first character is matched by the token.

```
p = token.match(s, p);
```

The **token.match** method receives the character in the string not as a character, but as the string and the index of the position in the string to start matching. The **token.match** method is responsible for performing the match test. It then returns the position of the match in **p**. If the match fails it returns the value **RegExpToken.MATCH_FAILED**.

We are assuming the match will succeed. The value in **p** will be the new index into the string: the position at the end of the previous match. Remember that the tokens are part of the regular expression, and although you have not seen exactly what **token.match** does yet, they might match more than one character.

For example, if the token is the **REmulitLiteral** token, then the token will match as many of the literal characters from the string as it can. It will then return the position after the last character was matched.

Avoiding Hard-Coded Numbers

To stop having to hard code in numbers, consider using a final static variable in the class. We use **RegExpToken.MATCH_FAILED** to avoid hard coding a number. It makes the code more readable, and it helps eliminate dependencies on specific values.

Gradually, we work our way through the tokens one at a time, matching the string. Eventually we will find that the complete list of tokens has been matched. Congratulations! A match has been found. The matched portion of the string is then added to a list of matches, and the algorithm trundles off to see if it can find more matches in the string.

Eventually, every character in the string will have been checked. If there has been at least one match added to the list of matches, the **match** method will return true.

REliteral.match

To understand more about the **token.match** call we saw earlier, let's look at the example from the **REliteral** class.

```
class REliteral extends RegExpToken {
    String literal;

    public REliteral(String pattern) {
        literal = new String(pattern);
    }

    final public int match(String s, int i) {
        if (s.startsWith(literal, i))
            return  i + literal.length();
        return RegExpToken.MATCH_FAILED;
    }
}
```

The fragment is from the **REliteral** class. The **match** method simply uses the **String.startsWith** method to determine if the literal matches the string at the position given by **i**. If the match success the method returns the position in the string after the match occurred; otherwise, it returns the value **RegExpToken.MATCH_FAILED**.

Backtracking

There is a wrinkle, though. We assume the match succeeded. What happens if the attempt to match a token against a string fails?

If we just keep stepping through until a match succeeds or fails we will miss some potential matches. To see what I mean, consider the example of trying to match **a+[a-b]** against the string **aaaaa**. In other words, we want a pattern that specifies that the string be at least one or more **a** characters followed by either, **a** or **b**. Remember that the plus sign means match one or more of the preceding characters, in this case **a**.

Figure 11.1 shows the first attempt at matching the string to the pattern. As you can see, the match fails; the **a+** has consumed too many a characters so there were none left in the test string for the **[a-b]** to match against.

The match we want is shown in Figure 11.2.

We need to be able to revisit the decision of how many **a** characters the **a+** matches. Ideally it should only match four, not five, which would leave one character for the **[a-b]** to match against.

This mechanism of revisiting the decision is called *backtracking*.

If you look at the code for the **match** method, you will see this is exactly what it does. If a match of a token against the string fails, the token's **backtrack** method is called. The **backtrack** method attempts to make a different decision on the match if that is possible. If the backtracking finds a new

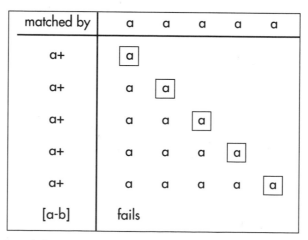

Figure 11.1   Bad match diagram.

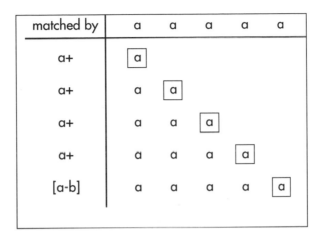

matched by	a	a	a	a	a
a+	[a]				
a+	a	[a]			
a+	a	a	[a]		
a+	a	a	a	[a]	
[a-b]	a	a	a	a	[a]

Figure 11.2   *Good match diagram.*

match, the forward-matching is started again from the new match point. This process carries on until either test succeeds or it fails.

Of course, it's not always possible for a token to be backtracked. For example, a literal at a given position in the string either matches or it doesn't—there is no backtracking for a single literal. In this circumstance or if a backtrackable token runs out of leeway, the backtracking continues from the next previous token. The backtracking continues back down the vector of tokens until a new match is found or until the beginning of the list of tokens is reached. If the beginning of the tokens if reached, the match has failed. At least it has failed at the given starting position.

So this is what backtracking is all about. We try to match the string, and as long as matches are found, all is well and good. As soon as a failure is found, we try to step backwards to see if there are any other ways to match the pattern against the string.

The Abstract RegExpToken Class

Let's talk now about the **RegExpToken** class. It is an abstract class. The parent of all of the token classes we have been looking at.

As you probably have noticed, the token classes do a lot of the work when it comes to matching the regular expression. The **RegExp** class is only responsible for sequencing through the test string and the tokens—it does not do the actual matching itself.

We have turned the tokens into active things—they are not just passive items holding information. The tokens do not just store the meta-character they represent. The tokens are actively controlling events. In a traditional programming language such as BASIC or C, the token would have been coded as data. There could have been functions written that use the data, but the functions would have had to have code for each of the possible types of tokens that it might meet. Here, though, the **RegExp.match** method knows very little about the **RegExpToken.match** methods. It just knows that it will get back the next position to start testing the sting at. This idea is a key principle in object-oriented design. This way of looking at a problem goes by the odd name of **noun-verb inversion**. We have turned the noun, the token, into the thing that does the work. So in more cryptic language, the noun has become inverted into a verb. Ah, how I love jargon.

If this last point has gone over your head, don't worry. It is not important that you understand the fine line differences between the various ways of doing things. All you really need to understand is that the tokens are playing an active role in the proceedings.

The code for the **RegExpToken** class is shown in Listing 11.5. I will not say much about it except that it provides some default implementations of some of the methods. For instance it provides a default implementation of **backtrack**. The default is to fail the backtrack. In other words, tokens that do not backtrack do not have to supply an implementation of the backtrack method. **RegExpToken** does it for them.

RegExpToken also supports a few convenience methods that the token classes can use such as the **save** method, which is used to save string position information when a match is made for a backtrackable token; and the debug methods to help debug the running of the regular expression package.

Oh, and you finally get to find out the value of the **RegExpToken. MATCH_FAILED** number. Yes, it is **-2**. Do you really care? Well, not much, probably. The value is chosen so that it is not a possible value that can occur in any of the string positions.

Listing 11.5   The RegExpToken class

```
abstract class RegExpToken {
    final static int MATCH_FAILED = -2;

    abstract int match(String s, int i);
```

```
int backtrack() {
    // DBG System.out.println("Token can't backtrack");
    return RegExpToken.MATCH_FAILED;
}

RegExpToken makeMulti(int min, int max)
    throws RegExpCompileException {
    // DBG System.out.println("Can't make multi");
    throw new RegExpCompileException();
}

String str;
int pos;

void save(String s, int i) {
    str = s;
    pos = i;
}

void DebugMatch(String s, String thing, int i) {
    DebugOp(">>>> ", s, thing, i, "");
}

void DebugBacktrack(String s, String thing, int i) {
    DebugOp("<<<< ", s, thing, i, "");
}

void DebugOp(String f, String s, String t, int i, String e) {
    System.out.println(f+" "+s + " at "+i+" by "+ t + " "+ e);
}
}
```

The inheritance tree of all of the tokens that the regular expression package age supports is shown in Figure 11.3. As you can see, there are a number of them.

The next few sections will give more of the code for the **REliteral** and **REmultiLiteral**. You have seen most of this already. For information on the other token classes, take a look at the RegExp.java file, which implements all the other regular expression tokens classes.

REliteral

Listing 11.6 shows the **REliteral** class, which handles straight character matches. As you can see, the **match** method here is quite simple. If the string at the position given by the index **i**, does not start with the literal, there is no match. If there is a match, the method returns the next index in the string after the match.

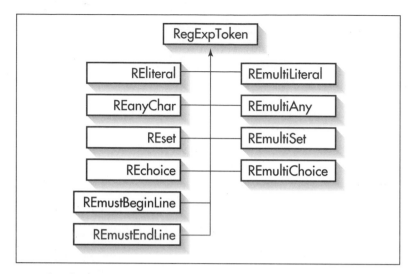

Figure 11.3 *The inheritance tree.*

Listing 11.6 REliteral Class

```
class REliteral extends RegExpToken {
    String literal;

    public REliteral(String pattern) {
        literal = new String(pattern);
    }

    final public int match(String s, int i) {
        // DBG DebugMatch(s,literal,i);
        if (s.startsWith(literal, i))
            return  i + literal.length();
        return RegExpToken.MATCH_FAILED;
    }

    final public RegExpToken makeMulti(int min, int max)
                    throws RegExpCompileException {
        return new REmultiLiteral(min, max, literal);
    }
}
```

Turning Debug Statements On and Off

A problem always crops up sooner or later is the need to debug or even just check a piece of code. A typical way of doing this is to instrument the code; that is, to add debugging statements which print out as the program runs. This can be very useful in situations when lots of data can go through a program. In these circumstances, using a debugger can be very cumbersome. The thing about instrumenting code is that, ideally, you want to be able to switch it on and off as and when needed. One way of doing this is to use **if** statements and switch it on and off at runtime—but often this is not really needed.

For those situations where switching on and off at compile time is sufficient, we use the following technique. First add a /* DBG */ to the beginning of the debug line. For example,

```
/* DBG */ System.out.println("My debug line");
```

The /* DBG */ does not interfere with the code. It is merely a comment. To switch debugging off, replace the /* DBG */ with a // DBG. This can be done globally with an editor—just search and replace. For example, the previous example line will change to

```
// DBG System.out.println("My debug line");
```

The whole line is now commented out and the debug statement will not get printed. You can use the reverse replacement to switch debugging back on.

REmultiLiteral

The **REmultiLiteral** class, on the other hand, provides a much more complicated implementation of the match method. The **REmultiLiteral** class handles the literals that have been matched up with a multiplier such as **a*** or **{3}**. This class has to deal with a number of things in its **match** method. First of all, it has a maximum count—a maximum number of matches that can be made, as well as a minimum count of the number of matches that must be made. Initially the maximum count is set at the maximum of integers—a rather large number that is pretty well guaranteed to be longer than the longest string we will encounter. However, when a match is made, the current number is recorded and this is then used as the maximum if a backtrack is needed. In this way the number of literals matched can be successively reduced as successive backtracks are called.

Listing 11.7 REmultiLiteral class

```
class REmultiLiteral extends RegExpToken {
    int minCount = 0;
    int matchCount = 0;
```

```
    int maxCount = Integer.MAX_VALUE;
    String literal;

public REmultiLiteral(int min, int max, String s)
                   throws RegExpCompileException {
    minCount = min;
    maxCount = max;
    literal= s;
    if (literal.length() == 0)
        throw new RegExpCompileException();
}

final public int match(String s, int p) {
    return match(s, p, maxCount);
}

final int match(String s, int p, int max) {
    save(s, p);
    int i;
    matchCount = 0;
    if (max < minCount)
        return RegExpToken.MATCH_FAILED;
    if (max == 0)
        return Math.max(p-1,0);
    for (i = p; i < s.length(); i+=literal.length()) {
        if (!s.startsWith(literal, i))
            break;
        if (++matchCount == max)
            break;
    }
    if (matchCount < minCount)
        return RegExpToken.MATCH_FAILED;
    return p+matchCount;
}

final boolean isBacktrackable() {
    return matchCount > minCount;
}

final public int backtrack() {
    if (isBacktrackable())
        return match(str, pos, matchCount-1);
    return RegExpToken.MATCH_FAILED;
}
}
```

The backtrack method will only attempt to operate if the current count is greater than the minimum count. If it is not greater than the minimum, the backtrack will fail. In this way, multipliers like the +, which sets a lower bound of at least one, can be implemented.

This termination characteristic of the backtrack method is exceptionally important for the correct operation of the whole regular expression classes. It is important that we can guarantee that the backtrack method will eventually terminate if no matches are found. If it does not the outer loop—the match method in the **RegExp** class will loop forever.

PUTTING THE CODE THROUGH ITS PACES

Now a piece of code like the collection of classes we have just written is a rather complicated beast. The likelihood of errors is high. We really must test this package before we can use it with any confidence. Also we need to write our tests in such a way as to be reusable, especially when, a few months down the road, we change the code. It is inevitable in a piece of code like this that the temptation to upgrade will strike—maybe to improve the performance, smarten up the algorithm, or add some whizzy new meta-character.

The code in Listing 11.8 is kind of a regression testing tool. It can be used in conjunction with a script or a command file to put the code through its paces—and to quickly tell us if something has gone out of whack.

The code is command-line driven. It takes as a minimum two parameters from the command line. The first parameter is the regular expression, the second is the string to match against the regular expression. A third parameter is used to determine what the results should be. It can take the values shown in Table 11.5.

The "true" value also takes some addition parameters. They are the actual expected match values when the string is matched against the regular expression.

If all the command-line parameters are correct, no output lines should be produced. This makes errors easy to detect: if there is some output, you have either put the wrong parameters on the command line or the regular expression code is wrong.

Table 11.5 *Command Line Parameters*

Command Line String	Meaning
"true"	The search should succeed.
"false"	The search should fail
"regerr"	The regular expression is wrong and should produce an error.

Listing 11.8 The TestRegExp Class

```
import java.util.*;
import java.lang.*;
import extension.*;i

public class TestRegExp {
    public static void main(String args[]) {
        try {
            RegExp re = new RegExp(args[0]);
            if (re.match(args[1])) {
                boolean force = false;
                if (args.length < 3 || !args[2].equals("true")) {
                    force = true;
                    System.out.println("Unexpectedly Found "+
                                    args[1] + " in " + args[0]);
                }
                int i = 3;
                for (Enumeration v = re.matches.elements();
                                v.hasMoreElements(); ) {
                    String s = (String) v.nextElement();
                    if (force || i >= args.length ||
                                    !args[i].equals(s)) {
                        System.out.println(s);
                    }
                    ++i;
                }
            } else {
                if (args.length < 3 || !args[2].equals("false")) {
                    System.out.println("Unexpected fail");
                }
            }
        } catch (RegExpCompileException e) {
            if (args.length < 3 || !args[2].equals("regerr")) {
                System.out.println("Error in Regular Expression");
            }
        } catch (ArrayIndexOutOfBoundsException e) {
            System.out.println("Bad number of arguments");
        }
    }
}
```

The code is driven by a script. An example script is shown on the next page. It is actually the first few lines of a test script included on the disk. The test script on the disk, however, contains a lot more tests. If you need to change the code we have developed here, I suggest you use the script to verify that your changes have not upset other areas of the code.

The format of the script as written here is for Windows, but it should not be too difficult to convert to your local machine format. For instance, only the comment lines that need to be changed to run under Unix.

```
REM two false positives to show that harness is detecting errors
java TestRegExp "a[]" "aba[]"  REM should be false
java TestRegExp "..." "abcdef" REM should be abc and def

REM These tests should not produce any output
java TestRegExp "^[ ]*$" "    " "true" "    "
java TestRegExp "^ $" " " "true" " "
java TestRegExp ".{8}\..{3}" "x.lis y.com" "true" "y.com"
```

WRITING GREP IN JAVA

Now that we have a fully working and tested regular expression package, we are finally ready to write our Grep tool.

Beyond performing regular expression searches, we are not going to write a particularly sophisticated Grep tool. It will simply take a regular expression as it parameter. It will then list all of the lines from standard input that match the given regular expression. It outputs, to standard output, matching lines prefixed by the line number that they are found on.

For example, the Grep command to list all the lines containing strings in the grep.java file, the source file for the Grep utility, along with the output from the real file on disk is shown here. The lines don't correspond to lines shown here in Listing 11.9, the code shown here has been compressed to save on space.

```
cmd>java grep "\".*\"" < grep.java
line 36: out.println("line "+line+": "+s);
line 53:    System.err.println("Bad regular expression: "+args[0]);
line 58: System.out.println("Usage:");
line 59: System.out.println("grep \"pattern\"");
```

Listing 11.9   The Grep Source Code

```java
import java.lang.*;
import java.io.*;
import explorer.regexp*;

public class grep {

    void grepStream(DataInputStream in,
                    PrintStream out, RegExp re) {
        String s;
        int line=0;
        try {
            while (true) {
                if ((s = in.readLine()) == null)
                    throw new IOException();
```

```
            ++line;
            if (re.match(s))
                out.println("line "+line+": "+s);
        }
    } catch(IOException e) {}
}

static public void main(String args[]) {
    try {
        DataInputStream ds = new DataInputStream(System.in);
        grepStream(ds, System.out, new RegExp(args[0]) );

    } catch (ArrayIndexOutOfBoundsException e) {
        System.out.println("Usage: grep \"pattern\"");
    } catch (RegExpCompileException e) {
        System.err.println("Bad regular expression: "+args[0]);
    }
}
}
```

The Grep program works by looping through each line of the file and comparing the line against the given regular expression. It reads lines by using the **readLine** method of a **DataInputStream**. **System.in** does not support the **readLine** concept, so it is first converted to a **DataInputStream** in the **main** method. The lines from the input are passed one at a time to the regular expression **match method**. If there is a match, the matching line is output prefixed by its line number. When all the lines on standard input have been used up, **readLine** returns null. The **while** loop throws an exception to terminate the loop.

To build the Grep utility, you will need the regular completed expression package. (instructions for building this package are in the chapter given earlier) Go to the java.dev/regexp directory and issue the command:

```
cmd> javac grep.java
```

A JAVA INTEREST MAIL SEARCHER

Here is a interesting variant on the Grep theme that might prove useful.

As a Java programmer, it's useful to sign up for the various Java Internet mailing lists. I prefer to subscribe to the digest lists so that I don't get my mail reader full of individual messages. I get one large message per day per mailing list.

The only problem is that searching the mailing lists can be a chore; my mail reader does not support very good searching facilities. I can save the digests to a file on disk and search it with the grep or with an editor, but it is difficult to get a good picture of the message.

What I really want is a tool that pulls out only the messages I am interested in. This was the motivation behind the **newsgrep** tool. The **newsgrep** tool will pick out the mailing list messages that contain the regular expressions I am interested in.

Most mailing lists have a common format. In addition, the digest mail messages are delimited by a run of hyphens. For example, a typical message might be:

```
From: neilb@the-wire.com Date: Mon, 11 Sep 1995 20:33:03 -0400
Subject: A questions

Hi,

Here is a question

Thanks
Neil
```

Now, it's fairly obvious that we have a simple way of recognizing the beginning and end of the messages: we can just look for the run of hyphens. So to construct a message extractor, we simply need to record the start position of a message, look for our string in the message, and output the message if the string is found.

This is effectively what the **newsgrep** program does. The **newsgrep** is similar to the grep program, except that the input stream is processed by a class called **NewsStream**. The **NewsStream** search looks for the regular expression we are searching for and, if it finds it, calls **messageBoundary** method.

The **messageBoundary** method, in turn, steps back to the beginning of the message and then prints the message out. It does so by printing out the input stream until it finds the delimiting hyphens.

The stepping back mechanism employs the mark and reset methods provided by the **FilterInputStream** class (the parent class of **DataInputStream**). The **FilterInputStream.mark** method records the current position in the file. It takes as a parameter the number of bytes to record before the mark becomes invalid. In other words, if the message is longer that the number of bytes passed to the **mark** method, the algorithm will throw a spanner.

The counterpart to the **mark** method is the **reset** method, which is used to reset the input stream to the previously marked position. All the bytes are replaced as if the stream were starting again at the marked position, as shown in Listing 11.10.

Listing 11.10   The NewsStream Class

```java
import java.lang.*;
import java.io.*;
import extension.regexp.*;

class NewsStream {
    RegExp re;
    DataInputStream in;
    PrintStream out;
    boolean outputMessage=false;
    String delimiter= new String("————————————");

    NewsStream(DataInputStream i, PrintStream o, RegExp pattern) {
        re = pattern;
        in = i;
        out = o;
    }

    void search() {
        String s;
        boolean done=false;
        messageBoundary(delimiter);
        while (!done) {
            try {
                if ((s = in.readLine()) == null)
                    throw new IOException();
                // DBG out.println("? "+s);
                if (s.equals(delimiter))
                    messageBoundary(s);
                else if (re.match(s))
                    messageMatched(s);
            } catch(IOException e) {
                done = true;
                messageBoundary(delimiter);
            }
        }
    }

    void messageMatched(String s) {
        // DBG System.out.println(">>"+s);
        outputMessage = true;
    }
```

```
        void messageBoundary(String boundary) {
            try {
                if (outputMessage) {
                    in.reset();
                    String s;
                    do {
                        if ((s = in.readLine()) != null)
                            out.println(s);
                    } while (s != null && !s.equals(boundary));
                }
                outputMessage = false;
                in.mark(10000);
            } catch(IOException e) { }
        }
    }

public class newsgrep {

    static public void main(String args[]) {
        try {

            String pattern = args[0];
            DataInputStream ds = new DataInputStream(System.in);
            NewsStream gs = new NewsStream(ds, System.out,
                                new RegExp(pattern) );
            gs.search();

        } catch (ArrayIndexOutOfBoundsException e) {
            printUsage();
        } catch (RegExpCompileException e) {
            System.err.println("Bad regular expression: "+args[0]);
        }
    }

    static void printUsage() {
        System.out.println("Usage:");
        System.out.println("newsgrep \"pattern\"");
    }
}
```

Again, you will need to have previously built the regular expression package using the instructions given earlier, then go to the java.dev/regexp directory and issue the command,

```
cmd> javac newsgrep.java
```

To run the newsgrep program, and print out a list of matching messages, enter

```
cmd>java newsgrep video < comp.lang.dec95.lis
```

at the command line.

The program performs reasonably well, as long as the message files are not too big. It takes about a minute to process a month's worth of files on my machine, although I've found that with very large files, the system tends to run out of juice. If this is a problem, you could use a different algorithm—a two pass algorithm, for example. First, search and find the start and end line numbers of the messages, then run through a second time, printing out the matching messages. I knocked out a short test of this method, and found that it was quicker than the method I've presented to you.

Taking Things Further

A project like the regular expression and grep tool project is almost a labor of love. It is the kind of thing that you can always tweak. There are always plenty of ideas to try out.

To prime the pump, here are a few obvious areas that could use some improvement.

- One useful change would be to add minimum count support for the {} multiplier meta-character. For instance, you could write a regular expression such as **[a-z]{0,8}\.[a-z]{0,3}** to match an alphabetic 8.3 filename. The improvement has been to add the support for the {min,max} rather than just {number}. Naturally, the regular expression should support both.
- Another useful meta-character change would be to allow meta-character support inside of a choice. For instance, we could write **([a-z]+|[0-9]+)** to match either a sequence of letters or a sequence of numbers.
- Beyond changes to the meta-characters, we could improve the matching algorithms. A number of sequences, as I pointed out earlier, can have poor performance speed. For example, think about testing **a+$** against a string like **aaaabaaaaabaaabaabaaab**. Our algorithm won't recognize that the search would be better conducted in reverse, as indicated by the **$** meta-character.

Beyond this, I'm sure that you can come up with plenty of improvements of your own!

If You Liked This, You'll Love These

By now, I am sure you can see the importance of regular expressions in the world of computers. If this chapter has whet your appetite and left you with more questions than it has answered then, well, good! That was my intent. For some Java-based material on regular expressions, check out:

http://www.cc.gatech.edu/gvu/people/Faculty/hudson/java_cup/home.html.

This Website has a parser generator capable for use in the Java language. Author Scott Hudson of the Graphics Visualization and Usability Center at Georgia Tech has used it to create a parser for the Java language itself. Very cool, if you are into parsers.

PROGRAMMING JAVA APPLETS

Neil Bartlett

Now that we can program in Java, let's look at putting our programs on the World Wide Web.

The programs we have written so far in the book have not differed much from programs we might write in any other language. Sure, we have been doing object-oriented stuff, but basically, we have been compiling programs and running them from the command line.

This command line stuff is probably not what attracted you to Java in the first place. In this chapter, we are going to take a look at a key feature that separates Java from other languages: applets.

This chapter is all about applets and how to program them. We take a look at a number of sample applets. We break them apart and we see what makes them tick. Then, when we have covered how to program applets, we move on to the very important issue of what we can *do* with applets. Applets have very strict security controls placed on them. We'll look closely at how restricting the controls are.

WHAT IS AN APPLET?

When we run Java programs, we run them using *java*, the Java interpreter. The Java interpreter runs a program by calling its **main** method. By doing so, it hands over control to the program. The program can then do whatever it likes: it can mess with strings, do some file I/O, or whatever it feels like doing. The program is in control. It is a master of its own destiny. Once the program decides it is finished, it stops.

Applets are different. They are run from within a Java-enabled program, such as a Web browser like Netscape Navigator. These Java-enabled programs contain a copy of the Java interpreter, and it is the interpreter that runs the applets. The applets are *interpreted* by the browser.

The key difference between a program and an applet is that a program is free to live its own life. An applet, on the other hand, is living inside of another program. It is kind of like a baby living inside of a mother. The baby is alive, but it is feeding and getting its essential nutrients from the mother.

The applet is conceived, so to speak, when the browser reads some HTML code with an **applet** tag. The **Applet** tag contains all the information necessary to bring the applet to life. The two main things it specifies are which Java applet to run and how big an area of screen space the applet wants for itself. The applet is just a .class file—the output of a compilation of a *.java* file by the Java Compiler, javac.

A typical **applet** tag from an HTML file might be,

```
<applet code=applet.class width=100 height=200>
```

This says that the applet is stored in the file applet.class and that it wants to use a screen area of 100 units by 200 units.

When the browser reads the Web page described by the HTML, it will load the applet code specified by the **applet** tag. Then, it will reserve a rectangular area of the Web page. The rectangle's size is determined by the **Width** and **Height** fields of the **applet** tag. Once the applet is loaded, the browser will start the applet and tell it to draw itself into the rectangular area it has had allocated to it.

A major difference from the command line program is that the browser retains significant control over the applet: it doesn't simply call the applet and tell it to do what it likes. Throughout the life of the applet, the browser will give the applet orders. For instance, as the user switches from one Web page to another, the browser will tell the applets on the new page to display themselves and the applets on the old page to go to sleep.

An applet, then, is responsible for what content goes into the area it has been allocated. The browser is responsible for managing the applet and providing guidance throughout its life.

"HELLO, WORLD" TO THE NTH POWER

As you have probably gathered from this book, you will know you are in the middle of a tutorial when you see the words "Hello" and "World" side-by-side. (Either that, or you're in the middle of a very bad 1950s science-fiction movie.)

This chapter is no different. We are exploring applet programming, so our first port of call must be the MinimalHelloWorldApplet. There is no arguing with tradition. Take a look at Listing 12.1.

Listing 12.1   MinimalHelloWorldApplet.java

```java
import java.awt.*;
import java.applet.*;

public class MinimalHelloWorldApplet extends Applet {

    public void paint( Graphics g) {

        g.drawString("HelloWorld", 160, 70);
    }

}
```

Compare this with the MinimalHelloWorld program, shown in Listing 12.2, which Steve showed us earlier in Chapter 3.

Listing 12.2   MinimalHelloWorld.java

```java
class MinimalHelloWorld {

  public static void main( String args[] ) {

    System.out.println( "Hello, World." );

  }
}
```

I'm sure you'll notice a few differences like the fact that *every* line of code is different between the two listings! About the only thing these two programs have in common is that they both say "Hello, World" to the user. That, and the fact they are written in Java.

Compiling and Running

Before we look at how our new Hello World applet works, let's take a look at how to get the program running. The applet programming really does change things: even how we run the program has changed.

The applet source code is contained on the book's CD-ROM in the file MinimalHelloWorldApplet.java. You will need to copy the file to a new directory on your hard disk. Then we can begin.

First of all, make sure you are in the directory that contains the copy of the source file, then (assuming that your Java directory is on your system path) type

```
cmd> javac MinimalHelloWorldApplet.java
```

to compile the program. This step, at least, is familiar to you. As before, compiling the .java file will produce a .class file. In this case, the .class file will be called MinimalHelloWorldApplet.class. Now let's run the applet.

This is where things start to get a little different. Previously, we ran our programs using the java command. As you know, the difference between an applet and a program is that the applet does not run standalone: it must be run from within a program such as a Web browser. Therefore, we will need a Web browser to run the program. However, the browser cannot run the .class file directly. It needs to be told about it in a language that it understands. Browsers typically talk HTML, so we will need to write some HTML to tell the browser about the applet we have just created. A typical piece of HTML to run the applet is show in Listing 12.3

Listing 12.3   Example.html, HTML to Run MinimalHelloWorldApplet

```
<applet code="MinimalHelloWorldApplet.class"
        width=400
        height=150>
</applet>
```

This HTML code consists of a single **applet** tag. The **applet** tag uses the **code** field to tell the browser the name of the .class file to run. It also tells the browser the width and the height of the area that it should allocate to the applet. The example.html file therefore tells the browser that it should run an applet called MinimalHelloWorldApplet.class in an area that is 400 units wide by 150 units high.

We can then view this HTML page using a Java-aware Web browser such as Netscape. We simply read the file with the browser. If we are using Netscape Navigator, for instance, and were running the HTML from a file on our machine, we would use the Open File... item from the File pull-dow menun. This would load in the applet as shown in Figure 12.1.

Of course, the HTML does not have to exist on the user's local disk. We could publish the HTML code on our home page, making it accessible to everyone with a Java-aware browser who accesses our home page. We have described this in more detail at the beginning of the book in *Chapter 2, Spicing Up Your Home Page*.

During development, it can be costly in terms of time and computer resources to run a large program such as Netscape just to see how the applet development is progressing. To save us some hassle, the JDK toolkit provides a minimalist browser which will just display the applet. The applet browser is called appletviewer. Unlike the Web browser, the appletviewer does not recognize all of the HTML tags, it only recognizes the **applet** tag. To use

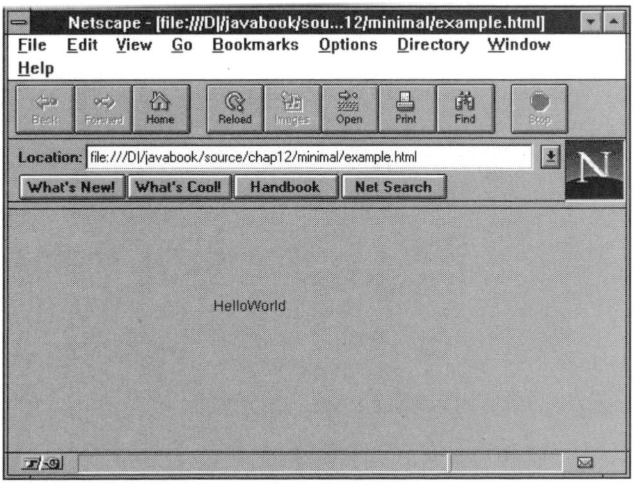

Figure 12.1 *Netscape running the MinimalHelloWorldApplet.*

appletviewer, we will need the example.html file we just created. We then type the command

```
cmd> appletviewer example.html
```

and the applet will popup. Remember, you need to run the **appletviewer** from the same directory where the MinimalHelloWorldApplet.class and the example.html file are located. The results of running the appletviewer with the example.html file are shown in Figure 12.2.

THE "HELLO, WORLD" APPLET EXPLAINED

Take a look at Listing 12.4. It is simply a repeat listing of the MinimalHelloWorldApplet.java.

Listing 12.4   MinimalHelloWorldApplet.java

```
import java.awt.*;
import java.applet.*;

public class MinimalHelloWorldApplet extends Applet {

    public void paint( Graphics g) {

        g.drawString("HelloWorld", 160, 70);
    }

}
```

Lets take a step-by-step look at this piece of code.

Figure 12.2   *The appletviewer running MinimalHelloWorldApplet.*

What, No main?

The first difference you'll notice is that there is no **main** method. As you know, the **main** method is the first method to run when a program is run from the command line.

Applets don't need a **main** method, because they are not run from the command line. They're run from within the context of another program.

One way that you can think of an applet is as a collection of methods that are called by the browser program. For example, in the applet we have one method, **paint**. It is the browser program, not the applet itself, that decides when the **paint** needs to happen. For instance, suppose the browser just loaded a new page containing our MinimalHelloWorldApplet. The **applet** tag tells the browser to allocate an area 400 by 150 to the applet named in the **code** field our MinimalHelloWorldApplet. The browser creates this area for the applet and calls the applet's paint method so that the applet can fill the space. In our case, the applet simply draws the *HelloWorld* string. Figure 12.3 shows this.

Naturally, there are a lot more methods that the browser and the applet can talk about. We will be looking at some more of these shortly.

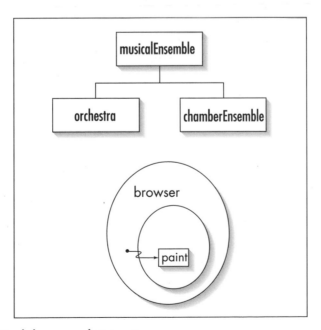

Figure 12.3 *Simple browser-applet interaction.*

The Applet Class

The **Applet** class is what converts our program from being a standalone program into being an applet. To make our program into an applet, we derive a class from the **Applet** class. When the browser runs a .class file, it expects to find an **Applet** class inside of the .class file. We derive the class by using the **extends** keyword to derive MinimalHelloWorldApplet from the **Applet** class as shown here:

```
public class MinimalHelloWorldApplet extends Applet {
```

If you have forgotten what *deriving* or *extending* from a class means, I recommend that you read the section on *inheritance* in Chapter 4. However, to recap briefly, the **extends** keyword means that the new class, in this case **MinimalHelloWorldApplet**, has all the same features as the class that it is extending from, the **Applet** class. So the **MinimalHelloWorldApplet** class has available to it all the methods and variables that the **Applet** class provides.

An important point to note is that the derived applet class must be declared with the **public** keyword. The **public** keyword declares this class to be visible to the browser. When the browser interprets the **code** field of the **applet** tag, it expects the .class file to contain a publicly visible applet class. If the browser does not find the public applet class, it will not be able to run the applet.

To get the applet code to compile, we also need to tell the compiler that we intend to use the **Applet** class. We do this by announcing at the beginning of the applet source code that we want to import the java.applet package into the program. To do this we use the **import** keyword. We use the simplest incarnation of this:

```
import java.applet.*;
```

This means import all the classes from the java.applet package.

Doing the Work

The applet we have put together does not do much. It simply prints out the *"Hello World!"* string whenever the **paint** method is called.

Previously, we used the **System.out.println** method to print output to the console window. This time, however, we want to draw onto the area that the browser has set aside for the applet. To do this, we need to use graphics drawing methods. The **System.out.println** method will not cut the mustard, because it is used only for outputting lines to a console. It does not have the smarts to print text into a graphical browser window.

When dealing with graphics, we need to know where to place a string. There are no line positions that we can fall back on. In Listing 12.1, we place the string at position (160, 70). In other words, in the 400-by-150 grid that the browser has allocated for the applet, the string *"HelloWorld"* is drawn at a point 160 units to the right of and 70 units down from the top-left corner of the applet area.

We will not dwell too much on the specifics of painting and drawing here. Chapter 14 is a tutorial on graphics. It will introduce enough fancy graphics ideas to let you indulge all your creative impulses. In this chapter, we want to concentrate on the applet side of things. We will deliberately keep the graphics stuff pared down to the bone.

Another point is that we aren't limited to graphics stuff only when we are programming applets. In fact, we have all the classes and methods of the entire Java toolkit available to us. We can use whatever classes we want to. Having said this, though, there are a few caveats. At the end of this chapter we will discuss these.

Let's briefly recap what we've discussed. Applets are programs that run inside other programs. To create applets, we must derive a public class from the **Applet** class. We override methods such as the **paint** method to control what the applet does in response to requests made by the browser.

THE BEGINNING AND THE END

Let's add a little bit more weight to our MinimalHelloWorldApplet. The changes we will make here will not seem like much, but they will reshape the code to prepare the way for some more interesting changes that are to come. Take a look at Listing 12.5 and compare it to Listing 12.1.

Listing 12.5   HelloWorld01Applet—Preparing for the Next Step

```
import java.awt.*;
import java.applet.*;

public class HelloWorld01Applet  extends Applet {
    String string;
    int xpos;
```

```
    int ypos;

    public void init() {
        string = "HelloWorld";
        xpos = 160;
        ypos = 70;
    }

    public void paint( Graphics g) {
        g.drawString(string, xpos, ypos);
    }
}
```

If you think that it looks as if I have not done much more than introduce a method called **init** and three variables to hold the constant values of **"HelloWorld"**, **160**, and **70**, then, you would be correct. However, the interesting thing is the **init** method itself.

init and destroy

The **init** method for the applet is rather like the **main** method for standalone programs. The **init** method is the first method that the browser will call for the applet, just as the **main** method was the first method that the java interpreter calls in an application.

Remember that the applet is being run from within the browser. This means that the browser will control when the applet is created and when it is destroyed. This is not controlled by the applet itself. However, the applet will often need to know when it is being created or destroyed so that it can perform important tasks. For example, the applet might need to read the settings from the nuclear reactor it is monitoring before it displays the flashing "Red Alert—Reactor has gone critical" warning message.

The **init** method and its death-bed counterpart, the **destroy** method, cover these bases. The **init** method is called when the applet is first created, and the **destroy** method is called when the applet is about to be destroyed. By overriding these methods, the applet can do what it needs to do when it is created or destroyed. In practice, it is not very often that you will end up using the **destroy** method. The **init** method, on the other hand, will be a mainstay and will often appear in your applet programs.

GETTING PARAMETERS

Often, an applet needs to accept some input from the HTML programmer to find out what to do. For instance, a pixel-board applet that features scrolling text might want to find out the text to display. It would be best if the HTML programmer could supply the text rather than the applet hard-wiring a constant value, such as the banal *"HelloWorld"*, for the text. This will make the pixel-board applet much more useful because the applet will not have to be recompiled just to change the text to be displayed.

The only way to get information from HTML into the applet is to use the **param** tag. The **param** tag is used to describe a named value called a *parameter*. As we have seen in the chapter on using applets, the **param** tag has the following format:

```
'<' 'param' 'name' '=' appletAttribute1 'value' '=' value '>'
```

The **param** tag has two fields: one called **name** and one called **value**. For instance, we might have a parameter named **GREETING** which we want to pass into our "Hello, World" applet. The value of the **GREETING** will be the text that we wish to display. The corresponding **param** tag would then be:

```
<param name="GREETING" value="Hello World!">
```

This will set the value of the **GREETING** parameter to the value *"Hello World!"*. An example of the complete HTML, including the **applet** tag, is shown in Listing 12.6.

Listing 12.6 helloworld02.html—HTML File with Parameter

```
<applet code="HelloWorld02Applet.class" width=400 height=300>
<param name="GREETING" value="Hello World!">
</applet>
```

Now that we have seen how the HTML writer can set the value of the **GREETING** parameter, let's look at the flip-side: the applet code that retrieves the parameter from the HTML file into the Java code.

The **Applet** class provides a single method which we can use to get the parameter. It is appropriately called **getParameter**. To use **getParameter** we supply it with a string that matches the name of field of the **param** tag we wish to retrieve. The **getParameter** method will return the value of the parameter as a **String**. Listing 12.7 is a new version of the Hello World applet. This version gets the parameter for us.

Listing 12.7   HelloWorld02Applet.java, Applet with a Parameter

```
import java.awt.*;
import java.applet.*;

public class HelloWorld02Applet extends Applet {
    String string;
    int xpos;
    int ypos;

    public void paint( Graphics g) {
        g.drawString(string, xpos, ypos);
    }

    public void init() {
        string = getParameter("GREETING");
        xpos = 160;
        ypos = 170;
    }
}
```

If you compare HelloWorld02Applet.java against the version shown in Listing 12.5, you will see that the only difference is that we are using the **getParameter(**"**GREETING**"*)* method call instead of using the constant value *"Hello World"* to set the initial value of the variable called **string**.

One Parameter or Two, Sir?

Of course, we don't have to limit ourselves to just one parameter. We can use the **getParameter** method to get more than one parameter, as long as each parameter has a different name. For instance, we might also want to get values for both of the **int** values, **xpos** and **ypos**. Listing 12.8 shows this happening.

Listing 12.8   HelloWorld03Applet.java—Accepting Multiple Parameters

```
import java.awt.*;
import java.applet.*;

public class HelloWorld03Applet extends Applet {
    String string;
    int xpos;
    int ypos;

    public void paint( Graphics g) {
        g.drawString(string, xpos, ypos);
    }
```

```
public void init() {
    string = getParameter("GREETING");
    xpos = Integer.parseInt( getParameter("XPOS") );
    ypos = Integer.parseInt( getParameter("YPOS") );
}
}
```

We also need to upgrade the HTML file to provide us with the extra parameters. Listing 12.9 shows this.

Listing 12.9   Helloworld03.html

```
<applet code="HelloWorld03Applet.class" width=400 height=300>
<param name="GREETING" value="Hello World!">
<param name="XPOS" value="160">
<param name="YPOS" value="70">
</applet>
```

Now we have all the applet variables' initial values being passed in from HTML. This technique is very flexible. It allows us to change the text and the position of the text simply by changing the HTML code. Certainly much easier than having to recompile the applet each time we want to make a change.

Converting Parameters

Listing 12.8 also raises a valuable point about the types of the parameters. The **getParameter** method always returns a **String** value. If we want a parameter to represent some other value such as an int value or a float value, we will need to convert the **String** value to the appropriate type value.

To do this, we will use the wrapper classes that we discussed at the end of Chapter 7. The wrapper classes, such as **Integer** and **Float**, provide methods to convert between **Strings** and the underlying type, for example, int for **Integer** and float for **Float**. In Listing 12.8, above, we use the **Integer.parseInt** method to convert the string returned from **getParameter** to an int.

Default Parameters

You might be asking yourself: "What happens if the HTML writer forgets to provide us with one of our **param** tags?" Good question. The answer is that the applet simply will not work.

If the **getParameter** method cannot find a parameter in the HTML file, it returns the value null. The null value is not particularly useful, because it does one of two unhelpful things: either it will cause **Integer.parseInt** to blow a gasket and throw the **NumberFormatException**, or it will cause the **drawString** method in the **paint** method to throw a **NullPointerException** because **string** will be null. Either way, it is bad news.

What's to be done? Well, we can put in some defensive code to protect ourselves.

I prefer to do this by providing what I call *parameter convenience* methods. I have a number of parameter convenience methods—one for each of the types to which a parameter might be converted.

The convenience methods try to convert the parameter to the appropriate type. If they fail, they return a default value. This ensures that, at the very least, the program will work. Listing 12.10 shows an updated version of the Hello World applet with two convenience methods: one for **Strings** and one for **ints**.

Listing 12.10   Using Parameter Convenience Methods

```
import java.awt.*;
import java.applet.*;

public class HelloWorld04Applet extends Applet {
    String string;
    int xpos;
    int ypos;

    public void paint( Graphics g) {
        g.drawString(string, xpos, ypos);
    }

    public void init() {
        string = getParam("GREETING", "Hello World!!");
        xpos = getParam("XPOS", 160 );
        ypos = getParam("YPOS", 70 );
    }

    public String getParam(String p, String d) {
        String s = getParameter(p);
        return s == null ? d : s;
    }

    public int getParam(String p, int d) {
        try {
            d = Integer.parseInt(getParameter(p));
        } catch (NumberFormatException e) {}
        return  d;
    }
}
```

The two convenience methods are both named **getParam**. The difference between them lies in the types that are passed into and out of the methods. The **getParam** method for **String** types takes a two-**String** type parameter and naturally returns a **String**; the **int getParam** method takes a **String** and an **int** and returns an **int**. The compiler will distinguish which version of **getParam** to call based on the different types. This behavior is an example of the *polymorphic overloading* behavior that we discussed in Chapter 6.

To use a **getParam** convenience method, we supply it with the name of the parameter and the default value to use if the parameter is not found.

The key to these methods is that they allow a default value to be passed in. If the conversion fails, then the default value is used. The means for detecting whether or not the conversion has failed is different for each type. For the **String** type, it just involves testing to see if the **getParameter** method returned null. For the **int** type, rather than testing for null, we pass the value to the **Integer.parseInt**. If, for any reason, the string is not a valid **int**, the **NumberFormatException** is thrown. The code catches this exception and returns the default value.

As a useful side effect, the numeric formats such as **int** are also protected against the HTML writer entering a badly formatted string for the number. In these instances, the wrapper class will throw the **NumberFormatException** and the default value will be used.

I have only shown two examples of the **getParam** method here. Each time I need a different type from a parameter, I write a corresponding version of **getParam**. For instance, you will probably find that you will need to get boolean or float values into the applet using the **param** tag. For each of these, you will need to write a version of the **getParam** method.

Advertising Your Parameters

The **Applet** class provides a simple method called **getParameterInfo** that you can use to record some usage information about the parameters the HTML writer can use with your applet. The **getParameterInfo** method returns an array of three strings (name, type, and description), each describing a single parameter. See the Java API reference for more information.

BRIEF REVIEW

Okay, it's time for breather and a brief review. The next section introduces a couple of sophisticated concepts so I want be sure that you understand what we have covered so far.

To build an applet and run it, we need to:

1. Use javac to compile the .java file and produce the .class file.
2. Write HTML code with an **applet** tag to reference the .class file.
3. Use the appletviewer or a Java-aware browser such as Netscape Navigator to view the applet.

To write an applet, we need to:

1. Derive a public class from the **Applet** class using the **extends** key word.
2. Provide an **init** method to do the setup and a **paint** method to draw the applet.

So far, so good. The only problem is that applet does not seem to do very much: the applet looks very dead. Let's breathe some life into it.

THE APPLET LIVES!

We are going to take a look at a useful applet. This applet is a scaled-down variant of the popular sideways scrolling text applet. The sideways scrolling text will continuously scroll a message sideways across the screen from right to left. When the scrolling message hits the left hand edge of the screen, it wraps around to the right-hand edge and starts scrolling again. The applet provides the effect of a pixel board with the text continuously scrolling right to left across the screen. Figure 12.4 shows the applet in action.

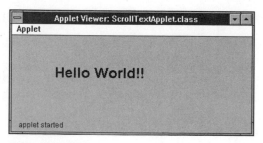

Figure 12.4 *Basic scrolling-text applet.*

Take a look at Listing 12.11. It is the complete listing of our scrolling text applet. It will scroll *"Hello, World!!"* across the screen.

Listing 12.11   A Scrolling-Text Applet

```java
import java.awt.*;
import java.applet.*;

public class ScrollTextApplet extends Applet implements Runnable {

    Thread workThread = null;
    String string;
    int xpos;
    int ypos;
    int leftedgepos;
    int pause;

    public void paint( Graphics g) {
        if (-xpos < leftedgepos)
            xpos = size().width;

        g.drawString(string, xpos, ypos);
    }

    public void init() {
        string = getParam("GREETING", "Hello World!!");
        xpos = getParam("XPOS", 160 );
        ypos = getParam("YPOS", 70 );
        leftedgepos = getParam("LEFTEDGEPOS", -100 );
        pause = getParam("PAUSE", 100 );
    }

    public String getParam(String p, String d) {
        String s = getParameter(p);
        return s == null ? d : s;
    }

    public int getParam(String p, int d) {
        try {
            d = Integer.parseInt(getParameter(p));
        } catch (NumberFormatException e) {}
        return  d;
    }

    public void start() {
        workThread = new Thread(this);
        workThread.start();
    }

    public void run() {
        while (true) {
            repaint();
```

```
        try {Thread.sleep(pause);}
        catch (InterruptedException e){ }
    }
}

public void stop() {
    if (workThread != null) {
        workThread.stop();
    }
}
}
```

As you can see, we have introduced a lot of new code. Let's go through this code step by step.

Red Light—Green Light

The **start** and **stop** methods are provided by the **Applet** class. An applet can override these methods to determine when it is active. We have already seen the **init** and the **destroy** methods. The **init** method is called when the applet is created, the **destroy** when it is destroyed. The **start** and **stop** are called are called to activate and deactivate the applet, according to the needs of the browser. The browser reserves the right to stop the applet whenever it thinks that the applet should not be running. For instance, when the browser changes pages, it wants to be able to start those applets on the new page and stop those applets on the old page that is no longer showing.

To understand what's written inside the body of the **start** and the **stop** methods, we need to understand *threads*.

Threads

The most important new concept needed to animate the applet is the thread. You will see the word "thread" scattered liberally throughout the code in Listing 12.11. The thread concept is exceptionally important to Java. As you read through this book, you will see that we talk about threads in lots of places for lots of different reasons. Hopefully, by the time you finish this book, you will have looked at threads from enough different angles to have a good appreciation of what they are. Here we are going to do a brief review of threads, but for the main story on threads, check out Chapter 20.

What is a thread?

A thread is a separate execution sequence. Creating a thread for the applet is like giving the applet its own CPU. Once the applet has created a thread, it works independently of the browser or any other applets that might be running.

Why do we need a thread?

The browser is responsible for calling the applet's methods to prompt it to do things. However, the browser does this from within its own execution sequence—it is running in its own thread. If the applet wants to do something time-consuming, it will end up stopping the browser in its tracks until the applet has finished. But suppose we have a number of applets on the same page. Ideally, we would like them all to run simultaneously. This is where threads save the day. The applet creates its very own thread so that it can do its own thing without interfering with the execution of the browser or any other applets that are running. However, the applet will still respond to the browser. For instance, it will repaint itself when instructed by the browser to do so.

Making a Thread for the Applet

To allow the applet to create its own thread of execution, we need to do a few things:

1. The new applet class must implement the Runnable interface. The **Runnable** interface requires that the class define a single method called **run**. When the thread is created and started, the thread will call the **run** method.

2. Create and start the thread. This happens inside the **start** method. The class maintains a single **Thread** object variable called **workThread**. Whenever the **start** method is called, a new **Thread** object is created and stored in the object **workThread** variable. The thread is then started so that it will call the **run** method.

3. Fill in the **run** method. The **run** method defines what the applet will do when it is running in its own thread. In Listing 12.11, we periodically repaint the applet. In other words, we cause the applet to call the **paint** method. Between the repaints, we put the thread to sleep—we stop it temporarily—for **pause** milliseconds. This controls the speed of the text scrolling.

4. Stop the thread when necessary. The **stop** method will stop the thread.

These steps are common to any applet using threads. In this particular case, we add one more step. We add some code to the **paint** method to ensure that the text moves across the screen.

Recapping How It Works

Well, we just introduced a lot of new concepts at the same time. Let's try to put it all in perspective.

Remember that the goal of **ScrollTextApplet** is to continuously move some text across the screen. At the same time, though, we want the browser to be responsive so that, for instance, the user can jump to a new Web page.

If the applet thread were not used when the browser called the applet's **start** method, the browser would stop working while the applet did its work. It would not respond to user requests. This is because the applet would have taken over the browser's thread. A thread can only do one thing at a time.

To allow the browser to continue working, we create a thread for the applet to use. We create this thread when the applet is started. The browser can then continue using its own thread while the applet runs in the newly created thread.

The threads do all of their work via the **run** method. Therefore, the applet implements the **run** method to do its stuff. When the thread is started, it will call the **run** method. The applet's **run** method will periodically call the **paint** method via a method called **repaint**. The **paint** method will move the text a little way across the screen each time it is called.

Eventually, when the browser calls **stop**, the applet thread is stopped and the text will stop moving. If the browser calls the applet's **start** method again, the applet creates another thread to start the text moving again.

Life-Cycle Methods

Four of the methods that we have covered (**init**, **start**, **stop**, **destroy**) are very important methods. These are the methods are commonly called the *life-cycle* methods.

By overriding the life-cycle methods, you can control what happens to the applet at the various stages of its life. You can imagine that the applet's life begins when the **init** method is called and ends when the **destroy** is called. In between, the **start** and the **stop** methods are called any number of times. Thus, the life-cycle of an applet will generally follow this pattern: **init**, **start**, **stop**, **destroy**. And some times it will go through a number of cycles of **start** and **stop** for instance: **init**, **start**, **stop**, **start**, **stop**, **destroy**.

Remember, though, that these methods are called by the browser to tell the applet where it is in its life; the applet does not call its own life-cycle methods.

Exploring the Applet Life Cycle

You might be curious as to when exactly the various phases of the life cycle are called. The **Applet** class itself does not really make any statements about when the various life-cycle methods are called. In many ways, it is not important to know *exactly* when they are called: it is only important to be ready to service them.

Having said this, though, it is useful to know on which occasions the browser calls the life-cycle methods. Let's look at what's going on behind the scenes in the appletviewer and Netscape Navigator. We are going to write a simple program to let us see the life cycle in operation.

Take a look at Listing 12.12. It will print out what is happening to the applet and when.

Listing 12.12   LifeCycle.html—A Life-Cycle Explorer

```
import java.applet.*;

public class LifecycleApplet extends Applet {

    public void init() {
        System.out.println("Init called");
    }

    public void start() {
        System.out.println("Start called");
    }

    public void stop() {
        System.out.println("Stop called");
    }

    public void destroy() {
        System.out.println("Destroy called");
    }
}
```

As you can see, this is a very simple applet. Whenever the browser calls any of the life-cycle methods, the method will print out a message to the console indicating that it was called.

This is an interesting point: you can still use the **System.out.println** to print out information to the console from within an applet. The **System.out.println** is a static method and is part of the java.lang package. The java.lang package is available to all Java programs or applets. Therefore even though the applet is running from within the context of a browser, the **System.out.println** will still be available. Of course, the browser's java interpreter can implement the method in a different way. For instance, the Netscape browser does not have to print the string to the command-line window. Netscape maintains its own special console window in which it writes the **println** strings.

To use the program, we will first need to compile it using javac. Then, we will need to write a simple HTML file to run the applet, as shown in Listing 12.13. Finally, we will need to run the applet.

Listing 12.13   Lifecycle.html

```
Listing <applet code="LifeCycleApplet.class" width=400 height=300>
</applet>
```

Try running the applet using both the appletviewer and Netscape Navigator. When you run the program using the appletviewer, the **println** methods will print to the command-line window that you ran the appletviewer from. When you use the Netscape browser, you will need to open the console window, shown in Figure 12.5, to see the output of the **println** methods.

And what will you discover?

Currently, when I run Netscape Navigator, I find that the **init** and the **start** methods are called whenever the HTML page with the applet is viewed. The **stop** is called when I stop viewing the applet page and the **start** is called when I switch back to viewing the applet page. The **destroy** is only called

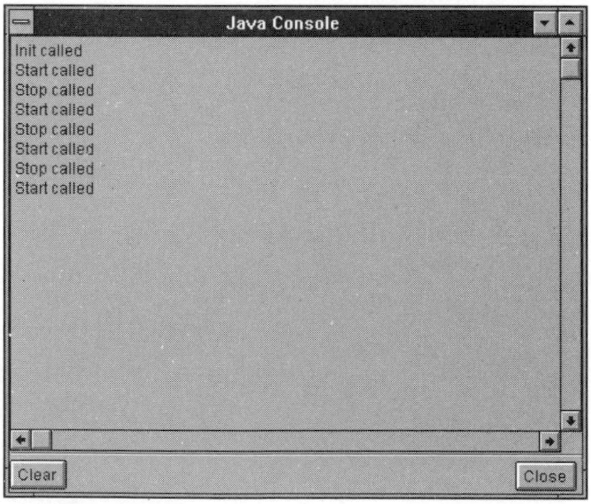

Figure 12.5 *The Netscape console window.*

when the browser is exited. Now, this behavior might change by the time you read this book; Java is still evolving. However, it's worth bearing in mind that currently you can write an applet that—if it disobeys the **stop** method and carries on processing—can run for the entire duration that the browser is up. Figure 12.6 shows a summary of these findings.

Shortly, in the chapter on graphics, we will see that we can construct separate windows called frame windows that have an existence outside of the applet area even though they can be controlled by an applet. This means that since the **destroy** method is not called, we can construct separate windows that remain up for the duration of the browser. This effect has endless possibilities. For example, consider an advertising applet: once someone has accessed your applet page, you can throw up a separate advertising frame. This advertising frame could continuously run advertisements.

THE APPLET IDIOM

To find out about how applets work, we have worked steadily from the ground up. We started with a very simple applet, and eventually arrived at a

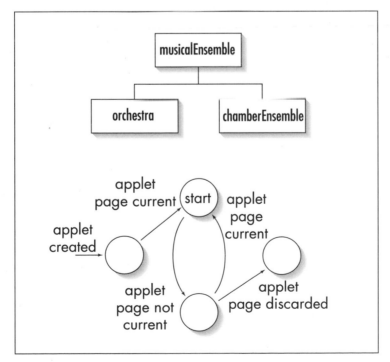

Figure 12.6 *State diagram of the life cycle.*

full-blown applet that uses threads. This process, though, was purely for the purposes of the tutorial. Whenever you start to write a new applet, you will discover that, time after time, you are using the same framework of code or subtle variants of it.

I call this base piece of code the *applet idiom*. It is like a phrase in English; it so often used that it is commonplace and widely understood. The applet idiom is shown in Listing 12.14. Of course, this is my favorite applet idiom. There are other ways of achieving the same effect, but they all amount to the same thing—so you might as well choose one and get on with life.

Listing 12.14   The Applet Idiom

```java
import java.awt.*;
import java.applet.*;

public class AppletIdiom extends Applet implements Runnable {

    Thread workThread = null;
    int sleeptime = 100;

    public void init() {

        // get parameters and set up variables
    }

    public void start() {
        workThread = new Thread(this);
        workThread.start();
    }

    public void run() {
        while (true) {

            // do some work e.g. repaint
            // then sleep for a useful amount of time

            try {Thread.sleep(sleeptime);}
            catch (InterruptedException e){ }
        }
    }

    public void paint(Graphics g) {
        // do some graphics work
    }

    public void stop() {
        if (workThread != null) {
            workThread.stop();
        }
```

```
    }

    public String getParam(String p, String d) {
        String s = getParameter(p);
        return s == null ? d : s;
    }

    public int getParam(String p, int d) {
        try {
            d = Integer.parseInt(getParameter(p));
        } catch (NumberFormatException e) {}
        return  d;
    }
}
```

You should recognize all the elements of the idiom. They are all methods we have presented before. There are just the life-cycle methods and the parameter convenience methods. I have put some comments in to show what goes where. To get an applet going, you will probably need to add code to the **init** and the **run** methods.

I use AppletIdiom as a code template. I just load the AppletIdiom.java file as the starting file for all new applets I write. When I start to program an applet, I read the file into the editor, customize it, and save it under a new filename.

TELLING THE USER WHAT'S HAPPENING

Earlier, when we looked at the applet life-cycle methods, we wrote a small applet to print out the stages of the applet's life cycle. We used the traditional **System.out.println** to do this. The trouble with using **System.out.println** though is that it doesn't put its output directly into the browser window. You need to bring up a separate console window to view the output. As far as applets are concerned, **System.out.println** is more of a debugging aid than as a way of presenting information to the user.

The way to present simple text information to the user is to use the **showStatus** method. I say simple text information because the **showStatus** method puts the text in the status bar of the browser window. This is just a one-line affair. It is not suitable for the output of large amounts of information. Later, in the chapter on components, we show how to use something called a *TextArea* as a way of presenting larger amounts of information to the user.

The **showStatus** method just takes a single string as a parameter. This string is displayed in the browser's status bar, replacing what was there before.

A good use of the **showStatus** method is to show the progress of an applet—especially if it is likely to take some time to run. You know how antsy users can get while they're waiting.

DEBUGGING APPLETS

My preferred method of debugging applets is to use **System.out.println** statements in the code. I use the **println** statements to tell me where I am in the program and what the values of various important variables are.

In addition to **println** statements, you can also use the Java debugger. Personally, I find the debugger unstable and cumbersome to use. As a result, I rarely use it. There is nothing worse that having a debugger giving you false information. Sun itself states that the current debugger is little more than a proof of concept: at the same time, Sun has laid down a challenge to tool writers to produce a better one. The bottom line is: don't expect too much from the debugger. However, for the brave of heart, here is some information on how to run it with applets.

Before using the debugger, it is best first to compile the .java file using the **-g** switch of javac. For example:

```
cmd> javac -g LifeCycleApplet.java
```

This is not an essential step. You can debug an applet that has been compiled without the **-g** switch, but you will not have variable information available.

To use the debugger, you must use the **-debug** switch of the appletviewer:

```
cmd> appletviewer -debug lifecycle.html
```

This command will then get you into the debugger.

The debugger is the same debugger we described in Chapter 3. Don't forget that a full set of debugger commands can be found on the Java Web page at http://java.sun.com.

APPLET LOCATION

We've talked a lot about programming in this chapter, but we haven't talked much about where the applet's .class files and the .html files reside.

The applets that we have discussed so far have all used one class to do their work. Often, though, you will want to use more than one class, which this means that a number of .class files will be produced—one .class file produced for each class in the applet.

One of the useful features of applets is that they can reside on one machine in a network and yet be run on another machine. The machine where the applet resides is referred to as the *server* machine, while the machine that runs the applet is called the *client.*

When the client machine loads an applet from the server machine, the applet needs to specify in which directory the applet .class files are located. It does this using the **codebase** field of the HTML **applet** tag. Listing 12.15 shows how to use the **codebase** field.

Listing 12.15   Using codebase

```
<applet codebase="http://java.sun.com/applets/applets/NervousText"
  code="NervousText.class" width=400 height=75 >
 <param name="text" value="Hello World">
 </applet>
```

codebase specifies the directory where all the .class files for the applet must exist. Meanwhile the **code** field specifies which .class file in the **codebase** directory contains the applet.

WHAT CAN WE DO WITH APPLETS?

We have covered the basics of how to program applets. Let's move on to look at what we can do with applets. As we will see in a moment, Java applets are highly restricted in what they are allowed to do.

Let's start off with a blanket statement: anything we *use* in a standalone program we can *use* in an applet. We can use any of the packages and classes provided by the Java toolkit in our applets. This means that we have access to graphics, imaging, sound, file I/O, data structures, and math classes. You name it, and you can use it in an applet. There is nothing inherent in an applet that stops these classes

Thus, you can use any of the JDK classes and methods that you want to in an applet. The applet will compile. However, many of the classes and methods will not work when you try to run the applet. You will receive a security exception from the applet. To understand why, we need to consider *applet security.*

Applet Security

If you have been following the doomsayers of the computer industry for the past few years you will quickly realize that unrestricted applets are really just an open door for an unscrupulous virus writer. If the applet could have un-limited access to all the toolkit features, such as file manipulation, library loading, and C program callouts, it would not be too difficult to write a very damaging virus.

To prevent this gloomy scenario from playing out, all java-aware browsers incorporate a piece of code called a *security manager*. The security manager is responsible for ensuring that applets cannot do anything damaging to a client system. In effect, the security manager disables certain methods of cer-tain Java classes. When the applet calls these methods, they either quietly fail or, more often, they throw a **SecurityException**.

Obviously, if you want to write applets that work correctly, you need to understand which methods you can use without concern and which methods might be disabled by the security manager.

Applet security is essentially a browser-based feature. Each browser imple-ments its own version of the security manager. We need to look at what a given browser will allow applets to do. Applets themselves do not have a built-in list of disabled methods.

In addition to the variation from one browser to another, security managers implement different policies, depending upon whether the applet was loaded over the network or from a local file. The presumption is that an applet loaded from a local file is less likely to be damaging than an applet loaded across the network.

Broadly speaking, the security managers will be concerned with the following activities of an applet:

- File manipulation
- Library loading
- Process control
- Property manipulation
- Network control
- Window creation

What do browser security managers actually let us do? Unfortunately, that isn't an easy question to answer. The security managers are undergoing some change, so anything I write now might not be correct by the time you read this.

Therefore, from here to the end of this section, be prepared to check what I say. And how might you check it? Well, currently there is only resource that has attempted to get a good handle on the security manager issue: the Security FAQ produced by Sun. It is available from http://java.sun.com/sfaq. If you want to get into some serious applet writing, then I suggest you become familiar with this resource.

A summary of the contents of the security FAQ is shown in Table 12.1. The table is essentially a comparison of what operations are allowed under what circumstances. The table shows what can be done with standalone programs, applets run under the appletviewer, and applets run under the Netscape browser. Then add into the mix the operations on applets, a split between network-loaded applets, and locally loaded applets. Table 12.2 shows the abbreviations used in the heading row of Table 12.1.

Table 12.1   *Summary of Applet Security*

Operation	NN	NL	AN	AL	JS
read file in HOME,acl.read=null	no	no	no	yes	yes
read file in HOME,acl.read=HOME	no	no	yes	yes	yes
write file in /tmp, acl.write=null	no	no	no	yes	yes
write file in /tmp, acl.write=/tmp	no	no	yes	yes	yes
get file infoacl.read=HOME					
acl.write=/tmp	no	no	yes	yes	yes
delete fileusing File.delete()	no	no	no	no	yes
delete fileusing Runtime.exec of					
/usr/bin/rm or equivalent	no	no	no	yes	yes
read the user.name property	no	yes	no	yes	yes
exit(-1)	no	no	no	yes	yes
import library	no	yes	no	yes	yes
connect to local port	no	yes	no	yes	yes
connect to foreign port	no	yes	no	yes	yes

Table 12.2 *List of Abbreviations from Table 12.1*

Abbreviation	Meaning
NN	Netscape Navigator 2.0 beta, loading applets over the Net
NL	Netscape Navigator 2.0 beta, loading applets from the local file system
AN	appletviewer, JDK beta, loading applets over the Net
AL	appletviewer, JDK beta, loading applets from the local file system
JS	Java standalone applications

The Netscape browser has the most severe security restrictions. The following comments apply to applets loaded over the network.

Netscape 2.0 does not allow any file manipulations on the client side. You cannot read or write files using applets running under Netscape, nor can you get information about any files on the system.

Netscape-run applets loaded over the Net cannot start other programs, nor can they do a **System.exit(-1)**. Applets also cannot load libraries, which means that you cannot use packages that are stored on the server side. For instance, you cannot do an

```
import test.*;
```

where the **test** package is found on the server side—even if it is in the **codebase** directory.

The appletviewer only fares a little better. The appletviewer observes a concept called the *access control list*. The access control list is a property that indicates what the appletviewer security manager allows. If you need more information on properties, you can find out more in the I/O system chapter.

Each access control list property is started with the *acl* prefix. There are several access control properties such as *acl.read* and *acl.write*. The values of these properties are a colon separated list of directories that can be accessed. For example

```
acl.read=/user/neilb:tmp
```

means that reading files that are stored in the user/neilb and tmp subdirectories, of the directory where the Web browser is installed, will be allowed. The access control properties themselves are set in a file called properties. The properties file is located in a directory called hotjava. This directory can be found in the user's home directory on Unix or in the top level directory of the drive where there the browser is installed on Windows and NT systems.

All of the preceding is true if the applet is loaded over the network. If the applet is loaded from the local file system, these restrictions do not apply.

Handling the Security Manager

If you intend to write an applet that will be used in widely varying circumstances, then you need to know how to recover from security manager violations. When the security manager finds a problem, it throws a **SecurityException**. Therefore, you will need to put the potentially dangerous method into a **try** clause and trap the security exception. Take a look at Listing 12.16. It shows an attempted read on a file. If the security manager does not allow the read, the **SecurityException** can be caught and appropriate action taken. For instance, if the read was to obtain some user preference information, default preferences could be used.

Listing 12.16   Handling Applet Security Violations

```
public void testRead() throws IOException {
    File f = new File(myFile);
    DataInputStream dis;
    if (f.exists()) {
        try {
            dis = new DataInputStream(new BufferedInputStream(
                            new FileInputStream(myFile),128));
            firstLine = "First line is: " + dis.readLine();
        } catch (IOException ioe) {
            System.out.println("testRead: caught IO exception");
        } catch (SecurityException se) {
            System.out.println("testRead: caught security  exception");
        }
    }
}
```

Programming with Your Hands Tied behind Your Back

Phew! As you can see, applets are highly restricted when loaded across a network and running under the browser. About the only things that you can do without concern are use Java's **Language** and **Graphics** classes. To use the other classes, you must understand thoroughly what you want to do.

It might seem to you that the browsers are being excessively restrictive. The answer to that question will only be discovered over time. If we can write all the useful programs that we need to write with the restrictions in place, then the restrictions are worthwhile. It would only take one major applet virus attack to knock the wind out of Java's sails.

However, the browser security policies do leave us with some problems to solve.

Probably the most important problem is how to record user information. For instance, how can we record that user Joe likes the color green for his background to our applet, while user Sally likes the color blue? To do this, we need to record the information in some persistent storage place such as a file. Clearly, we can't write a file via a browser on to the client side, so we will have to do something different.

One common solution that is emerging is to store the information on the server side and provide a mechanism to access the client side information. This topic, though, is not as straightforward as it might seem. We will need to cover some network-related issues to understand how to use the server side. These topics and more are covered in Chapter 21.

Other Security Features

The security manager is not the only security mechanism at work. There are two other security features built into Java: the *applet class loader* and the *verifier*.

The applet class loader is the part of the system that loads an applet. The class loader will ensure that the applet has all the classes that it needs to do its job. The class loader ensures that each applet loaded is maintained in a separate part of the system. It creates what is known as a *name space* to separate the classes loaded by one applet from the classes loaded by another applet. The name space is simply a list of the classes that each applet can access. The name space is private to the applet and is named according to the **codebase** from which the applet came. Therefore, it is not possible for applets to share classes. Each applet must be able, via its **codebase**, to reference any .class files its needs.

The verifier is a checker built into the Java interpreter. The verifier is a sophisticated piece of code that dynamically checks the .class file as the interpreter runs. It ensures that the .class file is properly compiled and does not contain any deliberate attempts to violate the system.

LET'S REVIEW

You now know how to write your own applets. In this chapter, we developed the applet idiom—the starting point of the code for most applets. The applet idiom is an important piece of template code, you will find yourself using it or something like it for most of the applets that you write.

To create an applet you need to:

- Use the applet idiom to construct an applet. According to the applet idiom, your applet will use a separate thread to run so that it doesn't block the browser.
- Use javac to compile the .java file in to a .class file.
- Write HTML code with an **applet** tag to use the .class file.
- Use the appletviewer or a Java-aware browser such as Netscape Navigator to view your applet.

The most important challenge in applet writing, however, is not the applet construction itself. The thorniest problems are to handle the restrictions placed upon applets by the security manager. The security manager restricts some of the fundamental operations that you would expect to be able to do with an applet—operations such as reading and writing files. The security manager does this to prevent applets from becoming dangerous computer viruses.

Java User Interface Tools

CHAPTER 13

Neil Bartlett

You've come this far, and we haven't even shown you the picture lounge! In this chapter, we'll show you how to paint. Soon you'll be painting pictures that you'll be proud of.

So far, we've dealt with the boring internal details of the language and the JDK. That's fine if we are interested in algorithms and the like—but ultimately, you want to impress your friends.

You want the cool stuff. And in today's visually-oriented world, you need to grab hold of your friend's visual cortex and give it a good shake—and then let him tell you what a good time he had.

Without these capabilities, you can bet that Java would not be creating as much noise as it is. The JDK, even in the early stages of its life, provides enough smarts to run animations, play sounds, and interact with the user with all the standard GUI interfaces, such as buttons and menus. Much of this ability is provided by the AWT. As you try the projects yourself, you'll see how it all works, right on your own computer screen.

Maybe Java isn't yet the tool that directly provides us with a William Gibson-style Cyberspace, but it might just be the tool that lets us programmers write it. If you'd like an example of what's possible, go

to the Web and check out Dimension X's Liquid Reality project at http://
www.dnx.com/lr/. You'll see where the future is going.

THE AWT

The AWT ("Another Widget Toolkit") is the part of the JDK that gives life to
our visual imaginings.

The AWT is a set of classes that provides all the building blocks you need to
do the cool stuff. At last count, there were over 50 classes in the AWT. You can
expect that this will be a growth area for the JDK as it evolves over the next
few years. A few rounds in the ring with the code will show you that you can
do plenty with it, but there is still lots of room for improvement. The AWT is
still missing a lot of the functionality you might expect to be present. It is a
curious mixture of high-level and low-level. There are a lot of cool features,
but you often end up writing code that you expect the toolkit to provide. Bear
with it, though: There is still plenty we can do. Sun has acknowledged a lot of
the toolkit's shortcomings and is working hard to improve the situation.

The AWT provides several useful classes:

- A set of control classes with which the user can interact
- Some layout classes to help lay out the controls
- Graphics classes to allow you to draw and paint your world
- Image manipulation classes to let you display and animate images.

The AWT does not do the sound handling for the JDK: that is handled by the
Applet code.

The truly cool thing about the AWT is that, like the rest of the JDK, it is multi-
platform. In other words, it works on all the different operating systems and
machines that Java does. The importance of this ability should not be under-
estimated. It is very hard work to write graphics code that runs on lots of
different platforms. The JDK does all the hard work for you. You only have to
code the graphics interface that you want—the JDK worries about making it
work on all the different machines. A true measure of its success is that you,
the AWT programmer, don't even care which system you are running on: You
just write an AWT program.

This is a tutorial chapter. I want to show you what the graphical part of Java
is all about. This is not an exhaustive-detail type of chapter. I will explain how
the fundamentals work and point out a few of the big features of the land-

scape. You will probably encounter some details along the way that I won't explain just yet. Beyond this chapter are the chapters that explore the various elements to a greater level of detail. At the end of this chapter is a recap of the important core things you must understand to program the AWT. Commit it to memory!

A QUICK TUTORIAL

Let's jump straight in and get something up on the screen. I want to show you a short program to get a window up on the screen.

A separate window, in AWT parlance, is called a **Frame** window. A **Frame** window is a window just like any other on your operating system desktop. It has the same window decoration—borders, minimize, maximize buttons, and so on—that your operating system provides. The AWT **Frame** class is handling the hard stuff for you. Later, we will look at how the AWT does this magic trick.

CREATING A FRAME WINDOW: THE ESSENTIALS

Frame windows are created by deriving from the **Frame** class. Listing 13.1 shows a short class that creates a **Frame** window.

Listing 13.1   Creating a Frame Window

```
import java.awt.*;

class TestFrame extends Frame {

    TestFrame() {
        super("Simple AWT Tutorial Example");
        resize(320, 150);
        show();
    }
}
```

The bare essentials of creating a **Frame** window are:

1. Import the AWT package so that we can use the AWT classes in our program. We have chosen to import all of the AWT facilities here. We could have just imported the **java.awt.Frame** class, but we are preparing ourselves for more graphics stuff to come.

2. Derive a window from the **Frame** class. We have called our derived class TestFrame. Ah, originality!

3. Provide a constructor. The constructor should call the **Frame** constructor with a **String**. The **String** is the title for the window. Here we have used the title "Simple AWT Tutorial Example."

4. Size the window how you want it. We use the **resize** method to do this. It takes the width and the height that you want for the window.

5. Call the **Frame** class's **show** method to make the window visible.

Of course, we need some kind of program to instantiate an object of the **TestFrame** class. Here we will simply write a Java class with a **main** function in it that will instantiate a TestFrame class for us. Listing 13.2 shows the class code.

Listing 13.2 Instantiating a TestFrame Class

```
public class Main {
    public static void main(String args[]) {
    Frame f = new TestFrame();
    }
}
```

The code should be placed in a file called Main.java, compiled, and run using the Java interpreter, as shown in the command lines below:

```
cmd> javac Main.java
cmd> java Main
```

The entire source code for this example is available in the SOURCE\CHAP13 directory on the book's CD-ROM.

Adding a Button

Let's add a button to the window. We will be sticking with the same program we had before and just adding a few extra lines. The source code for this is available in the Chapter 13 directory on the book's CD-ROM. Listing 13.3 demonstrates the technique.

Listing 13.3 Adding a Button

```
class TestFrame extends Frame {

    TestFrame() {
        super("Simple AWT Tutorial Example");
        setLayout( new FlowLayout());
        Button button = new Button("Press Me");
```

```
        add(button);
        resize(320, 150);
        show();
    }

    public boolean action(Event cvt, Object obj) {
        System.out.println("Button was pressed");
        return true;
    }
}
```

Compare the code with what we had before: You will notice that we have added a few new lines of code. There are several steps to follow:

1. **Set the layout.** The **setLayout** call sets the layout manager. The layout manager is an object that will control how things contained in the window are laid out. Here, we have used the **FlowLayout** manager. This layout manager arranges contained objects in lines.

2. **Create a button.** Here we create a button with the label "Press Me."

3. **Add the button to the Window.** Without the add, the button will not be displayed.

4. **Create an action method.** We have added a method called action. The action method will be called when the button is pressed. This method will print the line, "Button was pressed" whenever the button is pressed.

Low-Level Recky

We have done a quick fly-by and seen some of the basics in operation. Now, it's time to go in a little closer and see what is happening under the covers.

We will take what we have done so far and build on it some more. This time, rather than just telling you what we did to get the program to work, we will explore in detail what is happening behind the scenes.

The UI for this next program is very simple. It consists of a single window in which there is a button and a rectangular box. Each time the button is pressed, one thousand randomly placed lines are drawn in random colors into the box. A simple program, but one that will serve well as an introduction to the workings of the AWT.

To run the program, go to the simple1 subdirectory in the Chapter 13 directory of the CD-ROM. Type the following code at the command prompt. (Don't type the "cmd>" command prompt itself, of course.)

```
cmd> java TestFrame
```

The code for this program, shown below in Listing 13.4, can be loaded from the CD-ROM. It's in the file SOURCE\CHAP13\SIMPLE1\MAIN.JAVA.

Listing 13.4   Code for the TestFrame Program

```java
import java.awt.*;
import java.util.*;

class GraphicsCanvas extends Canvas {
    boolean dographics = false;
    private static Random r = new Random();

    void start() {
        dographics = true;
        repaint();
    }

    int rand(int i) {
        return Math.abs(r.nextInt()) % i;
    }

    public void paint(Graphics g) {
        Dimension d = size();
        g.setPaintMode();
    g.setColor(Color.black);
    g.drawRect(0, 0, d.width-1, d.height-1);

        for (int i = 0; dographics && i < 1000; ++i) {
            g.setColor(new Color(rand(256), rand(256), rand(256)));
            g.drawLine(rand(d.width), rand(d.height),
                        rand(d.width), rand(d.height));
        }

        dographics = false;
    }
}

class TestFrame extends Frame {
    GraphicsCanvas g;

    public TestFrame() {

        super("Simple AWT Tutorial Example");
        setLayout( new FlowLayout(FlowLayout.CENTER, 50,20));

        add(new Button("Start"));
        add(g = new GraphicsCanvas());

        resize(320, 150);
        show();
```

```
    }

    public boolean action(Event evt, Object obj) {
        if (evt.target instanceof Button) {
            String label = (String)obj;
            if (label.equals("Start"))
                g.start();
        }
        return true;
    }
}

public class Main {

    public static void main(String args[]) {
        Frame f = new TestFrame();
    }
}
```

GETTING DOWN TO DETAILS

The program consists of three classes: **Main**, **TestFrame** and **GraphicsCanvas**. You're already familiar with **Main** and **TestFrame**. **Main** is exactly the same as before: It just instantiates the **TestFrame** class.

TestFrame has been beefed up a bit. **TestFrame** still sets up the window. This time, though, it creates a button and a **GraphicsCanvas** object and displays them in the window. The action method has been upgraded to provide more features. It is responsible for calling the start method of the **GraphicsCanvas**.

The **GraphicsCanvas** object handles the drawing of the randomly generated lines.

The button and the **GraphicsCanvas** are placed on the window by first constructing the appropriate objects and then adding the objects to the window. The **add** method registers the objects as being for display in the frame window.

The class that is responsible for creating a button is the **Button** class. The constructor we have used here takes a string and uses that string as the label for the button. The **Button** class is one of a variety of user interface components that are provided by the AWT. In subsequent chapters, we will be looking in detail at the other components that are provided and what can be done with them.

The **GraphicsCanvas** is a subclass of the **Canvas** component. **Canvas** is another component, like button, except that the **Canvas** component—rather than displaying a button—provides a blank area of screen real estate into which drawing can be done.

Once the user interface objects have been created and registered with the frame, the frame is resized to an appropriate size and the **Frame**'s **show** method is called to display the entire ensemble. The display occurs by the **TestFrame** object displaying itself then requesting each of its contained objects—in this case the **Button** and the **GraphicsCanvas** objects—to display themselves. In this way the window is drawn first, then the button and the rectangle of the **GraphicsCanvas** are drawn into the window.

It's important to remember is that until the **show** method is called, the **Frame** window is not visible on the screen. All **Frame** objects are initially created as hidden. The show method is what finally makes the **Frame** visible. Prior to a **show**, you can manipulate characteristics of the **Frame** and the user will see none of the changes. For instance, the **resize** method does not cause any resizing that is visible to the user—the resize happens in the hidden state. After the **show**, all changes are visible as they happen. It we resized window after it had been shown, we would see the resize happen before our eyes.

It is possible to rehide a window. You can call the **hide** method to do this.

How Do These Objects Display Themselves?

All user interface graphics objects in the AWT have a method called **paint**, which is responsible for drawing the object of the screen. In the case of the **TestFrame** object, it does not explicitly code a **paint** method so it inherits it from the **Frame** object. The same is true for the **Button**. The button's **paint** method is supplied by the **Button** class. These inherited **paint** methods do the right thing for each of the objects. In the case of the frame, the window is drawn; in the case of the button, the button is drawn.

The fact that most of the displaying is handled for us is useful for us programmers; it means that most of the coding is done: We can just let it do its own thing. We don't really need to know how it all works to display buttons and other user interface objects.

However, the **GraphicsCanvas** is different. We want to code up our own **paint** method so that we can draw some lines into the Graphics **Canvas**. As you can see if you look at the **GraphicsCanvas**, we have created a method called **paint**. It is this **paint** method that is called when the frame's show method asks the **GraphicsCanvas** to display itself. The **paint** method we have written overrides the default **paint** method for **GraphicsCanvas** object that would have been that supplied by the **Canvas** object, the parent of **GraphicsCanvas**.

Mixing Your Own Paints

Let's get back to our example and look at the coding for **GraphicsCanvas**'s **paint** method. As we mentioned the decision to call the **paint** method is not the responsibility of the **GraphicsCanvas**—the **GraphicsCanvas** is told when to do the **paint** by the TestFrame. However, what the **GraphicsCanvas** object decides to do during the **paint** is its responsibility. The **GraphicsCanvas** overrides the **paint** method to implement what it wants to do.

The code for the **paint** method is shown in isolation below:

```
public void paint(Graphics g) {
    Dimension d = size();
    g.setPaintMode();
    g.setColor(Color.black);
    g.drawRect(0, 0, d.width-1, d.height-1);

    for (int i = 0; drawRandomLines && i < 1000; ++i) {
        g.setColor(new Color(rand(256), rand(256), rand(256)));
        g.drawLine(rand(d.width), rand(d.height),
                   rand(d.width), rand(d.height));
    }

    drawRandomLines = false;
}
```

A Key Concept

This ability to mix and match—to choose whether you let the default thing happen or whether you code your own thing—is at the heart of programming the AWT. The **paint** method is just one example of the many member functions that can be overridden to implement what you want to happen.

Much of AWT programming is about learning which classes to subclass and which member functions to code for yourself and which ones to leave be. There are a lot of classes and many more methods in the AWT. We won't be listing them all here. We expect you to be using the API documentation package that is available for the JDK. However, in this and later chapters we will be showing you who the important players are and how it all hangs together.

Doing the Painting

The **paint** method is passed an object of the class **Graphics**. The **Graphics** object is the object that allows us to draw into the screen real estate that the

GraphicsCanvas has been assigned. No, this is not the whole screen. It is not even the whole area of the window. It is just the area that has been given over to the **GraphicsCanvas**.

The **GraphicsCanvas** is an area with the origin of the rectangle as the upper left-hand corner of the rectangle. This origin is called (0, 0). The first value is called the x value and the second value is called the y value. If we take any point on the canvas, we can say that it is at point (x,y). The x value tells us how much across the canvas, the point is; the y values tells us how much down the canvas the point is. A point with positive x and y values would be a point more across to the right and further down the canvas than the top left-hand corner of the canvas.

The size of the area can be found out using the **size** method. The **size** method returns an object of type **Dimension**. The **Dimension** object is nothing much; it is currently coded as a storage area of the width and the height. We can access the width and height by directly accessing its public member variables, width and height. The **Dimension** object is useful because it allows the **size** method to return both the width and the height in one call.

The **setPaintMode** call just forces the **Graphics** area to be in **paint** mode. In other words, any drawing that happens in the **Graphics** area is destructive— it overwrites what is already there. As we will discover later, the **Graphics** system supports a number of different drawing techniques that can be used to support different types of drawing needs such as rubber banding.

Drawing a Border

Consider the lines in the code snippet below. The code lines draw a black rectangle around the border of the **GraphicsCanvas'** allocated area. Without the border we would not be able to differentiate the canvas from the rest of the window. When the **Canvas** is created, it is created by default with the same background color as the rest of the window.

```
g.setColor(Color.black);
g.drawRect(0, 0, d.width-1, d.height-1);
```

To set the drawing color, the **setColor** method is used. This sets the painting color, the color used to draw lines and other graphics shapes. The color is described using the objects of the **Color** class. The **Color** class provides several ways to define colors. We use two here. First of all, we use a predeclared color, in this case black. The documentation for the **Color** class lists all of the predefined colors. The second method we use is to specify the color using RGB (Red-Green-Blue) notation. For this call, we randomly choose colors by passing random numbers into the RGB color constructor.

The **drawRect** draws a rectangle into the graphics area in the current **paint** color. The **drawRect** and **drawLine** methods are two of a number of methods available to draw shapes using the **Graphics** object. When the **Graphics** object receives a request to do some drawing, it draws the object onto the appropriate area of the canvas. We specify the coordinates of the drawing by using the rectangular area we spoke about earlier—the one with its top left as (0,0). The **Graphics** object translates the positions that we give into the appropriate place on the canvas.

Drawing Lines

Once the rectangle has been drawn, the code goes into a **for** loop to try to draw 1,000 randomly placed rectangles on the screen.

We use the **drawLine** method to draw the lines. The **drawLine** method takes a start point and an end point for the line. Each point is given as a x value and a y value. The random positions are chosen so that they will fall in the **Graphics** rectangle. We take the height and the width and we produce random numbers that fall within these numbers, as shown in the code snippet below:

```
for (int i = 0; drawRandomLines && i < 1000; ++i) {
    g.setColor(new Color(rand(256), rand(256), rand(256)));
    g.drawLine(rand(d.width), rand(d.height),
            rand(d.width), rand(d.height));
}
```

Controlling Randomness

All of the randomness is being provided by the method called **rand**, shown at work in the code snippet below. **Rand** is providing the very useful function of returning us a random number that is between 0 and a value we supply. The **rand** method is using an object of the **Random** class to provide it with a random number. It is then restricting this random number to be between 0 and the number we want. We get a lot more into the random class in the chapter on **Graphics**.

```
private static Random r = new Random();

int rand(int i) {
    return Math.abs(r.nextInt()) % i;
}
```

Actually, this program is very useful for proving how good the random number generator is. As you can see when you hit the start button, the **Graphics** rectangle is evenly covered by the random lines. Had there been consistent gaps or holes, it would have been a sure sign that the random number generator was producing poor random numbers.

More on Paint Methods

The **paint** method should always be ready to draw the current state of the graphics window. Generally speaking, you cannot rely on the JDK code to draw the contents of the canvas.

As an interesting example of this, try running the program and using the start button to paint the lines, then cover the screen with another window. When the screen comes back, the lines will not be drawn. In effect, the **GraphicsCanvas** will have been cleared.

The reason for this behavior is that the operating system will clear the window, then it will call the **paint** method to redraw the window. If the **paint** method draws nothing, the window will remain cleared. In this case, we are using a **boolean** variable called drawRandomLines to determine when to draw the random lines. If drawRandomLines is **false**, which it is unless the button has just been pressed, the **paint** method will not redraw the lines.

Note that on some graphics systems, this effect will not be shown: For instance, under the Unix X-Windows system, it is possible to set a value called saveUnder that saves the contents of a window when it is covered by another window. Then, the contents of the window are automatically redrawn by the operating system and the **paint** method will not be called. This behavior is the exception rather than the rule.

The upshot of all this is that the **paint** method should always be ready to paint whatever should be in the canvas area.

Forcing a Repaint

Let's look more closely at the **runTest** method. It's shown in the code snippet below.

```
void runTest() {
   drawRandomLines = true;
   repaint();
}
```

Earlier, I rather glibly said that the decision of when to paint was made by the **Frame**. Well, that is true for the initial paint and most subsequent paints—such as when the frame window is revealed after having been hidden behind another window or when the frame window is repainted after a maximize. However, it is possible to force a paint to happen.

The best way of doing this, and the one that is used here, is to call the **repaint** method. The **repaint** method will eventually cause the **paint** method to be called. Notice that you can't call the **paint** method directly because the **paint** method needs a **Graphics** area object to draw into. One of the jobs of the **repaint** method is to get hold of the **Graphics** area object. When the **paint** is called by the **repaint** in the **runTest** method, the paint will draw the rectangle and all of the random lines since the **runTest** method has set the drawRandomLines to **true**.

How Does the RunTest Method Get Called?

Obviously, pushing the button causes the **GraphicsCanvas runTest** method to get called, but how does it all connect up?

Information about significant happenings is communicated by events. Events are objects that are generated when things happen, such as a button being pressed. Events are sent between components to communicate what has happened. The event objects hold information on exactly what occurred: information such as *what* happened, the *time* it happened, and *which component* it happened to. This information can be extracted from the event by the receiving component.

The exact method of how a component receives a particular event is a relatively complicated mechanism. It is a useful mechanism to understand, but we save the detailed discussion for Chapter 14. The important thing to understand is an object generates an event: The JDK then takes that event and passes it to any other objects it thinks might be interested in the event. If an object is interested in the event, that is, if it has coded a method to handle the event, it takes the event and decides what to do now that it knows the event has occurred.

There are many different types of events. The type of event that a button sends when it is pressed is called an action event. We can write code to wait for a button press by overriding the action method of the button's parent component—in this case the frame window.

A Brief Aside on Parenting

Before we discuss why the parent **Frame** window receives the action event, let's discuss the parent word a little more. This is a potentially confusing word. Parent can mean one of two things in a discussion of this sort. The first use of parent is the one we have used several times in the book so far—the parent class. So in the case of **TestFrame**, its parent class is **Frame**. However, in GUI circles, the parent can also mean the object or window that contains the object. For instance, we can imagine that the **TestFrame** object contains the **Button** and the **GraphicsCanvas** objects—after all, the **TestFrame** window houses both the **Button** and the **GraphicsCanvas** objects.

This double usage of parent can be confusing when discussing stuff with GUI-heads, especially on newsgroups where terse email is the order of the day. However, the context is usually adequate to work out which is which. To do that, you must be familiar enough with the AWT inheritance tree to know which classes are the parent classes of other classes. In Chapter 14, we will present an inheritance tree—learn this and you shouldn't have any problems.

Back to the Action Event

So the button has done the pressing, but the frame window receives the action event. Why does the frame window receive the event? Why doesn't the button receive the event? The answer is that the button could have. We just didn't code an action event for the button. We coded the action event for the TestFrame object because it holds the information about the **GraphicsCanvas** object and we want to call **runTest** against the **GraphicsCanvas** object when the button is pressed. The parent-child relationship between the TestFrame window and the **Button** is strong enough for the JDK to "offer" the event to the TestFrame after the **Button** has rejected processing the event. The **Button** rejected it by not coding an action event, but the TestFrame grabs it with open arms. This is illustrated in the code snippet below.

```
public boolean action(Event evt, Object obj) {
    if (evt.target instanceof Button) {
        String label = (String)obj;
        if (label.equals("Start"))
            g.runTest();
        }
        return true;
    }
}
```

So then, in our example, when the button press occurs, the **TestFrame** action method is called. Action methods can be called for a variety of reasons and by a variety of components, so the first thing that our action method does is to verify that the event was for a **Button**. It does this by looking to see if the target member variable of the event is an instance of the class **Button**. The target member variable stores the object for which the event occurred.

Once the code is sure that a **Button** action event has been received, it decodes the information stored in the event. **Button**s only send "pressed" actions, so the action method is now sure that it is a button-pressed event. However, it does not know which button sent the event. In our program, there was only one button, but the code here is written to support extension to multiple buttons, each button potentially doing different things. The action method decodes the name of the button by examining the **obj** parameter, which is set to the name of the button when the button-pressed event is sent.

Now, the action event knows it has a button-pressed event from a button with the name Start. The code then calls **runTest** against the **GraphicsCanvas** and so, as we discussed earlier, the random lines are drawn.

LAYOUTS

One of the rather elegant mechanisms at work in the AWT is the way objects are laid out on the screen.

Earlier, we mentioned the **setLayout** method, which is called in the constructor of the TestFrame class. The **setLayout** method, shown in the code line below, is at the heart of the layout mechanism.

```
setLayout( new FlowLayout(FlowLayout.CENTER, 50,20));
```

Some components, such as **Frames**, are special types of components in that they can contain other components. They are actually known as "containers." Components are added to a container by calling the container's **add** method. The container stores a list of all the components it contains. The **add** method adds a component to the container's list.

Before the **paint** method is called, the container object lays out the components under its control according to a layout controller. The layout controller is set using the container's **setLayout** method.

The layout controllers are classes such as **FlowLayout** and **BorderLayout**, which will lay out the components in a container according to certain rules.

The **FlowLayout** class, for instance, lays out components in rows. It adds the component in the container one by one on to a row until no more components will fit on the row. Then, it starts another row. The rows themselves are not drawn. The row concept is maintained by the **FlowLayout** object that is controlling the container. The height of the row, for instance, will depend on the height of the tallest component in the row.

Layout controller objects are very flexible. Most come with different options to control their particular formatting. For instance, we have use the **FlowLayout** in its centering mode. This will ensure that the components are evenly centered on the row. We have also set up the minimum sizes for the horizontal and vertical distances between the components. These are set to 50 and 20 respectively.

Layout controllers are an important topic in the AWT. We devote a whole chapter to them later in the book.

The Mystery of the Missing Event Loop

This next section provides some interesting insight into what is going on behind the scenes. If you find that you don't understand much of what is written in this small section here, don't worry too much. It is not essential that you understand this to be able to program the AWT. It is more to draw out some differences for those with a background in UI programming.

If you have ever done any GUI programming under other environments, you might be wondering what has happened to the event loop—or, as it is called under Windows, the "message loop."

Typically, in other GUI environments, there is a function or a **for** loop, which is the last thing in any program. The loop is called the event loop. The event loop is responsible for taking events such as button-press events and transferring them between components.

The event loop is the thing that holds the windows up on the screen. If the event loop were not there, the program would create the windows, put them up on the screen, and then immediately exit. Think about a non-GUI program for a moment. You create some classes, make objects of them, play with them for a while, then exit. When you have finished playing with the objects, the program exits. With a GUI, it is not certain when the play is over—that is controlled by the user. The event loop is the thing that waits for the user to finish. At each event the event loop will test if the "finish" event has been received. As soon as it has, the event loop will terminate and so will the program.

So where is the event loop in the AWT? Let's do a little experiment to find out.

The most natural place for an event loop would seem to be inside of the **show** method. If you carefully examine the program we have written, you will see that the **show** is the last method to be called before the program just sits and waits for the button to be pressed. Based on this, the **show** method would seem a good candidate for having an event loop hidden inside of it.

We are going to put in a couple of debugging statements to see where the event loop is hidden. We will put a couple of **System.out.println** statements one after the **show** method to tell us which parts of the program have been executed. The first will go after the **show** statement, as in the code snippet below:

```
public TestFrame() {
    super("Simple AWT Tutorial Example");
    setLayout( new FlowLayout(FlowLayout.CENTER, 50,20));
    add(new Button("Start"));
    add(g = new GraphicsCanvas());
    resize(320, 150);
    show();

    System.out.println("After the show method"); // Debugging
}
```

The second will go at the end of main just before the program exits, as shown in the code snippet below:

```
public static void main(String args[]) {
    Fame f = new TestFrame();

    System.out.println("About to exit main"); // Debugging
}
```

If you perform this experiment, you will discover the unexpected. Both **System.out.println** method calls happen as soon as the frame window is displayed—and before any buttons are pressed. There is no gap, no waiting for input. In other words, the program exits right out of main. What? Yes, the program exits main. If this were a non-GUI program, this would mean that the program would have stopped running. The event loop is not in the code we have written. It is elsewhere.

What is happening here is that the Java runtime is aware of GUI programs. When windows are created on the screen, the runtime will register this fact and on exit from the main. It will then drop into its equivalent of an event loop. The event loop will then wait, ready to dispatch events. This event loop is actually contained in a separate thread, commonly called the system thread.

So unlike other GUI systems, this system is doing the event loop work for you. Which is handy—it is one less thing to remember to code!

COMPONENT: THE AWT CHIEF

I hope you are getting the idea that there are a number of different user interface elements available with which you can design your user interface. I expect that you will be familiar with most of them well enough. There are menus, buttons, lists, dialogs, and most of the other GUI elements you know and love.

Remember that, earlier, we discussed several member functions of **Frame**, **Button**, and **Canvas**? We looked at the **paint** method, for instance. Each of the components had a **paint** method. The reason, naturally enough, is because they all descend from the same parent class.

Inside the AWT, all of the user interface elements ultimately have the **Component** class as a common parent. The **Component** class is, rather like the **Object** class, the mother of a whole bunch of other classes: in this case, all the UI classes such as **Button** and **Canvas**.

The **Component** class is one of those classes that never gets instantiated directly in a JDK programmer's code. It only ever exists as a parent to one of the familiar classes such as **Button**. Having said this, though, as an AWT programmer, you had better become mighty familiar with the **Component** class. If you take very few "big picture" concepts away from this chapter, the one thing you should get right is this: The **Component** class is *very important*. The **Component** class provides a lot of very useful methods. For instance, the **setLayout**, **show**, and **action** methods are all provided by the **Component** class.

One of the problems is that the **Component** class is a complicated class. It does have a lot of methods that do behind the scenes work. It can be difficult to determine which are the useful methods and which should be left alone. In Chapter 14, we will try to help you out with that question.

Controls, Widgets, and Components

One of the interesting side effects of the JDK being a multiplatform system is that the **Component** class and its descendants tend to get called names. I thought it best before we go any further to mention these names, because I am sure we will be using them from time to time. The **Component** and its concept are variously called "controls" and sometimes "widgets." You will read these terms in Java-related newsgroups and you will probably hear some Java people use them.

They all mean the same thing—they refer to **Components**. GUIs were one of the original beneficiaries of object-oriented coding, so it comes as no surprise that most GUI systems are OOP based. Therefore, they all tend to have groups of **Component**-like objects. Under Windows, these are called controls, while under Unix's Motif/X-Windows, these things are called widgets. Of course, you can tell from the name AWT—"Another Widget Toolkit"—that the JDK code had some origins with Unix programmers.

Containers

Very closely tied to the **Component** concept is the concept of a container. We have seen that a container is a special type of component that can contain other components. It is only the container classes such as **Frame**, **Applet**, and **Panel** that can contain, and hence lay out, other components.

The container classes have a very tight relationship with the **Component** and the **Layout** classes. We will be discussing this relationship much more in Chapter 14.

Graphics, UI, and Browsers

Suppose you want to do some UI work inside a browser. I hope you noticed earlier that the **Frame** class creates itself a new window in which to do its work. This could be rather inconvenient if you wanted to work inside of a window created by a browser. What we need is a container window that can be part of the browser window.

The **Applet** class is just such a thing. The **Applet** class operates in much the same way as the **Frame** class. You can add classes to an object of the **Applet** class and you can set up layouts to control the way that the objects are laid out inside of the applet. However, the applet does not create a separate window. It is an area inside of the browser. Also, because there is no window decoration, the applet classes do not support the concept of a window title.

You can still use **Frame** windows from within applets. However, these **Frame** windows will create separate windows that will be distinct from the browser window.

Another Mystery Unfolds...

Before we finally send our little program back to its maker, let's stick with it a little longer and see if there are any more insights it can provide. One word of warning: This section does contain information related directly to some aspects of the JDK running under Windows NT and even, occasionally, the machine I am running on; the results will not necessarily be the same on your version of the JDK. However, for all that, there is a mystery to be uncovered and solved before we can finally get a handle on how the JDK hangs together and, importantly, how it joins with the operating system to do its job.

The story starts innocently enough. Let's have a look, while we are here, at how well the graphics are performing. With a few simple tweaks we can get some information on the speed of the graphics engine. We can add some simple timing functions to find out precisely how long the graphics operations are taking. Listing 13.5 shows how it works.

Listing 13.5   Timing Graphics Operations

```
long startTime;
long endTime;

void runTest() {
   drawRandomLines = true;
   startTime = System.currentTimeMillis();
   repaint();
   endTime = System.currentTimeMillis();
   printTime();
}

void printTime() {
    System.out.println("Painted in "+(endTime-startTime)+
                                " millisecs");
}
```

Quite simply, we have added some code to record the time before the **repaint** and then record the time after the **repaint**. We then call the printTime method to print a message out to the console telling us how long the repaint took in milliseconds. The sample outputs from my first few presses of the button are shown in the snippet below:

```
cmd>java TestFrame
Painted in 0 millisecs
Painted in 0 millisecs
Painted in 0 millisecs
Painted in 0 millisecs
```

Hey! What gives? The code is registering that zero milliseconds were taken to draw the rectangle and the 1000 random colored lines. This does not correspond to what we are seeing on the screen. The graphics drawing is taking a lot longer. Also, it seems that the printing of the timing message is finishing before the line drawing finishes.

Let's change the code a little and see if we can't find out some more information on this mystery. Listing 13.6 shows how.

Listing 13.6   Better Graphics Timing Code

```
public void paint(Graphics g) {
    Dimension d = size();
    g.setPaintMode();
    g.setColor(Color.black);
    g.drawRect(0, 0, d.width-1, d.height-1);

    startTime = System.currentTimeMillis();
    for (int i = 0; drawRandomLines && i < 1000; ++i) {
        g.setColor(new Color(rand(256), rand(256), rand(256)));
        g.drawLine(rand(d.width), rand(d.height),
                        rand(d.width), rand(d.height)),
    }
    endTime = System.currentTimeMillis();
    printTime();

    drawRandomLines = false;
}
```

Here we have removed the timing stuff from runTest and put it into the **paint** method. We have just wrapped it around the **for** loop so as to concentrate on the timing of the line drawing.

Now, let's rerun the test. Some sample outputs from my humble home-made 486-100 machine running Windows NT 3.5 with an ATI GraphicsWonder are shown in the snippet below. How does your machine compare?

```
cmd>java TestFrame
Painted in 0 millisecs
Painted in 1873 millisecs
Painted in 1612 millisecs
Painted in 1613 millisecs
Painted in 1893 millisecs
Painted in 1592 millisecs
Painted in 1592 millisecs
```

Now that's more like it. Obviously, the first paint which draws no lines, the one before the first start button was pressed, is so fast as to not register on the millisecond scale. The initial test and fail of the **for** loop is obviously just a few instructions—and you would expect this to be rather fast.

After that, we settle into a timing roughly in the 1600-1900 millisecond range. The variation is due to many factors, such as system load. Perhaps the extra loud rock music playing on my CD-ROM was drawing valuable electrical current away from the video card. Who knows, but at least the results are reasonable and seem to correspond to what's happening on the screen.

So what was going on before? Why were we getting zero millisecond results from the first attempt at timing?

Well, the answer lies in how the graphics system works under the covers. It ties in with how the JDK achieves its remarkable multiplatform abilities. I want to take a quick peek at some of the Sun code and show you the culprit. It's in the code snippet below:

```
public void repaint(long tm, int x, int y, int width, int height) {
    ComponentPeer peer = this.peer;
    if ((peer != null) && (width > 0) && (height > 0))
        peer.repaint(tm, x, y, width, height);
    }
}
```

The code is from the Component.java file in the SRC/JAVA/AWT directory from the JDK source code. It is the code that is immediately called by the no-parameter version of **repaint** after it has worked out suitable values for the parameters.

The culprit for the zero millisecond timings is the little thing called a *peer*. The peer, as I explain in the next section, is the thing responsible for implementing the multiplatform stuff for the JDK. To keep performance fast, the peer runs some stuff in a separate thread—the system thread that we spoke about earlier. This means that the call to **repaint** will return pretty well immediately.

Therefore, our mystery is solved. The **repaint** is not doing the **repaint** at all. It is handing the hard work over to the peer. The peer is then running the code, which fires the **paint** method in a separate thread. This seems a bit contrived, so there had better be a good reason that it works the way it does. Before we talk about that reason, I want to make one more refinement in the timing we've been doing. After all, we originally set out to find out about graphics timing, not peers and their ilk.

The question is: Why does it take so long to draw 1000 lines? Is there anything we can do to improve the speed? Well, let's make one small change—we will comment out the line of code that changes the colors—and see what happens. The snippet below shows the effect of the change:

```
cmd>java TestFrame
Painted in 0 millisecs
Painted in 601 millisecs
Painted in 600 millisecs
Painted in 591 millisecs
Painted in 611 millisecs
Painted in 601 millisecs
```

Quite remarkable! The code is drawing lines three times faster—although admittedly only in black. The problem is that my graphics card is slow at changing colors compared to drawing lines. Actually, I should not be hard on my graphics card. This effect is common to most if not all graphics cards. So you are forewarned: If you want graphics performance, be careful with your color management.

Hmm. Did you notice that there was not much variance in the **paint** time this time round? Must be the CD-ROM. There is a quieter track playing at the moment and CD-ROM is probably drawing less current. Okay, let's stop the timing now and get on with looking at peers.

What Are Peers?

This was an area of discussion that I had originally planned to avoid. However, at the inaugural meeting of the Toronto Java Users Group, I changed my mind.

Alex and I attended the meeting in hopes that we could join up with a few friendly Java-heads—and boy, did we get more than we bargained for! The meeting gathered around 90 people, which for a first meeting of a group for a product that had not even been officially released, was an exceptional turnout. Our leader was Rick Yaswinski, a friendly, ear-ringed guy sporting a HotJava T-shirt. He had his work cut out, as 90 people crammed themselves into a space designed for 20 at the most.

During the course of a most enjoyable evening, the question arose: "What's a peer?" A few of the folks had obviously been reading the AWT source code and had come across the word "peer" scattered in the source for **Component** and its child classes.

It was then that I realized the source code does kind of lead you to water but it also stops you from drinking. The explanation of peers is not actually in the code, so to the uninitiated, it is all quite mysterious. A kind of thread left dangling—so to speak. To help put those inquiring minds to rest, here is a high-level explanation of peers.

As a Java programmer, the first thing you should remember about peers is that you need never concern yourself with them. They are underlying technology that helps provide the portability that is so important to Java and the JDK's success.

Having said that, peers do represent good object-oriented practice, so they are a useful study in their own right. Also, if you are intent on porting the JDK to another system, it's essential that you understand them. To find out more, let's first look at why peers exist.

The Java JDK is a portable technology that, among other things, provides a base set of graphics objects with which to develop user interfaces. The idea is that the JDK will eventually run on lots of different machines, under lots of different operating systems.

The trouble with portable technology is that unless you are very careful, you end up with a lot of code that looks like Listing 13.7.

Listing 13.7 "Yikes!" Code

```
if (machineX and operatingSystemY)
   do this
else if (machineX and operatingSystemZ)
  do somethingelse
else if (operatingSystem Y)
  do somethingcompletelydifferent
else if    // ..you get the picture
```

This can be a real headache to maintain. It can also perform slowly. The general solution to this problem is to provide a plug replaceable class or an API (Application Programming Interface) to hide the details of the implementation on any given machine.

Each machine has its own version of the class. The class will do the right thing for that machine. The caller of the replaceable class does not have to change its code. To, say, draw a line, it always calls the **drawLine** method. The replaceable class interprets this for the particular machine. In other words, we hide the specifics behind an interface. Programmers porting the JDK implement code to that interface; users of the JDK are none the wiser. So far, so good. We can hide the specifics behind an interface. However, we are still left with a number of problems.

First off, there's the class itself: As we have discussed, it is very monolithic. The interface to the class is very large—it must encompass all of the possible interactions between the JDK and the operating system. If we decide at some future date that we need to change the class or add to it, we are affecting the whole interface. This could lead to versioning problems. It also makes the class difficult to understand, because there are lots of methods and no grouping beyond the class itself.

Secondly, in the area of graphics, we are often dealing with objects such as buttons, which kind of have two existences. There is the JDK version of the button, the **Button** class, and there is the behind-the-scenes thing, the operating system button. The JDK does not re-invent the wheel. It wants to reuse the local operating system GUI features such as buttons. In this way, it can get the correct look and feel for each machine on which it runs.

This second problem raises the issue of keeping the two buttons in step. If the JDK button is resized, how do we communicate this information to the operating system side, and vice versa if the operating system needs to communicate the button-pressed event to the JDK **Button**?

The answer to all these problems is to use a peer.

Rather than some large monolithic class, peers are small. They don't provide an interface to the whole of the graphics system—only to a small part of it. For instance, the **ButtonPeer** only talks to the part of the operating system that deals with buttons. This makes individual peers easy to understand. It also makes them easier to evolve. Adding new functionality such as a spreadsheet control to the system only requires a new peer to be added. The spreadsheet peer can be distributed to users without affecting the entire system.

For each **Button** object you create in the JDK, a **ButtonPeer** object is created. This peer object will create the operating system button. The peer will also manage the communication of events between the **Button** object and the operating system button. In this way, the peer acts as a go-between. It moves information between the JDK **Button** class and the operating system button. It ensures that they are both in step with each other—that they have the same size and that events are sent between them. The peer also translates the information from the format required by the **Button** to and from the format required by the operating system button.

Actually, I should be careful here: I don't want to imply that there are two visible buttons on the screen. The visible button is the operating system button. The JDK **Button** class just contains information about the settings of the button.

The important thing to understand is that the **Button** class does not know anything about the operating system button and the operating system button knows nothing about the **Button** class. They each only know about the peer. In this way, the **Button** code can remain the same no matter what operating system is plugged in behind the scenes.

There are a lot of peer classes in the AWT. There is a separate source directory SRC/JAVA/AWT/PEERS where the interfaces to the peers are kept. To manage the creation of the peers, the JDK has a special class called the **Toolkit** class. The **Toolkit** class provides access to creating the peers. Even though a **Button** object knows the peer it wants to create, it will use the **Toolkit** object to create a peer for it. This allows the **Toolkit** to control the exact peer that is created and to do subtle stuff like manage the system resources. Remember, though, that the peers are tied up with threads—we saw that earlier with our 0-millisecond paint mystery—and might not be read at the same instant a creation is requested. For this reason, a special method called **addNotify** is used to inform the **Button** object when the **ButtonPeer** object is ready to do duty.

The peer mechanism is a well-known object-oriented technique for dealing with the problems we have discussed. It is variously called a "bridge" or a "handle/body" by O-O authors.

FINALLY

Let's summarize. The approach to writing a GUI is nearly always the same.

1. Decide on the top-level container object that will hold your GUI. This will probably be either an **Applet** or a **Frame**.
2. Decide on the components needed to make your GUI work. We discuss the avilable components in the next chapter, as well as what to do if the component that you want doesn't exist, and we'll show you how to make your own.
3. Decide how you want the components laid out. Remember that if you want to do layout, you will need to place the components that you want laid out inside of a container class.
4. Finally, code the events you want to handle. That includes decoding the exact events with which you want to deal. You will need to understand the event capabilities of each component, and you will need to understand the manipulation methods provided by each component to let you controls its appearance and behavior.

I hope you are starting to get a feel for the AWT now. The essential elements of **Component**, containers, events, and layouts will occur again and again in the chapters that follow. They are the core elements and we will need to look at them from different angles to get a fuller understanding of what they do.

USER INTERFACE COMPONENTS

Neil Bartlett

We've got menus, choice boxes, lists— take your pick! This chapter teaches you how to use them all.

In the last chapter, we almost ran our little test program into the ground. I think we made as much mileage (or "kilometerage," if you live in a country that uses the metric system) as possible out of the code. Now, let's broaden our horizons and look at all the standard user interface (UI) thingies—called *components*—provided by the AWT.

Before I can explain more about the various GUI components we have at our disposal, we will need to understand events. That understanding will enable us to harness the power of the components to do our bidding. Events are central to how the AWT works. So to start off, we are going to take a brief look at events.

Once we have a good handle on events, we will take a guided tour through the AWT user interface components. We will cover each component and take a look at it in action. We get into some typical uses of the components, such as a special text entry for getting user passwords, a form-entry system, and a debug output console. Watch out for these sections; they will prove especially useful as you progress in your Java programming.

Finally, I've put together a sample that shows a lot of the components in action. It's rather like a swatch of cloth from a clothing manufacturer. You can look at it and see what the various UI components can do for you.

THE STORY SO FAR

Last chapter, we discovered the four important food groups of UI programming:

- components
- containers
- events
- layouts

Components are the things with which the user can interact. We place the components on the screen in containers, which lay out the components in useful arrangements by using layout managers. The components communicate user requests to our Java program by using events.

This chapter will cover components, containers, and events in detail. Chapter 16 covers more stuff on events. Chapter 18 is devoted to layouts.

EVENTS

We mentioned events briefly in Chapter 13. We spoke about events being generated when things happen to GUI components. We took a look at how a button generates an event called an *action* event when the button is pressed.

Let's expand this concept a little more and look at what events are. As we said earlier, events are generated when things happen in the GUI. But it's even more fundamental than that. Events are what drive the GUI. Without events, a GUI would just be a lifeless drawing of buttons, menus, and lists. When the user clicked the mouse or entered data from the keyboard, the GUI would not respond.

Events are needed because of the hardware on your computer. The hardware, like the mouse, is operating very slowly compared to the speed of the CPU inside the computer. In the time between double clicks of a mouse, the average CPU could have done a million things—literally. To stop the CPU from having to wait for hardware like the mouse, the CPU does not wait at all. Effectively, it tells the mouse to send it events when it has something to say. Compared with what the CPU can do, there is nothing much happening in a GUI. The CPU is speeding along: As it sees things, mouse clicks and key presses are happening very infrequently.

This discussion has been low-level, but it is fundamental to why a GUI is driven by events. The GUI is written to wait around doing nothing—not consuming any of the computer's precious CPU cycles—until an event comes in. Then, the GUI springs to life and responds as quickly as possible to the event. This event thing is so fundamental that GUI software developers decided to push the concept even harder. They decided that anything that happens inside of a GUI should be controlled by events.

Today, not only do things like mouse clicks generate events, but more abstract things, like a button being pushed, will generate high-level events. Instead of making the GUI software detect the mouse, determine that it was the button that was clicked, process the state of the button, and so on, the GUI code just receives one event that says that the button was pressed. Obviously, the other stuff is still happening somewhere in the code, but the programmer does not have to write the code—it's already done.

As you can see, events are incredibly important to the life of a GUI. Events are like nerve impulses controlling the muscles of the GUI. A mouse press event comes in and the GUI button will move.

To become good AWT programmers, we really need to get a handle on what events we can use to control the life of the GUI. For instance, if you want to decide what happens when a user presses Enter within a text field, you have to know which events to look for. Once you know which events to look for, you will know which methods to override on which class to get the job done.

This, then, is one of the fundamentals of GUI programming. To make anything work that involves getting input from the user, you will need to determine the correct method to override. Table 14.1 shows a list of event methods that can be overridden.

This is not our last word on events. At the end of this chapter, we will be looking more deeply into how event processing works under the hood. And to really fill in the gaps, we even have a whole chapter (Chapter 16) devoted to handling mouse and keyboard events. That all adds up to event coverage to rival the Super Bowl.

Table 14.1 *Roles of Different Event Handlers*

Event Handler	Called When
mouseEnter	The mouse entered the component at the given position
mouseExit	The mouse left the component at the given position
mouseMove	The mouse moved to the given position
mouseDown	The mouse button was pressed
mouseDrag	The mouse was moved with the mouse button down
mouseUp	The mouse button was released
keyDown	A key was pressed
keyUp	A key was released
action	A high-level component specific event was generated. See the component tour later in this chapter for more information.
gotFocus	The component got the keyboard focus
lostFocus	The component lost the keyboard focus
handleEvent	Override this method to implement list and scrollbar event handling and to implement more complex event interactions. See the section on lists and the section on scrollbars toward the end of this chapter. Also see the section on user interaction in Chapter 16.

COMPONENTS

We have finished with events for the moment. Now, let's move along and look at each of the component classes. First of all, we will start at the beginning: with the **Component** class itself.

The Component Class

The **Component** class is the parent class of most of the user interface components. As we will see, menus are a little different. Figure 14.1 shows a diagram of all of the component classes and how they relate.

This means that all of the methods available in the **Component** class are available to each of the component classes. The **Component** class acts as a kind of repository for common methods.

The **Component** class, as we observed in the previous chapter, is a large class with a lot of methods. Last time I counted, there were around 75 public methods available in the component class. That's a *lot* of methods to learn. To

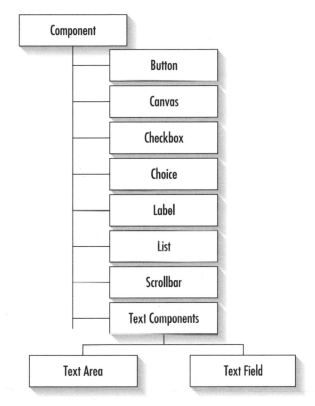

Figure 14.1 *The component hierarchy.*

help you see the wood for the trees, Table 14.2 shows my personal list of the most useful methods. That's not to say that other methods are not useful– merely that I have found that the other methods don't get used nearly as often. I've called it my "top 10" most useful component methods in honor of David Letterman. Why should we honor David Letterman? To be honest, I don't know: Could it be that endearing gap between his front teeth? His boyish Indiana charm? Decide for yourself. The component methods are listed alphabetically, not in order of their importance.

Roll Up For the Magical Component Tour

We are now going to step one-by-one through each of the components provided by the JDK. No need to get any more money out—this guided tour is free with the book. The full list of components on the tour is as follows.

- **Labels:** Labels display text strings. You can use labels to describe parts of your program's interface to the user. For instance, you can use labels

Table 14.2 *Neil's "Top 10" Most Useful Component Methods*

Method	Why and Where Used
getFont	Gets the current font setting for the component. Often used in conjunction with the getFontMetrics method. See the section on fonts in the Chapter 15.
getFontMetrics	Call this method to get a FontMetric object. See the section on fonts in the Chapter 15.
paint	Is the common method to override to implement custom drawing.
repaint	Call this method to force a paint of a component. Commonly used to redraw images and graphics when implementing movement or animation.
resize	Is the most common way of setting the size of a component.
setBackground	Sets the background color of the component.
setFont	Sets the current font for the component.
setForeground	Sets the foreground or graphics drawing color for the component.
show	Sets the essential method to call against a window component such as a Frame to get the window displayed on the screen.
size	Returns the size of the component; especially useful in the paint method to get the size of the available drawing area.

alongside text entry components to describe what type of information the user should enter into the text entry component.

- **Buttons:** Buttons let the user initiate some action. Buttons display text strings that tell the user what action is to be performed.
- **Menus:** Menus also initiate actions. However, menus provide a collection of actions to initiate.
- **Checkboxes:** Checkboxes allow the user to select one or more items from a group of items.
- **TextFields and TextAreas:** TextFields and TextAreas allow the user to enter text information. TextFields will accept one line of text; TextAreas accept multiple lines.
- **Lists:** Like Checkboxes, Lists allow the user to select from a group of items. Lists are generally used instead of Checkboxes when the items will vary or when the number of items is large.
- **Choices:** Choices are yet another variation on the selecting from a group of items theme. Choices are very similar to lists except that the complete list is not always visible.
- **Scrollbars:** Scrollbars allow the user to select a value from a range.
- **Canvas:** Canvases provide an area for drawing.

LABELS

Labels are text that can be placed on the background of the window. Labels are simple to use: You simply construct a label object and add it to the container in which you want to display it. Table 14.3 shows the various constructors for labels.

The user cannot interact with the text: It is for display only. The family, style, and size of the font can be set using the **setFont** method. Listing 14.1 shows the code for the labels shown in Figure 14.2.

Listing 14.1   Creating Some Labels

```
class LabelTest extends Panel {
    LabelTest() {
        setLayout( new GridLayout(4,1) );
        Label l = new Label("Helvetica 12");
        l.setFont(new Font("Helvetica", Font.PLAIN, 12));
        add( l );
        l = new Label("Helvetica 16 Italic");
        l.setFont(new Font("Helvetica", Font.ITALIC, 16));
        add( l );
        l = new Label("Helvetica 16 BOLD");
        l.setFont(new Font("Helvetica", Font.BOLD, 16));
        add( l );
        l = new Label("Helvetica 18");
        l.setFont(new Font("Helvetica", Font.PLAIN, 18));
        add( l );
    }
}
```

Labels also have alignment options. You can align labels to the left, center, or right. The values are:

- Label.LEFT
- Label.CENTER
- Label.RIGHT

Figure 14.3 shows the results of using the label alignment options.

Table 14.3   *Label Constructors*

Constructor	Produces
Label()	blank label
Label(String)	label with the string left-aligned
Label(String, int)	label with the string aligned using the given alignment

Figure 14.2 *Labels.*

Figure 14.3 *Label alignment.*

Don't Confuse Labels with Text Drawing

As we will see in Chapter 15, we can do magic with text drawing. Labels are controlled by the layout manager that manages the container in which the label is placed. Text is drawn onto a component such as a canvas. It is the canvas that is controlled by the layout manager, not the drawn text. Use labels when you want to place text alongside text fields and other UI components.

Roman Numeral Label

Let's design a simple variant of the **Label** class that displays Roman Numerals. We will need this type of label later, when we come to design our own component: a guitar chord component.

Roman Numerals

Okay, get out your slate and lend me your ears. We are going to take a dry subject and make it *really* dry. The topic for today is Roman numerals. You know—those confusing *Ms, Cs* and *Xs* that you see at the end of movie credits. The ones that you must decipher to win the bet over which year a movie was made. Yes, they really do mean something. They are not just random arrangements of characters.

Apart from their unfortunate choice of a metal (lead) for plumbing, the Romans were clever guys. They had a complete system of writing down numbers. The system the Romans employed was to use letters of the alphabet to stand for numerical values. Obviously, this was an early symbolic form of reuse and probably gave the chiselers more practice at getting the perfect V. The Arabic figures that we use today for our number system were still some centuries away from being developed when the Romans had their system. The values corresponding to letters of the alphabet in the Roman system are shown in Table 14.4.

Just in case you think that the Romans seemed to have a rather low limit on the largest numbers to which they could count, let me tell you that there are more numbers in the system. The Romans had single letter values up to one million. The next few in the sequence are rather difficult to type in modern type. They are the symbols V, X, C, and M with a bar over the top. They correspond to the unbarred figures multiplied by 1,000.

So, pray tell, what do we want Roman numerals for? Later in the book, we will be looking at chord diagrams. Yep: They use Roman numerals. Clock faces still employ the numerals on occasion, so a Java written clock, chock full of settings for the user to customize, is bound to provide a Roman numeral sequence. And naturally, since Java is in the business of bringing multimedia through the network, it seems only fitting to put a sequence of Roman numerals at the end of your home page—if only to carry on the obscure practice of the motion picture industry.

Table 14.4   *Values of Roman Numerals*

Letter	Value
I	1
V	5
X	10
L	50
C	100
D	500
M	1000

To save us the effort of always having to convert a number in our system to a Roman numeral, we can develop a simple class to do the conversion for us. I have only coded the conversion of a number in our system to a Roman numeral and not vice versa, since I have not yet had a need for the "vice versa."

First off, we need to understand how the Romans combined their numerals to form numbers. For the most part, you can simply work backwards. For instance, take a string like MCX; looking up the table gives us 1000+100+10 = 1110. So generally, numbers work by having the largest numbers on the left. To write in-between values, letters can be duplicated. MCC is 1000+100+100=1200. Naturally, the Romans used the shortest string, so MD = 1500 is used instead of MCCCCC—which looks more like a rapper with a stutter. (Sorry, Hammer.) The Romans did two other tricky things when they had numbers beginning with 4 and 9. To keep the chisel sequences short, they used IV for 4, IX for 9, XL for 40, XC for 90, and so on. In other words, when a lower symbol is to the left of a higher symbol, subtract the lower from the higher, for example, IV = 5-1.

The **RomanNumeral** class, shown in Listing 14.2, is a translation class. It translates from an **int** to a **String** that contains the sequence of Roman numerals corresponding to the **int**. I have skipped the error checking for underflow and overflow numbers. The methods of the RomanNumeral class will be called by the user when needed. To use the service, the user should not have to perform a **new** to create an instance of a RomanNumeral class. Therefore, I have created the required methods as static.

Listing 14.2 The RomanNumeral Class

```
public class RomanNumeral {

    private static void check( int i[], String s[], int value, String _
valueString) {
        while (i[0] >= value) {
            i[0] -= value;
            s[0] += valueString;
        }
    }

    public static String fromInt(int j) {
        String s[] = new String[1]; s[0] = "";
        int i[] = new int[1]; i[0] = j;

        check(i, s, 1000, "M");
        check(i, s,  900, "CM");
        check(i, s,  500, "D");
        check(i, s,  400, "CD");
```

```
check(i, s,  100, "C");
check(i, s,   90, "XC");
check(i, s,   50, "L");
check(i, s,   40, "XL");
check(i, s,   10, "X");
check(i, s,    9, "IX");
check(i, s,    5, "V");
check(i, s,    4, "IV");
check(i, s,    1, "I");

return s[0];
    }
}
```

I decided upon my algorithm, which is essentially to work sequentially from the high value symbols through to the low value symbols. However, when I came to implement the algorithm, I realized that I was going to end up writing a lot of long series of while statements of the form shown in the code snippet below:

```
while (i >= 1000){
    i -= 1000;
    s += "M";
}

while (i >= 500){
    i -= 500;
    s += "D";
}

while (i >= 100){
    i -= 100;
    s += "C";
}
```

Naturally, a method for factoring this stuff was called for. So I created one called *check*. However, there is a problem. I want my counter, **i**, maintained by the main method, and yet I want *check* to alter the counter. Now, as we know, methods are pass-by-value; for example, methods can't change the value of, say, an **int** that has been passed as an argument. I need pass-by-reference. I want the value to be changed. In Java, we need to fake this. The technique I have used is to pass the **int** (and also the **String**) in an array. The array is passed-by-value. It does not change, but the contents are free to change—so I can alter the contained values.

I would point out that I am not advocating this mechanism as a typical way to program Java code. Where possible, it is preferable to avoid this mechanism. For all that, where it is needed, it can prove a useful technique.

Putting all this together, we get a simple program to generate Roman numerals for given **int**s. Now that we have a way of generating Roman numerals, we are well on our way to developing a Roman numeral label class. All we have to do is extend the **Label** class to do what we need, as shown in the code snippet below:

```
import java.awt.*;

public class RomanNumeralLabel extends Label {
    public RomanNumeralLabel(int i) {
        super (RomanNumeral.fromInt(i));
    }

    public RomanNumeralLabel(int i, int s) {
        super (RomanNumeral.fromInt(i), s);
    }
}
```

We now have a component that we can use in place of the **Label** class whenever we need to display a Roman numeral. To use it, we simply use code similar to the code snippet below. Figure 14.4 shows the results.

```
new RomanNumberLabel(1168);
```

BUTTONS

We saw buttons in the last chapter. They are mouse-sensitive areas of the screen that send an action event when the mouse button is clicked in the area. We use the **Button** class to create a button and we use an action method

Figure 14.4   A RomanNumeralLabel.

Figure 14.5 *Some buttons.*

to intercept the button press. Figure 14.5 shows some buttons. Table 14.5 shows the various constructors for the **Button** class.

The **button pushed** action is the only *action* event generated by the **Button** class. All the events generated for a button are shown in Table 14.6.

The **button pushed** action is decoded using an action method. Typically, this action method is placed in the parent of the button, as we explained in the previous chapter. Listing 14.3 shows an action event that will respond to action events from buttons labeled "OK" and "Cancel."

Listing 14.3   Responding to OK and Cancel

```
public boolean action(Event evt, Object obj) {

    if (evt.target instanceof Button) {
        String label = (String)obj;

        if (label.equals("Cancel")) {
            cancel();
            return true;
        } else if (label.equals("OK")) {
            doSomething();
            return true;
        }
    }
    return false;
}
```

Table 14.5   *Button Constructors*

Constructor	Produces
Button()	blank button
Button(String)	button with the string centered

Table 14.6	Button Events	
Event	**Cause of Event**
Action Event	button pushed
KeyUp/Down	keyboard entry

When we construct the button, we pass in the label that will be displayed on the button. In this case, the buttons would have been constructed with the labels "OK" and "Cancel."

This is not shown in the code. When one of the buttons is pushed, the action event receives the button label. The action event first checks that the event is from a **Button**, then it works out which button was pushed by examining the name of the button.

MENUS

Menus are slightly different from the other components we have seen—they are not descendants of the **Component** class. Instead, they are derived from their own component parent, called **MenuComponent**. Menu support is provided by the **Frame** class. We met the **Frame** class, the class that creates a window, in the last chapter.

Menus are constructed using three classes: the **Menubar** class, the **Menu** class, and the **MenuItem** class. To make a menu, first construct a **Menubar** object. For each menu, construct a **Menu** object and add it to the **Menubar**. To create the items in the **Menu**, construct **MenuItem** objects and add them to the appropriate **Menu**. Then to make the **Menubar** appear, add the **Menubar** to the **Frame** window using the **setMenubar** method. The code to produce a simple menu with a quit entry is shown in Listing 14.4. Figure 14.6 shows the output when the example is run from the command line.

Figure 14.6   A simple menu.

Listing 14.4   A Simple Menu Example

```java
import java.awt.*;

public class SimpleMenu extends Frame {

    public SimpleMenu() {

        super("Simple Menu");
        resize(200, 100);
        makeMenus();

        show();
    }

    private void makeMenus() {
        MenuBar mb = new MenuBar();

        Menu mf = new Menu("File");
        mf.add( new MenuItem("Quit") );

        mb.add(mf);
        setMenuBar(mb);
    }

    public boolean action(Event evt, Object obj) {
        if (evt.target instanceof MenuItem) {
            String label = (String)obj;

            if (label.equals("Quit")) {
                System.exit(0);
                return true;
            }
        }
        return false;
    }

    public static void main(String args[]) {

        new SimpleMenu();
    }
}
```

The **makeMenus** method constructs the **Menubar** and a menu called "File." It adds an entry to the File menu called "Quit." When the Quit item is selected, the action method is called. The action method works in a similar fashion to the button action method. The action method first determines that the action method was indeed for a **MenuItem**; then, it casts the obj parameter—the label of the menu entry—to a label. It compares the label against the "Quit" string and, if there is a match, it calls the **System.exit** method to close down the program.

Table 14.7 *Menu Entries*

Entry	How to Place in Menu	What It Is
MenuItems	Add a MenuItem object to the menu	A Basic menu entry
Separators	Use the addSeparator	A dividing line used to aesthetically partition the menu entries
Checkboxes	Add a CheckboxMenuItem object to the menu	A choice between two states
Secondary Menus	Add a Menu object to the menu	A further menu that pops up when the menu is selected

---

You can put more than a simple menu entry into the menu. In fact, menus allow four types of things to be put into them. Table 14.7 shows each of the four types and the mechanism used to add them to the menu.

Listing 14.5 shows a more complex menu example that uses each of four types of menu entry. Figure 14.7 shows the program running.

Listing 14.5   A More Complex Menu Example

```java
import java.awt.*;

public class BigMenu extends Frame {

    public BigMenu() {
        super("Big Menu");
        resize(200, 100);
        makeMenus();
        show();
    }

    private void makeMenus() {
        MenuBar mb = new MenuBar();

        Menu ml = new Menu("Link");
        ml.add( new MenuItem("One"));
        ml.add( new MenuItem("Two"));

        Menu mf = new Menu("File");
        mf.add( new MenuItem("Open...") );
        mf.add( new MenuItem("Save") );
        mf.add( ml );
        mf.add( new MenuItem("Print") );
        mf.addSeparator();
        mf.add( new CheckboxMenuItem("Autosave"));
        mf.addSeparator();
        mf.add( new MenuItem("Quit") );
```

```java
        Menu mh = new Menu("Help");
        mh.add( new MenuItem("About..."));

        mb.add(mf);
        mb.add(mh);
        mb.setHelpMenu(mh);
        setMenuBar(mb);
    }

    public boolean action(Event evt, Object obj) {
        if (evt.target instanceof MenuItem) {
            String label = (String)obj;

            if (label.equals("Quit"))
                System.exit(0);
            else if (label.equals("One"))
                System.out.println("MenuItem One selected");
            else if (label.equals("Autosave")) {
                CheckboxMenuItem c = (CheckboxMenuItem)evt.target;
                System.out.println("Autosave is "+(c.getState()));
            }
        }
        return true;
    }

    public static void main(String args[]) {
        new BigMenu();
    }
}
```

This example is very similar to the previous example. We are still using the **makeMenus** method to create the menus and the action method to decode the user requests. However, this time the **makeMenus** method creates three different menus: File, which is the first menu on the menubar, Link, which is a secondary menu that pops up when the Link menu item is selected from the File menu, and Help, which is a help menu.

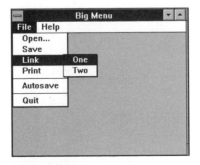

Figure 14.7 *A more complex menu example.*

The File menu contains one of each of the four types of menu entries. It uses the add menu to add three of them: **MenuItems** for menu entries, **Menu** for a secondary menu, and **CheckboxMenuItem** for a choice. The **addSeparator** method is used to add a separator to the menu.

The Help menu is set up much the same as any other menu. The only difference is that the **Menubar**'s **setHelpMenu** method is called to tell the **Menubar** which menu is the Help menu. This is necessary because on some systems, the Help menu is placed in a position separate from the rest of the menu entries.

The action method detects only three of the menu entries: the Quit entry from the File menu, the One entry from the Link menu, and the checkbox Autosave. The others are really just more of the same, so we do not need to show them here. The decoding of the Quit and the One entries are straightforward. We saw how to do this in the previous example. The checkbox is a little different.

Notice that we do not look for an instance of the **CheckboxMenuItem**. This is not necessary, as the **CheckboxMenuItem** class is a descendant of the **MenuItem** class. Once we have determined that the Autosave item has been chosen, we cast the **evt.target** variable to be a **CheckboxMenuItem** object. The **evt.target** item is an instance variable of the event object that tells us which item caused the event. Once we have a **CheckboxMenuItem**, we are free to use it. In this case, we just call the **getState** method to determine what state the **CheckboxMenuItem** is in.

CHECKBOXES AND RADIO BUTTONS

Checkboxes allow the user to select from a number of items. A checkbox consists of a label and an area with which the user can select the item with the mouse. Checkboxes come in two flavors. The first, shown in Figure 14.8, allows the user to select more than one of the items. The second flavor, shown in Figure 14.9, allows only one item to be selected—just like the Highlanders in the "Highlander" movies, "There can be only one." ("One what?"

Figure 14.8   *Checkboxes.*

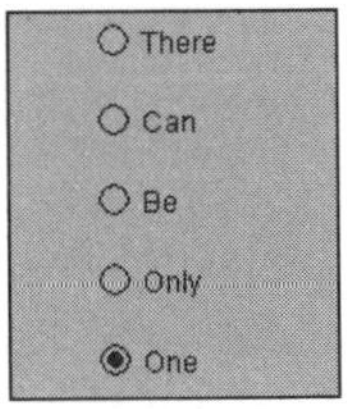

Figure 14.9 *Radio Buttons.*

Never mind. You had to be there.) If another item is selected, the original item is immediately deselected. The JDK itself does not provide a name for this second type, but to distinguish the two, I will refer to the first type as checkboxes and the second type as radio buttons. These are terms commonly employed by other UI programming systems, such as Microsoft Windows.

To create a checkbox, you instantiate a **Checkbox** object using a string. The string will be the label that sits alongside the selection area. The constructors for the **Checkbox** class are shown in Table 14.8.

To collect together checkboxes to, say, form the menu for an online pizza ordering service, you will need to use an appropriate layout manager to arrange the checkboxes in a pleasing fashion. This is no hassle. Generally, the best way to do this is to place the checkboxes in a **Panel** container using the **GridLayout** to control the layout of the checkboxes. In Listing 14.6, we show how to lay out the menu for pizza toppings.

Listing 14.6   Laying Out Groups of Checkboxes

```
class CheckboxTest extends Panel {
    CheckboxTest() {
        setLayout( new GridLayout(4, 1, 10, 10) );
        add ( new Checkbox("Onions") );
        add ( new Checkbox("Peppers") );
        add ( new Checkbox("Anchovies") );
        add ( new Checkbox("Pepperoni") );
    }

    public boolean action(Event evt, Object obj) {

        if (evt.target instanceof Checkbox) {
            Console.Print("Changed "+evt.toString()+ " to "+obj.toString());
            return true;
        }

        return false;
    }
}
```

Table 14.8 *Checkbox Constructors*

Constructor	Produces
Checkbox()	unselected, blank checkbox
Checkbox(String)	unselected checkbox labeled with the string
Checkbox(String, CheckboxGroup, boolean)	checkbox labeled with the string. The checkbox is selected if the boolean is true, unselected otherwise. The CheckboxGroup is used by radio buttons. If the checkbox is not a radio button, use the value null.

Table 14.9 *Checkbox Events*

Event	Cause of Event
KeyUp/Down	Keyboard entry
Action Event	Checkbox state changed

Checkboxes produce action events when they are selected and deselected. **Checkbox** events are shown in Table 14.9. The action event is decoded by checking the event for an instance of **Checkbox**.

The code for radio buttons is very similar, except that an object called a **CheckboxGroup** is used to group the radio buttons together. The **CheckboxGroup** ensures that only one of the checkboxes is selected at any moment. The presence of a **CheckboxGroup** object, as shown in Listing 14.7, also indicates to the checkboxes that they should display themselves in radio button format—assuming that the native operating system distinguishes between them.

Listing 14.7   Using a CheckboxGroup Object

```
class RadioButtonTest extends Panel {

    RadioButtonTest() {
        setLayout( new GridLayout(5, 1, 5, 10) );
        CheckboxGroup g = new CheckboxGroup();
        add ( new Checkbox("There", g, false) );
        add ( new Checkbox("Can", g, false) );
        add ( new Checkbox("Be", g, false) );
        add ( new Checkbox("Only", g, false) );
        add ( new Checkbox("One", g, true) );
    }

    public boolean action(Event evt, Object obj) {

        if (evt.target instanceof Checkbox) {
            Console.Print("Changed "+evt.toString()+ " to "+obj.toString());
```

```
        return true;
    }

    return false;
  }
}
```

TEXTFIELDS AND TEXTAREAS

Text fields and text areas are both used to display and gather text input from the user. There, however, the similarity ends. The two text components are designed for different uses, and one is not merely an extension of the other.

Both **TextField** and **TextArea** are derived from the **TextComponent** class as shown in Figure 14.10. The generic text capabilities available in both are the text manipulation capabilities provided by the **TextComponent**. The shared capabilities are support for selection and an editable switch that allows the text field to be used for display only.

There is also common support for a single action event that is sent whenever the Enter key is pressed when the keyboard focus is in the text component. This can be decoded by using the usual action key mechanism. Important events are shown in Table 14.10.

TextFields

The **TextField** object is useful for entry of a single line of text. The **TextField** supports a variety of constructors that allow control of the size

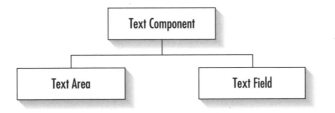

Figure 14.10 *TextComponent hierarchy.*

Table 14.10 *TextField and TextArea Events*

Event	Cause of Event
KeyUp/Down	Keyboard entry
Action	Enter key pressed

Table 14.11   *TextField Constructors*

Constructor	Produces
TextField()	blank TextField
TextField(int)	blank TextField with the given width in characters
TextField(String)	TextField displaying the given string
TextField(String, int)	TextField with the given width in characters displaying the given string

---

of the line of text and the initial contents of the line. The constructors are shown in Table 14.11.

A typical example for the TextField is forms entry. For example, it lets the program respond to a user name or a password entry, as shown in Listing 14.8.

Listing 14.8   Using the TextField Object

```
class TextFieldTest extends TextField {
    TextFieldTest() {
        super("Type here");
    }

    public boolean action(Event evt, Object obj) {
        System.out.println("Changed "+evt.toString());
        return true;
    }

    public boolean keyDown(Event evt, int key) {
        System.out.println(evt.toString());
        return false;
    }

    public boolean keyUp(Event evt, int key) {
        System.out.println(evt.toString());
        return false;
    }
}
```

The action event can be intercepted to determine when the user pressed the Enter key. Here, we do not do any detection of which object produced the action event; we just print an information string. As we have done for other components, we could test for an instance of the **TextField** object.

The keyboard events destined for the text components can be intercepted by overriding the **keyDown** and **keyUp** methods and returning **true**. For instance, suppose that you change the methods given above to be as shown in the following code snippet:

```
public boolean keyDown(Event evt, int key) {
    System.out.println(evt.toString());
    return true;
}

public boolean keyUp(Event evt, int key) {
    System.out.println(evt.toString());
    return true;
}
```

You will see the events being generated in the output console, but the **TextField** will not change. It will act as if it were a non-editable field. We can make use of this behavior to implement text validation fields. For instance, we could implement a numerical entry field by only returning **false** if the key value corresponded to a numerical key, as shown in the following code snippet:

```
public boolean keyDown(Event evt, int key) {
    if (Character.isDigit((char) key))
        return false;
    return true;
}

public boolean keyDown(Event evt, int key) {
    if (Character.isDigit((char) key))
        return false;
    return true;
}
```

Actually, there is slightly more work to do than this; we need to ensure that the text component will also see special keys, such as the Delete key or the navigation keys. Otherwise, the user will not be able to edit what was typed. We cover using the special keys in Chapter 16.

Password Entry Field

Figure 14.11 is a simple extension of the **TextField** to enable a password entry field.

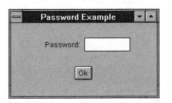

Figure 14.11   A password sample.

The essential ingredient of a password entry field is that it does not display the typed password to the user. It replaces the typed characters with a character such as an asterisk. The problem is that anyone looking over the password typist's shoulder can read the password directly off the screen if the password is not hidden. (This is called "shoulder surfing" a password, if you're interested.)

The **TextField** entry has direct support for this concept. It has a feature called an echo character. If the echo character is set, it is used to replace the characters typed by the user. This is illustrated in Listing 14.9. The test case driver code is shown in Listing 14.10.

Listing 14.9   Setting the Echo Character

```
package extension;
import java.awt.*;

public class PasswordField extends Panel {
    static int cols = 8;
    TextField p;


    public PasswordField() {
        configurePasswordField(cols);
    }

    public PasswordField(int c) {
        configurePasswordField(c);
    }

    void configurePasswordField(int c) {
        add( new Label("Password:"));
        add( p = new TextField("", c));
        p.setEchoCharacter('*');
    }

    public String getPassword() {
        return p.getText();
    }
}
```

Listing 14.10   The Test Case Driver Code

```
import java.awt.*;
import java.util.*;
import extension.*;


public class Password extends Frame {
    PasswordField pt;
```

```
   public Password() {

      super("Password Example");
      setLayout( new FlowLayout(FlowLayout.CENTER, 50,20));

      add(pt = new PasswordField());
      add(new Button("Ok"));

      resize(250, 150);
      show();
   }

  public boolean action(Event evt, Object obj) {
if (evt.target instanceof Button) {
    String label = (String)obj;
    if (label.equals("Ok"))
   System.out.println("Password is "+pt.getPassword());
}
return true;
   }

  public static void main(String args[]) {
Frame f = new Password();
   }
}
```

Form Processing

If you have ever filled in an on-screen computer form, you will probably know that computer forms processing is a remarkably standard entry system. Virtually all form processing systems will move you automatically on to the next field whenever you press Enter or the Tab key, and will allow you to move backward when you press Control+ Enter or Control+Tab. In addition, most dialogs (a type of form) support Tabbing to the next field. Like many things in the computer world, there is a standard for this stuff. The standard generally adopted for user interfaces is that designed by IBM. It's called "Common User Access" (CUA). This type of movement using keys on the keyboard to move between fields in a form is called *keyboard traversal.*

In a strange regression of the forms standard, Web browsers decided to only implement the Enter key shortcut for HTML-based forms. They do not support backward movement. This means that poor typists like myself who constantly make mistakes when filling in forms have to keep switching between the keyboard and the mouse just to fill in a dumb online form. I find filling out HTML-based forms much slower than filling out other forms of computer forms. Hmm-hmm, progress! *Vorsprung Der Technik* ("Progress through Technology"), as they used to say in Audi's television ads.

I suppose the simplest way to fix the problem would be to get better at filling in forms, but I'm a lazy programmer, so I set out to use Java to fix the problem. I wanted to design a text input field that would support moving backwards and forwards between input fields. Actually, I wanted to support moving onto buttons and other user interface components as well. I wanted to be able to use these fields to allow construction of online forms as good as those I find on most computer forms software.

I discovered that, at the moment, this isn't quite possible in Java. However, the code that I got going does have some useful features, so I present my findings here.

My first port of call was to determine which events I could rely on to move me to the next field. Naturally, I wanted to be able to process a keyboard event. Later in this chapter, I will be presenting a tool that will allow you to probe components for the events that they generate. So, to work out what events were generated when the keys were pressed, I got out the trusty event probe and eagerly pressed keys while the focus was on various components. Sadly, the only event I found that was of use to me was the Enter key sending the action event from a **TextField**.

Oh, well, *c'est la guerre*. At least we have an Enter key to work with. On this basis, I decided to put together a little **Form** system that will support movement to the next text field. I decided that I would design it as if the events I wanted to use were there. In this way, when Sun upgrades the capabilities of the components—which I'm sure it will—I will be in a position to capitalize on the change.

The basic idea is to wire up components so that when the Enter key is pressed, the focus will move to the next component. If the Control and the Enter key are both pressed, then the focus moves to the previous component in the sequence. To support the keyboard traversal mechanism, all components that want to take part must support the WireableComponent interface, shown in the code snippet below.

```
import java.awt.Component;

interface WireableComponent {
    public void wireUp(WireableComponent p, WireableComponent n);
    public Component getComponent();
}
```

The WireableComponent interface enforces the wireUp method, which will be used to link any **Component** object that conforms to WireableComponent into the keyboard traversal mechanism. Currently, I have only written up one component—the FormField component—that conforms to the interface. The FormField component is a version of the **TextField** component. Listing 14.11 shows the FormField component.

Listing 14.11   The FormField Component

```java
import java.awt.*;

public class FormField extends TextField implements WireableComponent {

    Component next=null;
    Component previous=null;
    boolean select;

    public FormField(int cols) {
        super("", cols);
    }

    public FormField(int cols, boolean select) {
        this(cols);
        this.select = select;
    }

    public void wireUp(WireableComponent p, WireableComponent n) {
        previous = p != null ? p.getComponent() : null;
        next = n != null ? n.getComponent() : null;
    }

    public Component getComponent() {
        return (Component) this;
    }

    public void setSelect(boolean s) {
        select = s;
    }

    public boolean getSelect() {
        return select;
    }

    public boolean gotFocus(Event e, Object arg) {
        if (select) {
            select(0, getText().length());
        }
        return true;
    }

    public boolean lostFocus(Event e, Object arg) {
        if (select) {
            select(0, 0);
```

```
        }
        return true;
    }

    public boolean handleEvent(Event e) {
        if (MovementHandler.moveField(e, previous, next))
            return true;
        return super.handleEvent(e);
    }
}
```

The wireUp method is supported by storing the previous and next components in the traversal sequence. The getComponent method simply returns this pointer.

The interesting stuff is what happens in the handleEvent method. The handleEvent method will filter all events through a method called moveField, which is supplied by the MovementHandler class.

The MovementHandler class is responsible for detecting the events that trigger the keyboard traversal. It is also responsible for doing the traversal to the next component. This class is shown in Listing 14.12.

Listing 14.12   The MovementHandler Class

```
import java.awt.*;

public class MovementHandler {
    static boolean moveField(Event e, Component p, Component n) {
        if (e.id == Event.KEY_RELEASE && e.key == 10) {
            if (e.controlDown()) {
                if (p != null) {
                    System.out.println("Move to: "+p.toString());
                    p.requestFocus();
                    return true;
                }
            } else if (n != null) {
                System.out.println("Move to: "+n.toString());
                n.requestFocus();
                return true;
            }
        }
        return false;
    }
}
```

The MovementHandler detects whether or not the keyboard traversal key has been pressed. If the key has been pressed, the MovementHandler checks further to see if the control key is down. If the Control key is not down, the

MovementHandler sets the focus to the next component in the traversal; otherwise, it sets the focus to the previous component in the traversal.

The FormField has a couple of extra smarts beyond the mere keyboard traversal mechanism. It can also be set up to automatically select the text in the FormField whenever it receives focus. This feature is implemented by detecting when the focus is gained and lost using the gainFocus and lostFocus event handlers.

The WireableComponent, FormField, and the MovementHandler are all part of a keyboard traversal "toolkit." We now need to implement something that actually uses the toolkit. Here, I have put together a simple questionnaire program. It displays three fields asking for some basic user information. As you can see in Listing 14.13, the code is a tad more complex than the same thing would be in HTML; but then, you *do* get the bonus of keyboard traversal.

Listing 14.13   A Simple Questionnaire Program

```
import java.awt.*;

public class Questionnaire extends Frame {

    public Questionnaire() {

        super("Please Complete Our Survey");

        GridBagLayout gridbag = new GridBagLayout();
        GridBagConstraints c = new GridBagConstraints();
        GridBagConstraints endline = new GridBagConstraints();
        Insets insets = new Insets(0, 0, 10, 10);
        c.insets = insets;
        endline.insets = insets;
        endline.gridwidth = GridBagConstraints.REMAINDER;
        endline.anchor = GridBagConstraints.WEST;

        setLayout(gridbag);

        WireableComponent f[] = new WireableComponent[3];
        Label l = new Label("First Name:");
        gridbag.setConstraints(l, c);
        add(l);
        f[0] = new FormField(10);
        gridbag.setConstraints(f[0].getComponent(), endline);
        add(f[0].getComponent());

        l = new Label("Last Name:");
        gridbag.setConstraints(l, c);
        add(l);
```

```
    f[1] = new FormField(20);
    gridbag.setConstraints(f[1].getComponent(), endline);
    add(f[1].getComponent());

    l = new Label("Age:");
    gridbag.setConstraints(l, c);
    add(l);
    f[2] = new FormField(5);
    gridbag.setConstraints(f[2].getComponent(), endline);
    add(f[2].getComponent());

    f[0].wireUp(null, f[1]);
    f[1].wireUp(f[0], f[2]);
    f[2].wireUp(f[1], null);

    resize(300, 250);
    show();
}

public static void main(String args[]) {
    Frame f = new Questionaire();
}
}
```

The key points are the array that is used to hold the WireableComponent objects and the bank of wireUp methods that join together the WireableComponents in the desired traversal order.

As you will see, there is a lot of stuff you can do with the **GridBagLayout** layout managers. This stuff is used to get the nice questionnaire-style layout of the components. If you want to know more, skip over to Chapter 18.

Figure 14.12 shows the results of running the questionnaire program that can be found in the \SOURCE\CHAP14 directory as the sourcefile Questionaire.java. When you run it; yourself, check out using the Enter and the Control+Enter keys to navigate between the fields.

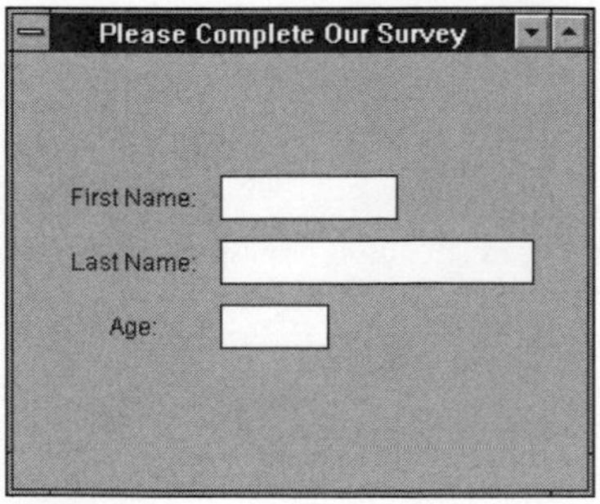

Figure 14.12   A simple questionnaire.

TextAreas

TextFields, as we have seen, are well-suited to accepting short, single lines of data. **TextArea**s, on the other hand, are better suited to the entry of more copious amounts of information. They support multi-line text. Also, **TextArea**s will display scrollbars when there is more text in the **TextArea** than can be displayed in the **TextArea** window.

Table 14.12 shows the **TextArea** constructors. Listing 14.14 shows each of the constructors in use. A screen capture from this program is shown in Figure 14.13.

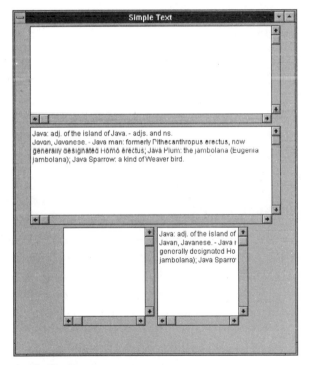

Figure 14.13 *Using the four TextArea constructors.*

Table 14.12 *TextArea Constructors*

Constructor	Produces
TextArea()	blank TextArea
TextArea(int, int)	blank TextArea with the given number of rows and columns
TextArea(String)	TextArea displaying the given string
TextArea(String, int, int)	TextArea with the given number of rows and columns displaying the given string

Listing 14.14   Using the TextArea Object

```
import java.awt.*;

public class SimpleText extends Frame {
    String s="Java: adj. of the island of Java. "+
        "- adjs. and ns.\nJavan, Javanese. - Java man: formerly"+
        " Pithecanthropus erectus, now\ngenerally designated Homo"+
        " erectus; Java Plum: the jambolana (Eugenia\njambolana);"+
        " Java Sparrow: a kind of Weaver bird.";

    public SimpleText() {

        super("Simple Text");
        setLayout( new FlowLayout());
        add( new TextArea());
        add( new TextArea(s));
        add( new TextArea(10, 20));
        add( new TextArea(s, 10, 20));
        resize(500, 600);
        show();
    }

    public static void main(String args[]) {
        new SimpleText();
    }
}
```

Creating a Debugging Console

I often find that, when I am debugging graphics or communications stuff, I would like to see more information about the finer details of what a program is doing. The debugger doesn't help much because, in graphics and communications, timing is a real issue. Setting and breaking on methods will disrupt the timing enough to alter the behavior of the program. The best way of debugging these kinds of programs is to output lines of debugging information using the **System.out.println** method. This is generally better than using the debugger because you are able to see bulk output, rather than breaking on individual methods and examining what is going on. The **System.out.println** has its limitations, though. For one thing, on systems like Windows NT, the console does not scroll backwards—so you cannot view previous output. Also, you can't resize the console window to a useful shape to see a lot of output at once.

I want to take the concept of **System.out.println** a little further and develop the idea of a debugging console–a little thing that can be flipped into a UI to provide on-screen information about what is happening. An example of what I intend is shown in Figure 14.14.

Figure 14.14   Using a message area.

Obviously, we are going to need a **TextArea** to do this kind of work. The **TextArea** will be the output area for the debugging information. This code snippet below shows a good place to begin:

```
public class DebugTextConsole extends TextArea implements ConsoleOutput {
    DebugTextConsole() {
        super("", 5, 60);
        setEditable(false);
    }

    void Print(String s) {
        insertText(s, getText().length());
    }
}
```

The **DebugTextConsole** class extends a **TextArea**. It provides some default size and also provides a **Print** method to put information into the output test area. Code wishing to output information to the window only has to call the **Print** method against the text area and a string will be output to the window.

This is fine, but it does have a number of drawbacks. First of all, code using the DebugTextConsole has to carry around a variable of a valid DebugTextConsole. Second, what if the code wants to switch off debugging and not have a DebugTextConsole at all?

To solve these problems, I've put together a wrapper class called **Console**. Notice that in the DebugTextConsole, we have the **implements ConsoleOutput** statement. Well, the ConsoleOutput interface is the one with the **Print** method in it.

The Console class is responsible for taking a string from the user and passing it out to an object that implements the ConsoleOutput interface. This output object is passed into the object either at Console construction time or dynamically, as necessary, using the **setOutput** method.

The Console class has a few smarts in it such as outputting directly to **System.out**, if there has been no ConsoleOutput object set up. This is shown in Listing 14.15.

Listing 14.15   Extra Smarts in the Console Class

```
package extention;

import java.awt.*;
import java.lang.*;

interface ConsoleOutput {
    void Print(String s);
}

public class Console {
    static ConsoleOutput consoleOutput = null;

    public static synchronized setOutput(ConsoleOutput co) {
        consoleOutput = co;
    }

    public static void synchronized println(String s) {
        if (consoleOuput != null) {
            consoleOutput.Print(s+"\n");
        } else {
            /* DBG */ System.out.println(s);
        }
    }
}
```

To use the Console class, it does not even have to be instantiated. Console.println will produce output using **System.out.println**. Adding in a DebugTextConsole is equally easy:

```
class MainPanel extends Panel {
    MainPanel() {
        DebugTextConsole d = new DebugTextConsole();
        Console(d);
        add(d);
    }

    dosomething() {
        Console.Print("Some useful output");
    }
}
```

I've set up the Console class to be thread-aware. The Console class setOutput and **println** methods are synchronized. This makes them useful for debugging situations such as multiple-thread code.

The Console object has a lot of advantages. For starters, it can be used directly in place of **System.out**. Anywhere you have **System.out.println**, you could just as easily have Console.print. Like **System.out**, Console is static so it can be called any time.

Another good thing is that is can support different output devices. At the moment, we have only written the DebugTextOutput class, but we could easily write, say, a file output class or even a communications output class to support remote debugging of our classes. And better yet, any code using the Console.Print will not need to change to take advantage of this.

This leads to the third advantage; we can dynamically switch the target of the output at runtime. This is shown in the code snippet below:

```
DebugFileOutput fo = new DebugFileOutput("debug.out");
DebugTextOutput to = new DebugTextOutput();

// Output via System.out.println
Console.println("Going graphical");

// switch over to outputting via the text area
Console.setOutput(to);
Console.println("Graphical mode");
Console.println("Dumping copious debug info to a file");

// switch over to file output
Console.setOutput(fo);
Console.println("copious info")l

// switch back to System.out.prinln
Console.setOutput(nill);
```

Console can be imbued with plenty more smarts. The key is, though, to ensure that the end-user classes don't have to know how Console does its work.

LISTS

Where would we be without lists? I'm currently surrounded by scraps of paper with ideas and things to do. Hmmm, I've got one here, "Remember to eat." Sounds like good advice. A typical **List** object is shown in Figure 14.15. It lists selections with a scrollbar that the user can use to scroll through the items.

Figure 14.15 A List.

Table 14.13   List Constructors

Constructor	Produces
List()	empty, single-selection List.
List(int, boolean)	empty List. The given number determines the number of items of the list that will be *visible*. The list allows multiple selections if the boolean is true.

Table 14.13 shows the constructors for the **List** class. There are two types of lists: lists that only allow the user to make one selection from the list of items, and lists that allow more than one selection to be made.

Listing 14.16 shows a simple extension of a **List**. It constructs a single selection **List** object with four items visible on the screen. The **List** itself, however, contains seven items—Richard, Of, York, Gave, Battle, In, Vain—which just happens to be the mnemonic used in English schools to remember the colors of the rainbow. Items are added to a list using the **addItem** method. The list maintains the items in the order in which they are entered: It does not sort the items.

Listing 14.16   A Simple List

```
class ListTest extends List {
    ListTest() {
        super(4, false);
        addItem("Richard");
        addItem("Of");
        addItem("York");
        addItem("Gave");
        addItem("Battle");
        addItem("In");
        addItem("Vain");
    }
}
```

Lists use events to communicate when the user makes a selection. **List** events are shown in Table 14.14.

Table 14.14 *List Events*

Event	Cause of Event
LIST_SELECT	A list entry was selected by the used
LIST_DESELECT	A list entry was deselected
KeyUp/Down	Keyboard entry

Lists have two special events that are used to indicate list changes. These are the LIST_SELECT and the LIST_DESELECT events. When the user selects an item in the list, the LIST_SELECT is sent; when the user deselects an item, the LIST_DESELECT is sent. There are no specific event handlers associated with the list events. You will need to override the **handleEvent** method to intercept the list events. In Listing 14.17, I have done this and I have added my own list event handlers methods in the style of the event handlers such as **mouseDown** and the like.

Listing 14.17   Intercepting List Events

```
class ListTest extends List {
    ListTest() {
        super(4, false);
        addItem("Richard");
        addItem("Of");
        addItem("York");
        addItem("Gave");
        addItem("Battle");
        addItem("In");
        addItem("Vain");
    }

    public boolean handleEvent(Event evt) {
        switch (evt.id) {
            case Event.LIST_SELECT:
                return listSelect(evt, evt.arg);
            case Event.LIST_DESELECT:
                return listDeselect(evt, evt.arg);
        }
        return false;
    }

    public boolean listSelect(Event evt, Object obj) {
        Console.Print(evt.toString());
        return true;
    }

    public boolean listDeselect(Event evt, Object obj) {
        Console.Print(evt.toString());
```

```
        return true;
    }

    public boolean action(Event evt, Object obj) {

        Console.Print("Dbl-Clicked "+evt.toString()+ " to "+obj.toString());
        return true;
    }
}
```

Once you have received a list event, you can examine the list using methods like **getSelectedIndexes** to find out what is the state of the list.

In addition, this is an action event generated when a list item is double clicked. Unfortunately, at the time of this writing, you cannot intercept this action event on the list; it is only available to the parent of the list. You can see this in the PeriodicTable program, which we develop later. When you double click on the list, the top-level window receives an uncaught action event. The **List**, which has an action event handler on it, does not see the action event. Hopefully, by the time you read this, this behavior will have changed so that the list will directly support the action event.

CHOICES

Lists have a counterpart called a **Choice**. A **Choice** is a drop-down combo box. These are fairly common user-interface components available on most systems. In essence, a **Choice** is a list that pops up when the user needs it. There are some differences, though. In particular, the list can be used to support multiple selections, while the choice list will only allow one selection to be made at a time, as shown in Figure 14.16.

Like the **List** box, the **Choice** list uses the **addItem** method to add items to its list. By default, the first item added to the list will be the one that it initially displayed as the current choice. This can be changed using the select mechanism. Choice events are shown in Table 14.15.

Figure 14.16   Using Choice lists.

Table 14.15 *Choice Events*

Event	Cause of Event
KeyUp/Down	Keyboard entry
Action Event	**Choice** changed

Despite the similarity in purpose of choice boxes and lists, they have very different event mechanisms. The choice list supports the action event mechanism. Whenever the choice is changed, the action event is generated. Listing 14.18 shows the techniques involved in using **Choice** lists.

Listing 14.18   Handling Choice Lists

```
class ChoiceTest extends Choice {

    ChoiceTest() {
        addItem("Variety");
        addItem("Is");
        addItem("The");
        addItem("Spice");
        addItem("Of");
        addItem("Life");
    }

    public boolean action(Event evt, Object obj) {

        if (evt.target instanceof Choice) {
            Console.Print("Selected "+evt.toString());
            return true;
        }

        return false;
    }
}
```

SCROLLBARS

Even though some components add scrollbars automatically, scrollbars can also be explicitly created as standalone components, as shown in Figure 14.17.

Scrollbars can be used for a number of purposes. Obviously, they can be used when constructing your own controls, such as writing sophisticated text components. However, they can also be used for implementing sliders and spin controls.

Figure 14.17   A Scrollbar.

Scrollbars maintain the idea of a minimum and maximum value and a current value. The scrollbar allows the user to select a value that is between the minimum and maximum value. The scrollbar can be moved in one of three ways: in line increments, in page increments, and to an absolute position.

Although these names do reflect the most common usage—text line scrolling—the names don't indicate very clearly how the different increment types are used. Essentially, the line increment is a small incremental change in position, the page increment is a more coarse change, and the absolute is a setting to a specific value. The scrollbar class provides methods that can be used to set the values of these increments. Table 14.16 illustrates this.

Like the list events, the scrollbar events do not have their own event handlers. You need to override the **handleEvent** method to receive scrollbar events. I have done this, and again—as I did with list events—I've created methods that mimic the event handler methods such as **mouseDown**. These are demonstrated in Listing 14.19.

Table 14.16   *Scrollbar Events*

Event	Cause of Event
KeyUp/Down	Keyboard entry.
SCROLL_LINE_UP	The scrollbar was scrolled up by the line increment.
SCROLL_LINE_DOWN	The scrollbar was scrolled by down by the line increment.
SCROLL_PAGE_UP	The scrollbar was scrolled up by the page increment.
SCROLL_PAGE_DOWN	The scrollbar was scrolled down by the page increment.
SCROLL_ABSOLUTE	The scrollbar was scrolled to a new position.

Listing 14.19 Using Scrollbar Events

```
class ScrollbarTest extends Scrollbar {
    ScrollbarTest () {
        super(Scrollbar.VERTICAL, 50, 500, 0, 1000);
    }

    public boolean handleEvent(Event evt) {
        switch (evt.id) {
            case Event.SCROLL_LINE_UP:
                return scrollLineUp(evt, evt.arg);
            case Event.SCROLL_LINE_DOWN:
                return scrollLineDown(evt, evt.arg);
            case Event.SCROLL_PAGE_UP:
                return scrollPageUp(evt, evt.arg);
            case Event.SCROLL_PAGE_DOWN:
                return scrollPageDown(evt, evt.arg);
            case Event.SCROLL_ABSOLUTE:
                return scrollAbsolute(evt, evt.arg);

        }
        return false;
    }

    public boolean scrollLineUp(Event evt, Object obj) {
        Console.Print(evt.toString());
        return true;
    }

    public boolean scrollLineDown(Event evt, Object obj) {
        Console.Print(evt.toString());
        return true;
    }

    public boolean scrollPageUp(Event evt, Object obj) {
        Console.Print(evt.toString());
        return true;
    }

    public boolean scrollPageDown(Event evt, Object obj) {
        Console.Print(evt.toString());
        return true;
    }

    public boolean scrollAbsolute(Event evt, Object obj) {
        Console.Print(evt.toString());
        return true;
    }
}
```

 **No Elevator Box?**

If you are having trouble creating **Scrollbars** with elevator boxes on them, make sure that you are not putting the **Scrollbar** into a **FlowLayout** controlled container. **Scrollbars** and **FlowLayouts** have strange encounters on some systems. This causes the scrollbar to appear without an elevator box. I generally try to use a **GridLayout** or a **GridBagLayout** instead. Another technique is shown in the Numerical Value Entry section.

Numerical Value Entry

It is common for the user to be required to enter numbers. Most online forms have some kind of numerical data to gather. The scrollbars provide a useful way of doing this. Listing 14.20 shows a short program that simulates the medical vital signs monitor from a science-fiction setting. The monitor is hooked up to the patient. The doctor has been tinkering—the monitor not only allows us to display the vital signs—it allows us to enter them as well.

Listing 14.20   A Science-Fiction SickBay Applet

```java
import java.awt.*;
import java.applet.*;

class Slider extends Panel {
    Scrollbar slider;
    Label value;

    Slider(int i, int min, int max) {
        setLayout(new GridLayout(1,2));
        add(value = new Label(String.valueOf(i)));
        add(slider = new Scrollbar(Scrollbar.HORIZONTAL,
                        i, 0, min, max));
    }

    public boolean handleEvent(Event evt) {
        if (evt.target.equals(slider)) {
            int i = slider.getValue();
            value.setText(i > slider.getMinimum() ?
                String.valueOf(i) :  "He's dead, Jim");
        }
        return true;
    }

    public Dimension preferredSize() {
        return new Dimension(400, 30);
    }
}
```

```
public class SickBay extends Applet {
    public void init () {
        add( new Slider(10, 1, 100));
        add( new Slider(70, 0, 220));
        add( new Slider(97, 80, 130));
        add( new Slider(201, 200, 1000));
    }
}
```

The SickBay applet is a grid of four vital-signs monitors. Each monitor is a combination of a **Label** and a **Scrollbar**, which are in turn arranged in a **Panel**.

The SickBay applet shows a number of very important **Scrollbar** programming techniques. Trying to size a scrollbar can be like trying to grab hold of an eel. Scrollbars, especially under Windows NT, do not provide enough information to the layout manager and frequently end up being the wrong size. I have fixed that problem in this applet by overriding the **preferredSize** method. This method is used by the layout manager to determine the ideal size of the component it is trying to layout.

Another technique is to use the event handler, **handleEvent**, to intercept any of the **Scrollbar** events. This intercepts all events, determines that the event was indeed for the scrollbar, and then sets the label according to the new value held by the scrollbar.

Figure 14.18 shows the output we would see if we run the applet using the appletviewer and the HTML file, slider.html, which can be found on the disk. The screen capture is of the patient's vital sings monitor. Unfortunately, he has died. But fear not, with a flick of the mouse, we can adjust the offending slider and magically bring him back to life. It *is* science fiction, after all.

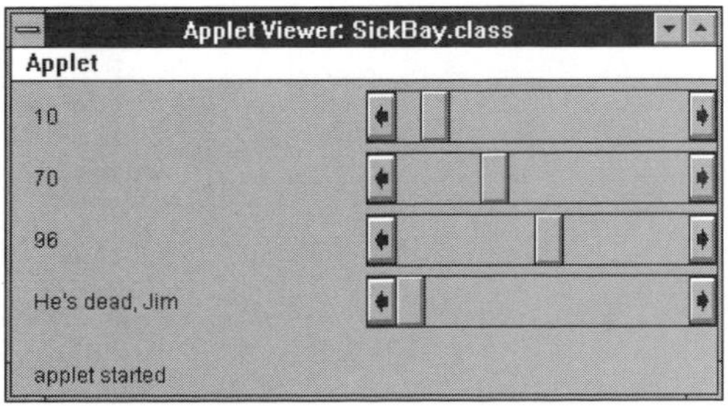

Figure 14.18 *An unlucky patient's demise.*

CANVAS

Canvases are designed for drawing on. Although it is possible to draw on other components and containers such as an **Applet** or a **Panel**, the Canvas' *raison d'etre* is to support drawing. A canvas itself does not do any drawing: It is the **Graphics** object that does the drawing, but the canvas provides a place where drawing can be done—a doodling area.

Listing 14.21 shows a **Canvas** object that will draw a rectangle. We have much more to say about drawing and **Canvas** objects in Chapters 15 and 16.

Listing 14.21 Drawing a Rectangle

```
class GraphicsTest extends Canvas {

    public void paint(Graphics g) {
        Dimension d = size();
        g.setColor(Color.darkGray);
        g.drawRect(0, 0, d.width-1, d.height-1);
    }
}
```

CONTAINERS

Containers are a type of **Component** that can be used as a layout area for other components. There are several container classes provided by the AWT.

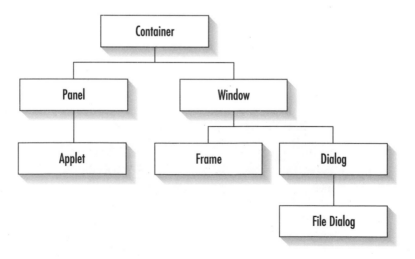

Figure 14.19   Container hierarchy.

They are the **Applet**, the **Frame**, the **Panel**, and the **Dialog**. Figure 14.19 shows how they are related.

In essence, they are all rather similar. They all provide a place to put components and a mechanism for arranging how those components get laid out. The differences among them depend on who they interact with and who created them. For instance, the **Frame** objects are containers that are independent windows, whereas **Applets** are containers that take up space in a browser window, and **Panels** are containers that can be used to provide finer degrees of layout support.

All components support the **add** method. The **add** method is the method that will add components to the container. Once the components have been added to the container, the container will lay out the components, using whichever layout manager has been installed.

APPLET

We have already met the **Applet** class. It is the class that allows us to create a container inside of a browser window. For more information about applets and their programming, see Chapter 12.

FRAME

The **Frame** allows us to create windows on the desktop. **Frame** windows can be created from standalone programs, but they can also be created from within applets.

We have seen a lot of examples of using the **Frame** window to create a window from a standalone program. The basic template for a standalone program with a **Frame** window is shown in Listing 14.22. This produces the window shown in Figure 14.20. With **Frame** windows, we must remember to call the **show** method to ensure that the windows are displayed.

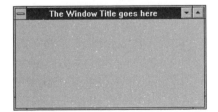

Figure 14.20   Simple window.

Listing 14.22 A Basic Frame Window

```
import java.awt.*;

public class SimpleWindow extends Frame {

    public SimpleWindow() {
        super("The Window Title goes here");
        resize(200, 300);
        show();
    }

    public static void main(String args[]) {
        new SimpleWindow();
    }
}
```

Frame windows can also be created from within applets. This allows us to create independent windows from within browsers. Listing 14.23 shows some code to create a separate, pop-up window.

Listing 14.23 Creating a Pop-Up Window

```
import java.awt.*;
import java.applet.*;

class SeparateWindow extends Frame {
    SeparateWindow(String s) {
        super(s);
        resize(200, 300);
        show();
    }
}

public class AppletWindow extends Applet {

    public void init() {
        new SeparateWindow("This is a separate Window");
    }
}
```

Figure 14.21 shows the window produced when the applet is run using the appletviewer. Notice that the separate window has a banner across the bottom of the window. The appletviewer, and, in fact, all browsers, regard separate windows created by applets as untrustworthy. The reason is that it is possible to create a window that looks like any other window on the desktop. This means that malicious beings can potentially create windows that mimic password entry screens or other sensitive application screens. The banner across the bottom of the window is a safeguard against such a masquerade.

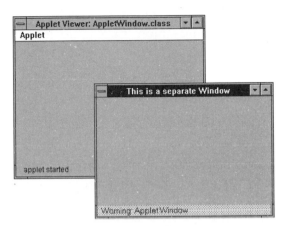

Figure 14.21 *A separate, pop-up window.*

Interchanging the Frame and Applet Classes

In this book's sample programs, we've generally used the **Frame** container class instead of the **Applet** container. The reason has been simply that it's easier to run programs that only use **Frame**; you don't need to mess with creating HTML files, as you would have to with applets. Still, we could have used the **Applet** class as the container wherever we have used the **Frame** class.

To do so, we would not have used the **main** method. We would have derived from **Applet** instead of **Frame**. We would have created a simple HTML file to run the applet, something along the lines of the following code line.

```
<applet code="ExampleApplet.class" width=400 height=300></applet>
```

We would need to run the applet with appletviewer and the HTML file rather than directly using the Java interpreter—java—on the .class file, as shown in the command line below:

```
cmd> appletviewer example.html
```

PANEL

Panels allow us to create complex layout arrangements. The **Panel** is the simplest form of container you can imagine. It provides some space to lay out other components. The **Panel** class is never used as the top-level container in the way that **Frame** and **Applet** are. The **Panel** container is always used as a component inside these other containers.

One of the really neat options is that panels can be nested inside other panels. We can use panels within panels more or less *ad infinitum* to create the layouts we desire. Each panel is free to use its own layout manager. We deal with the topic of layout more completely in Chapter 18.

Nested layouts affect event handling. As we will see at the end of this chapter when we develop the component event probe, the events are not necessarily passed directly to a component. Especially in the case of nested panels, the events are passed around between components.

At this point, just be aware that event handler methods, such as the **handleEvent** method, which we have seen several times in this chapter, should always try to determine if they are really interested in the event. The code for a component that handles the event should always be protected by **if** statements that determine if the event was really meant for the component. We have seen this technique several times: We use the **instanceof** operator or the **equals** method.

The other thing to be aware of is that the event handler methods should return **false** if they did not process the event. If they return **true**, the event will be stopped in its tracks and will not get passed on to other components that might be interested in the event. Event handlers should only return **true** if they have processed the event.

There are some special cases, but we won't deal with them here. However, do take a look at the event probe stuff at the end of this chapter and the JavaEyes application in Chapter 15. These sections show sample code and provide a lot more explanation about this issue.

One point we should talk about is drawing inside **Panel**s. It is perfectly possible to do this. As an example, in Listing 14.24, we have a class called EdgedPanel. This class draws a border around the container; it's useful to help differentiate it from other containers. It is rather like the Group box concept provided by various windowing systems, such as Microsoft Windows.

Listing 14.24   Drawing in a Panel

```
class EdgedPanel extends Panel {

   public void paint(Graphics g) {
   Dimension d = size();
   g.setColor(Color.red);
   g.drawRect(0, 0, d.width-1, d.height-1);
   }
```

```
public Insets insets() {
    return new Insets(10, 10, 10, 10);
}
}
```

Even though I've done it here, I'm not very sure about how appropriate it is to draw into a container class such as **Panel**. The problem is that the drawing might get "lost" in the work of the layout manager. The layout manager might lay out a component contained by the **Panel** large enough to overwrite the drawing. This is a potential problem. In this instance, I have fixed the "problem" by using the **insets** method, which we cover in Chapter 18. The **insets** method provides a border that will not be claimed by the layout manager. Therefore, we can draw our border around the panel, secure in the knowledge that the layout manager will not place a component over our border.

DIALOGS

The AWT provides some support for dialogs. In the AWT sense, dialogs are separate windows that are popped up to collect user input.

File Dialog

Currently, there is only one standard dialog supported. This is the File dialog, which allows the user to select a file name. The JDK implementation allows limited customization of the file dialog. It allows the programmer to set the directory to display and a filter to restrict the files listed in the dialog. To use the File dialog, you will need to instantiate it with a **Frame** window, as shown in Listing 14.25.

Listing 14.25   Using a File Dialog

```
class FileDialogTest extends FileDialog {

    FileDialogTest(Frame parent) {
        super(parent, "Test");
    }

    public boolean handleEvent(Event evt) {
        switch (evt.id) {
            case Event.LOAD_FILE:
                return loadFile(evt, evt.arg);
            case Event.SAVE_FILE:
                return saveFile(evt, evt.arg);
        }
        return false;
    }
```

```
public boolean loadFile(Event evt, Object obj) {
    Console.Print(evt.toString());
    return true;
}

public boolean saveFile(Event evt, Object obj) {
    Console.Print(evt.toString());
    return true;
}
}
```

You can decode the events using the **handleEvent** method. Note, however, that these events do not yet work on all platforms.

Writing Your Own Dialogs

To compensate for the relative lack of standard dialogs, you can write your own dialogs. To create a dialog, simply derive a class from the **Dialog** class. In use, dialogs are very much like **Frame** windows. You use the **show** method to pop up the dialog and you use the **hide** method to pop down the dialog.

A Quit Dialog

A Quit dialog is a simple dialog that asks if the user wants to quit an application. This type of dialog is not particularly useful from within an applet, but it is a very useful addition to a standalone window application. Listing 14.26 shows some code to build a Quit dialog.

Listing 14.26 A Quit Dialog

```
class QuitDialog extends Dialog {

    public QuitDialog(Frame parent) {
        super(parent, "Quit Application?", true);
        setLayout(new GridLayout(1,2));
        add(new Button("Yes"));
        add(new Button("No"));
        resize(200, 75);
        setResizable(true);
    }

    public boolean handleEvent(Event e) {
        if (e.id == Event.WINDOW_DESTROY) {
            hide();
            return true;
        } else {
            return super.handleEvent(e);
        }
    }
```

```
public boolean action(Event e, Object arg) {
    String label = (String)arg;

    if (label.equals("Yes")) {
        System.exit(0);
    } else if (label.equals("No")) {
        hide();
    }
    return true;
}
}
```

The Quit dialog is derived from the **Dialog** class. The dialog has the title "Quit Application?" and it creates two buttons: Yes and No. To pop up the dialog, we will need some code that will construct and show the dialog, such as the code in the code snippet below, where the parent is the **Frame** window. The dialog intercepts the user's response to the Quit by using the action method.

```
QuitDialog qd = new QuitDialog(parent);
qd.show();
```

Most GUI environments support the ability to close a window using a shortcut on the user interface. On the Windows and Motif systems, a control menu available from the top lefthand corner of the window will probably contain a Close choice. The AWT allows you to detect if the user has selected this entry and do clean-up processing. For example, with the Quit dialog, shown in Figure 14.22, we don't want the dialog to be destroyed. We only want the dialog to be hidden. We do this because we don't want to have to create the Quit dialog if it is called again—we want simply to be able to call the show method and have the Quit dialog appear again.

An About Dialog

No windowed application can be considered complete without the ubiquitous About dialog, shown in Figure 14.23. It is generally the place where we

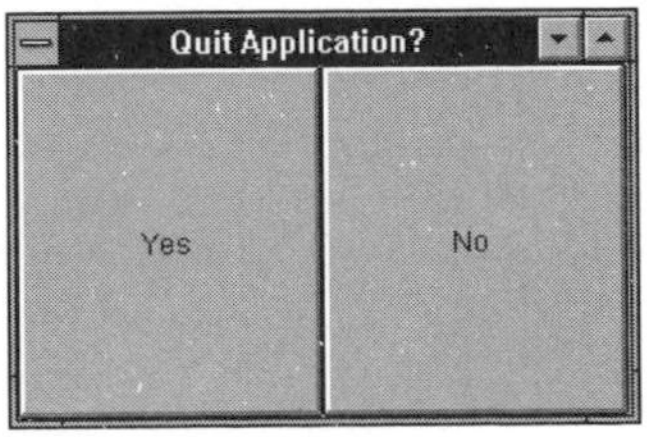

Figure 14.22 *Creating a Quit dialog.*

Figure 14.23   Creating an About dialog.

programmers get to sign our masterpieces: our equivalent of the artist scribbling his/or her name on the corner of a canvas.

The About dialog presented here is a simple affair: a collection of labels arranged in a dialog with an OK button to keep them company. The labels are generated as required. Labels do not seem to support multi-line text, so I generate a sequence of labels. The **String** passed in to the constructor of the About box is the **String** that will be displayed in the About box. I have put in "|" characters to denote where the next label line is to begin. I could just have easily used the newline character **\n**, but I decided to add some variety.

The About box dialog only processes one event—the OK button being pressed. When the OK button is pressed, the action method calls the **hide** method to hide the dialog box.

The **hide** method is the natural opposite of the **show** method. It makes the window, in this case the dialog, invisible. This means that the AboutBox object still exists, so a subsequent **show** call would make the AboutBox visible again. When a window is hidden, methods such as **resize** can still be called against the window. This is shown in Listing 14.27.

Listing 14.27   An "About" Dialog Box

```
class AboutBox extends Dialog {

    public AboutBox(Frame parent, String s) {
        super(parent, "About Box", true);
        StringTokenizer st = new StringTokenizer(s, "|");
        Panel pl = new Panel();
        pl.setLayout( new GridLayout(st.countTokens(), 1) );
        while (st.hasMoreTokens()) {
            pl.add(new Label(st.nextToken(),Label.CENTER));
        }
        add("Center", pl);
        Panel p = new Panel();
        add("South", p);
```

```
        p.add(new Button("OK"));
        resize(200, 175);
        setResizable(true);
    }

    public boolean action(Event e, Object arg) {
        hide();
        return true;
    }
}
```

A PERIODIC TABLE OF ELEMENTS

On the day I was born, a namesake of mine announced the discovery of the first known compounds of the so-called inert gases. In one of those true ironies of life, someone with the name "Neil Bartlett" did indeed discover that the so called "inert" gases, such as Neon, Argon, and Krypton, previously thought to be unreactive, could form compounds. What importance this has to the world, I am not chemist enough to know. To commemorate this rather odd correspondence, I decided to give our tutorial here a flavor of chemistry, as shown in Figure 14.24.

In my namesake's honor, this next tutorial is going to use the metaphor of the periodic table to group together the various UI components that are provided by the JDK. I am not claiming the originality of the idea of collecting together the elements of a UI as a periodic table. I believe that it was Digital Equipment Corp. (DEC) that originally produced the first periodic table of elements

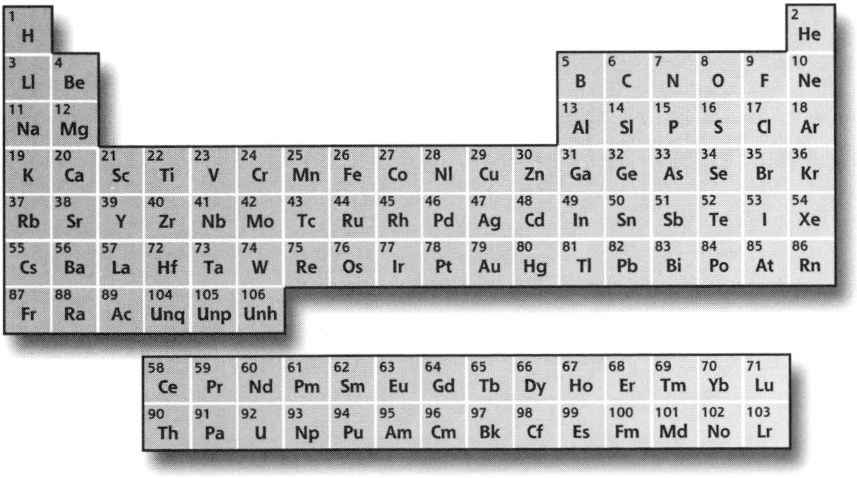

Figure 14.24 *The periodic table.*

for a UI. It did so for its DECwindows product, which, as all you graphics historians will be aware, is the essential technology behind X11/Motif, the windowing system on many Unix machines.

The Periodic Table of Java UI Components, like a periodic table of the chemical elements, is a grid that shows the basic building blocks of the Java UI. Each element of the grid is built using a different primitive UI component. However, unlike the periodic table of chemical elements, there are no implied relationships between elements in the same column.

The periodic table will form the basis of this section. I will walk through creating this program, after which you will have seen most of the graphics elements in the JDK. During the walkthrough, I will describe what the various components are and what they do.

Running the Tutorial Example

I encourage you to run the periodic table program. It is fully interactive and will allow you to play with each of the elements before moving on. There is a message screen at the bottom of the window that collects the output from the various elements as you move around and click on the elements. Those elements that produce output will print stuff in the message area. Also, don't forget to run your mouse pointer over the blank box near the center of the screen. It is an active area.

Most of the programs in this chapter have been written using frame windows rather than applets. As we have noted, and will mention several times in the next few chapters, these examples can be coded as either applets or frame windows. There is no inherent restriction on either.

To run the Periodic Table program, go to the \SOURCE\CHAP14\PT directory and use the following command from the command line:

```
cmd>java PeriodicTable
```

The program, as it stands, is designed for a minimum of 800x600 screen; I assume that most people reading this book would have at least that screen resolution. If you are one of the poor unfortunate souls still stuck with 640x480, you can resize the window. The program will still work, as shown in Figure 14.25, but it will not be as effective.

In case you are wondering, the screen captures for this tutorial were taken from JDK running under Windows NT 3.5.

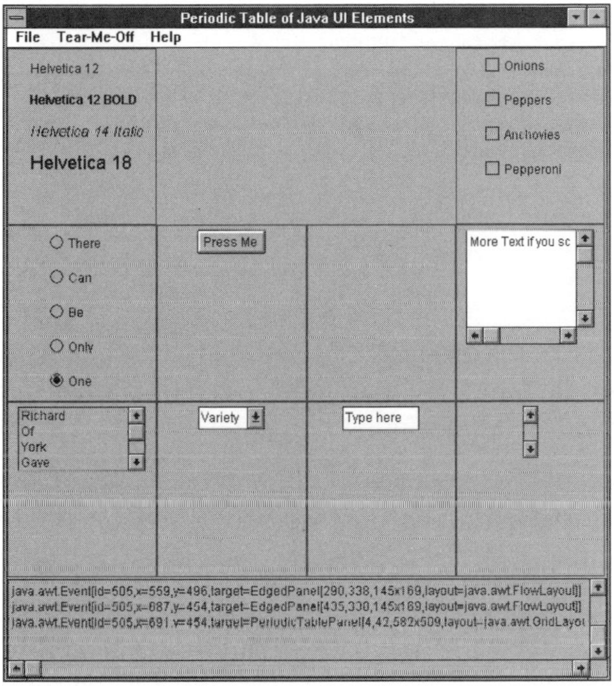

Figure 14.25   *Screen capture of the periodic table.*

The Design of the PeriodicTable

The main source for the PeriodicTable can be found in the file PeriodicTable.java. It is a large file—too big to present here in its entirety. I will describe the interesting points from the source as we proceed in the chapter.

The PeriodicTable is designed as a series of individual tests: one for each component. The table code provides a simple framework for these tests, as well as the window and layout. It also supports a generic output mechanism to which all components can output information. The framework approach is useful because it makes it easy to add more components as the AWT toolkit grows.

Each of the individual samples is provided as a class derived from the component we are adding to the PeriodicTable. For instance, the snippet below shows the code to test the **Button** class:

```
class ButtonTest extends Button {

    ButtonTest() {
        super("Press Me");
    }
```

```
    public boolean action(Event evt, Object obj) {
        if (evt.target instanceof Button) {
            String label = (String)obj;
            if (label.equals("Press Me")) {
                Console.Print("Pressed "+evt.toString());
                return true;
            }
        }
        return false;
    }
}
```

The class sets up a simple example of a button. It also supports the events that the button receives. When the button receives an event, it outputs information to the generic message window using the Console.Print call.

The ButtonTest is generally similar to all of the component samples. I added the word Test to the end of each of the derived classes to distinguish them from the rest of the classes in the PeriodicTable code.

One of the main uses for PeriodicTable.java is as a user interface code template. I have a copy of PeriodicTable.java sitting in an editor buffer. If I need any UI code, I just dip into PeriodicTable.java and pull out something close to what I need. This can be a real timesaver, especially for knocking up test harnesses for code fragments that you need to test in a hurry—just the thing for answering queries on the net. As I find new pieces of code that I need, I frequently code them up and place them in the file.

We can use the Periodic Table to do more. For instance, we can use it as a vehicle to find out more about how event handling works.

Documenting Events

The first problem I encountered with Java events is that the documentation was virtually non-existent. At the time this book was being written, there was no documentation of what to do to receive events when a list element is selected, no documentation of how to intercept the keyboard events as they are sent to a text control, and so on.

The problem in telling you about events is that by the time you get this book into your hot little hands, things are going to change. As I'm writing, the JDK event mechanism is still not perfect; actually I don't think the perfect piece of software has ever been written, but that's another story. I *know* that Java events are going to change because Sun has said so. Sun has admitted several times to frustrated developers on Internet newsgroups that it is actively trying to get things into better shape.

Here is a typical exchange between a developer and Sun, from the Internet newsgroup comp.lang.java:

```
From neilb@the-wire.com Wed Dec 06 12:21:43 1995
Path: psyche.the-
wire.com!fonorola!news1.toronto.fonorola.net!uunet!in2.uu.net!salliemae!newsfeed.internetmci.com!nntp-
hub2.barrnet.net!venus.sun.com!news2me.EBay.Sun.COM!handler.Eng.Sun.COM!news
From: Sami.Shaio@Eng (Sami Shaio)
Newsgroups: comp.lang.java
Subject: Re: Event gobbling?
Date: 30 Nov 1995 12:22:08 -0800
Organization: Sun Microsystems Inc., Palo Alto, CA
Lines: 25
Sender: daemon@handler.Eng.Sun.COM
Approved: mail2news@handler.eng.sun.com
Distribution: world
Message-ID: <199511301906.LAA27965@8183-news.ruffles.Eng.Sun.COM>
NNTP-Posting-Host: handler.eng.sun.com
To: java-interest@java.Eng.Sun.COM, daconta@PrimeNet.Com

This is a bug in the event-handling mechanisms that will be fixed
in the next release.

-sami

|From daconta@PrimeNet.Com Wed Nov 29 17:46:18 1995
|
|Hi fellow Java coders,
|
|Can anyone tell me how to access all the events?
|It seems that certain event types will get "gobbled"
|by a component.  For example, if you have a
|TextArea component in a Frame, it will gobble all
|the Key events.  I tried extending TextArea and
|using and overriding handleEvent() but that did
|no good.
|
|I must not understand the event passing methodology.
|
|All help is appreciated.
|
|- Mike Daconta
-
This message was sent to the java-interest mailing list
Info: send 'help' to java-interest-request@java.sun.com
```

This leaves me with a problem. I want to tell you all about events, but I only have so many to play with. I could skip the whole topic, but then I would leave you with a lifeless GUI. Since Sun has already said what will happen when it works, I could tell you that stuff. The problem then is that what I tell you might be wrong.

To solve these problems, I decided to build a tool. I decided to give you a tool and a little methodology to help you find out about events for yourself. We will develop a tool that will take us right inside the JDK so we can watch its nerve synapses firing and listen to its little electronic heart beating. This tool will do three things for us. First off, it will tell us which events are produced by which GUI occurrences. Second, it will identify for us the objects to which the events are sent. Finally, it will tell us which methods to override to pick up the events and implement our own ideas.

I figured that if I wanted to look at what happened when a button was pressed, I would be able to hook in my tool, click on the button, and it would tell me what method to override to control what happened when the button was pressed. Simple.

So, this tool is kind of a survivors' kit for the AWT. In the turbulent times of the development of a new piece of software, we are all, to a certain extent, testers. A piece of software of this kind will be in a constant state of evolution for some time to come. We are all riders on a wave—we are just hoping the wave is going in the right direction and that we don't hit a rock.

This is the kind of tool you can use again and again to find out what is happening inside the JDK and to verify that the documentation is correct. (What's that? You *believe* what you read in the documentation? Hmmm, I suggest you lie down for a while.) This, then, is the kind of tool that we can apply to any new release and find out useful information.

This section is going to be a journey of discovery. Later, we can categorize the results and you will find tables of events showing what caused the events. This, as we have discussed, is the essential information you will need to control the GUI to develop your own applications.

For instance, suppose we want to construct a drag-and-drop interface—maybe our aim is grand, and we want to develop a GUI interface that will let us drag and drop buttons onto a screen. We choose the buttons from a palette and drag them into position on our user interface. Can we do this with the current AWT? Well, the only way to answer this question is to see what events we can get from the button in the palette. We need to be able to receive an event to know that the button has been picked, and be able to receive events to know where the button is being dragged.

The tool itself will probably need to evolve as the AWT evolves, so I have included some stuff on helping you evolve the design of the tool. You can use this information to keep your tool up-to-date.

DEVELOPING THE EVENT PROBE

I have decided to call my tool the *Event Probe*. I was going to call it the Event Explorer, a name in keeping with the title of this book, but the name Event Probe popped into my mind and it stuck there.

The whole concept of the event probe is to override the methods inside of the JDK that are responsible for passing events around. However, we won't be disrupting the flow—we'll merely be listening in. When an event is received, we will decode the event, print out the interesting information, and then pass on the event just as if we weren't there. It does sound rather subversive, doesn't it? If you are not a subversive type of person, then don't worry: We aren't doing anything to "crack" the code. We are only trying to find information that we should already have.

The design of the event probe requires two steps. First, we need some code that, given an event, can reveal to us all the useful information that the event contains. Without this code, we could intercept all the events we want, but we would never know what they meant. This part of the tool, then, will be the event decoder.

Second, we need to design the code that lets us plug the event decoder in the JDK. It must be placed in the JDK in such as way that it can see all the events, yet still not disrupt the flow of events.

Decoding the Event

The first thing we are going to do is look at decoding an event. As we mentioned before, an event is itself an object that contains all the pertinent information about itself.

The information contained in the event can be found by looking at the JDK's **Event.java** source code. This is the class that is used to create all event objects. Event objects are not subclassed. Given a lot of what we have discussed recently, you might imagine that events are like say, components, in that there is a mother class called **Event** and then a whole bunch of child classes called things like MouseUpEvent and MouseDownEvent. However, this is not the case. There is only one event class, and this is used for *all* events.

To find out what sort of event an event is, we need to look inside of it and find out what information it is carrying inside. The key to what type of event we are dealing with is the **id** variable. The **id** variable is simply an integer that takes one of a set of values listed inside of the **Event** class. Table 14.17 shows the current values the event **id** can take. There is no need to commit this table to heart. It is just given to show you a flavor of what types of events you can expect to see when we go-a-probing inside the JDK. The exact numerical values don't matter to us—what the events mean is the information we are after.

Table 14.17 *Possible Values of the id Variable*

Event Name	Event id Value
ACTION_EVENT	1001
GOT_FOCUS	1004
KEY_ACTION	403
KEY_ACTION_RELEASE	404
KEY_PRESS	401
KEY_RELEASE	402
LIST_DESELECT	702
LIST_SELECT	701
LOAD_FILE	1002
LOST_FOCUS	1005
MOUSE_DOWN	501
MOUSE_DRAG	506
MOUSE_Enter	504
MOUSE_EXIT	505
MOUSE_MOVE	503
MOUSE_UP	503
SAVE_FILE	1003
SCROLL_ABSOLUTE	605
SCROLL_LINE_DOWN	602
SCROLL_LINE_UP	601
SCROLL_PAGE_DOWN	604
SCROLL_PAGE_UP	603
WINDOW_DEICONIFY	204
WINDOW_DESTROY	201
WINDOW_EXPOSE	202
WINDOW_ICONIFY	203
WINDOW_MOVED	205

When decoding events, we first look at the **id** value and convert it into a useful name. After that, we can display more information based on the actual type of the event. For instance, keyboard events will tell us which key was pressed. Our event decoder will need to identify the key and, if it's a special key such as PageUp, it should return its name. Also, the decoder should work out which modifier keys (for example, the control key) were being pressed at the same time as the main key. The code for the event probe is shown in Listing 14.28.

Listing 14.28 The EventProbe Class

```
package extension;
import java.awt.*;

public class EventProbe {

    public static void classifyEvent(String s, Event evt) {
        int i = evt.hashCode();
        Console.println("["+i+"]"+s+" "+classifyId(evt) +
                "-> "+evt.target.toString());
    }

    public static
    void classifyEvent(String s, Event evt, boolean b) {
        int i = evt.hashCode();
        Console.println("["+i+"]"+s+"->"+b+" "+classifyId(evt) +
                "-> "+evt.target.toString());
    }

    static String keyName(Event evt) {
        switch (evt.key) {
            case Event.HOME: return("HOME");
            case Event.END:  return("END");
            case Event.PGUP: return("PGUP");
            case Event.PGDN: return("PGDN");
            case Event.UP:   return("UP");
            case Event.DOWN: return("DOWN");
            case Event.LEFT: return("LEFT");
            case Event.RIGHT: return("RIGHT");
            case Event.F1: return("F1");
            case Event.F2: return("F2");
            case Event.F3: return("F3");
            case Event.F4: return("F4");
            case Event.F5: return("F5");
            case Event.F6: return("F6");
            case Event.F7: return("F7");
            case Event.F8: return("F8");
            case Event.F9: return("F9");
            case Event.F10: return("F10");
            case Event.F11: return("F11");
            case Event.F12: return("F12");
```

```
        }
        return(""+evt.key);
    }

    static String classifyKey(Event evt) {
        if (evt.key == 0)
            return ("");
        String str = new String();

        // classify the modifiers
        if (evt.shiftDown())   str += "shift+";
        if (evt.controlDown()) str += "control+";
        if (evt.metaDown())    str += "meta+";
        if ((evt.modifiers & Event.CTRL_MASK) != 0)  str += "alt+";

        return str;
    }

    static String classifyId(Event evt) {
        switch (evt.id) {
            case Event.GOT_FOCUS: return("GOT_FOCUS");
            case Event.LOST_FOCUS: return("LOST_FOCUS");
            case Event.KEY_ACTION: return("KEY_ACTION");
            case Event.KEY_ACTION_RELEASE:
                                return("KEY_ACTION_RELEASE");
            case Event.KEY_PRESS: return("KEY_PRESS");
            case Event.KEY_RELEASE: return("KEY_RELEASE");
            case Event.MOUSE_DOWN: return("MOUSE_DOWN");
            case Event.MOUSE_DRAG: return("MOUSE_DRAG");
            case Event.MOUSE_Enter: return("MOUSE_Enter");
            case Event.MOUSE_EXIT: return("MOUSE_EXIT");
            case Event.MOUSE_MOVE: return("MOUSE_MOVE");
            case Event.MOUSE_UP: return("MOUSE_UP");
            case Event.WINDOW_DESTROY: return("WINDOW_DESTROY");
            case Event.WINDOW_EXPOSE: return("WINDOW_EXPOSE");
            case Event.WINDOW_ICONIFY: return("WINDOW_ICONIFY");
            case Event.WINDOW_DEICONIFY:
                                return("WINDOW_DEICONIFY");
            case Event.WINDOW_MOVED: return("WINDOW_MOVED");
            case Event.SCROLL_LINE_UP: return("SCROLL_LINE_UP");
            case Event.SCROLL_LINE_DOWN:
                                return("SCROLL_LINE_DOWN");
            case Event.SCROLL_PAGE_UP: return("SCROLL_PAGE_UP");
            case Event.SCROLL_PAGE_DOWN:
                                return("SCROLL_PAGE_DOWN");
            case Event.SCROLL_ABSOLUTE: return("SCROLL_ABSOLUTE");
            case Event.LIST_SELECT: return("LIST_SELECT");
            case Event.LIST_DESELECT: return("LIST_DESELECT");
            case Event.ACTION_EVENT: return("ACTION_EVENT");
            case Event.LOAD_FILE: return("LOAD_FILE");
            case Event.SAVE_FILE: return("SAVE_FILE");
        }
        return ("UNKNOWN");
    }
}
```

The basis of the event probe is that all visible JDK event processing methods are *instrumented.* Instrumented means that we have included debug code to print out information we desire.

I have gone through the AWT and established the event processing methods. Where possible, I wrapped up these methods with instrumenting code—typically, this is the only possible way we can override the method.

Applying the Probe

Now that we have our event decoder, how are we going to fit it into event flow in the JDK?

Unfortunately, unlike the situation with a real-world electronic counterpart, we can't just point the probe at a component and have it give up its vital information. Rather, we need to unsolder the component and solder in our probe. This is unfortunate, but necessary.

Our approach will be more akin to measuring current flow in a circuit, which you're familiar with if you remember your school electronics. You *did* do electronics at school, I hope—if you didn't, you missed all the fun! There is a difference between measuring voltage and current. To measure voltage, you can touch your meter probes on any two points of a circuit, and you get your reading. To measure current, though, you have to break the circuit and put your meter to the circuit as a substitute for the wire you have just broken; you basically need to count the number of electrons flowing through the meter in a certain time.

So, we are going to be using our probe like a current meter. We are going to unhook part of the JDK event processing mechanism and hook our probe into the middle. How do we insert this probe? Well, there is a lot of hard work ahead, but don't worry: It's all been done for you. You can just read the files on the book's CD-ROM to get your hands on the code.

We have to develop probe-compatible versions of each of the GUI components. In Listing 14.29, I've printed out the probe version for the **Checkbox** component. I decided to prefix all of the probe versions with "EP"—for "Event Probe," naturally. This will give us a consistent naming convention, so that when we read code, we know which events are being probed. Also, I have put all the probe code into the extension package. This means that if you ever need to probe your own code, you will only need to prefix the names of the components you are using and you will have an event probe version of your own code.

Listing 14.29   The EPCheckbox Class

```
package extension;
import java.awt.*;

public class EPCheckbox extends Checkbox {

    public EPCheckbox(String s, CheckboxGroup g, boolean b) {
        super(s, g, b);
    }

    public EPCheckbox(String s) {
        super(s);
    }

    public void deliverEvent(Event e) {
        EventProbe.classifyEvent("deliverEvent", e);
        super.deliverEvent(e);
    }

    public boolean postEvent(Event e) {
        EventProbe.classifyEvent("postEvent", e);
        return super.postEvent(e);
    }

    public boolean handleEvent(Event e) {
        boolean ret;
        EventProbe.classifyEvent("handleEvent", e, ret = super.handleEvent(e));
        return ret;
    }
}
```

So what is all this stuff ? It certainly looks like a lot of code. You would kind of expect there to be one single line of code you could intercept and everything would be okay!

Before we get to a detailed discussion of how event passing works, I want to give you a high-level picture. First, there is an incoming event, and the idea is to find the component that wants to process this event. This means that the component will have an event handler for that event and that event handler will return **true**. An event handler? Yes, that's another way of referring to the method that processes the event. Once the component is found and the handler returns **true**, the process stops. The event has been processed.

The trick is to find the component that wants to process the event. This is where the fun begins. Figure 14.26 can help you find it.

Take a look at the diagram. It shows how events are propagated. Now you will need to bear with this for a moment. There are four layers to this event

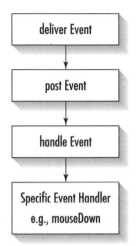

Figure 14.26 *The event method call sequence.*

propagation process: deliverEvent, postEvent, handleEvent, and the specific event method. It is quite detailed.

The deliverEvent passes an event to the postEvent, which hands it to the handleEvent method. Finally, the handleEvent method calls a specific method such as **mouseUp**. This final method processes the actual event.

Why do we use such as complicated mechanism? Why not just do a handle event—or even better, why not do a **mouseUp** straight away? Well, basically, it's for flexibility. The AWT developers want to retain the ability to let you change processing of each of these stages without affecting the others. Each method does a slightly different part of the processing.

First off, let's look at deliverEvent. This is responsible for finding the component for which the event is destined. Imagine that a mouse click occurs in a **Panel**. Now, the panel is a container. It can contain other objects. The panel needs to find out if the position of the click was in any of the components inside of it. It uses the deliverEvent method to burrow down to the next level of components. It uses the position of the event to do this. Look at the diagram. It shows a **Canvas** inside of a **Panel**. The deliverEvent burrows down to the **Canvas** component. It then calls the deliverEvent for the **Canvas**.

On the other hand, the deliverEvent of a *non*-container is very simple. It just calls postEvent. The postEvent method, in turn, will call handleEvent. HandleEvent decodes which specific method to call—for instance, the **mouseUp** function.

So why the postEvent? Well, postEvent is used to work back upwards if the handleEvent does not find a handler in this component. The process works the same was as when deliverEvent works in toward a more specific component. postEvent works outwards toward the outer window component. This is how we got the effect in the previous chapter of the button pressed action arriving at the **Frame** window. The button pressed event was first delivered to the button. The button did not want the event—its event hander returned **false**— so it used the postEvent to hand it back up to the parent—the TestFrame object.

Well, this has all been very involved. What do you really need to take away from this discussion? You don't need to understand all of it. You only need to understand that an event is processed by finding the component that wants to process the event. Once the component is found and the event method returns **true**, the event is processed and the GUI waits for another event to happen.

From this, we can understand how we can write code to process our events. First of all, we decide which component should process the event. Then, we write a handler for that component that returns **true**. This is simple enough.

The one problem we might encounter is if there are lots of event handlers. If, for instance, in our TestFrame and button example, the button and the frame both had an action event handler, we would need to ensure that the button did not absorb the event, for example, return **true**, before the frame action method got a chance to see it.

Our Own Probe Test Bed

Okay, our event probe is ready. We have an event decoder, we have created components that will transparently let the decoder see the events, and we have discussed how the events are passed around the system. We now know all we need to know about events. We are ready to plug in our probe and see what we see.

Since we don't really want to go a-fiddling with the our precious JDK source, we need a vehicle for doing our tests. We need our equivalent of the electronic circuit. Well, lordy, we just happen to have the PeriodicTable—that will do just fine.

The PeriodicTable is designed to present all of the components in the AWT, so building in the probe should enable us always to have a tool available that shows us which components are delivering which events. The event probe enhanced version of the periodic table can be found in the directory /SOURCE/ CHAP14/PTEV.

Running the Probe

Now that we've hooked up the probe, let's turn on the circuit and observe what happens.

The first time I did this, I had only coded up probe versions of a few of the components. I had done the likes of EPButton and EPCheckbox. As I moved around clicking buttons and typing and moving the mouse over the components, I felt like a SETI (Search for Extra Terrestrial Intelligence) observer looking through the starfields with my telescope on a hunt for little green people. (All right, all right, little *gray* people, for all you UFO purists.) It's so quiet out there. I was getting virtually no events back.

Then I added in the EPPanel stuff by hooking it into the EdgedPanel, as shown in the code snippet below.

```
class EdgedPanel extends EPPanel {

    public void paint(Graphics g) {
        Dimension d = size();
        g.setColor(Color.red);
        g.drawRect(0, 0, d.width-1, d.height-1);
    }
}
```

Suddenly, there was a plethora of events produced every time the mouse was moved. Obviously, the **Panel** supports the **mouseMove** event.

As more components start to support events such as the mouse and keyboard events, the event probe mechanism will start to produce more and more events. When full event support is in place, you will probably need to start filtering events to get an accurate picture of what is happening!

Keeping the Event Probe Up to Date

As I said earlier, things will change. The version of event processing I have described today is an internal concept of the AWT. It is an important concept to understand, but it is not one cast in stone. It is most likely subject to change. For instance, it is quite likely that the deliverEvent method might not be used. This would make things more efficient. The event would be delivered straight to the component's postEvent. In other words, the event mechanism shown here will not always be true.

To keep the event probe up-to-date, you will need to reverse engineer the event hierarchy to reconstruct the probe. The simplest way to do this is to start with the lowest level and work backwards. For instance, Sun recommends using the explicit mouse events **mouseUp**, **mouseDown**, and so forth when doing work based on events. So go into the code and work backwards—searching for the calls to these. They are currently all contained inside of the **Component** class. My personal feeling is that the event processing handling will always remain in the **Component** class. I base this on the fact that event handling is one of the main support tasks provided by the **Component** class, but I could be wrong.

As you skip back up the event processing method chain, you will need to write up appropriate probes. Use the current probe as a guide.

In this fashion, you should always be able to have at your fingertips a tool that will probe the event process. Eventually—hopefully soon—a list of which components produce which events will be given out by Sun. Until then, happy probing!

LET'S REVIEW

This has been a long chapter. We need to recap and see what we have learned.

In this chapter, we have taken a good look at the user interface facilities provided by Java. All user interaction takes place via user interface objects called components. We have seen that, to control components, we must override the component's event handlers. The event handlers are methods that are called in response to events. Events are the fundamental life force of the user interface system. Every user interaction will cause an event. Once we control the events, we can control how the programs we write react to the user input.

We have taken a complete tour of the user interface components. We stopped at each component and looked at the events to which it responds. We also looked at some useful code to see how we might use each component in practice.

Chapter 15

GRAPHICS: LEARNING TO SEW WITH SEQUINS

Neil Bartlett

You've already learned how to paint. Now, you learn about drawing, colors, text, and fonts.

This chapter is all about drawing. That means that it is also all about the **Graphics** class.

The **Graphics** class is a marvelous class. It is the class that allows us do drawing. Using the **Graphics** class, we can indulge the "artist-within" and create any manner of free-form drawings. We can draw shapes, splash color onto a canvas, crop the picture, and indulge in some calligraphy.

If you have been following what we have been saying about object-oriented programming, you will appreciate that object-oriented tools such as the JDK do not give all the work to one class. The same is true of drawing. The **Graphics** class itself does not do all of the work. There is a whole host of support classes that the **Graphics** object will call upon to get the drawing job done. We will be hearing about the **Canvas** class, the **Point** class, the Polygon class, the **Font** class, the **Text** class, the **Color** class and even the **Random** class. All these and more will be called upon to help us do some drawing.

We have already met the **Graphics** class several times—notably in Chapter 13, the graphics and user interface tutorial. If the **Graphics** class is entirely unfamiliar to you, I recommend that you read that chapter before this one.

SEWING WITH SEQUINS

My wife and I live in Ontario, Canada. My wife, Mary, works in a private school in the town of Oakville. Mary, who insists I mention her youth and boundless energy, teaches younger children. Among other things, she teaches them arts and crafts.

Recently, she decided that she wanted to teach her children how to sew designs onto fabric using sequins. She figured that sewing sequins would be good for their dexterity, while the pictures they formed would be helpful in teaching them about art.

Mary decided to practice a bit herself before she introduced her students to their new artform. It was not long before I started to notice little packets of sequins appearing around the house—and it was not long after that we had more sequins hidden in the couch than we had lost coins.

One evening Mary came home and started telling me about the difficulties some of the children were having when they tried to turn their hand-drawn designs into refrigerator-ready sequin art. Their hand-drawn designs looked good on paper, but when the kids tried to create them with the sequins, the designs became unrecognizable.

It was at this point that I decided to tell Mary that she was also teaching her children how to program graphics on a computer. Like the true computer-geek husband, I was delighted that Mary at last wanted to use my computer skills to help her, and it was not long before I was launching into a "here's the problem" spiel. For once, this was not met by a polite "yes, dear" smile, but by a look of genuine interest. Soon we had out sheets of graph paper and were looking at how to make shapes like circles appear circular when composed entirely of a grid of dots.

The fabric that is used for sequin sewing consists of a rectangular array of holes which, if you draw the parallel, is rather similar to the grid of pixels that make up a computer screen, as shown in Figure 15.1.

Back to Java. If you want an analogy, the pixels are sequins and the **Graphics** class is like the needle and thread that sews the sequins to the fabric. The component classes are like the fabric that the **Graphics** class sews the pixel to. There

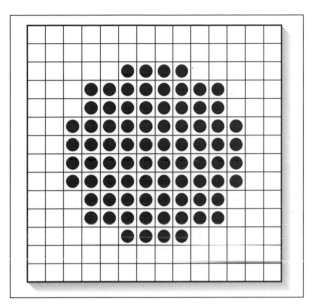

Figure 15.1 *A circle made of sequins.*

is plenty of fabric to choose from. The best quality fabric is the **Canvas** class, but the applet and the frame window also make good fabrics. Most of the component and container classes can be pushed into service as a fabric if need be.

THE COORDINATE SYSTEM

Objects of the "fabric" classes such as a **Canvas** object will arrange for an area of a window to be left clear, ready for a Graphics object to draw some graphics into it.

To determine where to place the things it wants to draw, the **Graphics** class uses a drawing grid called the *coordinate system* to position things in the window. The coordinate system is like the grid of the sequin fabric. It is a rectangular grid of points. Each point in the coordinate system is numbered. It takes two numbers to specify each point—the horizontal number and the vertical number. The horizontal number is called the x-coordinate and is the number of points the current point is from the left of the grid. The vertical number is called the y-coordinate and is the number of points the current point is from the top of the screen. This means that the origin of the coordinate system—the point labeled (0,0) is at the top-left of the grid. If you took (and, one hopes, passed) middle-school algebra, then Figure 15.2 should be quite familiar.

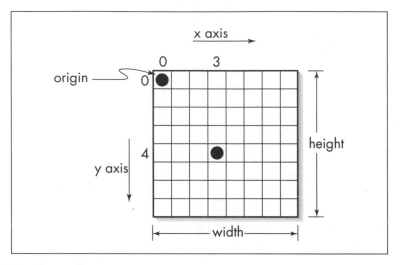

Figure 15.2 *The coordinate system.*

At school, you might have been used to drawing charts and graphs—maybe in math or physics. In these charts, the origin (0,0) was invariably at either the center or the bottom-left of the paper. It was never at the top-left of the paper. Computer graphics systems vary, but it is common to find the top-left corner as the origin of the system.

The Programs in this Section

All of the programs in this section are contained on the CD-ROM under the \SOURCE\CHAP15 directory. If you are interested in compiling and running these programs, you should first copy the programs to a directory on your hard disk, and then use the javac command to compile them. For example, to compile the ShapeTest.java program, which we'll see in a moment, you can do the following:

```
cmd> cd your-directory
cmd> javac ShapeTest.java
```

As you will be aware, there are several ways to run a java program, depending on whether the program is an applet or a standalone program. All of the techniques shown in this chapter can be applied to either type of Java program. Most sample programs shown in this chapter are standalone programs. You can run them using the java command. For instance, to run the ShapeTest program, use the following code line:

```
cmd java ShapeTest
```

You will find applet versions of some of the programs. The applet versions are named by appending the word "Applet" to the end of the program name. Naturally, applet files will need HTML files to run them—they are supplied as the *.html* file with the same "name" as the applet. The code snippet below shows an example of compiling and running the applet version of the shape test program:

```
cmd> javac ShapeTestapplet.java
cmd appletviewet ShapeTestapplet.html
```

LINE DRAWING: A RECAP

Before we go too far into this chapter, let's recap what we know about graphics drawing. We will look again at drawing a line on a canvas.

We first need to obtain a **Graphics** object. The **Graphics** object provides us with methods to do the drawing. Unfortunately, **Graphics** objects are not that forthcoming. The main way to get hold of one is via the **paint** method. The **paint** method is called each time the **Canvas** class must be redrawn.

To do our drawing, we code up the **paint** method to do the drawing we want to do.

Lines are possibly the simplest things that can be drawn using a **Graphics** object. To draw a line, we need to provide two points: the start point and the end point. We can draw lines using the **drawLine** method provided by the **Graphics** object. It takes the start and the end points as two sets of two numbers. In other words, we use four numbers (the x and y of the start point, and the x and y of the end point) to describe the line. For example, Listing 15.1 is a **Canvas** object with a **paint** method which will draw a line from the point (10, 20) to the point (190, 170).

Listing 15.1 Drawing a Line

```
class LineCanvas extends Canvas {
    public void paint(Graphics g) {
        g.drawLine(10, 20, 190, 170);
    }
}
```

Naturally, the **Canvas** object will need to be created inside of a program to be useful. As we have seen, we have a number of ways to set 11up the user interface program: we can use an applet, a frame window, or even a frame window from inside of an applet. In Listing 15.2, we use the **Canvas** object from Listing 15.1 in an applet. Listing 15.3 shows the HTML to drive the applet. Figure 15.3 shows the applet.

Listing 15.2   LineCanvasApplet.java

```java
import java.awt.*;
import java.Applet.*;

class LineCanvas extends Canvas {
    LineCanvas() {
        resize(200, 200);
    }

    public void paint(Graphics g) {
        g.drawLine(10, 20, 190, 170);
    }
}

public class LineCanvasApplet extends Applet {
    public void init() {
        add( new LineCanvas() );
    }
}
```

Listing 15.3   linecanvas.html

```html
<applet code="LineCanvasApplet.class" width=200 height=200>
</applet>
```

The LineCanvasApplet.java file draws the line into a **Canvas**. However, the canvas is contained inside of an applet.

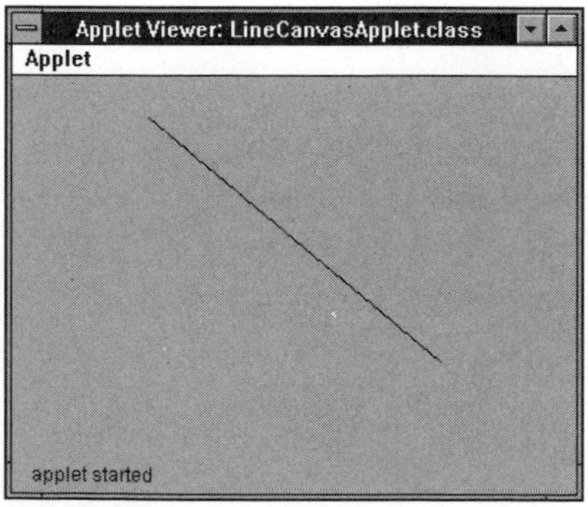

Figure 15.3   *LineCanvasApplet.java.*

FABRICS TO DRAW ON

The best class to draw on is the Canvas class. It has the very best support for drawing and it is likely to remain the best for drawing.

Other classes, such as those for the applet and frame window, are also good for drawing on. However, you must remember that these classes are also containers. Containers, as we saw in the last chapter, can be used to lay out other components inside of the area that the container has been allocated. Mixing containers' layout and drawing is not necessarily a very good idea. The layout manager in the container will lay out the components in potentially different places for different screen sizes.

When using the applet or the frame window as drawing areas, remember not to add other components into them. For instance, do not use code like that shown in Listing 15.4.

Listing 15.4   Bad Mix of Container and Drawing

```
public class BadDrawApplet extends Applet {
    public void init() {
        add( new Button("Press Me") );
    }
    public void paint(Graphics g) {
        g.drawLine(10, 20, 190, 170);
    }
}
```

Here the **Applet** class is being used as a place to draw on and as a container for a button. As you can see from Figure 15.4, this will produce some results, but they will not be consistent or reliable. If you want to mix components and drawing, it is far better to use a **Graphics** object, as illustrated in Listing 15.2.

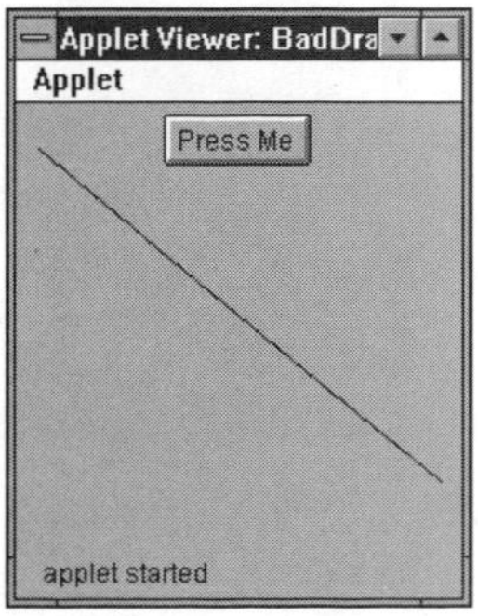

Figure 15.4   *Mixing components and drawing.*

However, if you do not intend to use the applet as a container, it makes as suitable place to draw on. Listing 15.5 shows drawing directly onto an applet. The result is shown in Figure 15.5.

Listing 15.5 LineDrawApplet.java—A Direct Drawing Applet

```java
import java.awt.*;
import java.Applet.*;

public class LineDrawApplet extends Applet {

    public void paint(Graphics g) {
        g.drawLine(10, 20, 190, 170);
    }
}
```

METHOD DRAWING

You cannot create a **Graphics** object yourself. You have to be given one at runtime. If you take the time to browse through the JDK AWT source, you will find that there are very few places where you can get hold of a **Graphics** object. The best place to get a **Graphics** object is to have one passed into a **paint** method of a suitable drawing object.

There are other ways of getting a **Graphics** objects. There is the **update** method of any component or container, and then there is the **getGraphics** method of the **Image** class. We will be looking at these methods later. In general, however, the best place to do drawing is in the **paint** method.

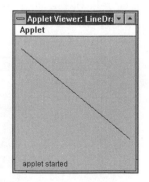

Figure 15.5   *Direct drawing Applet.*

Using the Point Class

The AWT provides us with a **Point** class. It is fairly bare bones. It provides a way of wrapping up the x and y coordinates of the point. You might be wondering, if you have looked at the **Graphics** class, why the **Graphics** methods do not use the **Point** class to specify points. You might also wonder why there is a **Point** class at all.

In fact, the **Point** class is used mainly as a class to return the x and y coordinates from a method. Recall that Java does not directly provide pass by reference; it is not possible to pass in a parameter to a method and get back the changed value in the same parameter. So you *can't* say things like

```
void method(int x, int y) {...}
```

where the method changes the values of x and y, and gets back the changed values in x and y. For this reason, **Point** objects are used as return values from these type of methods. So we could rewrite the above method as:

```
Point method(int x, int y) {... }
```

The method returns one thing: the **Point** object. The changed values of the x and y values would be returned in the **Point** object.

Conversely, to save us from having to construct unnecessary **Point** objects, the **Graphics** methods all take x and y coordinate parameters rather than **Point** objects.

A COMPENDIUM OF GRAPHICS OBJECTS

So that we can visualize the facilities provided by the **Graphics** class, let's put together a Graphics drawing compendium. It does for the methods of the **Graphics** class what the **PeriodicTable** did for the subclasses of the **Component** class. The directory for the compendium code is in the \SOURCE\CHAP15 directory. Refer to the instructions at the beginning of this chapter for running the programs.

Figure 15.6 shows the ShapeTest program running. The program consists of four rectangles (a drawn rectangle, two 3D rectangles, and a round-cornered rectangle), two polygons (one star and one filled star), a circle, an ellipse, and an arc. Some of these, you will notice, are not perfectly formed. We will be discussing why shortly.

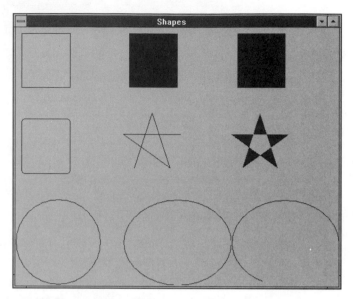

Figure 15.6 *The ShapeTest program.*

Listing 15.6 shows the ShapeTest program source code listing. The program is arranged as a grid of canvases inside of a frame window. Each canvas displays a different type of drawing object. There are rectangles, polygons, ovals, and arcs. To do the drawing, the **paint** method of each **Canvas** object is overridden and the appropriate **Graphics** method called to draw the required shape.

Listing 15.6 ShapeTest.java

```
import java.awt.*;
import java.lang.*;
import java.util.*;

class RoundRectCanvas extends Canvas {
    public void paint(Graphics g) {
        g.drawRoundRect(10, 10, 80, 90, 10, 10);
    }
}

class RectCanvas extends Canvas {
    public void paint(Graphics g) {
        g.drawRect(10, 10, 80, 90);
    }
}

class Rect3DCanvas extends Canvas {
    boolean raised;
```

```
    Rect3DCanvas(boolean b) {
        raised = b;
    }
    public void paint(Graphics g) {
        g.fill3DRect(10, 10, 80, 90, raised);
    }
}

class CircleCanvas extends Canvas {
    public void paint(Graphics g) {
        Dimension d = size();
        int diameter = Math.min(d.width, d.height)-2;
        g.drawOval(1, 1, diameter, diameter);
    }
}

class EllipseCanvas extends Canvas {
    public void paint(Graphics g) {
        Dimension d = size();
        g.drawOval(1, 1, d.width-1, d.height-1);
    }
}

class ArcCanvas extends Canvas {
    public void paint(Graphics g) {
        Dimension d = size();
        g.drawArc(1, 1, d.width-1, d.height-1, 0, 245);
    }
}

class PolygonCanvas extends Canvas {

    public void paint(Graphics g) {
        Polygon poly = new Polygon();
        poly.addPoint(18, 90);
        poly.addPoint(47, 0);
        poly.addPoint(77, 90);
        poly.addPoint(0, 35);
        poly.addPoint(95, 35);
        g.drawPolygon(poly);
    }
}

class FillPolygonCanvas extends Canvas {

    public void paint(Graphics g) {
        Polygon poly = new Polygon();
        poly.addPoint(18, 90);
        poly.addPoint(47, 0);
        poly.addPoint(77, 90);
        poly.addPoint(0, 35);
        poly.addPoint(95, 35);
        g.fillPolygon(poly);
    }
}
```

```
public class ShapeTest extends frame {

    public ShapeTest() {

        super("Shapes");

        setLayout( new GridLayout(3, 3) );

        add( new RectCanvas());
        add( new Rect3DCanvas(true));
        add( new Rect3DCanvas(false));
        add( new RoundRectCanvas());
        add( new PolygonCanvas());
        add( new FillPolygonCanvas());
        add( new CircleCanvas());
        add( new EllipseCanvas());
        add( new ArcCanvas());

        resize(550, 550);
        show();
    }

    public static void main(String args[]) {
    frame f = new ShapeTest();
    }
}
```

In the next few sections, we look at the **Graphics** drawing methods, shown in the ShapeTest program.

The Bounding Box

One thing that you will notice in common with most of the **Graphics** drawing methods is that they use the concept of a bounding box to specify the shape. The bounding box is a rectangle that encloses the shape to be drawn. For example, a circle can be drawn by using the **drawOval** method and using a square as the bounding box. The **drawOval** method will draw a circle so that the circle just touches the bounding box at the top, right, left ,and bottom.

The bounding box is specified using three facts: the upper-left corner of the rectangle, the width, and the height of the rectangle. The upper-left corner is used to position the rectangle and the width and the height are used to size the rectangle, as shown in Figure 15.7.

When supplying the bounding box as the parameter to the drawing methods, the JDK does not create a bounding box object. Instead, it requires the x and y coordinates of the bounding box and the width and the height. Each is passed as a separate parameter. The main reason for doing this is so as not to

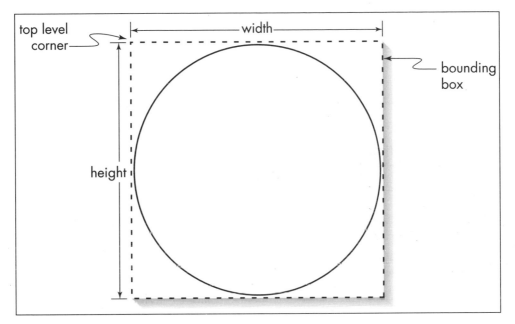

Figure 15.7 *A circle with its bounding box.*

incur the overhead of creating a separate bounding box object. This will give better performance when drawing.

The use of the bounding box may seem a little odd at first, especially if you are more accustomed to drawing circles on a piece of paper using compass needles or a coin. However, once you get used to it, it does seem very natural. Also, the bounding box concept has uses beyond the drawing of shapes. It is an important concept in many areas of graphics. We will return more to this subject later.

Rectangles

There are three types of rectangles that the **Graphics** object provides for us: rectangle, rounded rectangle, and 3D rectangle. Listing 15.7 shows a **paint** method that will draw a "regular" rectangle. The "regular" rectangle is drawn as an unfilled box.

Listing 15.7   An Unfilled Rectangle

```
class RectCanvas extends Canvas {
    public void paint(Graphics g) {
        Dimension d = size();
        g.drawRect(0, 0, d.width, d.height);
```

```
    }
}
```

All the rectangles are drawn using the bounding box for their size and position. The straight rectangles need no more information to specify them fully. The rounded and the 3D rectangles, though, are a little more complicated and will need some explanation.

Rounded Rectangles

Rounded rectangles are rectangles with rounded corners. The rounded rectangle is assumed to be equally rounded at each of the corners. You can imagine the rounded edges to be created by circles that are drawn at each of the four corners. The only difference is that the inner parts of the circles are not drawn. Only the parts that form a smooth curve between the sides of the rectangle are drawn. The corners do not have to be limited to circles. You can use ellipses if that is more the shape you need. An example is shown in Figure 15.8

Being able to use circles or ellipses means that you have full control over the amount of curve (by adjusting the size of the circle or the ellipse) and the shape of the curve (by adjusting the shape of the circle or ellipse).

Rounded rectangles need two extra facts to specify them: the width and height of the bounding box of the circle/ellipse. However, since the position of the bounding box is not needed—the drawing routines will draw them in the

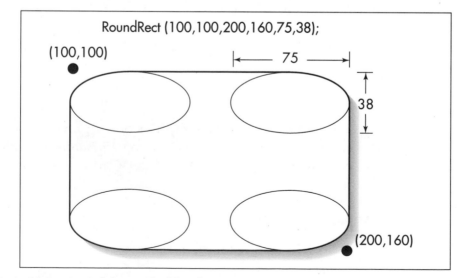

Figure 15.8 *A rounded rectangle with circles on its corners.*

correct positions in the corners—we need only specify the width and height of the bounding box.

In Listing 15.8, I chose to draw a rounded rectangle with rounded corners that are a tenth of the size of the rectangle's height and width.

Listing 15.8   Drawing a Rounded Rectangle

```
class RoundRectCanvas extends Canvas {
    public void paint(Graphics g) {
        Dimension d = size();
        g.drawRoundRect(0, 0, d.width, d.height,
                        d.width/10, d.height/10);
    }
}
```

3D Rectangles

3D rectangles are designed to give the impression of being either raised or lowered. This makes them useful for simulating buttons. 3D rectangles are best used as filled shapes rather than drawn shapes, though methods to draw both are provided. The 3D effect is not very strong in the drawn shape. Later we will write an improved version of the 3D rectangles. Listing 15.9 shows a sample piece of code to draw a 3D rectangle.

Listing 15.9   Drawing a 3D Rectangle

```
class Rect3DCanvas extends Canvas {
    boolean raised;

    Rect3DCanvas(boolean b) {
        raised = b;
    }
    public void paint(Graphics g) {
        Dimension d = size();
        g.fill3DRect(0, 0, d.width, d.height, raised);
    }
}
```

Another point to remember about 3D rectangles is the choice of colors. The algorithm that creates the 3D effect places darker or lighter colors at the edge of the rectangle to create the effect. However, because it is not possible to lighten white or to darken black. The effect will not look good for rectangles that are drawn in black or white—or colors close to them. For this reason, I generally choose **Color.lightGray** as the color when I am working with 3D rectangles. We will be looking at color management shortly.

Curved Shapes

The JDK has a number of methods for drawing curved shapes. The main method is a routine called **drawOval**. The JDK has decided to lump together all the circles and ellipse drawing routines and called them ovals. The circle is just an oval with a square bounding box. Listing 15.10 shows a canvas that will draw a circle.

Listing 15.10 Drawing a Circle

```
class CircleCanvas extends Canvas {
    public void paint(Graphics g) {
        Dimension d = size();
        int diameter = Math.min(d.width, d.height);
        g.drawOval(0, 0, diameter, diameter);
    }
}
```

Arcs

Arcs are provided by the **Graphics** object. They're interesting from several, pardon the expression, "points of view."

They are the only place in the AWT where angles are used. The angles used to specify arcs are measured in degrees. This contrasts with, say trigonometric methods in the **Math** class, which use radians as their way of specifying angles. The JDK does not provide a mechanism to convert between degrees and radians.

Arcs, as shown in Figure 15.9, are drawn using the **drawArc** method. It takes two parameters in addition to the bounding box: the starting angle and the

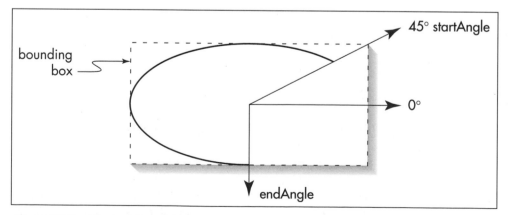

Figure 15.9 *The geometry of an arc.*

finishing angle of the arc. The starting and ending angles are measured starting from 0, which is at the three o'clock position (horizontally to the right). A positive number means a counter-clockwise rotation from three o'clock; a negative number means a clockwise rotation. Listing 15.11 draws the arc shape shown in the ShapeTest.

Listing 15.11   Drawing an Arc

```
class ArcCanvas extends Canvas {
    public void paint(Graphics g) {
        Dimension d = size();
        g.drawArc(0, 0, d.width, d.height, 0, 245);
    }
}
```

In addition to **drawArc**, there is a filled arc method, **fillArc**. This can be used to draw pie charts.

Polygons

In a book like this, I can't really resist the old joke:

Q: What shape is made by a parrot when it is squashed under the front wheel of a car?

A: A poly-gone.

Polygons, as you probably remember from school, are many sided shapes— the root word of "poly," of course, meaning "many" (in Greek) or "parrot" (in English). Here, we will only be concerned with the Greek meaning of the term.

The **Graphics** class allows us to describe a polygon using the points at the corners of the polygon. Polygon drawing departs from the bounding box mechanism of specifying shapes. There are two ways to specify the corners of the polygon. The first is to use two arrays of **ints**, the second is to use a **Polygon** object.

Using the array of **ints** technique is useful if we know how many points are in the polygon. We can then construct two arrays: one for the x coordinates and one for the y coordinates. For example, we can use

```
int xpoints[] = new int(5);
int ypoints[] = new int(5);
```

to construct an array ready for the points of a five-sided figure. This is not such a good technique if the number of points is unknown when the point arrays are constructed, because you will need to reconstruct the size of the arrays as you fill them.

Using the **Polygon** class is very handy since the class manages the construction and dynamic sizing of the point array for you. The **Polygon** class is the most sensible mechanism to use when dynamically constructing a polygon, especially when you don't know how many points will be required. I tend to use the **Polygon** class technique most of the time because it is so much simpler to use.

An important concept about specifying polygons is whether they are closed or not. A closed polygon is a polygon like a square: one in which all the sides join up. However, as we will see, the **Graphics** polygon drawing methods will *not* close the polygon *for* us. If we want to have the polygon closed, we have to repeat the starting point at the end of the list of points.

Drawing a Polygon

The **drawPolygon** method draws the points of a polygon. It connects the points by drawing lines between the points. It starts with the first point, then draws a line from the first to the second, from the second to the third, and so on, until it reaches the last point.

The example we will use here, shown in Figure 15.10, almost draws a five-pointed star. To show that the **drawPolygon** method does not close the polygon, we will not add the duplicated first point. The code is shown in Listing 15.12.

Listing 15.12   A Non-Closed Polygon

```
class PolygonCanvas extends Canvas {

    public void paint(Graphics g) {
        Polygon poly = new Polygon();
        poly.addPoint(18, 90);
        poly.addPoint(47, 0);
        poly.addPoint(77, 90);
        poly.addPoint(0, 35);
        poly.addPoint(95, 35);
        g.drawPolygon(poly);
    }
}
```

Now let's look at the same shape through the eyes of the **fillPolygon** method. The **fillPolygon** method will fill the shape that we have produced. Listing 15.13 shows this.

Figure 15.10 *A non-closed polygon.*

Listing 15.13 A Filled, Five-Point Star

```
class FillPolygonCanvas extends Canvas {

    public void paint(Graphics g) {
        Polygon poly — new Polygon();
        poly.addPoint(18, 90);
        poly.addPoint(47, 0);
        poly.addPoint(77, 90);
        poly.addPoint(0, 35);
        poly.addPoint(95, 35);
        g.fillPolygon(poly);
    }
}
```

If you look at Figure 15.11, you will notice that the star has a hollow center. This is because of the algorithm used to draw the polygon.

Polygons are filled by trying to determine if each point is inside or outside the polygon. If the point is inside, the area in which the point is contained is filled. Determining if a point is inside a polygon may seem intuitive to us humans, but the computer needs an algorithm to sort this out. The rule that decides if a point is inside of a polygon works like this: imagine a point inside of the polygon. Now draw a line out of the polygon from this point. Count the number of lines of the polygon that this escaping line crosses. If the escaping line crosses an odd number of lines then the area which contains the point is deemed to be inside of the polygon. If the count is even it is outside. This algorithm is shown in Figure 15.12.

Figure 15.11 *A filled, five-point star.*

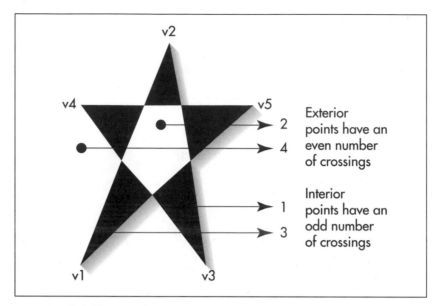

Figure 15.12   The odd-parity rule.

The reason this algorithm is used is that it runs fast. It works well for regular polygons such as squares, but crashes in pathological cases such as the five-point star. Some graphics systems, for example Windows, provide two polygon drawing algorithms that can be chosen by the programmer to correspond to the type of polygon being drawn. The **Graphics** class does not yet provide that degree of sophistication. Naturally, you could write your own, but we are talking very hardcore graphics here, so I wouldn't recommend it.

CREATING YOUR OWN SHAPES

The drawing methods we have looked at so far are the standard shape drawing methods provided by the **Graphics** objects. However, this does *not* mean that we are limited to these shapes. We are at liberty to construct our own shape drawing routines and use these in addition.

There are some notable examples of constructing shapes available on the Web. A good example is the Curve applet by Michael Heinrichs. This applet allows manipulation of various types of curves: Hermite, Bezier, and b-spline. It is available from **http://fas.sfu.ca:80/1/cs/people/GradStudents/ heinrica/personal/curve.html**

Let's go on to look at doing some shape creation of our own.

Improving 3D Rectangles

I don't know if you noticed, but the 3D effect of 3D rectangles is not that strong. The 3D effect is simulated by placing a border around the rectangle (actually, just inside the rectangle). This border is one color around the top and left edges, and another color around the bottom and right edges. The colors are chosen so that for a raised effect the color is lighter on the top and darker on the bottom; and vice versa for a lowered effect. The idea is to imagine that there is a light placed at the top left of the screen. Like an artist shading in a picture to create a 3D effect, the colors are shaded around the box.

The problem with the current JDK implementation is that the border width is chosen to be very small—one pixel of the screen. This has two effects: the first is to minimize the 3D effect, while the second is to generate a harder edge.

The mechanism used by our improved algorithm is to draw the borders as two rectangles and two polygons. These two polygons would have been rectangles but to get a nice beveled edge effect they are sawn off at the corners. Figure 15.13 shows what is happening.

The colors are chosen using the brighter and darker methods that the **Color** class provides. Listing 15.14 shows the code for the improved 3D rectangle. To use this code, you will need to add the method to a class derived from, say, the **Canvas** class.

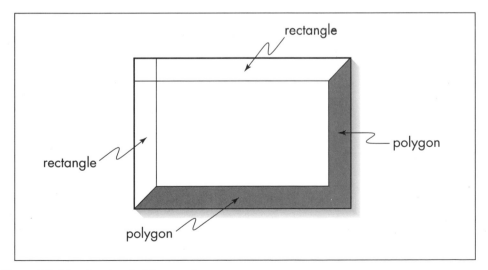

Figure 15.13   *Drawing the 3D rectangle.*

Listing 15.14 An Improved 3D Rectangle Drawing Method

```
public void
fill3DRect(Graphics g, int x, int y, int w, int h, int thick,
    boolean raised) {
    Color c = Color.lightGray;
    Color brighter = c.brighter();
    Color darker = c.darker();

    g.setColor(c);
    g.fillRect(x+thick, y+thick, w-(2*thick), h-(2*thick));
    g.setColor(raised ? brighter : darker);
    g.fillRect(x, y, w, thick);
    g.fillRect(x, y, thick, h);
    g.setColor(raised ? darker : brighter);

    int X[] = new int[4];
    int Y[] = new int[4];
    X[0] = x; Y[0] = y+h;
    X[1] = x+thick; Y[1] = y+h-thick;
    X[2] = x+w; Y[2] = y+h-thick;
    X[3] = x+w; Y[3] = y+h;
    g.fillPolygon(X, Y, 4);

    X[0] = x+w-thick; Y[0] = y+thick;
    X[1] = x+w; Y[1] = y;
    X[2] = x+w; Y[2] = y+h;
    X[3] = x+w-thick; Y[3] = y+h;
    g.fillPolygon(X, Y, 4);

    g.setColor(c);
}
```

Drawing Your Own Circles

This may seem like a particularly redundant thing to do, given that we can already draw good circles using the existing graphics routines. Writing our own routines, though, is useful as a way of learning how the system works. The programs in this section can be found in the \SOURCE\CHAP15\circle directory. Please refer to the beginning of the chapter for instructions on how to run them.

Okay, I admit what I am about to show you is a little hardcore. It is so hardcore that it might even be similar to an algorithm used deep down in the bowels of your operating systems graphics code, or possibly even hard-coded into the silicon on your graphics board.

In principle, the algorithm works like this. Imagine that you have a piece of graph paper. You stick a compass needle in the center of the circle and you draw a circle on the graph paper. You want to represent the circle just using filled in squares, so you will need to carefully choose which squares to fill to make the best-looking circle. The algorithm proceeds by starting at one point on the circle, then moving to the next point by working out which square to hop to next.

Now we know that the x and y points on a circle are given by

```
radius² = x² + y²
```

The cool thing about this algorithm—developed by a hot graphics expert called Bressenham in the 1970s—is that it does all its calculations using mainly adds and subtracts. It does not use squares and square roots, which are generally relatively slow on a computer. This makes the algorithm very fast. The algorithm I am using is taken from the book *Fundamentals of Computer Graphics* by Foley and Van Dam, second edition. The algorithm is in Chapter 3, pages 84-87. Listing 15.15 demonstrates the technique.

Listing 15.15 Drawing a Circle from Scratch

```java
public static void drawPoint(Graphics g, int x, int y) {
    g.drawLine(x, y, x, y);
}

static void
circlePoints(Graphics g, int cx, int cy, int x, int y) {
    drawPoint(g, cx + x,  cy + y);
    drawPoint(g, cx + y,  cy + x);
    drawPoint(g, cx + y,  cy -x);
    drawPoint(g, cx + x,  cy -y);
    drawPoint(g, cx -x,   cy -y);
    drawPoint(g, cx -y,   cy -x);
    drawPoint(g, cx -y,   cy + x);
    drawPoint(g, cx -x,   cy + y);
}

static void
fillCirclePoints(Graphics g, int cx, int cy, int x, int y) {
    g.drawLine(cx — x,  cy + y, cx + x,  cy + y);
    g.drawLine(cx — y,  cy + x, cx + y,  cy + x);
    g.drawLine(cx — y,  cy — x, cx + y,  cy — x);
    g.drawLine(cx — x,  cy — y, cx + x,  cy — y);
}

public static void
drawCircle(Graphics g, int cx, int cy, int r) {
    int x = 0;
    int y = r;
```

```
        int d = 1 - r;
        int deltaE = 3;
        int deltaSE = -2*r+5;
        circlePoints(g, cx, cy, x, y);

        while( y>x ) {
            if( d<0 ) {
                d += deltaE;
                deltaE += 2;
                deltaSE +=  2;
                x = x + 1;
            } else {
                d += deltaSE;
                deltaE += 2;
                deltaSE += 4;
                x += 1;
                y -= 1;
            }
            circlePoints(g, cx, cy, x, y);
        }
    }

public static void
fillCircle(Graphics g, int cx, int cy, int r) {
    int x = 0;
    int y = r;
    int d = 1 - r;
    int deltaE = 3;
    int deltaSE = -2*r+5;
    fillCirclePoints(g, cx, cy, x, y);

    while( y>x ) {
        if( d<0 ) {
            d += deltaE;
            deltaE += 2;
            deltaSE +=  2;
            x = x + 1;
        } else {
            d += deltaSE;
            deltaE += 2;
            deltaSE += 4;
            x += 1;
            y -= 1;
        }
        fillCirclePoints(g, cx, cy, x, y);
    }
}
```

I have written these methods so that they do not use the bounding box description mechanism that the other **Graphics** routines use. This makes these circle drawing routines more useful when we need to position a circle based on the center position. For instance, putting a centered circle at the end of a line is much easier using these circle methods.

One point to notice is that the **Graphics** class does not have a method to draw points (at least not yet, anyway). To simulate this, I have used a **drawLine** method with identical starting and end points. Another, and possibly better way, might have been to add the points into a **Polygon** object and then draw the object. This approach would have had additional performance advantages for drawing the filled circles.

The performance of these methods is slower but at least comparable on my machine to the native circle routines. Quite impressive. The Java code—a relatively high-level piece of code—is keeping up with code written with more machine-optimized methods.

Keeping Your Shapes Safe

A minor issue of writing your own graphics shapes is that you will probably want to use them in many circumstances, so there is the issue of how to package them. Obviously, it makes sense to put them in a central package such as our explorer package. However, how do we wrap up the method call?

There are three main options:

Option 1

We could write an extension of the **Graphics** class.

```
package explorer;
public class ExGraphics extends Graphics
```

This is not a particularly good option, because the **Graphics** class is an abstract class. This would mean that we would have to implement all of the **Graphics** methods or at the very least work out who would implement them.

Option 2

We could create a class which we initialize with a **Graphics** object. We would store this object inside the **ExGraphics** object. This has the advantage that we can override typical **Graphics** object methods by simply substituting the **ExGraphics** object for the **Graphics** object. We don't need to change the signature if the signature of our method is the same.

```
package explorer;

public class ExGraphics {
    Graphics graphics;
    ExGraphics(Graphics g) { ... }
}
```

The disadvantage is that we need to construct a separate **ExGraphics** object. If we are going to do a lot of graphics work with the **ExGraphics** object, then this could become an overhead.

Option 3
The third option is to define each new graphics shape-drawing method as static. These methods take an extra parameter, a **Graphics** object, which they will use to do the drawing.

This has the advantage that there is no extra construction involved. The **ExGraphics** simply becomes a collection of methods that can be called anytime without constructing a separate object.

```
package explorer;

public class ExGraphics {
    static drawFunc(Graphicsg, .... )
}
```

This last option is my personal preference. It does not suffer the potential overhead problems, though it does have the disadvantage of requiring the extra **Graphics** object in the parameter call.

CLIPPING

When a program draws lines, it can potentially draw very long lines: lines that could reach outside of the canvas. If these lines were completely drawn, then there could potentially be all kinds of interference between different components in a window. To stop this anti-social graphics behavior, a concept called *clipping* is used.

Clipping, as its name suggests, is the process that restricts the lines to make sure that they only display in the area where they are allowed. Clipping is normally done by using a *clipping rectangle*. All the lines and shapes are clipped so that only those portions that are in the rectangle are drawn, as shown in Figure 15.14. In this figure, only the solid black sections will be drawn the dotted sections will not be drawn.

When the AWT constructs a **Graphics** object to allow drawing to be done, it sets a clipping rectangle in the **Graphics** object, so that drawing done by the **Graphics** object will not affect other components in the same window.

This clipping rectangle is open for manipulation, using the **setClipRect** method. For instance, by reducing the size of the clipping rectangle, we can control

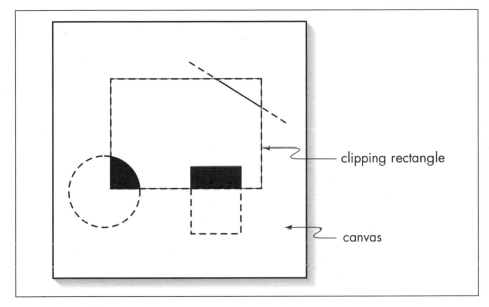

Figure 15.14   Clipping in action.

how much of the drawing we do actually gets to the canvas. This can be very useful when we want to do fast damage repair. For instance, if we are moving a rectangle around the screen, we might want to make sure that we only redraw the areas where the rectangle has moved from and which it has moved. This will probably result in faster and smoother movement of the rectangle.

CLEARING THE GRAPHICS

If you've played around a little bit with the canvas and graphics stuff, you've probably noticed that you do not have to clear the canvas before you do a paint. The act of repainting seems to clear the canvas to the background color.

This occurs because the canvas automatically draws the background just prior to doing a paint. The method that does the background clearing is the **update** method. The **update** method is also the method that calls the **paint** method. The purpose of separating the **update** and the **paint** method is precisely to do things that should happen before each paint, such as repaint the background.

If you don't want the background to be cleared each time, you can override the background drawing by overriding the **update** method with the following code:

```
public void update(Graphics g) {
    paint(g);
}
```

If you want to clear the graphics screen yourself, you use the **clearRect** method, which draws a rectangle in the background color. Here is some code to do that:

```
Dimension d = size();
g.clearRect(0, 0, d.width, d.height);
```

Transparent Backgrounds

There is a problem with the AWT if you want to have a transparent background. The problem is simple: you can't do it.

For instance, you might want to place an applet over a home page with a background image on it. You would like the home page background to show through as the background to the applet. In other words, you want to create a transparent applet background.

Currently, the background is drawn as a solid rectangle when the applet is first drawn. There is no way from the JDK to control this behavior, even by removing the "background" rectangle draw from the **update** method. Removing the background rectangle from the **update** does have other useful effects, which we will deal with later.

DRAWING MODES

The **Graphics** class provides two different types of drawing mode: the paint mode and the XOR mode.

Drawing mode refers to the way that the new shapes or lines being drawn interact with the things that have already been drawn. In paint mode, the new shape obliterates what was there before. The pixels that make up the shape are colored in the colors given by the new shape.

In XOR mode, this does not happen. The shape is drawn in a color that is dependent on the color of the shape to be drawn and the color of the shape that is already there. Where the shapes do not overlap, the shapes will be drawn in their own colors, but where they overlap a third color will be used to draw the overlap. The third color will be generated by XORing the pixel values of the colors.

Typically, when doing drawing, paint mode is the most common mode to use. However, XOR mode can be useful when moving objects around. We won't be using XOR mode in this book.

CHARTING YOUR PROGRESS

As an example of what we can do with our newfound knowledge, let's look at a program to draw graphs and charts. As a side effect, we will create a program to help us visualize some of the math functions provided by the JDK and we can experiment with some biological randomness.

The programs in this section can be found in the \SOURCE\CHAP15\graph directory. Please refer to the beginning of the chapter for instructions on how to run them.

The source for the graph program is rather large. It is stored in the file GraphTest.java. We will fragment it into three parts and discuss each of the parts individually. First, we will discuss the **Graph** class, which stores the points for the graph. Then, we will discuss the **GraphPlotter** class, which draws the graph. Finally, we will take a look at a class that tests the other two classes to make sure they work correctly.

The Graph Class

At the heart of our graphing program is a simple class called **Graph**. It will maintain all of the points that we will be using to draw our graph. Listing 15.16 shows the source for the graph.

Listing 15.16   The Graph Class

```
class Graph extends Observable {

    double xminimum=Double.POSITIVE_INFINITY;
    double xmaximum=Double.NEGATIVE_INFINITY;
    double yminimum=Double.POSITIVE_INFINITY;
    double ymaximum=Double.NEGATIVE_INFINITY;

    /**
     * The total number of points
     */
    public int npoints = 0;

    /**
```

```
    * the array of x coordinates
    */
   public double xpoints[] = new double[10];

   /**
    * the array of y coordinates
    */
   public double ypoints[] = new double[10];

   Graph() {}

   /**
    * appends a point to the graph
    * @param x the x coordinate of the point
    * @param y the y coordinate of the point
    */
   public void addPoint(double x, double y)  {
if (npoints == xpoints.length) {
      double tmp[];

      tmp = new double[npoints * 2];
      System.arraycopy(xpoints, 0, tmp, 0, npoints);
      xpoints = tmp;

      tmp = new double[npoints * 2];
      System.arraycopy(ypoints, 0, tmp, 0, npoints);
      ypoints = tmp;
}
xpoints[npoints] = x;
ypoints[npoints] = y;
npoints++;

      xminimum = Math.min(xminimum, x);
      xmaximum = Math.max(xmaximum, x);
      yminimum = Math.min(yminimum, y);
      ymaximum = Math.max(ymaximum, y);
   }

   double X(int i) {
      return xpoints[i];
   }

   double Y(int i) {
      return ypoints[i];
   }

   int numPoints() {
     return npoints;
   }

   public double xmin() {
      return xminimum;
   }

   public double xmax() {
```

```
        return xmaximum;
    }

    public double ymin() {
        return yminimum;
    }

    public double ymax() {
        return ymaximum;
    }

    public void plot() {
        setChanged();
        notifyObservers(this);
    }
}
```

The coordinates of the points are stored in separate arrays of doubles. The **Graph** class has an **addPoint** method which will add points one at a time onto the graph. The **addPoint** method handles the sizing of the coordinate arrays. If the arrays are not big enough to hold the points, the arrays are dynamically resized.

The code that handles the resizing is interesting. It is not possible in Java to dynamically resize an array. You need to create a new array of the new desired size and then copy the contents of the old array into the new array. This copy can be slow, so the JDK supplies an array copying function which is optimized to be as fast as possible on each platform. This copying is supplied by the **System.arraycopy** method. The array copy method takes parameters of the two arrays and the indices in the array to copy from/to plus the number of array elements to copy. The **System.arraycopy** method will detect array overflow and types mismatches between the two arrays.

The **Graph** class stores the model of the graph—the abstract information we want to store. For this reason, we have made the **Graph** an *observable*. We talk more about **Observable** classes later in the section on Color. The **Observable** class means that other objects can register their interest in a **Graph** object and so be told when the **Graph** object changes.

 ### Don't Hard-Code Numbers

Notice that we use the **Double.POSITIVE_INFINITY** and **Double.NEGATIVE_INFINITY** variables rather than hard coding the numbers directly ourselves. Whenever you need a mathematical number or a limit number, such as a maximum, for one of the built-in in data types, first try looking in the **Math** class or the number wrapper classes, such as **Double** or **Integer**.

Plotting the Graph

The **Graph** class is visualized using the **GraphPlotter** class. This will plot the points of the graph on a **Canvas**. Listing 15.17 shows the code for the **GraphPlotter** class.

Listing 15.17 The GraphPlotter Class

```
class GraphPlotter extends Canvas implements Observer {
    Graph graph;
    Dimension area;

    GraphPlotter(Graph g) {
        graph = g;
        g.addObserver(this);
    }

    public void update(Observable o, Object arg) {
        repaint();
    }

    Point plotPoint( double x, double y) {
        // DBG System.out.println("X:"+x+" Y:"+y);
        int offset = 10;
        int height = area.height - offset;
        int width = area.width - offset;
        int xpos = offset;
        int ypos = height;
        double xscale = width/(graph.xmax() - graph.xmin());
        double yscale = height/(graph.ymax() - graph.ymin());
        int px = (int) Math.round((x-graph.xmin())*xscale + xpos);
        int py = (int) Math.round(ypos - (y-graph.ymin())*yscale);
        return new Point(px, py);
    }

    public void paint(Graphics g) {
        area = size();
        Polygon poly = new Polygon();
        for (int i=0; i < graph.numPoints(); ++i) {
            Point p = plotPoint(graph.X(i), graph.Y(i));
            // DBG System.out.println(p.toString());
            poly.addPoint(p.x, p.y);
        }
        g.drawPolygon(poly);
    }
}
```

The main thing the **GraphPlotter** has to do is to convert the coordinate system. Currently the coordinate system for the canvas has the origin in the upper-left corner with the y values increasing down the screen. We want the origin to be near the lower left and have y values that increase up the screen not down. Also we want to scale the value of the graph so that we make good use of the available canvas space.

To do our conversion, we need to do two things: we need to scale the value and translate the point. To scale the value, we work out a ratio of how many points are required per graph unit. For instance, if we look at the horizontal value, we need to work out the difference between the smallest and the largest values in the x coordinates of the graph and divide this into the number of units that are in the width. Then we will have a number that we can multiply a value by to get the graph coordinate of the value.

The translation adjusts the point of the origin by adding some offset values. It also requires that we negate the y value so that it increases up the screen.

Once we have converted the points stored in the graph to their display positions, we can plot the graph. We plot the points here using the **drawPolygon** method. As I previously noted, the **drawPolygon** method does not automatically join up the first and last points, so in effect it is a *polyline* method. In other words, we can use the **drawPolygon** method to draw lots of linked lines rather than having to call **drawLine** to draw each line segment.

Testing the Graph

To put the graph through its paces lets us use it to visualize the **Math.sin** method. We will construct a simple frame-based interface and put the **GraphPlotter** at the center of a **BorderLayout** in the frame.

The **sin** function is plotted by incrementing the angle passed to the **sin** function from -2Pi to +2Pi. Remember that the **sin** function takes radians, so this is equivalent to two entire sweeps of the circle as 2Pi radians is the same as 360 degrees. Listing 15.18 shows the test program.

Listing 15.18   Testing the Graph

```
public class GraphTest extends frame {

    void plotSin(Graph g) {
        for (double d = -2*Math.PI; d < 2*Math.PI/2; d+=0.1) {
            g.addPoint(d, Math.sin(d));
        }
    }
    public GraphTest() {

        super("Graph Plotter");

    setBackground(Color.lightGray);
```

```
        setLayout( new BorderLayout());

        Graph g = new Graph();
        plotSin(g);

        add("Center", new GraphPlotter(g));

        resize(550, 550);
        show();
    }

    public static void main(String a[]) {
        count   = (a.length >= 1) ? Integer.parseInt(a[0]) : 50000;
        numBars = (a.length >= 2) ? Integer.parseInt(a[1]) : 100;
        frame f = new GraphTest();
    }
}
```

The program is a frame window which contains a **GraphPlotter**. The **GraphPlotter** is provided with a **Graph** object. The points to be plotted as added on the graph are added by the **Math.sin** method. The results of the program are shown in Figure 15.15.

A Biological Randomness

Now let's use our graph program to examine the output of the random number generator's **nextGaussian** method. The random number generator, which is provided by the **Random** class, provides a method called **nextGaussian**. This method is designed to provide a random number which conforms to the Gaussian normal distribution.

The Gaussian random number generator has a number of uses. It basically provides randomness near a number. The random number is more likely to

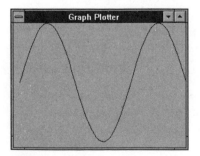

Figure 15.15 *Graph plot of the Math.sin method.*

be near the number that not near it. Let's run this through the graph and see what we get out. Listing 15.19 shows how to do it.

Listing 15.19   Plotting the Gaussian Distribution

```
public class GraphTest extends frame {
    static int count;
    static int numBars;

    void plotGaussian(Graph g, int n, int bars) {
        Random r = new Random();
        int values[] = new int[bars];
        for (int i= 0; i < n; ++i) {
            int value = (int) (bars/4*r.nextGaussian()+bars/2);
            value = Math.min(value, bars-1);
            value = Math.max(value, 0);
            values[value] += 1;
        }

        for (int i = 0; i < bars; ++i) {
            g.addPoint(i, values[i]);
        }
    }

    public GraphTest() {
        super("Graph Plotter");
        setBackground(Color.lightGray);
        setLayout( new BorderLayout());
        Graph g = new Graph();
        plotGaussian(g, count, numBars);
        add("Center", new GraphPlotter(g));
        resize(550, 550);
        show();
    }

    public static void main(String a[]) {
        count   = (a.length >= 1) ? Integer.parseInt(a[0]) : 50000;
        numBars = (a.length >= 2) ? Integer.parseInt(a[1]) : 100;
        frame f = new GraphTest();
    }
}
```

The **plotGaussian** method takes the output of the **Random.nextGaussian** method and counts the number of times that the Gaussian produces a particular number. In other words, we are trying to produce a histogram or a bar chart of the number of times a particular random number is produced. This is shown in Figure 15.16.

If we called the **nextGaussian** method enough times, we should eventually see that the shape of the graph starts to look more and more like the Normal or **Gaussian** curve, as shown in Figure 15.17.

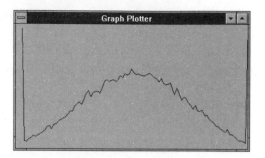

Figure 15.16 *Plotting the graph of the Gaussian distribution.*

So what's the big deal? For one thing, this Normal curve is very good at helping us simulate living things. The Normal curve has a tendency to a particular value—though it theoretically can be any value. Contrast this with other random numbers generated by the random number generator, which have equal likelihood of taking any number values.

A Better Graphing Program

The requirements I placed on our graph plotting program are rather arbitrary and restricting. I needed to produce particular types of graphs. As a conse-

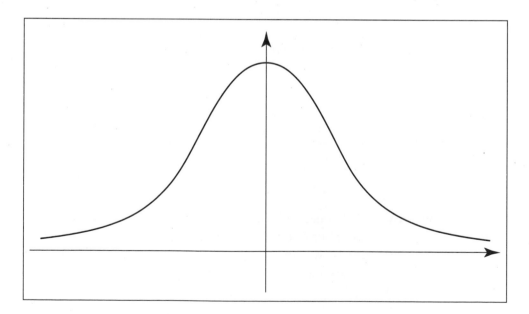

Figure 15.17 *Ideal Gaussian distribution.*

quence, the graphing program we have produced has lots of shortcomings: it plots graph shape rather than absolute values, which means that if the data is not ordered properly, a polygon will be drawn; and we have completely ignored cosmetics such as graph axes.

If you are after a good Java-based graphing package, there is one available on the Web at http://www-igpp.llnl.gov/people/brookshaw/java/. This package was written by Leigh Brookshaw. It has a lot of very interesting features and some of the test data that is displayed with the graph program is very interesting. I particularly like the volcano data. Take a look. I'm sure you will enjoy it.

THE RANDOM NUMBER GENERATOR

As we are here talking about parts of the random number generator, it is a good time to take a closer look at this beasty. The random number generator generates a sequence of random numbers. It can generate random number sequence for the following types found in Table 15.1.

To use the random number generator, you will need to construct an object of the **Random** class and call one of the methods shown in Table 15.1 to get a random number. Once the random number is constructed, you can use it to produces as many random numbers as you need by repeatedly calling any of the methods.

Restricting the Numbers

As you can see from the table, the Random class does not provide a way to generate a random number uniformly distributed over a range of values. To do this we need to do some work ourselves.

Table 15.1 *RandomNumber Generator Methods*

Method	Range Produced
nextInt()	Uniformly distributed over values possible from an int
nextLong()	Uniformly distributed over values possible from a long
nextFloat()	Uniformly distributed between 0.0 and 1.0; returned as a float
nextDouble()	Uniformly distributed between 0.0 and 1.0; returned as a double
nextGaussian()	Gaussian Normal distributed numbers with a mean of 0.0 and a standard deviation of 1.0; returned as a double

The simplest way to restrict numbers to a range of number is to use the modulus operator. Remember that the modulus operator provides the remainder when the number on the left is divided by the number on the right.

For instance, the code

```
result = x % 3
```

means that **result** can take the value 0, 1, or 2. The only proviso is that x must be greater than or equal to zero; otherwise, the modulus operator can't do its magic. To ensure that the value of x is not negative, we can use the **Math.abs** method.

A typical piece of code to get random numbers in the range 0 to n-1 is:

```
class someClass {
    Random r = new Random();

    int rand(int n) {
        return Math.abs(r.nextInt()) % n;
    }
}
```

Of course, there are more tricks we can play. For instance, if we want numbers in the range -(n-1) to (n-1), we will need to put back the sign information that the **Math.abs** method removed, as shown in this code snippet:

```
class someOtherClass {
    Random r = new Random();

    // assume that zero is a positive integer
    int sign(int i) {
        return (i <0) ? -1 : 1;
    }

    int rand(int n) {
        int i = r.nextInt();
        return sign(i) * Math.abs(i) % n;
    }
}
```

And that still leaves ranges like 1-5 to deal with! I'm sure you can cope with that though now.

A DICE PROGRAM

We can put the random number generator to good use to write a short dice program. The result of the program is shown in Figure 15.18. The program

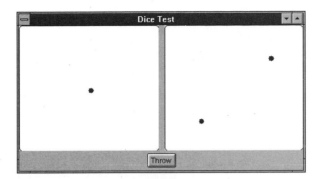

Figure 15.18 *Using the random number generator to create a dice program.*

consists of two die (yes, the plural of dice is die—isn't the English language wonderful) in a frame window. A button called Throw is also displayed. Each time the button is pressed, the die will randomly change their spots. The programs in this section can be found in the \SOURCE\CHAP15\dice directory. Please refer to the beginning of the chapter for instructions on how to run them.

How It Works

Listing 15.20 shows the complete source for the dice program. It consists of two classes: **DiceTest** and **Dice**. The **DiceTest** class constructs a frame window. The frame window is home to a panel that contains the two die and the Throw button. They are laid out using a **BorderLayout** class so that the button is placed at the bottom, the "South" of the window, while the Panel fills what is left of the window, the "Center." Each time the button is pressed, an action method is called. The action method will call the **throwDice** method for each of the dice.

Listing 15.20   DiceTest.java

```
import java.awt.*;
import java.util.*;
import java.lang.*;

public class DiceTest extends frame {
    Vector ds;

    public DiceTest() {

        super("Dice Test");
```

```
            setBackground(Color.lightGray);
            setLayout(new BorderLayout());
            Panel p = new Panel();
            p.setLayout( new GridLayout(1,2, 10, 10));
            ds = new Vector();
            for (int i = 0; i < 2; i++) {
                Dice d = new Dice();
                d.cheat(i);
                ds.addElement(d);
                p.add(d);
            }
            add("Center", p);
            p = new Panel();
            p.add( new Button("Throw") );
            add("South", p);
            resize(240, 140);
            show();
        }

    public boolean action(Event evt, Object obj) {
    if (evt.target instanceof Button) {
        String label = (String)obj;
        if (label.equals("Throw")) {
                for (Enumeration e=ds.elements();
                                 e.hasMoreElements(); ) {
                    Dice d = (Dice) e.nextElement();
                    d.throwDice();
                }
                repaint();
            }
    }
    return true;
        }

    public static void main(String args[]) {
    frame f = new DiceTest();
        }
}
class Dice extends Canvas {
    Random rand;
    int r;
    int value;

    Dice() {
        rand = new Random(hashCode());
        r = 10;
        setBackground(Color.white);
        setForeground(Color.black);
    }

    public synchronized void throwDice() {
        value = Math.abs(rand.nextInt()) % 6;
        // DBG System.out.println(toString());
        repaint();
```

```
    }

    void cheat(int n) {
        value = n % 6;
        repaint();
    }

    public int getNumber() {
        return value+1;
    }

    public String toString() {
        return new String("num="+value);
    }

    public void paint(Graphics g) {
        Dimension d = size();
        g.drawRoundRect(0, 0, d.width, d.height, 10, 10);
        switch ( value+1) {
            case 1:
                g.fillOval(d.width/2, d.height/2, r, r);
                break;
            case 2:
                g.fillOval(d.width/4, d.height*3/4, r, r);
                g.fillOval(d.width*3/4, d.height/4, r, r);
                break;
            case 3:
                g.fillOval(d.width/2, d.height/2, r, r);
                g.fillOval(d.width/4, d.height*3/4, r, r);
                g.fillOval(d.width*3/4, d.height/4, r, r);
                break;
            case 4:
                g.fillOval(d.width/4, d.height/4, r, r);
                g.fillOval(d.width*3/4, d.height/4, r, r);
                g.fillOval(d.width/4, d.height*3/4, r, r);
                g.fillOval(d.width*3/4, d.height*3/4, r, r);
                break;
            case 5:
                g.fillOval(d.width/2, d.height/2, r, r);
                g.fillOval(d.width/4, d.height/4, r, r);
                g.fillOval(d.width*3/4, d.height/4, r, r);
                g.fillOval(d.width/4, d.height*3/4, r, r);
                g.fillOval(d.width*3/4, d.height*3/4, r, r);
                break;
            case 6:
                g.fillOval(d.width/4, d.height/2, r, r);
                g.fillOval(d.width*3/4, d.height/2, r, r);
                g.fillOval(d.width/4, d.height/4, r, r);
                g.fillOval(d.width*3/4, d.height/4, r, r);
                g.fillOval(d.width/4, d.height*3/4, r, r);
                g.fillOval(d.width*3/4, d.height*3/4, r, r);
                break;
        }
    }
}
```

The heart of the dice program is the **Dice** class. This class is derived from the **Canvas** class. Each time the **throwDice** method is called, the dice will come up with a new number. When a **Dice** object is constructed, the dice will create a random number generator for itself. It will use this to determine how many spots to display on the dice. The **throwDice** method simple calls the random number generator to generate a new number, then calls a repaint. The **paint** method, which is called when the repaint happens, will draw the dice according to which number has been chosen by the random number generator. The **paint** method uses a **switch** statement to draw different patterns for each of the numbers. Each spot of the dice is drawn using a **fillOval** method set up to draw a circle.

Each dice class has its own **Random** object, which it uses to determine the dice value. As each dice has its own random number generator on-board, each dice should display an independent number. However, all is not as it appears. To find out more we need to understand a little more about random numbers.

Pseudo-Random Numbers

The numbers generated by the Java Random Number generator are what are termed *pseudo-random numbers*. Pseudo-random! How can a random number be pseudo? It sounds like the number is not random at all.

Actually, this is true. There is no way to produce a truly random number on a computer. The computer is what is termed a *deterministic* device. Deterministic means that if we do the same thing over and over again we always get the same result. If the computer were not deterministic it would not be so useful to us. After all, we want a device that will add two numbers up and for the same two numbers it will always give the same (hopefully, correct) answer.

However, this deterministic nature of the computer makes it difficult to produce a random number. After all, if it does the same thing over and over again—it is not random. To deal with this problem, pseudo-random numbers are produced.

Pseudo-random numbers are a long repeating cycle of numbers. The numbers are generated by a mathematical function that produces numbers appearing to be random. The pseudo-random numbers are *seeded* by an initial value. From there onwards, an algorithm will generate another number from the original number. The algorithm keeps generating pseudo-random numbers.

Eventually the numbers will cycle through and start over with the original value. Some random number generators have very long cycles—like 2 raised to the power 50—before they repeat the cycle. This does not mean that same numbers do not repeat themselves during the 2 raised to the power 50 sequence. It means that a guy, sitting trying to guess what the next number was, would have to memorize 2 to the power 50 numbers before he would know for certain what the next one was. A tall order—even for the famed Russian memory man, S.

The "randomness" is heavily dependent on the *seed* value. If two random number generators are started with the same seed value, then the random number generators will generate the same sequence of numbers. This would not be much use to us with the **Dice** class we created earlier. If we had two dice and the random numbers were generating the same sequence, we would keep throwing doubles. This is handy in a game of snakes and ladders but not much use elsewhere.

To stop two random number sequences being the same, we must ensure that their seed numbers are different. If you just use the code

```
new Random()
```

to construct a random number, the **Random** class uses the current system millisecond time to seed the random number generator. This can cause problems in some cases. For instance, if we construct two dice, one after the other, chances are that the two could easily be constructed within the same millisecond because a computer can execute a large number of instructions inside a millisecond.

The random number generator does allow you to provide your own seed value. So what we need then is a unique seed number for each **Dice** object. There are probably many ways to do this. The technique I most commonly use is the **hashCode** method. The **hashCode** method is supplied by the **Object** class. This is the class from which all other classes inherit, so the **hashCode** method is available in classes. As the source code for Object.java says, this number is generally unique for each object, so it serves our purpose.

How the pseudo-random number generator actually works is well out of the scope of this book. If you are interested in finding out more, here are a few suggestions. The source code for Random.java recommends Donald Knuth's *The Art of Computer Programming, Volume 2* , Section 3.2.1. Donald Knuth has played a major role in the development of computer algorithms. His books are a very valuable contribution to computer science. However, a word of warning: they are serious and demand a lot of reading. If you'd like a more readable book, you might try *Algorithms* by Robert Sedgewick.

COLORS

Support for colors is provided via the **Color** class. It has a number of different methods to allow us to create different colors. The programs in this section can be found in the \SOURCE\CHAP15\COLEDIT directory. Please refer to the beginning of the chapter for instructions on how to run them.

There are two types of objects for which we can set colors. We can set colors for components such as the **Canvas**, and we can set colors in the **Graphics** object.

Components maintain the concept of a *foreground* and a *background* color. These can be manipulated using the set and get foreground and background color methods that are part of all component objects. The background color is the color that is used for the background of the window; the foreground color is that color that all drawing will be done in.

The **Graphics** object on the other hand only supports one color. The color is set using the **setColor** method and all drawing and filling is done using that color. When the graphics object is set up for the **paint** method, it is preset to be the foreground color of the component object that owns the **paint** method. Therefore, if all your drawing is to be in a particular color, you can just set the foreground color in the component. However, if you will be frequently changing the color you want to draw in, the best scheme is to change the color on the **Graphics** object.

Creating Colors

When we want a color we must get an object of the **Color** class. The **Color** class provides three ways for you to create colors.

Option 1: Standard Colors

The **Color** class lets us choose from a standard set of colors. The standard set of colors are specified in the **Color** class as static objects so there is no need to instantiate a new color. You can just use a standard color straight in any of the color setting routines. For example, to set the color blue as the current graphics drawing color in a **paint** method we might use:

```
public void paint(Graphics g) {
    g.setColor(Color.blue);
}
```

As you can see, we have not constructed the color object, we have used a straight value. There are a number of colors in the standard set. These colors 1are shown in Table 15.2.

Option 2: RGB Color Naming Scheme

RGB stands for Red, Green, and Blue. The RGB color scheme works by combining different amounts of red, green, or blue to form the color that you want. If you remember your color wheel from school, you will know that you can form any color if you combine the right proportions of red, green, and blue. Arguments abound as to whether white and black are colors, but even they can be formed using RGB. White is the color that is formed when large, equal amounts of red, green, and blue are mixed together; black is formed when none of the colors are present.

There are three constructors that allow you to create a color using the RGB system. The first two are shown in the following code lines:

```
public Color(int r, int g, int b)
public Color(float r, float g, float b)
```

These first two constructors take individual values for each of the red, green, and blue values. Using the **int** constructor, you can specify the values using any number between 0 and 255. 255 represents the color

Table 15.2 *Standard Colors*

Color	Red	Green	Blue
white	255	255	255
lightGray	192	192	192
gray	128	128	128
darkGray	64	64	64
black	0	0	0
red	255	0	0
pink	255	175	175
orange	255	200	0
yellow	255	255	0
green	0	255	0
magenta	255	0	255
cyan	0	255	255
blue	0	0	255

being fully present. In other words, you can add no more of that particular color. Blue, for instance, would be constructed as shown in the following code line:

```
new Color(0, 0, 255)
```

As you will have gathered, 0 means that there is none of a particular color present. In the blue constructor, there is obviously no red and no green present in the color.

The second version—the float version—of the constructor can be used to specify colors using float values between 0.0 and 1.0 instead of 0 and 255. A point to notice is that even though you can give finer grained numbers using floats, the float values do not give more accurate colors. The floats are first converted into the closest 0 to 255 **int** value before the color is created. The float version is given more for convenience than for better accuracy.

This final constructor is, in some sense, the most raw way to specify RGB. You can imagine in the code

```
public Color(int rgb)
```

that the single **int** value, which is composed of 32 bits, allocated 8 bits to each of the colors. If you know your binary arithmetic, you will know that 8 bits can be used to represent 256 different values: hence, the 0..255 range we have been using, as shown in Figure 15.19.

The RGB naming convention can be a little confusing at times. The concept of a color being completely present is kind of bogus. For instance, which has more blue: white (red=255, green=255, blue=255), yellow (red=0, green=255, blue=255) or blue (red=0, green=0, blue=255) ? Well, obviously, blue is bluer, so it must have more blue in it, but the RGB value for blue is the same in each case. The important thing to consider with RGB is the ratio of the colors, as well as the colors themselves.

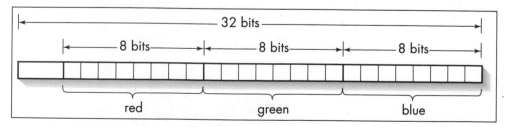

Figure 15.19   *Bit arrangement of an int RGB value.*

RGB is often represented as a cube, shown in Figure 15.20, with each of the colors taking a different axis of the cube. The color that you want is somewhere on the surface or on the inside of the cube.

Option 3: HSB Color Naming Scheme

HSB stands for Hue, Saturation, Brightness. It's another way of describing a color. Like RGB, the three HSB values can be used to describe any color. However, rather than break colors down in the three red, green, and blue colors, HSB uses a different mechanism.

The hue is the color or tint. Given a particular value for the hue, you would have a definite understanding of what the color was. Saturation is a measure of how strong the color is. It is a measure of the color purity. Brightness gives a measure of the lightness of the color. With a high brightness you can imagine a bright light being shone on the color, with a low brightness the color can be imagined as being viewed in a much darker setting.

The values for each of these numbers are floating point numbers between 0.0 and 1.0. Unlike the RGB values, the **Color** class does not provide a constructor; instead, a static method that will construct the color is provided, as shown in the code line:

```
public static Color getHSBColor(float h, float s, float b)
```

There are also several utility methods that allow conversion between the RGB naming scheme and the HSB naming scheme.

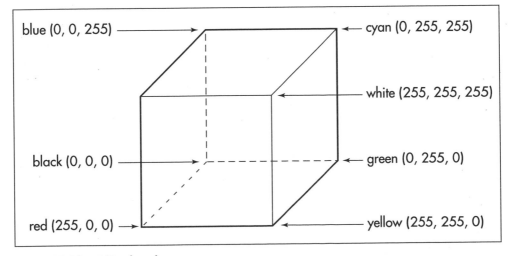

Figure 15.20 RGB color cube.

The HSB has a very interesting associated diagram, shown in Figure 15.21. RGB, we mentioned, can be viewed as a cube. HSB is typically imagined as a double cone with the points of the code being black and white. Like the RGB cube, the HSB color is either inside or on the surface of the cone.

These visualization techniques can come in very handy when you want to write color-selection programs. If you have done much work with good-quality painting programs you will probably recognize the visualization metaphor.

Why Three Ways to Create Colors?

So Java provides three ways to specify colors. One of them, the standard set of colors, is obviously provided as a convenience, but the other two seem to conflict. They both let us create a color using a combination of three values.

Having two color specification mechanisms seems like a certain amount of overkill. Surely one is enough. Well, sure, one *is* enough, but two are *very* useful. As it happens, there are numerous ways to specify colors in the computer world, but broadly speaking, they fall into two categories: those natural to the computer, and those useful to us humans.

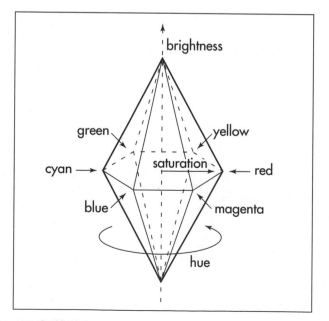

Figure 15.21   *HSB double cone.*

The **Color** class usefully provides one of each. The RGB format is the one closest to the computer way of using color. This probably comes as no surprise because TV sets use RGB guns to create a color picture. Most hardware graphics cards directly support the RGB format. You can load in the RGB value into a register in the card and the color is set.

The HSB value is much more in line with how we humans think.

Try this experiment: Below we present a program that lets us choose colors. Run the program, choose a color, then before changing, say, the brightness of the color, try to guess what the new color will look like. Try the same trick with RGB try to guess the outcome of changing one of the values. If you do this a number of times you will probably find that you can start to fairly accurately predict the new color using the HSB scheme, but using the RGB scheme it is much more difficult. Navigating your way around the RGB cube is a difficult process and one that takes a lot of learning. Moving around the HSB double cone is much easier even though the double cone sounds like a tough thing to say and the cube sounds easier :-)

If you want to know more about color representation on computers, I recommend that you take a look at the book, *Fundamentals of Computer Graphics* by Foley and Van Dam. It is a truly heavy weight computer graphics book, but it will cover most everything you need to know!

Altering Colors

Once you have a color object, you can't change the value of the color that it represents. To get a new color, you need to create a new color object. You can get red, green, and blue values from an existing color object to help you create your new color, as shown in this code snippet:

```
Color color = g.getColor();
Color newColor = new Color(color.getRed(), color.getGreen(), 255);
```

In addition to creating new colors by calculating values yourself, the **Color** class also provides two convenience methods, **brighter** and **darker**, which will create new color objects that are either lighter or darker versions of the current color, as shown in this code snippet:

```
Color color = g.getColor();
Color brighterColor = color.brighter();
Color darkerColor = color.darker();
```

Color Your World

Let's write a little explorer program that will let us see what colors are produced by the different creation options. It allows you to create colors based on the three color selection mechanisms that the JDK supports: choosing a standard color, using RGB to create a color, or using HSB to create a color. It also provides features to alter the brightness and the darkness of the color. Figure 15.22 shows the program running.

The color in the center of the window can be changed using any of the four mechanisms provided.

At the bottom of the screen is a row of buttons. These buttons let you choose one of the standard colors. The standard colors are supplied as part of the **Color** class. When you press one of the buttons, the color will change to the selected color.

At the top of the screen are two buttons: Brighten and Darken. These buttons, as their names imply, Brighten and Darken the color that is currently displayed. You can keep darkening or lightening the color until eventually the color turns to black or white. Obviously, brightening white or darkening black makes no difference to the color.

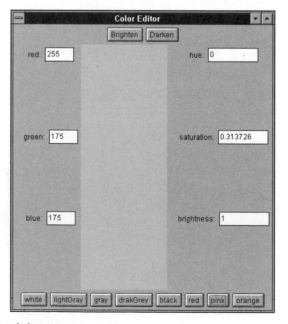

Figure 15.22   *The ColEdit program in action.*

The left side of the screen is used to set the color using the RGB color naming scheme. You will need to enter values between 0 and 255. The right side of the window is used to specify the color using the HSB. The values for each of these numbers are floating point numbers between 0.0 and 1.0. The code itself is shown in Listing 15.21.

Listing 15.21   ColEdit.java

```java
import java.awt.*;
import java.util.*;
import extension.*;

class ColorCanvas extends Canvas implements Observer {
    ColorSetting colorSetting;

    ColorCanvas(ColorSetting s) {
        colorSetting = s;
        s.addObserver(this);
    }

    public void update(Observable o, Object arg) {
        repaint();
    }

    public void paint(Graphics g) {
        Dimension d = size();
        g.setPaintMode();
        g.setColor(colorSetting.getColor());
        g.fillRect(0, 0, d.width-1, d.height-1);
    }
}

class ColorSetting extends Observable {
    private Color col;

    ColorSetting() {
        col = new Color(0,0,0);
    }

    public void setRed(int r) {
        col = new Color(r, col.getGreen(), col.getBlue());
        tell();
    }

    public void setGreen(int g) {
        col = new Color(col.getRed(), g, col.getBlue());
        tell();
    }

    public void setBlue(int b) {
        col = new Color(col.getRed(), col.getGreen(), b);
```

```
        tell();
    }

    public void setColor(Color c) {
        col = c;
        tell();
    }

    public int getRGB(String c) {
        if (c.equals("red")) return col.getRed();
        if (c.equals("green")) return col.getGreen();
        if (c.equals("blue")) return col.getBlue();
        return 0;
    }

    public void setRGB(String c, int i) {
        if (c.equals("red")) setRed(i);
        if (c.equals("green")) setGreen(i);
        if (c.equals("blue")) setBlue(i);
        tell();
    }

    public float getHSB(String c) {
        if (c.equals("hue"))
            return Color.RGBtoHSB(col.getRed(), col.getGreen(),
                                  col.getBlue(), null)[0];
        if (c.equals("saturation"))
            return Color.RGBtoHSB(col.getRed(), col.getGreen(),
                                  col.getBlue(), null)[1];
        if (c.equals("brightness"))
            return Color.RGBtoHSB(col.getRed(), col.getGreen(),
                                  col.getBlue(), null)[2];
        return 0;
    }

    public void setHSB(String c, float f) {
        float hsb[] = Color.RGBtoHSB(col.getRed(), col.getGreen(),
                                     col.getBlue(), null);
        if (c.equals("hue"))
            col = Color.getHSBColor(f, hsb[1], hsb[2]);
        if (c.equals("saturation"))
            col = Color.getHSBColor(hsb[0], f, hsb[2]);
        if (c.equals("brightness"))
            col = Color.getHSBColor(hsb[0], hsb[1], f);
        tell();
    }

    public void brighten() {
        col = col.brighter();
        tell();
    }

    public void darken() {
```

```
            col = col.darker();
            tell();
        }

    void tell() {
        setChanged();
        notifyObservers(this);
    }

    public Color getColor() {
        return col;
    }
}

class HSBField extends Panel implements Observer {
    String name;
    ColorSetting colorSetting;
    TextField fld;

    HSBField(ColorSetting cs, String s) {
        name = s;
        colorSetting = cs;
        add( new Label(name+":"));
        add(fld = new TextField(Float.toString(cs.getHSB(s)), 9));
        cs.addObserver(this);
    }

    public void update(Observable o, Object arg) {
        ColorSetting cs = (ColorSetting) arg;
        String s = Float.toString( cs.getHSB(name));
        if (!s.equals(field.getText()))
            fld.setText(s);
    }

    public boolean action(Event evt, Object what) {
        float value = Float.valueOf(fld.getText()).floatValue();
        colorSetting.setHSB(name, value);
        return true;
    }
}

class RGBField extends Panel implements Observer {
    String name;
    ColorSetting colorSetting;
    TextField f;

    RGBField(ColorSetting cs, String s) {
        name = s;
        colorSetting = cs;
        add( new Label(name+":"));
        add(f = new TextField(Integer.toString(cs.getRGB(s)), 4));
        cs.addObserver(this);
    }
```

```
    public void update(Observable o, Object arg) {
        ColorSetting cs = (ColorSetting) arg;
        String s = Integer.toString( cs.getRGB(name));
        if (!s.equals(f.getText()))
            f.setText(s);
    }

    public boolean action(Event evt, Object what) {
        if (evt.target == f) {
            int value = Integer.parseInt(f.getText());
            colorSetting.setRGB(name, value);
            return true;
        }
        return true;
    }
}

class BrightenButton extends Button {
    ColorSetting colorSetting;

    BrightenButton(ColorSetting c) {
        super("Brighten");
        colorSetting = c;
    }

    public boolean action(Event evt, Object what) {
        if (evt.target == this) {
            colorSetting.brighten();
            return true;
        }
        return false;
    }
}

class DarkenButton extends Button {
    ColorSetting colorSetting;

    DarkenButton(ColorSetting c) {
        super("Darken");
        colorSetting = c;
    }

    public boolean action(Event evt, Object what) {
        if (evt.target == this) {
            colorSetting.darken();
            return true;
        }
        return false;
    }
}

class RGBButton extends Button {
    ColorSetting colorSetting;
```

```
    Color color;

    RGBButton(ColorSetting cs, String name, Color c) {
        super(name);
        colorSetting = cs;
        color = c;
    }

    public boolean action(Event evt, Object what) {
        if (evt.target == this) {
            colorSetting.setColor(color);
            return true;
        }
        return false;
    }
}

public class ColEdit extends frame {

    ColorSetting cs;

    public ColEdit() {

        super("Color Editor");

    setBackground(Color.lightGray);
        setLayout( new BorderLayout());

        cs = new ColorSetting();

        Panel p = new Panel();
        p.setLayout( new GridLayout(3,1));
        p.add(new RGBField(cs, "red"));
        p.add(new RGBField(cs, "green"));
        p.add(new RGBField(cs, "blue"));
        add("West", p);

        add("Center", new ColorCanvas(cs));

        p = new Panel();
        p.setLayout( new GridLayout(3, 1));
        p.add(new HSBField(cs, "hue"));
        p.add(new HSBField(cs, "saturation"));
        p.add(new HSBField(cs, "brightness"));
        add("East", p);

        p = new Panel();
        p.add(new BrightenButton(cs));
        p.add(new DarkenButton(cs));
        add("North", p);

        p = new Panel();
        p.add( new RGBButton(cs, "white", Color.white));
```

```
        p.add( new RGBButton(cs, "lightGray", Color.lightGray));
        p.add( new RGBButton(cs, "gray", Color.gray));
        p.add( new RGBButton(cs, "drakGrey", Color.darkGray));
        p.add( new RGBButton(cs, "black", Color.black));
        p.add( new RGBButton(cs, "red", Color.red));
        p.add( new RGBButton(cs, "pink", Color.pink));
        p.add( new RGBButton(cs, "orange", Color.orange));
        p.add( new RGBButton(cs, "yellow", Color.yellow));
        p.add( new RGBButton(cs, "green", Color.green));
        p.add( new RGBButton(cs, "magenta", Color.magenta));
        p.add( new RGBButton(cs, "cyan", Color.cyan));
        p.add( new RGBButton(cs, "blue", Color.blue));
        add("South", p);

        resize(550, 550);
        show();
    }

    public static void main(String args[]) {
    frame f = new ColEdit();
    }
}
```

As you can see from Listing 15.21, the program is based on a **Frame** object which contains all the buttons, text fields, and the canvas area that make up the program. To keep the program short, each of the RGB and each of the HSB fields are provided by the same component. The constructor decides which one to build. **RGBButtons** provides access to the standard colors. The Darken and Brighten buttons are formed by deriving buttons from the **Button** class.

The whole thing is laid out using a combination of panels each arranged into a **BorderLayout** format.

What will probably be confusing to you is the way that the program hangs together. There is a central class called **ColorSetting**, which seems to be the thing that all of the buttons and text fields talk to.

To understand how the program works, we need to look at a couple of other classes called **Observer** and **Observable**.

OBSERVER AND OBSERVABLE

Did you notice that the numbers in the HSB and the RGB fields changed when different colors were selected? Take a look. Whenever you press one of the color buttons, the values in the RGB and the HSB fields will change. Also, if you change an RGB value, the HSB values will change to match the RGB, and vice versa.

It seems like the each of the different fields knows all about the other buttons and fields. For instance, if we press one of the standard colors buttons, it must set the values for the RGB and the HSB and set the color canvas to the correct color. Or when changing an HSB value, the HSB field must calculate the new RGB values and set the color in the center of the screen.

This sounds like a lot of work.

Actually the system does not work like this at all. I want to introduce you to two very useful and special classes: **Observer** and **Observable**. **Observer** and **Observable** are a great help in writing user interfaces on the screen that need to be kept instep with each other.

The idea is that the observable is managing some information that is being watched by the observers. When the observers want to watch an observable they register themselves with observable. They do this by calling the **addObserver** method of the **Observable** object, as shown in this code snippet.

```
s.addObserver(this);
```

The observable will maintain a list of all the observers that are watching it. When information held by the observable changes, the observable will call a method called **setChanged**, then a method called **notifyObservers**. This has the effect of calling an **update** method against each of the **Observer** objects, as shown in the code snippet below and in Figure 15.23.

```
setChanged();
notifyObservers(this);
```

The observers now know that the observable has changed and they are free to query the observable for more information.

Take the example we have here. We have a color that we are trying to change. We want to be able to alter that color, but we want all things that have an interest in the color to be told about the color.

You see, the color is something that is being changed. There are lots of things viewing this color though. The RGB fields are a view of the colors, as are the HSB fields, and the color canvas.

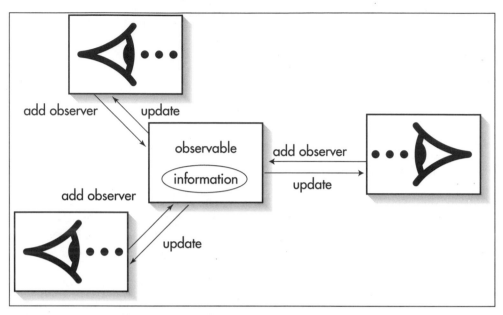

Figure 15.23 *The observer and observables.*

Confused? Well okay. A little confusion now and then is the hallmark of an active mind. Look at it this way: we have a concept called color; it is an abstract concept. We can't see the color, just a model of it. Now we can ask the color what its RGB values are and we can ask it what its HSB values are. We can also attach a view to the color. This color view will set the correct hardware values on our graphics card so we can see the color.

So the abstract color remains behind the scenes. We don't see it directly we only see it through the "eyes" of the RGB field, the HSB fields, and the color canvas. Take a look at the code back in Listing 15.21, the abstract color is represented by the class called **ColorSetting**.

The **ColorSetting** class extends the **Observable** class. In other words, it is being watched by other classes such as the **ColorCanvas** class.

The **ColorCanvas** class implements the **Observer** interface. That means that it must provide a method called **update**. When the **update** method is called the **ColorCanvas** knows that it observable, the **ColorSetting** object has changed, it can now update itself to be consistent with the new values stored in the **ColorSetting** object.

Take a good look at the two classes. Notice that the **ColorSetting** never calls the **ColorCanvas** class directly.

There are many uses for the **Observer** and **Observable** classes, but keeping the user interface up to date is probably the most common and the most useful. As an example of using **Observer** and **Observable,** take a look at the Visible Human applet, shown in Figure 15.24. This applet can be found at Web address http://www.npac.syr.edu/projects/vishuman/Visible Human.html.

The Visible Human applet shows a cross section of the human body at the top left of the screen. The cross section is governed by the two full views of the human body and by settings on the buttons and fields at the bottom of the screen. Given the interconnection between the various views and the various settings, how would you implement the Visible Human applet now that you know about the **Observer** and the **Observable** classes?

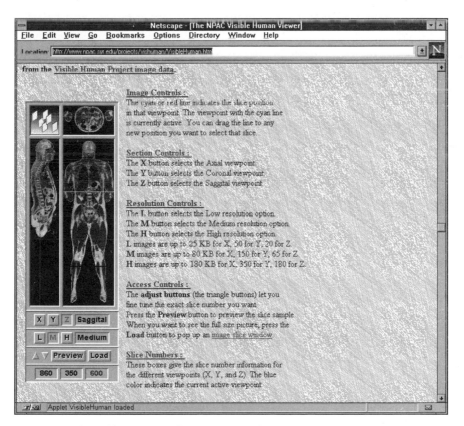

Figure 15.24   *The Visible Human applet.*

TEXT

The programs in this section can be found in the \SOURCE\CHAP15\TEXT directory. Please refer to the beginning of the chapter for instructions on how to run them.

Text can be drawn directly into the canvas using low-level text drawing methods provided by the **Graphics** class. These low-level text methods do not provide the support that a **TextArea** or a **TextField** component would provide. The **TextArea** component, for instance, knows about text lines and can be used to select text. The **Graphics** class text drawing methods do not support the newline mechanism. If the text runs off the edge of the canvas, it is clipped and will not be drawn: it does not start a new text line automatically.

The graphics text routines though have a lot of advantages. You can set the color of the text, you can control the text spaces, and best of all, you can write "Jiggly" text programs. "Jiggly" text programs are like a pet-rock fad among Java programmers. We will be looking at a "Jiggly" text program in a moment. Figure 15.25 shows a sample program that draws a few lines of text. It demonstrates how to draw text using the different drawing methods, and it shows how the newline character does not cause a newline on the screen. Listing 15.22 shows the code that produces the program.

Listing 15.22 TextTest.java

```java
import java.awt.*;

class TextCanvas extends Canvas {
    Font font1, font2;

    TextCanvas() {
        font1 = new Font("TimesRoman", Font.PLAIN, 36);
        font2 = new Font("TimesRoman", Font.PLAIN, 24);
    }

    public void paint(Graphics g) {
        Dimension d = size();

        g.setFont(font1);
        g.setColor(Color.red);
        g.drawString("Hello", 20, 30);
        g.setFont(font2);
        g.setColor(Color.yellow);
        // see how the character does not cause a newline!
        g.drawString("Here is a string with a newline\nin it",
                        20, 60);

        g.setColor(Color.blue);
```

```
            FontMetrics fm = getFontMetrics(getFont());
            String str = "Stepup";
            int height = fm.getHeight();
            char[] chars = str.toCharArray();
            for (int i = 0; i < str.length(); i++) {
                int xwidth = fm.charsWidth(chars, 0, i+1);
                g.drawChars(chars, i, 1, 20+xwidth+1, 120-i*height/2);
            }
        }
    }
}

public class TextTest extends frame {

    public TextTest() {
    setBackground(Color.lightGray);
        setLayout( new BorderLayout());
        add("Center", new TextCanvas());
        resize(550, 250);
        show();
    }

    public static void main(String args[]) {
    frame f = new TextTest();
    }
}
```

When text is drawn using the graphics text methods, you will need to specify the x and y coordinates of the baseline of the text. The baseline is like a line in a notebook: text without descenders sits on the line, characters with descenders such as g cross the line, as shown in Figure 15.26.

Currently, all individual characters are drawn in a left to right fashion. You cannot angle individual characters, though you can staircase the text to get a rising or descending text string. It is possible to rotate text, but it will require a lot of work on you part—you will need to draw the text into an image string then rotate the image string, then draw the image string in the correct place. There are a lot of issues involved here, so we will not cover this technique.

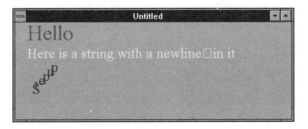

Figure 15.25 *The TestText program in action.*

Figure 15.26 *The baseline of text.*

FONTS

The programs in this section can be found in the \SOURCE\CHAP15\FONT directory. Please refer to the beginning of the chapter for instructions on how to run them.

The style and shape of the text that is drawn is controlled by the font of the text. There is always a default font available for text to be drawn in. The JDK provides a **Font** class which provides the main mechanism for describing fonts. You will need to construct a **Font** object if you want to change the font in use. Table 15.3 shows the attribute settings of the JDK fonts.

The font styles can be one or more of the following: Font.PLAIN, Font.BOLD, Font.ITALIC. To get a combination of the font styles, add together the styles. For example, to get a bold and italic font use the style shown in the following code snippet:

```
Font.BOLD+Font.ITALIC
```

Table 15.3 *Font Attributes*

Attribute	Set	Get	Description
Logical Name	setName	getName	The name of the font; the logical name is the same on all platforms
Family	setFamily	getFamily	Platform specific name of the font; this can be regarded as the font that 'implements' the logical font
Style	setStyle	getStyle	The style refers to the typeface of the font.
Size	setSize	getSize	The size of the font; the font size is given in point size

Listing All the Fonts Available on a Machine

A list of all the logical names available on a platform can be retrieved using the **Toolkit** class. The **Toolkit** class provides a method, **getFontList**, that will return a list of available logical font names as an array of Strings. We can get an object of the **Toolkit** class using the method shown in the code line:

```
Toolkit.getDefaultToolkit();
```

Listing 15.23 shows a short program to list the available fonts on to standard out.

Listing 15.23   Listing Available Fonts

```
import java.awt.*;
import java.lang.*;

public class FontList {

    public static void main(String args[]) {
    Toolkit tk = Toolkit.getDefaultToolkit();
        String[] fonts = tk.getFontList();
        for (int i=0; i < fonts.length; ++i)
            System.out.println(fonts[i]);
    }
}
```

When this program is run on my machine, I get the following list:

```
Cmdt>java FontList
Dialog
Helvetica
TimesRoman
Courier
Symbol
```

What Is a Toolkit?

In some sense, the **Toolkit** class is the creator class of the AWT. It is an interface to a lot of specific system information. For instance, we can get the screen size and a list of available fonts using the **Toolkit** class.

Most importantly, though, the **Toolkit** class is closely tied in with the peer classes we spoke about in a graphics tutorial chapter. The peer classes, you will recall, are the go-betweens that sit between the system-specific controls and AWT components. The **Toolkit** is the manufacturer of the peer classes. The **Toolkit** class is what is known as a factory class. In some sense, the **Toolkit** class is a stand-in for the operating system specifics. Each platform will have a different implementation of the **Toolkit** class, but because it provides the same interface on all platforms, the classes of the JDK can use the **Toolkit** class to get system-dependent things. For instance, components can use the **Toolkit** class to construct their corresponding peer class.

You might be tempted to ask: Why can't components just construct a peer class directly? The answer is that the **Toolkit** provides an extra degree of management. It can be used to ensure that system resources can be tuned. This enables the implementation of the platform specifics to retain a certain degree of control over the creation of system-specific resources.

Font Selection

Here is a simple program, demonstrated in Figure 15.27, to show the fonts that the JDK will let you use on your machine.

The idea of the program is that you can select a font using the three font description parameters: font name, style, and size. A string consisting of all the uppercase and lowercase characters in the font is drawn in that font. If the string will not fit on the screen, then as much of the string as possible will be shown. Below the string is a little information about the font.

When you take a look at the Font Selection program, be sure to try out different sizes and text styles. On my machine, this provided some very interesting information. Be careful how large a font size you choose. The program deliberately does not protect against large font sizes. I found on my machine that setting a large number—say 5000—as the point size was enough to hang my machine. This has a couple of impacts. First off, don't run the program when you have other programs with unsaved data. More importantly, you should consider providing limitations on the maximum size that can be set from programs that you write in which you allow your users to set the font size. If you do not, you will potentially run the risk of crashing user machines.

Figure 15.27   *The Font Selection program.*

Another aspect of setting the font size is so that you can see the effects of changing the size. Fonts generally come in two technologies—raster fonts and *vector* (or stroke) fonts.

Characters in raster fonts are just bitmaps which are drawn on to the screen. Raster fonts are fast to draw because it is fast to draw an image on the screen. However, raster fonts have a couple of draw backs. First, they are fixed size: a new raster font must be calculated for each new font size. Second, they require a lot of memory to hold all the bitmaps. A side effect of the raster fonts is that the description of the fonts is only done for certain point sizes. This means that in-between point sizes tend to be a bit jaggy, as shown in Figure 15.27.

Characters in vector fonts, on the other hand, are not stored as bitmaps. Instead, they are stored as a description the outline is a list of points that must be joined up, like a connect-the-dots puzzle, and then filled in. Obviously, vector fonts are slower to draw than bitmap fonts because each character must be calculated however; they have the advantage of being stored as a single description and that one description can be used to describe any size of font.

When you experiment with the font size you will discover which fonts are raster and which are vector.

Implementing the Font Selector

The complete source for the FontSelector program is on the disk as the file FontSelector.java. The code is shown in Listing 15.24.

Figure 15.27   *An in-between point size of a raster font.*

Listing 15.24 FontSelector.java

```java
import java.awt.*;
import java.util.*;
import extension.*;

class FontCanvas extends Canvas implements Observer {
    FontSetting fontSetting;
    int xoffset, yoffset;

    FontCanvas(FontSetting s) {
        fontSetting = s;
        s.addObserver(this);
        xoffset = yoffset = 10;
    }

    public void update(Observable o, Object arg) {
        // note setFont will cause a repaint
    setFont(fontSetting.getFont());
        // repaint()
    }

    public void paint(Graphics g) {
        Dimension d = size();
        g.setPaintMode();
        FontMetrics fm = getFontMetrics(getFont());
        g.drawString(
            "AaBbCcDdEeFfGgHhIiJjKkLlMmNnOoPpQqRrSsTtUuVvWwXxYyZz",
            fm.getMaxAdvance()+xoffset, fm.getAscent()+yoffset);
    }
}

class FontSetting extends Observable {
    private Font font;

    FontSetting() {
        font = new Font("Helvetica", Font.PLAIN,10);
    }

    public void setName(String s) {
        font = new Font(s, font.getStyle(), font.getSize());
        tell();
    }

    public void setType(String s) {
        if (s.equals("Font.PLAIN"))
            font = new Font(font.getName(), Font.PLAIN,
                            font.getSize());
        if (s.equals("Font.BOLD"))
            font = new Font(font.getName(), Font.BOLD,
                            font.getSize());
        if (s.equals("Font.ITALIC"))
            font = new Font(font.getName(), Font.ITALIC,
```

```
                                    font.getSize());
        tell();
    }

    public void setSize(int p) {
        font = new Font(font.getName(), font.getStyle(), p);
        tell();
    }

    void tell() {
        setChanged();
        notifyObservers(this);
    }

    public Font getFont() {
        return font;
    }
}


class FontInfo extends Panel implements Observer {
    FontSetting fontSetting;
    Label leading;
    Label ascent;

    FontInfo(FontSetting fs) {
        fontSetting = fs;
        add( leading = new Label("Leading:         "));
        add( ascent = new Label("Ascent:          "));
        fs.addObserver(this);
    }

    public void update(Observable o, Object arg) {
        FontMetrics fm = getFontMetrics(fontSetting.getFont());
        leading.setText("Leading: "+fm.getLeading());
        ascent.setText("Ascent: "+fm.getAscent());
    }
}
class FontName extends Choice {
    FontSetting fontSetting;

    FontName(FontSetting fs) {
        fontSetting = fs;
    Toolkit tk = Toolkit.getDefaultToolkit();
        String[] fonts = tk.getFontList();
        for (int i=0; i < fonts.length; ++i)
            addItem(fonts[i]);
    }

    public boolean action(Event evt, Object what) {
        if (evt.target == this) {
            fontSetting.setName(getSelectedItem());
            return true;
        }
```

```
            return false;
        }
}

public class FontSelector extends frame {

    FontSetting fs;

    public FontSelector() {

        super("Font Editor");

    setBackground(Color.lightGray);
        setLayout( new BorderLayout());

        fs = new FontSetting();

        Panel p = new Panel();
        p.add(new FontName(fs));
        p.add(new FontType(fs));
        p.add(new FontSize(fs));
        add("North", p);

        add("Center", new FontCanvas(fs));

        add("South", new FontInfo(fs));

        resize(500, 750);
        show();
    }

    public static void main(String args[]) {
    frame f = new FontSelector();
    }
}
```

The FontSelector program uses a number of the techniques we have explored so far. The font is drawn using a **FontCanvas** class. The **FontCanvas** class is a descendant of the **Canvas** class, as well as an observer of a **FontSetting** class. When the **FontSetting** class changes, the **FontCanvas update** method is called. The method will then set the font for the **FontCanvas** object to the **FontSetting** object's Font. The font is set using the **setFont** method included with all component objects. The **setFont** class immediately forces a repaint. A word of warning here though: The forcing of the repaint is handled by the peer class. It is not coded into the **Component** class. This might mean that on your machine it may behave differently. I think that the coding of a forced repaint on a change of setting is a rather dubious behavior. If you find that your fonts don't change when you change the settings, I would first put in an extra repaint at the end of the **update** method.

The actual drawing of the string is handled in the **paint** method. It uses the **Graphics** method **drawString** to draw the upper- and lowercase string. The **Graphics** object uses the font for the component object it is created by. In this case the **Graphics** object uses the **FontCanvas** font object.

To ensure that the string is usefully visible, the font is positioned so that it is Ascent units from the top of the screen and Leading units from the left of the screen. To prevent the font from touching the sides of the screen, a 10 unit offset is also added in.

The **FontSetting** class is very similar in concept to the **ColorSetting** we used for the color program. It is an **Observable** object which stores the current setting of the font. As the font is changed it notifies all the **Observer** objects that have registered interest in the font settings that things have changed.

In this case, the only other **Observer** object beside the **FontCanvas** is the **FontInfo** object. This is the object that prints the font information on the current font into the scrolling text window. Each time the font settings are changed, the text window will replace its text with the information on the current font.

The changing of the setting is done by a couple of choice controls and a text field. These items simply call the appropriate method of the font settings object when they change. For example, below is the class for the **FontName** object, which sets the logical name of the font. This is a **Choice** component. The **Choice** component is filled using the **Toolkit** mechanism we saw earlier. When the choice is selected, the action event is called. The action event decodes the request to change the font name, gets the chosen name, and informs the font setting object.

The whole program is strung together using a combination of layout managers. The **FontCanvas** is set as the center of a **BorderLayout** to ensure that when a resize happens, it will get as much of the space as possible.

Font Metrics

If you want to know all the specific details about a font you will need to use the **FontMetrics** class. The **FontMetrics** class can access a lot of interesting information about the font, as shown in Figure 15.28. The methods that can be used to access this information are shown in Table 15.4.

The **FontMetrics** class is an abstract class. It cannot be instantiated. To get hold of a **FontMetrics** object you will need to use the **getFontMetrics** method

Figure 15.28 *Font metric information for a string.*

provided by component objects. For instance, to get the font metrics for the current font in, say, a **Canvas** object we can use the code shown:

```
FontMetrics fm = getFontMetrics(getFont());
```

Writing Text That Jiggles

Nervous or jiggly text apps are quite a common site on the Java scene. The Nervous Text applet, which is provided as part of the JDK, was one

Table 15.4 *Font Metric Information Methods*

Method	Description
getLeading	This is the appropriate amount of space to leave between lines of the font
getAscent	This is the distance from the baseline to the top of a character
getDescent	This is the distance from the baseline to the bottom of a character
getHeight	This is the distance from the top to the bottom of a character
getMaxAscent	This is the maximum ascent for all characters in the font
getMaxDecent	This is the maximum descent for all characters in the font
getMaxAdvance	This is the maximum space before any character in the font
charWidth	This is the width of an individual character
stringWidth	This is the width of an entire string

of the original look-what-I-can-do-Ma applets, that showed how Java could be used to add some eye-catching interest to an HTML page. Other applets have since taken Nervous Text and expanded its capabilities. I figured I could not write a section on text handling without showing you how it is done.

We have covered all the stuff we need to understand how it all works. Nervous texts are simply graphics areas with text being repeatedly repainted. The position of the text is controlled by randomly adjusting the font metric information, such as the height position of the text. At each repaint, the position is altered slightly.

Listing 15.25 shows a version of the **paint** method of a jiggly text applet. It assumes that the text is in a variable called **text**. I have also placed information, such as getting the **FontMetrics** object, in the **paint** method. Typically, though, this information does not change between repaints, so it would have been placed in the constructor of the applet.

Listing 15.25   Code for Jiggly Text

```
public void paint(Graphics g) {
    FontMetrics fm = getFontMetrics(getFont());
    char chars[] = new char[text.length()];
    text.getChars(0, text.length(), chars, 0);
    int positions [] = new int[text.length()];
    for (int i = 0; i < text.length(); i++) {
        positions[i] = fm.charsWidth(chars, 0, i);
    }

    for (int i = 0; i < text.length(); i++) {
        int x = (int)(Math.random() * jiggleFactor) + positions[i];
        int y = (int)(Math.random() * jiggleFactor) + fm.getAscent() - 1;
        g.drawChars(chars, i, 1, x, y);
    }
}
```

LET'S REVIEW

We have covered a lot in this chapter, but it has all centered around the **Graphics** class. The **Graphics** class is the core class you need to know if you want to draw graphics. The **Graphics** class is supported in its work by other classes such as the **Font**, **Canvas**, and the **Color** classes, to name but a few. As a whole these classes give you full control over the drawing you want to do.

We have not finished with the **Graphics** class. It is so central to all graphics related stuff that it will be popping up from time to time as a star player in other chapters.

INTERACTING WITH THE USER

Neil Bartlett

Java makes it easy to handle mouse and keyboard events. In this chapter, we show you how.

In the chapter on components, we spent a lot of time on the event processing mechanism. We looked at how event processing works under the covers and how to use events to help us write user-interface programs.

In this chapter, we are going to continue looking at events. We are going to focus on handling mouse and keyboard events. We will be using the Canvas component for all of the examples because it provides the most complete support for mouse and keyboard handling. However, the techniques we deal with in this chapter can also be applied to other components such as TextArea.

Event handling is more than just reacting to events. It is a two-way process. It is important to be able to feed back information—especially graphics information—rapidly and in step with the event handling. For instance, we want to be able to perform drag-and-drop style operations so that as we move the mouse, the object we are dragging will be moved smoothly and in step with the mouse. This is an important issue. A lot of the JDK event han-

dling is thread based and therefore needs careful attention to stop mouse dragging and object movement from getting out of step.

EVENT HANDLING—A RECAP

User interactions such as keyboard keys being pressed, mouse buttons being clicked, or the mouse being moved, generate events. These events are transmitted to the component that the event happened in. For instance, if the mouse pointer is in a Canvas window, **mousemove** events will be sent to the Canvas component. Equally if the keyboard focus is set to a Canvas window, the Canvas component will receive keyboard events when keys are pressed.

For each hardware interaction that happens an event is generated. Events can be very granular. For instance, a keyboard event is generated on both the up stroke and the down stroke of a key. A keyboard event is also generated each time the keyboard auto-repeat happens.

Events can be received by a component by overriding *event handler* methods. Each event handler method corresponds to a specific user interaction. A list of the event handler methods for the mouse and for the keyboard is shown in Table 16.1.

If a component is interested in an event, it will implement the event handler method and return true; otherwise, the JDK will provide a default event handler that will return false, indicating that the component is not interested in the event.

Table 16.1   *Mouse and Keyboard Event Handler Methods*

Event Handler	Called When
mouseEnter	The mouse enters the Canvas window
mouseExit	The mouse leaves the Canvas window
mouseMove	The mouse is moved and no mouse button is pressed
mouseDown	The mouse button is pressed
mouseDrag	The mouse is moved with the mouse button down
mouseUp	The mouse is released
keyDown	A key is depressed
keyUp	A key is released
gotFocus	The keyboard focus is given to the Canvas window
lostFocus	The keyboard focus is removed from the Canvas window

When an event handler method is called, an object called an *event object* is passed in as a parameter to the method. The event object is an instance of the **Event** class. The event object contains information relating to the event. To react to an event, it is generally necessary to examine the event object. The event object has a number of methods that can help to work out why the event was generated. For instance, the keyboard event object will contain information such as whether the key was pressed or released, which key it was and which, if any, keyboard modifier keys, such as the control key, were pressed at the same time the key event occurred.

The basis of user interaction is therefore to override the event handlers for the events that need to be reacted to, do the work to react to the event, and then return true from the event handler.

SHE'S GOT "JAVA EYES"

The Austrian philosopher Ludwig Wittgenstein remarked that if people didn't sometimes do silly things, nothing intelligent would ever get done. In that spirit, here is a *very* silly program. Still, I like it a lot. It has entertainment value way beyond its worth. Just the thing to show your friends how human your computer can be. It's shown in Figure 16.1.

Yes, the program is JavaEyes. In case you hadn't guessed, the little white ellipses are eyes and the black dots are pupils. All the programs for this chapter can be found on the CD-ROM in the directory\SOURCE\CHAP16\. The JavaEyes program is written as a standalone Java program (not an applet),

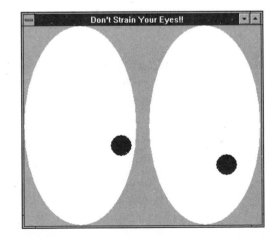

Figure 16.1   *JavaEyes in action.*

so you will need to run it from the SOURCE/CHAP16 directory using the java interpreter, **java**, comme ca,

```
cmd>java EyeTest
```

In the course of this chapter, as in many of the graphics and imaging chapters, we will be writing programs that can be equally well written as standalone programs or as applets. There is nothing special about these programs that forces them to be standalone. I will try to present a balance in the examples so that you can see the techniques from both sides. I have also put together an applet version of JavaEyes. You can run it as

```
cmd>appletviewer  eyetest.html
```

The applet version is shown in Figure 16.2.

What does it do? Well, try it and find out!

As you move the mouse inside of the window, the eyes follow the mouse—staring at it intently to ensure that it is not up to any mischief. Pretty basic, huh? But show it to your non-computer-literate friends and say to them, "I wrote this," and you'll get a surprising reaction: they love it! Funny how the simple things always get them. Show them your latest fadgadget applet and they would much rather be trying to hide from the eyes.

For all its simplicity, though, JavaEyes is a very interesting program. It will show us how to intercept mouse movement events and it will show us some of the problems of tracking mouse movements between Canvas components.

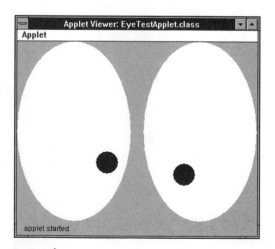

Figure 16.2   The JavaEyes applet.

How the Program Works

At the big-picture level, JavaEyes is tracking the **mouseMove** event. Whenever the mouse is moved inside of the window, the **mouseMove** event is sent to the window. The window takes this event and draws the pupils on the eyes so that the pupils track the eyes at all times.

The complete source code for this example is contained in the file JavaEyes.java. It is presented in the Listing 16.1.

Listing 16.1   JavaEyes.java—The Java Eyes Panel

```java
import java.awt.*;
import java.lang.Math;

class Pupil {
    Eye eye;
    Point p;
    int radius;

    Pupil(Eye e) {
        eye = e;
    }

    int setSize(int r) {
        return r/5;
    }

    Point setPosition(Point pt, Point center, int r) {

        Point p = new Point(pt.x-center.x, pt.y-center.y);

        if (p.x != 0 && p.y != 0) {

            int hypot = Math.min(r-radius,
                            (int) Math.sqrt(p.x*p.x + p.y*p.y));
            double angle = Math.atan2 (p.y, p.x);

            p.x = (int) (hypot * Math.cos (angle));
            p.y = (int) (hypot * Math.sin (angle));
        }

        p.x += center.x;
        p.y += center.y;
    return p;
    }

    void paint(Graphics g) {
        g.setColor(Color.black);
```

```
            radius = setSize(eye.radius);
            Point p = setPosition(eye.focus, eye.center, eye.radius);
            g.fillOval(p.x-radius, p.y-radius, radius*2, radius*2);
        }
}

class Eye extends Canvas {
    Point center;
    Point focus;
    Pupil pupil;
    int radius;

    Eye() {
        Dimension d = size();
        center = new Point(d.width/2, d.height/2);
        focus = new Point(d.width/2, d.height/2);
        pupil = new Pupil(this);
    }

    public void lookAt(Point p) {
        focus = p;
    }

    public void paint(Graphics g) {
        Dimension d = size();
        center = new Point(d.width/2, d.height/2);
        radius = Math.min(center.x, center.y);
        g.setColor(Color.white);
        g.fillOval(0, 0, d.width, d.height);
        pupil.paint(g);
    }
}

public class JavaEyes extends Panel {
    int numEyes;
    Eye eyes[];

    public JavaEyes(int n, int c, int r) {
        numEyes = n;
        setLayout( new GridLayout(c, r, 20, 20) );
        eyes = new Eye[numEyes];
        for (int i = 0; i < numEyes; ++i) {
            add( eyes[i] = new Eye() );
        }
    }

    public boolean mouseMove(Event evt, int x, int y) {
        for (int i = 0; i < numEyes; ++i) {
            Point offset = eyes[i].location();
            Point mouse = new Point(x-offset.x, y-offset.y);
            eyes[i].lookAt(mouse);
            eyes[i].repaint();
        }
```

```
        return true;
    }
}
```

The program defines a panel called **JavaEyes**, which lays out eye Canvas objects using a **GridLayout**. The number of eyes created by **JavaEyes** is passed into the constructor as is the number of rows and columns for the grid. The **GridLayout** object is created with a 20 unit border. This will prevent eyes from looking too close together.

The **Eye** class is called simply **Eye** and it is derived from the **Canvas** class. The **Eye** class is responsible for doing all the updates to the eyes. It has a helper class called **Pupil**, which contains the code to calculate the position of the pupils and draw them. The code contained in the **pupil** class could easily have been written into the **Eye** class, but I felt that it was appropriate to distinguish the two pieces of work. It is an example of how two classes can be used to break down a problem in to separate problems. The **pupil** code works on the problem of "given a mouse position where should the pupil be." The **Eye** class handles the whites of the eyes.

The position the eye is set by the **lookAt** method. As we shall see in a moment, the panel's **mouseMove** event will call the **lookAt** method to position the place where the eye will look. Then when the eye's **paint** method is called, the eye uses the **drawOval** method to draw the whites of the eye and then tells the **Pupil** object to position the pupil at the correct place to look at the eye.

The **Pupil** class has the code that, given a position for the pupil to stare at, determines where the pupil should be located on the screen. The **Pupil** code calculates where the pupil should be by applying some simple trigonometry. It first works out the angle between the horizon and the place where it needs to look at by using the arc tangent trigonometry function, which calculates an angle given the two non-hypotenuse sides of the triangle. The arc tangent trigonometry function is supplied by the **Math.atan** static method. Take a look at Figure 16.3 to see how this works.

The pupil now knows the line it needs to be on. It only needs to work out where to place itself on this line. We definitely know one thing about a pupil —it never leaves the eye! Therefore, at the very most, the pupil will only get to the radius of the eye. However, if the mouse point is inside of the eye, it will not need to go to the edge of the eye—it should sit under the mouse.

So now we have a pupil which, given a position to look at and an eye to position itself in, will position itself to be staring at the mouse.

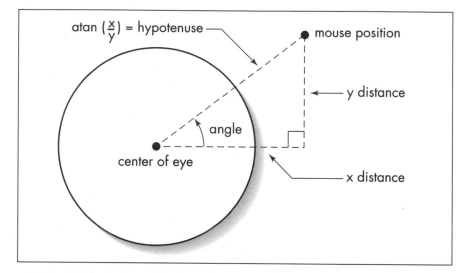

Figure 16.3 *Calculating the angle to the mouse.*

Handling the mouseMove Event

The first time I wrote this program, I put the **mouseMove** handler on the eye. Listing 16.2 shows my first attempt.

Listing 16.2 First mouseMove Attempt

```
class Eye extends Canvas {

    ...

    public boolean mouseMove(Event evt, int x, int y) {
        mouse = new Point(x, y);
        repaint();
        return true;
    }
}

public class JavaEyes extends Panel {

    public JavaEyes(int numEyes, int c, int r) {
        setLayout(new GridLayout(c, r, 20, 20));
        for (int i = 0; i < numEyes; ++i) {
            add( new Eye() );
        }
    }
}
```

This approach was very simple, except that it had one fatal flaw—only one eye tracked the mouse!

As we explained in the event section of the component chapter, an event is sent to the component that contains the event. So if a mouse movement occurs inside of one Canvas, that Canvas will receive the event. The other Canvas, meanwhile, will be blissfully unaware that the mouse has been moved at all. The problem is that there is only one event sent. It is received by one eye—not by both—so only one eye will move to track the mouse.

There are a number of ways to fix this problem, but they all revolve around the fact that both of the eye Canvases are contained within a single panel. We have to get the panel to receive the event. The panel can then either generate duplicate events and send one to each Canvas, or it can tell each eye where to look at and then tell the Canvases to repaint themselves.

If you look Listing 16.3, you will see that I chose the second method to fix the problem. Listing 16.3 is the **mouseMove** event handler from the JavaEyes **Panel** class.

Listing 16.3 JavaEyes mouseMove Event Handler

```
public boolean mouseMove(Event evt, int x, int y) {
    for (int i = 0; i < numEyes; ++i) {
        Point offset = eyes[i].location();
        Point mouse = new Point(x-offset.x, y-offset.y);
        eyes[i].lookAt(mouse);
        eyes[i].repaint();
    }
    return true;
}
```

The **Panel** class' **mouseMove** event calls the **lookAt** method for each eye to set the point that the eye is looking at and then it calls **repaint** to redraw the eye. Notice, though, that there is some trickery going on.

The **mouseMove** event has been received by the panel, so the mouse position held in the event is set up for the panel. Remember that each window has its own coordinate system so that a position set up for the panel will not necessarily be a correct window contained inside the panel. The problem is the mouse position is based on the origin of the panel. This means that the left-hand-side eye Canvas is okay. It just happens to have its left-hand corner at the same position as the panel. Remember that the origin of a component's coordinate system is given by the top-left corner. So, by coincidence, the position in the panel is correct for the position in the left-hand-side eye. However, the right-hand-side Canvas does not share the same original as the panel. Therefore the right-hand-side eye will look at the wrong place if it uses the panel position.

To fix this problem we must calculate a new position for the mouse for each of the eyes. To do this we need to recalculate the mouse position based on the origin of each Canvas not on the origin of the panel. We can do this using the **location** method, which is available for all **Component** class derived objects. The **location** method gives the position of the origin of the component within the **panel** class. We can then calculate the correct position of the mouse in the Canvas' coordinate system by subtracting the position of the origin of the Canvas from the mouse position for the panel. This will give the eye position for the Canvas. Figure 16.4 shows this calculation.

The Frame and the Applet

I have implemented the JavaEyes program as a panel to make it simple to switch it between being an standalone program, or being an applet. To make it into a standalone program, we can simply wrap a frame window with a main method around it; to make it into an applet, we can simply layout the panel in an applet class. Each program is built using javac to compile the JavaEyes.java program, shown earlier, and the appropriate test file: EyeTest.java for the standalone version and EyeTestApplet.java for the applet version.

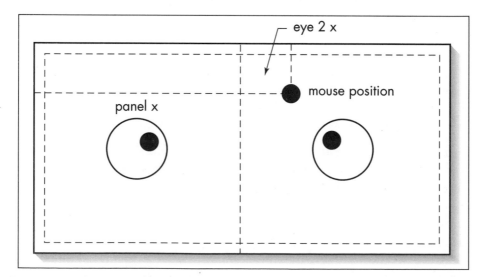

Figure 16.4   Mouse position for eyes and panels.

Listing 16.4 shows the Frame-based version of the program. It simply fills the frame window with a JavaEyes panel. The driver program uses a **BorderLayout** with the **JavaEyes** object added as the center of the layout.

Listing 16.4   EyeTest.java—Java Eyes Standalone Version

```
import java.awt.*;
import java.util.*;

public class EyeTest extends Frame {
    public EyeTest() {

        super("Don't Strain Your Eyes!!");
        setLayout( new BorderLayout(200, 200) );
        add("Center", new JavaEyes(2, 2, 1));

        resize(500, 400);
        show();
    }

    public static void main(String args[]) {
    Frame f = new EyeTest();
    }
}
```

Listing 16.5 shows the applet version of the JavaEyes program. It is far simpler than the frame version because the appletviewer or the browser handles construction of the applet rather than requiring a mainline. The HTML file shown in Listing 16.6 provides the sizing information.

Listing 16.5   EyeTestApplet.java—Java Eyes Applet Version

```
import java.awt.*;
import java.util.*;
import java.applet.*;

public class EyeTestApplet extends Applet {

    public void init() {
        setLayout( new BorderLayout() );
        add("Center", new JavaEyes(2));
    }

}
```

Listing 16.6   eyetest.html—Applet HTML File

```
<applet code="EyeTestApplet.class" width=400 height=300>
</applet>
```

Naturally, if we were specifically writing one of the other forms, we could avoid the panel step and layout each of the eyes directly onto either the applet or the frame window. As we discussed in the components and the layout chapter, both frames and applets can be containers for other components.

A New Species Evolves

You might have noticed that the number of eyes that JavaEyes displays is arbitrary. The code will create and layout as many eyes as is passed to the **JavaEyes** constructor. This makes for a very interesting test of the code.

Listing 16.7 is JavaEyes with 16 eyes. It is a frame window not an applet-based version.

Listing 16.7 JavaFly.java

```java
import java.awt.*;
import java.util.*;

public class JavaFly extends Frame {
    public JavaFly() {

        super("JavaFly");
        setLayout( new BorderLayout(200, 200) );
        add("Center", new JavaEyes(16, 4, 4));

        resize(500, 400);
        show();
    }

    public static void main(String args[]) {
    Frame f = new JavaFly();
    }
}
```

Figure 16.5 shows the JavaEyes program with 16 eyes in operation. I have called this program JavaFly. It is very eerie to have 16 eyes chasing the cursor around.

JavaFly does have a performance problem. It has a lot of trouble keeping up with the cursor. I am not going to fix this problem here, but a number of schemes could be employed to fix the problem. One is that we could stop using one **Canvas** per eye. One **Canvas** per eye is quite an overhead. Another problem you might notice is that there is a lot of flickering on the eyes as the mouse moves. Shortly after we have looked at little more closely at a few mouse and keyboard handling techniques, we will look at creating many objects inside of one Canvas. This technique could also help to fix these problems.

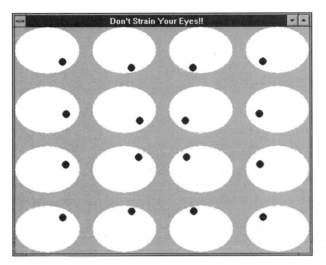

Figure 16.5 JavaFly creates 16 eyes to follow mouse movement.

MOUSE CLICKS

We have seen how to follow mouse movement. Now lets take a look at some fundamental techniques for handling mouse clicks using a few short programs and applets.

Detecting a Mouse Click

Mouse button clicking is detected by the **mouseDown** and **mouseUp** events. To process these events, simply override the **mouseDown** or the **mouseUp** methods to do what you want to do and then return a boolean value of **true**.

The published documentation, and indeed the AWT source code, makes no mention of how many mouse buttons are supported. There is no published mechanism of detecting which mouse button was clicked. You will find that on a multiple button mouse, the mouse button event handlers will be called regardless of the mouse button that is pressed. Listing 16.8 shows a workaround to this problem.

I recommend that you do not write programs or applets that are dependent on a multiple button mouse so that you can easily port your code to the Mac.

Note: At the time of this writing, the Mac port was underway but had not been completed.

Listing 16.8 An Attempt to Use Multiple Buttons

```
import java.awt.*;

class WhichButtonCanvas extends Canvas {

    public boolean mouseDown(Event evt, int x, int y) {
        System.out.println(evt.toString());
        System.out.println("Key "+evt.key);
        System.out.println("Modifiers "+evt.modifiers);
        if (evt.arg != null)
            System.out.println(evt.arg.toString());
        return false;
    }
}

public class WhichButtonTest extends Frame {

    public WhichButtonTest() {
        setLayout( new BorderLayout());
        add("Center", new WhichButtonCanvas());
        resize(550, 550);
        show();
    }

    public static void main(String args[]) {
    Frame f = new WhichButtonTest();
    }
}
```

The mouse button can be detected by looking at the event object's **modifiers** variable when the mouse event happens. The **modifiers** variable is set to 0 for the left mouse button and 2 for the right. However, this approach conflicts with the setting of the modifiers for some of the keyboard modifiers, so pressing the keyboard modifier and pressing the left mouse button will give a false right mouse button press. *But remember Caveat Emptor—this is undocumented.* This approach may not work on all machines, although it does on the ports I have tried, including NT, Windows 95, Solaris. However, I have presented it here in case anyone is interested.

Detecting a Mouse Double Click

You might have noticed that the mouse events are rather lacking in a double click event—and you would be correct. If we want to detect double clicks we have to do so ourselves. To do this we need to use the *timestamp* that it placed inside events. All events are timestamped with a count of the millisecond at which the event occurred. The timestamp is recorded by the **Event** class **when** public variable.

To detect a double click we can look at two incoming **mouseDown** events and determine if they happened inside of a brief enough period of time. If they did we can call this a double click. The typical maximum time interval for a double click is about 500 milliseconds. Listing 16.9 shows an example applet, DoubleClickApplet.java, that uses this technique. Listing 16.10 is the corresponding HTML file. DoubleClickApplet.java should be compiled using javac and the program should be run using the appletviewer and the HTML file. When you run the program try clicking the mouse quickly in the appletviewer window. A message indicating that the mouse was double clicked should be sent to the command line window.

Listing 16.9　Detecting a Double Click

```
iimport java.awt.*;
import java.applet.*;

public class DoubleClickApplet extends Applet {
    long lastDownTime = 0;
    final static long DOUBLE_CLICK_TIME = 500;

    public boolean mouseDown(Event evt, int x, int y) {
        if ((evt.when - lastDownTime) < DOUBLE_CLICK_TIME)
            mouseDoubleClick(evt, x, y);
        lastDownTime = evt.when;
        return false;
    }

    public boolean mouseDoubleClick(Event evt, int x, int y) {
        System.out.println("Mouse was double clicked");
        return true;
    }
}
```

Listing 16.10　Applet HTML File

```
<applet code="DoubleClickApplet.class" width=400 height=300>
</applet>
```

I have mimicked the format of the JDK mouse event handlers for the **mouseDoubleClick** method to give it an air of respectability.

Notice that this double click mechanism is really only detecting a mouse button press followed in short shift by another. On a multiple button mouse, if the one mouse button is clicked quickly followed by another mouse button, a double click will be registered.

One deficiency of this double click detection mechanism is that it is not integrated with the operating system. Quite often operating systems, such as

Windows, will provide a utility to set the double click duration, since the desired speed of a double click is often a matter of personal taste. The problem is that Java programs will not observe the settings provided by this utility. This is currently a hazard that is difficult to avoid.

KEYBOARD EVENTS

Handling keyboard input is not much different from handling mouse input. An event is generated when a key is pressed and another one is generated when the key is released. The two event handlers for the keyboard are **keyDown** and **keyUp**.

In addition to the physical movement of the keys, **keyDown** is also generated when the keyboard auto-repeat mechanism kicks in. The **keyDown** is generated without any extra **keyUp** events between the **keyDown** events. Therefore, code that wishes to detect repeated keys should not look for **keyUp** events. If you are writing code to do keyboard work if you were attempting to write a text editor component, for instance—you would generally use **keyDown** events as the basis for the keyboard detection mechanism.

Decoding Key Values

The keyboard events **keyDown** and **keyUp** get the parameters of the event object and the key that was pressed.

The key value itself is provided as a parameter to the **keyDown** and the **keyUp** events. It can also be found buried inside of the event object. The event object has a public variable called **key** which is the key value. The key itself is given as an **int** not a **char** value. The key value is potentially a full *Unicode* value. Unicode means that the key value can be used to decode keys on keyboards such as Chinese and Japanese Kanji keyboards. These keyboards can potentially generate several thousand different key values. Since there are so many possible values for the key, the key value must be processed to decode what the key actually is.

Let's look at some code that decodes the key value and prints the value of the key in a format we can read. Take a look at Listing 16.11. This program is an applet that will receive the key press and release events, decode the key value, and print out the value on to the command-line window. The program should be compiled using javac and run using the appletviewer using the HTML listed in Listing 16.12. The program is shown running in Figure 16.6.

Figure 16.6 *The KeyTestApplet.*

Listing 16.11   KeyTestApplet.java—Decoding Keyboard Input

```java
import java.awt.*;
import java.applet.*;

public class KeyTestApplet extends Applet {

    String isSpecial(int key) {
        switch(key) {

        case Event.HOME: return "HOME";
        case Event.END: return "END";
        case Event.PGUP: return "PGUP";
        case Event.PGDN: return "PGDN";
        case Event.UP: return "UP";
        case Event.DOWN: return "DOWN";
        case Event.LEFT: return "LEFT";
        case Event.RIGHT: return "RIGHT";
        case Event.F1: return "F1";
        case Event.F2: return "F2";
        case Event.F3: return "F3";
        case Event.F4: return "F4";
        case Event.F5: return "F5";
        case Event.F6: return "F6";
        case Event.F7: return "F7";
        case Event.F8: return "F8";
        case Event.F9: return "F9";
        case Event.F10: return "F10";
        case Event.F11: return "F11";
        case Event.F12: return "F12";
        }

        return null;
    }

    String haveModifier(Event evt) {
```

```
        if (evt.shiftDown())
            return "shift+";
        if (evt.controlDown())
            return "control+";
        if (evt.metaDown())
            return "meta+";
        return null;
    }

    public boolean keyDown(Event evt, int key) {
        String str = "Key Down ";
        String s;

        if ((s= haveModifier(evt)) != null)
            str+= s;

        if (key == 0)
            str+="Key value of 0";
        else if ((s=isSpecial(key)) != null)
            str+=s;
        else if (key >=32 && key <= 126)
            str += new Character((char) key).toString();
        else
            str += ""+key;

        System.out.println(str);
        return true;
    }

    public boolean keyUp(Event evt, int key) {
        System.out.println("Key Up");
        return true;
    }

    public boolean gotFocus(Event evt, int key) {
        System.out.println("Got Focus");
        return true;
    }

    public boolean lostFocus(Event evt, int key) {
        System.out.println("Got Focus");
        return true;
    }

    public void paint(Graphics g) {
        g.drawString("Click mouse and type here", 20, 100);
    }
}
```

Listing 16.12   keytest.html

```
<applet code="KeyTestApplet.class" width=300 height=300>
</applet>
```

The applet will print out when the **keyDown**, **KeyUp**, **gotFocus**, and **lostFocus** methods are called. It only decodes the key value when the **keyDown** is received.

Let's look at how the decode works step by step.

Decoding Special Keys

The first part of the decode is to look for the special keys. The source file Event.java, which is supplied as part of the Java Toolkit source in the **awt** directory, contains a list of special key values. Special keys, keys such as the Home key or the arrow keys, are shown in Table 16.2.

The special key decode method **isSpecial** simply uses a **switch** statement to test the key value for each special key value in turn. You may notice

Table 16.2 *Special Key Values*

Name	Value	Meaning
Home	1000	Home Key
End	1001	End of Line Key
PgUp	1002	Page Up Key
PgDn	1003	Page Down Key
Up	1004	Up Arrow
Down	1005	Down Arrow
Left	1006	Left Arrow
Right	1007	Right Arrow
F1	1008	Function Key 1
F2	1009	Function Key 2
F3	1010	Function Key 3
F4	1011	Function Key 4
F5	1012	Function Key 5
F6	1013	Function Key 6
F7	1014	Function Key 7
F8	1015	Function Key 8
F9	1016	Function Key 9
F10	1017	Function Key 10
F11	1018	Function Key 11
F12	1019	Function Key 12

that the table lacks a few interesting keys such as Enter and Tab. It is possible to decode these values we will look at this problem shortly.

Decoding the Key

The program here only attempts to decode the ASCII values. It does not attempt to decode the full Unicode character set. The main reason for this is that I have no way of testing Unicode stuff so I have not included Unicode information here.

ASCII values are a subset of the Unicode standard. ASCII values assign values to the first 256 characters to the Unicode standard. ASCII assigns values to all the standard keyboard keys such as a through z, 0 through 9, and all the punctuation characters. The ASCII values also assign separate values to the uppercase text values so A through Z have different values from a through z.

To save us having to translate between ASCII values and a string that we can read, the **Character** class has a method called **toString**. We can cast the key value to a char value and use the **toString** method to decode the value to a **String** value which we can recognize.

I have deliberately restricted the key values that get passed to the **Character.toString** method to be between 32 and 126 because the key values below 32 and key value 127 are kind of special values.

Some Other Useful Key Values

The ASCII character set defines some standard values for more keys than just the alphabetic, numeric, and punctuation keys. There are also predefined values for some more useful keys. Table 16.3 lists some of these keys.

Table 16.3 *Useful Values of Extra Keys*

Key	Decimal Value
Tab	9
Delete	8 (OR CONTROL-127)
Enter	10
Escape	27

Decoding the Modifiers

In addition to the key value, the event has a public variable called **modifiers** that shows which keyboard modifiers were depressed at the time the event happened. The **haveModifiers** method decodes which modifiers were in use by using several methods provided by the **Event** class. The modifiers recognized by the **Event** class are the shift, control, and meta modifiers. These can be detected using the **shiftDown**, **controlDown**, and **metaDown** methods.

DYNAMIC DRAWING OBJECTS

We have now looked at how to handle the mouse and the keyboard. Now let's move on to look at how we can mix graphics and event handling.

I want to show you a few techniques that will be very useful in lots of Java graphics programs that you will write. These are *picking* and *dynamic dragging* of objects. These two techniques kind of go hand in hand.

Take a look at the screen capture shown in Figure 16.7.

The figure shows the beginnings of a rudimentary electronics schematic program. Maybe we want to provide a schematics program that will let WWW people exchange their small electronics schematics. We are not going to get much into the electronic details of this program; we just want to get to grips with a couple of fundamental techniques of drawing, picking, and dragging. To do this we need a program that has things we can

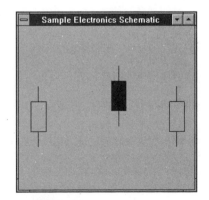

Figure 16.7 *The schematic program in action.*

pick up and put down. In other words, we need visual objects that we can interact with. The program could easily be a drawing package, or perhaps a solitaire card game. I have chosen an electronics schematic package just be to different.

I decided to write this program as a standalone program, although, again, it could equally be an applet.

Let's run the program. The program can be found in the SOURCE/CHAP16 directory. It is called SchematicTest. Use the **java** command to run the program.

When you have the program running, try to pick up one of the objects. The objects are representations of resistors. Pick up the resistor on the left by clicking on it with the mouse. Then while holding down the mouse button, drag the resistor to another position. Try the same with another resistor. You should be able to pick any resistor and drag it to wherever you want.

We are looking at resistors, but this could just as easily been any shape or it might have been cards in a game of solitaire or maybe it was objects in an adventure game, or, well, you get the idea.

How It Works

The complete source of the program is stored in the file SchematicTest.java. Before we get into the nitty-gritty of the program, let's take a look at the class that drives the program. Listing 16.13 shows the class.

Listing 16.13   The SchematicTest Class

```
public class SchematicTest extends Frame {
    Schematic s;

    public SchematicTest() {

        super("Sample Electronics Schematic");
        setLayout( new BorderLayout());
        add("Center", s = new Schematic());

        s.addDevice( new Resistor(s, new Point(20, 100)));
        s.addDevice( new Resistor(s, new Point(130, 100)));
        s.addDevice( new Resistor(s, new Point(250, 100)));

        resize(300, 300);
        show();
    }
    public static void main(String args[]) {
```

```
   Frame f = new SchematicTest();
     }
}
```

The driver class is a simple frame window that is created by a main method. The frame window contains an object of a class called **Schematic**. To the schematic three **Resistor** objects are added by using the method **addDevice**.

As you can see, this program is fairly simple and straightforward. Obviously the stuff that does the real work is elsewhere. The rest of the SchematicTest.java file, in fact the top half of the file, is shown in Listing 16.14.

Listing 16.14 Top part of SchematicTest.java

```
import java.awt.*;
import java.lang.*;
import java.util.*;

abstract class Device {
    Schematic schematic;
    Rectangle pickBox;
    Rectangle boundingBox;
    Color color;
    boolean highlighted;

    Device(Schematic s, Point p) {
        schematic = s;
        highlighted= false;
    }

    abstract public void draw(Graphics g);

    public boolean pick(Point p) {
        return boundingBox.inside(p.x, p.y);
    }

    public boolean isHighlighted() {
        return highlighted;
    }

    public void setHighlight(boolean b) {
        highlighted = b;
    }

    public void setPosition(Point p) {
        boundingBox.move(p.x, p.y);
    }

    public Point getPosition() {
        return new Point(boundingBox.x, boundingBox.y);
```

```java
    }

    public Rectangle getBoundingBox() {
        return boundingBox;
    }
}

class Resistor extends Device {

    Resistor(Schematic s, Point p) {
        super(s, p);
        boundingBox = new Rectangle(p.x, p.y, 25, 100);
    }

    public void draw(Graphics g) {
        g.setColor(Color.black);

        int x = boundingBox.x;
        int y = boundingBox.y;
        int width = boundingBox.width;
        int height = boundingBox.height;
        int halfWidth = boundingBox.width/2;
        int quarterHeight = boundingBox.height/4;

        g.drawLine(x+halfWidth, y, x+halfWidth, y+quarterHeight);
        if (highlighted)
            g.fillRect(x, y+quarterHeight, width, quarterHeight*2);
        else
            g.drawRect(x, y+quarterHeight, width, quarterHeight*2);
        g.drawLine(x+halfWidth, y+quarterHeight*3,
                   x+halfWidth, y+height);
    }
}

class Schematic extends Canvas {
    Vector devices;
    Device pickedDevice;
    Point offset;

    Schematic() {
        devices = new Vector();
        pickedDevice = null;
    }

    void addDevice(Device d) {
        devices.addElement(d);
    }

    void removeDevice(Device d) {
        devices.removeElement(d);
    }

    public void paint(Graphics g) {
        for (Enumeration e = devices.elements();
                         e.hasMoreElements(); ) {
```

```
            Device d = (Device) e.nextElement();
            d.draw(g);
        }
    }

    public Device pickDevice(Point p) {
        for (Enumeration e = devices.elements();
                             e.hasMoreElements(); ) {
            Device d = (Device) e.nextElement();
            if (d.pick(p)) {
                d.setHighlight(!d.isHighlighted());
                repaint();
                return d;
            }
        }
        return null;
    }

    public boolean mouseDown(Event e, int x, int y) {
        pickedDevice = pickDevice(new Point(x, y));
        Point p = pickedDevice.getPosition();
        offset = new Point(p.x-x, p.y-y);
        return true;
    }

    public boolean mouseDrag(Event e, int x, int y) {
        if (pickedDevice != null) {
            pickedDevice.setPosition( new Point(x+offset.x,
                                                y+offset.y) );
            repaint();
            return true;
        }
        return false;
    }

    public boolean mouseUp(Event e, int x, int y) {
        if (pickedDevice != null) {
            pickedDevice.setPosition( new Point(x+offset.x,
                                                y+offset.y) );
            pickedDevice.setHighlight(false);
            repaint();
            pickedDevice = null;
            return true;
        }
        return false;
    }
}
```

The main part of the program consists of three basic classes: **Device**, **Resistor**, and **Schematic**.

You can imagine the **Schematic** class is a piece of paper on which devices are drawn. All devices are objects of the class **Device**. **Resistor** is a class that is a type of Device, so resistors can be drawn on the schematic. If you think about this from the perspective of a drawing program you might call the **Schematic class**, the **Paper** class, the **Device** class would be a **Drawable**, and the **Resistor** class might be a **Circle** class.

In a full blown schematics program there might be several more classes like the **Resistor** class, you might have a Diode class, a Transistor class, etc.

The Schematic Class

The **Schematic** class—the paper—is a Canvas.

The **Schematic** class maintains a list of devices to be drawn. When its **paint** method is called, the **Schematics** class will ask each of the devices in its list to draw themselves at their positions in the schematics. The schematic does not actually know where the devices are placed. It only knows what devices it has.

The **Schematic** class maintains the list of devices in a vector, and provides **addDevice** to add a device into its list and **removeDevice** to remove the device from the list. The **Schematics** class also implements the mouse event handler methods. We will look at them more closely later.

The Device Class

The **Device** class is the basis for drawing our objects such as the resistors. As we saw earlier, the **Schematics** class does not know much about the devices. The devices are responsible for maintaining their own positions.

The **Device** class is an abstract class and cannot be instantiated. It defines a whole bunch of methods. There is one to set the position of the drawable object, one to highlight it, and so on. These are the base methods that all devices will need.

The **Device** class also defines one abstract method: the **draw** method. The **draw** method is the method that will be called when the device should draw itself.

Because the Device class cannot be we need to derive classes from the **Device** class if we want to be able to draw something on the schematic. The **Resistor** class is one such class.

The Resistor Class

The main thing that the **Resistor** class provides that the **Device** class does not provide is the **draw** method. The **draw** method is the method that the

Schematic class' **paint** method will call to draw the resistor. Obviously, a general class like the **Device** class would not know how to draw a resistor, so **Resistor** class itself implements the draw.

You can see that this is how you could simply extend the schematic to add in more types of electronic devices. You would create other classes, such as the Transistor class, which would only be responsible for doing what is different for that class—namely drawing the shape. All the other stuff, such as the positioning, would come from the **Device** class.

How Picking Works

Picking is the thing we do when we try to select something with the mouse button. The **pick** method needs to find out which object the user selected—in other words, which object was under the mouse pointer when the mouse button was clicked. Once the object has been determined, we can then call the highlight function against the object to select the object as having been picked.

Now, there are obviously several ways of doing picking. The simplest, though, is to give the point where the mouse was clicked to each device and ask the device if it contains the mouse point. Since we already have a vector of devices inside of the schematic canvas, when we get a mouse click we can simply enumerate through each of the elements of the vector and ask the device if it contains the mouse point.

We use the **pick** method of the device to determine if the device contains the mouse point.

The pick method itself potentially can be a fairly complex piece of code. For instance, how do we know if the user picked a point on the lead of the resistor or on the body of the resistor. It sounds like a fair amount of complicated geometry even for something as simple as a resistor. Besides being a headache for us to work out, it also runs the risk of being slow. Suppose we had a lot of resistors in the schematic and we were trying to work out which resistor had been picked. We might have an awful lot of geometry calculations to plow through. This might not have the performance we need.

In Leaps the Bounding Box

The "Keep It Simple, Stupid" answer to this problem is to use a bounding box. Each device object carries with it a rectangle which completely encloses the device. For instance, the bounding box for the resistor would look like Figure 16.8.

Now, checking if a point is inside of a rectangle is easy. It is very easy for us because the **Rectangle** class supplies a method called **inside**, which does just the job we need. All we need to do is create the bounding box as a rectangle object, then whenever we get a mouse click we can query if the mouse click is inside the rectangle.

Testing if a point is inside a rectangle is very fast—it only requires four **if** statements. So the bounding box test besides being simple will also be fast.

Refining the Bounding Box

Of course, the bounding box will not always provide us with the most accurate information. For instance, suppose we had a cross shaped object, as shown in Figure 16.9.

The bounding box for this shape would have to enclose more than just the cross. We could choose a point in the corner of the bounding box and the cross would still be picked.

So obviously for some objects we'll have to go beyond the bounding box scheme.

However, we will still use the bounding box, which enables us to quickly reject a lot of objects. If their bounding boxes don't match then we don't consider them further. This rejection of objects will save us an awful lot of work.

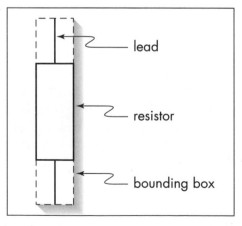

Figure 16.8 *Bounding box of a resistor.*

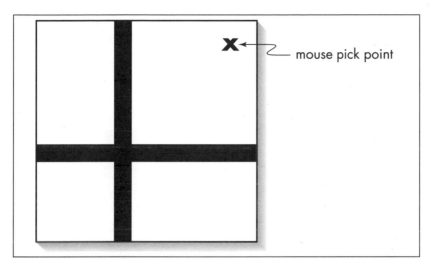

Figure 16.9 *An alternative to a bounding box.*

A good picking scheme is, therefore, to apply the bounding box first and then, if necessary, further refine the bounding box. The can be done with multiple bounding boxes to save us from further complicated geometry.

As you can see from the cross example in Figure 16.10, we can use the big box to do the coarse elimination followed by using the two smaller boxes to pinpoint the cross.

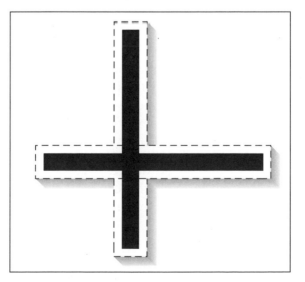

Figure 16.10 *Using a bounding box to enclose a cross shape.*

Finding If a Point Is Inside of a Shape

The AWT provides a number of shape-representing classes such as **Rectangle** and **Polygon**. These provide a method, generally called **inside**, which will determine if a point is inside of the shape. Using this method generally saves a lot of heartache and time. It is often very worthwhile constructing **Rectangle** and **Polygon** objects for this reason.

Moving the Device

Now that we can actually pick a device from out of the masses, we will look at moving the device around.

The basic principle is to look at the **mouseDrag** event. The **mouseDrag** event is sent whenever the mouse button is held down when the mouse is moved. The **mouseDrag** event can be used to continuously update us on the position of the mouse. Therefore, to move a device around all we need to do is to override the **mouseDrag** event hander, get the new position of the mouse, set the position of the currently selected device to the mouse position, and then repaint the scene.

Smooth Movement

Moving the device around smoothly depends a lot on how complex the drawing of the device is. We need to look at a number of repainting mechanisms if we are going to get our movement to be smooth.

Mechanism 1: Full repaint

The first and most obvious method is to simply use a repaint. In this scheme, a complete repaint of the whole schematic is done each time a **mouseDrag** is received. This is the method I have used in the code. It is very simple but it does tend to have performance problems.

Suppose we had a number of devices on the schematic, say 100 devices. If we are doing a full repaint, every single device must be drawn each time the mouse is moved. As you can imagine, this can be a slow process and it will make the motion look jerky. Also the schematic will appear to flash as it is constantly being redrawn.

Mechanism 2: Partial repaint

Another mechanism we can employ is to not repaint the whole schematic, but only repaint the parts of the schematic that are changed.

A typical way of doing this is to provide **erase** and **draw** functions. The **erase** function will redraw the section of the screen where the device was, which has the effect of removing the device. The **draw** function only redraws the device. Once we have these two functions we can set the clipping rectangle of the schematic in the **paint** function. This will then allow us to draw only the sections of the schematic that have changed.

The big gain from all this seemingly extra work, is that the graphics card receives far fewer draws to perform, so the net effect is that the whole thing moves a lot more smoothly. Also, since the sections of the schematic where the movement is not taking place are not redrawn, the rest of the picture does not appear to flicker.

The bad news about attempting to do this is that we open up a whole can of worms.

Previously, we discovered that the **repaint** and the **paint** methods did not directly call each other, but were in fact operating in different threads. The **repaint** method will return almost immediately having set up the **paint** method to be called by another thread. This means that the call to **repaint** in the **mouseDrag** event handler and the actual **paint** do not necessarily get handled synchronously. It is possible—and in fact it nearly always happens—that when the mouse is moved quickly, several **mouseDrag** events will be received before a **paint** gets done.

The net effect is that the current position of the mouse and the drawing of the mouse get out of synch. We need to be very careful to ensure that we do not do calculations that set up the new drawing positions, bounding boxes, and such and then do the **repaint**. If we take this approach, then the calculations will probably be incorrect by the time the **paint** method is called. We will then be treated to some strange effects as the clipping rectangle and the drawing code compete—only fragments of the device will be drawn as it moves.

The solution to all this is to take the mouse position and set it as the last known mouse position. Then do the repaint. All calculations, such as calculating bounding box values, must take place inside of the **paint** method. It is only once inside the **paint** method that you are sure that everything is happening synchronously (well, almost!).

Mechanism 3: Other techniques
There are plenty of other techniques for achieving smooth movement. We will be looking at another one of them—double buffered image redraw—

when we get to the images chapter. Of all the techniques, the double buffer redraw will produce the smoothest results. However, it takes some work to set it up and we need to look at some more stuff before we are ready to tackle double-buffered drawing.

Setting the Correct Position

One interesting wrinkle we did not discuss earlier is how to get the initial mouse move to look correct.

If you look at the code for **mouseDown**, you will see that it records a variable called **offset**. You can then see that this variable that is used when calculating the new position to set the device to in the **mouseDrag** method. Why do we need this offset?

The problem is that when we were moving the object around, we were setting the top-left position of the device. At each **mouseDrag** we reposition the top-left position of the device to be where the mouse is. Now think about the initial pick of the device. If the mouse is not at exactly the top-left corner of the device when the first pick is made, the top-left corner of the device will be positioned at the mouse position. This will happen even if the mouse has not moved. The effect will be that the top-left corner of the device will jump to mouse position.

To prevent this sudden jump from happening, we record the position, the offset, of the mouse from the top-left corner of the device. When we move the device we make sure that we always correct for an initial offset. Then at the first pick the top-left corner of the device does not appear to jump to the mouse position. Figure 16.11 shows how the offset is calculated.

To cure this effect, we need to work out where the mouse was in relation to the top-left position when the original pick took place. Then, we always need to maintain this as an offset when we move the object around the window.

Wrapping up on Dynamic Objects

All this stuff we have been discussing such as devices, picking, and moving are fairly generic things. If you take a good look at the **Device** class you will see that there is nothing specific to electronics. These techniques can be applied in any circumstances in which we have a drawing composed of a collection of things that we want to be able to manipulate independently.

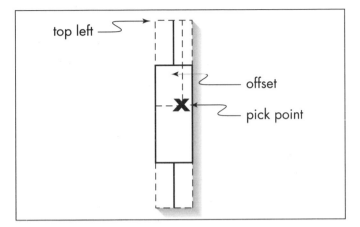

Figure 16.11   *Initial offset calculation.*

You might be tempted to think that this drawable stuff could be accomplished using a Canvas for each of the objects. However, this is far from the case. There are a number of reasons. One is that you can't have overlapped **Canvas** objects on the screen. Another is that, as we saw earlier, **Canvas** components bring with them a certain amount of baggage which can slow down performance. Finally, even if we did not want to do overlapping, the layout support that places and sizes component objects is not designed for dynamic manipulation.

LET'S REVIEW

Keyboard and mouse handling is part of the event handling mechanism. We can override the mouse and the keyboard event handler method to intercept the mouse and keyboard events.

We have looked at a number of techniques for handling the mouse and the keyboard. We have also looked at how to mix graphics and user interaction. We implemented a simple drawing package that allow object picking and smooth dragging.

IMAGES AND SOUND

Neil Bartlott

Can you say "Lights, Camera, Action?" We go for an in-depth look at the making of images and sounds.

In Chapter 15, we saw how to use the JDK to draw things. The **Graphics** class provides a whole bunch of methods that let us draw pictures using basic drawing techniques such as drawing lines, circles, and so on. Now, we are moving on to explore images.

You are probably very familiar with images through your Web browser. Any graphics picture displayed on a Web page is an image. Images are like camera pictures. The Web page does not draw an image as a series of points, lines, and circles. It treats an image as a whole. It reads a complete picture into memory from a file and then displays the picture. This whole process is called *loading* the image.

The JDK provides a lot of image manipulation classes. You can load images, apply image filters, crop images, alter pixel values—the works. Don't be fooled, though. All is not as it seems. The image manipulation classes have a number of interesting quirks. I recommend that you read this chapter very carefully. The whole concept of loading and drawing images in Java is a paradigm shift. Even if you are a veteran graphics programmer, some of the concepts and techniques will probably seem new to you. Stay tuned.

LOADING AN IMAGE

The centerpiece of image handling is a class called **Image**. Objects of the **Image** class contain the image that is to be displayed. If we want to load and draw an image file we need to perform these two basic steps:

1. Create the **Image** object and load it from the file.
2. Display the image in the **Image** object.

Let's look at each of these steps in more detail.

Creating and Loading an Image Object

The simplest way to load in an image from a file is to use the **getImage** method. The **getImage** method does it all in one: it creates an **Image** object and then loads the object with an image from a specified file on disk.

There are two classes that provide the **getImage** method: the **Toolkit** class and **Applet** class. The **Applet.getImage** method is used from applets to create an image object; the **Toolkit.getImage** method is used to create an image for non-applet programs. For example, to create an image from a file named fancy.gif in a standalone program we would write the code shown here:

```
Image i = Toolkit.getDefaultToolkit().getImage("fancy.gif");
```

The JDK does not let us just instantiate an **Image** object. The **Image** class is defined as an abstract class. The JDK provides several service methods, like **getImage**, to allow us to get our hands on an **Image** object. The service methods will construct an image object on our behalf.

The JDK does not do this from overt paranoia. It does this because images are highly platform-dependent things. The JDK wants to retain the right to implement different image algorithms and storage mechanisms on different platforms. It does not want you to create an image intended for a Mac on a Windows machine—so it hides the image creation from you.

Later in this chapter, we will see other techniques for loading images besides the **getImage** method. For the time being, though, we will restrict ourselves to loading images stored in files on disk.

Display the Image

The image is displayed using the **Graphic's** class **drawImage** method. This method is used in much the same way as the shape drawing methods, such as **drawRect**, that we saw in Chapter 16. To use the **drawImage** method, we need to be in possession of a friendly **Graphics** object. The best place to meet one of these little darlings is in the **paint** method.

VIEWING A GIF FILE

That is enough theory for the moment. This is a tutorial book, so let's break the wrapping on the box and dive in. Listing 17.1 shows a simple applet that displays a GIF (Graphics Interchange Format) file. All programs in this chapter are found in the \SOURCE\CHAP17 directory.

Listing 17.1   A GIF Viewer Applet

```
import java.awt.*;
import java.applet.*;
import java.awt.image.*;

public class GifViewerApplet extends Applet {
    Image curimage;

    public void init() {
        curimage = getImage(getDocumentBase(), "cactus.gif");
    }

    public void paint(Graphics g) {
        g.drawImage(curimage, 0, 0, this);
    }
}
```

You can compile and run the applet as usual, as shown in this snippet:

```
cmd> javac GifViewerApplet.java
cmd> appletviewer gifviewer.html
```

The code for gifviewer.html is shown in Listing 17.2.

Listing 17.2   Code for the GIF Viewer

```
<applet code="GifViewer.class"width=640 height=480></applet>
```

The code in Listing 17.1 is straightforward. It consists of an applet class, **GifViewerApplet**, which overrides the **init** and **paint** methods.

Inside of the **init** method, the **getImage** method is called to load a file called cactus.gif. The **getImage** method does a lot for us. It creates an **Image** object, reads in the cactus.gif file, and converts it into an internal format used by the **Image** object. All in one shot. The image is then stored in an instance variable, **curimage**. It will remain in safekeeping till we need it in the **paint** method.

There are several versions of the **getImage** method. Check the API documentation for each of them. Each version has a slightly different way of specifying the location from which to load the image file. This version takes two parameters to locate the image file. The first parameter is the URL location at which to find the file; the file itself is named in the second parameter. Therefore, in this case, cactus.gif is located at the URL location that the **getDocumentBase** method returns. The **getDocumentBase** method returns the URL of the HTML document in which the applet is embedded. In other words, gifviewer.html and cactus.gif file are in the same network directory.

Now that we have an image, let's display it on the screen. This happens in the **paint** method. As we know, the **paint** method is called when the applet is first displayed.

In the **paint** method, the image stored in **curimage** is passed to the **drawImage** method. The **drawImage** method takes four parameters. The first is the image. The next two are the x and y coordinates at which to place the top-left corner of the image. The fourth and final parameter is the applet **this** pointer. Here we have used the (0,0) origin point for the x and y coordinates. This will cause the image to be placed at the top-left corner of the applet.

Figure 17.1 shows the GIF viewer applet in operation displaying an image of some cacti. The image is copyrighted by Aris Entertainment.

While we are looking at GIF viewers, let's look at the frame window version shown in Listing 17.3. This is very similar to the applet version.

Listing 17.3   Standalone GIF Viewer

```
import java.awt.*;
import java.awt.image.*;

public class GifViewer extends Frame {
    Image curimage;

    GifViewer(String s) {
        super("GifViewer - "+s);
        curimage = Toolkit.getDefaultToolkit().getImage(s);
        resize(640,480);
```

```
        show();
    }

    public void paint(Graphics g) {
        g.drawImage(curimage, 0, 0, this);
    }

    public static void main(String args[]) {
        Frame f = new GifViewer(args[0]);
    }
}
```

The main differences between the applet and the standalone frame window version are typical of the differences between such programs: The differences lie in how the initial object is created. The frame window uses the **main** method and a constructor to create itself. The applet is created by the browser that it runs inside of—it only has to override the **init** method to do the work it wants to do when it starts.

From the perspective of images, the differences are that we use the **Toolkit** version of **getImage** for the frame window program. The **Toolkit** version has a slightly different set of parameters for the **getImage** method. It supports a

Figure 17.1 *GIF viewer applet in operation.*

single parameter version of **getImage**. The single parameter version takes a string which is the file name. There are no URLs to worry about here.

As a bonus, I have altered the frame window-based viewer so that it can read any image file passed in via the command line. Therefore, to use the program, compile it with javac, and run it with java as follows:

```
cmd> java GifViewer dunes3.gif
```

The result of doing this is shown as Figure 17.2. The image shown is copyrighted by Aris Entertainment.

The Unfolding Image

The programs we have written seem simple enough, but there is a problem.

When you run either of the viewer programs, take a careful look at the image as it is loaded in. Do you notice a delay when the image is loaded and some flickering as the image is drawn? Well, this is caused by the paradigm shift I spoke about at the beginning of the chapter. The image is being loaded *asynchronously*.

Looking at the code in, say, Listing 17.1, it might *seem* like the image was completely loaded at the **getImage** method call, but it wasn't. It seems like the image was loaded because of our expectations. We expect that each method call will do all its business before it returns back. We expect the **getImage** method to have loaded the image before it returns. Here, though, this is not the case. The **getImage** method returns before the image is fully loaded. There is some *thread* trickery going on.

There are *two* threads operating. One thread runs the applet, while another thread works at loading in the image. This second thread is started by the **getImage** method call. It will start loading the image and repeatedly call the **paint** function to display the image bit by bit until the image is fully loaded.

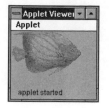

Figure 17.2   *GIF viewer program in operation.*

You will probably recognize that this is exactly the behavior required by a browser. Typically, the image being loaded by a browser will take a fair amount of time to load, because it is being loaded across the network. As the image is loaded by the browser, as much of the image as can be displayed is displayed. The user then does not have to wait for the complete image to be loaded to get an idea of what the image is.

Let's put a simple **println** call into the **paint** method and see how many times it is called. When I did this on my machine I got the output shown in the following snippet:

```
cmd>appletviewer example.html
status: applet loaded
status: applet initialized
status: applet started
Called Paint
Called Paint
Called Paint
Called Paint
...
```

This is very interesting: on my machine, the **paint** method is called over 10 times before the image is fully displayed. Now, if you do this on your machine, you will almost certainly get a different number. You might even get just one **paint**. The point, though, is that **paint** is called potentially as many times as is required to load in the full image.

Image Observers and the imageUpdate Method

To understand more fully what is going on, we need to take a look behind the scenes.

Let's recap. Image loading is an asynchronous activity. The image is not loaded when we actually do the **getImage** call in the applet. The **getImage** call primes the pump for image loading. The image is loaded by a separate image-loading thread that operates behind the scenes to load the images for us. This thread, like all threads, is operating on its own time and consequently might not have the image ready by the time we come to do a **paint**—not even when we are loading the image from our local machine. Therefore, we need a way of determining when the image has been loaded, so that we know when to repaint the complete image.

The solution the JDK uses to synchronize the image loading and the **paint** method is to use image observers. Image observers are employed to *watch* the image loading. As the image loads, **ImageObserver** will repeatedly call repaints to keep the viewing window up to date with the image as it loads.

All components are image observers: they derive from the **ImageObserver** interface. The **ImageObserver** interface defines a method called **imageUpdate**. The image loading thread will periodically call the **imageUpdate** method to tell the **ImageObserver** the status of the loading image. The **imageUpdate** method can then call a repaint when it thinks that the image should be repainted.

The connection between the image-loading thread and the **ImageObserver** is done by the **drawImage** method. Recall that the **drawImage** method takes the **this** pointer as its fourth parameter. In our applet case, the **this** pointer is the applet. This works because all components, including applets, support the **ImageObserver** interface. Under the covers, the **drawImage** method introduces thread and the **ImageObserver**.

Now, notice that we did not provide an **imageUpdate** method in our code. We do not have to provide one, because all components get a default **imageUpdate** method, which they inherit from the **Component** class. The "problem" with the default **imageUpdate** method, from our perspective, is that it's designed to display the image each time the **imageUpdate** method is called.

Stopping the Flicker

We want to stop the flickering and have the image display only once—when it has finished loading. To do this we must override the **imageUpdate** method. We can use the **imageUpdate** method to inform us when the image has been fully loaded and then, when it has been fully loaded, we can repaint the image. Of course, we now have a slight delay before the image is finally drawn. Sometimes there is no win-win. Listing 17.4 shows some code to do this—to *synchronously* load the image.

Listing 17.4 One-Shot Image Loading

```
public boolean imageUpdate(Image img, int flags, int x, int y, int w, int h) {
    if ((flags & ALLBITS) != 0) {
        repaint();
    }
    return (flags & (ALLBITS|ERROR)) == 0;
}
```

This **imageUpdate** is overridden on the **Applet** class. The method is called each time the image loading status changes. Our overridden method checks the status flags, **flags**, to see if the **ALLBITS** bit has been set. If the **ALLBITS** bit has been set, then the image has been successfully loaded, and so should be redrawn. The return value of the **imageUpdate** method should be **true** if further updates are needed; **false** otherwise. The code here returns **false**, which means it stops further **imageUpdate**s being called, if the **ALLBITS** or the **ERROR** bits have been set.

The **imageUpdate** method provides us with six parameters: the image object, the flags that indicate the status of the loading of the image, and the x, y, width and height parameters. These final four need to be interpreted according the status flags. Table 17.1 shows the possible flag values.

The table of **imageUpdate** values shows the various bits of the flags that are passed into the **imageUpdate** method. These flag values should all be decoded using the bitwise-and operator, **&**, as shown in Listing 17.4. To get more than one value, use the bitwise-or operator, |, to join together the bit values.

Is the Image File There?

There are several ways of detecting if the file is not there. One way is to check that the file exists beforehand. Another way, and one that deals with other potential image file loading errors, is to use the ERROR bit of the flag in **imageUpdate**. For instance

```
if ((flags & ERROR) != 0) {
    System.out.println(" Error Loading Image" );
}
```

will print out an error if the image loading fails.

Table 17.1 *ImageUpdate Flag Values*

Bit Value	Meaning
WIDTH	Width information is ready for the image
HEIGHT	Height information is ready for the image
PROPERTIES	Property information is ready for the image
SOMEBITS	Extra information for scaling the image is available
FRAMEBITS	Provides support for images with multiple images; it indicates that another image is available
ALLBITS	The image is complete
ERROR	The image loading failed

The New and Improved Image Applet

Let's pull together some of the stuff we have looked at to make a new and improved, whiter-than-white, version of the GIF viewer. Listing 17.5 shows the file ImageViewerApplet.java. It will load an image in any of the file formats supported by the JDK (the JDK currently supports only JPG and GIF). The ImageViewerApplet will load the image with one **paint** method, without any intervening paints. It detects if the file loading was in error and prints out a suitable error message using **showStatus**.

Listing 17.5   ImageViewerApplet.java

```java
import java.awt.*;
import java.applet.*;
import java.awt.image.*;

public class ImageViewerApplet extends Applet {
    Image curimage;
    String imageName;

    public void init() {
        imageName = getParam("IMAGE", "");
        curimage = getImage(getDocumentBase(), imageName);
    }

    public void paint(Graphics g) {
        g.drawImage(curimage, 0, 0, this);
    }

    public boolean imageUpdate(Image img, int flags, int x, int y, int w, int h)
{
        if ((flags & ALLBITS) != 0) {
            repaint();
        }
        if ((flags & ERROR) != 0) {
            showStatus("Error Loading Image named "+imageName);
        }
        return (flags & (ALLBITS|ERROR)) == 0;
    }

    public String getParam(String p, String d) {
        String s = getParameter(p);
        return s == null ? d : s;
    }
}
```

Listing 17.6 shows an HTML file that uses the image viewer applet.

Listing 17.6   Imageviewer.html

```
<applet code="ImageViewerApplet.class"width=640 height=480>
<param name="IMAGE"value="atlantis.jpg">
</applet>
```

This HTML code will load in a file called atlantis.jpg. It is a picture of the space shuttle Atlantis blasting off. The output running the appletviewer with this HTML file is shown in Figure 17.3. Once again the image file is copyrighted by Aris Entertainment.

AN IMAGE LOOP

A very useful variation on displaying a single image file is to display a sequence of image files. This is like an image slide show. In Web CGI parlance, this is commonly called a *GIF animation*. The images are displayed one after the other, with a suitable delay in between each image. Sun's Tumbling Dukes and their animated Java coffee cup from the Java homepage are examples of image loops. The effect is a smooth animation—a very close approximation to video.

Figure 17.3   Image viewer applet in operation.

Listing 17.7 shows my first shot at an image loop. It reads in a list of image names from the HTML file, which then calls the applet, loads in each of the images, and displays them one by one in an endless loop.

Listing 17.7 An Image Loop

```
import java.awt.*;
import java.applet.*;

public class ImageLoop1 extends Applet implements Runnable {

    Thread workThread = null;
    int sleeptime;
    Image images[];
    int numImages;
    int cnt=0;

    public void init() {
        numImages = getParam("NumImages", 0);
        images = new Image[numImages];
        sleeptime = getParam("Delay", 100);

        for (int i = 0; i < numImages; ++i) {
            images[i] = getImage(getDocumentBase(),
                            getParam("Image"+(i+1), ""));
        }
    }

    public void paint(Graphics g) {
        cnt = cnt % images.length;
        g.drawImage(images[cnt++], 0, 0, this);
    }

    public void start() {
        workThread = new Thread(this);
        workThread.start();
    }

    public void run() {
        while (true) {
            repaint();
            try {Thread.sleep(sleeptime);}
            catch (InterruptedException e){ }
        }
    }

    public void stop() {
        if (workThread != null) {
            workThread.stop();
        }
    }

    public String getParam(String p, String d) {
        String s = getParameter(p);
```

```
        return s == null ? d : s;
    }

    public int getParam(String p, int d) {
        try {
            d = Integer.parseInt(getParameter(p));
        } catch (NumberFormatException e) {}
        return  d;
    }
}
```

This program loads several images into an array of images and then displays these images in sequence one at a time. The image display is controlled by a secondary thread, which generates a timed sequence of repaints. The **paint** method maintains a count of where it is in the image sequence. When a repaint is called, the **paint** method picks the next image from the array to paint.

As I mentioned, the image loop is running in a secondary thread. To create the secondary thread, I used the applet idiom we discussed in Chapter 13. The thread's **run** method calls **repaint**, then **sleep** for a delay period called **sleeptime**, then repeats the cycle.

To produce an image loop, we need a sequence of images to display. This sequence is provided by the HTML file shown in Listing 17.8. The HTML file supplies the names of the images as parameters to the **applet** tag. One parameter, **NumImages**, provides a count of the number of images in the file. A **for** loop then reads the images in one at a time. As a convenience to the HTML writer, the image counts start at 1, not at 0.

Listing 17.8   Imageloop1.html

```
<applet code="ImageLoop1.class"width=321 height=321>
<Param Name="NumImages"value="12">
<Param Name="Image1" value="images\cntdwn1.gif">
<Param Name="Image2" value="images\cntdwn2.gif">
<Param Name="Image3" value="images\cntdwn3.gif">
<Param Name="Image4" value="images\cntdwn4.gif">
<Param Name="Image5" value="images\cntdwn5.gif">
<Param Name="Image6" value="images\cntdwn6.gif">
<Param Name="Image7" value="images\cntdwn7.gif">
<Param Name="Image8" value="images\cntdwn8.gif">
<Param Name="Image9" value="images\cntdwn9.gif">
<Param Name="Image10" value="images\cntdwn10.gif">
<Param Name="Image11" value="images\cntdwn11.gif">
<Param Name="Image12" value="images\cntdwn12.gif">
<Param Name="Delay"value="1000">
</applet>
```

When the sequence is run using the appletviewer, a countdown timer is displayed. The counter counts from 12 down to 1, then starts recounting down from 12. Figure 17.4 shows the counter on the number ten.

Try running the program yourself using the command line below:

```
cmd> appletviewer imageloop1.html
```

and take a look at how well it works.

Well, it does work—kind of. The image loop has a hard time getting started. For the first minute or so, there are a lot of half drawn pictures. Eventually, though, the loop starts working properly, and then the animation effect starts to run smoothly.

So what is wrong with the first minute or so of the image loop? Why are we getting half-drawn pictures?

If you were following what was happening in the GIF viewer program, you will realize that the problem is that the images are being loaded asynchronously. The initial paints are performed on half-loaded pictures. The **getImage** calls all happen quickly—they set up a thread to load the images; then they return pretty well immediately. The **paint** method is called before the images have finished loading, and the result is half-drawn images. It is not until all the images have been loaded that we get to running the image loop correctly.

Figure 17.4 *The countdown timer counts down while the image sequence is running.*

There are a number of ways of fixing this problem. One solution is to use the **imageUpdate** method we looked at earlier. However, it is a bit more complicated because we have to record what is happening to a lot of images at once. Also, we don't really want the images to redraw until all of the images have been loaded: otherwise, we will have a stop/start motion effect as the images are loaded.

Using the **imageUpdate** method to check on the status of the images loading is a flexible approach, but it can cause a bit of a headache. The Tylenol for the headache is the **MediaTracker** class.

Media Tracking

The **MediaTracker** class provides a service that watches images as they load. You can register images with a **MediaTracker** object, then use the **MediaTracker** to tell you when the images have finished loading. It is far simpler than having to write a lot of **imageUpdate** code. Listing 17.9 shows the **init** method from Listing 17.7 upgraded to use the **MediaTracker**. On the disk, there is a new version of the image loop called ImageLoop2.java which contains the enhanced **init** method. There is also a corresponding HTML file call imageloop2.html.

Listing 17.9 Using MediaTracker

```
public void init() {

    MediaTracker tracker = new MediaTracker( this);

    numImages = getParam("NumImages", 0);
    images = new Image[numImages];
    sleeptime = getParam("Delay", 100);

    showStatus("Loading images...");

    for (int i = 0; i < numImages; ++i) {
        images[i] = getImage(getDocumentBase(),
                            getParam("Image"+(i+1), ""));
        tracker.addImage(images[i], 0);
    }

    try {
        tracker.waitForAll();
    } catch (InterruptedException e) {
        showStatus("Interrupted while loading images.");
    }

    showStatus("Images Loaded");
}
```

The extra enhancements are made by creating a **MediaTracker** object, **tracker**, and registering images for it to watch. The method **addImage** is used to register images with the tracker. Once all the images have been registered, the **waitForAll** method is used to wait until all the images have been loaded. Once all the images have been loaded, the image loop functions as normal.

Now, of course, we have replaced our initial image-drawing problems with a delay while the images load. We can view this as a user-interface problem and simply put up a message—something like "Loading images"—as we did in Listing 17.9. However, we can try to get a bit fancier.

One thing we can do is to display the first picture as soon as it is loaded. This will at least overlap the drawing of the first picture with the loading of subsequent pictures.

The **MediaTracker** makes this easy to do. We have only used one of the many **MediaTracker wait** facilities. The **MediaTracker** supports a whole range of **wait** options. However, in order to use them to solve our delay problem, we need to change more than just the **init** method. Listing 17.10 shows the complete source of ImageLoop3.java, which has been enhanced to load just the first image and display it, then wait for the rest of the images to load before starting the image loop.

Listing 17.10 ImageLoop3.java

```java
import java.awt.*;
import java.applet.*;

public class ImageLoop3 extends Applet implements Runnable {

    Thread workThread = null;
    int sleeptime;
    Image images[];
    int numImages;
    int cnt=0;
    MediaTracker tracker;

    public void init() {

        tracker = new MediaTracker( this);

        numImages = getParam("NumImages", 0);
        images = new Image[numImages];
        sleeptime = getParam("Delay", 100);

        showStatus("Loading first image...");

        for (int i = 0; i < numImages; ++i) {
            images[i] = getImage(getDocumentBase(),
```

```
                                    getParam("Image"+(i+1), ""));
        tracker.addImage(images[i], i==0 ? 0 : 1);
    }
    Thread.currentThread().setPriority(Thread.MIN_PRIORITY);

    try {
        tracker.waitForID(0);
    } catch (InterruptedException e) {
        showStatus("Interrupted while loading images.");
    }

    Thread.currentThread().setPriority(Thread.NORM_PRIORITY);
    showStatus("First images loaded");
}

public void paint(Graphics g) {
    cnt = cnt % images.length;
    if (tracker.checkID(1, true)) {
        g.drawImage(images[cnt++], 0, 0, this);
    } else if (tracker.checkID(0)) {
        g.drawImage(images[0], 0, 0, this);
    }
}

public void start() {
    workThread = new Thread(this);
    workThread.start();
}

public void run() {
    try {
        showStatus("Loading rest of the images...");
        tracker.waitForID(1);
        showStatus("All images loaded");
    } catch (InterruptedException e) {
        showStatus("Error loading images");
    }
    while (workThread != null) {
        repaint();
        try {
            Thread.sleep(sleeptime);
        } catch (InterruptedException e){}
    }
}

public void stop() {
    if (workThread != null) {
        workThread.stop();
    }
}

public String getParam(String p, String d) {
    String s = getParameter(p);
    return s == null ? d : s;
}
```

```
    public int getParam(String p, int d) {
        try {
            d = Integer.parseInt(getParameter(p));
        } catch (NumberFormatException e) {}
        return  d;
    }
}
```

In this version, we use the **MediaTracker**'s **ID** facility. The **ID** facility allows us to group together one or more images. The loading status of each group can then be individually waited upon or checked. Here, we have partitioned the images into two groups: the first group, with the ID of 0, contains the first image. The second group, with the ID of 1, contains the rest of the images.

Three methods have changed compared to ImageLoop2.java shown in Listing 17.9: **init**, **paint**, and **run**. **init** has been changed to put the first picture in group **ID** 0 and put all the rest of the images in group ID 1. Then, instead of waiting for all the images to be loaded, the code only waits for the images in group **ID** 0. In other words, it waits for the first image to load, then it proceeds.

The **paint** method, meanwhile, checks on the loading status of the images using the tracker's **checkID** method. It will only display the first image until all the images have been loaded.

The **run** method waits for the rest of the images before going into a continuous repaint loop.

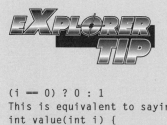

Using the ?: Syntax

You might have noticed that to partition the images into the two groups, we used the shorthand **if** statement

```
(i == 0) ? 0 : 1
This is equivalent to saying
int value(int i) {
    if (i==0)
        return 0;
    else
        return 1;
}
```

using **value**(i) instead of the ?: stuff.

The ?: syntax is very useful in circumstances where you want to return one of two values depending on some boolean condition. It keeps the code terse yet readable.

Of course, if we don't need a smooth animation effect—if we are genuinely just cycling through a few of our snaps from our summer vacation in the Bahamas—we can go one step further. We can overlap the display of all the images with the loading of the other images. In this way, the images will appear one by one at the loading speed. Once they are all loaded, the image loop will then proceed at the speed we want to run the loop at. Listing 17.11 shows ImageLoop4.java, which does this.

Listing 17.11   ImageLoop4.java

```java
import java.awt.*;
import java.applet.*;

public class ImageLoop4 extends Applet implements Runnable {

    Thread workThread = null;
    int sleeptime;
    Image images[];
    int numImages;
    int cnt=0;
    MediaTracker tracker;
    int lastLoaded=0;

    public void init() {

        tracker = new MediaTracker( this);

        numImages = getParam("NumImages", 0);
        images = new Image[numImages];
        sleeptime = getParam("Delay", 100);

        for (int i = 0; i < numImages; ++i) {
            images[i] = getImage(getDocumentBase(),
                            getParam("Image"+(i+1), ""));
            tracker.addImage(images[i], i);
        }
    }

    public void paint(Graphics g) {
        if (lastLoaded == images.length -1 ) {
            cnt = cnt % images.length;
            g.drawImage(images[cnt++], 0, 0, this);
        } else if (tracker.checkID(lastLoaded)) {
            g.drawImage(images[lastLoaded], 0, 0, this);
        }
    }

    public void start() {
        workThread = new Thread(this);
        workThread.start();
    }
```

```
public void run() {
    try {
        for (int i=0; i < images.length; ++i) {
            tracker.waitForID(i);
            lastLoaded = i;
            repaint();
        }
    } catch (InterruptedException e) {
        showStatus("Error loading images");
        System.exit(0);
    }
    while (workThread != null) {
        repaint();
        try {
            Thread.sleep(sleeptime);
        } catch (InterruptedException e){}
    }
}

public void stop() {
    if (workThread != null) {
        workThread.stop();
    }
}

public String getParam(String p, String d) {
    String s = getParameter(p);
    return s == null ? d : s;
}

public int getParam(String p, int d) {
    try {
        d = Integer.parseInt(getParameter(p));
    } catch (NumberFormatException e) {}
    return  d;
}
}
```

To do this, we track each image as a separate group. Then, until all the images are loaded, we only display the last loaded image. To place each image in a separate group of the tracker, we use the **for** loop variable, i, as the group ID. The **run** method has a **for** loop of its own. The **for** loop loops through each of the images waiting for each one to individually load. Previously, we had waited for a whole bunch to load with one method, **waitForAll**. This time, however, we wait for one at a time using the **waitForID** method. As each image is loaded, a variable called **lastLoaded** is incremented. The **paint** method will only display images that have been loaded. It uses **lastLoaded** to ensure this.

Surprisingly, when you run this program, the effect is a smooth sequence of images that starts almost immediately. Contrast this with other versions, we have had long delays between the loading of the images.

To avoid confusing the issue, I kept a lot of the error checking out of the **MediaTracker** examples. The **MediaTracker** does provide a good set of error-tracking features. It provides a public variable called **ERRORED,** which can be tested to find out if the loading of the images registered with the tracker produced an error. The **getErrorsAny** method can then be used to get an array of images that failed to load properly.

Useful Sources for GIF Animations

There are a number of sites on the Web that are home to collections of royalty-free GIF animations. To find them, simply search for "GIF animation" using your favorite Web crawler. My favorite GIF animation site is http://member.aol.com/royalef/gifanim.htm, which bills itself as the "1st Internet Gallery of GIF Animation." Figure 17.5 shows a gratuitous screen shot of the Web page.

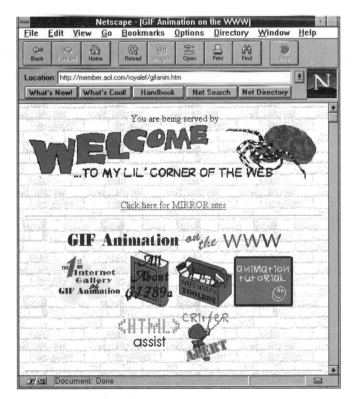

Figure 17.5 *The 1st Internet Gallery of GIF Animation.*

STOPPING THE FLICKER REVISITED

We now have the basic format of the image loop going. We can start the sequence of images cleanly. But the animation effect isn't smooth. The images load well enough, but the animation flickers.

The flickering happens because an erase rectangle is drawn between each image of the animation. The erase rectangle is drawn to clear the previous image. The erase rectangle is drawn by a method called **update**. The purpose of the erase rectangle is to ensure that drawing applications get a clean slate to draw on each time. The JDK provides this as a default because it usually produces the "correct" result. Unfortunately, the *one* time of 10 where it is *not* the best thing to do is for image loops. Therefore, to fix the flickering problem, we need to override the **update** method to call just the **paint**,

```
public void update(Graphics g) {
    paint(g);
}
```

If we add this overridden method to any of the image loop applets and run the animations we have been using, we get a smooth, flicker-free animation. On the disk, ImageLoop5.java is a version of the image loop with the erase rectangle removed. It you run it using the appletviewer and the imageloop5.html file, you will see the fruits of our labor—so far.

Did you notice the "so far" comment? Sounds like even after five times around the "loop" we still haven't got to the final version of the image-loop code. I'm afraid that's true. There are a few other situations we need to look at before we are finished with image loops. Read on.

DRAWING IRREGULARLY SHAPED OBJECTS

So far, all the images I have used have been rectangular images. In other words, when you draw them, they completely eliminate what was there before. Wouldn't it be great if we could draw more realistic images, in which the outline of the image follows the shape of the image we want to display, or where the background shows through "holes" in the image, like the center ring of a donut?

The answer is: we can. We just need to learn how to use transparent GIF images.

Transparent GIF Files

The GIF format is a graphics file format first developed by CompuServe around 1987. Since then it has undergone a number of revisions. In 1989 the GIF file format acquired the concept of a transparent color. Any pixels drawn in an image using the color are transparent—if the GIF is drawn over the top of a background, then the background will show through the GIF for all pixels drawn in the transparent color.

The transparent color is not fixed. It can be different for each GIF file. The GIF file header contains the information on which color, if any, is the transparent color for the GIF image contained in the GIF file. It is not actually necessary for the GIF file to use the transparent color. In fact, a lot GIF files do not use the transparent color. None of those rectangular GIFs we used in the image loops use transparent colors. Moreover, a lot of GIFs are still in the original 1987 format, and the GIF file must be in the 1989a format to be able to use the transparent color concept.

Transparent GIFs are useful in a number of places. They are directly supported by browsers such as Netscape. Using transparent GIFs can be a very useful way of adding some interest to images on your home page. For example, red_ball.gif is a transparent gif that produces the little red bullets common on home pages.

Actually, GIF files are a source of some controversy on the Net. With the growing popularity of the Net and the popularity of exchanging graphics information, a lot of programs started using the GIF format as a de facto graphics format. The problem was that the technology was and is owned by CompuServe. CompuServe decided that they were none too happy with the free use of their technology, so they started making rumblings. A number of defenders jumped to the Internet's rescue but the net effect (so to speak) is that the GIF format is now tainted with a proprietary label (since it is proprietary), and other graphics formats are now being groomed as the de facto standard. If you are interested in finding out more, take a look at http://www.xmission.com/~mgm/gif/summary.html.

Making a Transparent GIF

Now that we know it is possible to create transparent GIFs, we still need to learn *how* to create them. Creating transparent GIF images is highly machine-specific, and we are trying to avoid being machine specific in this book (after all, that's one of the advantages of the JDK).

At the very least, you will need a graphics package that supports 1989a GIF format. Two possible choices are Paint Shop Pro or Ximage. If the package you have can write 1989a GIF files, but does not directly support the transparent file images, you can use a background color instead of the transparent color and then use a tool such as **giftrans** to set the background color to be the transparent color, using the command shown here:

```
cmd> giftrans -T file.gif
```

For a good explanation of how to make transparent GIFs and where to obtain tools, consult the following URLs:

```
http://melmac.corp.harris.com/transparent_images.html
http://exodus.mit.edu/transparent.html
```

For tools to handle GIF files, go to the following Web page:

```
http://www.public.iastate.edu/~stark/gutil_sv.html
```

The result of all that hard work is that we can now use irregularly shaped images and place them over interesting backgrounds.

DOUBLE BUFFERING

Irregularly shaped GIFs look great. We can start to do some interesting image loops now, ones where we can draw an image over the top of a background and have the image animated on the background. If we can do that, we aren't too far away from being able make animated short films using Java. Now that seems like an interesting direction to be heading, so let's try it. Let's try using a GIF sequence of irregularly shaped GIFs and see if we can't get an animated character to move over the top of an interesting background.

I tried it, and I got into a mess. Figure 17.6 shows the effect of doing this on the image loop and running the Sun's Duke animation GIFs that are supplied with the JDK toolkit under the DEMO\ANIMATOR\IMAGES\DUKE directory. Messy, huh?

We now see why the erase rectangle, which we cleverly removed a couple of sections ago, was there in the first place. The erase rectangle was protecting us against doing this type of drawing.

We have a problem, though. We can go back to the old way, which used the

Figure 17.6   Bad image loop.

erase rectangle, or we can stick with what we have: a mess. Clearly, the old way wins. But why can't we have a flicker-free, irregularly shaped GIF animation? I really want to have my cake and eat it, too.

Well, here in computer land, we can do whatever we like. We are Masters of our Domain (and I don't mean that in the sense of the classic "Seinfeld" episode). We just need to learn one more technique—then, we will be home and dry.

This new technique is called *double-buffering*. It's a kind of "computer graphics sleight of hand"—a variant of the shell game. We only let the viewer of the animation see what we want him to see. With any luck, the viewer won't catch on to our little game, and we will have a smooth, flicker-free animation once again.

The essence of double buffering it to prepare each "frame" of the animation in an offscreen area where the user can't see it. By the frame, I just mean the next complete image we want to display including the background. Then when the frame is required, it is drawn onto the screen.

To achieve double-buffering, we create a temporary offscreen Graphics object. We do all our drawing into that Graphics object, including the erasing rectangle. Finally, we replace the on-screen Graphics with the off-screen Graphics contents. This final operation is very fast and produces a smooth change. So all the changes are made behind the screens and the user only sees one change—the final swap of the contents.

Image Loop: The Last Version. (Honest)

Let's put double buffering to work in our image loop program. Listing 17.12 shows a listing of the program.

Listing 17.12 Using Double Buffering

```java
iimport java.awt.*;
import java.applet.*;

public class ImageLoop6 extends Applet implements Runnable {

    Thread workThread = null;
    int sleeptime;
    Image images[];
    int numImages;
    int cnt=0;
    MediaTracker tracker;
    Dimension offscreenSize;
    Image offscreenImage;
    Graphics offscreenGC;
    int lastLoaded=0;

    public void init() {

        tracker = new MediaTracker( this);

        numImages = getParam("NumImages", 0);
        images = new Image[numImages];
        sleeptime = getParam("Delay", 100);

        for (int i = 0; i < numImages; ++i) {
            images[i] = getImage(getDocumentBase(),
                             getParam("Image"+(i+1), ""));
            tracker.addImage(images[i], i);
        }
        makeDoubleBuffer(800, 600);
    }

    public void update(Graphics g) {
        paint(g);
    }

    public void paint(Graphics g) {
        Dimension d = size();
        Image image=null;

        if (lastLoaded == images.length -1 ) {
            cnt = cnt % images.length;
            image = images[cnt++];
        } else if (tracker.checkID(lastLoaded)) {
            image = images[lastLoaded];
        }

        if (image != null ) {
            offscreenGC.setColor(getBackground());
            offscreenGC.fillRect(0, 0, offscreenSize.width,
                                   offscreenSize.height);
```

```
                offscreenGC.drawImage(image, 0, 0, this);
                g.drawImage(offscreenImage, 0, 0, this);
            }
        }

        void makeDoubleBuffer(int width, int height) {
            offscreenSize = new Dimension(width, height);
            offscreenImage = createImage(width, height);
            offscreenGC = offscreenImage.getGraphics();
        }

        public void start() {
            workThread = new Thread(this);
            workThread.start();
        }

        public void run() {
            try {
                for (int i=0; i < images.length; ++i) {
                    tracker.waitForID(i);
                    lastLoaded = i;
                    repaint();
                }
            } catch (InterruptedException e) {
                showStatus("Error loading images");
                System.exit(0);
            }
            while (workThread != null) {
                repaint();
                try {
                    Thread.sleep(sleeptime);
                } catch (InterruptedException e){}
            }
        }

        public void stop() {
            if (workThread != null) {
                workThread.stop();
            }
        }

        public String getParam(String p, String d) {
            String s = getParameter(p);
            return s == null ? d : s;
        }

        public int getParam(String p, int d) {
            try {
                d = Integer.parseInt(getParameter(p));
            } catch (NumberFormatException e) {}
            return  d;
        }
    }
```

So what have we added to get double buffering going? Whenever we are using double buffering, the following things always need to be done:

1. Set up an offscreen image.
2. Ensure that the **update** method only calls the **paint** method.
3. Do all the drawing into the offscreen image.
4. Draw the offscreen image into the onscreen graphics.

The offscreen image is created using the **makeDoubleBuffer** method. The **makeDoubleBuffer** method creates an image using a method called **createImage**. Previously, we used the **getImage** method to create an image by loading in a file. The **createImage** method just creates an image with nothing in it. We just tell it how big an image to create and out pops an image object.

Images provide a mysterious method called **getGraphics**. This method is very useful to us. It will create a graphics object which we can use to draw into the image. We can treat the image as if it were a window. We can use all the **Graphics** object drawing methods to draw into the image. The only thing is that we won't see what is happening. Why? Well, the image is not drawn to the screen. Therefore all the drawing we do to the image is hidden from the user. The image becomes a virtual screen we can draw on. Cool!

So the **makeDoubleBuffer** method has created us a virtual screen. In the **paint** method, we do all the drawing to the virtual screen, then once all the dust has settled, we draw the virtual screen onto the real screen—with no erase in between. The virtual screen completely replaces what was there before. The viewer just sees a seemly replacement of the next frame. There is no flicker.

Figure 17.7 shows the Earth rotating. The images for this figure were created by Alex, who painstakingly captured all 72 images—one for each 5 degree rotation of the Earth—from a program called xearth, a Unix program of a rotating Earth. Now there's dedication!

Figure 17.7   Rotating Earth.

Film Speed

In the image loop, we left the choice of the delay between the frame of the image loop to the HTML. The choice of loop speed is obviously based on our needs from the image loop. If we are looping through unrelated pictures—for a slide show effect—we will need to slow down the loop speed. If the effect we are after is to achieve an animation, because we are looping through consecutive images of an animation, then we need to approach film speed refreshes. This means that we need to draw 25 frames per second. This entails a delay of only 40 milliseconds between frames.

For animations, there is little point in exceeding film speed. If we do try to do this, we will be sucking precious resources away from other parts of the system.

The Animator Demo Program

We have spent a lot of time developing our image loop program. It's become quite sophisticated. We have seen a lot of different techniques. Now that you know what is going on, you might like to see some other examples of image looping. Included as a part of the JDK demonstration programs is a demo called Animator.java. This applet is a variation on the image-looping program. Actually, it is unfair to call it a variation; it's more like the grandfather image loop. Most image loops, including the ones we've developed here, owe at least a passing nod to the techniques used in the animator program.

Now that you understand the basics of image looping, reading the source code for the animator should be a doddle. The code itself is relatively early Java code, so it does not make full use of some of the features we've discussed here, such as the **MediaTracker**. Nevertheless, it is still worth a look for some of the techniques it illustrates.

Beyond Image Loops

The image loops we have been developing are really "a poor man's video." In fact, if you look at our rotating Earth image sequence, you can see that the performance of the images loops is good enough for video. The only difference is that the GIF and JPG file formats are designed for individual images, not for long sequences. According to the newsgroups, Sun has been working on some MPEG video classes which, with any luck, will be ready soon. Keep a look out—they will be fun to play with.

Scaling an Image

It is very easy to change the size of an image. You can draw the image using the **drawImage(x, y, width, height, observer)** method. If you compare this to the version of the **drawImage** method we have been using, you will see that it has two extra parameters: **width** and **height**. These are the width and height that the new image should be drawn into. If necessary, the image is *scaled* (its size is altered) to fit into the new size.

As an exercise, you might try using this technique to resize an image in one of your own Java practice programs.

IMAGE MANIPULATION

We've done a fair amount of image playing, haven't we? We have taken images for a bit of a spin and we've learned the basics of displaying images. However, we have seen surprisingly little about what is going on under the covers. For instance, how is the image stored inside an **Image** object? How do I change the color of a pixel on the screen? How can I fade images? How can I apply color filters to an image? Curious? Read on.

To answer these questions, we need to descend deep into the bowels of the imaging system. The JDK way of doing things is very different from any other system you will have encountered. Even if you class yourself as a graphics whiz, be careful with this section. There are a lot of objects at play. The whole assembly resembles a client/server network more than it resembles what you might think of as graphics programming.

That does not mean that the concepts are difficult. Far from it. They are just different. The concepts are easy enough to understand as long as you are not expecting them to be something else. If you do not approach the explanations with an open mind, you might get the wrong end of the stick. Okay: you have been prepped. Let's play ball.

Two New Friends

We have mentioned several times in this chapter that images are loaded asynchronously. The loading does not actually take place when a call to, say, **getImage** is made; rather, loading is done by a loading thread. The loading thread is free to take its own time about loading images, so we have to be prepared that an image might not be loaded when we want to draw it. Obviously, the loading thread will not deliberately take its time. It is not slouching.

It is just that the image loading process can take a while—especially when it's being done across the network. The loading thread allows the rest of the program or applet to get on with its life without having to hang around, waiting for the image to be completely loaded.

So how does the loading actually work?

To understand this, we need to meet two new players, core players who act at the very heart of the imaging system—**ImageProducer** and **ImageConsumer**.

Given the names I bet you can guess what each of these things does. Yes, the **ImageProducer** produces an image, while the **ImageConsumer** consumes the image. You can imagine that the producer feeds the consumer with the image. Loading in an image consists of an **ImageProducer** feeding the pixels of the image from, say, a file to an **ImageConsumer,** which stores the pixels in the image.

The image-loading process proceeds as follows. The image is loaded from the source, such as a file using the **ImageProducer**. An **ImageConsumer** registers itself with the **ImageProducer** and asks it to get the representation of the image. The **ImageProducer** goes to the source and transfers the information to the **ImageConsumer**. The image is transferred between the **ImageProducer** and the **ImageConsumer** in chunks. This whole process is watched by the **ImageObserver**, which we saw earlier. The **ImageObserver** watches the **ImageProducer** sending stuff to the **ImageConsumer**. It watches each image chunk go across from the **ImageProducer** to the **ImageConsumer**. Each time it sees a chunk go across, it calls the **imageUpdate** method.

Take a look at the diagram shown in Figure 17.8. It shows an image being loaded. The **ImageProducer** is sending the **ImageConsumer** the pixels of the image from a file, circle.gif. The **ImageConsumer** is taking these pixels and storing them in an internal representation format inside of an image. The whole process is watched by an **ImageObserver**. Once the process is finished, the **imageUpdate** method will be called by the **ImageObserver**. The image is now ready to be drawn by a **Graphics** object.

Circle.gif contains the image of a circle. The **ImageProducer** is reading the file in GIF format but it is converting the bits into an array of pixels. The **ImageConsumer** expects the image to be sent to it in this array-of-pixels format. The **ImageConsumer** then stores the image inside of the **Image** object in an internal representation format. Strictly speaking, we don't know—and we don't need to know—how the internal **Image** format works. It is

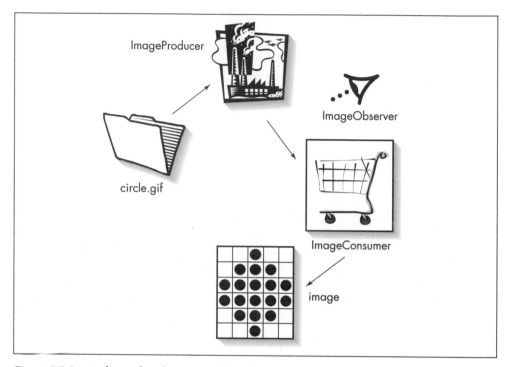

Figure 17.8 *Understanding the ImageProducer/ImageConsumer relationship.*

hidden from us. As we will see shortly, if we want to see the pixels of the **Image**, we have to use an **ImageConsumer** to get the pixels from the **ImageProducer** for us.

It's important to understand the array of pixels format. Each pixel is stored as an **int**. Each **int** stores the color information for one pixel on the screen. The **int** array contains the horizontal lines of the picture joined together. In other words, the start of the first line of the picture is at the start of the array, the second line is width pixels into the array, the third two width pixels and so on. Take a look at Figure 17.9. It shows a long array of pixels.

Thus, the process is not so difficult to understand, but I'm sure you have a few questions. For example, who creates these **ImageProducer** and **ImageConsumer** things? And when does all this stuff happen?

For simple image stuff such as the GIF Viewer and image loop we have looked at so far, the **ImageProducer** and **ImageConsumer** are created and the process is started behind the scenes by either **getImage** or **drawImage**. I say "either" because they might *both* do it. The point is that the image is loaded on demand.

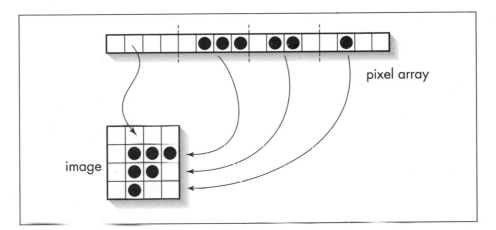

Figure 17.9   *A long array of pixels.*

Look at it this way. Consider that the image is never actually stored on your system. Each time the image is loaded, the producer-consumer thing happens. The **ImageObserver** sees it happen, watches it complete, and draws the image on the screen. Then, the image is thrown away. Just discarded. The next time we draw the image, we go through the same process: producer consumer, observer, paint.

This sounds extreme, doesn't it? It certainly grates on our finely tuned sense of performance. It appears that we do an awful lot of work each time we want to draw an image. Why not save the image and redraw it each time from an internal store? Well, in truth, that's what *does* happen, but the point is you can't *count* on it.

The reason for using this process is that images are potentially large bulky things. They consume a lot of memory space. The runtime implementation retains the right to throw the image representation away in order to regain space if space is tight. To retain this right, the producer-consumer things might be needed at any time.

For this reason, you should assume that the image is always loaded on demand by the producer-consumer each and every time the **drawImage** is needed. In practice, the image will usually be in memory ready and waiting for fast performance. However, you should not write code that assumes this.

A Quick Recap

Phew! I think we need to draw breath here for a moment. We have talked about three types of object: the **ImageProducer**, the **ImageConsumer**, and the

ImageObserver. Their purpose is to implement the asynchronous loading of images. In principle, the **ImageProducer** supplies the image information, the **ImageConsumer** prepares it for the screen, and the **ImageObserver** is told when the image is ready for the screen and then draws it.

They work as a tightly coupled arrangement. Like a fine hockey team, they work well together, each player doing its allocated task.

Ready for Some More?

We have talked about loading, but there is more. Think about this for a moment. If we can never *guarantee* that the image is in-memory, how do we know how big the image is? How do we know its height or its width? Surely, it must be loaded for us to know this information.

This is true. If you look at the methods that get the image size, **getWidth** and **getHeight**, you will see that they, too, take an **ImageObserver**. If they return -1, then the information is not ready and the **imageUpdate** is only called when the information is ready.

Thus, you can see that this asynchronous image-loading is very insidious. It touches all aspects of image handling. You need always to have your wits about you when you code images. The information you need might still be a producer-consumer away.

Well, I think we have had more than enough theory. We could go on about this producer-consumer stuff into the wee hours of the night. Now it is time to fulfill a promise. I said earlier that we had to cover *this* stuff before we would be able to do the *interesting* stuff. In the next few sections, I hope to fulfill that promise.

Creating In-Memory Images

We can break free of the limitations of having to use graphics files to create our images by creating them dynamically.

A very useful **ImageProducer** is the **MemoryImageSource** class. This enables us to construct an image directly from an array of **int**s. Listing 17.13 shows a simple applet that generates an image from an array of **int** values.

Listing 17.13   MemoryImageApplet.java

```
import java.awt.*;
import java.awt.image.*;
import java.applet.*;
```

```
public class MemoryImageApplet extends Applet {
    Image image;

    public void init() {
        Dimension d = size();
        image = makeImage(d.width, d.height);
    }

    public void paint(Graphics g) {
        g.drawImage(image, 0, 0, this);
    }

    public Image makeImage(int w, int h) {
        int pixels[] = new int[w * h];
        int index = 0;
        for (int y = 0; y < h; y++) {
            int red = (y * 255) / (h - 1);
            for (int x = 0; x < w; x++) {
                int blue = (x * 255) / (w - 1);
                pixels[index++] = (255 << 24) | (red << 16) | blue;
            }
        }
        return createImage(new MemoryImageSource(w, h, pixels, 0, w));
    }
}
```

The interesting stuff takes place inside of the **makeImage** method. Given a width and a height, this method will create an image with colors graduating from red in the bottom-left to blue in the top-right. In between are various shades of red and blue mixed together. The image is created by first constructing the array of color values. The array is called **pixels**. It is constructed by creating an array of **int**s that holds width pixels multiplied by height pixels. The dual **for** loops in the middle of the **makeImage** method poke color values into the pixels array.

Once the pixels array has been set up, a **MemoryImageSource** object is created using the pixel array as input. The **MemoryImageSource** acts as an image producer. The **createImage** method is called to create an **Image** object using the **MemoryImageSource** as its producer. When the **drawImage** is called, the **drawImage** will create an **ImageConsumer** to get the pixels from the **Image** and store the pixels in an internal format inside of the **Image**. Once the image is loaded, the **imageUpdate** method for the applet is called. The default operation of this method is to repaint the newly read image. And so the image is displayed on the screen.

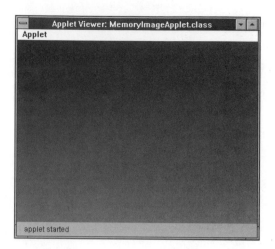

Figure 17.10   *An in-memory image.*

Figure 17.10, which unfortunately is in black and white, shows this program running.

An Image Consumer

There is one **ImageConsumer** that you should be aware of. It is the **PixelGrabber**.

You might notice that there is no direct way of getting the pixels of an image out of an image. This is where the **PixelGrabber** comes in. It is an **ImageConsumer** that attaches itself to an **ImageProducer** object and records the pixels that the producer generates in an array.

There are a couple of things you should be aware about a **PixelGrabber**, though. For one thing, it can take some time to do its work, so you should create a separate thread in which to run the **PixelGrabber**. Another thing: you should not really carry around the pixels yourself. It is not generally a good idea to maintain a shadow buffer of pixels within your own application. It is much better to grab them when you need them and then let them go. You can do this by making the pixel buffer a local variable in the method that works on the pixels. The reason that holding on to the pixels is bad is that you are not giving the memory manager a chance to make the best use of memory.

IMAGE FILTERING

Some of the coolest effects can be achieved using image filters. Image filters are a type of image consumer. The image filters attach themselves to the producer and as they receive the pixels of the image, then they alter the pixels according to how they want to alter the image.

Image filters allow us to take an image and create another image from it. This second image is similar to the original but has some aspects of it changed. For instance, there is a type of image filter called the **RGBImageFilter**. This filter will alter the RGB values of each of the pixels of an image. Using the **RGBImageFilter** it is possible to give the whole image, say, a red tint. Or, by using double buffering and red and green filters, it would be possible to develop a stereoscopic drawing package—one which, when viewed with red-green glasses, would give a 3D impression.

Ghosts and Fade-Ins

Here is a very nice little applet. It can be just the thing to add as an eye-catching applet for a Web page.

An image is loaded and instead of immediately being drawn, the image fades into existence. The image starts from nothing then gradually appears from the background until it is fully visible. Then, it slowly fades away. It then repeats this sequence. The image will appear to pulse like a ghost trying to break through from the Nth dimension. Yes, it is yet another variant on the image loop—but this loop is based on only one image! Figure 17.11 shows three screen shots of an image appearing.

The code for creating the Fader applet is shown in Listing 17.14.

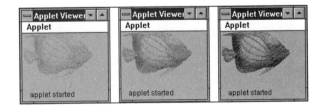

Figure 17.11   Image fading in.

Listing 17.14   Fader.java

```java
import java.awt.*;
import java.applet.*;
import java.awt.image.*;

class AlphaFilter extends RGBImageFilter {

    int alpha;

    public AlphaFilter(int a) {
        alpha = a;
        canFilterIndexColorModel = true;
    }

    public int filterRGB(int x, int y, int rgb) {
        return ((rgb & 0x00ffffff) | (alpha << 24));
    }
}

public class Fader extends Applet implements Runnable {

    Thread workThread = null;
    int sleeptime;
    Image images[];
    int numImages;
    int cnt=0;
    int incr=-1;
    Dimension offscreenSize;
    Image offscreenImage;
    Graphics offscreenGC;

    public void init() {

        MediaTracker tracker = new MediaTracker( this);
        numImages = getParam("NumLevels", 0);
        images = new Image[numImages];
        sleeptime = getParam("Delay", 100);

        showStatus("Loading "+numImages+"images...");

        images[0] = getImage(getDocumentBase(),
                        getParam("Image", ""));
        tracker.addImage(images[0], 1);

        for (int i = 1; i < numImages; ++i) {
            ImageFilter filter =
                        new AlphaFilter(256-(i*256/numImages));
            ImageProducer src = images[0].getSource();
            ImageProducer producer =
                        new FilteredImageSource(src, filter);
            images[i] = createImage(producer);
            tracker.addImage(images[i], 1);
```

```
        }

        try {
            tracker.waitForID(1);
            showStatus("Images loaded");
            makeDoubleBuffer(800, 600);
            cnt = numImages-1;
        } catch (InterruptedException e) {
            showStatus("Error loading images");
        }
    }

    public void update(Graphics g) {
        paint(g);
    }

    public void paint(Graphics g) {
        offscreenGC.setColor(getBackground());
        offscreenGC.fillRect(0, 0, offscreenSize.width,
                                    offscreenSize.height);
        offscreenGC.drawImage(images[cnt], 0, 0, this);
        g.drawImage(offscreenImage, 0, 0, this);

        if (cnt == numImages-1) incr=-1;
        if (cnt == 0) incr=1;
        cnt += incr;
    }

    void makeDoubleBuffer(int width, int height) {
        offscreenSize = new Dimension(width, height);
        offscreenImage = createImage(width, height);
        offscreenGC = offscreenImage.getGraphics();
    }

    public void start() {
        workThread = new Thread(this);
        workThread.start();
    }

    public void run() {
        while (workThread != null) {
            repaint();
            try {
                Thread.sleep(sleeptime);
            } catch (InterruptedException e){}
        }
    }

    public void stop() {
        if (workThread != null) {
            workThread.stop();
        }
    }
```

```
public String getParam(String p, String d) {
    String s = getParameter(p);
    return s == null ? d : s;
}

public int getParam(String p, int d) {
    try {
        d = Integer.parseInt(getParameter(p));
    } catch (NumberFormatException e) {}
    return  d;
}
}
```

To use the applet, try running the appletviewer with the HTML file shown in Listing 17.15.

Listing 17.15   Fader.html

```
<applet code="Fader.class"width=200 height=200>
<Param name="NumLevels"value="16">
<Param name="Image"value="images\fish.gif">
</applet>
```

The heart of the applet in Listing 17.14 is an image loop. We need to use an image loop because, although we seem to just be changing the characteristics of one image, we actually create a new image for each of the different stages of the fade. The number of stages in the fade is controlled by the **numImages** variable.

To create each new image, we pass the original image to an object of a class called **AlphaFilter**. The **AlphaFilter** class is very simple. It is a child of the **RGBImageFilter** class. It only has two methods: one is the constructor, the other is called **FilterRGB**. The purpose of the **RGBImageFilter** class is to convert RGB values of each of the pixels of the image. The **FilterRGB** method alters the RGB values to achieve the translucence. We will look more at how it does this in a moment.

As I mentioned earlier, **ImageFilter** classes are derived from **ImageConsumer**. This means that it is going to be fed some pixels of an image by an **ImageProducer**. Take a look at this snippet of Listing 17.14:

```
ImageFilter filter =
new AlphaFilter(256-(i*256/numImages));
ImageProducer src = images[0].getSource();
ImageProducer producer =
new FilteredImageSource(src, filter);
images[i] = createImage(producer);
```

It is the code required to produce one of the intermediate frames of the fade. As you can see, it constructs the filter and gets the **ImageProducer** from the original image, **images[0]**. However, it does not stop there. It constructs yet another producer using a class called **FilterImageSource** and then uses this producer to construct an image. In effect, it is constructing two producer-consumer pairs. One pair constructs a kind of virtual image source, the other constructs the image. The virtual image source is a replacement for the GIF file. In this case, the virtual image source is the filtered image.

Once each of the frames has been produced, we use a **MediaTracker** to track the generation of the images, then we go into a straightforward double-buffered image loop which continuously cycles through each of the filtered images.

Alpha Values

The fading effect is achieved using what are called *alpha values*. When we spoke in Chapter 16 about the RGB settings for colors, we weren't telling the complete story. There is an extra dimension in the RGB concept—the alpha value. The alpha value is a blending factor. It does not change the color, but it affects how the image is blended with the background onto which it is drawn.

By changing the alpha value, we can create different blendings of the image with the background. The alpha value, like the values for RGB takes a value between 0 and 255. The value 255 represents a solid image—there will be no background showing through. The value 0 represents pure background and no image. Values in between 0 and 255 represent varying degrees of image and background blending.

When we construct the AlphaFilter shown in Listing 17.14, we construct it with a suitable alpha value. When the filter is passed pixels by the producer, the filter sets the alpha value of each of the pixels to the value passed into the constructor. To ensure an even fade, the values for the constructor are chosen so that they evenly cover the range 0 to 255, given the number of images that will be in the fade.

In this case, the filter sets the alpha value of each pixel to be the same as all the others. The filter does not enforce this. It is just what we need to do for image fading. You can set different alpha values for different pixels and achieve all manner of weird and wacky effects.

This whole RGB and alpha concept is commonly called the RGBA model.

RELIEVING YOURSELF IN THE FISH TANK

It is time now to relax a bit and bring together some of the techniques we have been discussing and create ourselves a truly mindless applet.

Us programmers tend to suffer a lot of stress. We have unreasonable coding deadlines and coffee addiction so intense they named a programming language after it—Java. And that doesn't even mention the long hours we spend trying to stay afloat on our Internet surf boards.

To help you relieve your stress and unburden your load, we are going to present a truly mindless applet. There is nothing like a pet to relieve stress, so here we present the first Java pets: Java fish. They swim in their little Java fish tank. Watching the little fish swim around the tank is such a mind-numbing exercise that after a few minutes you will be itching to get back to work!

Fish watching on the Web has a lot of historical precedent. You probably have heard of—and hopefully have seen—the amazing Fish Cam (http://www.netscape.com/fishcam/) which was one of the original experiments in tele-presence. You can see full-motion video of a fish tank in another part of the world from the comfort of your own browser.

Our fish tank program uses most of the techniques we have learned in this chapter: threads, doubled-buffered image loops, media trackers, and so on. Actually, this project is shown in two parts of the book. Alex discusses the fish tank in Chapter 20. There, he plays an omnipotent being and breathes some life into the fish—giving the fish individual behaviors and more fish-like lifestyles. In this program, I have contented myself with just making the fish swim soothingly through the virtual water. Figure 17.12 shows the java fish in action.

Figure 17.12 *JavaFish is a wonderful stress reducer!*

Take a look at Listing 17.16. It is the complete listing of the JavaFish code. I'll meet you in a few pages at the other side of the listing.

Listing 17.16   The JavaFish Program

```
import java.awt.*;
import java.applet.*;
import java.awt.image.*;
import java.util.*;

interface Sprite {
    void nextFrame(Graphics g);
}

class Direction {
    final static int left=-1;
    final static int right=1;
}

class OffScreen {
    public Dimension size;
    public Image image;
    public Graphics GC;

    OffScreen(Dimension s, Image i) {
        size = s;
        image = i;
        GC = i.getGraphics();
    }
}

class Fish implements Sprite {
    Rectangle r;
    FishTank tank;
    int direction;
    Image fwd[];
    Image bkwd[];
    Image images[];
    int imageSelector;

    Fish(FishTank t, Image ir[], Image il[], int x, int y) {
        tank = t;
        fwd = ir;
        bkwd = il;
        images = fwd;
        r = new Rectangle(x, y, images[0].getWidth(tank),
                                images[0].getHeight(tank));
        direction = Direction.right;
        imageSelector = 0;
    }

    public void nextFrame(Graphics g) {
        updatePosition();
```

```
            selectImage();
            paint(g);
    }

    void paint(Graphics g) {
        g.drawImage(images[imageSelector], r.x, r.y, tank);
    }

    void updatePosition() {
        Dimension d = tank.size();

        switch (direction) {
            case Direction.left:
                if (r.x == 0)
                    direction = Direction.right;
                break;

            case Direction.right:
                if ((r.x + r.width) == d.width)
                    direction = Direction.left;
                break;
        }
        r.move(r.x + direction, r.y);
    }

    void selectImage() {
        images = (direction == Direction.right) ? fwd : bkwd;
        imageSelector = (imageSelector==0) ? 1 : 0;
    }
}

class FishTank extends Canvas implements Runnable {
    Vector fish;
    int sleep=40;
    Thread simulation=null;
    OffScreen offscreen;
    Image background;

    FishTank(Image b, OffScreen os) {
        fish = new Vector();
        offscreen = os;
        background = b;
    }

    void addFish(Fish f) {
        fish.addElement(f);
    }

    void removeFish(Fish f) {
        fish.removeElement(f);
    }

    public void init() {}
```

```
    public void start() {
        if (simulation == null) {
            simulation = new Thread(this);
            simulation.start();
        }
    }

    public void stop() {}

    public void run() {
        while (true) {
            repaint();
            try {
                Thread.sleep(sleep);
            } catch (InterruptedException e){}
        }
    }

    public void update(Graphics g) {
        paint(g);
    }

    public void paint(Graphics g) {
        offscreen.GC.setColor(getBackground());
        offscreen.GC.drawImage(background, 0, 0, this);
        for (Enumeration e = fish.elements();
                        e.hasMoreElements(); ) {
            Fish f = (Fish) e.nextElement();
            f.nextFrame(offscreen.GC);
        }
        g.drawImage(offscreen.image, 0, 0, this);
    }
}

public class JavaFish extends Applet {
    Image background;
    Image imageFwd[] = new Image[2];
    Image imageBkwd[] = new Image[2];
    String imageFwdNames[] = { "coll_1rt.gif", "coll_2rt.gif"};
    String imageBkwdNames[] = { "coll_1lt.gif", "coll_2lt.gif"};
    MediaTracker tracker;
    FishTank ft;

    public void init() {

        tracker = new MediaTracker( this);
        background = getImage(getDocumentBase(),
                                "gifs/background.gif");
        tracker.addImage(background, 1);

        for (int i = 0; i < imageFwdNames.length; ++i) {
            imageFwd[i] = getImage(getDocumentBase(),
                                "gifs/"+imageFwdNames[i]);
```

```
            tracker.addImage(imageFwd[i], 1);
        }

        for (int i = 0; i < imageBkwdNames.length; ++i) {
            imageBkwd[i] = getImage(getDocumentBase(),
                                    "gifs/"+imageBkwdNames[i]);
            tracker.addImage(imageBkwd[i], 1);
        }

        try {
            tracker.waitForAll();
        } catch (InterruptedException e) {
            showStatus("Error loading images");
            System.exit(0);
        }

        setLayout(new BorderLayout());
        ft = new FishTank(background, makeDoubleBuffer(700, 300));
        ft.addFish( new Fish(ft, imageFwd, imageBkwd, 100, 60));
        ft.start();
        add("Center", ft);
        show();
    }

    OffScreen makeDoubleBuffer(int w, int h) {
       return new OffScreen(new Dimension(w,h), createImage(w,h));
    }
}
```

This program is an applet. The applet can be compiled with javac and run using the appletviewer with the HTML code shown in Listing 17.17.

Listing 17.17   Javafish.html

```
<applet code="JavaFish.class"width=623 height=238>
</applet>
```

We are going to spend the rest of this chapter discussing the implementation of JavaFish.

Sprite

The main code for the fish is based around the concept of a sprite. A sprite is an independently moving animation. Each sprite is responsible for maintaining its own position and drawing its own image onto the canvas.

To give an extra sense of reality, the fish sprite swims by using a sequence of images. Each image is slightly different from its neighbors. The images are cycled through as the sprite moves around. This creates a more realistic swimming effect than just repositioning the same image around the tank. For JavaFish,

I have only used two images to create the swimming effect, but it looks good just the same.

The implementation of sprites I use here is not a full implementation. To do that, each fish would need to be running in its own thread. Alex discusses this technique in Chapter 20. Here, all fish are running in the thread maintained by the fish tank. We will discuss the fish tank shortly.

The sprites assume that the time has changed when their **nextFrame** method is called. When the **nextFrame** method is called the fish sprites calculate themselves a new position, calculate which image in the sequence to draw next, then draw the image at the new position. They assume that they are living in a double-buffered world—they do not have to erase their old position.

All sprites are descendants of the **Sprite** interface, which is simply an obligation to provide a **nextFrame** method, as shown in the following code snippet.

```
interface Sprite {
    void nextFrame(Graphics g);
}
```

There are a number of different fish images. Each fish image is stored as a GIF with a transparent border. The images of the fish come from a public domain fish tank written for the X-Windows system called "xfishtank." A good starting place for adding even more fishy pictures is FINS, the Fish Information Service, maintained by Mark Rosenstein at http://www.actwin.com/fish/. There, you can find a whole catalog of fish GIFs.

Fish Tank

The fish tank is the world in which the sprites live. The fish are maintained in the tank as a vector of fish. Fish can be added and removed from the tank using the **addFish** and **removeFish** methods.

The fish tank also provides *time*. It is the fish tank that controls when the fish sprites draw their next frame. The fish tank runs in a separate thread. The thread is a typical animation loop of the kind we looked at earlier. It repeatedly calls the **paint** method. The **paint** method is double buffered. It calls the **nextFrame** method of each of the fish in the tank with the offscreen image for the fish sprites to draw into.

The background of the fish tank is maintained as a separate image, which is drawn onto the offscreen image before the fish sprites draw themselves.

There is plenty more we can do to improve upon this fish tank design. In Chapter 20, we make some improvements in the movement of the fish to create that extra sense of realism.

SOUND

So far, all we've talked about are applets and images and mediatrackers. We need to add some sound into the mix. The basic unit of sound support is the **AudioClip,** which is played by an applet. **AudioClip**s only allow you to do two things: play them or loop them. The applet shown in Listing 17.18 will play a sound as the applet loads.

Listing 17.18   Playing an AudioClip

```
import java.awt.*;
import java.applet.*;

public class Sound extends Applet {

    AudioClip sound;

    public void init() {
        sound = getAudioClip(getDocumentBase(), "applause.au");
        sound.play();
    }
}
```

The sound is stored in a sound file, called applause.au. The **getAudioClip** method is a parallel to the **getImage** method. It reads the sound file from a location relative to a URL and creates an object of the class **AudioClip**. The **AudioClip** object provides the methods to control playing the sound. Once the audio clip has been loaded, the sound is played using the **play** method. The **play** method will play the sound once from the beginning of the clip.

At present, that's really all there is to the Java sound system.

There are two other methods that the **AudioClip** class supports: **loop** and **stop**. **loop** is like **play** except that it will endlessly cycle playing the sound. It is definitely not recommended for short sound bytes. It is a sure way to burn the ears of a user. The **stop** method, as its name suggests, stops an audio clip playing.

Creating Your Own Sounds

To play a sound, you will need to create an *.au* format sound file. The JDK works best with 8-bit .au files.

If you want to detect whether or not a bad audio format has been supplied to your code—for instance, you might have an applet in which the name of the audio is passed as a parameter to the applet—there is currently no "official" way to do it. However, it does appear that all machines (at least all that I have tried) will throw a **InvalidAudioFormatException** if the format of the audio clip file is not supported.

LET'S REVIEW

Despite all that we have covered, we have still only just touched the surface of what can be achieved with images. There are plenty more very interesting effects that we could have looked at. For instance, we barely touched on filters. Filters can easily form a chapter in their own right. However, the very real time and space constraints on book writing don't let us get into these topics just now.

I hope, though, that you have gained enough from this chapter to enable you to progress further. We have covered the very basic stuff, such as image drawing, but more importantly, we got in under the hood and saw **ImageProducer**s and **ImageConsumer**s in action. The key to progressing in JDK image programming will depend on how well you understand these two classes and all their offspring, such as the **ImageFilter**.

Good luck. Make sure you invite me to the premier of your first Web movie.

Layout Management

Chapter 18

In this chapter, I'll show you how to arrange your components in their containers.

I must tell you about my favorite architecture book. It's called *Why Buildings Fall Down,* and was written by Matthys Levy and Mario Salvadori. The book is a catalog of architectural disasters from ancient to modern times. I suppose it shows my perverse nature that I should choose such a book as my favorite. It covers disasters from the Greek Parthenon destruction (27 B.C.E.), through the Tacoma Narrows bridge disintegration (July, 1940), up to the worst structural disaster in U.S. history—the Hyatt Regency Ballroom collapse (July, 1980).

Reading the book makes you feel that we should stick to dwelling in mud huts and maybe just wade through rivers rather than trying to cross them without getting our feet wet. The book also has a few cool moments of architectural survival. For instance, it tells of several incidents in which planes have hit New York skyscrapers. Yet the skyscrapers still stand! The most spectacular of these incidents was the impact of a B-25 bomber with the 79th floor of the Empire State building in 1945. Until I read about this, the closest I thought a plane

The book also has a few cool moments of architectural survival. For instance, it tells of several incidents in which planes have hit New York skyscrapers. Yet the skyscrapers still stand! The most spectacular of these incidents was the impact of a B-25 bomber with the 79th floor of the Empire State building in 1945. Until I read about this, the closest I thought a plane had come to the Empire State was in the 1933 RKO film classic, "King Kong," when assorted aviation weaponry was focused on a giant gorilla as he perched on top of the building. It shows how truth can be as spectacular as fiction.

So why am I talking architecture? Well, I want to introduce the topic of layout management.

Layout management is the group of concepts and techniques used to lay out Java UI components on the screen. It is rather like laying out the floor plan of a building. We assign space to rooms we want to include in the building. We need to arbitrate between each of the rooms to ensure that they do not exceed the size of the building, but at the same time each gets the space it needs to be useful. After all, putting a washroom the size of a filing cabinet in the corner of a busy restaurant would upset a lot of people with, shall we say, urgent problems from drinking too much coffee. The same is true of components. We need to arrange them in a container so that each gets the space it needs to do its job properly.

All the source and programs in this chapter can be found on the accompanying CD-ROM in the directory /SOURCE/CHAP18. As usual, compile all programs using javac, and run the programs using either java for frame window-based programs or appletviewer for applets. All techniques discussed in this chapter will work in both standalone and applet programs.

A BRIEF RECAP

In previous chapters, we've already met some layout stuff, so let's have a recap of what we have discussed so far. To lay out components in a container, we need to do the following:

- Set up a container to hold the components. **Applet**, **Frame**, and **Panel** are suitable choices for containers.
- Decide on the layout manager. The layout manager is responsible for positioning the components inside the container. We use the container's **setLayout** method to select which layout manager to use. We pass **setLayout** the layout manager object. We will be looking at the available layout managers shortly.
- Call the container's **add** method to place components into the container. Remember, though, that there are some subtly different forms of **add**—some take extra parameters—and those differences depend on which layout manager you decided to use. We will cover this more thoroughly when we look at the individual layout managers.

Putting all this together is Listing 18.1, which is a simple example of a column of **Button** objects laid out in a **Panel**.

Listing 18.1 Sample Three-Button Layout

```
class SimpleArrangementOfButtons extends Panel {
    SimpleArrangementOfButtons() {
        setLayout( new GridLayout(1, 3) );
        add( new Button("One") );
        add( new Button("two") );
        add( new Button("three") );
    }
}
```

A CONSTANT STATE OF FLUX

When we design a grouping of components such as buttons, lists, and text fields, we lay out the components in a way that makes sense to us. For example, we might group together some UI components to make a dialog box. Typically, we spend time on the layout of the components to help with usability and to obtain a pleasing layout. However, with a lot of graphics systems, if the window is resized, then the pleasing layout is lost.

The JDK helps us with this problem: it makes possible automatic layout managers which maintain the layout we want, despite changes in the dimensions of the window displaying the layout. The components of the layout are not just anchored in position—they can change position. Even when they change position, however, they always remain in a fixed relationship to each other. For example, a title might always remain above a picture. This is an essential feature for laying out components on, say, a home page. As an example consider your favorite home page, go there and resize it. Most home pages will shuffle about a bit but will still be readable after the resize. HTML provides implicit layout management. The JDK, which aims to extend the features available, also needs this layout feature.

To provide layout management, the JDK uses the idea of a layout manager—an object that controls the layout of the components in a container. The layout manager dictates the position of each of the components according to own its internal algorithm. For example, the **Applet** container uses the **FlowLayout** layout manager as a default. This makes sense, because applets are placed on home pages and home pages are typically laid out in a left-to-right, top-to-bottom fashion. **FlowLayout** lays out the components under its control in the same way.

If you have done much UI programming in, say, MOTIF or TCL/TK, you should be fairly at home with the concept of layout management, which is sometimes also called "geometry management." However, if you come from Windows or OS/2 programming, this feature might be new to you. For example, Windows and OS/2 use fixed positions to describe the layout of elements in dialog windows. This is the reason you are not given the option to resize dialogs under these environments.

THE STANDARD LAYOUT CLASSES

The task of writing layout managers is fairly complicated. The layouts must be predicable in their behavior at different window sizes and they should be general enough to create a wide variety of layouts. To relieve the burden of every single programmer having to master the intricacies of layout management, some standard layout managers are provided. These standard layout managers can be used to create most of the layouts you will encounter.

Each standard layout manager lays out the components in a different arrangement. As we will see later, you can combine the layout managers to construct a wide range of different layout arrangements.

The next few sections cover the standard layout managers and how to use them.

BorderLayout

BorderLayout, one of the standard layout managers, can be used to lay out up to five components. The components are placed according to a compass-setting paradigm. Each position in the layout is assigned a name: **North**, **East**, **South**, **West**, or **Center**. The names determine where the component is placed in the layout. To add components to the layout, you use the **add(String, Component)** format of the **add** method. The **String** parameter is the desired position of the component according the compass-setting paradigm. In addition, horizontal and vertical gaps between the components can be set. Table 18.1 shows the possible values of the string parameter.

The example code shown in Listing 18.2 shows a **BorderLayout** object with each of its sections filled with a button. Each button carries the label of the section of the **BorderLayout** it is placed in.

Table 18.1   *BorderLayout Positions*

North	Drawn full width across the top of the container
South	Drawn full width across the bottom of the container
East	Drawn on the right between the bottom of North and the top of South
West	Drawn on the left between the bottom of North and the top of South
Center	Drawn with whatever space is left in the middle

Listing 18.2   BorderLayoutTest.java

```java
import java.awt.*;

public class BorderLayoutTest extends Frame {
    public BorderLayoutTest() {
        super("BorderLayoutTest");
        setLayout(new BorderLayout());
        add("North", new Button("North"));
        add("Center", new Button("Center"));
        add("South", new Button("South"));
        add("West", new Button("West"));
        add("East", new Button("East"));
        resize(200, 200);
        show();
    }

    public static void main(String args[]) {
        new BorderLayoutTest();
    }
}
```

When this program is run, using java, a frame window will be created as shown in Figure 18.1.

Figure 18.1   *BorderLayout test program.*

Be Careful Spelling Compass Names

Be careful when typing the position names such as North. The exact spelling, especially the capital letter at the start of the word, is required.

Note that not all the compass positions need to be assigned a component. You can use as many or as few of the components as you need. For instance, a very useful technique to completely fill a window with a component is to add the component as the Center of a **BorderLayout**. We do not supply a North, East, South, or West component when we do this. We discuss some more useful layout techniques shortly.

If two or more components are set with the same name, the last component to be set with that name is the only component displayed in the layout for the given position; the others are not included as part of the layout. It is not an error to add a component that does not have one of the position names. However, the component will not be controlled by the layout manager and will appear seemingly at random within the container. Not recommended!

The **BorderLayout** is very useful for many things, including constructing dialog boxes and combining titles with pictures.

FlowLayout

FlowLayout, another one of the standard layout managers, lays out components much like a word processor lays out words. It takes each component in the container, one at a time, and tries to place it on the same horizontal line as the previous component. If there is enough width left on the current line to contain the component, the component is put on the line; otherwise, a new line is started. Components are added to the container using the **add(Component)** format of the **add** method.

Listing 18.3 shows a sample test applet using the **FlowLayout** manager. It lays out three button components. Figure 18.2 shows the results of running the applet using the appletviewer with the sample HTML file in Listing 18.4.

Listing 18.3   FlowLayoutApplet.java

```
importjava.awt.*;
importjava.applet.*;
public class FlowLayoutApplet extends Applet {
    public void init() {
        setLayout(new FlowLayout());
```

```
        add(new Button("One"));
        add(new Button("Two"));
        add(new Button("Three"));
    }
}
```

Listing 18.4   Flowlayout.html

```
<applet code="FlowLayoutApplet.class" width=100 height=200>
</applet>
```

FlowLayout also provides alignment options, which, like word-processor paragraph options, allow the components on a given line to be left-, center-, or right-justified. Horizontal gaps between the components and vertical gaps between the lines can also be set. Be careful, though, when using the **FlowLayout**. If you do not specifically size the container, the **FlowLayout** will take the minimum size available. This generally gives a component of zero size — a rather unnerving result, because it looks as if the component was not drawn at all.

FlowLayout is useful for arranging buttons in a sequence and for the general layout of components and applets.

GridLayout

A **GridLayout** layout is like a spreadsheet of components. **GridLayout** lays out the components in a container as a rectangular grid with one component in each entry in the grid. Each entry in the grid is given the same amount of space. **GridLayout** will dynamically calculate the size of the entry by dividing the total amount of space in the container by the size in the grid.

The size of the grid is fixed in advance when the **GridLayout** object is created. It is given in terms of the number of rows and the number of columns in the grid. In addition, the horizontal and vertical gap between each of the grid entries can be set. You add components to the container using the **add(Component)** format of the **add** method. The **GridLayout** layout is demonstrated in Listing 18.5.

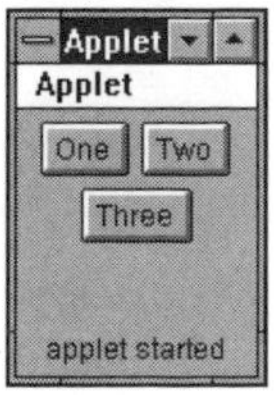

Figure 18.2   FlowLayout test applet.

Listing 18.5 GridLayoutTest.java

```java
import java.awt.*;

class GridLayoutTest extends Frame {
    GridLayoutTest() {
        super("GridLayoutTest");
        setLayout(new GridLayout(4,2));
        for ( int i = 0;  i < 7; ++i )
            add(new Button(""+i));
        resize(200, 200);
        show();
    }

    public static void main(String argv[]) {
        new GridLayoutTest();
    }
}
```

This program creates a grid layout with four rows and two columns that has seven buttons placed in it. The buttons are arranged in a top-down, left-to-right order. Figure 18.3 shows the results of running this program using java.

Converting an int into a String

Did you notice the strange looking **""+i** in the constructor for the button in Listing 18.5? Well, Java does not allow you to cast an **int** to a **String** directly. For instance, it will not let you say

```java
String s = (String) i;
```

For this reason, you can use the trick of forcing the **int** to be a **String** by using the **""+i** syntax.

Figure 18.3 *GridLayout test frame.*

GridLayout can be very picky. The actual layout can be dependent on the number of components in the container, which can give unusual results. You can set the rows and columns and have the layout obey neither. For example, try adding more components than the number of entries in the grid. I typically use the **GridLayout** with the row value set to zero. This forces the **GridLayout** to use the specified number of columns but to *dynamically* calculate the number of rows it requires. By the way, it is an error to have both the row and the columns set to zero: the Java runtime throws an exception.

GridBagLayout

The **GridBagLayout**, like the **GridLayout**, lays out components in a spreadsheet arrangement. However, unlike the **GridLayout**, the entries in the **GridBagLayout**'s grid do not have to be the same size. The **GridBagLayout** can be used to create grids that have rows with varying numbers of columns in each row, rows with differing heights, and entries with different widths. It is a very flexible grid layout manager.

The **GridBagLayout** controls its layout differently from the other layout classes. The **GridBagLayout** has a sister class called the **GridBagConstraints** class. The sister class is responsible for gathering all the settings that the **GridBagLayout** needs. The settings are used to control how components are added to the container. Each time a component is added to a **GridBagLayout**-controlled container, the **GridBagLayout** object will consult a **GridBagConstraints** object to find out where in the grid to place the component.

To use **GridBagLayout**, you will need to construct both a **GridBagLayout** object and a **GridBagConstraints** object. You set the **GridBagLayout** object as the layout manager using the **setLayout** method. Then, before you add each component to the container, you call the **GridBagLayout**'s **setConstraints** method, passing the component to be added and the **GridBagConstraints** object. The current values set in the **GridBagConstraints** will be assigned to control the position of the component. You then call the container's **add** method using the **add(Component)** format to add the component to the container.

The code in Listing 18.6 produces the output shown in Figure 18.4. A frame window container displays three buttons. The layout of the buttons is controlled by a **GridBagLayout**. A convenience method called **button** is used to add the button to the frame window container. Before each button is added, the appropriate settings are made on the constraints. These settings ensure that the first button is two rows high, while the second and third buttons are each one row high.

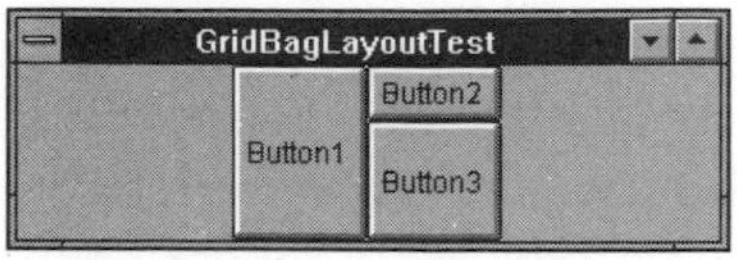

Figure 18.4 *GridBagLayout example.*

Listing 18.6   GridBagLayoutTest.java

```java
import java.awt.*;

public class GridBagLayoutTest extends Frame {

    void button(String n, GridBagLayout gb, GridBagConstraints c) {
        Button b = new Button(n);
        gb.setConstraints(b, c);
        add(b);
    }

    GridBagLayoutTest() {
        super("GridBagLayoutTest");

        GridBagLayout gridbag = new GridBagLayout();
        GridBagConstraints c = new GridBagConstraints();

        setLayout(gridbag);

        c.fill = GridBagConstraints.BOTH;
        c.gridheight = 2;
        c.weighty = 1.0;
        button("Button1", gridbag, c);

        c.weighty = 0.0;
        c.gridwidth = GridBagConstraints.REMAINDER;
        c.gridheight = 1;
        button("Button2", gridbag, c);
        button("Button3", gridbag, c);

        resize(300, 100);
        show();
    }

    public static void main(String args[]) {
        Frame f = new GridBagLayoutTest();
    }
}
```

The first button is given a gridheight of 2, whereas the second and third buttons each have a gridheight of 1. Therefore, the first button has twice the height of the second two buttons. The default for a **GridBagConstraints** object is to place one component in each row. Thus, if you were to add a lot of components to a **GridBagLayout** using a default **GridBagConstraints** object, the components would be laid out in a single column.

Notice that the constraints for the first button do not set any values for **gridwidth**. Therefore, it has the value 1 and the first row only contains the first button. The next two, however, use a **gridwidth** value of **REMAINDER**, which forces the second and third buttons to be laid out on the same row.

Table 18.2 shows the possible **GridBagConstraints** settings and values. Note that all settings, such as CENTER and RELATIVE, will need to be specified as **GridBagConstraints.CENTER** and **GridBagConstraints.RELATIVE** because they are all static variables inside of the **GridBagConstraints** class.

Table 18.2 *GridBagConstraints Values*

Values	Default	Purpose
gridx	RELATIVE	The upper-left x position. Use RELATIVE to position the component to the right of the previous component.
gridy	RELATIVE	The upper-left y position. Use RELATIVE to position the component to below the previous component.
gridwidth	1	The number of cells in a row. Use REMAINDER to specify a cell as being the penultimate cell in a row. Use RELATIVE to specify the last element in the row.
gridheight	1	The number of cells in a column. Use REMAINDER to specify a cell as being the penultimate cell in a column. Use RELATIVE to specify the last element in the column.
weightx	0	This determines how the horizontal space is distributed amongst the cells in the row.
weighty	0	This determines how the vertical space is distributed amongst the cells in the column.
anchor	CENTER	If a component is smaller than the grid area allocated to it, anchor says where to place the component in the grid.
fill	NONE	This determines whether and how to fill the grid cell. NONE indicates that the component should not be forced to fill the cell. HORIZONTAL and VERTICAL mean fill the appropriate direction. BOTH means fill the entire available space.
insets	(0, 0, 0, 0)	This value is the border around the component in the cell.
ipadx	0	This value is the internal width padding.
ipady	0	This value is the internal height padding.

Why use this sister class mechanism? There are plenty of reasons. There are a lot of customizable settings. This means that the constructor for the **GridBagLayout** would need to define a lot of potential values. Secondly, the settings can be changed fairly frequently, and so there would be a lot of changes against the main classes. Thirdly, and most importantly, it is possible to create a preset object that is used repeatedly. We use this approach in the form layout we describe later.

You might be wondering about the need for two classes, **GridLayout** and **GridBagLayout**, which both lay out components in a grid format. It does seem like a certain amount of overkill, doesn't it? Well, we are dealing here with convenience versus power. The **GridLayout** class is simple to use. However, it does have a lot of limitations. **GridBagLayout**, on the other hand, is pure power. It has lots of smarts but it takes some learning to use. Also, even if you know how to use **GridBagLayout**, it does tend to eat up code lines.

CardLayout

The **CardLayout** manages the collection of components in a container so that only one component is visible at any time. The best way to think of this, and the reason it is so named, is as a set of cards. Imagine a deck of cards with the top one turned over, obscuring the rest.

The cards in the **CardLayout** are ordered. There is a first and last card. The **CardLayout** provides member functions to move to the first card, move to the last card, move to the next card, and move to the previous card. **Previous** and **next** are cyclic: calling **previous** card on the first card will take you to the last card. Similarly, using **next** on the last card will take you to the first.

Good uses for the **CardLayout** might be a tabbed dialog, a database record viewer, or a multimedia player.

Listing 18.7 shows a simple example applet that uses the **CardLayout**. Listing 18.8 shows the HTML file that runs the applet. Figure 18.5 shows the applet in action.

Listing 18.7   CardLayoutApplet.java

```
import java.awt.*;
import java.applet.*;

public class CardLayoutApplet extends Applet {
    CardLayout cards;
    Panel cardsPanel;

    public void init() {
        cardsPanel = new Panel();
```

```
    cards = new CardLayout();
    cardsPanel.setLayout(cards);
    cardsPanel.add(new Label("Card One"));
    cardsPanel.add(new Label("Card two"));
    cardsPanel.add(new Label("Card three"));

    setLayout( new BorderLayout() );
    add("Center", cardsPanel);
    add("South", new Button("Move To Next Card"));
    }

    public boolean action(Event e, Object arg) {
        cards.next(cardsPanel);
        return true;
    }
}
```

Listing 18.8   CardLayout.html

```
<applet code="CardLayoutApplet.class"   width=100 height=200>
</applet>
```

This example is a little more complicated than the other examples. The actual use of the **CardLayout** is inside of another layout. The outer layout contains a panel and a button. The panel is the container that is controlled by the **CardLayout**. The button is used to cycle between the cards in the card layout. When the button is pushed, an action event handler method is called which then calls the **next** method of the **CardLayout**. The **next** method cycles to the **next** card in the card layout stack of cards.

When the panel is created, three buttons are added to the panel. These buttons, though, are controlled by the **CardLayout**, so only one of the buttons will show at a time.

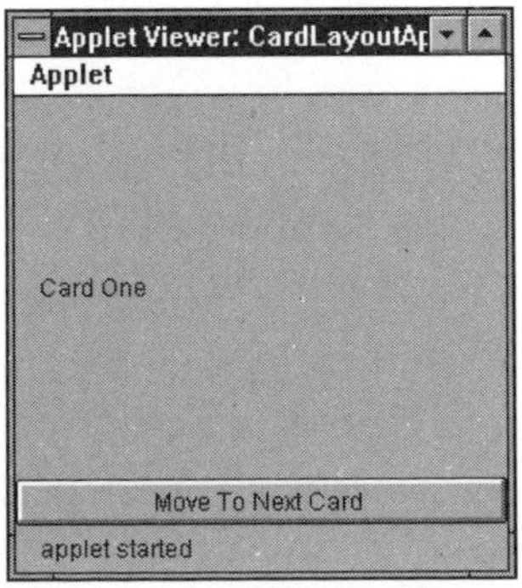

Figure 18.5   *CardLayout example.*

The layouts that can be placed inside a **CardLayout** can be as complicated or as simple as necessary. The example in Listing 18.7 only shows buttons being controlled by the **CardLayout**, but the buttons could equally have been panels with lots of components on them. Any layout that can be placed inside of a container can be placed as a card in a **CardLayout**.

The add Method

As we have seen, you use the **add** method to add components to a container. There are, however, several forms of the **add** method. When using the layout managers you should be aware of which type of **add** method to use.

When adding components to a container, you need to know whether to add using a *named* add or not. Some layouts—like the **BorderLayout**—require extra information to know where to place the components within the container. For these layout managers, you add components to the container using the named **add** method, **add(String, Component)**. For other layout managers, you can add using the simple **add(Component)** method. The difference between these two forms of adding can lead to some confusion. For instance, it is not an error to add to a named layout manager using a non-named add. This simply means that a container can contain components that are not part of the layout.

By default, all components are maintained in the container's internal list in the order in which the **add** methods are called. It is, however, possible to insert a component into the list in a different place using the **add(Component, int)** method. The **int** value specifies the position in the list.

Predefined Layouts of Containers

Each container class comes with a default layout manager. Table 18.3 shows the default layout managers for each of the major containers.

Changing a Layout Manager

In general, it is best to set the desired layout for a container before you add any components to the container. Although you can change the layout of a container at any time, it is not necessarily a good idea to do so. Things will work well as long as the layout managers do not use named adds. These layout managers simply lay out the components of the container. However, there will be problems when you switch to and from layout containers that use named adds. Some layouts also require more information than others. For instance, the **BorderLayout** needs to know the names of the components. In this instance, you will have to remove and then read the components.

Table 18.3 *Default Layout Managers*

Container	Default Layout Manager
Applet	FlowLayout
Frame	BorderLayout
Panel	FlowLayout

MIXING LAYOUTS

One of the neat features of the layout management system design is that you can effectively join layouts together. The design of the layout managers is a good example of power through simplicity. Rather than one large layout manager that supports a bewildering array of options, there is a small number of layout managers, each layout manager handling only one type of layout. The power lies in being able to combine the layouts to produce more complex layout arrangements. Once you understand the basic working of each layout type, the only limitation is your imagination—not the imagination of the designer of the JDK.

The **Panel** class makes this all work smoothly. The **Panel** class is a container that can be nested inside of another container. The nesting can go as deep as you need to achieve your layout.

This nesting feature is very powerful. For instance, to design a typical file dialog box arrangement, you can use the **BorderLayout** to split the dialog into two horizontal parts. The code is shown in Listing 18.9.

Listing 18.9   A Sample File Dialog Box Layout

```
import java.awt.*;
import java.applet.*;

public class FileNameApplet extends Applet {
    public void init() {
        setLayout(new BorderLayout());
        Panel top = new Panel();
        top.setLayout(new GridLayout(0, 2, 20, 5));
        top.add(new Label("Files"));
        top.add(new Label("Directories"));
        top.add(new List());
        top.add(new List());
        add("Center", top);
        Panel bot = new Panel();
        bot.setLayout(new FlowLayout());
        add("South", bot);
        bot.add(new Button("Ok"));
        bot.add(new Button("Cancel"));
```

```
        bot.add(new Button("Help"));
    }
}
```

The bottom part will be used for displaying the buttons. Inside the bottom section, we set up a center-justified **FlowLayout**. When we add buttons to the container for the bottom section, they are a neatly arranged set of OK, Cancel, and Help buttons. Inside the top half, we can arrange a **GridLayout** with two columns. We can put in the labels first, followed by the lists to create our desired layout. The layout is shown in Figure 18.6.

Having used a number of systems, I truly appreciate the simplicity of this approach, and I am impressed by the number of stable layouts that can be configured. With the basic layout classes, it is possible to construct a wide variety of layouts that operate very well, and over a wide range of screen sizes.

GUIDELINES FOR DESIGNING LAYOUTS

When faced with a layout problem, try to decompose the arrangement into large groups, then model the large groups. Follow this by decomposing any components contained inside the groups into groups themselves. Continue this process until all components are laid out. Using this technique, most everyday layouts can be created.

Once in a while, it will not be possible to achieve your desired layout using the standard layouts. Then, it's time to consider writing your own layout. In a moment, we will see how to do this.

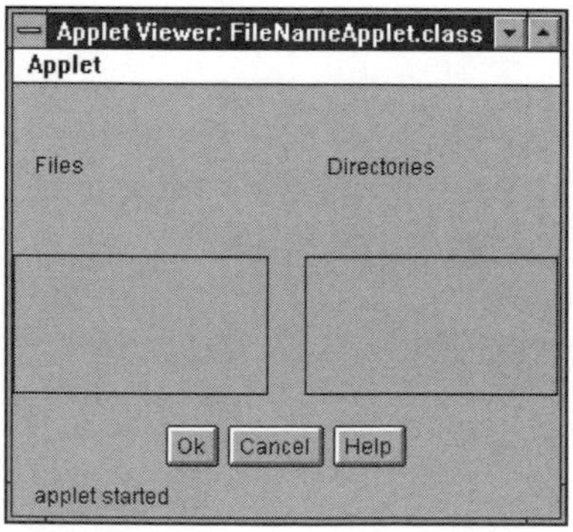

Figure 18.6   Sample file dialog style layout.

SOME USEFUL LAYOUTS

Here are a few simple but frequently occurring layouts. You can use these to help you create your own layouts more efficiently. They are:

- Completely filling the window
- OK and Cancel buttons
- Form entry layout

Completely Filling the Window

Quite often, you need to fill the entire available space in the container with a component. There are a number of ways of doing this. My favorite, though, is to use the center of a **BorderLayout**. The **Center** section of a **BorderLayout** will completely fill the available space. This can be very useful within an applet. Listing 18.10 shows some sample code to do this.

Listing 18.10   Completely Filling a Window

```
class AppletButton extends Applet {
    init() {
        setLayout( new BorderLayout());
        add("Center", new Button("hit me!"   ) );
    }
}
```

The OK/Cancel Button Idiom

OK and Cancel buttons are truly a must for dialog boxes. Virtually all dialog boxes have them. Typically, they are placed along the bottom of the dialog box in a single row. Listing 18.11 is a generic piece of code to construct the OK and Cancel buttons.

Listing 18.11   OK and Cancel Buttons

```
class DialogButtons extends Panel {
    DialogButtons() {
        setLayout(new FlowLayout());
        add(new Button("Ok"));
        add(new Button("Cancel"));
        add(new Button("Help"));
    }
}
```

The **FlowLayout** is used because it does not attempt to size the buttons—it simply places them. Compare this with the behavior of, say, the **GridLayout** class, which would resize the buttons to fill the available space. We could use insets, but the buttons would still grow as the window was resized. This would not look correct to the user.

Form Entry Layout

Often, it is useful to lay out text fields and labels as if they were in an online form. To do this, we could use **FlowLayout**, but it is heavily dependent on the size of the available space. I recommend using the **GridBagLayout**. When you set the **gridwidth** to be **GridBagConstraints.REMAINDER**, then the next component to be added will be the end of the row. Listing 18.12 shows a form entry for a questionnaire.

Listing 18.12   Form Entry Layout

```
class Questionaire extends Panel {

    Questionaire() {

        GridBagLayout gridbag = new GridBagLayout();
        GridBagConstraints c = new GridBagConstraints();
        GridBagConstraints endline = new GridBagConstraints();

        endline.insets = c.insets = new Insets(0, 0, 10, 10);
        endline.gridwidth = GridBagConstraints.REMAINDER;
        endline.anchor = GridBagConstraints.WEST;

        setLayout(gridbag);

        Label l = new Label("First Name:"   );
        gridbag.setConstraints(l, c);
        add(l);
        TextField t1 = new TextField(10);
        gridbag.setConstraints(t1, endline);
        add( t1 );
        l = new Label("Last Name:");
        gridbag.setConstraints(l, c);
        add(l);
        TextField t2 = new TextField(20);
        gridbag.setConstraints(t2, endline);
        add( t2 );
    }
}
```

I prefer not to use a single constraint in these circumstances. I generally set up a constraint called **endline** which has all the constraints required of the line ending component. This approach saves having to keep resetting the values within the single constraint.

Taking this form layout one step further, it is often useful to make the actual rows of the form into separate panel objects. The objects are then easier to lay out, as shown here:

```
class LabelledText extends Panel {
    LabelledText(String s, int i) {
        add(new Label(s));
        add(new TextField(i);
    }
}
```

The Insets Method

A very useful aid to laying out components is the **insets** method. Each container maintains an inset, which is the size of the edging between the container and its parent. For instance, in the case of a frame window, this is the margin between the operating-system window and the inner container where the UI components are laid out.

If you want to set the insets for a container yourself, you can simply override the **insets** method. For instance, we can create a 10-unit margin around the container as shown in the code snippet below:

```
public Insets insets() {
    return new Insets(10, 10, 10, 10);
}
```

HOW LAYOUT MANAGEMENT WORKS

Now that we've had a good look at what layout management does for us, it is time to go under the covers and look at the inner workings of layout management. This will prepare us to write our own layout managers.

The Principal Players

The three principal classes in the layout management pattern are **Component**, **Container**, and **LayoutManager**. The first two classes have been encountered in previous chapters and so should be familiar to you. For the purposes of a layout discussion, though, the roles played by these classes are as follows:

- **Component** objects are the things to be positioned in the layout.
- **Container** class records which layout manager is being used and maintains a list of components.

- The **LayoutManager** class is responsible for the algorithm that lays out the components.

There is a slight wrinkle. If the layout manager is using the named add technique used by the likes of **BorderLayout**, then the layout manager will also contain a separate list of the components that it will lay out. This is in addition to the list maintained by the **Container** object.

The layout manager has no part in saying when a layout occurs. It is the container that tells the layout manager to do its work.

Placing the Components

When the layout manager is told to perform the layout, it either uses the named list that it contains or the components contained in the container. It performs its layout algorithm, calling placement member functions such as **reshape** on each component in the container. The layout algorithm will normally use the **preferredSize** member function of the component to discover a reasonable size for each component in the container. The **preferredSize** is one of the keys to the recursive nature of the layout management scheme. If a component of the container is itself a layout mechanism, then, the **preferredSize** will eventually call the layout manager's **preferredLayoutSize** method. This can then leave enough space for itself to perform its own management.

Most of this stuff is fairly complicated. There are a large number of potential interactions between the principal players that make layout management work. The good news is that to design your own layout manager, you only need an appreciation of the types of interaction—the main task is to implement a derived class of the **LayoutManager** class. Next, we take a look at what is needed to derive a class from the **LayoutManager** class.

The Layout Manager Abstract Class

The **LayoutManager** class is the abstract class for all the layout classes. The layout classes such as **BorderLayout** implement the functionality described by the abstract class. The code for this class can be found in source that comes with the JDK as the file LayoutManager.java.

The first thing to note is that currently all layout management is based on rectangles.

There are three main methods that must be fully implemented by all **LayoutManager**-derived classes.

- **Dimension preferredLayoutSize(Container parent)**

  This is a very important method. It should always be implemented. It should return the dimension of the box that the layout will need when it comes to place the components. This method will call the **preferredSize** method of each of the components when determining its preferred dimensions.

- **Dimension minimumLayoutSize(Container parent)**

  This method is similar to the **preferredSize** method except that it calculates the minimum size that the layout can take. This method will call the **minimumSize** method of each of the components when determining its minimum dimensions.

- **void layoutContainer(Container parent)**

  This method actually places the components. This method should ensure that it lays itself out according to the dimensions provided by the **preferredLayoutSize** method. Once the position of a component is determined, the component's **reshape** method is called to place the component.

In addition, there are two methods that must be supplied but only have code if the named method of adding components to the container is supported.

- **void addLayoutComponent(String name, Component comp)**

  This method is implemented only if the layout uses named items. Most simple layouts will not provide an implementation for this method. One example of the use of this method is the **BorderLayout** class. In this case, the **BorderLayout** class maintains a list of the North, East, South, West, and Center components within itself.

- **void removeLayoutComponent(Component comp)**

  This method is only implemented when the **addLayoutComponent** method is implemented.

DESIGNING YOUR OWN LAYOUT MANAGER

In addition to using the standard layout managers, it is possible to write your own layout manager. This requires some thought, but in the long run, it can make you more productive—if you needed a customized layout manager once, you will probably need it again. Actually, writing and publishing layouts—like writing and publishing applets and components—is a useful way of helping the Java community as a whole to grow.

Once in a while, you'll find you have a layout that cannot be constructed using the standard managers. Under these circumstances, you will probably be tempted simply to use each component's **draw** routine to custom-position it. However, it is much more useful to write a **LayoutManager**-derived class.

 **Pitfalls of Layout Management**

One thing to be careful about when writing layout managers is that you should *only* use them to lay out components. Sometimes, it is tempting to try to do more work in the layout manager. For example, if we were laying out a hierarchy chart, where each component was a member of the hierarchy, we might be tempted to draw the lines between each component. Resist this temptation to complicate the layout manager. It's a prescription for trouble.

CenterLayout

Let's write our own layout manager. This layout manager will lay out a single component. It will ensure that no matter what the container size, the contained component will always be square and perfectly centered within the container. In addition, the centering layout will maintain the concept of a margin. The margin is the minimum distance that must be maintained between the component being laid out and the edge of the container.

The layout management provided by **CenterLayout** overlaps with what can be achieved using **GridBagLayout**. However, **CenterLayout** is very simple to use, and it certainly makes an interesting introduction to designing your own layout managers.

The **CenterLayout** class is derived from the **LayoutManager** class. It implements the three most important methods: **preferredLayoutSize**, **minimumLayoutSize**, and **layoutContainer**. The code for the **CenterLayout** class is shown in Listing 18.13.

Listing 18.13 CenterLayout Layout Manager

```java
import java.awt.*;

public class CenterLayout implements LayoutManager {

    int margin=0;

    public CenterLayout() {
    }
```

```
public CenterLayout(int margin) {
    this.margin = margin;
}

public void addLayoutComponent(String name, Component comp) {
}

public void removeLayoutComponent(Component comp) {
}

public Dimension minimumLayoutSize(Container target) {
    Dimension dim = new Dimension(0, 0);
    Component m = target.getComponent(0);
    if (m != null && m.isVisible()) {
        Dimension d = m.minimumSize();
        int s = Math.min(d.height, d.width);
        dim.height = dim.width = s + 2*margin;
    }
    Insets insets = target.insets();
    dim.width += insets.left + insets.right;
    dim.height += insets.top + insets.bottom;
    return dim;
}

public Dimension preferredLayoutSize(Container target) {
    Dimension dim = new Dimension(0, 0);
    Component m = target.getComponent(0);
    if (m != null && m.isVisible()) {
        Dimension d = m.preferredSize();
        int s = Math.min(d.height, d.width);
        dim.height = dim.width = s + 2*margin;
    }
    Insets insets = target.insets();
    dim.width += insets.left + insets.right;
    dim.height += insets.top + insets.bottom;
    return dim;
}
public void layoutContainer(Container target) {
    Insets insets = target.insets();
    Dimension size = target.size();
    int top = insets.top;
    int bottom = size.height - insets.bottom;
    int left = insets.left;
    int right = size.width - insets.right;
    Component m = target.getComponent(0);
    if (m != null && m.isVisible()) {
        int h = bottom-top;
        int w = right-left;
        int s = Math.min(h, w) - 2 * margin;
        int d = Math.max(0, s);
        int oleft = left + margin + ((w > h) ? (w-h)/2 : 0);
        int otop  = top  + margin + ((h > w) ? (h-w)/2 : 0);
        m.reshape( oleft, otop, d, d);
    }
```

```
        }

    public String toString() {
        return getClass().getName() + "[margin=" + margin + "]";
    }
}
```

The **preferredLayoutSize** and the **minimumLayoutSize** methods are broadly similar. They get the first component from the container and, if it is visible, they try to calculate a size for the component. They try to make a square size for the component. The size of the side of a square will be the smallest of either the height or the width. Once a size for the square has been calculated, the **insets** for the container are added to the dimension to get the overall size of the container. This is returned to the calling method as a **Dimension** object.

The **layoutContainer** method works like the layout sizing methods, except that it will call the component's **reshape** method to give it a size. Notice also that the component is reshaped according to the current dimensions and position of the container. There is no attempt to resize the container itself. This is good practice. It is best if the algorithm works by accepting the given size of the container.

Now that we have our layout manager, we need to test it. Listing 18.14 shows some sample code that will draw a black rectangular canvas on the screen. The output from this code is shown in Figure 18.7.

Listing 18.14 Test Code for CenterLayout

```java
import java.awt.*;

class Box extends Canvas {
    public void paint(Graphics g) {
        Dimension d = size();
        g.setColor(Color.black);
        g.fillRect(0, 0, d.width-1, d.height-1);
    }
}

public class CenterLayoutTest extends Frame {

    public CenterLayoutTest() {
        super("CenterLayout Test");
        setLayout(new CenterLayout(10));
        add( new Box() );
        resize(234, 127);
        show();
    }
```

```
    public static void main(String args[]) {
        Frame f = new CenterLayoutTest();
    }
}
```

This code simply creates a frame window to display a canvas called **Box**. As the frame window is resized, the **CenterLayout** layout manager will ensure that the **Box** is kept square and centered in the window.

IF YOU LIKED THIS, YOU'LL LOVE THESE

There are several custom-designed layout managers floating around the World Wide Web. Here are two that you might be interested in.

XYLayout

If you want to nail your components at a fixed point in the container, take a look at http://www-elec.enst.fr/java/XyLayout.java. The **XyLayout** positions the components at the given locations no matter how the window is resized. In the eyes of some people, this is a step backward from the dynamic layout scheme provided by typical layout managers. However, if you feel you need to fix a component at a given position, take a look.

PackerLayout

The **PackerLayout** layout is somewhat similar to the **GridBagLayout**. It lets you lay out components in rows, columns, and other similar arrangements. Check it out at http://www.geom.umn.edu/~daeron/apps/ui/pack/gui.html.

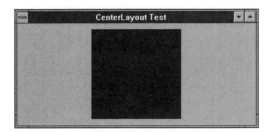

***Figure 18.7**   Testing the CenterLayout.*

LET'S REVIEW

To arrange components in containers, we use layout managers. Different layout managers provide different arrangements of the components. The JDK provides a standard set of layout managers. They can be used singly or in combination to provide most of the component layouts you will ever need. For situations that the standard layout managers do not cover, you can create our own layout managers.

CREATING YOUR OWN COMPONENTS

Neil Bartlett

If the standard UI components are not to your liking, you can make your own.

Sometimes, you are just not content with what you are given. You just want more —plain and simple. The AWT and graphics packages in general are kind of like that. You are given a rich set of components to play with: there are buttons to push, menus to navigate, and text fields to type into. But then, you that find you need, say, a spreadsheet component —and you don't have one. Going back a decade, a set of components similar to those provided by the AWT would have appeared as manna from heaven. Now, they are the building blocks of the user interfaces we create: essential tools to create the essential interfaces demanded of us by our users.

The problem with user interfaces is that they are always evolving. Users are very demanding people. They want our interfaces to be intuitive and easy to use. Today, users will enter a date into a text field. They are content with understanding the date format, content with typing in the date. Tomorrow, though, they will want graphical input. A full calendar should pop-up allowing them to navigate using the mouse to the month and day they want to enter. Naturally, the calendar will provide them with full feedback on the day of the week they are choosing and indications of national holidays: all the information they need to make a good choice of the date to enter. There will be no more remembering the number of days in a month, no more wondering if next Tuesday is the first or the second of the month. The calendar will do all that for them. No typing, just mouse clicking.

What we are talking about here are custom-designed components or, as they are often known, custom controls. We are talking about extending the GUI to provide a richer set of components than is provided by the default installation. These demands are placed on us by our own imagination—and the imagination of others. These things tend to evolve rapidly and, once one toolkit has them, all toolkits need them. By the way, a small word of warning: I will be using the terms "component" and "control" interchangeably for the rest of the chapter.

Think about the date example. Am I being far-fetched? Not at all. Controls like this are starting to appear for Rapid Application Development (RAD) database tools. Entering dates into databases is quite a commonplace need, so the RAD programmers have taken the lead. Maybe national holidays are not yet part of the make up of the RAD date entry controls, but they do provide the rest of the stuff I spoke about.

So where does that leave you and I—Java GUI programmers? Do we want to be left out in the cold? No, we want to be able to innovate for ourselves. We want to create GUI controls that create waves.

The really good news is that Java makes GUI component writing rather easy. We have already covered most of the techniques we need to make our controls work: we have looked at existing components, we have looked at event handling, we have looked at drawing graphics—we have looked at everything required to make virtually any GUI control we desire.

In this chapter, we go under the hood and take a look at GUI control writing. We will start off writing our own custom control and then we will look at what makes it tick. Later, we will talk about some of the more philosophical issues involved in writing your own controls.

GUITAR CHORDS

We talked about a date control earlier. When I first began writing this chapter, I decided to tell you about the design of a date control I had put together.

Then I thought about it some more. I wanted to be a bit more unusual. I fancied doing something that you will probably not read about anywhere else.

After a bit of thought, I decided to create a guitar chord control. This control will enable the display of guitar chord diagrams in Java windows. The idea is to provide a chord diagram that guitarists can use to publish their strummings on the Web.

The published page will look just like that in a music magazine, albeit minus the admittedly rather useful music staves. If you look around the Net, you will find countless tunes published. Generally, these tunes are written in a very cryptic, but eventually decipherable format, such as songwriter format. Some of them are free-form attempts to capture the music in text format. For example, check out OLGA, the OnLine Guitar Archive, at ftp://ftp.nevada.edu/pub/guitar. OLGA stores thousands of songs transcribed for guitarists. Figure 19.1 shows a typical attempt to represent chords in OLGA.

Sometimes, to get over the hurdles of printing the music, the musician will resort to drawing out the chords, scanning them in, and placing them on the Web as GIFs. Fine, but this is a lot of work and the GIFs take a relatively long time to download.

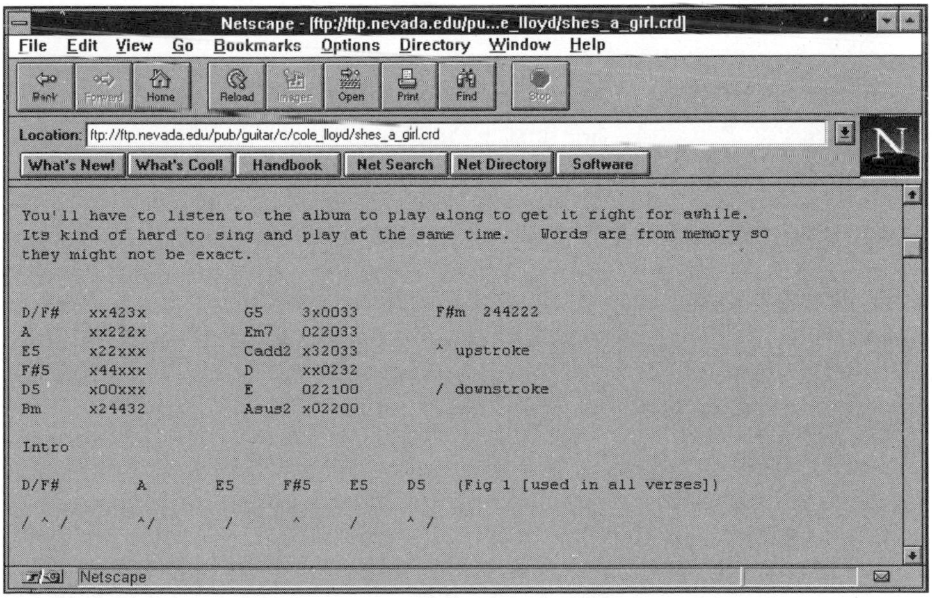

Figure 19.1 *OLGA contains an archive of transcribed songs for guitarists.*

I wanted to design something that would be fast and effective. Something as visual as GIFs, but with simpler creation and better download performance. However, I am getting a bit ahead of myself. Before we conquer the world, let's simplify things. Let's start by designing ourselves a chord diagram control that will allow us to display a single chord.

I suppose I should take a bit of time out here for the non-musicians among us. Yes, I am indulging my interest in music, but I hope I am not doing so at your expense. I have put together a small sidebar to tell you what guitar chords are all about. You only need to understand the terms I will use: you don't need to know what the chords are used for. I recommend that you glance over the sidebar to familiarize yourself with the essential elements of the diagram.

For the purposes of this chapter, you don't have to be a musician to follow what's going on. The chord diagram is just a vehicle to explain the principles of custom component writing. As it happens, writing a chord diagram will exercise most of the skills you will need to write any control. In fact, as I discovered while writing it, the chord diagram control takes more skills to write than a date control does. So even if you are a non-musician, read on. The techniques you pick up will keep you in good stead for most of the controls you care to write.

 ## What's a Chord Diagram?

First of all, for those non-strummers among us, let's review a chord diagram.

A chord is simply a collection of music notes. For stringed instruments, such as guitars, chords are played by placing fingers on the strings at the frets—the little metal bars running across the neck of the guitar. The exact position of the fingers determines the chord played. Generally, for a right handed guitarist, the fingers of the left hand will hold down the chord. The right hand is used to pluck the strings. Sometimes, a string must not be played. In this case, the right hand will avoid playing that string.

All the information to describe the chord is contained in a chord diagram. A typical chord diagram is shown in Figure 19.2.

The D7 label across the top of the diagram is the name of the chord. Chord diagram names are abbreviations of the full chord names. In this case, D7 is the D dominant

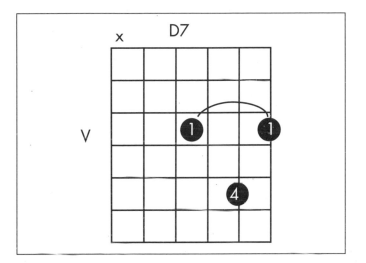

Figure 19.2   *A chord diagram.*

seventh chord. The Roman numerals are used to locate the position of the frets. The Roman numeral V on the left side of the diagram says that the chord is to be played at the fifth fret. The first fret is at the top of the guitar neck furthest away from the body of the guitar. If the top of the chord diagram is the first fret, no Roman numeral is used. The words under the chord diagram are the lyrics of the song. Figure 19.3 shows the chord diagram with annotations.

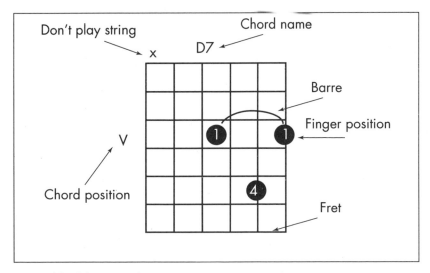

Figure 19.3   *Chord diagram with annotations.*

The chord diagram itself is a grid of lines. The vertical lines are strings and the horizontal lines are frets. The black dots are fingers. The little Xs over the strings are strings that are not played. Strings with no X or finger marks are called open strings.

The looping arc between the fingers is called a barre and is used to indicate that a single finger is placed as a bar over the strings between the two fingered positions.

WHAT WILL IT DO?

Well, obviously, the chord diagram component must be able to draw chord diagrams like those shown in Figures 19.2 and 19.3. I have decided not to implement the barre part of the chord diagram—not because it is difficult to code, but because it would add little to the discussion and I want to keep the code as focused as possible. Adding the barre is left for you as a fun exercise.

In addition to drawing the chord, I want to be able to change the chord diagram settings using the mouse. Although I don't cover it in the book, I am writing a simple song writing program for publishing your own songs. So, as part of that exercise, I need to be able to interact with the chords to change their settings dynamically.

I want to be able to click the mouse over an empty fret of a string and have that string marked with a finger at that fret. At the same time, if there are any other marks on the string, I want them to be cleared. To clear the mark, I want simply to click on the mark. Finally, if the mouse is clicked over the top of a string, outside the grid, I want the don't-play-the-string symbol, the X, to be placed over the string. If there is an X there already, I want it to be cleared.

If this description of events is confusing to you, then you can try running an example of the chord diagram control. The source is on the disk at \SOURCE\CHAP19\FINAL.VER. You can run, say, the test02.html sample as

```
cmd>appletviewer test02.html
```

Try clicking the mouse over the example chord. It won't be long before you work out what is happening.

IMPLEMENTING THE CHORD DIAGRAM CONTROL

Okay, that gets the specification of the user needs of the chord diagram out of the way. Our task is clear enough for us to begin to design the chord diagram.

The first thing we need to do is to develop the overall design of the chord diagram control. My first step is generally to separate the visuals from the underlying thing that is being displayed. What do I mean by this? Well, take, for example, the idea of a UI Label. The Label will display a string. The string itself can be considered to be an abstract entity. After all, we can manipulate the string without displaying it. We don't *have* to display the string. The Label, though, exists to display the string. In this sense, the label gives a visual representation of the string.

So what are the visual and non-visual parts of the chord diagram? The equivalent of the Label's string, the non-visual part, is the chord itself. The chord does not have to be visible for us to be able to use it. For instance, we might want to play the sounds of the chord, or we might want to convert the chord into some other musical notation. To do these things, it is not necessary for us actually to display the chord. The chord has a life of its own aside from any visual representation.

The visual part is the chord diagram. It will take a chord and turn it into a visual reality. It will use the chord to determine what to display. The visual part will be responsible for tracking all the information associated with the visual aspects—such as the dimensions of the chord grid and so on. The non-visual part will not retain any of this information.

This separation of the abstract chord from the visual chord diagram is called *separating the model from the view.* The model, the chord, is abstract and can be developed independently from the view, the chord diagram. The model-view is a very important concept in GUI programming.

Let's take a look first at developing the chord model. We need to understand this before we can understand how to display it. The source code for the chord diagram component and its test files can all be found on the CD-ROM in the directory \SOURCE\CHAP19.

The Chord Model

As I mentioned earlier, the chord is just a collection of notes. In its purest musical form, a chord can be played on any musical instrument. For example, an A minor chord can be played on any instrument you wish. When developing a chord model, the most natural idea would be to design the model to record the chord in its rawest form, the collection of notes.

The trouble with this approach is that just as different musical instruments have different mechanisms to produce the sounds, the chords played on each instrument need different information to produce them. The guitar has strings. It is really a multi-input device—several strings can produce the same note. So, for a guitar, we need to specify on which string the note is to be produced. This fact makes sight-reading guitar music without chord diagrams a matter of interpretation. On a piano, for instance, this would not be necessary. For each note, there is only one possible piano key to press. A chord for a piano can be written in pure music notation. It is not open to interpretation. All piano players would press the same keys—without the benefit of additional chord diagrams.

The chord model we are developing, then, is one in which the strings of the chord are modeled.

If you have read anything so far about inheritance, you will realize that the chords are prime candidates for a complete family of chords. However, as you will see from the design. I have not done this. I decided against inheritance for this project. I reasoned that I am only trying to describe guitar chords—not the entire spectrum of musical instruments. However, bear this thought in mind: if we intended to put this chord into a full music program—one with complete music staves, and with parts for different instruments —we would definitely need to consider using inheritance.

Thus, we will be implementing our chord model using a single class. We will call it **Chord**. Actually, despite what I was saying about different musical instruments needing different chord information, the **Chord** class will do better than just hold guitar chords. Instruments like banjos use the same chord diagramming technique as guitars. The only difference is the number of strings; the concept of frets is pretty much the same. This means that the class must contain strings and the frets that are used on the strings. Also we need to represent when a string is not played.

The simplest representation for this is to have the **Chord** class contain an array of integers. Each element of the array represents a guitar string. The number stored in an element of the array is the fret position at which the string is played. A number of 0 represents an open string and -1 represents a string that is not played.

We spoke about position, the fret at which the chord diagram will be drawn. Now, strictly, this is not in the domain of the chord, because the chord should not contain any visual information. However, as will become clearer in a moment, we need to construct the chord from some user information. This information is easier for the user to provide if the position is provided first. Therefore, we will be storing the position in the chord.

Finally, the name of the chord is something that is also independent of the visuals, so the chord will store the name of the chord.

Listing 19.1 shows the **Chord** class. It should make sense from our previous discussion. I have added a few support functions to return information to the outside world. However, we have not yet discussed how the creator of the chord will supply the chord details. We need to discuss the input format. We do that in the next section.

Listing 19.1   Chord.java

```java
public class Chord {

    Integer strings[];
    String chordname = "";
    int pos=0;

    Chord( String n, int p, String s) {
        pos = p;
        chordname = n;
        string2Strings(s);
    }

    void string2Strings(String s) {
        // format "0-123-"
        strings = new Integer[s.length()];

        for (int i=0; i < s.length(); ++i) {

            if (s.charAt(i) == 'X')
                strings[i] = new Integer(-1);
            if (s.charAt(i) == '-') // same as 0
                strings[i] = new Integer(0);
            else if (Character.isDigit(s.charAt(i)))
                strings[i] = new Integer(
                    Character.digit(s.charAt(i), 10));
            else
                strings[i] = new Integer(-1);
        }
    }

    public int numberOfStrings() {
        return strings.length;
    }

    public boolean fingered(int i) {
```

```
        return strings[i].intValue() != -1;
    }

    public int fret(int i) {
        return strings[i].intValue();
    }

    public String name() {
        return chordname;
    }

    public int position() {
        return pos;
    }
}
```

Input Format

I am guilty here of not having given enough information in the spec—okay, so sue me. The chord could quite simply have taken an array of integers along with the name. In fact, my initial test version of the chord did just that. The code is still in the source on the disk, if you care to look. However, the main description of the chord diagram, for the uses to which I will put the chord diagram control, is a string describing the chord. A typical string might be "—231-" which represents the A minor chord shown in Figure 19.4.

Table 19.1 shows the meaning of the characters in the string.

The advantage of the string approach is that the chord is easily readable in human format and it takes up little space in the source code. Compare the

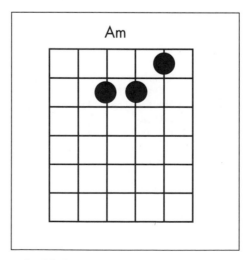

Figure 19.4   *An A minor chord diagram.*

Table 19.1   *Chord Representation String*

Symbol	Meaning
1 to 9	Fret to play
- or 0	Open string
X	Don't play string

"—231-" to the equivalent for a Integer array format shown in the following code snippet:

```
array[0] = new Integer(0);
array[1] = new Integer(0);
array[2] = new Integer(2);
array[3] = new Integer(21);
array[4] = new Integer(1);
array[5] = new Integer(0);
```

and I am sure you will see what I mean.

Take a look back at Listing 19.1. The **Chord** class constructor will take three things: the description string, the position of the chord, and the name of the chord. The constructor calls the **string2strings** method to convert the string into an array of integers. I use a very simple error-handling scheme—if the string is supplied in the wrong format, I supply a wrong diagram. This simple scheme, while not good at alerting the user to the potential failure, is at least robust.

Well, that about does it for the **Chord** class. We have now created a model that represents the abstract information in the chord diagram. The abstract information is tuned to the application we have at hand—the chord diagram control—but there is no reason we can't tune it to a different need just by changing the internals. For instance, we could add more methods to the **Chord** class to support, say, playing the chord. But that is for another day. Now let's move on and take a peek at the visual side of things.

The Chord Diagram

In the sidebar at the beginning of the chapter, I explained the elements that make up a chord diagram. Let's look at the diagram now from a GUI programmer's perspective to see what components it has inside of it.

What we are looking for is the potential for reuse. Are there any GUI components we can reuse to construct the chord diagram? Often, a custom control can be completely designed using existing controls. The custom control does not use any new GUI interface: it just reuses existing ones—perhaps laid out in a particular fashion or interacting in a particular way. This might not seem like much of a gain until you consider that the aim of the game is to emphasize reuse and, if you are designing a lot of products using this custom control, to ensure consistency. Controls that are formed from a combination of other controls are often termed *composite controls.*

So back to our chord diagram, can we identify existing components? Figure 19.5 shows a component breakdown of the chord that we will be using.

As you can see, we have two **Label**s, one **RomanNumeralLabel** and one new control. I have called the new control the **UndecoratedChordDiagram**. It is a bit of a mouthful, but at least it describes what its does. I toyed with class names such as ChordGrid and the like but they did not capture what I was after. Naming classes was never my strong suit.

One thing about the **UndecoratedChordDiagram** class is that it is the core difference we are providing here. **The UndecoratedChordDiagram** is itself a useful control. Some applications might not want the full **ChordDiagram**. These applications could potentially use the **UndecoratedChordDiagram** class directly. However, we will have more to say on customizing the **ChordDiagram** class later.

This knowledge enables us to describe what is called a *control hierarchy:* the hierarchy of controls that make up our composite control. The control hierarchy for the chord diagram is shown in Figure 19.6.

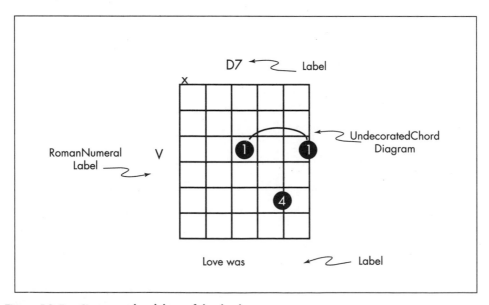

Figure 19.5   Component breakdown of the chord.

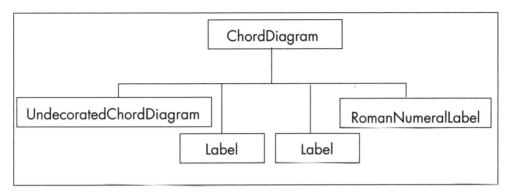

Figure 19.6 *Control hierarchy diagram.*

If we assume some details for the **UndecoratedChordDiagram** class, we can go ahead and write the **ChordDiagram** class. Take a look at Listing 19.2.

Listing 19.2 ChordDiagram Class

```
public class ChordDiagram extends Panel {

    UndecoratedChordDiagram cp;
    Chord chord;

    ChordDiagram( int w, int h, Chord c, String lyric) {
        chord = c;
        cp = new UndecoratedChordDiagram(c);
        arrange(w, h, c.name(), lyric);
    }

    void arrange( int w, int h, String title, String lyric) {

        GridBagLayout gridbag = new GridBagLayout();
        GridBagConstraints c = new GridBagConstraints();
        setLayout(gridbag);

        Label l = new Label(title);
        l.setFont(new Font("Helvetica", Font.PLAIN, 8));
        c.gridwidth = GridBagConstraints.REMAINDER;
        gridbag.setConstraints(l, c);
        add(l);

        c.gridwidth = GridBagConstraints.RELATIVE;
        c.anchor = GridBagConstraints.NORTHEAST;
        RomanNumeralLabel r = new RomanNumeralLabel(
                            chord.position(), Label.CENTER);
        r.setFont(new Font("Helvetica", Font.PLAIN, 6));
        gridbag.setConstraints(r, c);
        add(r);
```

```
        int savey = c.ipady; c.ipady = 50;
        int savex = c.ipadx; c.ipadx = 50;
    c.gridwidth = GridBagConstraints.REMAINDER;
        c.anchor = GridBagConstraints.CENTER;
        gridbag.setConstraints(cp, c);
        add(cp);
        c.ipadx = savex;
        c.ipady = savey;

    c.gridwidth = GridBagConstraints.REMAINDER;
        l = new Label(lyric, Label.CENTER);
        l.setFont(new Font("Helvetica", Font.PLAIN, 10));
        gridbag.setConstraints(l, c);
        add(l);

        resize(w, h);
    }
}
```

The first important thing to notice about the **ChordDiagram** class is that it is a descendent of the **Panel** class. This gives the **ChordDiagram** class the ability to lay out the components that it is controlling. In this case, we use a **GridBagLayout** class to lay out the components.

The **GridBagLayout** allows fine control and placement of controls arranged as a grid. It has the important property that the components in the grid can be different sizes. As we discussed we have two **Label**s, one **RomanNumeral Label**, and the **UndecoratedChordDiagram**. The **GridBagLayout** uses a series of constraints to control the size and position of the components. We add the first **Label**, the name of the chord, into the grid with the **gridwidth** constraint set as **REMAINDER**. This instructs the **gridbag** to treat this as the last, in this case the only, component in current row. The component takes the entire width of the control and, because it is a centered label, the label is positioned in the middle of the top row. We use the same technique for the lyric, which is the last row of the control.

The middle row is formed by the **RomanNumeralLabel** and the **UndecoratedChordDiagram**. The **RomanNumeralLabel** is placed first on the row. Its constraint settings place it at the top of its allocated area in the top-right corner of the area. The chord diagram, meanwhile, is placed as the last component on the row. It is forced to have a minimum size.

Finally, the **ChordDiagram** control is forced to the size given by the creator of this class.

As you can see, the **ChordDiagram** class is a true composite component class. All it is doing is arranging its composite components in the desired layout. It does not directly process any events or do any drawing. For its simplicity, though, it is doing a very useful job. This is typical of composite controls.

The UndecoratedChordDiagram

We have seen the composite technique. Now, let's get to the meat of the chord diagram: a fully interactive chord diagram control written directly in Java.

The **UndecoratedChordDiagram** class will be drawing the chord diagram and it will be interacting with the user. It will take an instance of the model **Chord** class and make a visual version of the chord. It will get the information from the **Chord** object directly.

I decided to make **ChordDiagram** class the one that does the drawing. This might seem obvious, but it would be possible to fragment the problem even further and create a grid of components that could be laid out as the grid of frets and strings. However, we would be getting into a number of problems such as deciding who draws the edges of the boxes to prevent double thickness. In addition, we would start to get into performance problems, since we would be adding over 30 extra objects per chord diagram. All these problems and very little gain! For these reasons, I decided the buck stops with the **UndecoratedChordDiagram** class. There is no benefit in any further application of divide and conquer.

Control Hierarchy

Now that we have decided that this class is going to do all the drawing work, we still need to decide upon the parent component for the chord diagram.

Obviously, the chord diagram will need to override the **paint** method and it will need to override event handling. Therefore, the most natural choice for the parent is a **Canvas** or a **Panel** component. I have chosen **Panel** here, even though **Canvas** would seem to be the most appropriate fit. The reason is a simple real-world fact. When I ran my test harness under an earlier version of the JDK, the **Canvas** would not work under the appletviewer whereas changing the parent class from **Canvas** to **Panel** set things up just fine. So **Canvas** it should be—but **Panel** it is. In general, I would recommend using the **Canvas** class and not the **Panel** class.

Now that we have the parent, there are only two things left to do to get the chord diagram going. First, we need to handle drawing the chord and its elements. Then, we need to deal with interacting with the user.

Drawing the Diagram

The first task is to look at the diagram and work out the information we need to describe it.

An initial decision is whether the diagram will have its overall size given to it, or whether it will get its overall size from within itself. After all, the diagram itself has a certain minimum size to which it can be reduced, beyond which it becomes just a single black blob with no defining information.

To make life simple, I decided to implement it as sizing from within. I would point out, though, that this decision is not one I have fixed in stone for myself. At a future date, I will probably review this decision. Given the current uses to which I have put the chord diagram, the decision has worked out well.

Instead of using a resize, another useful way of managing the size is to override the minimum and preferred size methods. This works well because it works directly with the layout management classes, as shown in the code snippet below:

```
public Dimension minimumSize() {
    return new Dimension(80, 80);
}

public Dimension preferedSize() {
    return minimumSize();
}
```

Figure 19.7 shows the various internal variables that we will need to capture in the class.

The main information we are capturing is the distance between strings, the distance between frets, and the information on the margins around the grid.

The source code for the class is quite straightforward. We construct the class with a **Chord** class. Then, we size the chord diagram, setting up the parameters we require for later drawing. The purists among you will notice that I have hard-coded a few variables in place. Well, don't worry—we will be getting rid of them very soon. They are just placeholders to keep the development steps in sequence. I will be removing them when we deal with customization.

Once the **UndecoratedChordDiagram** class has been constructed, it does nothing until the runtime calls the overridden **paint** method. The **paint** method

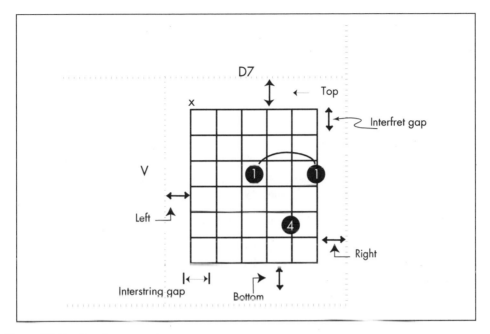

Figure 19.7 *Drawing parameters.*

draws the chord grid, then it paints the rest of the chord. The fingers and the other symbols are calculated by querying the chord for the information. The **UndecoratedChordDiagram** source code is shown in Listing 19.3.

Listing 19.3   The UndecoratedChordDiagram Class

```
class UndecoratedChordDiagram extends Panel {
    Chord c;
    int interstringgap;
    int interfretgap;
    int numberOfFrets;
    int left;
    int right;
    int top;
    int bottom;

    UndecoratedChordDiagram(Chord in) {
        c = in;
        sizeChord();
    }

    void  sizeChord() {

        interfretgap = 9;
        interstringgap = 8;
```

```
        numberOfFrets = 6;
        left = interstringgap/2+1;
        right = left+interstringgap*(c.numberOfStrings()-1);
        top = interfretgap;
        bottom = top+interfretgap*(numberOfFrets -1);

        resize( 80, 80);
    }

  void drawDiagramBackground(Graphics g) {
        int i, x, y;
Dimension d = size();
        for (y = top, i=0; i<numberOfFrets; y+=interfretgap, ++i) {
            g.drawLine( left, y, right, y);
        }
        for (x = left, i = 0; i < c.numberOfStrings();
                              x+=interstringgap, ++i) {
            g.drawLine(x, top, x, bottom);
        }
    }

  void drawCross(Graphics g, int x1, int y1, int w, int h) {
        g.drawLine(x1, y1, x1+w, y1+h);
        g.drawLine(x1+w, y1, x1, y1+h);
    }

  void drawNoPlayIndicator(Graphics g, int i) {
        drawCross( g, left+interstringgap*i-interstringgap/2+1+1,
                      top-interfretgap+1,
                      interstringgap-2-1, interfretgap-3-1);
    }

  void drawFinger(Graphics g, int i) {
        g.fillRect( left+interstringgap*i-interstringgap/2+1,
                    top-interfretgap+interfretgap*c.fret(i)+2,
                    interstringgap-2, interfretgap-3);
    }

  void drawFingers(Graphics g) {
        for (int i=0; i < c.numberOfStrings(); ++i) {
            if (!c.fingered(i)) {
                drawNoPlayIndicator(g, i);
            } else if (c.fret(i) != 0) {
                drawFinger(g, i);
            }
        }
    }

  public void paint(Graphics g) {
g.setPaintMode();
    drawDiagramBackground(g);
    drawFingers(g);
    }
}
```

Interacting with the User

The interaction we need is to check when the mouse is clicked over a finger position.

This gives us two choices for events: The **mouseUp** event or the **mouseDown** event. The **mouseDown** event would mean that the change of finger position would happen when the mouse is depressed; the **mouseUp** event would change the finger position when the mouse button is lifted.

It is safest for us to use the **mouseUp** event because it allows users to change their mind by moving the mouse out of the chord diagram before lifting the mouse button up if they unintentionally depress the mouse button over the chord diagram. For additional safety, we could detect that the **mouseDown** event actually occurred inside the chord and only allow those **mouseUp** events that occurred when the **mouseDown** event occurred in the chord diagram.

Listing 19.4 shows the overridden event handler for the chord diagram.

Listing 19.4   Event Handler for a Chord

```
public boolean mouseUp(Event e, int x, int y) {
        if (!waitingForMouseUp)
            return false;
        waitingForMouseUp = false;
        Rectangle r = new Rectangle();
        for (int i=0; i < c.numberOfStrings(); ++i) {
            for (int j = 0; j < numberOfFrets; ++j) {
                r.reshape( left+interstringgap*i-interstringgap/2+1,
                        top-interfretgap+interfretgap*j+2,
                        interstringgap-2, interfretgap-3);
                if (r.inside(x, y)) {
                    c.setFinger(i, j);
                    repaint();
                    return true;
                }
            }
        }
        return false;
    }

    public boolean mouseDown(Event e, int x, int y) {
        waitingForMouseUp = true;
        return true;
    }
```

The code for the **mouseUp** event uses the variable **waitingForMouseUp**. The variable has been declared and assigned an initial value to prevent incorrect operation for an uninitialized variable.

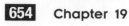 

Initialize Class Variables

One of the useful features of the Java compiler is that it does try to detect uninitialized values for variables that are declared inside a method. However, it doesn't perform the same trick for class variables. So take care when creating class variables to assign initial values, at least, when you do not assign them directly in a constructor of the class.

Once a **mouseDown** event occurs inside of our chord diagram control, the mouse button is grabbed. In other words, all mouse events will be sent to the **ChordDiagram** object, even if the mouse moves out of the window. We do not have to worry about the mouse being moved out of the window and the mouse button being lifted up. We will see the mouse up event and so clear the flag correctly, as shown in the code line below:

```
boolean waitingForMouseUp=false;
```

Once the **mouseDown** event has been detected, we need to determine where the mouse button was pressed. There are two main techniques for doing this. One uses what is called a "hit list"—a list of objects against which we wish to check. We could have used this strategy if we had stored the possible finger positions as a list of rectangles. Recall that this was the mechanism we used when picking devices in a schematic in Chapter 15.

I have used a different method here. I dynamically calculate the rectangles for each of the finger positions. One by one, each of these rectangles is tested to see if the **mouseUp** position is inside of the rectangle. If the **mouseUp** position is inside of the rectangle, we call a new method, **setFinger**, on the chord to set the new finger position. Finally, we call **repaint** to ensure that the chord redraws itself with the correct updated information.

I am using the **repaint()** function, which repaints the complete chord, rather than **repaint(x, y, w, h)**, which just repaints a rectangle. I am using this approach because the chord might change in areas other than the rectangle containing the current finger position. For instance, setting a finger value will clear the X at the top of the string and the finger setting to be drawn. However, flickering can be a problem.

For instance, if you had a very slow graphics card, or if you wanted to create a very large chord on a screen, you could optimize the **repaint** by repainting the rectangle for the entire string rather than the entire chord. Alternatively, you could have the chord return a list of finger positions that have changed, calculate the rectangle for each finger position, and then just repaint those. As it stands, given the size at which I have fixed the chord, the current **repaint** mechanism works just fine.

On the subject of performance, the algorithmically minded will no doubt have spotted a much faster way to detect which finger position the **mouseUp** position is in. A faster method would have been to subtract the **interstringgap** from the x position and **interfretgap** from the y position, counting how many subtractions of each are needed to move beyond the top-left corner.

Fastest of all would be to use left shift to binary-chop the grid in both the horizontal and vertical axes—but then who needs the performance of a Ferrari in a simple piece of mouse code like this? The simplicity of using the operating system's mouse-button detection will far outweigh any performance gains that could be achieved. I have presented what I consider to be the easiest-to-understand algorithm and also satisfied a hidden agenda of wanting to use the **Rectangle** class, which at the time of writing this chapter I had not shown in any code. So now you know!

In addition, we need to add the **setFinger** method to the chord class to enable it to change the finger positions.

```
public void setFinger(int s, int f) {
    if (strings[s].intValue() == f)
        f = -1;
    strings[s] = new Integer(f);
}
```

Now, **setFinger** starts to open up some interesting questions. We will ask the questions here and later we will consider fixing them.

The questions are first, "Who created the **Chord** object?" and second, "Who needs to know that the **Chord** object has changed?" To see more of what I am talking about, think about how chords are used. If you are a non-musician this might not be obvious. The problem is that a given chord will be used a number of times in a song.

Now suppose we were writing a songwriting tool in which we dragged various chords on to a sheet of music. Now holding that idea in your mind, suppose we want to change a chord. Of course, if the chord is incorrect throughout the song, we'd want the change to affect all instances of the chord. This would seem entirely reasonable from the end user's perspective. As you can see, though, the **setFinger** code merely changes the underlying data structure—it does not cause any repaints of any other chord diagrams that might be viewing the **Chord** class.

As you will probably have guessed if you have read Chapter 15, this would be an ideal situation to use the **Observable** and the **Observer** classes.

Making It Customizable

So now, we have a functionally complete piece of code. The essence of the control is now written. Before we write the test harness code that will run a test case, I want to add one more thing in to the mix.

You might recall, that earlier, I had a few hard-coded values in the code with no way for the user to change them. Let's look at replacing those values with user-customizable values. The simplest solution would be to add extra parameters to the **ChordDiagram** class.

```
ChordDiagram(int w, int h, Chord c, int isg, int ifg)
```

However, this quickly becomes unwieldy, especially when you have a large number of chords. It becomes difficult to assign default values, because they have to be passed in the creation of the **ChordDiagram**—which is getting cluttered with a large number of parameters.

The solution to our problems is to use a **parameterizing class**. This is a fancy way of saying: *put the data we want to customize into an object, then pass the object to a **ChordDiagram** object when it is constructed.* This might seem a little over the top, but it has a lot of advantages. It simplifies the interface to the **ChordDiagram** and to the **UndecoratedChordDiagram**. It enables the settings to reside in one place. The settings class can provide user-friendly setting methods that can take input and convert it into appropriate settings for the **ChordDiagram**. An example might be where the **Chord Diagram** were part of an applet and we were are using the Param part of the HTML **applet** tags to pass in data. This could be fed directly to a settings object rather than expecting the user program to interpret and manipulate the information.

The settings class is shown in Listing 19.5.

Listing 19.5 ChordDiagramSettings.java

```
public class ChordDiagramSettings {

    public int width;
```

```
    public int height;
    public int interstringgap;
    public int interfretgap;
    public int numberOfFrets;
    public int left;
    public int top;
    public int fingerStyle;
    public final static int ROUND_FINGER=1;
    public final static int SQUARE_FINGER=2;

    ChordDiagramSettings() {
        width = 200;
        height = 200;
        interfretgap = 9;
        interstringgap = 8;
        numberOfFrets = 6;
        left = interstringgap/2+1;
        top = interfretgap;
        fingerStyle=SQUARE_FINGER;
    }
}
```

To use the **ChordDiagramSettings** class, we need to introduce a few changes into the constructors for the **UndecoratedChordDiagram** and the **ChordDiagram** classes, as shown in Listing 19.6.

Listing 19.6   Modifying the Constructors

```
UndecoratedChordDiagram(Chord in, ChordDiagramSettings csdin) {
    c = in;
    csd = csdin;
    sizeChord();
}

ChordDiagram(ChordDiagramSettings csd, Chord c, String lyric) {
    chord = c;
    cp = new UndecoratedChordDiagram(c, csd);
    arrange(csd.width, csd.height, c.name(), lyric);
}
```

Naturally, we need to update the **sizeChord** to remove the hard-coded values we had. This is shown in Listing 19.7.

Listing 19.7   Updating the sizeChord

```
void  sizeChord() {

    interfretgap = csd.interfretgap;
    interstringgap = csd.interstringgap;
```

```
numberOfFrets = csd.numberOfFrets;

left = csd.left;
right = left+interstringgap*(c.numberOfStrings()-1);
top = csd.top;
bottom = top+interfretgap*(numberOfFrets -1);

resize( 80, 80);
}
```

Finally, we upgrade the **drawFinger** method to add in the extra ability to draw rounded as well as square finger styles. This is shown in Listing 19.8.

Listing 19.8   Upgrading the drawFinger Method

```
void drawFinger(Graphics g, int i) {

    switch (csd.fingerStyle) {

        case ChordDiagramSettings.SQUARE_FINGER:
            g.fillRect( left+interstringgap*i-interstringgap/2+1,
                top-interfretgap+interfretgap*c.fret(i)+2,
                interstringgap-2, interfretgap-3);
            break;

        case ChordDiagramSettings.ROUND_FINGER:
            g.fillOval( left+interstringgap*i-interstringgap/2+1,
                top-interfretgap+interfretgap*c.fret(i)+2,
                interstringgap-2, interfretgap-3);
            break;

    }
}
```

The parameterizing class might seem like a mere convenience for storing the settings for the chord diagrams' visual properties. In this example, that is true. But consider what happens when we have a number of chord diagrams in a music sheet. Suppose we want to change all of them to use round finger styles rather than square finger styles. It would make a lot of sense if we could just change the settings on the **ChordDiagramSettings** class and let all the chord diagrams update themselves from the class directly without any extra work on behalf of the programmer. You might recognize this need as being similar to the need of a single abstract chord being used by a number of visual chords. In effect, it's the same problem. They both are situations in which there is one thing with many things interested in what its settings are. And yes, this is yet *another* case for the **Observable** and **Observer** classes.

Testing the Code

So, now we have a functionally complete piece of code. I still have a few changes I want to show you, but the essence of the control is now written. Let's write some simple test code to draw a single chord up on the screen. My primary use for the chord diagram is going to be to publish stuff on the Internet, so I want to ensure that it works when used as part of an applet. This is shown in Listing 19.9.

Listing 19.9 Test01.java

```java
import java.awt.*;
import java.applet.*;
import java.lang.*;
import java.net.*;

public class Test01 extends Applet implements Runnable {

    public void init()
    {
        ChordDiagramSettings s = new ChordDiagramSettings();
        s.fingerStyle = ChordDiagramSettings.ROUND_FINGER;

        add( new ChordDiagram(s,
                    new Chord("Am", "-221-"), "Yesterday") );
    }
}
```

The full code for the control is available in the /SOURCE/CHAP19/FINAL.VER directory

To run the test applet, simply use the appletviewer on the test01.html file. You should see a single chord control with rounded finger styles, as shown in Figure 19.8. Try clicking the mouse over the chord diagram to change the fingering positions of the chord.

REVIEWING WHAT WE HAVE ACCOMPLISHED

We have taken a complete trip through writing a control in Java. The chord diagram is a relatively complicated control: it makes use of composition of other controls, it draws a complicated diagram, it interacts with the user, and it provides a settings mechanism to change visual aspects of the control. Not bad. When you look at the chord control in this light, you realize that it is of similar complexity to any of the controls in an everyday GUI.

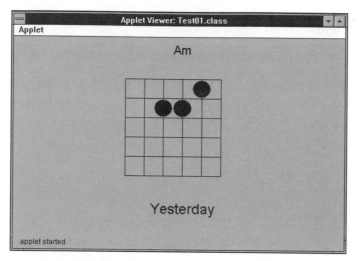

Figure 19.8   *Running Test01.html.*

Writing controls in Java is a natural extension of everyday Java programming. Control writing demands a certain understanding of the internal classes that constitute the Java JDK, but using those classes is no more difficult than, say, reading in a file. If you have ever written any controls for Windows or widgets for X-Window/MOTIF or any other GUI for that matter, I am sure you will appreciate the simplicity of the Java approach.

So, if this is so easy, what have we lost? As currently written, the JDK does have its limitations. We have discussed its shortcomings with the completeness of its event handling and with its controlling some of the finer features of the GUI. These shortcomings, though, are not inherent limitations of the Java JDK: they are just examples of the incompleteness typical of the first version of a toolkit. It won't be long before these features are up to par with any of the existing operating systems. The peer component approach to interfacing with the operating system should enable the JDK developers to rise above the "lowest common denominator" approach.

My favorite benefit from writing controls in Java is the multiplatform flexibility. It is very handy to be able to write a control once and then have it run on multiple machines. Having written controls for a number of different operating systems, I can tell you from experience that it's a chore to have to manage the ports between the machines.

IS THIS APPROACH THE ONLY WAY?

You know, I'm glad you asked that. All right, so *I* asked it. One of us asked it, and that's all that really matters.

The general principle used was to subclass our control from an existing Java component. We have stayed completely within Java for our programming. We have not had any need to use techniques or tools outside the Java system.

However, there is another way. I want to talk about that for a while because it is interesting to consider.

Previously, in Chapter 13, we mentioned peer classes. These are classes that wrap up the interface between the native operating system and the JDK classes. The peer classes are responsible for implementing a lot of the standard controls that are used by the JDK. For instance, the **button** class is not implemented directly in Java; instead, the JDK uses the same button code that your operating system GUI uses. The advantage of this, from the JDK's perspective, is that tools written using the JDK look and feel just like native operating system tools.

So if the JDK's native components are written using peers, can't we use the same technique?

The answer is yes—you most certainly can! There are a number of plus sides to using peers to develop controls.

If you already have a control that you want to use, and it's running on several operating systems, you might be in a good position to use a peer. You could write a peer to interface to your control and rapidly incorporate it into Java. Secondly, using peers, you can gain access to the full set of events provided by the operating system. This might be necessary when writing certain types of controls.

So what is the downside of writing controls using peers? Probably the biggest negative is having to write the control for each platform on which the JDK runs. Naturally, a point of success for the JDK will be its coverage of operating systems. It is essential that the JDK operate on a wide range of operating systems if it is to gain acceptance as the Internet programming tool of choice. The cost of ensuring that your own control runs on all these operating systems is probably enough to put you off using the peer approach. This is very likely to be a rather large chore involving investment in many machines and operating systems—not to mention your own knowledge of the various operating systems themselves. This might sound like fun—and it is, at least for the first go-round the loop, but believe me, it won't be long before it becomes a burden.

If you are prepared to bite the cherry and write for multiple operating systems, are there any other problems? Well, another problem is understanding the peer classes themselves. These are not, strictly speaking, part of the JDK. They are only available from Sun if you get hold of the source code for the runtime system. It is available only by request at Sun's discretion. And, naturally, there is a learning curve beyond basic Java programming to learn how the peer classes work.

I hope this has successfully put you off considering the peer class method. If not, give me a call: you sound like just the kind of off-the-wall character I like to work with!

WHY WRITE OUR OWN CONTROLS?

It might seem like an odd question to ask at the end of a chapter on writing controls, but why should we write our own controls?

The prime reason for writing a control is that you have a user entry or user interaction that you want to use a lot of. Rather than writing this interaction a lot of times in different places, you write a control to do the interaction and then use the control in a number of places in your code. This is, after all, what the operating system does. The code for buttons is written once in the operating system. All applications are then able to use this code and they do not have to reinvent the wheel every time. Equally important, the operating system provides a consistent look and feel to enable the user to learn new applications much more quickly. Think about it: suppose that for each application on a system you had to work out how to activate a button. It would make using windowing systems very unfriendly.

Whether you should write a control is a matter of taste and time. I tend to write most of my user interactions like controls. In this way, if I need a similar interaction later, I can just include the package containing the appropriate control, and I am up and running.

You should definitely be writing you own controls if you're finding that you are using an existing JDK control, but you are often using it in the same way or getting information from the same place. The **RomanNumeralLabel** control is a very simple example. It only performs one function beyond that provided by a

Label—it writes its label as a Roman numeral. Not much, but it does it every time you use it, so you are not having to remember the code to call to perform the translation. A simple saving, but as they say in Scotland, "Many a mickle makes a muckle." In other words, every little bit counts.

You should also consider writing your own control if you are doing complicated combinations of controls and layouts and maybe even mixing in a little custom drawing. Often, there is a control in there waiting to get out. And when it does, it generally simplifies matters no end.

Actually, I am forgetting some prime motivations to writing your own controls: yes the old favorites, fame and fortune. It's inevitable that a healthy industry in Java control writing will develop quickly. Already, there are controls available for various things. Writing a useful control for the Java community and publishing it on the Web is a very rewarding thing to do. You might not get much cash out of it (or you might), but you will at least develop a group of users, which is always fun to have.

SETTING UP FOR WRITING YOUR OWN CONTROLS

Now that I have encouraged you to write your own controls, is there anything you can do to make control writing easier?

One thing I'd encourage you to do is to start putting your code into a package of its own. You will probably read advice like this at several places in this book—and with good reason. Starting to reuse what you write is important if you want to progress. Java gives us the packaging concept—so use it! We place a lot of our code in the explorer package. This makes it always on hand. It is just "an import away."

Another thing you should consider is documenting your code with the /** syntax. Then you can run javadoc and have Web-ready information pages on how to use your code.

This is especially important with controls. Controls are developed to be reused. They are also developed to centralize the code that runs the control. If you are in the habit of copying classes into a directory whenever you decide you need the code, you will end up with a collection of code that's tough to maintain.

In addition, I strongly recommend getting a good make system, such as GNU make. It will make mundane tasks (such as copying class files to you package

class directory) much easier. Also, a version control system such as RCS is very useful for maintaining versions of your controls. Steve, Alex, and I used those tools when writing the code for this book. RCS is the reason for the strange headers at the top of the source code on the accompanying CD-ROM.

Choosing Your Own Parent

An important part of writing a control is to decide which class should be the parent class of the control. This is important, because we will be inheriting the behavior and appearance of the parent control. It is also important because we want to reuse as much existing code as possible.

One problem in the JDK is that native controls tend to usurp the system. They especially hold on to events, which it would be nice to get hold of for other purposes.

In Chapter 14, we discussed how the event production mechanism works. We also noted there that controls such as **button** hold on to events and only produce action events when they decide to do so. This can make things difficult for the control writer. Before you wander off writing controls that sub-class from parent controls, it's a good idea to establish that the control does indeed generate the event you are hoping to use. For instance, if we want to create a button that changes its label when the user moves the cursor over the button, we are out of luck with the JDK **Button** class. It does not generate mouse enter and leave events, so we can't detect when to change the button.

IF YOU LIKED THIS YOU WILL LOVE THESE

The chord diagram we have produced is a typical example of the kind of code that you need to write when you want to write your own controls. There are a number of examples available on the Web. The Gamelan site lists a few. Here are a few that are worthy of note:

Slider is a control that allows a slide to be used to specify value. This can be more useful than entering numbers into a textfield, when the values are from a range of numbers. The slider widget can be found at http://www.cs.brown.edu/people/amd/java/Slider/.

The *spreadsheet* control, which is part of the JDK demo package, is worth looking at. It makes a good starting point for developing your own spreadsheet-style controls.

Nice Threads, Javaman!

Alex Leslie

Take a deep breath and get ready to dive into something totally new. It'll free your mind and your Java programming will follow.

Java has been lauded in the press as few other developments in the computer industry ever have. I've seen it called *the* programming language of the Internet in more than one publication. It has been endorsed by Borland, Netscape and—yes, believe it or not—even Microsoft, a company better known for driving the tractor that pulls the PC software technology bandwagon than riding in the bandwagon itself.

You already know that Java is object-oriented. And you've learned that Java has a lot of graphical windowing capabilities that make it easy to whip up sexy user interfaces. And, as you'll soon see, it has advanced built-in networking abilities. The Internet is its oyster. All these features alone represent a formidable package—but to top it off, Java is *multithreaded*, too.

This chapter is divided into two parts. The first part is devoted to revisiting the essentials of Java threads. The second part deals with issues that are more complex. It is the sort of material that you can read after you have experimented with Java threads for a while.

BACK TO BASICS

I know that Java threads aren't totally new to you. It's been necessary to use them in several examples in previous chapters already. That's okay. Because threads were not the focus in those other chapters, the treatment was brief. In this chapter, I'll bring you up to speed by going back to the basics. That way I know you'll be ready for the fancy stuff.

The Simplest Thread of All

Actually the simplest thread of all is the main program thread. It's something so ubiquitous that you take it for granted. The main program thread is just the single sequence of execution that you should be familiar with by now: a program running one line at a time. Every program has to have at least this lone thread. Figure 20.1 illustrates what I mean.

Listing 20.1 contains such a program. Each line is executed in turn by what is called a *single thread of execution.*

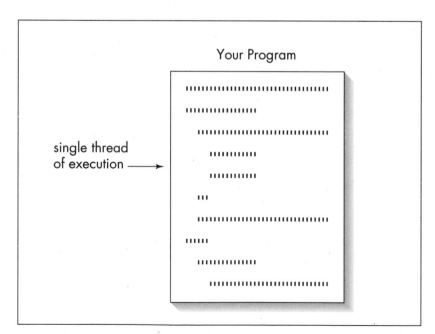

Figure 20.1   A single-threaded program.

Listing 20.1   HelloWorld.java

```
public class HelloWorld {
    public static void main( String args[] ) {
        System.out.println( "Hello World!" );
    }
}
```

```
cmd> java HelloWorld
Hello World!
```

When this minimal program is run, the **main** method is executed by the program thread. That thread executes the one and only line of real code in the program. The thread reaches the end of the method and dies. The program exits. Even if I were to write a million lines of Java code without using threads, only one line at a time would be executed.

One Thread Plus Three

Listing 20.2 includes a *Hello World* program that has tired of doing all the greeting by itself and has delegated the job to several other threads. The **main** method only instantiates the other threads and starts them on their way. This program has more to say than just *Hello World*. Each **Thread** pipes in and extends the salutation.

Listing 20.2   SayHelloThreads.java

```
public class SayHelloThreads {
    public static void main( String args[] ) {
        new Greeter1().start();
        new Greeter2().start();
        new Greeter3().start();
    }
}

class Greeter1 extends Thread {
    public void run() {
        System.out.println( "Hello World from me" );
    }
}

class Greeter2 extends Thread {
    public void run() {
        System.out.println( "and me" );
    }
}

class Greeter3 extends Thread {
    public void run() {
```

```
        System.out.println( "and me too" );
    }
}

cmd> java SayHelloThreads
HelloWorld from me
and me
and me too
```

The main program thread stills dies at the end of its **main** method just the same, but not before getting a chance to create and start three other threads. In each line in the **main** method, two operations are performed. The expression is just a compact way of dispatching a thread, but let's break it down for discussion purposes. I think it might help to see the "what's going on" expressed in two separate lines, as in the code snippet below:

```
Thread thread = new Thread();
thread.start();
```

The first line instantiates a new object of class **Thread**. Note that this instantiation just creates the object—the thread that will run this object is not yet running.

Let's look at the new classes that were introduced. *Greeter1* is one of three classes that was written specifically to do work for the *MainThread* class. Note that each of the three Greeter classes extends **Thread**. Remember from Chapter 4 that *extends* means one class is derived from the other. Therefore, each of the Greeter classes is a **Thread**.

It is the **start** method that causes each Greeter thread to begin running. Immediately after the first Greeter thread is started, there will be two threads running in the program: the main application thread that's always there, and the just-started thread. By the time the main thread has reached the end of its **main** method, there are a total of four separate threads running. Technically, the **run** method of each Greeter thread is so short that there is a possibility that one of the earlier threads has already run and died. But let's just assume that hasn't happened yet. Figure 20.2 illustrates multiple threads in a single program.

Note, incidentally, that there was no **import** statement at the beginning of this application. The class **Thread** is a part of the **java.lang** package. You might remember from Chapter 4 that it is unnecessary to explicitly import that package.

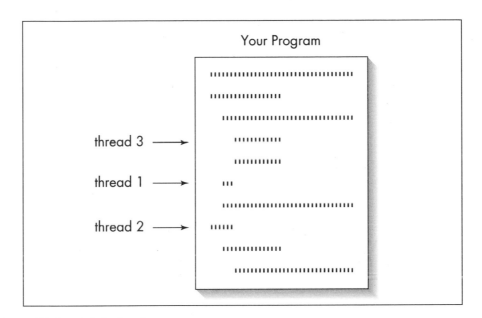

Figure 20.2 *Multiple threads in one program.*

Racing Threads

In the first example, each Greeter thread just printed out a message and that was it. Even though you saw how to write a simple class derived from Thread and how to start it running, the example failed to demonstrate convincingly that multiple threads can actually run simultaneously. Listing 20.3 contains a little program in which two Threads race with each other. The race just involves a *for* loop in each thread that prints out messages indicating the *step* in the race that each thread is at. The output you get when you run this program clearly indicates that the two threads are running at the same time, racing to see which can finish first.

Listing 20.3 Race.java

```
class Racer1 extends Thread {
    public void run() {
        for( int i = 1; i <= 10; ++i )
            System.out.println( "Racer1: step " + i );
    }
}

class Racer2 extends Thread {
    public void run() {
        for( int i = 1; i <= 10; ++i )
            System.out.println( "Racer2: step " + i );
```

```
        }
    }

public class Race {
    public static void main( String args[] ) {
        new Racer1().start();
        new Racer2().start();
    }
}

cmd> java Race
Racer1: step 1
Racer2: step 1
Racer1: step 2
Racer2: step 2
Racer1: step 3
Racer2: step 3
Racer1: step 4
Racer2: step 4
Racer1: step 5
Racer1: step 6
Racer1: step 7
Racer1: step 8
Racer2: step 5
Racer2: step 6
Racer2: step 7
Racer2: step 8
Racer2: step 9
Racer2: step 10
Racer1: step 9
Racer1: step 10
```

Each racer is implemented as a new class derived from **Thread**. Each racer class implements just one method called **run**. Both racer classes are local to the program. The class *Race*, on the other hand, is public and it conducts the race. In one line each, the racers are instantiated and started with a call to the **Thread** method **start**—and off they go! The race is neck-and-neck until the end, where *Racer2* takes a few quick steps in sequence across the finish line.

Looking back at the program, a few things might puzzle you. You're probably wondering how it is that calling **start** in the **main** method ends up calling the **run** method in each racer, which is clearly what is happening. That's a feature implicit to the operation of Java threads that you need to appreciate right away. You must always call **start** to start a **Thread**. The method **start** goes off hunting for a **run** method that it can execute. Once it finds it and gets the **run** method going, it returns just as any other method would. In fact, it will usually return long before the **run** method is finished. That's how it is that *Racer2* can get instantiated and started after *Racer1*—*Racer1's* **start** method is called by the main program thread but it returns, allowing **main** to **start** *Racer2*.

THE LIFE AND TIMES OF A THREAD

Threads have just been introduced, and already you've encountered three phases of the thread life-cycle. These phases, or *states*, are distinguished by a set of characteristics that uniquely identifies it and differentiates it from all other states. Calling **Thread** methods can change the state of a thread, as you'll see.

You saw already how to instantiate a new thread. That was really no different from instantiating an object of any other Java class. We can call this *instantiated yet unrun* state the *New Thread* state. After the thread is started, it is in the *Runnable* state. When the end of the thread's **run** method is reached, the thread passes into the *Dead* state. Figure 20.3 illustrates the life cycle of threads in Java.

The lines connecting the three states are annotated with several **Thread** methods, which you might recognize. Think about the example in Listing 20.2. Each racer was instantiated and started life as a new thread. Remember that at that **stage**, start had not yet been called so the racer thread could not yet run. However, once **start** was called, the thread went to work, trying to win the race. Once it reached step ten, it reached the end of the loop and the end of the **run** method and promptly died without even being told to.

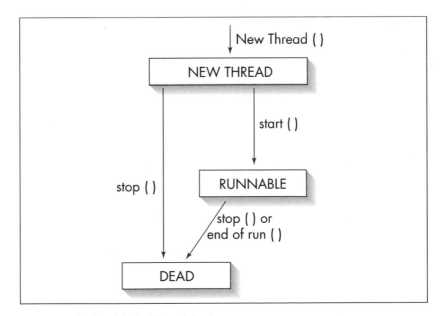

Figure 20.3   Simple thread birth, life, and death.

Listing 20.4 introduces an unfamiliar method called **stop**. This is the way to stop a Thread dead in its tracks.

Listing 20.4   Thread stop Method Example

```
Thread aThread = new Thread();
thread1.start();
...
while( true ) {
    ...
    boolean stopThread1 = ...;
    if( stopThread1 ) {
        thread1.stop();
    }
    ...
}
```

This is an example of how **stop** could be used. Imagine that this code is part of a method of another class. That class instantiates and then starts a new thread. The main thread, at some time later, enters a processing loop. On each iteration, a **boolean** is returned from a call to a method that will tell whether or not to stop the other thread.

Once the **stop** is called, *Thread1* will soon die. It dies *asynchronously*. That just means that the first thread doesn't wait for the contract to be carried out. The dirty deed gets done whenever it gets done. Technically, what happens involves a **ThreadDeath** exception that is received by the second thread but we're not going to get into those sorts of details here. In Chapter 5, you should have learned how to throw and catch exceptions like a major-leaguer.

Let's pick apart the first program introduced, in order to see what else we can learn about threads.

Execution Order

When you ran the program in Listing 20.2, would it surprise you if, instead of what you saw on the screen, the snippet below appeared on your screen?

```
and me
Hello World from me
and me too!
```

Not exactly the order in which you expected the lines to appear, is it? "How did the second thread gets its greeting out ahead of the first?" I can hear you asking. You can never rely on the exact execution order of Java threads. Let that sink in. You can, however, takes steps to control the order using differential thread priorities. Priorities are introduced later.

The truth is that *Runnable* threads are not exactly running simultaneously. All *Runnable* threads are in contention for time on the processor. Java currently only runs on operating systems that support multiple threads. The reason for this limitation is that it is much more difficult to implement threads on an operating system that doesn't provide a thread execution scheduler. The scheduler is a part of the kernel which in turn is a part of the operating system. The scheduler is responsible for regulating the assignment of threads to the processor. The scheduler might be pre-emptive or non-pre-emptive in the way it shifts threads off the processor to make room for some other thread. Most schedulers are pre-emptive. That means the scheduler says *ready or not, here I come* to the running thread and boots it off—it doesn't wait for the thread to finish in its own sweet time. In addition to being pre-emptive, most schedulers divide the processor's time fairly equitably among all *Runnable* threads. This process is calling *time slicing*. This is certainly necessary with single-processor computers. Lucky readers with computers that have multiple processors will be happy to find out that it is possible that different threads could be scheduled on different processors, though Java, currently, makes no guarantees that it will actually happen. So don't hold your breath.

The puzzling order of execution represents the sometimes unpredictable nature of multiple threads. When each thread was started, the thread moved from the *New Thread* state to the *Runnable* state. To emphasize: *Runnable* does not necessarily mean *Running*. That's an important distinction. As mentioned above, a computer with a single processor can run only one thread at a time. Any other threads in a *Runnable* state, will spend that time waiting for the current thread to finish so they can get another kick at the can.

An explanation that might account for the *out of order* greetings I illustrated at the top of this section is this: Somehow the first thread that was started, though *Runnable*, simply missed being scheduled into the processor until after the second thread was both scheduled and run. It's totally unintuitive, but think of it as a gentle introduction to the capricious nature of thread execution order. Once started, all bets are off as to the exact order in which each thread will get scheduled to run.

Down But Not Out

There are cases where you want to halt the execution of a thread temporarily. Your first impulse might be to use the **stop** method. Note from the diagram,

though, that there are no arrows leading away from the *Dead* state. This indicates that you should **stop** threads only after you are really finished with them, because there's no returning from the dead. Luckily there are a pair of methods available for the specific purpose of stopping a thread's execution temporarily: **suspend** and **resume**. Figure 20.4 includes a new thread state called *Not Runnable*.

One of the arrows joining *Runnable* and *Not Runnable* represents the **suspend** method. You've probably guessed that resuming is the opposite of suspending, and that it makes the thread *Runnable* again. Note that the thread won't necessarily start running immediately.

A thread might be suspended and it will not run until it is resumed. However, Java provides you with no way of checking whether a thread is suspended or not. There is just a method called **isAlive** that will tell whether a thread is *Dead* or not. Note that an *unstarted* thread is not considered alive. Therefore, there is no way to determine if a thread is dead or if it has just been recently instantiated yet unstarted. Listing 20.5 contains a code snippet using the **suspend** method.

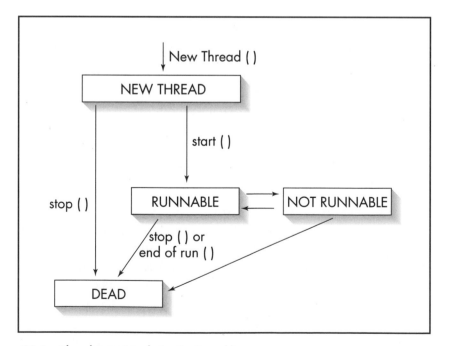

Figure 20.4 *Thread states introducing Not Runnable.*

Listing 20.5 Thread Suspend Example

```
if( thread.isAlive() ) {
    thread.suspend();
} else {
    ...     // too late - it's already dead
}
```

The second arrow connecting *Runnable* and *Not Runnable* in Figure 20.4 represents another, time-related way of making a thread *Not Runnable*: putting the thread to **sleep**. There are two **sleep** methods. Both take a **long** argument, representing time expressed in milliseconds. The second **sleep** method takes an additional integer parameter that can be used to express nanoseconds.

This is typical code in which a thread is put to sleep for a time. In this case, the code has been taken out of the **run** method of a Thread class. After doing something in each iteration of the *while* loop, the thread will go to sleep for 2000 milliseconds—that's two seconds. During that time, the thread is *Not Runnable*. After the two seconds are up, the thread will automatically wake up and become *Runnable* again. Note that if you use either **sleep** method to put a thread to sleep, not even **resume** will wake it up until it's ready to wake up and the time entered has elapsed. Listing 20.6 shows a typical *while* loop that includes a **sleep**.

Listing 20.6 Thread Sleep Example

```
while( true ) {
    ...     // do something
    sleep( 2000 );
}
```

How to Create a Thread

There are two ways of creating a new **Thread**. You've seen the first several times already but there it is again in Listing 20.7. You just instantiate an object of a class that is derived from the class **Thread**. You know how to start such a thread too, so I'm not even going to bother repeating it.

Listing 20.7 Thread Creation by Thread Extension

```
class DerivedThread extends Thread {
    public void run() {
        // ...
    }
}
```

There is a second way to create a thread. This time, you use the **Runnable** interface as I have done below. Listing 20.8 implements the previous example with **Runnable** instead of **Thread**.

Listing 20.8   Thread Creation by Runnable Implemention

```
class NewRunnable implements Runnable {
    public void run() {
    }
}
```

Note that while this class will contain the body of the thread that we're creating, it is not a **Thread**. There's one more step. You create a **Thread** and pass a new instance of the **Runnable** class as the only parameter:

```
NewRunnable runnable = new NewRunnable();
new Thread( runnable ).start();
```

The result is nearly the same for both methods. You will have created a new thread that runs the **run** method of either the *DerivedClass* object or the *NewRunnable* object.

Thread Identity and Construction Technique

There are several very important differences that you must take into account when deciding which Thread creation technique to use. For example, each Thread has a unique name. Eventually you will want to be able to distinguish one Thread from another. You will need to determine a running thread's name from within the run method.

If you implemented your class by implementing Runnable, you'll be out of luck. There's simply no way to call the Thread method getName from within a class that just implements Runnable. An object of that class doesn't even realize that it is living in the belly of a Thread object. The only way around this limitation is to include a constructor for the Runnable class that takes a String that will substitute for the name of the Thread. Then all you need to do is to construct the Thread with an instance of that Runnable class that was itself constructed with some unique name.

Another guideline is that if you want to write a class that extends some other class—say, for instance, **Applet,** since it's a common one—you should implement **Runnable**. You probably already know that Java does not allow multiple inheritance. A class can implement multiple interfaces but can only extend one other class. If you did want to implement the threaded class by deriving from Java **Thread,** you would have to add a second step—a second level of derivation. It's simpler to just use the **Runnable** technique with the proviso mentioned above.

THE RUN METHOD

The **run** method is the heart and soul of any **Thread**. It makes up the **Thread** class's entire body. It is the one any only method in which you can implement your **Thread**'s behavior. Often the **run** method contains a loop. Sometimes, it's even an endless loop as in Listing 20.9.

Listing 20.9   Typical run Method

```
public void run() {
    ...
    while( true ) {
        ...     // do something
    }
    ...
}
```

Though the issues of data and method locking and synchronization are covered later, it is worth mentioning here that the **run** method should not be *synchronized* in a **Thread**. All threads that are constructed from the class will need to have simultaneous access to the method, which the modifier *synchronized* would prevent.

THE STANDARD THREAD'S IDIOM

The idiom that I'm about to introduce is something that you will use over and over with Java threads. It is implemented with two methods and a special **Thread** object. This technique is used within a class that itself is not derived from **Thread** but that you, nevertheless, want to run in a separate thread. The first new method is **start**. It has the same name as a **Thread** method you've met already but it is very different in operation.

Listing 20.10 contains a simple Java program that illustrates the use of the standard idiom.

Listing 20.10 Idiom.java

```
public class Idiom implements Runnable {
    Thread threadRef = null;

    public static void main( String args[] ) {
        new Idiom().start();
    }

    public void start() {
        if( threadRef == null ) {
            threadRef = new Thread( this );
            threadRef.start();
        }
    }

    public void stop() {
        if( threadRef != null ) {
            threadRef.stop();
            threadRef = null;
        }
    }

    public void run() {
        System.out.println( "Hi There!" );
    }
}
```

```
cmd> java Idiom
Hi There!
```

In **start**, a check is made to see if *threadRef* is *null*. It will be *null* the first time that **start** is called. If **start** were to be called a second time, *threadRef* would likely have been set to a thread already and it would fall through without creating a second incarnation of *Idiom*. A single parameter—*this*—is passed to the **Thread** constructor. Just to remind you, the variable *this* refers to the object in which it is found. In this case, *this* refers to the current instance of *Idiom*. *Idiom* implements **Runnable** so the **Thread** constructor has all it needs.

After being constructed, the method **start** is called against *threadRef*. This is the real **Thread** method **start**. Note that *threadRef* is an instance of **Thread**, not *Idiom*. Calling **start** against a **Thread** instance means: Call the **run** method of the **Runnable** instance passed in the constructor. In this case, that is the **run** method of *Idiom*.

The **stop** method demonstrates the second half of this idiom. If you want to stop the Idiom after it has been started, you call **stop** against the instance. The method **stop** checks that *threadRef* is set *non-null*—that means that the *threadRef* was assigned and it is safe to assume that it is running. Then the

stop method of *threadRef* itself is called. That means the **Thread** method **stop**, not the Idiom **stop**. The distinction is important. They are very different functions. Finally, *threadRef* is set to *null* so that the *Idiom* could be re-started if necessary.

ADVANCED THREAD ISSUES

This second half of the chapter discusses more advanced issues than you've encountered so far. In fact, you might need to spend some time experimenting with threads before proceeding. This experience will help you appreciate how these issues fit together in thread programming.

I/O Blocking

A very common application of multithreading involves interacting with the data input and output system of your computer. Typically, this means peripherals such as a hard disk. Whenever you access peripherals with system calls, there is the possibility of getting "hung up" and having to wait for the call to return. There are several system calls that behave this way. They return only after the data that is to be returned has become available and has been assembled. If you wrote an application with a single thread of execution, everything would grind to a halt during such waits. This enforced suspension is known as *I/O blocking*.

While it is inevitable that such system calls will cause whichever thread is executing them to block and become *Not Runnable*, you have the ability with multithreading to make sure that a secondary thread gets waylaid, and not the main thread. Often you'll find it helpful to create a thread just for such occasions. A blocking system call is an example of a *synchronous* call. Synchronous means the client of the system service—your program—waits for the service to return with the data. Figure 20.5 illustrates how the main thread avoids being blocked.

You can improve overall system throughput by reducing the effect of synchronous calls. Multithreading lets you overlap blocking system calls with the main thread of your program. The net effect is that your application has the benefits of *asynchronicity*, but you don't have to write the sort of complicated code that is necessary to implement *asynchronous I/O*.

The **Thread wait** method causes a thread to become *Not Runnable*. "Why would I ever want a thread to wait?" The answer is that the wait is done while waiting on the value of a variable to change. Listing 20.11 illustrates an advanced use of the **Thread** method **wait**.

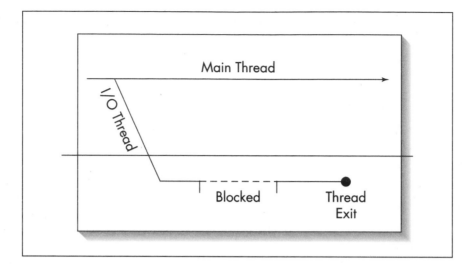

Figure 10.5 *I/O blocking avoided with a thread.*

Listing 20.11 A Guard Action Example

```
synchronized void waitForCond() {
    while( checkCondition() == false ) {
        wait();
    }
}

void someMethod {
    waitForCondition();
    ... // continue with code for which the
        // condition needed to be true
}
```

This sort of method is used by another method as a means of halting until the condition being checked becomes *true*. Note that this *while* loop doesn't spin away out of control as it might appear to do. Once the **wait** method is hit, execution will halt until this thread is *notified*, as you'll soon see.

This code mechanism is sometimes called a *guard action*. Java doesn't have such a mechanism built-in. You have to associate a condition with an action yourself. The other half of the technique involves the use of the **notifyAll** method. The method **notifyAll** wakes up all threads in the object that is waiting. See Listing 20.12 for a method that will do the awakening.

Listing 20.12 Wake Up Example

```
public synchronized void wakeMe() {
    notifyAll();
}
```

A simple way to see how this mechanism works is as follows. You have written code for your thread with the understanding that it will be executed by multiple threads. At the appropriate places in your code, you have placed *guards*. They operate just like real guards that ask to see your security badge before permitting entry to a restricted area. These code guards check a condition. That condition is just the *boolean* result of an expression. If that condition is not satisfied, execution enters the *while* loop and hits the **wait** method.

While your application runs, there could be several threads that get halted at the guard station, so to speak. They will remain there until you wake them up and the condition in the *while* loop is again evaluated. Only if the condition has become *true* does execution pass out of the method that contains the **wait**. In this case, the method was called *waitForCond*. Elsewhere in the program, you'll have methods that followed the call to *waitForCondition* and were being guarded. The guard ensured that the operations they were to perform were not executed until the condition became *true*. Figure 20.6 illustrates all the Thread states and method transitions.

This is the entire **Thread** state diagram. The only part we haven't discussed is that little loop labeled *yield* that exits and immediately re-enters the state

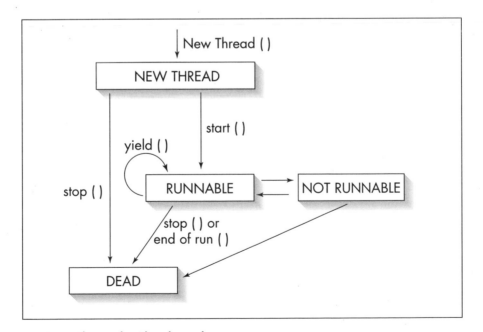

Figure 20.6 *The complete Thread state diagram.*

Runnable. Have you ever been running off a large photocopying job when someone with only a few pages to copy comes to the machine and you decide to yield it to them? If so, your good manners captured the essence of yielding. You often need to include strategically placed *yields* in the multithreaded program that you write. These yields will cause the scheduler to go out and see if another thread of the same priority is *Runnable* and waiting to run. If so, the current thread is pre-empted and another waiting thread gets to run. It's the responsible thing for a thread to do periodically.

Synchronization

We use threads only to the extent that they improve performance or make the task of programming easier. Performance means getting the most out of limited resources. Threads generally improve performance when carefully applied. There are pitfalls to avoid, though. Failure to do so can lead to mysteriously disappointing performance, or even erroneous operation.

All the threads running in a program can share the same code and data space. That's tight quarters indeed. Threads can cause each other problems by modifying the same data nearly simultaneously. Synchronization is a big issue that you must master before you can feel confident with threads. Therefore any thorough discussion of threads would certainly be incomplete without discussing how to keep threads from tripping each other up.

Threads are capable of data modification far beyond merely assigning a value to a variable. That minimal operation is discrete and is likely performed by the processor in very few cycles. The chance of thread conflict doesn't really exist.

What happens, though, when we extend the discussion to non-trivial data such as a Java **Vector** or even one of our own data structures? Operations that modify a **Vector** object cannot be completed as discretely as an **int** assignment, for example. The duration of the operation might span several processor cycles. You could consider that time period *a window of vulnerability.* It is possible that, during that operation, some other thread is scheduled into the processor and the current thread scheduled out. The first operation remains partially completed. Loose ends have been left hanging. The operation will get finished successfully, if the original thread can get back in without the other thread screwing up the data. It should be able to pick up where it left off. Unfortunately, in the meantime, the interrupting thread might attempt an operation that is intimately related with the operation that the original thread was performing. It might even perform the very same operation. Nothing prevents it from corrupting the data.

To solve this dilemma, the thread needs a way to grab exclusive control of a method (or even just a block of code) just long enough to complete the operation that is vulnerable to uncoordinated modification by other threads. The Java keyword **synchronized** gives you that ability. Synchronization is the act of locking data or a method so uninterrupted access is guaranteed.

You can add the synchronized modifier to a method declaration, as shown in the code snippet below. Threads have synchronized methods all to themselves for as long as they run in the method. All other threads that want to access the method have to wait. They end up *camping on the threshold*. When the first thread leaves the method, another thread is scheduled and gets access to the synchronized block.

```
public synchronized void someMethod() {
    // ...
}
```

Data alone can be synchronized too, as shown in the code snippet below:

```
synchronized( someData ) {
    // some operation on that data
}
```

This use of **synchronized** might look like a method call until you get used to it. It is a synchronization command that is in effect for the duration of the code block that follows. As with synchronized methods, threads in contention for synchronized data end up waiting. Note that the same data variable might be synchronized in different methods and even in different classes. It's all the same as long as the data variable is the same. A thread in one section of code can synchronize on a data variable causing threads elsewhere to wait, so be careful and thoughtful.

Locking Granularity

You will eventually grapple with the issue of how to choose the optimal *granularity of locks* using **synchronized**. The balance you are trying to achieve is between *coarse-grained* locking and *fine-grained* locking.

Coarse-grained locking involves a few, large blocks of synchronized code. Such a block would likely include some lines of code that don't need to be synchronized but are, since they are interspersed among lines of code that legitimately do need the lock. The benefits of such a coarse-grained approach is that there are fewer synchronized blocks for you to manage. Also, locking data has an associated processing time cost, so by reducing the number of blocks you minimize that cost. The negative consequences of coarse-grained locking are that data or methods spend more time unavailable to other threads, sometimes unnecessarily. Performance can therefore suffer using this approach.

The opposite of coarse-grained locking is fine-grained locking. Fine-grained means that only the lines that strictly need the lock get synchronized. This approach is characterized by numerous small locks. Synchronization ends up being performed multiply throughout your code. From a programmer's point of view, there is also the extra burden of managing numerous small locks. Figure 20.7 contains a diagram that illustrates in simple terms the differences between the two types of locking.

To find the proper granularity for your application, try coding it with coarse locks first. Later, try to determine if and where performance bottlenecks are occurring as a result of inefficient coarse-grained locks. Replace only the problematic coarse-grained locks with finer-grained locks and hope for the best. Performance should improve.

Deadlocks

A *deadlock* occurs whenever a thread tries to lock data that is already locked but cannot be freed up by the other thread because it itself is blocked from

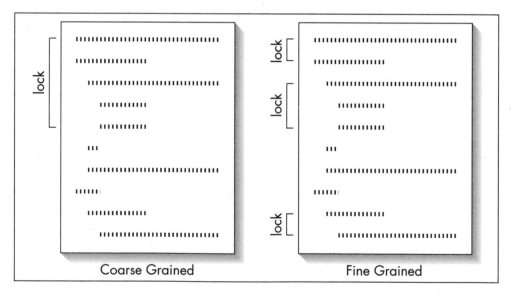

Figure 20.7 *Comparing coarse-grained locking to fine-grained locking.*

doing so, because it is waiting for the first thread to free up its data. It's a vicious cycle. Both threads just sit there waiting for the other but neither blinks. Processing grinds to a halt. Figure 20.8 shows how each thread ends up waiting for the other's data to be available.

Imagine a situation where one thread is executing code like the snippet that follows in which two different data objects are synchronized in nested blocks in a specific order. A deadlock problem can occur if some other thread adopts a different order of synchronization in a similar nested block, as illustrated in the second part of the snippet. Listing 20.13 contains two blocks that, if they occurred in separate threads, would present the potential for a thread deadlock.

Listing 20.13 Deadlock Potential Example

```
synchronized( a ) {
    synchronized( b ) {
        . . .
    }
}
synchronized( b ) {
    synchronized( a ) {
        . . .
    }
}
```

In a deadlock problem, each thread blocks the other. For instance, let's say the top thread locks data *a* and is about to lock *b*. However, the bottom thread locks *b* first. The top thread is blocked. The bottom thread, though, can never free up data *b* because, in order to do so, it must be able to lock data *a* and do some processing. The top block prevents this from happening:

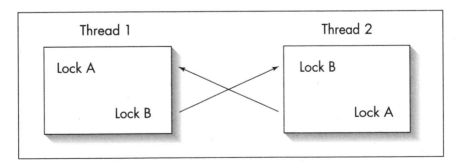

Figure 20.8 *Common deadlock condition.*

Deadlock! Each block is in contention for the other's resource. This condition—commonly called an *out-of-order* deadlock—is permanent, unless something supernatural happens.

The imperfect solution to this problem is to ensure that data objects are synchronized in the same order wherever they are used. Unfortunately, this isn't always possible.

It's also possible to have a condition called a *recursive* deadlock. A thread locks certain resources and then tries to access those same resources indirectly through a method call. Due to code complexity, it might be extremely difficult for the programmer even to know about the potential for this kind of deadlock.

Again, there is an imperfect solution. You must try to ensure that a thread never calls methods that might call back into the thread itself without first determining that there is no risk of a recursive deadlock. If you're not sure—don't do the call. If you feel absolutely compelled to do it, you must make sure that, before that call outside, the thread leaves the synchronized block and all locks are dropped, thus preventing the possibility of deadlock altogether.

A final note about deadlocks will explain how you can sometimes get a thread that fails to progress through its code. This situation can occur if a thread locks data and then releases the lock only briefly by leaving the synchronized data or method for a very short time before quickly re-locking. Another thread might not have time to acquire the lock and might remain blocked. It's something that you will need to keep an eye out for, too.

Thread-Specific Data

Using threads doesn't have to mean surrendering individuality. You will often encounter instances where it's necessary to store data that belongs uniquely to one thread. The intimacy of threads means that you'll have to take some special steps to ensure that only the appropriate thread gets access. You have to create a data structure in which you'll store any such data. Note that you certainly can't use static class variables to achieve the same end since such variables actually belong to the class and not to any particular instance. Neither will non-static instance variables work without synchronization. All of the threads in a class are equally able to see the data encapsulated in the class code in which they are active.

One solution is to use a Java data structure called a **Hashtable**. Chapter 9 gave you the details on **Hashtable** and other Java data structures but, to review, a **Hashtable** stores key/object pairs. The keys and values are non-primitive types. You can add key/value pairs as needed since the **Hashtable** object will grow automatically to accommodate. You can retrieve an object using its key.

In this example, we'll use the **Thread** name as the key. You could encapsulate any thread-specific data into a separate class. An instance of that class would be the value associated with the key. It is then simple for any thread to retrieve its own specific data since it knows its own name. It is not even necessary to encapsulate the **Hashtable** in the thread class itself. I've coded a simple thread-specific data class in Listing 20.14.

Listing 20.14   Thread-Specific Data Example

```
class ThreadSpecificData {
    String name;
    float  data;

    ThreadSpecificData( String n, float f ) {
        name = n;
        data = f;
    }

    float getData() {
        return data;
    }
}
```

This is an example of a class derived from a thread that uses thread-specific data. Any use of the table containing thread-specific data is synchronized because you never know what other threads are lurking out there. Remember that an alternative to locking the data would be to include the block that modifies the data in a separate method and to synchronize that entire method. In Listing 20.15, I illustrate the use of the thread-specific data introduced in Listing 20.14.

Listing 20.15   Thread-Specific Data Use Example

```
class ThreadSpecificDataUser extends Thread {
    static Hashtable          table;
    static ThreadSpecificData data;

    ThreadSpecificDataUser( String n, float f, Hashtable t ) {
        table = t;

        synchronized( table ) {
            ThreadSpecificData data = new ThreadSpecificData( n, f );
            table.put( data );
```

```
            }
        }
    public void run() {
        ...
        synchronized( table ) {
            Object object = table.get( getName() );

            if( object != null ) {
                data = ( ThreadSpecificData )object;

                float f = data.getData();
            }
        }
    }
}

class MainClass {
    Hashtable threadSpecificDataTable;

    MainClass() {
        threadSpecificDataTable = new Hashtable();
    }

    someFunction() {
        new ThreadSpecificDataUser( "First Thread",  1.2,
            threadSpecificDataTable ).start();
        new ThreadSpecificDataUser( "Second Thread", 7.6,
            threadSpecificDataTable ).start();
    }
}
```

Thread Priorities

All threads might be created equal, but it is sometimes necessary to favor some threads over others. You exercise such control by setting the *priority* of the thread.

All threads begin life with their priority set to the priority of the thread that created them. It is unnecessary and even unwise to change the priority without good reason. The default setting is **NORM_PRIORITY**. There are two other priority settings defined in **Thread**: **MAX_PRIORITY** and **MIN_PRIORITY**. They define the upper and lower bounds of Thread priority. Thread priority, by the way, is expressed as a simple integer value.

Just because a thread starts life with one priority doesn't mean it's stuck with that priority forever. You are free to set a thread's priority to any integer value between MIN_PRIORITY and MAX_PRIORITY. The only exception comes when a thread is included in a **ThreadGroup** that has a limited maximum priority. **ThreadGroups** are covered later.

"Why would I ever want to change priority?" The most common answer is that your program provides a service that is time-critical. Sometimes certain input will need to be answered as quickly as possible. Naturally, a thread that is monitoring for such service requests could benefit from a priority boost to a value above that of the other common threads.

The execution of threads is automatically scheduled on a priority basis. The scheduling is pre-emptive. That means that as soon as a thread with a higher priority comes along, any lower priority threads are bumped off the processor. The higher priority thread then hops in and starts executing. It'll continue until it finishes and relinquishes the *Running* state voluntarily, or until an even higher priority thread comes along and bumps it. That's worth repeating: The highest priority thread always pre-empts any lower priority threads on a pre-emptive multithreading scheduler.

Don't Let Your Threads Be Hogs

Threads will execute until they yield or sleep unless pre-empted. Make sure that each thread gets a chance to run from time to time. Use **yields** and **sleeps**. This is especially true when threads with a mixture of priorities are running. The high priority thread will always pre-empt any lower ones. If you let one thread dominate, your application might take on a particularly single-threaded performance appearance.

ThreadGroups

ThreadGroup is a new Java class. You commonly use a **ThreadGroup** to organize several threads together for a joint purpose. A **ThreadGroup** might contain just threads or even other **ThreadGroups**. Meet your first **ThreadGroup** example in Listing 20.16.

Listing 20.16   ThreadGroup1.java

```
public class ThreadGroup1 {
    public static void main( String args[] ) {
        ThreadGroup topGroup = new ThreadGroup( "Top Group" );
        Thread          thread1 = new Thread( topGroup, "Thread1" );
        ThreadGroup subGroup = new ThreadGroup( topGroup, "SubGroup" );
    }
}
```

You can create entire hierarchies of **Threads** and **ThreadGroups** if needed. Figure 20.9 shows a sample hierarchy of **Threads** and **ThreadGroups**.

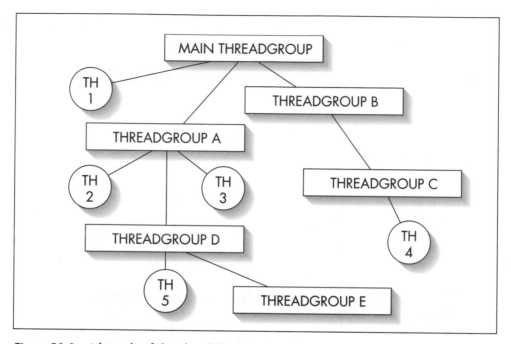

Figure 20.9   *A hierarchy of Threads and ThreadGroups.*

Listing 20.17 contains an example that demonstrates the sort of centralized control **ThreadGroup**s make possible.

Listing 20.17   ThreadGroupStop.java

```
class RunawayThread extends Thread {
    RunawayThread( ThreadGroup g, String n ) {
        super( g, n );
    }

    public void run() {
        while( true ) {
            System.out.println( getName() + " is running..." );
        }
    }
}

public class ThreadGroupStop {
    public static void main( String args[] ) {
        ThreadGroup group = new ThreadGroup( "RunawayGroup" );
        new RunawayThread( group, "Thread1" ).start();
        new RunawayThread( group, "Thread2" ).start();
        new RunawayThread( group, "Thread3" ).start();

        for( int i = 0; i < 5; ++i ) {
```

```
                System.out.println( "Main thread counting: " + i );
            }

            group.stop();
        }
    }

cmd> ThreadGroupStop
Main thread counting: 0
Main thread counting: 1
Thread1 is running...
Thread2 is running...
Main thread counting: 2
Thread3 is running...
Thread1 is running...
Thread2 is running...
Main thread counting: 3
Thread3 is running...
Thread2 is running...
Thread1 is running...
Main thread counting: 4
Thread3 is running...
```

Note that there is no constructor for **Thread** that takes just a **ThreadGroup**. That is why I was obliged to add a **String** representing a name for each **Thread**.

It is also possible for a **Thread** within a **ThreadGroup** to retrieve its **ThreadGroup** in order to access other **Threads** in the same **ThreadGroup**. See Listing 20.18 for an example of how one **Thread** can communicate with another in the same **ThreadGroup**.

Listing 20.18   HeyNeighbor.java

```
interface Neighbor {
    void LendAHand( Thread t );
}

class Neighbor1 extends Thread implements Neighbor {
    Neighbor1( ThreadGroup t, String n ) {
        super( t, n );
    }

    public void run() {
        ThreadGroup group = getThreadGroup();
        Thread[] list = new Thread[ group.activeCount() ];

        group.enumerate( list );
        for( int i = 0; i < list.length; ++i ) {
            Thread t = ( Thread )list[ i ];

            if( t.getName().equals( "Neighbor2" )) {
```

```
                    System.out.println( "Neighbor1 found Neighbor2" );
                    if( t instanceof Neighbor ) {
                        Neighbor neighbor = ( Neighbor )t;
                        neighbor.LendAHand( this );
                    }
                }
            }
        }
    }

    public void LendAHand( Thread t ) {}
}

class Neighbor2 extends Thread implements Neighbor {
    Neighbor2( ThreadGroup t, String n ) {
        super( t, n );
    }

    public void run() {
    }

    public void LendAHand( Thread t ) {
        System.out.println( "Neighbor2 lends " +
                            t.getName() + " a hand" );
    }
}

public class HeyNeighbor {
    public static void main( String args[] ) {
        ThreadGroup neighborhood = new ThreadGroup( "The Neighborhood" );
        new Neighbor1( neighborhood, "Neighbor1" ).start();
        new Neighbor2( neighborhood, "Neighbor2" ).start();
    }
}

cmd> java HeyNeighbor
Neighbor1 found Neighbor2
Neighbor2 lends Neighbor1 a hand
```

As easily as you created the **ThreadGroup**, you can destroy it with the method **destroy**. Note that destroying a **ThreadGroup** destroys only the association among the threads. It does not destroy the threads themselves. Nor does it affect their state.

The only limitation placed on threads within a **ThreadGroup** is that a thread cannot access the parent of the **ThreadGroup** itself. This encapsulation promotes good programming style. You can **suspend**, **resume,** and **stop** all the **Threads** within a **ThreadGroup** with **ThreadGroup** class methods. This is the centralized control I referred to earlier. You even have the ability to set a maximum priority that will apply to all threads in the **ThreadGroup** with **setMaxPriority**.

The method **setMaxPriority** has a grandfather clause in that any threads already in a **ThreadGroup** that might have their priority set to a value higher than that set in the **setMaxPriority** call, are unaffected. They will continue to operate at that higher priority until death. The setting only affects threads that are added later. You've already seen that, like **Threads** themselves, **ThreadGroups** have names. And they also have a method called **getName** for retrieving their name.

Threads within **ThreadGroup** objects see each other by retrieving a Java array containing all their co-inhabitants, be they threads or other **ThreadGroups**. To do this, you can use a method called **enumerate**. This is an example of retrieving the threads that you already saw in Listing 20.18, part of which is reproduced in the code snippet below:

```
ThreadGroup group = getThreadGroup();
Thread[] list = new Thread[ group.activeCount() ];
group.enumerate( list );
```

You can then find whichever thread you wish to interact with by iterating through the array and checking the identity of each thread with the method **getName** as I did in Listing 20.18, part of which is reproduced in the code snippet below:

```
for( int i = 0; i < list.length; ++i ) {
    Thread t = ( Thread )list[ i ];

    if( t.getName().equals( "Neighbor2" )) {
        System.out.println( "Neighbor1 found Neighbor2" );
        if( t instanceof Neighbor ) {
            Neighbor neighbor = ( Neighbor )t;
            neighbor.LendAHand( this );
        }
    }
}
```

There are times when you might find it necessary to spin off a new thread in response to user requests. The number of threads created this way might not necessarily be limited. Use a **Vector** object to keep track of them all. It'll make life simpler. You can use a **ThreadGroup** object to exercise central control.

Thread Guidelines

There is an elegance to using multiple threads. Often, too, the code can be easier to write, understand, and maintain.

The event loop is implemented as a separate thread because it is imperative that the user's interface is reliably serviced. User interface events must be handled promptly. The alternative—dropping events altogether—is simply unacceptable. Another related example is a service thread that gets created in response to an intermittent requirement. A new communications session with a remote computer over the Internet might merit a separate thread to manage the connection.

Finally, and it was touched on in regards to I/O blocking, it is wise to anticipate system calls that could block. Instead you can create a new thread specifically to wait out the block. By effectively changing a *synchronous* interaction into an *asynchronous* one, performance should improve.

Threads are a wonderful innovation and hold the potential for enabling programmers to write software that is both more efficient and easier to understand. However, threads have their limitations. They cannot be applied blindly to every problem. Now that you've learned about all the good things you can do with threads, your first temptation might be to run to your computer and write everything using them. Resist the urge until you have gained some experience through experimentation. The contrived use of threads just leads to poor-quality software.

I don't want you to have any bad experiences right at the start. I hope you put threads into proper perspective. To that end, I've prepared Table 20.1 to serve as a simple guide to differentiating between good multithreading candidates and bad.

LET'S REVIEW

You will come to find threads nearly indispensable. Java was designed to exploit the power of the multithreaded programming that your computer's advanced operating system allows. Not only will multithreaded programming open up the potential of writing code that matches how you think about problem solutions, but you can begin to realize significant performance increases, too. You've been warned about some of the pitfalls but you also know how to work around them.

Programming with threads takes practice. You should always be ready to roll up your sleeves and fine-tune your application if its performance is disappointing. There are advanced uses of multithreaded programming that are beyond the scope of this chapter, but I hope it has laid a good foundation for your explorations.

Table 20.1 *What Makes a Good Thread?*

Threading Candidate?	Identifying Qualities	Examples
Yes	Contains operations that are naturally or conceptually concurrent already. Greater performance is often a coincidental benefit.	GUIs, Communications programs.
Maybe	Contains operations that can be threaded only through careful analysis to yield greater performance. Sometimes performance comes at the cost of comprehensibility.	Many numerical calculations,such as Matrix operations.
No	Anything for which threading would work already but difficult or unnatural. Few performance gains to be recognized.	Programs that offer satisfactory performance. Programs that require separate processes. Large existing programs.

IF YOU LIKED THIS, YOU'LL LOVE THESE

There are two more great Web sites that provide helpful information on multithreading.

comp.programming.threads

This is the newsgroup to follow to learn more about multithreaded programming. It's the best way to learn new techniques and follow new developments. Also, you can always draw on the talents of the individuals who are active on the newsgroup if you run into difficulties.

Sun's Threads Page

There is a Web page at Sun Microsystems devoted to multithreading issues. Though a lot of the information doesn't necessarily pertain to Java threads, there are still links that are worth checking out. See: http://www.sun.com/sunsoft/Developer-products/sig/threads.

Do-it-Yourself Internet

Alex Leslie

This chapter goes way beyond putting the good stuff on your homepage. It's a taste of real Net programming. You'll learn how Java makes it easy to communicate over the Internet.

Everyone's heard of the Internet, but what most people have actually *seen* is the World Wide Web. Most of those people view the Web with a software program called a browser. No doubt, you've heard of Netscape *Navigator* and the meteoric rise of its company's stock in recent months.

Without a doubt, the explosive growth of the Internet is due to the early wide availability of such an easy-to-use, well-written program. There are other excellent Web browsers besides: Microsoft's *Internet Explorer* and NCSA *Mosaic,* to name just two. See Figure 21.1 for a shot of your favorite publisher's homepage displayed in the most popular Web browser of them all.

Web browsers have brought the Internet to life. The Internet was always a useful tool, but no Internet services previously available can compare to the impact of the Web. Even television watching is down among Web-surfers. It's likely the single

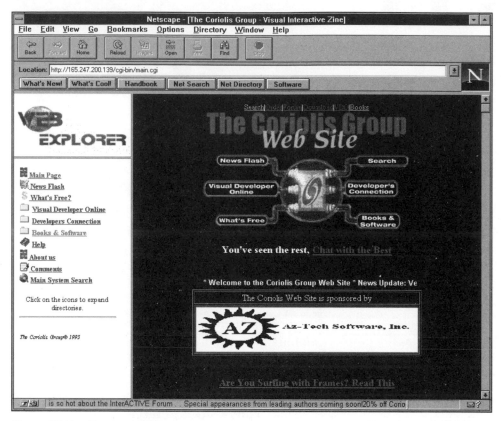

Figure 21.1   Netscape in action.

biggest motivation for getting online. Roaming the Web is currently the most engaging way to explore cyberspace.

But aren't you tired of taking such a passive role sitting on the sidelines? Maybe you have a homepage that you are proud of. You've got a handle on *HTML*. That's excellent! You're contributing to Internet content—self-publishing, as it were.

Surely, you must be curious about how all this Internet stuff is really done, though. You're tired of always being a tool-user. You want to know how to build the tools. Perhaps you have an idea for an Internet program that you would like to try to implement. The good news is that Java makes it all extremely easy, as you'll find out in this chapter. Figure 21.2 is an Internet program that, in Java, was a piece of cake to write.

```
─                        Who Is...                    ▼  ▲
coriolis.com
The Coriolis Group,Inc. (CORIOLIS-DOM)                        ▲
      7339 E. Acoma Drive, Suite 7
      Scottsdale, AZ 85260

      Domain Name: CORIOLIS.COM

      Administrative Contact:
          Duntemann, Jeff  (JD131)  jeffd@CORIOLIS.COM
          (602) 483-0192 x3 ext. 3
      Technical Contact, Zone Contact:
          Fisher, William  (WF17)  hilfish@INDIRECT.COM
          602-274-0100

      Record last updated on 24-Jun-95.
      Record created on 28-Jun-94.

      Domain servers in listed order:

      NS1.INDIRECT.COM              165.247.1.3
      NS2.INDIRECT.COM              165.247.1.17

The InterNIC Registration Services Host contains ONLY Internet
(Networks, ASN's, Domains, and POC's).
Please use the whois server at nic.ddn.mil for MILNET Informat ▼
◄                                                              ►

                   Search   Clear   Quit
```

Figure 21.2 *A Java Internet application.*

This is a real Internet program that will be developed in this chapter. You'll find out many other useful techniques that will open up the full potential of Internet programming with Java.

The aim of this chapter is to show you some practical—and often, surprisingly easy—techniques for Internet programming. I will be demonstrating several practical Java code examples. Several different important protocols and techniques will be explored as well. You'll get a taste of the future.

The Great Besides

The fact is that there is a lot to the Internet besides the Web. You might have heard of a few of the services: FTP and electronic mail (email) are the best-known ones, but there are many others. Each one was designed to operate separately. The specifications for these services were laid down in documents that detailed exactly how each service would operate. That's commonly called the "RFC." It contains the protocol details for that service.

Not so long ago, in order to use email or FTP, you had to use separate software tools. Now, many Internet services are being integrated into single larger tools, such as Web browsers. The current crop of browsers usually include email and access to the newsgroup service.

The differences among different Internet services have become blurred in many people's minds, since most browsers support them in addition to the Web. We'll be looking at a few services in this chapter.

It is the protocols that distinguish one Internet service from another. To a casual user, the fact that the browsers offer integrated access to functions has been a tremendous boon. To somebody programming for the Internet, it is still necessary to appreciate the differences. This chapter is for the programmer who wants to know how to apply Java within the context of the Internet and its protocols.

I love Web browsers. They combine power and simplicity. Armed with a browser, the most difficulty anyone now faces is trying to remember Internet addresses. The @ symbol, colon, and forward slash seem to have become the holy trinity of Internet addressing. You might have felt bewildered when first confronted with all those odd characters combined with seemingly-redundant prefixes and a generous dose of non-standard abbreviation. Sometimes, it almost seems it would be easier to memorize your car's serial number than the cryptic address of some Web pages. Isn't it amazing how almost over-night Internet addresses have started showing up in TV commercials, maga-zine ads, even in the credits of day-time talk shows! I still wonder what the Internet-illiterate think of it all.

We're going to dive right into the middle, and I'm going to satisfy that promise I made to fill in the details about protocols.

PROTOCOLS DEMYSTIFIED

There's going to be a lot of talk about protocols in this chapter, but maybe the only protocol you have ever heard of is the set of guidelines that specifies how to interact with royalty. It's a guide that you start studying once it's announced that you're going to be knighted. I bet Paul McCartney's got it beside his bed—fine-tuning his "Would your Highness care to jam?"

An Internet protocol is only slightly different from that. It's a specification of how two computers should interact over the Internet to cooperatively to achieve some common goal.

Protocols exist for transferring data files or email, or even just retrieving a timestamp from an Internet site that has a particularly accurate clock. Generally, one computer provides a *service* and the other is a *client* of that service. Email is an example of a service. The Internet is the delivery mechanism for a veritable cornucopia of services. Protocols are central, so don't be surprised that most of the acronyms you come upon end in *P* for protocol.

The computer-to-computer interaction takes the form of messages that are passed back and forth. One computer initiates the dialog by connecting to another and sending some sort of introductory message. Perhaps that message introduces the client computer by stating its Internet address. The other computer—the server—may respond in turn by answering and indicating its willingness to provide a service.

The set of valid prompts and answers is strictly defined by the protocol. It's not a free-for-all, though even within a protocol, there are certainly different options: different queries that may be posed and a variety of potential answers that may be used to respond.

It will help to examine a real protocol. The one I've chosen is SMTP—*Simple Mail Transfer Protocol*—and it is used for email. It is not implemented in this chapter and the description here is brief and non-technical. We'll just pretend we've got some mail to send. Let's listen in on the conversation. It's shown in Listing 21.1.

Listing 21.1 Protocols in Action

```
import java.net.*;

public class MyIPAddress{
  public static void main( String args[] ) {
    InetAddress localAddress = null;
    try {
      localAddress = InetAddress.getLocalHost();
    } catch( UnknownHostException e ) {
    }
    System.out.println( localAddress );
  }
}
```

Most protocols are made up of simple messages that are just as straightforward as in this example. This kind of back-and-forth is commonly called handshaking.

Note that, in reality, the format of the messages sent back and forth is very strictly specified according to a syntax that is much more terse than the example above. But that's just details. The only difficulty in implementing any protocol is writing an program that is robust and meets the demands of the entire protocol—not just the part that gets used 90 percent of the time.

Internet Addresses

Although you're justifiably proud of mastering the colons and slashes of Web addresses, you might not realize that *real* Internet addresses don't include any letters. Raw Internet addresses—IP addresses—are expressed as just a series of four integers separated by dots. It's not surprising that it's come to be called *dotted-decimal notation.* The integers are limited in range from zero to two-hundred fifty-five, which just happens to be two to the eighth power, minus one. It's all binary, which means that an Internet address is currently a *32-bit binary word.* See Figure 21.3.

If you are already registered on the Internet, you have your own unique Internet address in addition to your more familiar email address. Very likely, you had to enter that number when you were setting up the various Internet tools that you use.

You can use the Java class **InetAddress** to find out what your local address is with the program in Listing 21.2.

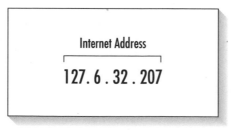

Figure 21.3   Internet address.

Listing 21.2   What's My IP Address?

```java
import java.net.*;

public class GetIPAddress {
  public static void main( String args[] ) {
    InetAddress address = null;
    try {
      address = InetAddress.getByName( args[ 0 ] );
    } catch( UnknownHostException e ) {
    }
    System.out.println( address );
  }
}
```

If you run the program, you'll get your own IP address back:

```
cmd> java MyIPAddress
187.45.68.112
```

There is a set of rules that describes how Internet addresses are distributed and assigned. The details are the subject of other books. The important thing is that often you don't need to deal with Internet addresses expressed this way. In most cases, Java takes the familiar textual Internet addresses you might love or hate.

Another neat thing you can do with **InetAddress** is use it to get the Internet address of some other computer that you know. Let's take a peek and see what this book's publisher's Internet address is with the program in Listing 21.3.

Listing 21.3   What's Someone Else's IP Address?

```java
public class getIPAddress {
  public static void main( String args[] ) {
    String address;
    try {
      address = InetAddress.getByName( args[ 0 ] );
    } catch( UnknownHostException e ) {
    }
    System.out.println( address );
  }
}
```

```
cmd> java getIPAddress coriolis.com
```

To protect the innocent, I didn't give you my Internet address when I ran the program in Listing 21.2, but the line below shows what you'll get as *coriolis.com*'s IP address:

```
coriolis.com/165.247.200.139
```

This brings up an issue that I'll mention but won't explain in detail. One of the things that has to happen whenever you use a textual Internet address, such as *coriolis.com,* is called address resolution. To be useful in locating the computer they identify, textual Internet addresses always have to be converted into the 32-bit binary word mentioned above. Perhaps you have noticed while using a browser such as Netscape Navigator that the status line near the bottom of the pane will display the textual address for a moment after you click on a site but it is then sometimes replaced by the real 32-bit address of the site. That's just a visible reminder of the resolution that is taking place. Sometimes that 32-bit address is even postfixed with colon and a number like *:8080.* That is called the *port number.* Figure 21.4 adds the port number to the Internet address.

Internet Address Shortage Looming

It is interesting to note that the world is quickly running out of Internet addresses! Hard to imagine, considering it is such a big number, but it's true. The upcoming replacement for the current Internet protocol is called *IPng: Internet Protocol—next generation.* I guess the cat's out of the bag: The design of the Internet is being left up to a bunch of *Trekkers.* Live long and prosper.

Much of this new protocol is already specified. It will sport 128-bit addresses. That works out to something like over a billion addresses for each-and-every square yard of the surface of the earth. That should do for a while—or will it?

URLs and Other Internet Denizens

The Web itself follows a protocol called the *HyperText Transmission Protocol.* That little **http** at the beginning of each Web site address is not as redundant as

Figure 21.4   Internet address and port.

you might have thought. It tells your computer which protocol to use when trying to communicate with that site. Sometimes you will encounter other prefixes. The prefix **ftp** is a common one. They, too, are important parts of the address.

An entire Internet address has the form shown in the line below:

```
http://www.coriolis.com
```

The address is called a URL. That stands for *Uniform Resource Locator.* All valid URLs include two main parts. The first part—everything up to the first colon—is called the **protocol** prefix.

The second part is everything following that colon. That last bit is called a URI. It stands for *Universal Resource Identifier.* Here it is from the example above:

```
//www.coriolis.com
```

I break apart a URL in Figure 21.5.

Note that you never see whitespace in a URI. It is forbidden. And there is a small set of characters that cannot be part of a URI. They are reserved: See Table 21.1 for the complete list.

Protocol History

The URL is so named because by combining an address uniquely identifying something with a protocol that specifies the mode of access, you have a neat, uniform way of expressing a wide variety of things. Internet addressing is just one potential application of such a naming scheme.

Though the Web has become nearly synonymous with the Internet, it is not the whole Internet. In fact, it is a relatively new development. It dates from 1992. That's recent history for the Internet, which is already over 20 years old.

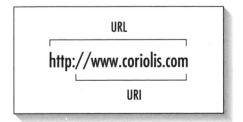

Figure 21.5 *URLs and URIs.*

Table 21.1 *URI Reserved Characters*

Character	Description
/ - forward slash	separate directory and file components
? - question mark	identifies a query and precedes a search term
# - pound sign	separates fields
% - percent sign	identifies specially-encoded characters
* - asterisk	reserved
! - exclamation point	reserved

If you ever use email, you're not using the Web, even if you are using a browser. It is interesting to note that email still represents perhaps the single most used program on the Internet. The primary protocol is called SMTP, which we saw in the simple handshaking example earlier. SMTP dates way back to before 1983. Most people who use it can't imagine life without it. This book likely couldn't have been written without it.

If you've ever retrieved files from a remote site, you likely used yet another important protocol. Not surprisingly, the protocol is called *FTP*, which stands for File Transfer Protocol. These three represent the lion's share of Internet traffic by number of messages sent—though the Web, with its affinity for expensive, high-grade content, is growing much faster than the other two. FTP is likely to hang on as number one in terms of sheer demand for bandwidth—at least, for a while longer.

HOW THE INTERNET DEVELOPED

A little background on the Internet might give you a better appreciation why the Internet has proved so successful.

Significantly, the Internet does not follow the typical development process of other less successful projects. The Internet uses a form of natural selection. The "survival of the fittest" protocol is a good way to describe the development of the Internet.

Protocols Are the Key

You probably already know that the Internet is actually an inter-net: a net consisting of connections among other computer networks. Contrast that with *intranets,* which we are starting to hear about. They are generally limited, internal corporate networks.

Internet Power

The power of the Internet is due to its extreme connectivity. A computer industry guru once said that the real power of a network is proportional to the *square* of the number of computers connected. Just as a nuclear pile reaches critical mass, the Internet has exploded in the past year as the number of computers connected has rapidly increased.

Aside from the connectivity of the Internet, the common services it provides really run on only a couple of dozen popular protocols that have been refined over the years. Like I said, the protocols that exist in common use today are the survivors. We are the beneficiaries of that process of technological "natural selection."

Granted, most of the protocols were written by individuals in academia or some high-tech company, but did you know that anyone can write his or her own protocol? That's right—even you, as long as you follow the right procedure.

The protocol that drives the Web was written as a side effort by Tim Berners-Lee, a scientist at CERN ("Conseil Europeen pour la Recherche Nucleaire," the European Council for Nuclear Research) in Europe. He is a nuclear scientist, so perhaps he appreciated the parallels with nuclear reactions that would result once Marc Andreessen, now of Netscape fame, got hold of his specification.

Don't be discouraged that most of the obvious protocols are already claimed. There will always be new protocols under development. Maybe you've got a special insight you want to indulge. It's a rare honor to be the inventor of something so intangible yet with such a great potential impact on computers and even on human society.

The Birth of a Protocol

Let's go back to the beginning and pretend that we're looking over the shoulder of someone who has written a specification. Anyone would need to start by writing the details of the protocol. Then, it is necessary to develop a working program that uses the protocol. It's part of the process. Your protocol must be demonstrated with practical implementations that you hope will catch on in the Internet community.

The process runs on RFCs: *Requests For Comment*. They are documents that are published with either a specification or just a perspective on some issue for which the author is seeking feedback. RFCs are submitted by mailing them to *internet-draft@cnri.reston.va.us*. They are then placed in public directories at two sites. Those sites are *ds.internic.net* and *nri.reston.va.us*. You'll be re-introduced to the *InterNIC* site in the *WhoIs* program later.

As I implied earlier, a protocol must be implemented to qualify. If it is a useful protocol, it will likely become informally popular and other Internet users will adopt it. If it stands the test of time, and proves to be well-designed and complete, it stands a chance of becoming official.

Note that any RFC is first "published" in this way so that it can be reviewed by other interested parties. The entire process often takes years. There are several boards and task forces that have a say in the proposal. Note that unlike other protocols, Internet protocols are not designed by committee. Although the groups involved have no interest in standing in the way of legitimate qualifiers, any Internet standard might still end up going around and around through repeated reviews and revisions before being accepted.

The bottom line is that many submissions simply don't survive to become standards. The evolutionary approach ensures that only those most widely useful are ultimately adopted.

THE WhoIs PROTOCOL

In this chapter, we're going to start with a protocol that is under-appreciated. You might have never even heard of it. It is called the *Nicname* or, more commonly, the **WhoIs** protocol.

You use this protocol in a program to find out who someone is. It works as long as that person is registered with InterNIC—the Internet address assignment agency. It applies to organizations and companies as well. We're going to write such an program together, so once it's done, you can try all sorts of names.

A strong motivation for introducing this particular protocol is its simplicity. Other protocols are introduced later, and they generally involve significantly more detail. Once you know the basic techniques, you can load on the details in any other protocol without much difficulty.

All the important **WhoIs** details are contained in one brief document called RFC954. At just four pages, it is very brief indeed by Internet standards. The specifications of several other protocols span hundred of pages.

Exotic Ports of Call

Part of any protocol specification spelled out in an RFC is a port number. Over the past 20 years, a list of unique port numbers and corresponding Internet services has been developed. Each service follows a distinct protocol. A port is identified by just an integer between 0 and 65535—it's a *16-bit number*.

In order to understand how to program for the Internet, you have to understand *ports* and *sockets*. Your Java program communicates via a **Socket** object. In order to do that, a **Socket** object must be created. Its constructor expects an IP address and a port number. The IP address indicates with which computer you want to establish communication.

A Port Definition

A port is an abstract creation, not a physical port like something into which you'd be able to stick a plug or a bus card. Because ports and their associated Internet services have been standardized, think of ports as just a way of choosing to access a particular service offered by some computer on the Internet.

You can create your own service by choosing a port number that is not yet officially assigned. One computer could have several valid ports to which you could connect. Listing 21.4 shows an example that introduces the Java class **ServerSocket**:

Listing 21.4   Listening on Port 77

```
try {
  ServerSocket serverSocket = new ServerSocket( 77, 16 );
} catch( IOException e ) {
}
serverSocket.accept(); // this blocks while waiting for connection
```

In the code fragment in Listing 21.4, I created a **ServerSocket** attached to port 77. This code causes your program to establish a port to which some other computer could connect using a **Socket** object that it created with your IP address and port 77. But before you are prepared to accept a connection from some other computer, you have to call the **accept** method to begin waiting for a client to come along and connect.

In order for your program to start communicating with a computer that is waiting to **accept** a connection, it must use a **Socket**. I'll show you all about these new Java networking classes after I tell you more about port numbers and Internet services.

Common Port Numbers

WhoIs's port number is 43. There are several computers on the Internet around the world that provide the **WhoIs** service. All are listening on port 43. The computers are likely listening on other ports, too, since they almost certainly offer services other than just **WhoIs**. Table 21.2 lists some common port/service pairs.

There is a computer that you can be guaranteed is listening on port 43. It is *whois.internic.net*. There is a long list of other computers that provide the service but this is the grand-daddy of **WhoIs**.

The line below shows the simple Java code you'd use to connect to *whois.internic.net* on port 43.

```
Socket socket = new Socket( "whois.internic.net", 43 );
```

Okay, now it's time to explore **Sockets** and **SocketServers** and ports in more detail.

Socket Science

Talking about ports and sockets at the same time certainly sounds like a serious case of mixed metaphors. The names suggest the basic operation of each entity, though they leave many questions unanswered.

You've already been introduced to the **Socket** and **ServerSocket** classes. Do you appreciate the difference between them?

You can use **Socket**s for both ends of a communications session. When you instantiate a **Socket**, what you are really doing is creating an association with a

Table 21.2   *Internet Services and Ports*

Internet Service	Port Number
Time	37
WhoIs	43
Finger	79
SMTP	25
POP3	110
NNTP	119

particular port on some remote computer. You've already seen how to instantiate a **Socket** and connect to a computer above. The mere act of constructing a **Socket** will attempt a connection. That is why it is necessary to be prepared to catch an **IOException** at the constructor, as shown in the code snippet below:

```
try {
  Socket socket = new Socket( "...", 43 );
  // do something clever
} catch( IOException e ) {
}
```

Once a connection is established, either an input stream or an output stream, or both; can be assigned, as shown in the code snippet below:

```
InputStream is = socket.getInputStream();
OutputStream os   socket.getOutputStream();
```

You can then read and write via the stream to your heart's content. Just remember to close the **Socket** when you're done, as shown in the code line below:

```
socket.close();
```

Note that many of the **Socket** methods can throw **IOException**, so you should be prepared with a **try/catch** block. Figure 21.6 shows how each *peer* computer has a socket on either end of the connection. By peer, I mean that there are no assumptions about which computer is providing a service and which is a client. It is a communication between equals.

Back to ServerSocket Again

You can see the difference for yourself between this technique and the one just introduced by comparing the methods in **Socket** with those in **ServerSocket**. What you are doing when you instantiate a **ServerSocket** is establishing a port to which other computers can connect. Do you notice the subtle but important difference between that and **Socket**?

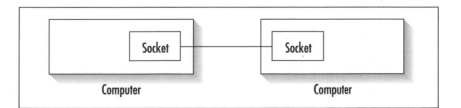

Figure 21.6 *Socket-to-Socket.*

The mere instantiation of a **ServerSocket** doesn't automatically connect to any other remote computer, as happens with **Socket**. Instead, after creating a **ServerSocket**, you must use the method **accept** to agree to connect with another computer attempting connection. This is shown in the code snippet below:

```
ServerSocket serverSocket = new ServerSocket( 77. 16 );
Socket   client;
while( true ) {
 try {
  client = serverSocket.accept();
  // do something with the client socket
 } catch( IOException e ) {
}
```

The act of accepting the connection returns a **Socket** object. It is that **Socket** you then use to communicate with the new correspondent. Figure 21.7 shows that you now consider the computer that has the **ServerSocket** as the service server. Clients are users of the service. They still use a **Socket** to connect to the server's **ServerSocket**.

The Internet Who's Who Explored

Now that I've given you a brief **WhoIs** backgrounder, it's time for the real thing. This Java program consists of a simple interface with a **TextField** at the top and a **TextArea** filling most of the rest of the area. There are three buttons along the bottom, labeled Search, Clear, and Quit.

To use the program, you just type some text into the field and press the Search button. That string will be packaged and passed out over the Internet to the computer that provides the **WhoIs** Internet service. The response is read and displayed in the **TextArea**. You might wish to clear that area from time to time with the Clear button. Figure 21.8 is a shot of the Internet program that I introduced at the beginning.

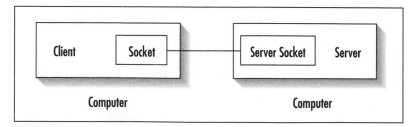

Figure 21.7 *Socket-to-SocketServer.*

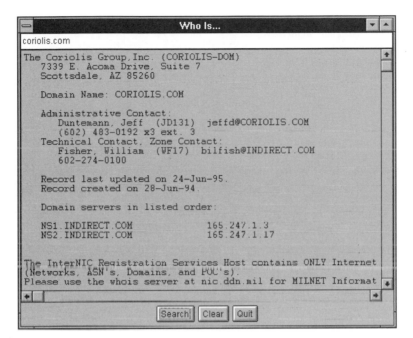

Figure 21.8 The WhoIs program again.

The source for a simple yet graphical **WhoIs** program that really works is found in Listing 21.5.

Listing 21.5 A Working WhoIs Program

```
import java.awt.*;
import java.io.*;
import java.net.*;
import java.util.*;

class InputField extends TextField {
 InputField() {
  super( 60 );
 }
}

class InfoBox extends TextArea {
 InfoBox() {
  super( "", 10, 60 );
  setEditable( false );
  setFont( new Font( "Courier", Font.PLAIN, 12 ));
 }

 void Print( String s ) {
  insertText( s, getText().length() );
 }
}
```

```
class Controls extends Panel {
 public Controls() {
   add(new Button("Search"));
   add(new Button("Clear"));
   add(new Button("Quit"));
 }
}

public class WhoIs extends Frame {
 InputField inputField;
 InfoBox infoBox;

 WhoIs() {
  super( "Who Is..." );

  setBackground( Color.lightGray );
  setLayout( new BorderLayout() );

  inputField = new InputField();
  add( "North", inputField );

  infoBox = new InfoBox();
  add( "Center", infoBox );
  add( "South", new Controls() );

  resize( 400, 300 );
  show();
 }

 public String goSearch( String query ) throws UnknownHostException {
  String  s = null;
  StringBuffer sb = new StringBuffer();

  try {
   Socket socket = new Socket( "whois.internic.net", 43 );

   DataInputStream dis = new DataInputStream( socket.getInputStream() );
   DataOutputStream dos = new DataOutputStream( socket.getOutputStream() );

   dos.writeBytes( query + "\r\n" );
   dos.flush();

   int c;
   while( ( c = dis.read()) >= 0 ) {
    sb.append( ( char )c );
   }

   s = new String( sb.toString() );

   socket.close();
  } catch( IOException e ) {
   System.out.println( "ERROR: IO Exception" );
  } finally {
   if( s == null || s.length() == 0 ) {
```

```
    s = new String( "Sorry, nothing found..." );
  }

  return s;
 }
}

public synchronized boolean handleEvent( Event e ) {
 if( e.id == Event.WINDOW_DESTROY ) {
  return true;
 }
 else {
  return super.handleEvent( e );
 }
}

public boolean action( Event evt, Object obj ) {
  if( evt.target instanceof Button ) {
   String label = ( String )obj;

   if( label.equals( "Quit" )) {
    System.exit( 0 );
   } else if( label.equals( "Search" )) {
    try {
     infoBox.Print( goSearch(inputField.getText()));
    } catch( UnknownHostException e ) {
     System.out.println( "ERROR: Unknown Host" );
    }
   } else if( label.equals( "Clear" )) {
    infoBox.setText( "" );
   }
  }

  return true;
}

public static void main( String args[] ) {
 new WhoIs();
}
}
```

The essential part of this example is enclosed with the **WhoIs** method *goSearch*. The query string that is passed in is just the exact string that you typed into the field at the top of the interface.

This protocol is so simple that after you have created a **Socket** and created an **InputStream** and an **OutputStream** stream attached to that socket (as shown in the snippet below), you need only send a string containing the query and terminated by a *Carriage-Return, New-Line* combination, as shown in the following code snippet:

```
Socket      socket = new Socket( "whois.internic.net", 43 );
DataInputStream dis = new DataInputStream(
          socket.getInputStream() );
DataOutputStream dos = new DataOutputStream(
          socket.getOutputStream() );
```

Note that all of these I/O operations using **Stream**s can throw **IOExceptions** that must be caught and handled or re-thrown. The code to do that is included in the example above, but in the code snippet below, has been omitted for the sake of compactness.

```
dos.writeBytes( query + "\r\n" );
dos.flush();
```

The characters representing *Carriage-Return, New-Line* are "\r\n". They are known as *special characters*. If they don't look familiar, you can review the section on special characters in Chapter 4.

Once the string is written to the **OutputStream** attached to the **Socket** with the method **writeBytes**, you just need to read what is eventually returned from the computer, as shown in the code snippet below:

```
StringBuffer sb = new StringBuffer();
int c;
while( ( c = dis.read()) >= 0 ) {
 sb.append( ( char )c );
}
```

This particular technique—of reading from the **InputStream** one-character-at-a-time—is recommended. An alternative method would be to read an entire array of bytes with a single read. The latter approach, shown in the code snippet below, depends on successful blocking of the incoming I/O and is sometimes unreliable.

```
int numAvailable = dis.available();
byte[] buffer = new byte[ numAvailable ];
try {
 dis.read( buffer );
} catch( IOException e ) {
}
```

Using a **StringBuffer** is easy. You can convert it to a Java **String,** which can then be returned and displayed, as shown in the code snippet below:

```
s = new String( sb.toString() );
```

This program just pumps the string straight into the **TextArea** for viewing. That's all there is to it.

The **WhoIs** program might be simple, but it is a real Internet program. If you run it, you will actually communicate over the Internet to some far off computer using an official Internet protocol. You should be able to write any other programs based on the techniques used here—plus, of course, a little creativity.

OTHER POPULAR PROTOCOLS

Besides **WhoIs**, there are numerous other protocols for the Internet. Note that not all that are specified in an RFC are in widespread use. There are a smaller number that are used extensively and represent the underlying protocols used in popular Internet tools.

Time

The **Time** protocol is as simple as **WhoIs**, if not simpler. It is defined in RFC868. Its port is 37. It dates back to 1983. You use it to get the current time—if that comes as a surprise.

Once you are connected to the **Time** port of some computer, you simply need to send an empty datagram. That just means send an empty buffer of data. You can immediately read the time.

The time is encoded as a 32-bit binary number. The number represents the number of seconds since 00:00 on 1 January 1900 GMT. Negative values represent dates and times prior to that baseline date.

Finger

This is a protocol that is graced with a name that has potentially vulgar interpretations. It's funny how many bashful grins appear when it is introduced for the first time. **Finger**'s port is 79. Its modern incarnation dates from just 1990.

You **Finger** someone to retrieve data that they have earmarked for public availability. The kind of information usually includes such things as a user's name, address, phone number, and perhaps even office hours. Think of it as retrieving someone's business card—it's usually that sort of thing. If you want to write your own finger, first read RFC1288.

Email

The protocol for email, as you likely use it, is actually a combination of three different protocols. The primary protocol is **SMTP**. It was developed in 1982.

Associated protocols are **POP3** and **MIME**. **POP3**—which stands for **Post Office Protocol**—is necessary because most Internet users are not continuously connected to the Internet and instead their mail accumulates at their Internet provider's site—essentially their post office. The protocol covers the handshaking between your computer and another computer that is connected directly to the Internet. It dates from 1984, but newer enhancements have occurred as recently as just a few years ago. Check out RFC1724.

Finally, **MIME**—Multipurpose Internet Mail Extensions, which dates from just 1992—extends email to be able to transmit, within mail messages, special types of data such as sound files or image data. **MIME** is described in RFC1521 and some other subsequent RFCs.

FTP

FTP is a service that enables you to transfer files to and from your computer and some other computer. It is one of the keystone Internet services and it still sucks up the most bandwidth on the Internet. It dates from 1985 and has reserved port 21. RFC0959 spells out the details.

News

Who could live without Internet newsgroups? They are an incredibly up-to-date way to stay abreast of issues on a wide variety of topics. If you've got a nagging question, you can often find the answer by posting it to the appropriate newsgroup: Other Internet users are more than happy to answer you. I encourage you to start following the discussions in comp.lang.java. It is one of the most active comp.lang groups, and with good reason. It is the number one source for Java information. There are so many eyes and ears out there attached to people with similar interests that nothing gets missed. Every periodical gets read and every conference gets attended by at least one member of the newsgroup.

The protocol that drives newsgroups is **NNTP**—Network News Transfer Protocol. It dates from 1986 and the details are in RFC0977. A computer providing Network News does so on port 119.

APPLET ISSUES

There are several Internet issues that you need to consider if you are planning to write Java applets. They are the Applet Context, controlling the browser, loading a remote applet, and letting applets communicate with each other.

The Applet Context

The Applet Context is defined as the environment in which the Applet operates. It is defined by the Java class **AppletContext**. Briefly, the Applet Context is important here because it gives any applet access to other applets and to other documents on the Internet via the method **showDocument**.

Controlling the Browser

A common thing that you might want to do from with an **Applet** is direct the browser to a different URL. This is really easy to do, but seems to have caused confusion for many new Java users.

Directing the browser to a different URL is possible because you have access to the Applet Context. From within an **Applet**, you can call something as shown in the code snippet below:

```
URL newURL = new URL( "http://www.interlog.com" );
showDocument( newURL );
```

The method call, via the Applet Context, directs the browser to replace the current document, including the applet itself, with a new document from somewhere else on the Internet. Note that you can only do this once from an applet.

Loading a Remote Applet

The Internet enables you also to do some things with applets that you might have not even considered. For instance, you can point to Java applets that actually reside on other computers and reference them in an HTML page.

You're probably already familiar with the syntax of the **Applet** HTML tag. It's actually the **CODEBASE** parameter that gives it the power to point wherever you choose, as shown in the code snippet below:

```
<applet code="AFriendsApplet.class"
HEIGHT=200 WIDTH=400
CODEBASE="http://www.myfriend.com/applets/>
</applet>
```

Though not strictly Internet programming, I included it nevertheless. I believe that this is something that you will eventually want to do.

Talk Amongst Yourselves, Applets

A final useful technique you might employ is allowing **Applets** on one of your Web pages to talk to each other. Another one of the things that **AppletContext** gives you access to is an **Enumeration** of Applets. **Enumeration**s are discussed in much more detail in Chapter 9. For now, just think of it as a list. That list will contain references to all the other **Applets** in the same context. You can then iterate through the **Enumeration** and locate any particular applet.

If you're working within a class derived from **Applet**, you'll use the kind of code structure in Listing 21.6 to find the applet with which you want to communicate.

Listing 21.6 Applet-to-Applet Communication

```
for( Enumeration e = getApplets(); e.hasMoreElements(); ) {
 Applet applet = ( Applet )e.nextElement();

 if( applet instanceof GraphicsDrawingApplet ) {
  GraphicsDrawingApplet graphApplet =
        ( GraphicsDrawingApplet )applet;
  // communicate via
  // the GraphicsDrawingApplet interface
 } else if( applet instanceof SoundPlaying Applet ) {
  SoundPlayingApplet soundApplet =
          ( SoundPlayingApplet )applet;
  // communicate via
  // the SoundPlayingApplet interface
 } else ...
 // ...
}
```

Once you have the **Applet** reference, you use the **instanceof** keyword to determine the real class of the **Applet** you've got. Then, with the appropriate cast, you have access to that **Applet's** public methods. The rest is up to you.

HANDLING A VARIETY OF CONTENTS

An important issue that you have to tackle when writing Internet Java programs is handling different types of content. You might want to handle contents that are not supported by Java.

Possibly you will even have the need or inclination to define content of your own and will need to write Java code that can interpret it.

Content Defined

A simple definition of content is the format of some data. Different documents can be classed according to their content. For instance, files containing graphical information encoded in the GIF format all have one type of content. Different audio or video formats are considered different contents. Program files are yet another content type. Even plain text files are considered a distinct content type.

Different contents are really just different media types. Not surprisingly, content itself is defined in an RFC, just as Internet protocols are. Check out RFC1521 for all the details.

Table 21.3 contains the complete list of standard Internet content types and subtypes.

Table 21.3 *Standard Content Types/Subtypes*

Type	Subtype
text	plain
	richtext
	enriched
	tab-separated-values
	sgml
mulitpart	mixed
	alternative
	digest
	parallel
	appledouble
	header-set
	form-data
	related
	report

Continued

Table 21.3   *Standard Content Types/Subtypes (Continued)*

Type	Subtype
message	rfc822
	partial
	external-body
	news
program	octet-stream
	postscript
	oda
	atomicmail
	andrew-inset
	slate
	wita
	dec-dx
	dca-rtf
	activemessage
	rtf
	applefile
	mac-binhex40
	news-message-id
	news-transmission
	wordperfect5.1
	pdf
	zip
	macwriteii
	msword
	remote-printing
	mathematica
	cybercash
	commonground
	iges
	riscos
	eshop
	x400-bp
	sgml

Continued

Table 21.3   *Standard Content Types/Subtypes (Continued)*

Type	Subtype
image	jpeg
	gif
	ief
	g3fax
	tiff
	cgm
	naplps
audio	basic
video	mpeg
	quicktime

You can always get an up-to-date list of content types from ftp://ftp.isi.edu/
in-notes/iana/assignments/media-types.

Determining Different Contents

Despite having learned the details of Internet contents, you may not know
how to make your programs determine the content type of a particular file.

The primary method used to determine content is the filename extension.
Java uses an extensive list of recognized extensions and corresponding content type and subtype. This will be introduced later.

There exists a second method that can be used if the first method is considered unreliable in a particular case. It involves actual inspection of the contents of the file. This method is often effective because in many different file
formats, an identifying header must occur first in the file. So if you know what
to look for, you might be able to determine the content of the file.

Content Details

There are only seven different content types defined in the RFC. They are
text, multipart, message, program, image, audio, and video. Content of one
type is further distinguished by numerous subtypes. There is a different list of
subtypes for each type.

The content of a file is commonly expressed as a combination of type and
subtype. Type and subtype are usually separated by a forward slash.

Plain text is of type text and subtype plain for a content of "text/plain." This distinguishes it from "text/sgml," which is also text. It is also readable just like plain text. The difference is that the text represents Standard Graphics Markup Language (commonly expressed as simply "SGML") specifications instead.

There is a long list of program subtypes. These are not programs themselves, but files containing data requiring a specific program or type of program. Two examples are "program/postscript" and "program/zip."

Finally, you might recognize image content in "image/gif" or video in "video/mpeg."

A Content Handler Framework

The program in Listing 21.7 can be used as a framework that you can extend.

Listing 21.7   A Custom ContentHandler Framework

```
import java.io.*;
import java.net.*;

class MyObject {
  String string;

  MyObject( String string ) {
    this.string = string;
  }

  public String toString() {
    return new String( "MyObject:\n" + string );
  }
}

class MyHandler extends ContentHandler {
  public Object getContent( URLConnection urlConnection ) {
    String   string;
    MyObject  mailObject = null;
    URL    url  = urlConnection.getURL();
    StringBuffer sb   = new StringBuffer();

    try {
      InputStream is = url.openStream();

      int c;
      while(( c = is.read() ) >= 0 ) {
        sb.append( ( char )c );
      }

      myObject = new MyObject( sb.toString() );
    } catch( IOException e ) {
    } catch( Exception e ) {
```

```
      }

      return myObject;
   }
}

class MyContentHandlerFactory implements ContentHandlerFactory {
   public ContentHandler createContentHandler( String type ) {
      ContentHandler handler = null;

      if( type.equals( "text/plain" )) {
         handler = new MyHandler();
      }

      return handler;
   }
}

public class ContentDemo {
   public static void main( String args[] ) {
      try {
         URL url =
            new URL( "http://www.../SomeContentFile.txt" );
         URLConnection connection = url.openConnection();

         MyContentHandlerFactory myFactory =
            new MyContentHandlerFactory();

         connection.setContentHandlerFactory( myFactory );
         connection.connect();
         Object object = connection.getContent();

         if( object instanceof MyObject ) {
            MyObject myObject = ( MyObject )object;
            System.out.println( myObject );
         }
      } catch( Exception e ) {
      }
   }
}
```

The first step is to create a **URL** object and establish a connection to that **URL**.

Make the Connection

You first need a **URL**. They've been introduced already. And hopefully you consider ports your friends, too, so you should have no problem with this code line:

```
URL url = new URL( "...", 43 );
```

Note that this does nothing more than define an instance variable. There is no Internet activity going on yet. You have to take the **URL** and create another instance variable of class **URLConnection**, as shown in the code line below.

```
URLConnection connection = new URLConnection( url );
```

You are yet one step away from actually making a connection. You still have to explicitly connect, as shown in the code snippet below:

```
try {
 connection .connect();
} catch( IOException e ) {
 // connect failed
}
```

Even the best-laid plans can fail, and the same is true of any attempt to connect. Even though the **URL** is correct and you are attempting to connect to a legitimate port, the connection might fail: Perhaps that server is temporarily down. There are numerous potential causes. The bottom line is that you must try to connect and be prepared for an **IOException** that might get thrown your way in the event of failure.

ContentHandlers Off the Assembly Line

Well, **ContentHandler**s are strictly the product of **ContentHandlerFactories**. Other Factories can produce anything imaginable in the intangible software realm.

A **Factory** is an abstract design pattern. Its implementation is disarmingly simple so you're probably wondering about the fancy name. The fact is that one deficiency of software development has been the lack of consistent patterns of design and accompanying consistent nomenclature. It was difficult to talk about designs without a whiteboard handy and a willingness to fire off code examples to demonstrate where verbal explanations failed. I hope that you read Chapter 6 for an introduction to O-O programming.

A **Factory** object takes a parameter that is used to determine an appropriate class instance to create and return. The **Factory** can return instance variables of differing classes, since its return value is a base class of the derived classes the **Factory** actually produces. Here's a simple example in Listing 21.8.

Listing 21.8   A Factory Pattern

```
class MyDataClass {
 // ...
}
class MyStringClass extends MyDataClass {
 // ...
}

class MyNumberClass extends MyDataClass {
 // ...
}
class MyFactory {
 MyFactory() {
 }

 MyDataClass getClass( String type ) {
  MyDataClass myClass = null;

  if( type.equals( "String" ) ) {
   myClass = new MyStringClass();
  } else if( type.equals( "Number" ) ) {
   myClass = new MyNumberClass();
  }

  return myClass;
 }
}
```

The interface of the class MyDataClass might be all that you need to use. By calling any method of MyDataClass that is overloaded by MyStringClass or MyNumberClass—and to be useful they most certainly will be—you are actually calling the methods of the derived classes.

The power of polymorphism in Java means that you can also use **instanceof** to determine the real class of the instance variable that is returned. After the appropriate, legal cast, you have access to any methods that are only available to the derived class.

Note that in the example above, even before the attempt to connect to the **URL** was made, a **ContentHandlerFactory** was created and assigned to the **URLConnection** with the method **setContentHandlerFactory**, as shown in the code snippet below:

```
MyContentHandlerFactory myFactory =
      new MyContentHandlerFactory();

connection.setContentHandlerFactory( myFactory );
```

This is the standard way of creating your own **ContentHandlerFactory**.

Getting a Handle on Handlers

Here, I define a simple **Factory** that only looks out for "text/plain" and creates a very simple **ContentHandler** for just that type of data content. See Listing 21.9.

Listing 21.9   A New ContentHandler

```
class MyHandler extends ContentHandler {
  public Object getContent( URLConnection urlConnection ) {
    String   string;
    MyObject  mailObject = null;
    URL    url  = urlConnection.getURL();
    StringBuffer sb   = new StringBuffer();

    try {
      InputStream is = url.openStream();

      int c;
      while(( c = is.read() ) >= 0 ) {
        sb.append( ( char )c );
      }

      myObject = new MyObject( sb.toString() );
    } catch( IOException e ) {
    } catch( Exception e ) {
    }

    return myObject;
  }
}
```

In a real-world handler, where the data received is to be processed in a non-trivial way, the body of this class would contain several more methods that the method **getContent** would use to assemble the new object. That's left as an exercise.

What ContentHandler Recognizes

Remember that the filename extension is often used to determine the type of the content contained in a data file. In Java, it's up to the **ContentHandler** to do the inspection. Table 21.4 lists the extensions that Java's **ContentHandler** recognizes.

Table 21.4   *Java-Recognized Content Types/Subtypes*

Filename Extension	Content Type/Subtype
<blank>	"content/unknown"
.uu	"program/octet-stream"
.saveme	"program/octet-stream"
.dump	"program/octet-stream"
.hqx	"program/octet-stream"
.arc	"program/octet-stream"
.o	"program/octet-stream"
.a	"program/octet-stream"
.bin	"program/octet-stream"
.exe	"program/octet-stream"
.z	"program/octet-stream"
.gz	"program/octet-stream"
.oda	"program/oda"
.pdf	"program/pdf"
.eps	"program/postscript"
.ai	"program/postscript"
.ps	"program/postscript"
.rtf	"program/rtf"
.dvi	"program/x-dvi"
.hdf	"program/x-hdf"
.latex	"program/x-latex"
.cdf	"program/x-netcdf"
.nc	"program/x-netcdf"
.tex	"program/x-tex"
.texinfo	"program/x-texinfo"
.texi	"program/x-texinfo"
.t	"program/x-troff"
.tr	"program/x-troff"
.roff	"program/x-troff"
.man	"program/x-troff-man"
.me	"program/x-troff-me"
.ms	"program/x-troff-ms"
.src	"program/x-wais-source"

Continued

Table 21.4 *Java-Recognized Content Types/Subtypes (Continued)*

Filename Extension	Content Type/Subtype
.wsrc	"program/x-wais-source"
.zip	"program/zip"
.bcpio	"program/x-bcpio"
.cpio	"program/x-cpio"
.gtar	"program/x-gtar"
.shar	"program/x-shar"
.sh	"program/x-shar"
.sv4cpio	"program/x-sv4cpio"
.sv4crc	"program/x-sv4crc"
.tar	"program/x-tar"
.ustar	"program/x-ustar"
.snd	"audio/basic"
.au	"audio/basic"
.aifc	"audio/x-aiff"
.aif	"audio/x-aiff"
.aiff	"audio/x-aiff"
.wav	"audio/x-wav"
.gif	"image/gif"
.ief	"image/ief"
.jfif	"image/jpeg"
.jfif.tbnl	"image/jpeg"
.jpe	"image/jpeg"
.jpg	"image/jpeg"
.jpeg	"image/jpeg"
.tif	"image/tiff"
.tiff	"image/tiff"
.ras	"image/x-cmu-rast"
.pnm	"image/x-portable-anymap"
.pbm	"image/x-portable-bitmap"
.pgm	"image/x-portable-graymap"
.ppm	"image/x-portable-pixmap"
.rgb	"image/rgb"
.xbm	"image/xbitmap"

Continued

Table 21.4   *Java-Recognized Content Types/Subtypes (Continued)*

Filename Extension	Content Type/Subtype
.xpm	"image/xpixmap"
.xwd	"image/xwindowdump"
.htm	"text/html"
.html	"text/html"
.text	"text/plain"
.c	"text/plain"
.cc	"text/plain"
.c++	"text/plain"
.h	"text/plain"
.pl	"text/plain"
.txt	"text/plain"
.java	"text/plain"
.rtx	"appication/rtf"
.tsv	"text/tab-separated-values"
.etx	"text/x-setext"
.mpg	"video/mpeg"
.mpe	"video/mpeg"
.mpeg	"video/mpeg"
.mov	"video/quicktime"
.qt	"video/quicktime"
.avi	"video/x-troff-msvideo"
.movie	"video/x-sgi-movie"
.mv	"video/x-sgi-movie"
.mime	"video/rfc822"

Any extension not listed will not be recognized, and a call to the **URLConnection** class method **getContentType** will return a null. Listings 21.10 and 21.11 contain code for checking content type.

Listing 21.10   Checking Content Type

```
URLConnection connection = new URLConnection( new URL( "..." ));
String type;
if( (type = connection.getContentType) != null ) {
// recognized type
} else {
```

```
// unrecognized type
}
```

Being ready to handle a string containing the standard content type/sub-type is especially important for the **ContentHandlerFactory**. Here's the method createContentHandler defined for the class MyContentHandler that you've already seen:

Listing 21.11 Check for "text/plain"

```
public ContentHandler createContentHandler( String type ) {
  ContentHandler handler = null;
  if( type.equals( "text/plain" )) {
   handler = new MyHandler();
  }
  return handler;
}
```

This being by necessity a simple example, myContentHandler just handles the type/subtype "text/plain." The file that I accessed over the Internet had an extension ".txt" so the **URLConnection** was able to make positive determination. Note that it is certainly possible to trick the **URLConnection**, because there is nothing preventing you from accidentally or maliciously misnaming data files. You might even want to write code that verifies the contents, if that is possible with the format of data in question.

Objects of Your Own Design

The ultimate goal of using a **ContentHandler** is to be able to read data over the Internet and convert that data into an appropriate object. That object will be an instance variable of a Java class that you have defined. Note that it is possible to load Java classes over the Internet, too.

Once you have the instance variable, you will then use that object's methods to access the data. You could display an image, play a sound, or feed the data to some other program. The potential is really wide open.

Granted, the object that I created in the above example was really basic, but it demonstrated the essentials. Listing 21.12 contains the simple object that gets created.

Listing 21.12 My Simple Object

```
class MyObject {
 String string;
```

```
MyObject( String string ) {
 this.string = string;
}

public String toString() {
 return new String( "MyObject:\n" + string );
 }
}
```

Data was passed to a new instance in the form of a Java **String** as its one-and-only parameter. The only other method is the **toString** method overloaded from class **Object** that lets me later pass the instance of this class to an output function, such as **System.out.println**.

A TASTE OF CLIENT-SERVER

Guess what? *You've already been soaking in it, as Madge would say.* By using **Socket**s, you are effectively implementing Client-Server. And not unless you have been living on Mars for the past five years could you have escaped hearing at least *something* about Client-Server.

If you've heard of Client-Server but the significance is not clear, it might help to contrast it with what preceded it. It wasn't long ago when all processing was centralized. In many cases, this meant a mainframe or some other large computer. All programs and data resided on that computer. A user accessed the programs via a dumb terminal. The key aspect was that there was really no interaction between computers in the client-server sense. The terminal, even if it was a workstation operating essentially like a terminal, was just a window to the program on the main computer.

One of the drawbacks often cited about this approach was that it was limited by the power of the central computer. Also, as users began to be tempted with more sophisticated graphical interfaces, the demand for network bandwidth skyrocketed.

Fortunately, about the same time, along came capable workstations that possessed significant processing power themselves. The solution was to off-load some of the processing onto the workstations. The program that would be run on the workstation was dubbed the Client. The original main computer would still be part of the process. It would provide services to the Client and it was therefore dubbed the Server. The data that would have to traverse the network could then be reduced by establishing a protocol that the Client and Server could use to communicate. This abstracted the relationship. No longer were individual pixel instructions needed to repaint screens being sent over

the network, for instance. The communication could be conducted at a higher level and based on the assumptions implicit in the protocol. The Client essentially included most of the functionality of any program, but relied on the server for the data.

You can easily implement Client-Server in Java, as you've briefly seen. I am going to take it a step further by introducing a simple program. You can take it from there.

The Relationship

The relationship between a client and a server is defined by a protocol. It defines what is called the "handshaking" that will take place between the two computers. The **WhoIs** protocol is a simple Client-Server implementation, though there was minimal interaction.

Most other protocols involve a lot more details regarding the interaction. Instructions are passed from one computer to the other and the listening computer responds to the message and returns a message that contains information requested. It is like choreography, though it certainly does not dictate exactly how every session will be conducted. It just specifies messages that can be passed and valid replies. At each stage, there are usually several options for replies. Each computer must be prepared to handle all potential responses to be considered a faithful implementor of the protocol.

Here's a typical, generic client-server interaction:

1. The server waits listening on the appropriate port.
2. A client sends a request that is received by the server.
3. The request is processed by the server and the result is sent back to the client.
4. Repeat until the client is satisfied.

There are always going to be a lot of specific details that make one protocol different from another, but this simple interaction will be common.

I'm Hearing Voices

One of the practical problems related to programming client-server programs with Java is the fact that you probably only have one computer. You might find it enlightening to note that you can *talk to yourself* using Java. Effectively, it is the same as if you were communicating over the Internet. The server can be coded identically. The only change needed is to the client-side program.

The client will connect to its own IP address. Both the server and the client will be at the same address. It's called *loopback,* because the communication will connect back to your computer without going out onto the Internet. It's an easy way to test even your most elaborate networking programs. The following client-server example shows how easy it is to have both client and server programs running on the same computer.

Then, all that's required to go from your program "talking to itself" to talking to some other computers over the Internet is to change the **InetAddress** to which you connect its **Socket**.

Getting It Humming...

All that really happens in *ClientServerTest's* constructor is that both server and client are instantiated and, because they implement **Runnable**, they are each passed into a new **Thread** object. That object is immediately started without looking back. That's all there is to it. Start the thread and off it goes. The complete listing of a very simple client-server program is found in Listing 21.13.

Listing 21.13   A Client-Server Example

```
import java.io.*;
import java.net.*;

public class ClientServerTest {
 ClientServerTest() {
  new Thread( new MyServer() ).start();
  new Thread( new MyClient() ).start();
 }

 public static void main( String args[] ) {
  new ClientServerTest();
 }
}

class MyServer implements Runnable {
  public void run() {
    ServerSocket server  = null;
    Socket  serverSocket = null;
    OutputStream os   = null;

    try {
      server = new ServerSocket( 77, 16 );
      serverSocket = server.accept();
      System.out.println( "Connect on the Server side" );
      os = serverSocket.getOutputStream();
      os.write( 42 );
    } catch( IOException e ) {
```

```
      }
    }
  }
}

class MyClient implements Runnable {
  public void run() {
    Socket clientSocket = null;
    InputStream is      = null;

    try {
      clientSocket =
        new Socket( InetAddress.getLocalHost(), 77 );
      is = clientSocket.getInputStream();
      System.out.println( "client reads: " + is.read() );
    } catch( UnknownHostException e ) {
    } catch( IOException e ) {
    }
  }
}
```

When we run this program, it's easy to see that the int *42* was successfully transmitted from the *server* to the *client* object once the connection was established, as shown in the snippet below. You could extend this example for two-way communication without difficulty.

```
cmd> java ClientServerTest
Connect on the server side
client reads: 42
```

Are You Being Served?

Both the server and the client are very short, as you can see. Both are implemented as **Runnable**. That is especially important here since I want the client and server to both be running simultaneously on my computer. The only way to do that is to use Java **Threads**. Chapter 20, which you might have just read, was devoted exclusively to threads. Hopefully, at least, you understand the motivation for including that **implement**s extension.

The server establishes a ServerSocket on port 77.port77 was just picked out of the air, but try to choose numbers that don't interfere with standard ports already in common use. The **accept** method of **ServerSocket** is called. It blocks. Blocking occurs when execution is suspended typically waiting for some I/O to occur. In this case, the server is waiting for some client to come along and connect. Listing 21.14 contains the server code.

Listing 21.14   SimpleServer.java

```
class MyServer implements Runnable {
  public void run() {
    ServerSocket server  = null;
    Socket  serverSocket = null;
    OutputStream os   = null;

    try {
      server = new ServerSocket( 77, 16 );
      serverSocket = server.accept();
      System.out.println( "Connect on the Server side!" );
      os = serverSocket.getOutputStream();
      os.write( 42 );
    } catch( IOException e ) {
    }
  }
}
```

Naturally, the server doesn't wait. Eventually, **accept** will unblock and a message will be printed to the screen indicating success.

Remember that **accept** returns a **Socket** object. The server uses that object to get its associated output stream with **getOutputStream**. Finally, the server sends the number 42 out onto the output stream. You know why I chose 42, don't you? If you've ever read Douglas Adam's *Life, The Universe and Everything* you'll know what I mean. The main character in the book, after many misadventures, discovers that *42* is the ultimate answer to life's greatest questions.

The Client

The client is also an implementation of a **Runnable**. Listing 21.15 contains the code for the simple client. It connects to the server. That unblocks the server's **accept** call and allows the server to print the message that confirms connection.

Listing 21.15   SimpleClient.java

```
class MyClient implements Runnable {
  public void run() {
    Socket clientSocket = null;
    InputStream is    = null;

    try {
      clientSocket =
        new Socket( InetAddress.getLocalHost(), 77 );
```

```
      is = clientSocket.getInputStream();
      System.out.println( "client reads: " + is.read() );
   } catch( UnknownHostException e ) {
   } catch( IOException e ) {
   }
 }
}
```

The line that I mentioned that would need to be changed to stop talking to yourself would be the line in which the client's **Socket** is instantiated. In order to talk back to the server that is also running on the same computer, I used the technique for retrieving your own Internet address that I introduced earlier in the chapter. Again, you must match port numbers, so the 77 appears again.

All the client does is pick up the input stream from the **Socket** once connection is established and read one byte of whatever comes down the line. It gets set up just in time to receive the answer to life, the universe and everything: 42. It's so proud of this discovery that it displays the information on the screen.

You can take it from here. You know as much as you'll need to do a lot of interesting network programming with just what was covered here. The next section introduces some issues that you should be aware of as you begin your explorations.

Issues to Anticipate

While engaging, this example is very simple and certainly doesn't implement any real protocol. As I said, once you see the framework, the details are just a matter of coding. There are some additional techniques that I should introduce, because you'll need a little more sophistication with the more powerful and robust client-server programs you might write with Java.

I included a brief, non-technical example of an exchange between a client and a server of Internet services near the beginning of this chapter. Remember that I said I had omitted the exact syntax of the messages passed. If you take the time to study a protocol such as **SMTP**, you'll find that there are special tags that prefix most messages and help the receiver to determine how to respond. For instance, when the sender in the example introduced itself to the receiver, it would have actually sent something like that shown in the code line below:

```
HELO abc-corp.com
```

The receiving system then responds in turn with something like the code line shown below:

```
250 mail.mega-u.edu
```

The *250* is actually a reply code number. There are numerous reply codes that can be returned in response to different messages, subject to such things as availability or success of services.

In order to handle a real exchange such as this, you'll need to write Java code that uses the classes **String** and probably **StringTokenizer**, rather than just integers and bytes as I did in the example. Brush up on both in Chapter 7. Once you've retrieved the data from the socket and assembled it into a string, you might use something like the code snippet below to check for the **INFO** tag:

```
String line = readSocket();
if( line.indexOf( "HELO" ) == 0 ) {
 // continue
} else {
 // perhaps disconnect the socket since
 // an incorrect message was received
}
```

Perhaps you want to write a server that must be prepared to handle service requests from more that one client at a time. Some of the issues that you will encounter can be solved by using a data structure such as a **Hashtable** to store references to clients.

A strategy that is often adopted to handle multiple clients is to use the published port only for initial communication. The server will tell the client an alternate port to which it should attempt to reconnect. Typically, this port is some distance numerically from the original. The server starts listening on the port. The client disconnects and attempts to connect to that new port.

You will find that threads come in handy when you want to create independent data readers and writers. These can be simple classes that run in their own thread. The reader would just sit and monitor a socket, reading anything that comes in and writing the data into a storage structure and notifying all interested objects of the new arrival. The data writer does just the opposite. Conceptually, this approach is simple and avoids the problem of I/O blocking interfering with the operation of the mainline of your program. Check out the last section for a reference to some excellent development work that has been done with Java and client-server programming in the Netherlands.

Finally, I want to conclude by introducing something that will have a great impact on computing in the not-too-distant future.

THE GLOWING ORB

You might not have noticed it but there is a glow beginning in the east. Much like a new day about to break, it signifies the dawning of the age of *distributed object programming.*

Distributed object programming is about encapsulation on a grand scale: *Have data and methods—will travel.* Maybe you've already heard of agents. They are software entities popularized as the little electronic pixies that scamper across the net and do your banking or buy airline tickets or negotiate the schedule for a meeting. Generally, they are just called objects. They are objects in your computer, so why not just call them objects if they have skipped across the Internet to some other computer? By the way, ORB isn't just an allusion to the sun—it stands for *Object Request Broker.* They're the things that will act in part like the gate-keepers and manage the objects traveling the net. There are several distributed object architectures—one you might have heard of is called CORBA (Common Object Request Broker Architecture). OpenDoc and Microsoft's OLE can be considered others.

Sun Microsystems has this motto that has often been the source of confusion on the part of customers and competitors: *The Network is the Computer.* That is coming true. Java is one step in that direction. The time is coming when it will be unimaginable not to have your computer continuously connected to some network like the Internet. You will never give a thought to how or where things get done on your computer. If you were to look, you'd find that the lines around everyone's computer had blurred. That will really be the age of the network.

It's beyond the scope of this chapter to discuss the details of this emerging area. Just note that Java is well-positioned to enable you to program for distributed objects when the time comes—and it will.

LET'S REVIEW

You've tackled a lot of subject matter in this chapter. Granted, a lot of descriptions were brief and the implications of some of the material might just now be starting to sink in. Programming for the Internet might be relatively easy with Java, but there are details inherent in the operation that you must be prepared to handle. Java helps you in this regard. Just ask anyone who has ever tried doing what we did here with some other programming language. You should feel confident that you can sit down with one of the protocol RFCs not implemented and bang out some Java code that does the trick.

IF YOU LIKE THIS, YOU'LL LOVE THESE

These three Web sites will show you what some pioneering developers have done with Java's networking capabilities.

VPRO's Java Pages

Some ambitious Java programmers at the Dutch National Public Radio have written some excellent client-server programs that support Internet chat and could serve as the base for an Internet-based game-playing application. Check out: http://www.vpro.nl/htbin/scan/www/object/VPRO/JAVA/BETA/OBJECT.

JIDL

JIDL is a CORBA interface definition compiler with Java as the target language. Unless you know a bit about distributed objects this might not mean much to you but, the page has links to information resources you'll need to learn more. JIDL will allow Java applets to manipulate CORBA objects remotely. It's the future, now! Find all the goods at: http://herzberg.ca.sandia.gov/jidl.

Mapplet

Andrew L. Wick has developed a networked applet called Mapplet that illustrates beautifully a really innovative use of Java. He has generously included the source, so you can find out how it all works! Find it at: http://maps.purple.org/map/index.html.

INTERFACING WITH C

CHAPTER 22

Neil Bartlett

Java is a friendly programming language. We look at how it talks to its fellow programming language, C.

The hallmark of a good language is the ability to coexist peacefully with other languages. One of the great successes of C++ was that it seamlessly absorbed C programming. Moving to C++ is a path of least resistance for C programmers.

Java, of course, is a departure from C and C++, but the designers felt—and rightly so—that it was important to allow programmers to bind in C programs. For instance, Java allows legacy (previously written and tested) code to be used. This can jump-start programmers. They can keep library packages they have developed from going stale.

This chapter is aimed very squarely at C programmers. I've put a nightclub bouncer on the door. He is standing at the door looking mean—don't mess with him. He is not checking for jeans—he's checking for suits. One sign of a non-tekkie in a suit and you're barred. He wants to see you wearing your frayed jeans and your hang-dog, "I'm a C programmer" look. Anyone else, and he knows

you will be in for a fight if he lets you in. So do yourself a favor, don't try to get in without your jeans.

YOU'RE IN

So you passed the entry criteria and got past the bouncer at the door. Let's look at how we can make Java and C coexist peacefully.

If you think about what it means to join two languages such as Java and C, you will appreciate that you need to be able to do four things: Call C from Java, pass values from Java to C, pass values from C to Java, and finally call Java from C. If we can do all this, we can write a program in any combination of Java and C.

The Java interface mechanism lets us do all these things. The first thing we need though is to do the part that links Java and C. The other parts will be done from the C side (no pun intended). We will see how these other parts are accomplished later in the chapter. For now, we are going to concentrate on calling a C function from a Java method. The key to doing this is a thing called a *native method.*

What Is a Native Method?

A native method is a Java method without any implementation code. It is placed in a class like any other method, but is used solely as a placeholder to tell the Java interpreter to go and look for a C function instead of some Java code. When the Java interpreter encounters a call to a native method, it calls a corresponding C function.

This is a very simple mechanism to describe, but like a lot of simple things, it is backed up by some more complicated stuff. Let's look at how we can program native methods.

PROGRAMMING BASICS

For this first section, we are going to take a tutorial example. This is the last chapter in the book, but we will be sticking with our "Hello World" tutorial example. We will connect a native method called **printHelloWorld** from a class called **HelloWorld** with a C function that just performs a simple **printf**,

```
printf("Hello World\n");
```

If you ever take a trip through Sun's online documentation, you will notice that this example bears a remarkable similarity to the native method tutorial found there. This is not an attempt to rip off some one else's tutorial: Rather, it is a testimony to the uniformity of writing Java native methods. There really is only one way to do it. Once you have decided to connect a native method that calls a C **printf**("Hello World\n") statement, you have, apart from the names, pretty well pre-ordained the exact lines of code that you will need.

The Six Steps to Heaven

Let's look at how you can take the two pieces—the Java native method and the C implementation function—and join them.

The idea is to create a library that contains the C function. When the Java interpreter encounters a call to a native method, it will search for a C function with a name that corresponds to the native method. It will search through its list of known libraries, checking each library to see if it contains the C function.

The process of creating the library ensures that the C function is named correctly so that the Java runtime can find it. The process uses some bridge code to do this. The bridge code creates a function entry in the library that can be searched for by the runtime. The function entry will then call our C function to do the work. The six steps are:

1. Write the Java native method.
2. Compile the Java native method.
3. Create the bridge .h file.
4. Create the bridge .c stubs file.
5. Implement the C function.
6. Create a library.

Once you have completed these six steps, you will have a Java native method that you can use in the same way as any other Java method. The Java code that calls the native method will not have to know that the method is native: that is transparent to the Java code.

Let's look at each of the steps in more detail. A number of these steps are platform dependent. I will try where possible to give examples and gotchas for Windows 95/NT and Solaris versions of Java. I have also tried to make it clear what the step is trying to do, so that you might be able to work out what to do on other platforms. If you do want to use native methods on other platforms, you will probably need to contact the vendor of the platform port.

The source code for this section can be found in the directory \SOURCE\CHAP22\BASIC.

Step 1: Write the Java Native Method

Listing 22.1 shows the Java native method we will be using for our example. The native method is called **printHelloWorld**. It takes no parameters and it returns no values. It is defined in a class called **HelloWorld**.

Listing 22.1   HelloWorld.java

```
class HelloWorld {
    public native void printHelloWorld();

    static {
        System.loadLibrary("helloworld");
    }
}
```

Native methods are defined by using the **native** keyword in the definition of the method. A native method does not provide any code to implement the method. It is rather like an abstract method: The native method only defines the signature of the method. For example, if we were going to write the code in Java, we might enter something like the code snippet below:

```
abstract class HelloWorld {
    public abstract void printHelloWorld();
}
```

Then, we would have left the writing of the body of the method to some other class that is derived from the **HelloWorld** class.

Although the concept is similar, the native methods are not implemented by a derived class. The bridging between the native method and the C implementation function is done by the Java runtime. The runtime will hunt for the native method in all of the libraries that have been loaded. Now, look at the code snippet below:

```
    static {
        System.loadLibrary("helloworld");
    }
```

This is where the part of the program in the code snippet comes into play. It does not do the searching, but it ensures that the library that contains the C function has been loaded. The library is forced to load by including the code that loads the library in a static block inside of the class. The library is loaded using the **System.loadLibrary** method. As you can see, I have decided to call the library **helloworld**. We will see more about the name of the library later.

Now, when the Java runtime encounters the native method, it will have the **helloworld** library loaded.

Forcing Code to Run Once

You might not have seen the use of the static block shown in Listing 22.1 before. It is not a technique specific to just native methods. You can use it any time you want to force some code to run once when the class is first referenced. Another example of this type of code can be found in the JDK source code in the file JAVA\LANG\CHARACTER.JAVA.

The **HelloWorld** class shows an example of only one native method being created. A class can have as many native methods defined in it as it needs. The C implementation of these native methods is defined in one library.

Step 2: Compile the Java Native Method

The Java native method and the class that contains it are treated no differently from any other Java code. To compile them, you must use the Java compiler, **javac**. To compile the HelloWorld.java file to the HelloWorld.class file, use the command line below:

```
javac HelloWorld.Java
```

Step 3: Create the Bridge .h File

The bridge code—the code that wraps up our C implementation—is defined in two parts: a header file and a C file. These two parts will then be combined with our C implementation to make the native method library.

Both the .h and the .c files are generated by using the *javah* tool. We have not encountered the javah tool before. It takes a .class file and scans it for definitions of native methods. For each native method definition it finds, it will create the appropriate entries in the .h and .c bridge code files.

The javah tool does not create both the header and the C file at the same time, however. When called without any switches, it will generate an .h bridge file for a .class file. To generate the .h file for our HelloWorld example, we simply type the command line:

```
javah HelloWorld
```

This will cause the javah tool to scan the HelloWorld.class file for native methods. This is why we need to compile the native method class before we create the bridge code. The bridge code generation scans the .class file—not the .java file—for native methods, so we need the .class file available.

Javah names the .h file "HelloWorld." by default. You can override the name by using the **-o** switch of javah.

Let's take a brief look at the .h file produced. I will use the Windows NT version of the .h file to illustrate the principles. Other platforms will have different entries. Listing 22.2 shows the HelloWorld.h file. Note this listing has been edited slightly to fit in the book.

Listing 22.2   HelloWorld.h (Windows NT Version)

```
/* DO NOT EDIT THIS FILE - it is machine generated */
#include <native.h>
/* Header for class HelloWorld */

#ifndef _Included_HelloWorld
#define _Included_HelloWorld

typedef struct ClassHelloWorld {
    char PAD; /* ANSI C requires at least one member */
} ClassHelloWorld;
HandleTo(HelloWorld);

#ifdef __cplusplus
extern "C" {
#endif
__declspec(dllexport) void
    HelloWorld_printHelloWorld(struct HHelloWorld *);
#ifdef __cplusplus
}
#endif
#endif
```

Even if you aren't a Windows NT C programmer, I'm sure you'll recognize the two essential parts: a structure called **ClassHelloWorld** and a function definition called **HelloWorld_printHelloWorld**. These two parts will be common to all HelloWorld.h files produced by javah on all platforms. These two things are the only parts of the .h file you need to understand:

- **ClassHelloWorld** This structure mirrors the instance variables in the **HelloWorld** class from the HelloWorld.java file. The **ClassHelloWorld** structure is used to communicate the values of instance variables between the **HelloWorld** class and our C implementation. The **HelloWorld** class does not contain any instance variables so the **ClassHelloWorld** contains nothing more than a placeholder required by ANSI C.

- **HelloWorld_printHelloWorld** This is the definition of the function where our implementation must reside. If **HelloWorld.class** contained any other native method definitions, these definitions would also have been listed here. We will talk more about this function when we implement the body of the function.

When Javah Won't Work

On some systems, when you try to run javah, you will encounter a rather unfriendly error messsage: "java.lang.object: not found - aborting." Don't panic! You just need to do a little more setup work to get things going. I have found that, especially on NT, javah cannot find the .class files for the system. There are a number of ways to fix this problem. I have found the simplest solution is to create a directory called classes under the java installation directory. Then unzip the classes.zip file—found in the lib directory of the java installation directory—into the classes directory. Like magic, everything will work when you next use javah.

Step 4: Create the Bridge .c File

We will also need to generate a .c bridge file. This is done using the javah tool with the **-stubs** switch. For example, to generate the .c bridge code for the HelloWorld example, we would use the command line shown below:

```
javah -stubs HelloWorld
```

This will take the **HelloWorld.class** file and scan it for any native method definitions. The Windows NT version of the resulting file, HelloWorld.c, is shown in Listing 22.3. Note this listing has been edited slightly to fit in the book. It is not necessary to understand the contents of HelloWorld.c to be able to program native methods. It is shown for interest only.

Listing 22.3   HelloWorld.c (Windows NT Version)

```
/* DO NOT EDIT THIS FILE - it is machine generated */
#include <StubPreamble.h>

/* Stubs for class HelloWorld */
/* SYMBOL: "HelloWorld/printHelloWorld()V",
                    Java_HelloWorld_printHelloWorld_stub */
```

```
__declspec(dllexport) stack_item *
    Java_HelloWorld_printHelloWorld_stub(
                        stack_item *_P_,struct execenv *_EE_) {
  extern void HelloWorld_printHelloWorld(void *);
  (void) HelloWorld_printHelloWorld(_P_[0].p);
  return _P_;
}
```

Step 5: Implement the C Function

Finally, now that we have created all the bridge code, we only have to implement the C function. We already know the name and the signature of the C function from the bridge.h file. Listing 22.4 shows the code for the C function.

Listing 22.4   HelloWorldNative.c

```
#include <StubPreamble.h>
#include "HelloWorld.h"
#include <stdio.h>

void HelloWorld_printHelloWorld(struct HHelloWorld *this) {
    printf("Hello World\n");
    return;
}
```

I have named the file HelloWorldNative.c. The *Native* suffix is a convention I adopted to tell me that the .c file contains the implementation of a native method. You are free to choose any name you want.

The file contains three header files and the function body. Of the header files, two will be familiar to you. The stdio.h file is the header file we need to use **printf**, while HelloWorld.h is the bridge header file we created earlier. The StubPreamble.h header file is a required header file. It is found in the include directory of the Java installation. It contains a lot of useful structures and macros. However, we will not use any of the values here.

The function body is very simple. We call the **printf** to do the work and then return.

The function passes in a pointer called **this**. We will not be using the **this** pointer here. Later, when we look at passing values, we will use it.

Step 6: Create a Library

We now have all the ingredients necessary to make the library: the bridge header file, the bridge C file, and the implementation C file. Now comes the most platform-dependent part of it all. We need to combine the ingredients.

I will just give you the command lines you will need for the various platforms. You will need to take them as given. I am assuming here that the variable JAVAHOME is set to the root directory of your Java installation.

Step 6a: For Windows 95/NT

Set up the following variables from the command line (I prefer to use the control panel System tool to do this permanently). The variables are shown in the snippet below:

```
cmd> set INCLUDE=%JAVAHOME%\include;%INCLUDE%
cmd> set LIB=%JAVAHOME%\lib;%lib%
```

These two lines will set up the INCLUDE path so that the compiler can find the necessary include files like StubPreamble.h. It will also set up the library path to find the javai.lib file.

Use the following command to make the library (it has been split in two to fit the typesetting margins in this book). It will make a library called helloworld.lib.

```
cmd> cl HelloWorld.c HelloWorldNative.c -Fehelloworld.dll -MD
          -LD javai.lib
```

If you encounter problems with the command line, you can try some of the following. If the compile is having problems finding header files, try adding %JAVAHOME%\include\win32 to the include path. If you are having problems with OLE or the MFC, try using the define -DWIN32_LEAN_AND_MEAN on the compile line.

Make Sure You Have the Right Windows Compiler

You will need a Microsoft Visual C++ version 2.X compiler to write native methods. You can also use the Borland C++ 4.3 compiler to produce a 32-bit DLL.

Step 6b: For Solaris

Use the following command line to compile the library (the command line has been split in two to fit the typesetting margins in this book). This will produce a file called libhello.so.

```
cmd> cc -G -I$JAVAHOME/include -I$JAVAHOME/include/solaris
              HelloWorld.c HelloWorldImp.c -o libhello.so
```

Using the Native Method

The native method can be used just like any other method in Java. Listing 22.5 shows a test program called TestHelloWorld.java.

Listing 22.5   TestHelloWorld.java

```
class TestHelloWorld {
    public static void main(String args[]) {
        HelloWorld h = new HelloWorld()
        h.printHelloWorld();
    }
}
```

This file can be compiled using javac and run using java from the console. The words "Hello World" should be output to the console. Figure 22.1 shows the output from doing this.

You should have no problems if you do this from the directory where the code is; however, if you want to create the library in a central place so that you can use it in a number of programs, you will need to ensure that the Java runtime can find it. To do this, make sure that it is either in the Java installation lib directory or it is on the PATH for Windows NT, or the LD_LIBRARY_PATH for Solaris. I am assuming that you know how to set environment variables for your shell under Solaris.

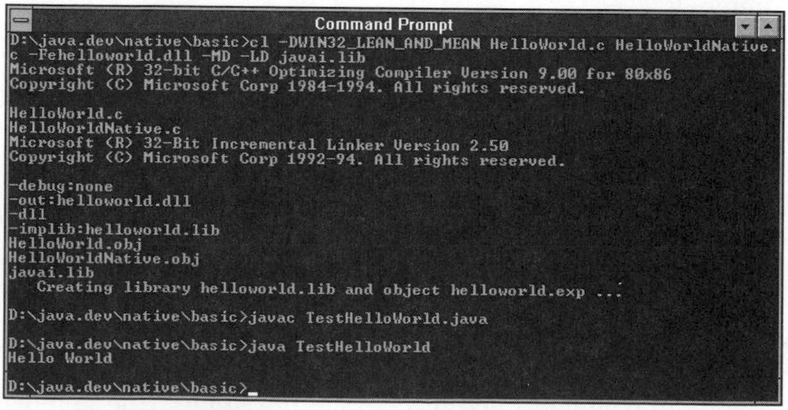

Figure 22.1   Running TestHelloWorld.

Robust Library Loading

If you are planning to distribute code that contains custom-written native methods, it is probably a wise idea to protect the library-loading code. The System.loadLibrary will generate an UnsatisfiedLinkError if it cannot resolve the library name. You can use code such as the following to help users with their installation problems:

```
try {
    System.loadLibrary("mylibrary");
} catch (UnsatisfiedLinkError e) {
    System.err.println("Please ensure that mylibary.lib is on the PATH");
}.
```

Recap

That is all there is to the basics of implementing a native method. Just follow the six steps and you should have perfect native methods every time.

The six steps will not change in anything else we talk about in this chapter. We now move on to look at some more programming techniques. I have refrained from trying to create some large artificial example to show all of the techniques. This is not supposed to be an exercise in C programming. I want to show the techniques pure and simple. Their usage is up to you.

I will be assuming from now on that you are familiar with these six steps. You will have to apply the six steps to each of the examples that follow to get the code to run.

Using Instance Variables

In Step 5, we did rather conveniently pass over the concept of accessing instance variables from the Java class in the C implementation. I wanted to keep things simple. Now, let's move on to a natural extension to the "Hello, World" example. Let's look at a general output native method that can print any string that we give it.

To show how instance variables work, we won't be passing the string to print as a parameter; we will pass it as an instance variable. The C implementation function will need to access the instance variable and print it out. Listing 22.6 shows the file Output.java. It defines a class called **Output**, which contains a native method called **print**. All the code for this section can by found under the directory \SOURCE\CHAP22\OUTPUT.

Listing 22.6   Output.java

```
class Output {
    String outputString;

    Output(String s) {
        outputString = s;
    }

    public native void print();

    static {
        System.loadLibrary("print");
    }
}
```

The **Output** class is used in Listing 22.7. Listing 22.7 shows the file TestOutput.java. It prints out the words "Hi There!" using the **print** method of the **Output** class. The words "Hi There!" are passed in to the constructor to the **Output** object when it is created. The **Output** object will store the string ready for the print method to be called.

Listing 22.7   TestOutput.java

```
class TestOutput {
    public static void main(String args[]) {
        Output o = new Output("Hi There!");
        o.print();
    }
}
```

Now, it should be obvious that our C implementation needs to eventually call **printf** on the "Hi There!" string. The question is: How do we connect the Java String with a C character pointer? Before I explain the answer, let's work through Step 3 of the six steps. So compile Output.java and run javah against Output.class. This will produce the header file shown in Listing 22.8.

Listing 22.8   Output.h

```
/* DO NOT EDIT THIS FILE - it is machine generated */
#include <native.h>
/* Header for class Output */

#ifndef _Included_Output
#define _Included_Output
struct Hjava_lang_String;

typedef struct ClassOutput {
    struct Hjava_lang_String *outputString;
```

```
} ClassOutput;
HandleTo(Output);

#ifdef __cplusplus
extern "C" {
#endif
__declspec(dllexport) void Output_print(struct HOutput *);
#ifdef __cplusplus
}
#endif
#endif
```

Remember that previously I said the structure in the bridge header file is used to mirror the instance variables in the object. If you look at Listing 22.8, you will see that the structure contains a member defined by the code line below:

```
struct Hjava_lang_String *outputString;
```

Notice that it has the same name as the instance variable shown in Listing 22.6. Take a close look at the type. It is called **struct Hjava_lang_String**. This is the native method type for a string. Remember we are in C code here. The **Hjava_lang_String** structure allows us to access Java Strings in C. As you will see in a moment, we can access each of the Java types via a C struct or C data type.

Now, let's take a look at Listing 22.9. Obviously this file must contain the function, **void Output_print(struct HOutput *)**. This was dictated by the bridge header file in Listing 22.8. This is the function that we must implement to print the string.

Listing 22.9   OutputNative.java

```
#include <StubPreamble.h>
#include "Output.h"
#include <stdio.h>

void Output_print(struct HOutput *this) {
    int len = javaStringLength(unhand(this)->outputString);
    char *buffer = malloc(len+1);
    javaString2CString(unhand(this)->outputString,
                       buffer,
                       len);
    buffer[len] = '\0';
    printf(buffer);
    return;
}
```

You can see that I have called the struct **HOutput** parameter, **this**. The **HOutput** parameter contains all the information relating to the Java object that contains the native method that this C function implements. The information is wrapped up in such a way that we can access all the variables from the C code.

The most important thing we will need to do is get at the instance variables for the object. We can do this by using the **unhand** function passing the **this** pointer as an argument. This will return us a pointer to the **ClassOutput** structure shown in the header file in Listing 22.8. Therefore we can get at the **outputString** variable by simply accessing the outputString member of the **ClassOutput** structure. For example, to get at the **outputString** variable, we use the code line below:

```
unhand(this)->outputString
```

The **outputString** variable is not a C character array. It is a thing of type **Hjava_lang_String**. How do we handle this thing? Well, there are a number of functions we can apply to it to perform conversions and other useful manipulations. The functions we can use are all defined in the header file javaString.h, which is found in the include directory of the Java installation directory.

One of the functions we can apply is called **javaString2CString**. This function takes a **Hjava_lang_String** and copies characters into a character array that must be supplied. Therefore if we malloc ourselves a character buffer of a size big enough to hold the outputString, we have a C character array that we can then pass directly to **printf**. The only thing we need to know is the length of the character array to create. We use the function **javaStringlength** to do this.

So now we have a working function. We simply create a C character array from the Java String and pass the character array to **printf** to be printed. Java and C both use the same line termination characters so the **printf** will correctly honor the '\n' passed in by the Java String.

As you will have guessed, **Hjava_lang_String** is one of a number of types that the native system supports. Table 22.1 shows a list of all the main types. The table shows the Java type and the resulting C type that is produced with javah. The definition of most of the C data structures for the types, such as **HArrayOfChar,** can be found in the file oobj.h in the include directory of the Java installation.

Table 22.1   *Java Types and Native Types (Windows NT)*

Java Type	C Native Type
char	unicode
short	short
int	long
long	int64_t
float	float
double	double
String	struct Hjava_lang_String *
boolean	/*boolean*/ long
char[]	HArrayOfChar *
short[]	HArrayOfShort *
int[]	HArrayOfInt *
long[]	HArrayOfLong *
float[]	HArrayOfFloat *
double[]	HArrayOfDouble *
String[]	HArrayOfString *
boolean[]	HArrayOfInt *

If you want to change the values of the instance variables from within the C implementation function, you can simply assign the new value you want to the instance variable accessed via the **this** pointer, which is easy for simple data types such as **int**s—you just equate the value as is done in the code line below:

```
unhand(this)->ianIntValue = 10;
```

For strings, this is slightly more difficult, because we need to construct a new string. We do this using **makeJavaString**. An example is shown in the code line below:

```
unhand(this)->aStringValue= makeJavaString("Hello", strlen("Hello"));
```

You have to do a similar thing for arrays, except in this case you will use the **ArrayAlloc** function.

PASSING PARAMETERS

In the previous example, we chose to pass the string to be printed via an instance variable. Obviously, this is not a very satisfactory way of passing a string for printing. The best way is to pass the string as a parameter to a Java native method and have the C implementation function receive the parameter as an argument. All the code for this section can by found under the directory \SOURCE\CHAP22\PARAMETER.

Listing 22.10   Parameter.java

```
class Parameter {

    public native void print(String s);

    static {
        System.loadLibrary("print");
    }
}
```

Listing 22.10 shows a native method called **print**, which is set up to do just that. When we run javah against the Parameter.class file produced when we run javac on the Parameter.java file, we get the header file shown in Listing 22.11.

Listing 22.11   Parameter.h

```
/* DO NOT EDIT THIS FILE - it is machine generated */
#include <native.h>
/* Header for class Parameter */

#ifndef _Included_Parameter
#define _Included_Parameter

typedef struct ClassParameter {
    char PAD; /* ANSI C requires structures to have a least one member */
} ClassParameter;
HandleTo(Parameter);

#ifdef __cplusplus
extern "C" {
#endif
struct Hjava_lang_String;
__declspec(dllexport) void Parameter_print(struct HParameter *,struct
Hjava_lang_String *);
#ifdef __cplusplus
}
#endif
#endif
```

Careful scrutiny of Parameter.h will show that the parameter to the print method is appearing as a second parameter to the C implementation function. The type of the parameter, predictably enough, is the **Hjava_lang_string** type. In general, the parameters to the Java native method become arguments to the C implementation function with their position offset by one to make way for the **this** pointer.

ParameterNative.c, shown in Listing 22.12, now becomes pretty straight forward. We just take the technique used in the OutputNative.java, Listing 22.9, and apply it to the parameter that is passed in. Naturally we do not need to use the **unhand** function since the parameter is already in the correct format.

Listing 22.12   ParameterNative.c

```
#include <StubPreamble.h>
#include "Parameter.h"
#include <stdio.h>

void Parameter_print(struct HParameter *this, struct Hjava_lang_String *string)
{
    int len = javaStringLength(string);
    char *buffer = malloc(len+1);
    javaString2CString(string,
                        buffer,
                        len);
    buffer[len] = '\0';
    printf(buffer);
    return;
}
```

To finish things up, Listing 22.13 shows a test class that will print out the string "Hello Again!" using the native method we have just developed.

Listing 22.13   TestParameter.java

```
class TestParameter {
    public static void main(String args[]) {
        new Parameter().print("Hello Again!");
    }
}
```

RETURN VALUES

So we can pass stuff in and access instance variables. The only thing we need to be able to do now is return values. Then, we'll be pretty well set to exchange data fully between the Java and the C implementations. All the code for this section can by found under the directory \SOURCE\CHAP22\RETURN.

Listing 22.14   Return.java

```
class Return {
    public native int theAnswer();
    public native String myName();

    static {
        System.loadLibrary("return");
    }
}
```

Listing 22.14 shows Return.java. By way of a change, it implements two native methods: **theAnswer** and **myName**. The method **theAnswer** returns an **int**; **myName** returns a **String**. Again, using the javah program of the Return.class file, we get the header file shown in Listing 22.15.

Listing 22.15   Return.h

```
/* DO NOT EDIT THIS FILE - it is machine generated */
#include <native.h>
/* Header for class Return */

#ifndef _Included_Return
#define _Included_Return

typedef struct ClassReturn {
    char PAD; /* ANSI C requires structures to have a least one member */
} ClassReturn;
HandleTo(Return);

#ifdef __cplusplus
extern "C" {
#endif
__declspec(dllexport) long Return_theAnswer(struct HReturn *);
struct Hjava_lang_String;
__declspec(dllexport) struct Hjava_lang_String *Return_myName(struct HReturn *);
#ifdef __cplusplus
}
#endif
#endif
```

As you can see, the C implementation functions that correspond to the native methods each return the C type that corresponds to the Java type, as indicated in Table 22.1. Therefore, in the C implementation functions, shown in Listing 22.16, all we have to do is return the values we want as the appropriate types.

Listing 22.16   ReturnNative.c

```
#include <StubPreamble.h>
#include "Return.h"
#include <stdio.h>
```

```
long Return_theAnswer(struct HReturn *this) {
    return 42;
}

struct Hjava_lang_String *Return_myName(struct HReturn *this) {
    char* name = "Slartibartfast";
    return makeJavaString(name, strlen(name));
}
```

The only slight wrinkle is that objects such as strings need to have space created. We can simply use the function **makeJavaString** to create a **struct Hjava_lang_String** * for a character array.

Listing 22.17   TestReturn.java

```
class TestReturn {
    public static void main(String args[]) {
        Return r = new Return();
        System.out.println("The Answer is "+ r.theAnswer());
        System.out.println("My name is " + r.myName());
    }
}
```

The **Return** class can be tested using the program TestReturn.java, shown in Listing 22.17. When this program is run, we get the output shown in the snippet below:

```
The Answer is 42
My name is Slatibartfast
```

Calling Java Methods

Once in a while, you will want to call a method in the Java code from within your C code. It is possible to do this. You should probably not make a habit of it. I feel it is more of a technique to get you out of a jam than a technique that should be a mainstay of your design.

Keep Your Code as Java Code

Instead of using a callback from C code to Java code, it often makes more sense to rewrite the code so that the bulk of the work is done inside of the Java code with the native method as just a small service. If you find yourself getting into a situation where your C code is calling your Java code a lot, you probably have a big mess on your hands. As a rule of thumb, try to keep as much work as possible done in Java code and as little work as possible done in C code.

If you take a look in the header file interpreter.h in the Java installation in-clude directory, you will find a number of functions that are prefixed with "execute_java_". These are helper functions that you use to call back into Java code. There are three "execute_java_" functions: **execute_java_constructor**, **execute_java_static_method**, and **execute_java_dynamic_ method**. The names give a clear indication of what type of java method they are designed to call—constructor, static method, and dynamic method, respectively.

All the code for this section can by found under the DIRECTORY \SOURCE\CHAP22\METHOD.

Listing 22.18   Method.java

```
class Method {
    public native int roundTripPrint();
    public void callback() {
        System.out.println("Hiya old buddy");
    }

    static {
        System.loadLibrary("method");
    }
}
```

Take a look at Listing 22.18. It shows a class called **Method**, which has two methods in it. One method is a native method called **roundTripPrint**, the other is a Java method called **callback** that prints the phrase "Hiya old buddy" to standard output. In the style in which we have presented the last few examples, let's take a look at the bridge header file, shown in Listing 22.19.

Listing 22.19   Method.h

```
/* DO NOT EDIT THIS FILE - it is machine generated */
#include <native.h>
/* Header for class Method */

#ifndef _Included_Method
#define _Included_Method

typedef struct ClassMethod {
    char PAD; /* ANSI C requires structures to have a least one member */
} ClassMethod;
HandleTo(Method);

#ifdef __cplusplus
extern "C" {
#endif
__declspec(dllexport) long Method_roundTripPrint(struct HMethod *);
```

```
#ifdef __cplusplus
}
#endif
#endif
```

This header file should be very familiar because it is similar to the header file for our very first HelloWorld example. The names have changed, but the essence is the same. We are calling a C implementation function named **Method_roundTripPrint** with no parameters from a class with no instance variables.

Take a look at Listing 22.20. It is the implementation of the **roundTripPrint** method. It does just one thing: calls the **callback** method from the **Method** object.

Listing 22.20   MethodNative.c

```
#include <StubPreamble.h>
#include "Method.h"
#include <stdio.h>

long Method_roundTripPrint(struct HMethod *this) {
    return execute_java_dynamic_method(0, (HObject*) this, "callback", "()V");
}
```

The **execute_java_dynamic_method** function takes four parameters. The first is a pointer to the environment. We are not concerned with this, so we pass in a null value. The second parameter is the object that the method is contained in. Obviously, we will be using the **this** pointer. The third parameter is the name of the method. The fourth parameter is a little more complicated: It is the signature of the **callback** function. The "()V" signifies that the callback function takes no parameters "()" and that the function returns a void, "V".

Listing 22.21   TestMethod.java

```
class TestMethod {
    public static void main(String args[]) {
        new Method().roundTripPrint();
    }
}
```

When you put all this together, you have a function that calls the method called **callback** on the **Method** object. So if we drive the code with a test class, such as that shown in Listing 22.21, we get the phrase "Hiya old buddy!" output to the command line window.

Each of the **execute_java** methods has the same signature. If you want to get picky, the only difference is the type of method they can call.

The fourth parameter has a wide range of possible values. It describes the calling syntax of the called Java method. Obviously, Java methods have parameters and return codes. The signature string can take care of these.

The signatures use a coded value for each of the types that Java can support. Table 22.2 shows a list of the possible values. The signature combines these values like so: The parameters are shown between the brackets. For instance, "(I)" means a parameter taking an **int**, while the value after the brackets indicates the return type. Therefore "()I" is a function returning an **int**. To pass more than one parameter, you must string together a list of parameters—for instance, "(IF)V" is a method taking two parameters: an **int** and a **float**. Finally an array can be defined using the "[]" after a type.

As an example, Listing 22.22 shows a different version of Method.java.

Listing 22.22   Method.java with Parameters and Return

```
class Method
    public native int roundTripPrint();
    public int retmulticallback(int i, float f) {
        System.out.println("got value "+i+" " +f);
        return 42;
    }

    static {
        System.loadLibrary("method");
    }
}
```

This has a corresponding version of MethodJava.c shown in Listing 22.23.

Listing 22.23   Calling Method with Parameters and Return

```
#include <StubPreamble.h>
#include "Method.h"
#include <stdio.h>

long Method_roundTripPrint(struct HMethod *this) {
    long i = execute_java_dynamic_method(0, (HObject*) this, "retmulticallback",
"(IF)I", 10, 1.0);
    printf("return value = %d\n", i);
    return i;
}
```

Table 22.2 *Signature Values*

Java Datatype	Signature Character
boolean	Z
byte	B
char	C
class	L
double	D
float	F
int	I
long	J
short	S
void	V

The signature of the Java method is given as "(IF)I". This means that it is a method taking an **int** and a **float** as parameters and returning an **int**. The parameters are passed in as extra parameters to the **execute_java_dynamic_method** function. The return value is passed back from the **execute_java_dynamic_method** function.

We have only used the one execute function here, but they each have the same calling signature. The only difference is the type of the method that they call.

SHOULD YOU USE NATIVE METHODS?

The phrase "native method" kind of implies that the method is indigenous to the local computer. This is wholly correct: Native methods can only be run from the local disk—they can't be run over a network. Unlike vanilla Java methods, native methods, must be located on the hard drive of the local machine. It is not possible to locate a native method in a class on a network and have the native method used.

This imposes severe limitations on using native methods. For instance when you hear about native methods the first thing that might jump into your mind is something like: "Great! Now, I can use that superb piece of 3D graphics code to write a cool network app." Stop. Sit down. Native methods aren't like that.

If you want to use native methods, you will need to distribute them yourself. You will have to make sure that each user has a copy of the native method residing on his or her machine. Also you will be responsible for ensuring that the C implementation code works correctly on all platforms that your users have. You can't take advantage of Java's multi-platform nature. You have to do the porting yourself. In short, you have lost all the advantages of Java applets.

Having poured this cold water on native methods, I should point out that they *are* useful if you have decided to use Java as a programming language rather than an applet writer. For instance, it does make an awful lot of sense to start using Java as a multiplatform user interface. The user interface can be written in Java. Existing legacy "service" code written in C can then be bound in to the Java code. Frequently, legacy service code is much more portable than user interface code. This gives you the best of both worlds: retained investment in existing code and portability.

IF YOU LIKE THIS, YOU WILL LOVE THESE

For a very good example of native methods in action, check out JavaMIDI, http://www.users.interport.net/~mash/java.html. It is an implementation of a MIDI interface. It only runs under Windows. Even if you are not a Windows user, it is worth a look to pick up a few tips on programming native methods. Michael St. Hippolyte, the programmer behind JavaMIDI, has kindly provided the source.

LET'S REVIEW

This chapter has been short, sweet, and to the point— the way it should be. Interfacing Java with C is a simple, straightforward process: Just follow the six steps.

The big issue with writing C interface code is whether you should do it. It *is* a useful tool if you have decided to make Java the language you want to program in and you have some C legacy code that you want to use. However, this approach does not work well with applets. If you want an applet to use the code, you will have to distribute your interface code and your C code to each and every user that you want to use the code. This is an especially large hassle when you consider that you will also have to perform a port of your C code to each type of machine that the applet will run on.

Java 'n C++

Alex Leslie

SHORTCUT

Does this Appendix have *shortcut* written all over it or what? Be forewarned that this Appendix is aimed squarely at programmers with significant C++ experience. If you don't qualify, don't be surprised if some of the descriptions seem a bit disjointed and confusing. You'd be better off starting with Chapter 4.

If you're still reading, get ready for a quick dash—helter-skelter—across a lot of territory. I won't go too deeply into any subject—just in and out. I'll only discuss as much as I believe is necessary to make a point.

WHY WE LOVE JAVA SO MUCH

I've been up to my elbows in Java for several months writing this book and still I can sing its praises. Java combines in one package much of what programmers have been searching for in recent years.

C++ programmers will feel immediately at home. The syntax is familiar. Numerous keywords are shared. Java is, in fact, based on C++ in large part. The designers retained what they felt would add value and discarded features of C++ that had proved to be more problematic than useful. There's no question it was a wise move to base Java on such a popular existing language rather than writing it from scratch—especially considering just how many C++ programs are roaming the earth!

There's no better way to extol the virtues of Java than to start with a punchy little list of criteria that I've adapted from Sun's "Java Language Environment White Paper." The list goes beyond mere syntax, and lists features that make programmers more productive, creative, and safe. The list is loaded with a set of keywords that you will encounter whenever you read about Java. I've used each as the basis of a head-to-head comparison of Java and C++. See Table A.1. You'll find that Java stands tall in the saddle.

Table A.1   *Java and C++ Compared*

Criteria	Java	C++
Object-oriented	Trimmed to the essentials	More features but more responsibility too
Speed	Impressive considering it's interpreted—shorter turn-around time during development since no linking necessary	The winner in sheer execution speed
Portability	Compile code portable to Solaris, Windows NT, and Mac.	Only source code is portable and with several caveats
Robustness	At a minor performance cost	Only as robust as the programmer's code
Multithreaded	By nature	Operating system-dependent
Dynamic	Very adaptable—able to load new classes at runtime	Not
Security	Security Manager class built-in	What's security?
Richness	Built-in Toolkit includes graphics, networking, I/O, data structures and more	Depends on your third-party library

Consider your own situation. You're a C++ programmer and you're reading this Java stuff, so you must be convinced there's something real behind all the hype. Java might not change "the economics of software," as some have predicted. Even with a lesser bang, Java is going to be a major player in software development in the short- to medium-term at least. You're wise to investigate. There's certainly a fire that burns in the heart of Java after you've blown away the smoke.

BUILDING PROGRAMS

The compile-link-test three-step process that you have been iterating for years is broken with Java, which has a new rhythm. It goes like this: compile-interpret. That's right, Java is interpreted. Actually, bytecodes are interpreted, but this is part of what makes Java's platform-independence possible.

I guess you can consider the interpretation of the bytecodes as a form of linking, but it's linking "on the fly." In fact, Java goes one step further. You can even pull other new classes into the runtime while a program is running! The source of the other classes is only limited by the connectivity of the Internet. You've never figured out how to do that with C++, have you?

Executable content is a buzzword that captures the exciting promise of Java. It encapsulates the concept of programs that can be packaged and shipped over the Internet, then re-assembled on the other end into programs that can be executed. This feature alone is largely responsible for the frenzy Java has spawned. Java breaks out of the static mold into which the World Wide Web had sunk.

Businesses had been starting to lament that it was difficult to differentiate their Web presence from that of an ambitious and creative individual on the Web. They felt severely limited by the static presentation format. Everyone is excited about Java because you can create a real value-added Web product that is not limited by HTML. You're only limited by your creativity and the content that you have to offer.

All this talk of free-and-easy sharing of programs over the Internet might raise a red flag in your mind if you are security conscious. It certainly does look to be an excellent avenue of exploitation. Unfortunately, Java has been labeled the "Virus Propagation Language" by some who don't fully appreciate the security balance that Java has had to strike. Before you make up your mind, examine the Java Security Manager. It's covered later in this Appendix.

Stepping back to basic issues, we compile our code as shown in the command line below:

```
cmd> javac MyFirstJavaApplet.java
```

The compiler—**javac**—takes the name of your Java code. It's expecting a file name with a .java extension. The compiler does what it does best and produces several .class files. Each .class file contains the bytecodes corresponding to each class that you created in the original .java file. One of the .class files will have the same name as the .java file being compiled.

To run your newly compiled Java program, use the Java interpreter that's just called **java**. It takes, as its parameter, the name of the original .java file less the extension, as shown in the command line below:

```
cmd> java MyFirstJavaApplet
```

DATA TYPES

There are four kinds of data in Java. You're already familiar with two of them from C++: **class** types and **primitive** types. The other two—**interface** types and **array** types—are new to Java. It is important to note that all types but the primitive ones covered immediately below are objects first-class. Yes, that includes **arrays**.

The Usual Suspects

Since Java is platform-independent, the primitive types in Java are standard and have a standard size for any platform your Java code could ever run on. Table A.2 has the specifics.

In Java, a **boolean** is just a boolean. It cannot do double-duty as an integer, as it is often encouraged to do in C++. A **null** cannot masquerade as **false**. You'll have to dispense with some of the exceedingly compact expressions you might now commonly use in C++.

Casting About

Java is above automatic coercion, so don't even try it. You cannot coerce one type into another without an explicit cast. Note that it is legal to cast in certain circumstances where precision will be lost, as shown in the code snippet below:

```
int i = 1234567890;
short s = ( short )i;
```

Table A.2 *Primitive Java Types*

Type	Description
byte	8-bit signed two's-complement integers
short	16-bit signed two's-complement integers
int	32-bit signed two's-complement integers
long	64-bit signed two's-complement integers
float	32-bit IEEE 754 floating-point
double	64-bit IEEE 754 floating-point
char	16-bit Unicode
boolean	true or false

This is legal, but loses precision because **short**s can only hold values up to 32767. The variables in this case will equal 722, somewhat less than 1234567890. Obviously, you're likely only to try this trick with integer values when you expect to fall within the legal range of a **short**.

Without the explicit cast, you'd get a compiler error, as shown in this snippet:

```
Incompatible type for declaration. Explicit cast needed to convert int to short.
```

Don't worry—the Java language does a pretty good job of keeping you on the straight-and-narrow.

First-Class Arrays

Finally, with Java, **array**s join the ranks of first-class types. **Arrays** consist of an indexed collection of objects of some other type. You can instantiate an **array** without defining it, by using either of the techniques shown in the code snippet below:

```
String[] array;

String array[];
```

Assignment to an **array** is easy, too, as shown in the code line below:

```
String[] array = new String[ 10 ];
```

Java **array**s are single-dimensional. However, you can create arrays of **array**s, as shown in the code line below:

```
Point array[][] = new Point[ 5 ][ 5 ];
```

Finally, you can allocate **array** objects at the same time, as shown in the code snippet below:

```
int array[] = { 1, 10, 100, 1000 };
String[] array = { "Header", "Body", "Footer" };
```

Because **array**s have a runtime representation, it is possible to check the length of the array by simply using an array's length field, as shown in the following code:

```
int length = array.length;
```

No longer do you have to keep track yourself. No more iterating through the **array** just to count the elements contained within.

While we're on the subject of **array** sizes: How many times have you accidentally misjudged the size of an **array** and wrote code that waltzes off the end like Wile E. Coyote off a cliff until—too late—you realized your predicament? Negative array indices aren't too friendly, either. Again, the designers of Java have anticipated many of the difficulties that C++ programmers have faced and have provided a simple solution.

Java **array**s automatically perform bounds checking for you. Maybe you've had a taste of this when you've used third-party C++ libraries. In Java, bounds-checking is already built in. The first step that you code that takes off either end of an **array** will cause an **ArrayIndexOutOfBoundsException** to be thrown. Do with it what you will. Either **catch** it and handle the consequences or re-**throw** it and let some other code handle it.

CLASSES

Every bit of code that you write in Java has to be in a **class**. *There are no ifs, ands, or buts.* Java requires a full commitment to object-oriented programming. Even the trivial "Hello, World" program needs to be in its own **class**, as shown in the code snippet below:

```
public class HelloWorld {
    public static void main( String args[] ) {
        System.out.println( "Hello World" );
    }
}
```

Yes, that's right: There are no functions as there are in C++. However, they are easy enough to fake with a small **class**, as shown in the code snippet below:

```
class FunctionClass {
    static void function() {
    }
}
```

You can then call the function with code like that shown in the line below:

```
new FunctionClass().function();
```

Notice that it is possible to instantiate a **class** that has no defined constructor.

One Parameter too Few?

The spry among you might immediately recognize what the parameter to the **main** method in the "Hello, World" program above is all about. The parameter name—**args**—should have given it away.

In Java, the command-line parameters are passed in as an **array** of Java **String**s. Since it's an **array**, you can use **args.length** to find out how many to expect. Up to this point, it's really not much different from **argc** and **argv** in C++.

However, you might be disappointed to find out that the first element in the **array** is the first command-line parameter that's not the name of the application. This is a significant divergence from **argc** and **argv**. Program accordingly.

The general form of a **class** is nearly identical to what you use in C++, as shown in the code snippet below:

```
class MyClass {
    MyClass() {
    }

    void someMethod() {
    }
}
```

Note there is no destructor and no semicolon at the end of the class definition. Listing A.1 introduces some simple Java code that illustrates derivation and class **interface**s. Each is described in more detail following the listing.

Listing A.1   Implements and Extends

```
interface AnInterface {
    void anInterfaceMethod(int i);
}

class Parent {
    private int hiddenVariable;

    private void hiddenMethod() { }

    Parent(int 1) {
        hiddenVariable = 1;
    }

    protected int childAccessibleMethod() {
        return hiddenVariable;
    }
```

```
    public void EvrybodyCanUseMethod() {
    }
}

class Child extends Parent implements AnInterface {

    Child() {
        super(10);
    }

    public void anInterfaceMethod(int i) {
    }

    void aMethod() {
    }
}
```

One Parent Only, Please

I hope you haven't become a multiple-inheritance addict. Just when you thought you had it all figured out in C++, Java comes along and yanks it all away. Only single inheritance is permitted via the **extends** keyword.

Good thing, actually. Multiple inheritance in C++ is unwieldy, so it didn't make the Java cut.

Mixins

The restriction on inheritance might leave you wondering how you are ever going to implement your clever designs. Perhaps you've been using **pure virtual** classes and multiply inheriting them in order to yield the effect of mixing an interface into another class.

With Java, you can do just that, but express it more clearly by implementing an **interface**. A Java **interface** is a type. You won't find anything much defined in the **interface**—just one or more method declarations. The only variables in an **interface** must be defined as **final** and **static**. That means that they can't be changed, and they apply to the class as a whole rather than any particular instance.

My Parent Is Super

From C++, you are already familiar with **this**. Java adds **super**. You use **super** to make explicit calls to the constructor of your superclass. You'd only need to do this if you were passing some parameters. If present in your code, the call to **super** must be the first line in the constructor for the derived class. You might have noticed its use illustrated in Listing A.1.

The MetaClass

Something that is new to C++ programmers is the concept embodied in the Java class called **Class**. Every Java class has such a runtime representation. Despite not knowing the name of a class that gets passed in a reference to one of that class's superclasses, you can still find out by using one of the methods of **Class**, as shown in the code line below:

```
String name = object.getClass().getName();
```

The Java runtime system maintains a list of the names of all the **classes** in the scope of the program. You can identify a class directly by name and then instantiate it to boot, as shown in the code line below. This kind of thing is simply not possible in C++.

```
Object object = Class.forName( "MyClass" ).newInstance();
```

MODIFIERS GALORE

Java introduces several new modifiers to accompany the ones that have been lifted from C++. See Table A.3.

There are a lot of details regarding the modifiers, covering such issues as exactly what they mean in particular cases, or when they are combined with other modifiers. It is beyond the scope of this Appendix to repeat what you can find detailed in the official Java language specification from Sun, or (hint,

---

Table A.3   *Java Modifiers*

abstract

final

native

synchronized

private

protected

public

static

transient

volatile

---

hint) in *The Java Programming Language* (Coriolis Group Books, 1996). I'll just highlight a few of note.

In the Abstract

The keyword **abstract** is used to achieve what you would call an abstract base class in C++. You might recognize it as making a class into what's called a *pure virtual* class. It can be applied to either a method or an entire class. Note that if it is applied to a method, you have to make the class abstract, too.

You cannot directly instantiate an abstract class. You must derive another class from the abstract class.

The Holy Trinity

I guess the Java designers recognized the C++ **private**, **protected**, and **public** modifiers as being access control mechanisms worth retaining.

The new **package** concept in Java introduces a fourth access control method. Without including any of these access control keywords explicitly, all the **classes** within one **package** can see each other's variables. Each class is said to be *friendly* with all the others in the same **package**. This makes sense, assuming you'll always use a **package** to contain related classes that need the privilege.

The **public** keyword can be applied to a **class** as well as a method. If applied to a **class**, it had better be the one-and-only **public class** in the file or else the compiler will complain. Applied to a method or instance variable, **public** makes the entity in question available to all other **classes**. This is roughly the same as in C++.

The keyword **protected** limits visibility to classes that are derived from the **class** in question.

By using the **private** keyword, you really pull down the blinds. The method or variable is only visible inside the **class** in which it is defined.

None of this is news to you since you are already comfortable with the similar concepts in C++.

Let's Synchronize Our Watches

Java includes a new keyword called **synchronized**. I think it probably qualifies as a control structure, because it does regulate access to blocks of code. If you are familiar with multithreaded programming, you would recognize it as a monitor. You use **synchronized** to ensure that only one thread at a time has access to code that cannot tolerate multiple threads. Methods themselves may be defined with the **synchronized** modifier or you can use **synchronized** with blocks of code within methods.

OBJECTS AND POINTERS

Remember how as a kid you hated having to pick up your toys? Still harbor that same temptation to avoid dirty jobs? You'll love Java because it spoils you. You'll only have to write constructors for your classes. Kiss destructors goodbye. The clean-up job is performed by the Java **Garbage Collector**— "GC," for short.

Finally, after all those years, there's no longer any need to clean up after yourself.

Leave Your Pointers at the Door

There are no pointers in Java. Java only allows operations on references.

Pointers—their misuse actually—have been arguably the prime cause of C++ programmers becoming prematurely gray. As you already know, errors with pointers rank as the most difficult to track down.

Pointers are often praised because of the power they place in the hands of the programmer. They're what connect the language to the *bare metal* of the computer. What made it unlikely that pointers would be included in Java was that they also give programmers the power to breach the security of an application's code or data space. Because they are not explicitly limited in scope, pointers can be used to pry into data without permission.

Note that in Java, the absence of pointers means there's no longer a call for "->." You'll only use "." from now on.

The instanceof Operator

The **instanceof** operator is one Java keyword that merits its own section. It's something that you won't be familiar with in C++, but you'll recognize its value immediately.

You use **instanceof** to determine if an object is derived from a particular **class**. This applies no matter how distant the relation. And with **interface**s,

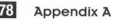

instanceof lets you check to see if an object implements a certain **interface**. This determination also checks to see if any of the object's superclasses ever implemented the **interface**.

The standard form goes like that shown in the code snippet below:

```
if( myObject instanceof SomeClass ) {
    SomeClass someClassInstance = ( SomeClass )myObject;
}
```

This will be used extensively in all your Java code without question. It's obligatory if you want to take advantage of some of the dynamic class-loading capabilities of Java.

Goodbye NULL, Hello null

Though Java has no pointers, you'll still find the **null** concept. However, unlike the **NULL** value from C++, **null** is a first-class concept in Java. The value **null** is assigned to a reference to indicate that there is no reference to anything. Note that, in Java, **null** no longer qualifies as a **false** in an expression, so you'll have to get used to explicitly spelling out what you mean each time. Only a **boolean** can qualify as true or false.

Garbage Man

Soon you'll wonder how you ever lived without curbside pickup. Sure, you should take pride in being able to write clever, bulletproof code that can allocate memory for complex data structures and then, after twisting and spindling the data and copying it from here to there, can disassemble the structures and put the memory away. But it's not always that simple. Programmers aren't infallible—not even you, I'd venture.

That's why it is convenient to offload the entire responsibility for cleanup. Java lets you get away with it. In fact, you don't have a choice. Just start coding and forget about thinking about how this or that variable is going to be put away after no longer being needed. It sounds lazy, and there are some penalties in performance, but at the end of the day, it's a small price to pay for the freedom.

OPERATORS AND EXPRESSIONS

Java's C++ roots really show through when you take a look at its operators. Table A.4 shows the complete list of Java operators.

Table A.4   *Java Operators*

=	>	<	!	~	?	:				
==	<=	>=	!=	&&	||	++	—			
+	-	*	/	&	|	^	%	<<	>>	>>>
+=	-=	*=	/=	&=	|=	^=	%=	<<=	>>=	>>>=

The only new operator in the bunch is **>>>** and its cousin **>>>=**. They are included in Java simply because Java has only signed data types. **>>>** performs an unsigned right shift. I'll let you figure out what **>>>=** does. Three guesses, and the first two don't count.

After all this good news, you're likely going to be disappointed to hear that you cannot overload operators for classes as you did in C++. Get used to slightly more verbose expressions from now on.

CONTROLLING PROGRAM FLOW

You'll be happy to learn that all the old favorites are included in Java.

    if
    switch
    while
    do
    for
    break
    continue

And Java still lets you return values with a **return** keyword.

Exception Handling

There are a couple of new keywords that you'll need to get accustomed to using. Java makes heavy use of **exception**s. Most of the useful methods of the JDK classes you'll use throw some sort of **exception**.

Code that can throw something must be enclosed in a **try** block. The **try** block must be followed by a **catch** clause and block. The **catch** clause just includes a parameter name and type, which is the type of the **exception** that you are prepared to handle. The code that goes in the **catch** block is the code that you deem is up to the job. Finally, you have the **finally** keyword. You sometimes tack a **finally** clause and block onto the end of a series of **try**, **catch**, **catch**, **catches**. See, if the code in the **try** were to throw an **exception** that you handle in one of the **catch** clauses, any code following that **catch** block will not get executed—unless you had the foresight to include a **finally** clause and block on the end. You place into the **finally** block just the stuff that you can't leave in a hurry without getting done. You'll generally find that **finally** will be used to put away complex data structures or make sure that connections or streams are shut down properly.

PACKAGES

All Java source code is found in **package**s. These **package**s have names that indicate a hierarchy. For example, there is a **package** called **java.io.InputStream** and it contains the JDK's **InputStream** class. You can and likely will put your own code into **package**s, too. The **package** name can even include an Internet address. If it does, the rule for naming the **package** states that the name is formed by reversing the order of the components in the name and then tacking on the path to your Java code. What you end up with is a series of components separated by dots. There are no slashes. The whole point is to ensure that package names are unique.

When Java goes hunting for **packages**, which might include classes that you are using but haven't defined in your code, it starts by using each of the paths defined in the **CLASSPATH** environment variable. So, **java.io.InputStream** would cause Java to look for JAVA/IO/INPUTSTREAM.CLASS from each of those root directories defined in **CLASSPATH**.

You create your own package by including the keyword **package** followed by a name you've chosen. That information goes at the beginning of the code. You can omit this, and often you will. In that case, your code is placed in a default package that has no name.

The Import Business

Import replaces the C++ keyword **include**. It's your way of telling Java where to look to find the classes that you use but do not define in your code.

One important effect of importing rather than including is that it avoids the need to constantly relink. As you already know, you can't avoid relinking in C++ if the source code that belongs to one of the included headers is changed. It's a fact of life that you've gotten used to as you've had to struggle with make files and file dependencies.

When a Java program is run, it dynamically imports all the code components it needs. If some have changed since your code was compiled originally, it makes no difference. You'll just end up **importing** newer code. It as simple as that. That new code could even include new methods in classes that you are already using. Everything will work the same. And those components may be sourced from far across the net so it would really be impossible to keep track of code changes if it were any other way.

C++ STUFF THAT GOT DROPPED

Several other "superfluous" features were dropped from C++ during the development of Java. They are as follows:

- Structures and unions: Java classes have rendered C++-style **structure**s and **union**s unnecessary. Classes can be used to the same effect. Remember that in C++, **classe**s and **structure**s were closely related and differed primarily in the default levels of visibility of their data members.
- Global variables: Java introduces you to a whole new way of thinking about programming and that way has no room for global variables. You have to settle with defining variables within classes to achieve the same end. There are no global variables.
- Default values: No default values are allowed in Java methods.
- The pre-processor: Kiss the pre-processor goodbye. You'll just have to learn to live without defines and pragmas. There is no substitute for pragmas, but defines can be faked. The modifier **final** can be used to effectively create a variable that behaves as a define:

```
final int token = 47;
```

- Goto hell: I know nobody will admit it now but, as surely as Java is another name for Borneo, some of you were fond of **goto** and sprinkled it generously in your code. **Goto** has gone away. Good riddance. You still have multilevel **break**s, so dry your tears.

ENVIRONMENT

The Java developers seem to have been so proud of the name they used it as the prefix on the name of every tool. Table A.5 lists the tools and what each is for.

Prior to the introduction of other development tools or environments, these are all you have to work with.

THE JDK TOOLKIT

Unlike C++, Java comes with a standard set of libraries for such things as graphics, networking, data structures, and input/output. It's the kind of stuff that you'd only have with C++ if you were to combine several third-party libraries and hope for the best.

Much of the subject of the rest of this book is a tutorial exploration of these toolkits, so it's inappropriate to go into much detail here. You'll be able to find a chapter that covers the details of any of these toolkits.

Toolkits

All of what you'd call libraries in C++ are included in the JDK—the Java Developer's Toolkit. Toolkit is a new Java word, so you may as well start using it. The Toolkit is threadsafe. If that means anything to you, good—if not, don't worry about it.

Table A.6 lists the Java toolkits and a description of their contents.

Table A.5 *Java Tools*

Tool	What It's For
javac	compiling
java	running the compiled code by interpreting bytecodes
jdb	debugging (so I lied about the java prefix)
javah	generating C-style headers and stub code
javadoc	generating the cool HTML documentation for your own classes
javap	disassembling compiled code and displaying bytecode representation
appletviewer	in lieu of using a Web browser—leaner and relaxed security

Table A.6   *Java Toolkits*

Toolkit	Description
java.applet	Applet-related classes
java.awt	The Java Abstract Windowing Toolkit—all the graphics classes
java.awt.image	A subset of AWT that contains image manipulation classes
java.awt.peer	A subset of AWT that contains classes that bridge to platform-specific graphics entities
java.io	Input/Output classes including streams
java.net	Networking classes
java.lang	The basic Java classes
java.util	The Java data structures and a few others

Data Structures

Reinvent the wheel no longer: Java provides you with a good set of data structures. It doesn't include everything you'd find in a good third-party C++ library, but it's more than sufficient for most uses. And best of all, it is a standard.

Here's the complete list. You'll likely understand what each is by its name:

Vector
Stack
Dictionary
Hashtable
BitSet

Stack is derived from **Vector**, as is **Hashtable** from **Dictionary**. The **BitSet** is just a bitmap data structure. **Vector** is an especially rich class. You'll be able to easily derive new classes such as Queues from it.

Threads

Perhaps you are among the few who are already programming with threads. The good news for you is that Java has threads. Java threads don't offer the extensive API that you might be used to in other multithreading environments.

Your Java programming will likely make heavy use of threads, because a lot of what you are going to be doing is user-interface related. The news for the rest of you who aren't so well acquainted with threads is that it's time to learn something new.

Security

Security is a non-issue with C++ because there was really no thought given to security in the design of C++. Many C++ programmers don't even appreciate the concept. Perhaps one of the things you appreciated about C++ was that it didn't tie your hands. It's a sacrifice you'll have to make with Java.

Security issues in Java are related to two different issues. The first is security of program and data space. That issue is dealt with nicely by stripping Java of pointers.

The second issue was introduced earlier, and it's related to the close relationship Java has with the Internet. Java has a Security Manager class that you can use to regulate the kind of access an untrusted Java program has to your file system and computer resources. Generally, you'll trust your own code, but what you need to be on the lookout for is malicious code from afar.

GO AND TELL THE WORLD

Java's obviously the product of some bright minds who were able to sift through competing language features and produce a language that makes good sense. Java has shed the shortcomings of C++ and has picked up new features that C++ was missing.

And you—as an accomplished C++ programmer—will certainly find it gratifying to be able to write code that cleans up after itself, never fails because of screwed-up pointers, allows you to port your code without much thought—and comes complete with a rich toolkit of handy classes that include multithreading and sophisticated graphics.

Once you try Java, you'll never look back.

Obtaining Java and Java Resources

Neil Bartlett

All the Java code in this book is written to the Java 1.0 release API. If you want to run any of the Java programs and applets that come with this book, you will need to obtain a copy of Java. Java is currently only available via download from the Internet. The good news is that it is *free*. Yes, not many things in life are free, so grab it while you can.

Your first port of call should be to the Java Home Page. This is found at http://java.sun.com. Choose the downloading section, and from there you will find instructions on how to download Java for your particular machine.

To use Java, you will need to be running one of its supported operating systems. Sun and other companies are trying to port Java to as many operating systems as possible. At the time of writing, Sun supplies Java on only the Windows 95, Windows NT, and Solaris operating systems. However, a number of other vendors are working on or have running ports for other operating systems, notably Linux, Apple Macintosh, and Digital Equipment Corp.'s Alpha. For up-to-date information, try http://java.sun.com/Mail/external_lists.html. Currently, Windows 3.1 is not listed as an operating system for running Java.

Not listed by Sun is a very interesting version of Java that is available for the proud possessors of Silicon Graphics workstations running Irix 5.3. Check out http://www.sgi.com/Products/cosmo/cosmo_instructions.html.

INSTALLING JAVA

Once you have downloaded a copy of the Java JDK, you will need to install it. I will not cover the process of installation here. It is too dependent on operating system type and version numbers. You should carefully follow the installation instructions given on the page from which you downloaded your copy of Java.

Once you have Java installed, you might like to verify that you have all that you need. Java comes with a collection of tools, which are typically found in the \BIN directory. You should have the programs java, javac, appletviewer, and javadoc, among others. You should also have a \LIB directory and an \INCLUDE directory. There is also a \DEMO directory where you can play with the demo applets that Sun has supplied.

I suggest that you run some of these demos to check that your installation is correct. If you read the file index.html in the top-level installation directory using a Java-aware browser such as Netscape 2.0, you can click on the "example applets" link to run the applets. Try Bouncing Heads: It is very surreal.

Java also comes with complete source code for the JDK. The source code is sometimes supplied as a separate ZIPed file within the Java installation. You will need to unzip this file. We recommend that you read the source as much as possible. From time to time in the book, we point you to source code for the JDK. It is this source code to which we are referring.

DOCUMENTATION

We do not supply any Java API documentation with this book. The book would have been too bulky and, given the rapid pace of Java releases, we did not want to give incorrect information.

We recommend that you download a copy or create a copy of the Java documentation for yourself. To download a copy, go to the Java Home Page at http://java.sun.com and go to the Documentation section. Download a copy of the API documentation to your own disk. You can view the documentation using a suitable HTML browser such as Netscape. To view the online documentation, start with the file called packages.html. This is shown in Figure B.1. You can then navigate through the API by clicking with the mouse.

Also, if you wish, you can generate your own documentation from the source code provided with the JDK. The javadoc tool will let you do this. Steve shows you how to use javadoc in Chapter 3. Use the javadoc tool on each of the source code .java files and store the HTML files that are produced in a single directory.

JAVA BROWSERS

The premier Java-related browser is Netscape 2.0. You will need this browser if you wish to run any Java applets. Go to http://www.netscape.com to get it.

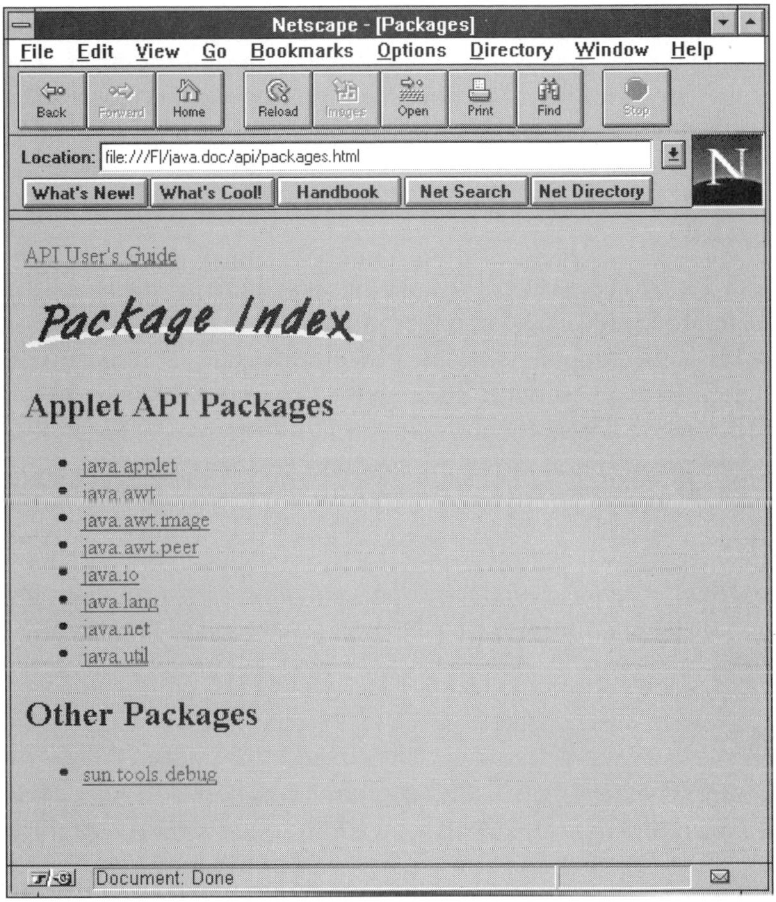

Figure B.1   *Viewing the Java API documentation.*

Another Java-aware browser is HotJava, available from Sun. Meanwhile, Microsoft is rumored to be incorporating Java into its "Internet Explorer" Web browser, so you might check out http://www.microsoft.com.

RESOURCES

There are plenty of resources available for Java programmers. The rest of this chapter is devoted to a tour through the various resources.

The central resource for Java-related information is the Java home page, maintained by Sun at http://java.sun.com. This site contains all the official Java information. Links from this site lead to places for release information, documentation, demos, and so on.

Yahoo, a Web search engine, maintains a Java entry in its subject index. It can be accessed in the Language subsection of the Computer section. If any of the URLs that are given in this Appendix have gone stale, I suggest that you use Yahoo to locate the latest URL.

WEB PAGES

There are a lot of Java-related Web Pages out there. Here is a list of a few developer-related pages. These pages change frequently. To save you from having to keep checking the sites for new information, I suggest that you use a URL change detector service, such as the URLminder. URLminder is available at http://www.netmind.com/URL-minder/URL-minder.html. This service will send you email when the Web page you are interested in changes.

JavaSoft

Obviously, Sun's Web Page at http://java.sun.com is a premier site for Java developers. Here, main resources such as documentation can be found. There are also sample applets, mailing lists, developer resources, and all things Java.

Gamelan

It is pronounced "Gam - uh - lon." Nothing will peg you as a Java newbie faster than pronouncing it "game-lan." It is the social *faux pas* of the Java age.

Gamelan is a superb resource for the Java programmer. It is a collection of applets from Java programmers around the world. Many of the applets come with complete source. The applets are categorized, so you should have no trouble finding the applet you need. You will find Gamelan at http://www.gamelan.com.

Digital Espresso

Digital Espresso is a Web page run by our fellow Toronto JUG member David Forster. It achieved fame under the name J*** Notes. Then, late in 1995, the site was renamed to Digital Espresso.

Digital Espresso is a kind of summary of Java happenings. Its mainstay is a weekly compilation of the newsgroup comp.lang.java, but it is so much more. It is a great place to pick up advice and meet people. There are announcements, features, and a class exchange to name a few of the useful topics it covers. You can find Digital Espresso at http://www.io.org/~mentor/phpl.cgi?J_Notes.html.

JARS

JARS is the Java Application Rating Service—which does exactly as its name implies—rates Java applets. The ratings are determined by a panel of judges drawn from a number of different spheres of expertise. Of course, in the interest of fairness, I must point out that I (Neil) am on the judges' panel. Check out the home page at http://www.surinam.net/java/jars/jars.html. It is a useful way to find applets to give your home page that little extra. The JARS team also maintains a Web page with a lot of Java-related material on it. Find it at http://www.surinam.net/java.

The Java Developer

This is a useful compilation of Java-related material maintained by a company called Digital Focus. It is billed as a public service FAQ (Frequently Asked Questions), but there is a FAQ, some job listings, and plenty of other Java-related stuff. The Java Developer can be found at http://www.digitalfocus.com/digitalfocus/faq/index.html.

MAILING LISTS

Sun provides a number of different Java-related mailing lists. They cover announcements about Java through to hard-core porting issues.

- **java-announce:** This mailing list is used by Sun to communicate releases and changes to Java and the Java toolkit.
- **java-interest:** This is the main programming list. It covers all aspects of programming Java and the JDK. The mailing list has a lot of throughput. I recommend that you do not subscribe to the java-interest mailing list itself, but subscribe instead to java-interest-digest. This reduces the number of mail messages to about one per day.
- **java-porting:** This mailing list covers issues about porting Java to other platforms. It is not intended for the general programmer.
- **hotjava-interest:** This mailing list is devoted to HotJava, where you can find out the latest developments for this very interesting browser.

Probably the easiest way to join these mailing lists is to surf over to the Sun mailing list homepage, http://java.sun.com/mail.html. You can also subscribe directly via email.

To subscribe via email, send the word "subscribe" in the *body* of a message sent to *listname*-request@java.sun.com, where *listname* is the name of the mailing list that you wish to join. For example, to join the java-interest group you would send the word "subscribe" in a message to java-interest-request@java.sun.com. If you are successful, you will receive an automated message telling you that you have been accepted. Save this message: It tells you how to unsubscribe if you ever decide to do so. Once you have subscribed, prepare for an onslaught of messages.

Each of the mailing lists provides a digest version. The digest mailing list will send a new mail message when enough messages have been sent to its corresponding mailing list. This can be very handy for large throughput mailing lists such as java-interest and java-port. These mailing lists produce an annoyingly large number of mail messages per day in the non-digest version. Avoid the hassle and start off with the digest version.

JUG Mailing List

Many Java Users Groups maintain their own mailing lists. These can be useful, because they tend to be slightly more personable than the main Sun-related mailing lists. For instance, the Toronto JUG maintains a mailing list. You can join it at http://www.jug.org.

NEWSGROUPS

The following two newsgroups provide plenty of up-to-date information on Java and Java programming.

comp.lang.java

This is the main newsgroup for Java language programming. It is a very popular newsgroup and covers all issues of Java programming. One of the major problems here is the heavy traffic. Ideally, this group should be broken into more focused newsgroups. However, at this stage in the development of Java, it does make sense to put everybody into one big pool and see what swims out. Personally, though, I find it too much to read daily—unless you have a couple of spare hours on your hands. I prefer to track this newsgroup using the mailing list digests or Digital Espresso. Both of these compress the newsgroup into a digested form. If you want to find specific information from the newsgroup, you can always use Asknpac, discussed in the next section.

Asknpac: A Newsgroup Searcher

The Northeast Parallel Architecture Server at Syracuse University tracks comp.lang.java, among other newsgroups. This is a handy way to get all of the comp.lang.java postings regarding "garbage collection," for example. You will find this very useful resource at http://asknpac.npac.syr.edu/.

USER GROUPS

We, the authors, are members of the Toronto Java Users Group. The Web page for the users group can be found at http://www.jug.org. Java Users Groups are affectionately known as JUGs. There are a number of JUGs located around the world. A useful list can be found at http://www.surinam.net/java/group.htm.

Java-SIG

Most of the important areas of computer technology are covered by a SIG or Special Interest Group. The special interest groups are like "super" user groups. They hold conferences, produce periodicals, maintain and develop standards, and are generally responsible for helping shape the direction of the area of computer technology with which they are associated. Java now has its own SIG: the Java SIG. Take note, though, that this SIG is run by Sun. It is not part of the umbrella SIGs group that traditionally has sponsored SIGs.

You have to join the Java-SIG if you want to be a part of it. It is not free. However, by joining, you can often get discounts on things like books and computer hardware, which significantly, if not completely, offset the cost of membership. For more information, contact office@sug.org or call 617-232-0514.

MAGAZINES AND PERIODICALS

The mainstream computer magazine press is heavily covering Java. Periodicals such as *Visual Developer Magazine, Dr. Dobbs Journal,* and *Byte* now regularly carry Java articles. Here are a few more Java-targeted periodicals.

Java-SIG _README_ Periodical

When you join the Java-SIG, you will receive the Sun User Group newsletter called _README_. It is not devoted entirely to Java, but it will cover Java issues regularly.

Java Report

There is some competition in the SIGs marketplace. The Java Report is a publication from the SIGs group. It is due to be launched in March 1996 at the Java conference in New York. The magazine sounds very interesting, and should prove to be diverse and useful. It is preceded by the high reputation of other SIGs publications, such as *The C++ Report*.

Visual Developer Magazine

Okay, this is a shameless plug for a Coriolis Group publication, *Visual Developer Magazine*. It will carry regular Java articles. You can order the magazine online from http://www.coriolis.com. If you do so, you'll also get some freebie issues. Now, *there's* a deal!

THIRD-PARTY VENDORS AND TOOLS

The market for Java-related tools is booming. Vendors such as Symantec and Borland have announced support for Java:

- **Borland:** Borland has set up JavaWorld, an electronic community for developers. It has a list-server and some general information on how Borland is supporting Java. Check it out at http://www.borland.com/Product/java/java.html.
- **Symantec:** Symantec has launched Espresso. It has been announced as the first Windows 95/NT third-party tool. At present, Espresso is an add-in to the Symantec C++ development environment. The add-in supports full graphical development and project management. You can get Espresso from Symantec's Java Central at http://www.symantec.com/lit/dev/javaindex.html.
- **Silicon Graphics:** Back in December 1995, Silicon Graphics announced its intention to catch the Java wave. It has a development system called "Cosmo," which is integrated with Java. Take a look at http://www.sgi.com/Products/cosmo/index.html for more information.

TRAINING

There are plenty of Java training centers springing up. Here are two that might interest you:

- **Sun Courses:** Sun runs courses in a variety of locations. Surf over to Sun's Sales and Service Web page for more information at http://www.Sun.COM/sunservice/suned/.
- **The NetExcel Java Training:** Yes, we run a Java training center ourselves. For more information, you can contact me at neilb@the-wire.com or go to our new Web page, which should be set up by the time you read this at http://www.netexcel.com.

The JDK Packages

Neil Bartlett

The Java Development Kit is composed of eight java packages. Each package contains classes and interfaces. We have grouped these as interfaces, abstract classes, and non-abstract classes. We have also provided diagrams of the more complex class hierarchies.

java.applet

This package holds all the applet information.

Interfaces	Description
AppletContext	Accesses a browser's environment
AppletStub	Accesses a non-browser's environment, for example, appletviewer
AudioClip	Provides audio capability

Class	Description
Applet	Base class for Applets

java.awt

This package holds all the windowing and graphics classes.

Interface	Description
LayoutManager	Interface for all layout managers
MenuContainer	Interface for all menu containers

Abstract Class	Description
Component	Base class for all UI components
Container	Base class for UI containers
FontMetrics	Accesses font information
Graphics	Provides graphics routines

Class	Description
Image	Represents an image
MenuComponent	Base class for all menu components
Toolkit	Represents the operating system
AWTError	An AWT error
AWTException	An AWT exception
BorderLayout	Layout components according to a compass paradigm
Button	A labeled button component
Canvas	A drawing area
CardLayout	A stack of cards layout metaphor
Checkbox	A checkbox component
CheckboxGroup	Group that turns checkboxes into radio buttons
CheckboxMenuItem	A two-state menu entry
Choice	A drop-down combo box, or pop-up list, component
Color	Encapsulates RGB colors
Dialog	Base class for all Dialogs
Dimension	Encapsulates width and height

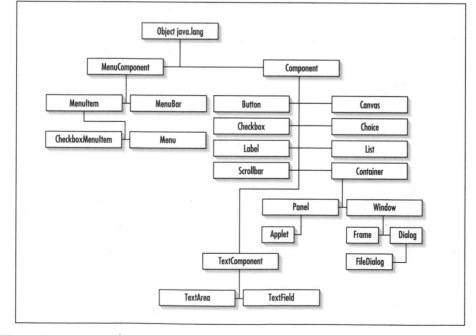

Figure C.1 *Diagram of java.awt.*

Class	Description
Event	Platform-independent component messages
FileDialog	File open and save component
FlowLayout	Word-processor-like layout manager
Font	Represents a Font
Frame	An operating system window
GridBagConstraints	Settings for GridBagLayout
GridBagLayout	A flexible grid layout manager
GridLayout	A simple, easy-to-use grid layout
Insets	Window border information
Label	A text display component
List	A list component
MediaTracker	An image loading monitor
Menu	A menu component
MenuBar	A menu bar component
MenuItem	A menu entry component
Panel	A container allowing nested layouts
Point	A graphics coordinate pair
Polygon	A series of points describing a polygon
Rectangle	Holds rectangle information
Scrollbar	A scrollbar component
TextArea	A scrollable, row and column text entry component
TextComponent	A base class for Text components
TextField	A single line text entry component
Window	A base class for windows such as Frames and Dialogs

java.awt.image

This package provides low-level image manipulation services classes.

Interface	Description
ImageConsumer	Pairs with ImageProducer to load an image
ImageObserver	Monitors an image being loaded
ImageProducer	Image loader

Class	Description
ColorModel	Low-level color representation
CropImageFilter	Allows an image to be cropped
DirectColorModel	A particular low-level color model
FilteredImageSource	Provides a source for an image to be filtered
ImageFilter	An image consumer that allows filtering to occur
IndexColorModel	A particular low-level color model
MemoryImageSource	An in-memory image loading mechanism
PixelGrabber	Gets a pixel based representation of an image
RGBImageFilter	Allows an image's colors to be manipulated

java.awt.peer

This package provides classes that act as intermediaries between the JDK and the operating system UI components.

Interface

ButtonPeer

CanvasPeer

CheckboxMenuItemPeer

CheckboxPeer

ChoicePeer

ComponentPeer

ContainerPeer

DialogPeer

FileDialogPeer

FramePeer

LabelPeer

ListPeer

MenuBarPeer

MenuComponentPeer

MenuItemPeer

MenuPeer

PanelPeer

ScrollbarPeer

TextAreaPeer

Interface

TextComponentPeer

TextFieldPeer

WindowPeer

java.io

This package provides classes that allow input and output.

Interface	Description
DataInput	An input stream of machine independent data
DataOutput	An output stream of machine independent data
FilenameFilter	A filter interface for file names

Abstract Class	Description
InputStream	An input stream of bytes
OutputStream	An output stream of bytes

Class	Description
BufferedInputStream	A buffered input stream
BufferedOutputStream	A buffered output stream
ByteArrayInputStream	An input stream from a byte array
ByteArrayOutputStream	An output stream to a byte array

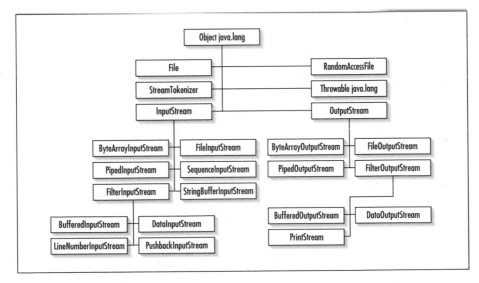

Figure C.2   *Diagram of java.io.*

Class	Description
DataInputStream	Input stream of primitive Java data types
DataOutputStream	Output stream of primitive Java data types
EOFException	End-of-file exception
File	Represents an operating system file
FileDescriptor	Identifier for a file
FileInputStream	Input stream from a file
FileNotFoundException	Unable to find a file exception
FileOutputStream	Output stream to a file
FilterInputStream	Filtered input stream of bytes
FilterOutputStream	Filtered output stream of bytes
IOException	An input output exception
InterruptedIOException	Input and output was interrupted
LineNumberInputStream	Input stream that keeps track of line numbers
PipedInputStream	Combines with PipedOutputStream to allow inter-thread communication
PipedOutputStream	Combines with PipedInputStream to allow inter-thread communication
PrintStream	Formattable output stream
PushbackInputStream	Input stream with a single byte pushback stream
RandomAccessFile	Seekable file
SequenceInputStream	Combines input streams
StreamTokenizer	Chops input stream into tokens
StringBufferInputStream	A string buffer used as an input stream
UTFDataFormatException	A UTF-8 format was in error

java.lang

This package provides all the Java language-related classes.

Interface	Description
Cloneable	Cloneable objects are able to be copied
Runnable	Interface for threads

Abstract Class	Description
ClassLoader	Defines policy for loading classes into the runtime environment
NumberBase	Class for number wrappers
Process	Encapsulates the operating system process

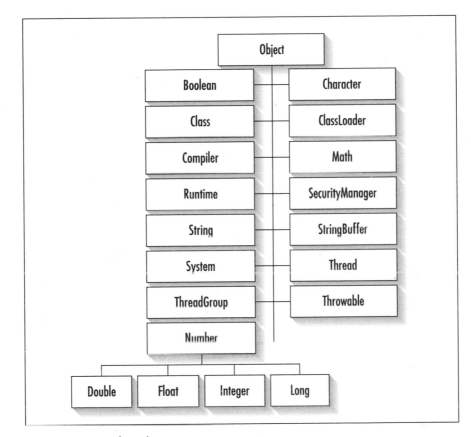

Figure C.3 *Diagram of java.lang.*

Abstract Class	Description
Runtime	Access to the operating system environment
SecurityManager	Defines policy security management
VirtualMachineError	A very low-level exception occurred

Class	
AbstractMethodError	Attempt to call an abstract method
ArithmeticException	Arithmetic error occurred
ArrayIndexOutOfBoundsException	Index was out of array bounds
ArrayStoreException	Attempt to store the wrong type of object into an array
Boolean	Wrapper class for booleans
Character	Wrapper class for chars
Class	Meta class representing other classes
ClassCastException	Attempt to illegally cast a class to another class

Class	Description
ClassCircularityError	Attempt to construct an incorrectly defined class
ClassFormatError	Class file format was incorrect
ClassNotFoundException	Unable to find a class
CloneNotSupportedException	Attempt to clone a class that does not implement Cloneable
Compiler	Provides access to a Java compiler
Double	Wrapper class for doubles
Error	Base class for errors
Exception	Base class for exceptions
FloatWrapper	Class for floats
IllegalAccessError	Illegal access to a class
IllegalAccessException	Illegal access to a class
IllegalArgumentException	Illegal number of arguments to method
IllegalMonitorStateException	Illegal attempt to access data
IllegalThreadStateException	Thread is not in the correct state for the requested operation
IncompatibleClassChangeError	Illegal attempt to change a class
IndexOutOfBoundsException	Base class for index out of bounds exceptions
InstantiationError	Interpreter tried to instantiate an interface or an abstract class
InstantiationException	An attempt to instantiate an interface or an abstract class
Integer	Wrapper class for ints
InternalError	Java is FUBAR! Email Sun.
InterruptedException	Another thread has interrupted this thread
LinkageError	Linkage failed due to an error
Long	Wrapper class for longs
Math	Assorted mathematical functions
NegativeArraySizeException	Attempt to construct an array of negative size
NoClassDefFoundError	Unable to find the class definition
NoSuchFieldError	A class loading was in error
NoSuchMethodError	Attempt to call a method that does not exist
NoSuchMethodException	Attempt to call a method that does not exist
NullPointerException	Attempt to use a null pointer as a reference
NumberFormatException	A string was in the wrong format to convert to a number wrapper class

Class	Description
Object	The mother of all other classes and objects
OutOfMemoryError	Close some applications or buy some more memory!
RuntimeException	Special silent exception class
SecurityException	Security manager did not allow the operation
StackOverflowError	Memory overrun
String	An immutable first-class text class
StringBuffer	A mutable first-class text class
StringIndexOutOfBoundsException	Attempt to access beyond the limits of a string
System	Wraps the system dependent methods
Thread	A single path of execution and its related method and data
ThreadDeath	A class that is thrown when a thread dies
ThreadGroup	A collection of Threads and other ThreadGroups
Throwable	The base class for errors and exceptions
UnknownError	Your guess is as good as the interpreter's
UnsatIsfiedLinkError	A link was unsatisfied during linking
VerifyError	Some necessary verification failed

java.net

This package provides all the network-related classes.

Interface	Description
ContentHandlerFactory	Represents the ability to create ContentHandlers
SocketImplFactory	Represents the ability to create SocketImpls
URLStreamHandlerFactory	Represents the ability to create URLStreamHandlers

Abstract Class	Description
ContentHandler	Interprets data in a specific format from a stream and creates the appropriate object
SocketImpl	Encapsulates a specific implementation of a socket
URLConnection	Encapsulates a connection to a URL
URLStreamHandler	Encapsulates methods for managing data from a URL

Class	Description
DatagramPacket	A datagram packet
DatagramSocket	A datagram socket
InetAddress	An Internet address

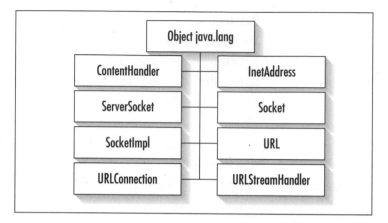

Figure C.4 *Diagram of java.net.*

Class	Description
MalformedURLException	URL string was incorrectly formatted
PlainSocketImpl	The default socket implementation
ProtocolException	A protocol was violated
ServerSocket	A connection-oriented, server socket
Socket	A socket
SocketException	An error occurred while using a socket
SocketInputStream	An input stream connected to a socket
SocketOutputStream	An output stream connected to a socket
URL	A Uniform Resource Locator representation
URLEncoder	Converts a String of text into x-www-form-urlencoded format
UnknownHostException	A failed attempt to connect to an unknown host
UnknownServiceException	An unknown service use was attempted

java.util

This package provides useful utilities.

Interface	Description
Enumeration	Allows the elements of a data structure to be accessed one by one
Observer	Represents a viewer of an object of the Observable class

Abstract Class	Description
Dictionary	A data structure containing key-value pairs

Class	Description
BitSet	A data structure to store bits
Date	A date and time implementation
EmptyStackExccption	The stack is empty
Hashtable	A hashtable
NoSuchElementException	The desired element could not be found
Observable	A model that is viewed by one or more objects of class Observer
Properties	A hashtable of operating system properties
Random	A random number gonorator
Stack	A last-in-first-out data structure
StringTokenizer	A class to chop up a String into tokens
Vector	A universal growablc list data structure

Using the CD-ROM

Neil Bartlett

The CD-ROM contains the complete source code examples for the book. It is under the top-level directory, *source*. The source code is divided by chapter: Thus, for example, the source code for Chapter 17 is found in the directory SOURCE\CHAP17 (or SOURCE/CHAP17 depending on your system's directory convention). Under the chapter directories, there are occasionally sub-directories that provide further division of the sample code as necessary.

Each directory contains two additional files: make.bat and run.bat. These directories will build the examples program and run the program examples, respectively. These programs should work correctly on most types of machine that support Java. On PCs with Microsoft Windows, it's only necessary to type the name of the file without the extension. On Unix machines, however, you must type the full name of the file including the extension. Other operating systems have their own rules; check your system documentation.

The directories on the CD-ROM contain fully-built source code examples. In general, the run.bat files should work directly from the CD-ROM, but there are a couple of instances where this is not true. In Chapter 8, some sample programs write to the disk and therefore cannot run from the CD-ROM. Typically the run.bat files contain more than one sample program to run. This can cause a problem. When you run some run.bat files, you will find that it is not possible to close some windows—especially Frame windows—of the sample programs on some operating systems. To get around this problem, try typing Control+C on the command window from which you ran the run.bat command. Windows NT, for example, allows you to go to the next program to run. If your operating system does not allow this, you will need to run each of the sample programs individually from the command line. Use the run.bat file as a guide.

The make.bat files will not work at all from the CD-ROM, because they are designed to write to the disk. To use the make.bat files, you will need to copy the complete directory that contains the make.bat file to your hard disk. You will also need to copy any subdirectories. You will be able to use the make.bat file from the directory on your hard drive.

Note: You will need to install the Java JDK to use the run.bat and make.bat files. See Appendix B for more information.

INDEX

-D-

-H-

Y